Lecture Notes in Computer Science

Lecture Notes in Artificial Intelligence   15979

Founding Editor

Jörg Siekmann

Series Editors

Randy Goebel, *University of Alberta, Edmonton, Canada*
Wolfgang Wahlster, *DFKI, Berlin, Germany*
Zhi-Hua Zhou, *Nanjing University, Nanjing, China*

The series Lecture Notes in Artificial Intelligence (LNAI) was established in 1988 as a topical subseries of LNCS devoted to artificial intelligence.

The series publishes state-of-the-art research results at a high level. As with the LNCS mother series, the mission of the series is to serve the international R & D community by providing an invaluable service, mainly focused on the publication of conference and workshop proceedings and postproceedings.

René Thiemann · Christoph Weidenbach
Editors

Frontiers of Combining Systems

15th International Symposium, FroCoS 2025
Reykjavik, Iceland, September 29 – October 1, 2025
Proceedings

 Springer

Editors
René Thiemann
University of Innsbruck
Innsbruck, Austria

Christoph Weidenbach
Max-Planck-Institut für Informatik
Saarbrücken, Germany

ISSN 0302-9743   ISSN 1611-3349 (electronic)
Lecture Notes in Artificial Intelligence
ISBN 978-3-032-04166-1   ISBN 978-3-032-04167-8 (eBook)
https://doi.org/10.1007/978-3-032-04167-8

LNCS Sublibrary: SL7 – Artificial Intelligence

This Springer imprint is published by the registered company Springer Nature Switzerland AG
The registered company address is: Gewerbestrasse 11, 6330 Cham, Switzerland

If disposing of this product, please recycle the paper.

Preface

These proceedings contain the papers selected for presentation at the 15th *International Symposium on Frontiers of Combining Systems* (FroCoS 2025). The symposium was held during September 29 – October 1, 2025 at ICE-TCS, the theoretical computer science lab of Reykjavik University, Iceland. It was co-located with the 34th *International Conference on Automated Reasoning with Analytic Tableaux and Related Methods* (TABLEAUX 2025) and the 16th *International Conference on Interactive Theorem Proving* (ITP 2025).

FroCoS is the main international event for research on the development of techniques and methods for the combination and integration of formal systems, their modularization and analysis.

FroCoS 2025 received 32 submissions. Each paper was evaluated by the members of the Program Committee who did a great job at thoroughly evaluating these submissions regarding their technical and presentational quality and providing helpful feedback to the authors. Reviewing was single-blind and each paper was subject to at least three reviews, followed by sometimes extensive discussions within the Program Committee. In the end, 21 papers were selected for presentation at the symposium and for publication. We have grouped them in this volume according to the following topic classification: (1) description logics, (2) beyond classical logic, (3) satisfiability modulo theories (SMT), (4) term rewriting systems, (5) theorem proving, (6) specific reasoning procedures, and (7) proof checking.

Together with the Program Committee, we considered suitable candidates to give an invited talk, and were delighted to find two outstanding invited speakers:

- Kaustuv Chaudhuri, LIX, Inria/École Polytechnique (joint with TABLEAUX)
- Carsten Fuhs, Birkbeck, University of London

We would like to thank all the people who contributed to making FroCoS 2025 a success. In particular, we thank the members of the Program Committee and the external reviewers for their excellent, timely work and for providing the authors with insightful feedback. Of course we thank the authors for submitting high-quality papers, taking the reviewers' feedback into account, and presenting their work in a way that is accessible to the broad FroCoS audience. Next, we thank the invited speakers for their inspiring talks. Moreover, we thank the local organizers and the theoretical computer science lab of Reykjavik University for organizing and supporting FroCoS. Finally, we gratefully acknowledge financial support from Springer.

July 2025

René Thiemann
Christoph Weidenbach

Organization

Program Committee Chairs

René Thiemann	University of Innsbruck, Austria
Christoph Weidenbach	Max Planck Institute for Informatics, Germany

Steering Committee

Franz Baader	TU Dresden, Germany
Andreas Herzig	University of Toulouse, France
Boris Konev	University of Liverpool, UK
Andrei Popescu	University of Sheffield, UK
Giles Reger	Amazon Web Services, USA & University of Manchester, UK
Ulrike Sattler	University of Manchester,UK
Martin Suda	České vysoké učení technické v Praze, Czech Republic

Program Committee

Franz Baader	TU Dresden, Germany
Haniel Barbosa	Universidade Federal de Minas Gerais, Brazil
Jasmin Blanchette	LMU München, Germany
Cyril Cohen	Inria, ENS de Lyon, France
Clare Dixon	University of Manchester, UK
Mathias Fleury	Universität Freiburg, Germany
Silvio Ghilardi	Università degli Studi di Milano, Italy
Jürgen Giesl	RWTH Aachen, Germany
Alberto Griggio	Fondazione Bruno Kessler, Italy
Andreas Herzig	IRIT, CNRS, University of Toulouse, France
Boris Konev	University of Liverpool, UK
Georg Moser	University of Innsbruck, Austria
Lawrence Paulson	University of Cambridge, UK
Elaine Pimentel	University College London, UK
Andrei Popescu	University of Sheffield, UK
Andrew Reynolds	University of Iowa, USA

Christophe Ringeissen	Inria Nancy, France
Philipp Rümmer	University of Regensburg, Germany
Uli Sattler	University of Manchester, UK
Renate A. Schmidt	University of Manchester, UK
Roberto Sebastiani	Università di Trento, Italy
Viorica Sofronie-Stokkermans	Universität Koblenz, Germany
Martin Suda	České vysoké učení technické v Praze, Czech Republic
Akihisa Yamada	AIST, Japan

Local Organizers

Tarmo Uustalu	Reykjavik University, Iceland
Antonis Achilleos	Reykjavik University, Iceland
Bjarki Gunnarsson	University of Iceland, Iceland
Vasiliki Kyriakou	Reykjavik University, Iceland
Calvin Santiago Lee	Reykjavik University, Iceland
Yasuaki Morita	Reykjavik University, Iceland
Jacob Neumann	Reykjavik University, Iceland

Additional Reviewers

Carlos Aguilera Ventura	IRIT, CNRS, University of Toulouse, France
Mauricio Ayala-Rincón	Universidade de Brasília, Brazil
Bartosz Bednarczyk	Uniwersytet Wrocławski, Poland
James Brotherston	University College London, UK
Martin Desharnais	LMU München, Germany
Zafer Esen	Uppsala University, Sweden
Tiago Ferreira	Universidade Federal de Minas Gerais, Brazil
Carsten Fuhs	Birkbeck, University of London, UK
Alessandro Gianola	Universidade de Lisboa, Portugal
Roland Herrmann	University of Regensburg, Germany
Ullrich Hustadt	University of Liverpool, UK
Jan-Christoph Kassing	RWTH Aachen, Germany
Christian Lidström	Fondazione Bruno Kessler, Italy
Luca Maio	LMU München, Germany

Albert Oliveras	Universitat Politècnica de Catalunya, Spain
Magdalena Ortiz	TU Wien, Austria
Pedro Quaresma	Universidade de Coimbra, Portugal
Gianluca Redondi	Fondazione Bruno Kessler, Italy
Balazs Toth	LMU München, Germany
Hongkai Yin	Central European University, Austria

Abstracts of Invited Talks

Towards a Universal Interactive Theorem Proving Interface

Kaustuv Chaudhuri

Inria & LIX, Institut Polytechnique Paris

Abstract. Interactive theorem provers are usually designed to use formal languages for expressing proofs and commands. Such languages are rarely portable across different systems, which leads to fragmentation in the community, duplication of effort, and an incumbency bias for existing systems. One way to address this incompatibility is to design an interactive proving interface where proof and command languages have a negligible role. Instead, users build proofs by manipulating the theorem itself using interaction devices such as mice and touch screens, and interaction mechanisms such as clicking, selection, dragging-and-dropping, etc.; in other words, using *direct manipulation*. There have been a number of proposals for such interfaces, most famously the *proof by pointing* approach of the 1990s [1], with several other approaches since then [8, 2, 3, 9].

This talk presents a foundational, proof theoretic, and system independent view of direct manipulation interfaces that generalizes these earlier attempts to *proof by linking* [5], which has been implemented in the interfaces *Profound* [6] and *Actema* [7] for first-order intuitionistic logic. These interfaces are intended to be compatible with arbitrary backend proof systems, either as plugins or as certifying procedures. For example, *Profound* can be used to produce proofs for Lean 3, Lean 4, Rocq (Coq), Isabelle/HOL, and HOL4 [4]. Linking requires the use of proof calculi of *deep inference*, which are proof systems where logical inferences are allowed in arbitrary formula contexts. This talk presents a particular kind of deep inference called *open deduction*, which was originally developed for classical logic but which is now extended and adapted to intuitionistic logic. In addition to linking, open deduction is suitable for a variety of other front-end features such as hierarchical levels of detail and refactoring by sharing subproofs. We will also discuss current work on extensions of open deduction (and linking) to support dependent type theory and induction.

References

1. Bertot, Y., Kalın, G., Théry, L.: Proof by pointing. In: Hagiya, M., Mitchell, J.C. (eds.) International Conference on the Theoretical Aspects of Computer Software TACS. TACS 1994. LNCS, vol. 789, pp. 141–160. Springer, Heidelberg (1994). https://doi.org/10.1007/3-540-57887-0_94
2. Breitner, J.: Visual theorem proving with the incredible proof machine. In: Blanchette, J.C., Merz, S. (eds.) Interactive Theorem Proving, pp. 123–139. Springer, Cham (2016). https://doi.org/10.1007/978-3-319-43144-4_8

3. Callies, E., Laurent, O.: Click and coLLecT an interactive linear logic prover. In: 5th International Workshop on Trends in Linear Logic and Applications (TLLA 2021). Rome (virtual), Italy (2021), https://hal-lirmm.ccsd.cnrs.fr/lirmm-03271501

4. Chaudhuri, K., Donato, P., Massacci, L., Werner, B.: Certifying proof-by-linking. Technical report, INRIA (2022). https://inria.hal.science/hal-04317972

5. Chaudhuri, K.: Subformula linking as an interaction method. In: Blazy, S., Paulin-Mohring, C., Pichardie, D. (eds.) Proceedings of the 4th Conference on Interactive Theorem Proving (ITP). LNCS, vol. 7998, pp. 386–401. Springer, Cham (2013)

6. Chaudhuri, K.: Subformula linking for intuitionistic logic with application to type theory. In: Platzer, A., Sutcliffe, G. (eds.) 28th International Conference on Automated Deduction. LNCS, vol. 12699, pp. 200–216. Springer, Cham (2021). https://doi.org/10.1007/978-3-030-79876-5_12

7. Donato, P., Strub, P., Werner, B.: A drag-and-drop proof tactic. In: Popescu, A., Zdancewic, S. (eds.) 11th ACM SIGPLAN International Conference on Certified Programs and Proofs, pp. 197–209. ACM (2022). https://doi.org/10.1145/3497775.3503692

8. Lerner, S., Foster, S.R., Griswold, W.G.: Polymorphic blocks: formalism-inspired UI for structured connectors. In: 33rd Annual ACM Conference on Human Factors in Computing Systems, pp. 3063–3072. Association for Computing Machinery, New York, NY, USA (2015). https://doi.org/10.1145/2702123.2702302

9. Reis, G., Naeem, Z., Hashim, M.: Sequoia: a playground for logicians - (system description). In: Peltier, N., Sofronie-Stokkermans, V. (eds.) 10th International Joint Conference on Automated Reasoning (IJCAR). LNCS, vol. 12167, pp. 480–488. Springer, Cham (2020). https://doi.org/10.1007/978-3-030-51054-1_32

Automated Static Program Analysis via Constrained Term Rewriting

Carsten Fuhs 🆔

University of London, UK
c.fuhs@bbk.ac.uk

Abstract. Static program analysis is a way of determining whether a program has certain desirable properties without actually running the program. Over the last decades, static analysis has made massive strides forward thanks to the ready availability of tools like SAT and SMT solvers. In this talk, I will sketch a systematic way of constructing a tool for static program analysis based on constrained rewriting, with a focus on program termination as the property of interest.

In the first part of the talk, I will discuss Logically Constrained Simply-typed Term Rewriting Systems (LCSTRSs) as an intermediate verification language that extends classic term rewriting in several directions relevant to program analysis. LCSTRSs as a form of constrained rewrite systems allow for expressing many features of real-world programming languages:

- algebraic data types;
- built-in data types (e.g., integers, arrays) and their standard operations and constraints;
- higher-order types, as used in functional programs.

I will describe a Dependency Pair Framework for compositional analysis of termination of call-by-value evaluation for LCSTRSs. Its automation heavily benefits from existing off-the-shelf SMT solvers to tackle the search problems inherent to automated termination proving.

In the second part of the talk, I will describe a translation from a subset of Scala to constrained rewrite systems such that termination of the rewrite system implies termination of the original Scala program. In combination with a termination tool for constrained rewriting as a back-end, this approach allows for proving termination of real-world programs via tools designed for the analysis of constrained term rewriting.

This talk is based on joint work with Liye Guo, Cynthia Kop, Viktor Kunčak, and Dragana Milovančević.

Contents

Term Rewrite Systems

Theorem Proving

Specific Reasoning Procedures

Proof Checking

Description Logics

The Concrete EVONNE: Visualization Meets Concrete Domain Reasoning

Christian Alrabbaa[1]($^{(\boxtimes)}$) (iD), Franz Baader[1]($^{(\boxtimes)}$) (iD), Raimund Dachselt[2]($^{(\boxtimes)}$) (iD),
Alisa Kovtunova[1]($^{(\boxtimes)}$) (iD), and Julián Méndez[2]($^{(\boxtimes)}$) (iD)

[1] Institute of Theoretical Computer Science, TU Dresden, Dresden, Germany
{christian.alrabbaa,franz.baader,alisa.kovtunova}@tu-dresden.de
[2] Interactive Media Lab Dresden, TU Dresden, Dresden, Germany
{raimund.dachselt,julian.mendez2}@tu-dresden.de

Abstract. EVONNE is a web application primarily designed to explain Description Logic (DL) entailments using an interactive visualization approach for proofs. This paper introduces an extension of EVONNE to DLs with concrete domains, which are needed for formalizing concepts whose definitions involve quantitative information. Specifically, we focus on two extensions of the DL $\mathcal{EL}_\perp$: one with constraints formulated as linear equations and the other with difference constraints. First, we have extended EVONNE to enable the generation and presentation of proofs involving these concrete domains. Then, leveraging the unique properties of each domain, we have designed and incorporated alternative visual explanations for the numerical parts of the proofs. Finally, we have assessed the effectiveness of these visual explanations through qualitative user studies and a performance benchmark. While opinions on one of these explanations varied, the other was widely recognized for its clarity and ease of understanding.

Keywords: Explainable AI · Description Logic · Concrete Domains · Visualization · Linear Equations · Difference Constraints

1 Introduction

Due to the opacity of many machine learning approaches such as deep neural networks [27], explainability (xAI) has become a major research field in Artificial Intelligence [18,19]. Symbolic AI approaches based on logic have the advantage over subsymbolic approaches that they are explainable by design. a consequence computed by an automated reasoner can in principle be explained using a proof, which demonstrates how the consequence can be derived from given axioms by applying simple inference rules, and the non-derivability of a statement can (for some logics) be explained by showing a finite counter-interpretation, which is a model of all axioms, but not of the non-derivable statement. However, to leverage this advantage of logic-based approaches in practice, one must be able to produce proofs (counter-interpretations) that are appropriate for explanation purposes and present them in a comprehensible and cogent way.

© The Author(s) 2026
R. Thiemann and C. Weidenbach (Eds.): FroCoS 2025, LNAI 15979, pp. 3–21, 2026.
https://doi.org/10.1007/978-3-032-04167-8_1

In ongoing work, we address these issues in the context of Description Logics (DLs) [12], which are a prominent family of logic-based knowledge representation languages frequently used to formalize ontologies for various application domains. The computation of appropriate proofs and counter-interpretations has been tackled in [3,4] and [8,9], respectively. Both means of explanation can be presented in our interactive visualization tool EVONNE[1][2,23], but the proof-presentation facilities are considerably more mature. Since the publication of the EVONNE system description [2] and a journal paper emphasizing its visualization components [23], this tool has been extended by new features and the look and feel of the system has been improved considerably.

Here we concentrate on the extension of the proof visualization facilities of EVONNE to DLs with so-called concrete domains [11,22]. In particular, we consider extensions of tractable DLs of the $\mathcal{EL}$ family [10] with two p-admissible concrete domains based on rational numbers, one ($\mathcal{D}_{\mathbb{Q},lin}$) that can use linear equations to formulate constraints [13] and another ($\mathcal{D}_{\mathbb{Q},diff}$) based on difference constraints [10]. Such numerical constraints turn out to be very useful for describing concepts whose definition involves quantitative information, such as the battery capacity of a drone, its flight time, and weather conditions including temperature, which may influence the battery discharge rate. The exact definition of p-admissibility is not relevant for this paper (see [10,13] for details), but note that it is needed to preserve tractability. Both mentioned concrete domains are p-admissible, but their combination is not, though they can both be integrated into the same DL as long as they do not interact. In [5], we have addressed the problem of generating proofs for consequences derived from knowledge bases formulated in such DLs. Basically, the proof system for the extended DL as introduced in [10] uses entailment between and unsatisfiability of sets of concrete domain constraints as applicability conditions. The idea is then to explain the satisfaction of such side conditions by a proof of the entailment (unsatisfiability) if this is requested by the user. The first important new feature of EVONNE described in this paper is the extension of its proof presentation facilities by such concrete domain proofs and their interaction with the abstract DL proofs.

However, the most original contribution of this work lies in its introduction of novel visual explanations for unsatisfiability and entailment in the considered numerical concrete domains. These visualizations are designed to reflect the unique properties of the domains and offer more intuitive insight into the underlying numerical reasoning. In the case of $\mathcal{D}_{\mathbb{Q},lin}$, unsatisfiability of a set of constraints using only two variables can be visualized in the 2D Euclidean Space by showing that the lines corresponding to the constraints do not intersect in a single point. Here, we address the challenge of extending this idea to higher dimensions. For $\mathcal{D}_{\mathbb{Q},diff}$, unsatisfiability of a constraint set corresponds to the existence of a negative cycle in the difference graph induced by these constraints. Thus, we developed a visual explanation based on such cycles. A priori, it is not clear how these visual explanations compare to numerical proofs.

---

[1] EVONNE's source code, documentation, and evaluation material (user studies, benchmark) are available at: https://imld.de/evonne.

For this reason, we conducted qualitative user studies to investigate the user reception of these visualization techniques.

In summary, this paper presents the latest extension of EVONNE, enabling interactive visualization of proofs for DLs with concrete domains—crucial for modeling concepts involving quantitative constraints. We contribute: (1) the *first* proof visualization tool supporting DLs with linear equations and difference constraints, (2) novel domain-specific visual explanations tailored to enhance comprehension of numerical reasoning, and (3) empirical validation through user studies and benchmarks, demonstrating the effectiveness of our approach. Our assessments showed that the proposed visualizations supported users in understanding conclusions more effectively than when no explanation was provided.

2 Description Logics and Concrete Domains

In this section we recall the Description Logic $\mathcal{EL}_\perp$ [12], and its extension $\mathcal{EL}_\perp[\mathcal{D}]$ with a concrete domain $\mathcal{D}$ [10]. We focus on two particular concrete domains $\mathcal{D}_{\mathbb{Q},diff}$ and $\mathcal{D}_{\mathbb{Q},lin}$ [10,13], both defined over the rational numbers $\mathbb{Q}$.

2.1 Concrete Domains

Concrete domains integrate reasoning about quantitative attributes of objects into DLs [11,13,22]. Let $\mathsf{N}_\sqcap$ be a set of *concrete predicates*, where every $\sqcap \in \mathsf{N}_\sqcap$ has arity $n_\sqcap \in \mathbb{N}$. A *concrete domain (CD)* $\mathcal{D} = (\Delta^\mathcal{D}, \cdot^\mathcal{D})$ over $\mathsf{N}_\sqcap$ consists of a set $\Delta^\mathcal{D}$ and relations $\sqcap^\mathcal{D} \subseteq (\Delta^\mathcal{D})^{n_\sqcap}$ for all $\sqcap \in \mathsf{N}_\sqcap$. We assume that $\mathsf{N}_\sqcap$ always contains predicates $\perp$ and $\top$, interpreted as $\perp^\mathcal{D} := \emptyset$, and $\top^\mathcal{D} := \Delta^\mathcal{D}$. Let N_V be a set of *variables*. A *constraint* $\sqcap(x_1, \ldots, x_{n_\sqcap})$, with $\sqcap \in \mathsf{N}_\sqcap$ and $x_1, \ldots, x_{n_\sqcap} \in \mathsf{N}_\mathsf{V}$, is a predicate with variables as arguments. A constraint $\alpha = \sqcap(x_1, \ldots, x_{n_\sqcap})$ is *satisfied* by an assignment $s: \mathsf{N}_\mathsf{V} \to \Delta^\mathcal{D}$ if $(s(x_1), \ldots, s(x_{n_\sqcap})) \in \sqcap^\mathcal{D}$. An *implication* is of the form $\mathfrak{C} \to \alpha$, where $\mathfrak{C}$ is a conjunction (set) of constraints. The implication is *valid* if all assignments satisfying all constraints in $\mathfrak{C}$ also satisfy α. A conjunction $\mathfrak{C}$ of constraints is *unsatisfiable* iff $\mathfrak{C} \to \perp$ is valid.

The CD $\mathcal{D}_{\mathbb{Q},diff}$ contains predicates $\top$, $\perp$, $x = q$, $x > q$, and $x + q = y$, for constants $q \in \mathbb{Q}$, with their natural semantics [10]. For instance, the constraint $x + q = y$ is interpreted as $(x + q = y)^{\mathcal{D}_{\mathbb{Q},diff}} = \{(p, r) \in \mathbb{Q} \times \mathbb{Q} \mid p + q = r\}$.

Example 1. Assume a delivery drone with bp representing its current *battery percentage*. The percentage is measured at multiple checkpoints, denoted as bp_0, bp_1, bp_2, with constraints: $bp_0 - 0.25 = bp_1$, $bp_1 - 0.2 = bp_2$, $bp_1 > 0.3$ and $bp_2 > 0.25$. If the initial percentage (bp_0) equals 0.65, then not all the constraints hold, and the drone is not permitted to fly.

For $\mathcal{D}_{\mathbb{Q},lin}$, besides $\top$ and $\perp$, the predicates are given by linear equations $\sum_{i=1}^n a_i x_i = b$, for $a_i, b \in \mathbb{Q}$, with their natural semantics [13]. For instance, $x + y - z = 0$ is interpreted as $(x + y - z = 0)^{\mathcal{D}_{\mathbb{Q},lin}} = \{(p, q, s) \in \mathbb{Q}^3 \mid p + q = s\}$.

Example 2. Assume nr and hr represent the average $\underline{n}ormal$ and $\underline{h}igh$ battery *discharge $\underline{r}ates$*, respectively. Under normal conditions, the delivery drone can fly for 8 hours on a single charge with a 30Ah battery, i.e., $8nr = 30$. In cold conditions, one hour of flight increases the battery consumption such that $4nr + hr = 30$. Therefore, if a delivery requires at most 2 hours in cold temperatures, the drone can complete it on a single charge.

2.2   Description Logics

DLs are decidable fragments of first-order logic (FOL) with a special, variable-free syntax and use only unary and binary predicates, called *concept names* and *role names*, respectively. These are used to build *complex concepts*, which correspond to first-order formulas with one free variable, and *axioms*, which correspond to first-order sentences. In this paper we consider the lightweight DL $\mathcal{EL}_\perp$. We use the usual notion of *entailment*, denoted $\mathcal{O} \models A \sqsubseteq B$, where Aand Bare concept names, and $\mathcal{O}$is a finite set of axioms, called an *ontology*. For more details about the syntax and semantics of DLs, see [12].

The extension of $\mathcal{EL}_\perp$ with a concrete domain $\mathcal{D}$, i.e., $\mathcal{EL}_\perp[\mathcal{D}]$, is obtained by allowing constraints α in $\mathcal{D}$ to be used as $\mathcal{EL}_\perp$ concepts. As in [5], we use the notation $[\alpha]$ to distinguish between constraints and classical concepts. For instance, the statement that a $\underline{d}elivery \ \underline{d}rone$ has a battery with a battery percentage greater than 0.25 can be expressed in an $\mathcal{EL}_\perp[\mathcal{D}_{\mathbb{Q},diff}]$ axiom as DD $\sqsubseteq \exists$has.(Battery $\sqcap [bp > 0.25]$).

3   Combined Proofs

EVONNE is a web application designed to explain DL entailments. It supports multiple proof types [2] and enhances them with interactive visualizations, helping users understand entailments and debug ontologies [23]. Proofs in EVONNE are generated using the EVEElibrary [7], and follow the notion introduced in [3]: A proof $\mathcal{P}$of $\mathcal{O} \models A \sqsubseteq B$ is a finite, acyclic, directed *hypergraph*, where each vertex v is labeled with an axiom $\ell(v)$. Hyperedges are of the form (S, d), where S is a set of vertices and d is a vertex such that $\{\ell(v) \mid v \in S\} \models \ell(d)$. The leaf vertices of a proof are labeled with axioms from $\mathcal{O}$, and the root with $A \sqsubseteq B$. EVONNE visualizes the proof hypergraphs using *tree* structures. In this paper, we extend EVONNE's proofs to cover *combined proofs* for $\mathcal{EL}_\perp[\mathcal{D}_{\mathbb{Q},diff}]$ and $\mathcal{EL}_\perp[\mathcal{D}_{\mathbb{Q},lin}]$ entailments. The following example demonstrates the approach, as introduced in [5].

Let $\mathcal{O} = \{A \sqsubseteq [\alpha_1], A \sqsubseteq [\alpha_2], A \sqsubseteq [\alpha_3], [\beta] \sqsubseteq B\}$ be an ontology such that $\mathcal{O} \models A \sqsubseteq B$. First, we identify the relevant constraints in $\mathcal{O}$ and establish implications between them in order to build the subsumption hierarchy of abstract concepts. By using an appropriate CD reasoner, we test relevant implications such as $\{\alpha_1, \alpha_2\} \rightarrow \beta$. The ontology is then extended with axioms that encode all the valid relevant implications, i.e., $\mathcal{O}' = \mathcal{O} \cup \{[\alpha_1] \sqcap [\alpha_2] \sqsubseteq [\beta], \ldots\}$. By classifying $\mathcal{O}'$ we obtain $\mathcal{O}' \models A \sqsubseteq B$. Lastly, by integrating the proof of $\{\alpha_1, \alpha_2\} \rightarrow \beta$

in the proof of $\mathcal{O}' \models A \sqsubseteq B$ as a proof for $[\alpha_1] \sqcap [\alpha_2] \sqsubseteq [\beta]$, we obtain the combined proof for $\mathcal{O} \models A \sqsubseteq B$.

Example 3. Consider the delivery drone (DD) from Example 2, along with the concept name *large battery drone* (LBD). Additionally, assume the following information is given. First, if operating at a high discharge rate for two hours draws 30Ah, this implies that a drone has a large battery, i.e., $[2hr = 30] \sqsubseteq$ LBD. Second, the delivery drone satisfies the constraints shown in Example 2, i.e., DD $\sqsubseteq [8nr = 30] \sqcap [4nr + hr = 30]$. From these two axioms, it follows that the delivery drone is a large battery drone, i.e., DD $\sqsubseteq$ LBD. An explanation of this conclusion is provided by the combined proof shown in Fig. 1a, where the proof in Fig. 1b shows the inferences at the level of equations.

To complete the picture of how concrete domain-dependent entailments are proven, we now describe the procedures that handle the CD reasoning steps.

Reasoning in $\mathcal{D}_{\mathbb{Q},lin}$. Deciding the validity of $\mathfrak{C} \to \beta$ is achieved by identifying *linear combinations* that allow β to be derived from the equations in $\mathfrak{C}$. For instance, the implication $\{8nr = 30, 4nr + hr = 30\} \to hr = 15$ can be shown by multiplying $8nr = 30$ by $-\frac{1}{2}$ and adding it to $4nr + hr = 30$. Similarly, the unsatisfiability of a system of equations can be shown by providing a linear combination that results in the derivation of $0 = c$, where $c \neq 0$. In [5], determining the coefficients for the linear combinations is achieved using *Gaussian Elimination*, and these coefficients are used to build the inferences that constitute the proof. An example of a $\mathcal{D}_{\mathbb{Q},lin}$ proof in EVONNE is shown in Fig. 1b

Reasoning in $\mathcal{D}_{\mathbb{Q},diff}$. Unlike the reasoning process in $\mathcal{D}_{\mathbb{Q},lin}$, deciding the validity of $\mathfrak{C} \to \beta$ is based on the *saturation* of $\mathcal{D}_{\mathbb{Q},diff}$ constraints, using the rules shown in [5, Fig. 1]. Thus, checking whether $\mathfrak{C} \to \beta$ is valid is done by checking if the implication is present in the result of the saturation. In addition, if β is of the form $x > q$, then the implication is valid if either (i) $x = q'$ where $q' > q$ or (ii) $x > q'$ where $q' \geq q$ are derived with the saturation rules. A proof of $\mathcal{D}_{\mathbb{Q},diff}$ entailment is thus built using the instantiations of saturation rules directly. An example of such a proof in EVONNE is shown in Fig. 1c

Combined proofs do not depend on the nature of the domains, making them versatile explanations that can be applied to various logics and concrete domains. However, their level of detail can result in large structures with potentially complicated inferences. For instance, the more variables and constraints involved in an entailment, the larger the resulting proof. To address this, we introduce alternative visual explanations, which we discuss in Sect. 4.

4   Domain-Specific Visualizations

In this section, we introduce two alternative visual explanations that leverage the specific characteristics of each concrete domain to present numerical entailments differently. These explanations do not rely on the DL part of the ontology, making them applicable to other logics or formalisms that incorporate these domains.

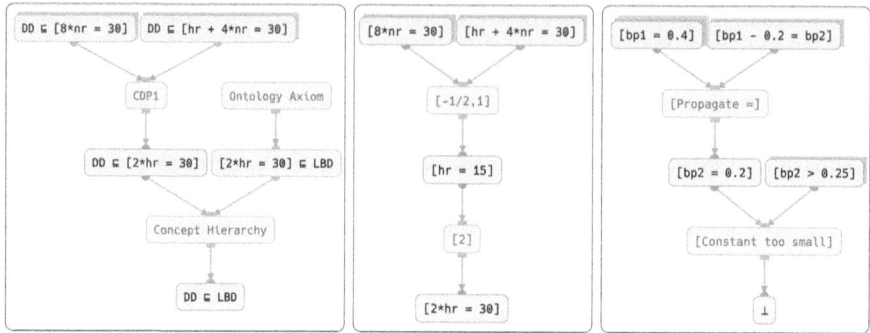

(a) Combined proof from Ex. 3   (b) CD proof from Ex. 2   (c) CD proof from Ex. 1

Fig. 1. Examples of proofs in EVONNE.

4.1   Explanations of $\mathcal{D}_{\mathbb{Q},lin}$ Entailments

Let β be a linear equation, and $\mathfrak{C}$ be a set of linear equations such that $\mathfrak{C} \rightarrow \beta$. The implication means that every *assignment* satisfying all the constraints in $\mathfrak{C}$, i.e., every *solution*, also satisfies β. A proof explains the implication by showing how the conclusion β is derived from equations in $\mathfrak{C}$, i.e., showing that all solutions to $\mathfrak{C}$ are also solutions to β. Hence, a compact representation showing every solution to $\mathfrak{C}$ is a solution to β offers an alternative way to explain the implication.

If we consider systems of linear equations with at most two variables, which are shared across all equations (e.g., $\{\alpha_1, \ldots, \alpha_n, \beta\}$), then we can use *lines* in the 2D *Euclidean Space* to achieve a compact representation of all solutions to the equations, as each solution corresponds to a point in the 2D space. For example, assume $\{\alpha_1, \ldots, \alpha_n\} \rightarrow \beta$. If $\beta = \bot$, this means that the system $\{\alpha_1, \ldots, \alpha_n\}$ has *no solutions*. In other words, the lines corresponding to $\alpha_1, \ldots, \alpha_n$ neither intersect at a single point nor overlap. On the other hand, if $\beta \neq \bot$ and $\{\alpha_1, \ldots, \alpha_n\}$ is satisfiable, then the system $\{\alpha_1, \ldots, \alpha_n, \beta\}$ either has a *unique solution*, i.e., exactly one point where all the lines intersect, or *infinitely many solutions*, i.e., all lines overlap. Therefore, by demonstrating the existence or absence of such intersections, we can explain entailments effectively.

Using *dimensionality reduction*, we can apply the same idea to equations with more than two variables. While there are multiple ways to achieve dimensionality reduction [15], we utilize the solution space of a system of equations to project the n-dimensional equations to 2D. Let $\mathfrak{C}$ be a set of equations where $\mathfrak{C} \rightarrow \beta$, let s be a solution to $\mathfrak{C}$, and let x and y be any two variables appearing in β. By replacing all the variables, except x and y, in all equations with their corresponding values in s, we obtain equations involving at most two variables. The resulting equations can be viewed as a snapshot of $\mathfrak{C}$ with respect to s, focusing on x and y. Therefore, in a plane defined by x and y, and since s is a solution, all the lines must intersect. Hence, we can explain $\mathfrak{C} \rightarrow \beta$ by showing that for every solution s and every plane

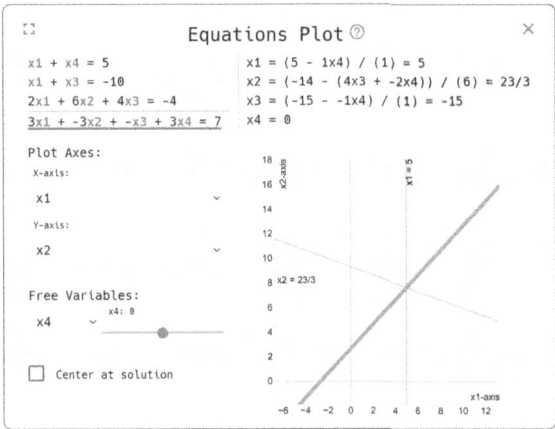

Fig. 2. $\mathcal{D}_{\mathbb{Q},lin}$ implication of $3x_1 - 3x_2 - x_3 + 3x_4 = 7$ in EVONNE.

defined by x and y, the intersection of all the lines of $\mathfrak{C}$ is the same intersection of the line corresponding to β and the lines of $\mathfrak{C}$.

To explain unsatisfiability, we can use a similar approach. If $\mathfrak{C} \rightarrow \bot$, then there must be a contradiction in $\mathfrak{C}$. More specifically, at least two contradictory equations must be derivable from $\mathfrak{C}$, i.e., equations of the form $X = q$ and $X = p$, where X is a sum of terms and $p, q \in \mathbb{Q}$, $q \neq p$. Thus, in any 2D plane defined by variables appearing in $\mathfrak{C}$, with at least one variable appearing in X, the lines corresponding to $X = q$ and $X = p$ do not intersect. Consequently, in a plane where all the equations in $\mathfrak{C}$ needed to derive $X = q$ and $X = p$ can be plotted, these lines must also not intersect. Therefore, we can explain $\mathfrak{C} \rightarrow \bot$ by highlighting these contradictory equations in $\mathfrak{C}$ and showing that their lines never intersect, regardless of variable assignments.

Figures 2 and 3 show examples of $\mathcal{D}_{\mathbb{Q},lin}$ explanations in EVONNE. The system of equations is shown in the top left. Hovering over an equation highlights its corresponding line in the 2D plot, and vice versa, helping users connect the algebraic and geometric views of the constraints. In Fig. 2 the top right displays an instantiation of the system's solution based on the chosen value for the free variable. Since this system has one degree of freedom, setting $x4 = 0$ uniquely determines the remaining variables. Hovering over the question mark icon reveals the solution without the variable assignment. In contrast, in Fig. 3, the top right shows the system of equations with respect to the currently chosen variable assignment. Additionally, users can manipulate the visualization directly by switching between different planes and assigning values to (free) variables using the controls beside the plot. In the case of unsatisfiability, the visualization makes contradictions immediately apparent: if a user assigns a value that causes an equation to evaluate to $p = q$ with $p \neq q$, then this inconsistency is highlighted in red, as illustrated by $3 = 0$ in Fig. 3.

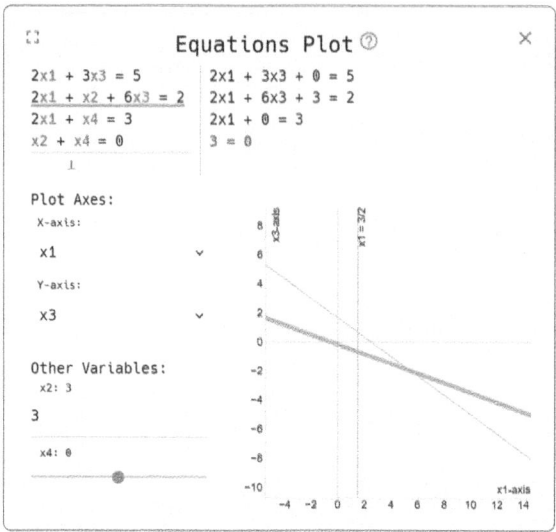

Fig. 3. DQlin implication of ⊥ in EVONNE

4.2 Explanations of $\mathcal{D}_{\mathbb{Q},\textit{diff}}$ Entailments

It is well established that *difference constraints* (i.e., $x-y \leq q$) can be represented as graphs such that every variable corresponds to a vertex and every constraint to a weighted edge [14]. Given a set of difference constraints, deciding whether it is *unsatisfiable* can be reduced to finding a *simple cycle* in the corresponding graph with a *negative weight* [14]. Therefore, we use graphs and negative cycles to explain implications in $\mathcal{D}_{\mathbb{Q},\textit{diff}}$. However, since predicates in $\mathcal{D}_{\mathbb{Q},\textit{diff}}$ express more types of constraints, we first need to introduce some necessary transformations.

Let $\mathfrak{C}$ be a set of difference constraints. A *difference graph* is a weighted directed graph $G = (V, E)$, where each variable x_i in $\mathfrak{C}$ corresponds to a vertex $v_i \in V$, and each constraint $x_j - x_i \leq q_{ij}$ corresponds to an edge $(v_i, v_j) \in E$ with weight $q_{ij} \in \mathbb{Q}$. A *path* $\pi(v, u)$ from v to u is a sequence of edges:

$$v \xrightarrow{q_0} v_1 \xrightarrow{q_1} v_2 \ \dots \ v_n \xrightarrow{q_n} u,$$

with weight $\pi^w(v, u) = q_0 + q_1 + \dots + q_n$. A path is *simple* if all vertices, with the possible exception of v and u, are distinct. A *negative cycle* is a simple path $\pi(v, v)$ where $\pi^w(v, v) < 0$. A set of difference constraints is unsatisfiable iff the corresponding difference graph contains a negative cycle ([14, Theorem 24.9]).

Constraints in $\mathcal{D}_{\mathbb{Q},\textit{diff}}$ of the form $y - x = q$ can be rewritten as two difference constraints: $y - x \leq q$ and $x - y \leq -q$. Additionally, the *unary* $\mathcal{D}_{\mathbb{Q},\textit{diff}}$ constraints, i.e., constraints of the form $x \bowtie q$, where $\bowtie \in \{=, >\}$, can be represented as $x - z_0 \bowtie q$ where z_0 is a fresh variable. This formulation is sound because $x \bowtie q$ is satisfiable iff $\{x - z_0 \bowtie q, z_0 = 0\}$ is satisfiable ([14, Lemma 24.8]).

Lastly, we rewrite $x - z_0 > q$ as $z_0 - x \leq -q - \epsilon$, where ϵ is a placeholder for some small positive value. This rewriting is sound for the following reason:

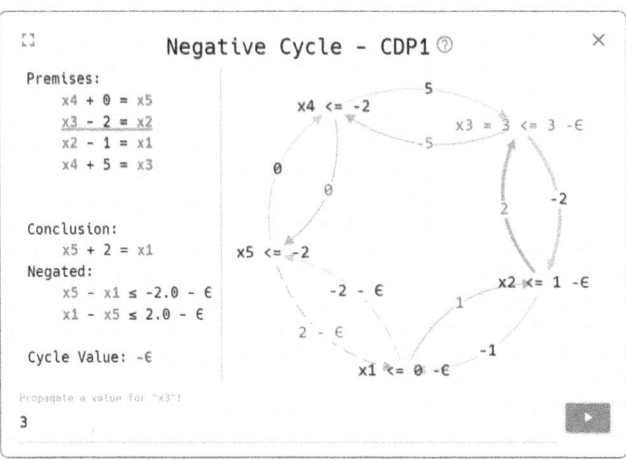

Fig. 4. Example of an explanation for $\mathcal{D}_{\mathbb{Q},diff}$ implications in EVONNE.

If $\mathfrak{C}$ is satisfiable and $\mathfrak{C} \cup \{x - z_0 > q\}$ is unsatisfiable, then for any positive $e \in \mathbb{Q}$, the constraints $\mathfrak{C} \cup \{x - z_0 \geq q + e\}$ are also unsatisfiable, which is equivalent to $\mathfrak{C} \cup \{z_0 - x \leq -q - e\}$. Meanwhile, for any assignment satisfying $\mathfrak{C} \cup \{x - z_0 > q\}$, there exists a positive $e \in \mathbb{Q}$ such that the same assignment also satisfies $x - z_0 \geq q + e > q$. Thus, $\mathfrak{C} \cup \{z_0 - x \leq -q - e\}$ is also satisfiable. Since such a small positive rational number e can always be found, we use ϵ symbolically as a reference to e whenever we need to transform a constraint with a $>$-predicate, rather than computing the specific value e for each set of constraints.

Consequently, we can represent any set $\mathfrak{C}$ of $\mathcal{D}_{\mathbb{Q},diff}$ constraints as a difference graph, and if $\mathfrak{C} \rightarrow \bot$, we can explain the contradiction in $\mathfrak{C}$ by identifying the negative cycle in the graph. However, if $\mathfrak{C}$ is satisfiable and $\mathfrak{C} \rightarrow \beta$, an additional step is required. In particular, we can explain that $\mathfrak{C}$ implies β by showing that $\mathfrak{C} \cup \{\neg\beta\} \rightarrow \bot$, which allows us to effectively use the notion of negative cycles to explain the implication. If β is of the form $x > q$, then the negative cycle in the difference graph corresponding to $\mathfrak{C} \cup \{x - z_0 \leq q\}$ shows that whenever an assignment satisfies all the constraints in $\mathfrak{C}$, the value of x must be greater than q. If β is of the form $x + y = q$, then $x + y \neq q$ is transformed into $x - y \leq q - \epsilon \vee y - x \leq -q - \epsilon$, leading to two negative cycles in the graph corresponding to $\mathfrak{C} \cup \{x - y \neq q\}$ These cycles explain $\mathfrak{C} \rightarrow x - y = q$ by demonstrating that no satisfying assignment for $\mathfrak{C}$ exists unless $x - y = q$ holds.

Figure 4 shows an example of a negative cycle in EVONNE. Hovering over a constraint highlights its corresponding edge(s) in the graph, and vice versa. The dotted edges represent the negated conclusion. Furthermore, the negative cycle is animated, allowing users to visually follow its progression. This animation can be triggered by clicking on a vertex or a constraint; the clicked element then determines the starting point of the animation in the graph. Additionally,

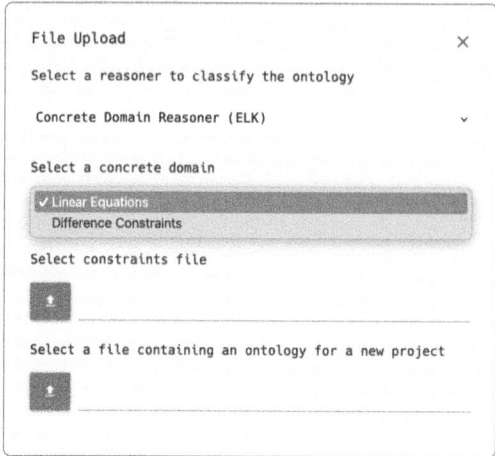

Fig. 5. Popover for specifying new project information in EVONNE.

users have access to a feature that lets them assign concrete values to variables by double-clicking on them. These values are then automatically propagated along the negative cycle, allowing users to observe how the set of constraints behaves under such assignments. In particular, this makes it possible to see exactly how the cycle leads to logical inconsistencies, which are highlighted in red. An example of such a contradiction is $x_3 = 3 \leq 3 - \epsilon$, as shown in Fig. 4.

5   Numerical Explanations in EVONNE

The first step to using EVONNE to generate CD explanations is to create a new project. As shown in Fig. 5, users must first specify which reasoner they would like to use—which, in our case, is the CD reasoner. This selection prompts the user to choose one of the two supported domains. Since the OWL 2 standard [28] does not support all predicate types used in our concrete domains, EVONNE requires the user to provide two files for an ontology: one text file that contains the CD constraints of the ontology, and one OWL file that contains the DL part. Once the files are loaded, the user is asked to provide an axiom (concept inclusion) that they would like to have proven. If proving this axiom depends on the concrete domain part of the ontology, then a combined proof is generated and displayed.

By default, all numerical subproofs within a combined proof are collapsed into single inferences. Each of these inferences is labeled with a unique rule identifier—for example, the label *CDP1* used in the proof shown in Fig. 1a—which allows for a more compact presentation of the proof. However, users can expand these subproofs to reveal all intermediate inferences. The visual explanations are accessible by clicking the labels of the numerical subproofs, which appear as popovers, as shown in Figs. 2, 3, and 4). It is worth noting that visual explanations rely only on the constraints within the corresponding subproofs and do not use additional constraints from the ontology.

The CD explanations in EVONNE use function-plot and cytoscape.js to render the 2D plots and difference graphs, respectively. To handle numerical precision in JavaScript, we represent rational numbers as fractions, using Fraction.js. We implemented a Gaussian elimination solver for evaluating $\mathcal{D}_{\mathbb{Q},lin}$ equations, and a Hamiltonian cycle detector for animating the negative cycles. In our difference graphs, a negative-weight Hamiltonian cycle is guaranteed. This is because our graphs are based on minimal proofs, ensuring that (i) all necessary constraints for constructing the negative cycle are present, and (ii) no constraint is superfluous, as the proof's leaf constraints correspond to a justification, i.e., a minimal set of constraints entailing the proof's root constraint [3].

The current version of EVONNE is accessible through https://imld.de/evonne, where all the examples used in the user studies (Sect. 6.1) and the benchmark (Sect. 6.2) are listed under the *Play Around* tab of EVONNE.

6   Evaluation

We conducted two experiments to evaluate different aspects of our approach. The first experiment consists of user studies that assess the effectiveness of the numerical explanations in terms of user understanding and perceived helpfulness. The second experiment is a benchmark that evaluates the efficiency of rendering these explanations.

6.1   User Studies

To assess the CD explanations we conducted two qualitative studies—one for $\mathcal{D}_{\mathbb{Q},diff}$ and the other for $\mathcal{D}_{\mathbb{Q},lin}$—using online structured interviews. Both studies compared the classical proofs (e.g., Figs. 1b, and 1c) with their respective alternative CD explanation (e.g., Figs. 2, 3, 4). The goal was to compare the effectiveness of the explanations and collect feedback to improve them.

To ensure adherence to best scientific practices, we preregistered the studies. The preregistration, an extended report, and detailed user feedback are available online [20].

Study Design. We employed a 2x2 factorial design with two independent variables: **representation** (i.e., *plot/cycle* or *proof*), and **task type** (i.e., *unsatisfiability* or *entailment*). The task type condition was necessary due to slight differences in plot and cycle representations between cases. Within each domain, four visual explanations of comparable difficulty were created with EVONNE. Each task in $\mathcal{D}_{\mathbb{Q},lin}$ involved 3–4 linear equations and, for $\mathcal{D}_{\mathbb{Q},diff}$, 4–6 difference constraints. We used a within-subjects design with a randomized order: all participants experienced all conditions and examples. The dependent variables included ease of use (measured using Single Ease Question, SEQ [24]), user experience (assessed with User Experience Questionnaire, UEQ-S [21,26]),

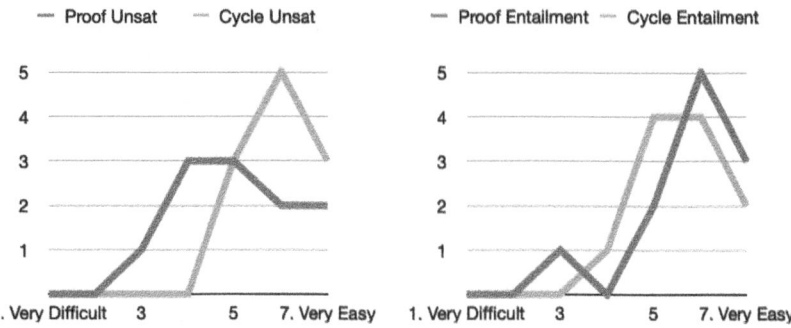

Fig. 6. Distribution of SEQ responses in $\mathcal{D}_{Q,diff}$: X-axis represents how difficult it was to understand an explanation, and Y-axis indicates the number of participants who selected each class.

and subjective preference. These dependent variables are interrelated. As demonstrated further, subjective preferences consistently aligned with the results from SEQ and UEQ-S, reinforcing the validity of our findings. The online surveys were hosted on LimeSurvey [1] and included an introductory video for each domain. The $\mathcal{D}_{Q,diff}$ study averaged just 35 minutes, whereas the $\mathcal{D}_{Q,lin}$ study required an average of 50 minutes.

We recruited eleven participants (2 female, 9 male), aged 18–44, from among colleagues familiar with logic and linear algebra, of whom seven were Ph.D.s, two M.Sc.s, and one B.Sc. Participants were informed about the objective of the studies and consented to the use of anonymous data for scientific purposes.

Results for $\mathcal{D}_{Q,diff}$. First, SEQ shows how difficult the explanation is to understand on a Likert scale from 1 "very difficult" to 7 "very easy". Figure 6 demonstrates the following findings: For an *entailment* task, *cycles* and *proofs* received similar evaluations (*cycles*: average 5.6, sd. = 0.9; *proofs*: average 5.8, sd. = 1.2, respectively). However, for *unsatisfiability*, *cycles* received an average score of 6, sd. = 0.8, and were unanimously perceived as more intuitive than *proofs* (average 5, sd. = 1.3).

In addition to SEQ, participants briefly explained why they found a task difficult. They generally found *cycles* and their animations clear and understandable, particularly because the visualization automated calculations, highlighted negative cycles, and helped relate edges to constraints. However, a few participants noted that understanding the interface and interpreting the information required some initial effort, explanations, and practice, as in *"It took me a moment to understand the tool. Once I was given the explanation, I could understand how it works"*. On the other hand, *proofs* were perceived slightly less positively. While participants appreciated the ability to inspect inference steps, clearly identify which equations to combine, and the simplicity of step verification, they also noted some challenges. These included uninformative or redundant information (e.g., repetitive left-hand sides of axioms and overly lengthy node labels), the need for manual calculations, and difficulties with the semantics of edge opera-

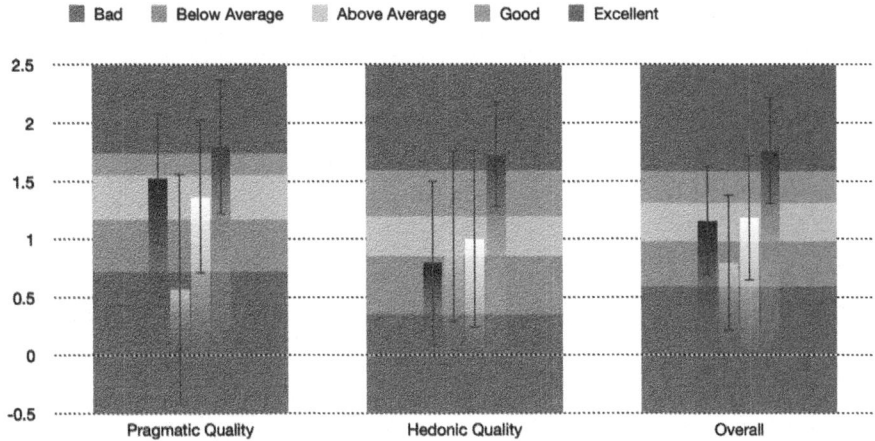

Fig. 7. $\mathcal{D}_{\mathbb{Q},lin}$ proof (in blue), plot (in cyan), $\mathcal{D}_{\mathbb{Q},diff}$ proof (in white), and cycle (in gray) UEQ-S scores, their interpretation, and confidence intervals. (Color figure online)

tions. For instance, a participant remarked: *"Proofs take a lot of space, and the edge labelings are unfamiliar"*.

Overall, both methods were well received, with participants appreciating their different strengths. As one participant summarized: *"A positive implication is actually very well represented in a proof. Cycle highlighting, hovering and animation are super cool"*.

Next, we assessed the user experience using the UEQ-S [25], by calculating *pragmatic* and *hedonic* quality scores. Pragmatic usability focuses on the task-oriented nature of an experience, whereas hedonic usability reflects non-utilitarian aspects such as appeal, originality, and joy of use. The white and gray bars in Fig. 7 correspond to the following results: *Proofs* received an "above average" rating across all qualities, with scores of 1.364 (pragmatic quality, e.g., usability and functionality), 1 (hedonic quality, e.g., enjoyment and stimulation), and 1.182 (overall quality). In contrast, *cycles* were rated as "excellent" in all three categories, with scores of 1.795 (pragmatic), 1.727 (hedonic), and 1.761 (overall).

After each task, participants were asked whether the explanation service was useful for understanding. All but one participant responded "yes" across both task types and both representations. The outlier cited confusion related to the naming of *proof* edges.

Finally, in the post-test assessment in $\mathcal{D}_{\mathbb{Q},diff}$, most participants preferred *cycles* (8 vs. 2 for *proofs*, 1 for both). This preference grew stronger with more constraints (9 vs. 2 for *proofs*).

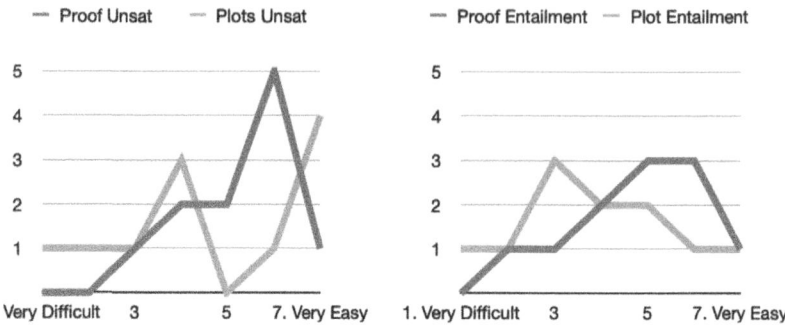

Fig. 8. Distribution of SEQ responses in $\mathcal{D}_{\mathbb{Q},lin}$: The X-axis represents how difficult it was to understand an explanation, and the Y-axis indicates the number of participants who selected each class.

Results for $\mathcal{D}_{\mathbb{Q},lin}$. Regarding SEQ, Fig. 8 demonstrates that, across both task types—*unsatisfiability* and *entailment*—*plots* (with average scores of 4.7, sd. = 2.2, and 3.9, sd. = 1.8, respectively) were perceived as less intuitive than *proofs* (with average scores of 5.3, sd. = 1.2, and 4.8, sd. = 1.5, respectively). In the case of *plots*, participants found them useful and enjoyable but also cognitively demanding to combine and interpret multiple variables displayed simultaneously, in particular when dealing with a higher number of dimensions. A respondent highlighted this point: *"The projection made me think that the solution was a point at first, before I realized that the solution is higher dimensional"*. Unsatisfiability tasks are perceived slightly easier than the *entailment* ones. Over time, familiarity with the visualization also improved, aided by provided instructions. For *proofs*, some participants found the step-by-step approach helpful, as it made the task easier to follow and verify compared to *plots*. They appreciated the ability to trace each step and felt confident in the overall result due to its clear mathematical foundation. However, the mental calculations required for verifying were quite challenging, as one participant noted: *"For proofs, I like that they show each individual step, but I did not figure out the solution myself from proofs, instead I trusted the system"*. Many participants found the notation less accessible, in particular: *"Too many symbols and too long node labels so it was hard to parse"*.

With respect to user experience, the blue and cyan bars in Fig. 7 illustrate the following findings: *Proofs* received an overall rating of "above average" (1.159). Specifically, they scored "above average" (1.523) for pragmatic qualities (e.g., usability and functionality) but "below average" (0.795) for hedonic qualities (e.g., enjoyment and stimulation). In contrast, *plots* were rated overall as "below average" (0.795). They scored "bad" (0.568) for pragmatic qualities but achieved an "above average" (1.023) rating for hedonic qualities.

After each task, we asked if the explanation was helpful. For *proofs*, the response was unanimously positive across both task types. Feedback on *plots* varied: for *unsatisfiability*, 10 said "yes" and 1 was "not sure"; for *entailment*, 6 said "yes", 4 were "not sure", and 1 said "no".

Subjectively, most participants preferred *proofs* (8 vs. 2 for *plots*, 1 for both). However, when linear equations involved only 2–3 variables, preference shifted to *plots* (8 vs. 3 for *proofs*).

Discussion. The user studies demonstrate that concrete domain-specific visualizations can significantly enhance the understanding of numerical reasoning, especially in the case of $\mathcal{D}_{\mathbb{Q},diff}$, where animated cycles were preferred for their clarity and intuitiveness. While proof trees were appreciated for their structure and detail, the choice between concrete domain visualizations and proofs appears task-dependent and influenced by numerical complexity. For simpler $\mathcal{D}_{\mathbb{Q},lin}$ entailments involving few variables, users preferred plots; however, for more complex cases and even with the added cognitive load, proofs were still preferred, as they were perceived as more trustworthy. These insights suggest that offering multiple, complementary explanation forms—proofs and CD visualizations—can accommodate diverse user preferences and experience levels. Future iterations of Evonne could build on this by incorporating adaptive explanation strategies based on characteristics of entailments or user feedback. Additionally, enabling users to adjust the existing visual explanations—or even extend them with user-defined visualizations, as supported by systems like Sterling [17]—could further accommodate individual preferences.

6.2   Performance Benchmark

We measured the response times for rendering the concrete domain explanations using combined proofs from the dataset provided in [5]. To automate the process, we used cypress.io, a testing framework, to load these proofs and open the corresponding CD explanations. Since the goal of the benchmark is to assess the rendering overhead introduced by the visual explanations, we do not measure the time required to compute the combined proofs, as this has already been reported in [6].

On average, response times were 18.32 ms for $\mathcal{D}_{\mathbb{Q},lin}$ and 8.7 ms for $\mathcal{D}_{\mathbb{Q},diff}$. The slowest times were 180.4 ms for $\mathcal{D}_{\mathbb{Q},lin}$ and 124.8 ms for $\mathcal{D}_{\mathbb{Q},diff}$, which correspond to large proofs that push the browser's resources considerably. These higher initial times occur when a CD explanation is opened for the first time, as the required HTML DOM elements are created and the relevant libraries are loaded. However, subsequent renders within the same proof are significantly faster. In the slowest cases, follow-up renders took 44.4 ms in $\mathcal{D}_{\mathbb{Q},lin}$ and 9.3 ms in $\mathcal{D}_{\mathbb{Q},diff}$. Note that all response times are within the 200ms threshold for perceived responsiveness [16].

7   Conclusion

We have extended Evonne to generate and present proofs for $\mathcal{EL}_{\perp}[\mathcal{D}_{\mathbb{Q},diff}]$ and $\mathcal{EL}_{\perp}[\mathcal{D}_{\mathbb{Q},lin}]$. Additionally, we have designed and developed alternative visual explanations for numerical entailments, taking into account the characteristics of each concrete domain. Specifically, we illustrate $\mathcal{D}_{\mathbb{Q},diff}$ entailments using negative cycles and $\mathcal{D}_{\mathbb{Q},lin}$ entailments with 2D plots. These visual explanations are specific to the concrete domain yet independent of the underlying logic, making them adaptable and applicable to other formalisms. Furthermore, the visual display of the CD explanations scales better than that of the combined proofs. For instance, in the case of $\mathcal{D}_{\mathbb{Q},lin}$, adding more constraints simply results in additional lines in a 2D plot, without significantly affecting the overall layout. In contrast, increasing the number of equations in a proof expands the entire proof structure, which can make navigation more difficult due to increased scrolling and zooming.

We conducted qualitative user studies to assess the effectiveness of numerical explanations in EVONNE. For $\mathcal{D}_{\mathbb{Q},lin}$, participants' opinions varied, though most alluded to a trust factor favoring proofs over visual explanations, suggesting that, in this case, such visual explanations might not be necessary. In contrast, for $\mathcal{D}_{\mathbb{Q},diff}$, participants highly valued the clarity and ease of understanding provided by the animated cycles, making them a more preferred form of explanation.

As future work, we plan to address issues raised by the participants' feedback on both proofs and the visual CD explanations. Additionally, we will refine EVONNE's capabilities for explaining non-consequences through counter-interpretations and extend them to support DLs with concrete domains.

Acknowledgments. This work is funded by Deutsche Forschungsgemeinschaft (DFG) under Germany's Excellence Strategy: EXC 2050/1, 390696704 – "Centre for Tactile Internet" (CeTI); by DFG grant 389792660 as part of TRR 248 – CPEC, see https://perspicuous-computing.science; and by Bundesministerium für Bildung und Forschung (BMBF) and Saxon State Ministry for Science, Culture and Tourism (SMWK) in Center for Scalable Data Analytics and Artificial Intelligence (ScaDS.AI, SCADS22B). The authors extend gratitude to Dr. Ida Sri Rejeki Siahaan and Nicolás Rojas for their support in the early design and implementation of CD visualizations.

References

1. Der Umfragedienst für sächsische Hochschulen und Berufsakademien. https://bildungsportal.sachsen.de/umfragen/
2. Alrabbaa, C., Baader, F., Borgwardt, S., Dachselt, R., Koopmann, P., Méndez, J.: Evonne: interactive proof visualization for description logics (system description). In: Automated Reasoning - 11th International Joint Conference, IJCAR 2022, Proceedings. Lecture Notes in Computer Science, vol. 13385, pp. 271–280. Springer (2022). https://doi.org/10.1007/978-3-031-10769-6_16
3. Alrabbaa, C., Baader, F., Borgwardt, S., Koopmann, P., Kovtunova, A.: Finding small proofs for description logic entailments: theory and practice. In: LPAR 2020: 23rd International Conference on Logic for Programming, Artificial Intelligence and Reasoning, Alicante, Spain, May 22-27, 2020. EPiC Series in Computing, vol. 73, pp. 32–67. EasyChair (2020). https://doi.org/10.29007/NHPP

4. Alrabbaa, C., Baader, F., Borgwardt, S., Koopmann, P., Kovtunova, A.: Finding good proofs for description logic entailments using recursive quality measures. In: Automated Deduction - CADE 28 - 28th International Conference on Automated Deduction 2021, Proceedings. Lecture Notes in Computer Science, vol. 12699, pp. 291–308. Springer (2021). https://doi.org/10.1007/978-3-030-79876-5_17

5. Alrabbaa, C., Baader, F., Borgwardt, S., Koopmann, P., Kovtunova, A.: Combining proofs for description logic and concrete domain reasoning. In: Rules and Reasoning - 7th International Joint Conference, RuleML+RR 2023, Proceedings. Lecture Notes in Computer Science, vol. 14244, pp. 54–69. Springer (2023). https://doi.org/10.1007/978-3-031-45072-3_4

6. Alrabbaa, C., Baader, F., Borgwardt, S., Koopmann, P., Kovtunova, A.: Combining proofs for description logic and concrete domain reasoning (technical report) (2023). https://arxiv.org/abs/2308.03705

7. Alrabbaa, C., et al.: Explaining reasoning results for OWL ontologies with Evee. In: Proceedings of the 21st International Conference on Principles of Knowledge Representation and Reasoning, KR 2024, Hanoi, Vietnam. November 2-8, 2024 (2024). https://doi.org/10.24963/KR.2024/67

8. Alrabbaa, C., Hieke, W.: Explaining non-entailment by model transformation for the description logic $\mathcal{EL}$. In: Proceedings of the 11th International Joint Conference on Knowledge Graphs, IJCKG 2022, pp. 1–9. ACM (2022). https://doi.org/10.1145/3579051.3579060

9. Alrabbaa, C., Hieke, W., Turhan, A.: Counter model transformation for explaining non-subsumption in $\mathcal{EL}$. In: Proceedings of the 7th Workshop on Formal and Cognitive Reasoning co-located with the 44th German Conference on Artificial Intelligence (KI 2021). CEUR Workshop Proceedings, vol. 2961, pp. 9–22. CEUR-WS.org (2021). https://ceur-ws.org/Vol-2961/paper_2.pdf

10. Baader, F., Brandt, S., Lutz, C.: Pushing the EL envelope. In: IJCAI-05, Proceedings of the Nineteenth International Joint Conference on Artificial Intelligence, Edinburgh, Scotland, UK, July 30 - August 5, 2005. pp. 364–369. Professional Book Center (2005). http://ijcai.org/Proceedings/05/Papers/0372.pdf

11. Baader, F., Hanschke, P.: A scheme for integrating concrete domains into concept languages. In: Proceedings of the 12th International Joint Conference on Artificial Intelligence. Sydney, Australia, August 24-30, 1991, pp. 452–457. Morgan Kaufmann (1991). http://ijcai.org/Proceedings/91-1/Papers/070.pdf

12. Baader, F., Horrocks, I., Lutz, C., Sattler, U.: An Introduction to Description Logic. Cambridge Univ. Press (2017). https://doi.org/10.1017/9781139025355

13. Baader, F., Rydval, J.: Using model theory to find decidable and tractable description logics with concrete domains. J. Autom. Reason. **66**(3), 357–407 (2022). https://doi.org/10.1007/s10817-022-09626-2

14. Cormen, T., Leiserson, C., Rivest, R., Stein, C.: Introduction to Algorithms, third edition. Computer science, MIT Press (2009). https://books.google.de/books?id=i-bUBQAAQBAJ

15. Cunningham, J.P., Ghahramani, Z.: Linear dimensionality reduction: survey, insights, and generalizations. J. Mach. Learn. Res. **16**, 2859–2900 (2015). https://doi.org/10.5555/2789272.2912091

16. Dabrowski, J.R., Munson, E.V.: Is 100 milliseconds too fast? In: CHI 2001 Extended Abstracts on Human Factors in Computing Systems, CHI Extended Abstracts 2001, Seattle, Washington, USA, March 31 - April 5, 2001. pp. 317–318. ACM (2001). https://doi.org/10.1145/634067.634255

17. Dyer, T., Jr., J.W.B.: Sterling: a web-based visualizer for relational modeling languages. In: Rigorous State-Based Methods - 8th International Conference, ABZ 2021, Ulm, Germany, June 9-11, 2021, Proceedings. Lecture Notes in Computer Science, vol. 12709, pp. 99–104. Springer (2021). https://doi.org/10.1007/978-3-030-77543-8_7

18. Gunning, D., Stefik, M., Choi, J., Miller, T., Stumpf, S., Yang, G.: XAI – explainable artificial intelligence. Sci. Robotics **4**(37) (2019). https://doi.org/10.1126/SCIROBOTICS.AAY7120

19. Holzinger, A., Saranti, A., Molnar, C., Biecek, P., Samek, W.: Explainable AI methods - a brief overview. In: xxAI – Beyond Explainable AI - International Workshop, Held in Conjunction with ICML 2020, Revised and Extended Papers. Lecture Notes in Computer Science, vol. 13200, pp. 13–38. Springer (2020). https://doi.org/10.1007/978-3-031-04083-2_2

20. Kovtunova, A., Alrabbaa, C., Baader, F., Dachselt, R., Méndez, J.: The Concrete Evonne (2025). https://doi.org/10.17605/OSF.IO/Y4X5T

21. Laugwitz, B., Held, T., Schrepp, M.: Construction and evaluation of a user experience questionnaire. In: HCI and Usability for Education and Work, 4th Symposium of the Workgroup Human-Computer Interaction and Usability Engineering of the Austrian Computer Society, USAB 2008, Graz, Austria, November 20-21, 2008. Proceedings. Lecture Notes in Computer Science, vol. 5298, pp. 63–76. Springer (2008). https://doi.org/10.1007/978-3-540-89350-9_6

22. Lutz, C.: Description logics with concrete domains-a survey. In: Advances in Modal Logic 4, papers from the fourth conference on "Advances in Modal logic," held in Toulouse, France, 30 September - 2 October 2002, pp. 265–296. King's College Publications (2002). http://www.aiml.net/volumes/volume4/Lutz.ps

23. Méndez, J., Alrabbaa, C., Koopmann, P., Langner, R., Baader, F., Dachselt, R.: Evonne: A visual tool for explaining reasoning with OWL ontologies and supporting interactive debugging. Comput. Graph. Forum **42**(6) (2023). https://doi.org/10.1111/CGF.14730

24. Sauro, J., Dumas, J.S.: Comparison of three one-question, post-task usability questionnaires. In: Proceedings of the 27th International Conference on Human Factors in Computing Systems, CHI 2009, Boston, MA, USA, April 4-9, 2009 pp. 1599–1608. ACM (2009). https://doi.org/10.1145/1518701.1518946

25. Schrepp, M.: User Experience Questionnaire Handbook (2015). https://doi.org/10.13140/RG.2.1.2815.0245

26. Schrepp, M., Hinderks, A., Thomaschewski, J.: Design and evaluation of a short version of the user experience questionnaire (UEQ-S). Int. J. Interact. Multim. Artif. Intell. **4**(6), 103–108 (2017). https://doi.org/10.9781/IJIMAI.2017.09.001

27. Søgaard, A.: On the opacity of deep neural networks. Can. J. Philos. **53**(3), 224–239 (2023). https://doi.org/10.1017/can.2024.1

28. W3C OWL Working Group: OWL 2 Web Ontology Language Document Overview (Second Edition) - W3C Recommendation 11 December 2012 (2012). http://www.w3.org/TR/owl2-overview/

The Expressive Power of Description Logics with Numerical Constraints over Restricted Classes of Models

Franz Baader[1,2] and Filippo De Bortoli[1,2(✉)]

[1] Institute of Theoretical Computer Science, TU Dresden, Dresden, Germany
franz.baader@tu-dresden.de
[2] Center for Scalable Data Analytics and AI (ScaDS.AI), Dresden/Leipzig, Germany
filippo.de_bortoli@tu-dresden.de

Abstract. Standard Description Logics (DLs) can encode quantitative aspects of an application domain through either number restrictions, which constrain the number of individuals that are in a certain relationship with an individual, or concrete domains, which can be used to assign concrete values to individuals using so-called features. These two mechanisms have been extended towards very expressive DLs, for which reasoning nevertheless remains decidable. Number restrictions have been generalized to more powerful comparisons of sets of role successors in $\mathcal{ALCSCC}$, while the comparison of feature values of different individuals in $\mathcal{ALC}(\mathfrak{D})$ has been studied in the context of ω-admissible concrete domains $\mathfrak{D}$. In this paper, we combine both formalisms and investigate the complexity of reasoning in the thus obtained DL $\mathcal{ALCOSCC}(\mathfrak{D})$, which additionally includes the ability to refer to specific individuals by name. We show that, in spite of its high expressivity, the consistency problem for this DL is ExpTime-complete, assuming that the constraint satisfaction problem of $\mathfrak{D}$ is also decidable in exponential time. It is thus not higher than the complexity of the basic DL $\mathcal{ALC}$. At the same time, we show that many natural extensions to this DL, including a tighter integration of the concrete domain and number restrictions, lead to undecidability.

1 Introduction

Description logics (DLs) [6,13] are a prominent family of logic-based knowledge representation languages, which can be used to formalize the terminological knowledge of an application domain in a machine-processable way. For instance, the standard Web Ontology Language OWL[1] is based on an expressive DL and the large medical ontology SNOMED CT[2] has been developed using a rather inexpressive DL. The *expressive power* of a DL is determined by the constructors that are available for building complex concept descriptions out of concept

---

[1] https://www.w3.org/TR/owl2-overview/.
[2] https://www.snomed.org/.

© The Author(s) 2026
R. Thiemann and C. Weidenbach (Eds.): FroCoS 2025, LNAI 15979, pp. 22–39, 2026.
https://doi.org/10.1007/978-3-032-04167-8_2

names (unary predicates) and role names (binary predicates). For example, the concept description Person $\sqcap$ $\exists$pet.Dog, describing persons that have a dog as a pet, uses conjunction ($\sqcap$) and existential restriction ($\exists r.C$) as constructors, where Person and Dog are concept names and pet is a role name. To show that a given DL $\mathcal{L}_1$ can be expressed by another DL $\mathcal{L}_2$ using the same concept and role names, we can provide a semantic-preserving translation of $\mathcal{L}_1$ concept descriptions into $\mathcal{L}_2$ concept descriptions. Proving inexpressivity is more challenging. The first formal investigation of the expressive power of DLs was performed in [1,2], but in a rather ad hoc manner. More fundamental characterizations of the expressive power of various concept description languages up to the DL $\mathcal{ALC}$ based on the model-theoretic notion of *bisimulation* are given in [20]. Basically, this approach (pioneered by van Benthem [28] for the modal logic K, which is a syntactic variant of $\mathcal{ALC}$) characterizes a given DL as the fragment of first-order logic (FOL) that is invariant under an appropriate notion of bisimulation.

The expressive power of $\mathcal{ALC}$ can, for instance, be extended by enabling the use of numerical constraints within concept descriptions. In the extension $\mathcal{ALCQ}$ of $\mathcal{ALC}$, qualified number restrictions [18] can be employed to constrain the number of role successors belonging to a certain concept; e.g., Person $\sqcap$ ($\geq$ 3 child.Female) $\sqcap$ ($\leq$ 2 pet.Dog) describes persons that have at least 3 daughters and at most 2 dogs as pets. The DL $\mathcal{ALCSCC}$ [3] extends $\mathcal{ALCQ}$ with very expressive counting constraints on role successors expressed in the logic QFBAPA [19]. Since QFBAPA only considers finite sets and their cardinalities, the semantics of $\mathcal{ALCSCC}$ is restricted to finitely branching interpretations, where each element can have only finitely many role successors. In $\mathcal{ALCSCC}$ one can, e.g., describe persons that have more daughters than they have dogs as pets, without using specific numbers as upper/lower bounds for the numbers of pet dogs and daughters. Bisimulation-based characterizations of $\mathcal{ALCQ}$ (or its modal logic variant of K extended with graded modalities) can be found in [22,25,26]. In [7,8], we have investigated the expressivity of DLs with expressive counting constraints. However, to dispense with the requirement that interpretations be finitely branching, we used an infinite variant QFBAPA$^\infty$ of QFBAPA to formulate these constraints, which yields the variant $\mathcal{ALCSCC}^\infty$ of $\mathcal{ALCSCC}$. We were able to show that $\mathcal{ALCSCC}^\infty$ is not a fragment of FOL and characterized the first-order fragment of this logic ($\mathcal{ALCCQU}$ or equivalently $\mathcal{ALCQt}$) using a form of counting bisimulation [22]. The *first major contribution* of the present paper is to prove the same results for $\mathcal{ALCSCC}$, where only finitely branching interpretations are available. The proof techniques used in [7,8], which were inspired by the ones in [22], cannot be employed in this setting since they depend on compactness of FOL, which does not hold for the restriction of FOL to finitely branching interpretations. Instead, we employ a proof technique inspired by [25,27], which utilizes locality properties of FOL rather than compactness. Interestingly, this approach can deal with arbitrary interpretations, finitely branching interpretations, and finite interpretations in a uniform way.

An orthogonal approach for employing numerical constraints within concept descriptions is the use of numerical concrete domains [14,21]. In a DL with a concrete domain, concrete objects such as numbers or strings can be assigned to individuals using partial functions called *features*. For example, the concept description Person $\sqcap$ $\exists$child age, pet age.$<$ describes persons that have a child that is younger than one of their pets. Here, age is a feature that assigns a rational number, their age, to some of the elements of the interpretation domain, and $<$ is the usual smaller relation between rational numbers. In [9,10], we have investigated the abstract expressive power of DLs with concrete domains, which only considers the abstract part of interpretations, i.e., ignores the values assigned to features. We have shown that the abstract expressive power of $\mathcal{ALC}(\mathfrak{D})$, i.e., $\mathcal{ALC}$ extended with the concrete domains $\mathfrak{D}$, is contained in FOL for certain concrete domains, but have also exhibited a large class of concrete domains for which this is not the case. The *second major contribution* of the present paper is to introduce a notion of concrete expressive power for DLs with concrete domains that also takes the feature values into account. For example, if we take two concrete domains over the rational numbers, where one has as only predicate $+_1$ (relating $q \in \mathbb{Q}$ with $q + 1$) and the other $+_2$ (relating $q \in \mathbb{Q}$ with $q + 2$), then the extensions of $\mathcal{ALC}$ with these concrete domains have the same abstract expressive power, but their concrete expressive power is incomparable. Using proof techniques similar to the ones employed for $\mathcal{ALCSCC}$ we can characterize $\mathcal{ALC}(\mathfrak{D})$ as the fragment of $\mathrm{FOL}(\mathfrak{D})$ (i.e., FOL extended with the concrete domain $\mathfrak{D}$) that is invariant under an appropriate notion of bisimulation.

A technical report containing detailed proofs of all the results introduced in this paper is available online [11].

2   Preliminaries

We start by introducing the base logic $\mathcal{ALC}$ before defining its two orthogonal extensions with numerical constraints. Since here we focus on the expressivity of concept description languages, we do not introduce TBoxes, ABoxes, or reasoning problems (see [13] for more details on $\mathcal{ALC}$ and other classical DLs).

The classical DL $\mathcal{ALC}$ Given disjoint, at most countable sets N_C and N_R of *concept* and *role names*, $\mathcal{ALC}$ concept descriptions (*concepts* for short) are built from concept names using negation ($\neg C$), conjunction ($C \sqcap D$), and *existential restrictions* ($\exists r.C$), where $r \in N_R$ and C, D are $\mathcal{ALC}$ concept descriptions. As usual, we define $C \sqcup D := \neg(\neg C \sqcap \neg D)$ (disjunction), $\forall r.C := \neg\exists r.\neg C$ (value restriction) and $\top := A \sqcup \neg A$ (top concept). An *interpretation* $\mathcal{I}$ consists of a non-empty *domain* $\Delta^{\mathcal{I}}$ and a mapping $\cdot^{\mathcal{I}}$ assigning a set $A^{\mathcal{I}} \subseteq \Delta^{\mathcal{I}}$ to $A \in N_C$ and a binary relation $r^{\mathcal{I}} \subseteq \Delta^{\mathcal{I}} \times \Delta^{\mathcal{I}}$ to $r \in N_R$. For $d \in \Delta^{\mathcal{I}}$, we define $r^{\mathcal{I}}(d) := \{e \in \Delta^{\mathcal{I}} \mid (d, e) \in r^{\mathcal{I}}\}$. We extend $\cdot^{\mathcal{I}}$ to concepts by $(\neg C)^{\mathcal{I}} := \Delta^{\mathcal{I}} \setminus C^{\mathcal{I}}$, $(C \sqcap D)^{\mathcal{I}} := C^{\mathcal{I}} \cap D^{\mathcal{I}}$ and $(\exists r.C)^{\mathcal{I}} := \{d \in \Delta^{\mathcal{I}} \mid r^{\mathcal{I}}(d) \cap C^{\mathcal{I}} \neq \emptyset\}$. In this DL, the concept of a person not having a dog as a pet can be written as Person $\sqcap$ $\forall$pet.$\neg$Dog.

The DL $\mathcal{ALCSCC}$ This DL employs the logic *QFBAPA* [19] to state cardinality constraints on role successors that are more expressive than existential and value restrictions. In QFBAPA, *set terms* are built from *set variables* and the constants $\emptyset$ and $\mathcal{U}$ using intersection $\cap$, union $\cup$ and complement ^{c}. A *QFBAPA formula* is a Boolean combination of *atomic formulae* of the form

$$m_0 + m_1|s_1| + \cdots + m_k|s_k| \leqslant n_0 + n_1|t_1| + \cdots + n_\ell|t_\ell| \tag{1}$$

where each s_i, t_j is a set term and each m_i, n_j is a natural number.[3] A *solution* σ of a QFBAPA formula ϕ assigns a *finite* set $\sigma(\mathcal{U})$ to $\mathcal{U}$, the empty set to $\emptyset$ and subsets of $\sigma(\mathcal{U})$ to set variables such that ϕ is satisfied by σ, in the standard way. Checking if a QFBAPA formula has a solution is an NP-complete problem [19]. The logic QFBAPA$^\infty$ [7] has the same syntax as QFBAPA, but solutions may assign infinite sets to $\mathcal{U}$. Its satisfiability problem is also NP-complete [7].

$\mathcal{ALCSCC}$ extends the syntax of $\mathcal{ALC}$ with the new constructor *role successor restriction* (or succ-*restriction*) succ(con), where con is an atomic QFBAPA formula with role names and $\mathcal{ALCSCC}$ concept descriptions as set variables [3]. For instance, the concept of all persons that have more daughters than they have dogs as pets can be expressed in $\mathcal{ALCSCC}$ as succ($|\text{pet} \cap \text{Dog}| < |\text{child} \cap \text{Female}|$). Note that existential restrictions $\exists r.C$ are not needed as explicit constructors in this DL since they can be expressed as succ($|r \cap C| \geqslant 1$).

When defining the semantics of $\mathcal{ALCSCC}$, interpretations $\mathcal{I}$ are required in [3] to be *finitely branching*, i.e. such that the set of all role successors $\text{ars}^\mathcal{I}(d) := \bigcup_{r \in \mathsf{N_R}} r^\mathcal{I}(d)$ is finite, for all $d \in \Delta^\mathcal{I}$. Then, each $d \in \Delta^\mathcal{I}$ induces a QFBAPA assignment σ_d, where $\sigma_d(\mathcal{U}) := \text{ars}^\mathcal{I}(d)$, $\sigma_d(r) := r^\mathcal{I}(d)$ for $r \in \mathsf{N_R}$ and $\sigma_d(C) := C^\mathcal{I} \cap \text{ars}^\mathcal{I}(d)$ for concepts C. The mapping $\cdot^\mathcal{I}$ is extended to succ-restrictions by defining $d \in \text{succ}(\text{con})^\mathcal{I}$ iff σ_d is a solution of con.

The DL $\mathcal{ALCSCC}^\infty$ is defined in [7] with the same syntax as $\mathcal{ALCSCC}$, but in the semantics arbitrary interpretations are allowed. Consequently, the assignment σ_d may be such that $\sigma_d(\mathcal{U})$ is infinite, and thus satisfaction of the constraint con by σ_d is evaluated in QFBAPA$^\infty$ rather than QFBAPA.

In the definitions of $\mathcal{ALCSCC}^\infty$ and $\mathcal{ALCSCC}$, we considered two classes of first-order interpretations: the class $\mathbb{C}_{\text{all}}$ of all interpretations and the class $\mathbb{C}_{\text{fb}}$ of finitely branching interpretations. Later on, we will also consider the class $\mathbb{C}_{\text{fin}}$ of all finite interpretations, which is also of interest in DL research [17,23]. Our results on the expressive power will be parameterized with a class $\mathbb{C}$ of interpretations satisfying certain restrictions. Since the syntax of $\mathcal{ALCSCC}^\infty$ and $\mathcal{ALCSCC}$ coincide, we will in the following always talk about $\mathcal{ALCSCC}$ concepts. However, if $\mathbb{C}$ contains interpretations that are not finitely branching, then the semantics uses QFBAPA$^\infty$ rather than QFBAPA.

DLs with Concrete Domains. Following [12,14,21], we use the term *concrete domain* to refer to a relational structure $\mathfrak{D} = (D, \ldots, P^D, \ldots)$ over a non-empty, at most countable relational signature, where D is a non-empty set, and each predicate P has an associated arity $k_P \in \mathbb{N}$ and is interpreted by a relation $P^D \subseteq D^{k_P}$. An example is the structure $\mathfrak{Q} := (\mathbb{Q}, <, =, >)$ over

---

[3] Following [8], we use a streamlined definition of QFBAPA that does not explicitly introduce set constraints and divisibility constraints.

the rational numbers $\mathbb{Q}$ with standard binary ordering and equality relations. Given a countable set V of variables, a *constraint system* over V is a set $\mathfrak{C}$ of constraints $P(v_1, \ldots, v_k)$, where $v_1, \ldots, v_k \in V$ and P is a k-ary predicate of $\mathfrak{D}$. We denote by $V(\mathfrak{C})$ the set of variables that occur in $\mathfrak{C}$. The constraint system $\mathfrak{C}$ is *satisfiable* if there is a mapping $h \colon V(\mathfrak{C}) \to D$ such that $P(v_1, \ldots, v_k) \in \mathfrak{C}$ implies $(h(v_1), \ldots, h(v_k)) \in P^D$. The *constraint satisfaction problem* for $\mathfrak{D}$, denoted $\mathrm{CSP}(\mathfrak{D})$, asks if a given finite constraint system $\mathfrak{C}$ over $\mathfrak{D}$ is satisfiable. The CSP of $\mathfrak{Q}$ is decidable in polynomial time, by reduction to $<$-cycle detection: for example, the system $\{x_1 < x_2,\ x_2 < x_3,\ x_3 < x_1\}$ is unsatisfiable over $\mathfrak{Q}$.

When integrating such a concrete domain into the DL $\mathcal{ALC}$, it needs to satisfy certain restrictions to obtain a decidable DL. Without a TBox, admissibility is required in [12] whereas in the presence of a TBox the stronger ω-admissibility is required in [14,21]. In the context of our investigation of the expressive power of DLs with concrete domains, it is sufficient to assume that negated constraints can be expressed using one or more non-negated ones.

Definition 1. *A structure $\mathfrak{D}$ is* weakly closed under negation (*WCUN*) *if for all $k \geqslant 1$ and all k-ary relations P of $\mathfrak{D}$ there are k-ary relations $P_1, \ldots, P_{n_P}$ such that $(d_1, \ldots, d_k) \notin P^D$ iff $(d_1, \ldots, d_k) \in \bigcup_{i=1}^{n_P} P_i^D$ for all $d_1, \ldots, d_k \in D^k$.*

It is easy to see that both admissible and ω-admissible concrete domains satisfy this property. Examples of ω-admissible, and thus WCUN, concrete domains are Allen's interval algebra, RCC8 and $\mathfrak{Q}$ [14,21]. For example the negated predicate $\neq$ in $\mathfrak{Q}$ is obtained as the union of $<$ and $>$.

To integrate a given concrete domain $\mathfrak{D}$ into $\mathcal{ALC}$, we complement $\mathsf{N_C}$ and $\mathsf{N_R}$ with a finite set $\mathsf{N_F}$ of *feature names* that connect individuals with values in D [12]. A *feature path* p is of the form f or rf with $r \in \mathsf{N_R}$ and $f \in \mathsf{N_F}$. For instance, age is a feature name as well as a feature path, while child age is a feature path including the role name child. The DL $\mathcal{ALC}(\mathfrak{D})$ extends $\mathcal{ALC}$ with *concrete domain restrictions* (or *CD-restrictions*) of the form $\exists p_1, \ldots, p_k.P$ and $\forall p_1, \ldots, p_k.P$, where p_i are feature paths and P is a k-ary predicate of $\mathfrak{D}$. An interpretation $\mathcal{I}$ assigns to $f \in \mathsf{N_F}$ a *partial* function $f^{\mathcal{I}} \colon \Delta^{\mathcal{I}} \rightharpoonup D$. A feature path p is mapped to $p^{\mathcal{I}} \subseteq \Delta^{\mathcal{I}} \times D$ by defining[4] $p^{\mathcal{I}}(d) := \{f^{\mathcal{I}}(d)\}$ if $p = f$ and $p^{\mathcal{I}}(d) := \{f^{\mathcal{I}}(e) \mid e \in r^{\mathcal{I}}(d)\}$ if $p = rf$. Then we can define

$$(\exists p_1, \ldots, p_k.P)^{\mathcal{I}} := \{d \in \Delta^{\mathcal{I}} \mid some \text{ tuple in } p_1^{\mathcal{I}}(d) \times \cdots \times p_k^{\mathcal{I}}(d) \text{ is in } P^D\}$$

$$(\forall p_1, \ldots, p_k.P)^{\mathcal{I}} := \{d \in \Delta^{\mathcal{I}} \mid every \text{ tuple in } p_1^{\mathcal{I}}(d) \times \cdots \times p_k^{\mathcal{I}}(d) \text{ is in } P^D\}.$$

For example, one can describe individuals having a child that is younger than one of their pets using $\exists$child age, pet age.$<$.

3   The Expressive Power of $\mathcal{ALCSCC}$

In this section, we first introduce a notion of bisimulation, called Presburger bisimulation, such that $\mathcal{ALCSCC}$ concept descriptions are invariant under such

---

[4] In a slight abuse of notation, we view $f^{\mathcal{I}}(d)$ both as a value and as a singleton set.

bisimulations, i.e., bisimilar elements belong to the same $\mathcal{ALCSCC}$ concept descriptions. Next, we consider an approximate variant of Presburger bisimulation and show that, while not all $\mathcal{ALCSCC}$ concept descriptions are invariant under this notion, the ones that are expressible in first-order logic are. This shows that there are $\mathcal{ALCSCC}$ concept descriptions that are not expressible in FOL. Finally, we characterize the fragment of $\mathcal{ALCSCC}$ that is first-order definable as the logic $\mathcal{ALCQt}$, for which successor constraints have a restricted form.

Presburger Bisimulation. Assume that N_C and N_R are finite. We base our definition of Presburger bisimulations on the notion of *safe role types*, which are non-empty subsets of N_R. Intuitively, such a role type stands for the intersection of its elements intersected with the complements of the non-elements. For example, if $N_R = \{r, s, t\}$, then the safe role type $\{r, s\}$ corresponds to the set term $r \cap s \cap t^c$. More formally, safe role types τ are interpreted in an interpretation $\mathcal{I}$ as the binary relation

$$\tau^{\mathcal{I}} := (\textstyle\bigcap_{r \in \tau} r^{\mathcal{I}} \setminus (\bigcup_{r \in N_R \setminus \tau} r^{\mathcal{I}})) \subseteq \bigcup_{r \in N_R} r^{\mathcal{I}}.$$

The fact that safe role types are non-empty sets of role names ensures the inclusion stated above, i.e., any $\tau^{\mathcal{I}}$ is an $r^{\mathcal{I}}$ successor for at least one role name r, which justifies the name *safe*. Consequently, for all $d \in \Delta^{\mathcal{I}}$, the set $\tau^{\mathcal{I}}(d) := \{e \in \Delta^{\mathcal{I}} \mid (d, e) \in \tau^{\mathcal{I}}\}$ is a subset of $\mathsf{ars}^{\mathcal{I}}(d)$, and every $e \in \mathsf{ars}^{\mathcal{I}}(d)$ belongs to $\tau^{\mathcal{I}}(d)$ for exactly one safe role type τ. The set N_R must be finite, in order to encode safe role types as well-defined set terms. For $\mathcal{ALCSCC}^{\infty}$ it was shown in [7] that each set term s occurring within a succ-restriction can be rewritten as the disjoint union of terms of the form $\tau \cap C$ where τ is a safe role type and C an $\mathcal{ALCSCC}^{\infty}$ concept [7]. The same also holds for $\mathcal{ALCSCC}$. Following [7], we modify the notion of *counting bisimulation* from [22] by using safe role types in place of role names to obtain Presburger bisimulations (called $\mathcal{ALCQt}$ bisimulations in [7]).

Definition 2. *Let N_C and N_R be finite and $\mathbb{C}$ a class of interpretations. The binary relation $\rho \subseteq \Delta^{\mathcal{I}} \times \Delta^{\mathcal{J}}$ is a Presburger (Pr) bisimulation between the interpretations $\mathcal{I}$ and $\mathcal{J}$ if for all $A \in N_C$ and all safe role types τ over N_R the following properties are satisfied:*

Atomic *$(d, e) \in \rho$ implies $d \in A^{\mathcal{I}}$ iff $e \in A^{\mathcal{J}}$;*
Forth *if $(d, e) \in \rho$ and $D \subseteq \tau^{\mathcal{I}}(d)$ is finite, then there is a set $E \subseteq \tau^{\mathcal{J}}(e)$ such that ρ contains a bijection between D and E;*
Back *if $(d, e) \in \rho$ and $E \subseteq \tau^{\mathcal{J}}(e)$ is finite, then there is a set $D \subseteq \tau^{\mathcal{I}}(d)$ such that ρ contains a bijection between D and E.*

We call $d \in \Delta^{\mathcal{I}}$ and $e \in \Delta^{\mathcal{J}}$ Pr bisimilar if $(d, e) \in \rho$ for some Pr bisimulation ρ between $\mathcal{I}$ and $\mathcal{J}$. A concept C is $\mathbb{C}$-invariant under Pr bisimulation if $d \in C^{\mathcal{I}}$ iff $e \in C^{\mathcal{J}}$ holds for all Pr bisimilar individuals $d \in \Delta^{\mathcal{I}}$, $e \in \Delta^{\mathcal{J}}$ with $\mathcal{I}, \mathcal{J} \in \mathbb{C}$.

In [7] we proved that $\mathcal{ALCSCC}^{\infty}$ concepts are $\mathbb{C}_{\mathsf{all}}$-invariant under Pr bisimulation. A very similar proof (by induction on the structure of concept descriptions) can be used to show the corresponding result for $\mathcal{ALCSCC}$, where only finitely branching interpretations are considered.

Theorem 1. *Every $\mathcal{ALCSCC}$ concept is $\mathbb{C}_{\mathsf{fb}}$-invariant under Pr bisimulation.*

Proof. Let $\mathcal{I}, \mathcal{J} \in \mathbb{C}_{\mathsf{fb}}$ and ρ a Pr bisimulation relating $d \in \Delta^{\mathcal{I}}$ and $e \in \Delta^{\mathcal{J}}$. We show by induction on the structure of an $\mathcal{ALCSCC}$ concept C that $d \in C^{\mathcal{I}}$ iff $e \in C^{\mathcal{J}}$ holds. The cases where C is a concept name, a conjunction of concepts or the negation of a concept are similar to the analogous cases in the proof of a corresponding result for $\mathcal{ALC}$ [13], and are omitted.

Thus, we focus on the case $C = \mathsf{succ}(\mathsf{con})$, where we inductively assume that every subconcept of C is $\mathbb{C}_{\mathsf{fb}}$-invariant under Pr bisimulation. Recall that con is of the form (1). By applying distributivity of set intersection over set union, it is easy to show that any set term occurring in con can be written as the disjoint union of set terms of the form $\tau \cap F$ where τ is a safe role type and F is a Boolean combination of concepts to which the induction assumption applies. The reason we can restrict the attention to safe role types here lies in the semantics of $\mathcal{ALCSCC}$, which considers only role successors when evaluating set terms. We provide for every $\mathcal{ALCSCC}$ concept F and safe role type τ over $\mathsf{N_R}$ an injective mapping from $D := \tau^{\mathcal{I}}(d) \cap F^{\mathcal{I}}$ to $E := \tau^{\mathcal{J}}(e) \cap F^{\mathcal{J}}$ and vice versa. This proves that these sets have the same size, and thus that con is evaluated equally w.r.t. d and e. Note that, since $\mathcal{I}$ and $\mathcal{J}$ are finitely branching, the sets D and E are both finite. Overall, this implies that $d \in C^{\mathcal{I}}$ iff $e \in C^{\mathcal{J}}$.

The required injections are obtained as follows. Thanks to the forth property, we find a set $E' \subseteq \tau^{\mathcal{J}}(e)$ such that ρ contains a bijection between D and E'. By our induction hypothesis, the concept F is $\mathbb{C}_{\mathsf{fb}}$-invariant under Pr bisimulation, so we obtain that $E' \subseteq C^{\mathcal{J}}$. Then, $E' \subseteq E$ holds, and the bijection between D and E' is the sought injective mapping from D to E. Using the back property, we similarly prove that there is an injective mapping from E to D.

Together with the other cases, this concludes our proof, and thus we conclude that every $\mathcal{ALCSCC}$ concept is $\mathbb{C}_{\mathsf{fb}}$-invariant under Pr bisimulation.   □

Since finite interpretations are finitely branching, this also implies $\mathbb{C}_{\mathsf{fin}}$-invariance of $\mathcal{ALCSCC}$ concepts under Pr bisimulation.

As usual, such invariance results can be employed to prove that a certain DL $\mathcal{L}$ cannot be expressed in $\mathcal{ALCSCC}$. For this, it is sufficient to find an example of an $\mathcal{L}$ concept that is not invariant under Pr bisimulation. In [11], we apply this approach to show that the abstract expressive power [10] of $\mathcal{ALC}(\mathfrak{Q})$ is not contained in that of $\mathcal{ALCSCC}$ on finitely branching interpretations, and that $\mathcal{ALCSCC}^{++}$ [4] is a strict extension of $\mathcal{ALCSCC}$ on finite interpretations.

$\mathcal{ALCSCC}$ goes beyond FOL $\mathcal{ALC}$ and many other DLs are fragments of first-order logic (FOL) [15], in the sense that for every concept description C of the given DL there is a FOL formula $\phi(x)$ such that $\phi^{\mathcal{I}} = C^{\mathcal{I}}$ for all interpretations $\mathcal{I}$, where $\phi^{\mathcal{I}} := \{d \in \Delta^{\mathcal{I}} \mid \mathcal{I} \models \phi(d)\}$. This notion of definability of a concept description by an FOL formula in one free variable can be relativized to a class of models $\mathbb{C}$ in an obvious way. $\mathbb{C}$-invariance of an FOL formula in one free variable under a given notion of bisimulation is also defined in an obvious way.

In [7], we have shown that there are $\mathcal{ALCSCC}^{\infty}$ concepts that are not FOL-definable in this sense w.r.t. $\mathbb{C}_{\mathsf{all}}$. However, since the semantics of $\mathcal{ALCSCC}$ is defined w.r.t. a restricted class of interpretations, this result does not directly transfer to $\mathcal{ALCSCC}$. Our tool for showing non-FOL-definability for $\mathcal{ALCSCC}$ (and incidentally also for $\mathcal{ALCSCC}^\infty$ w.r.t. other classes of interpretations) is a bounded version of Pr bisimulation where one makes only a bounded number ℓ of steps into the interpretation and bounds the cardinalities of the sets considered in the back and forth conditions by a number q. This notion of bisimulation is obtained by adapting the bisimulation-based characterization of modal logic with graded modalities w.r.t. finite models in [25] to our more expressive logic.

Definition 3. *Let* N_C *and* N_R *be finite and* $q, \ell \in \mathbb{N}$*. The relation* $\rho \subseteq \Delta^{\mathcal{I}} \times \Delta^{\mathcal{J}}$ *is a Pr* $(q,0)$*-bisimulation between the interpretations* $\mathcal{I}$ *and* $\mathcal{J}$ *if it satisfies the (atomic) condition of Definition 2, and it is a Pr* $(q, \ell+1)$*-bisimulation if it is a Pr* (q,ℓ)*-bisimulation that satisfies the following for all safe role types* τ*:*

> (q,ℓ)**-forth** *if* $(d, e) \in \rho$ *and* $D \subseteq \tau^{\mathcal{I}}(d)$ *with* $|D| \leqslant q$*, then there are* $E \subseteq \tau^{\mathcal{J}}(e)$ *and a Pr* (q,ℓ)*-bisimulation* ρ' *that contains a bijection between* D *and* E*;*
> (q,ℓ)**-back** *if* $(d, e) \in \rho$ *and* $E \subseteq \tau^{\mathcal{J}}(e)$ *with* $|E| \leqslant q$*, then there are* $D \subseteq \tau^{\mathcal{I}}(d)$ *and a Pr* (q,ℓ)*-bisimulation* ρ' *that contains a bijection between* D *and* E*.*

The notions of Pr (q,ℓ)*-bisimilarity and* $\mathbb{C}$*-invariance w.r.t. Pr* (q,ℓ)*-bisimulation are defined similarly to how it was done in Definition 2.*

Theorem 1 states that all $\mathcal{ALCSCC}$ concepts are invariant under Pr bisimulation. For Pr (q,ℓ)-bisimulation, this need not hold, as stated in the next theorem.

Theorem 2. *There is an* $\mathcal{ALCSCC}$ *concept* C *such that, for all values of* q *and* ℓ*, the concept* C *is not* $\mathbb{C}_{fb}$*-invariant under Pr* (q,ℓ)*-bisimulation.*

Proof. Consider the $\mathcal{ALCSCC}$ concept $C := \mathsf{succ}(|r \cap A| = |r \cap \neg A|)$, which has been used in [7] to show that $\mathcal{ALCSCC}^\infty$ is not a fragment of FOL. For $n, m \in \mathbb{N}$, let $\mathcal{I}_{m,n}$ be the finitely branching interpretation containing individuals d and d_i for $i = 1, \ldots, m+n$, where r is interpreted as the set of tuples (d, d_i) for $i = 1, \ldots, m+n$, every d_i with $i = 1, \ldots, m$ is in A and every other individual is not in A. Given $q \in \mathbb{N}$ we consider $\mathcal{I}_{q,q}$ and $\mathcal{I}_{q,q+1}$, and notice that $d \in \Delta^{\mathcal{I}_{q,q}}$ and $d \in \Delta^{\mathcal{I}_{q,q+1}}$ are Pr (q,ℓ)-bisimilar: the relation mapping $d \in \Delta^{\mathcal{I}_{q,q}}$ to $d \in \Delta^{\mathcal{I}_{q,q+1}}$ and $d_i \in \Delta^{\mathcal{I}_{q,q}}$ to $d_i \in \Delta^{\mathcal{I}_{q,q+1}}$ is a Pr (q,ℓ)-bisimulation for all $\ell \in \mathbb{N}$. However, $d \in C^{\mathcal{I}_{q,q}}$ holds, whereas $d \notin C^{\mathcal{I}_{q,q+1}}$.   □

Our goal is now to show that this cannot happen for $\mathcal{ALCSCC}$ concepts that are FOL-definable w.r.t. $\mathbb{C}_{fb}$ or $\mathbb{C}_{fin}$ (or more generally a class $\mathbb{C}$ of interpretations satisfying certain closure properties). The proof of this result uses certain locality properties of FOL formulae that are invariant under Pr bisimulation.

Definition 4. *Let* $\mathcal{I}$ *be an interpretation. The* distance *of* d *and* d' *in* $\mathcal{I}$ *is the smallest value* $\ell \in \mathbb{N}$ *for which there is a sequence of elements* $d_1, \ldots, d_{\ell+1} \in \Delta^{\mathcal{I}}$ *where* $d_1 = d$*,* $d_{\ell+1} = d'$ *and* d_i *is a role successor or predecessor of* d_{i+1} *for* $i = 1, \ldots, \ell$*, or* ∞ *if such a number does not exist. The* ℓ*-neighborhood* $\mathcal{N}_\ell^{\mathcal{I}}[d]$

of d is derived from $\mathcal{I}$ by taking the substructure consisting of all individuals with distance at most ℓ from d.

The class $\mathbb{C}$ of interpretations is *closed under neighborhoods* if $\mathcal{N}_\ell^{\mathcal{I}}[\![d]\!] \in \mathbb{C}$ for all $\mathcal{I} \in \mathbb{C}$, $d \in \Delta^{\mathcal{I}}$ and $\ell \in \mathbb{N}$. The FOL *formula $\phi(x)$ is ℓ-local w.r.t.* $\mathbb{C}$ if for all $\mathcal{I} \in \mathbb{C}$ and all $d \in \Delta^{\mathcal{I}}$ we have that $\mathcal{I} \models \phi(d)$ iff $\mathcal{N}_\ell^{\mathcal{I}}[\![d]\!] \models \phi(d)$.

Interestingly, there is a close relationship between ℓ-locality of FOL formulae and invariance under finite disjoint union.

Definition 5 (Disjoint union). *Given a finite index set $\mathbb{I}$ and a family of interpretations $(\mathcal{I}_\nu)_{\nu \in \mathbb{I}} \subseteq \mathbb{C}$, their* finite disjoint union $\mathcal{I}$ *is defined by:*

$$\Delta^{\mathcal{I}} := \{(d, \nu) \mid \nu \in \mathbb{I} \text{ and } d \in \Delta^{\mathcal{I}_\nu}\},$$
$$A^{\mathcal{I}} := \{(d, \nu) \mid \nu \in \mathbb{I} \text{ and } d \in A^{\mathcal{I}_\nu}\} \quad \text{for all } A \in \mathsf{N_C},$$
$$r^{\mathcal{I}} := \{((d, \nu), (e, \nu)) \mid \nu \in \mathbb{I} \text{ and } (d, e) \in r^{\mathcal{I}_\nu}\} \quad \text{for all } r \in \mathsf{N_R}.$$

The FOL formula $\phi(x)$ is $\mathbb{C}$-invariant under finite disjoint unions if, for any finite disjoint union constructed as above, $\mathcal{I}_\nu \models \phi(d)$ iff $\mathcal{I} \models \phi((d, \nu))$ holds for every $\nu \in \mathbb{I}$ and $d \in \Delta^{\mathcal{I}_\nu}$. We say that $\mathbb{C}$ is closed under finite disjoint unions if $\mathcal{I}_\nu \in \mathbb{C}$ for all $\nu \in \mathbb{I}$ implies that the disjoint union of $(\mathcal{I}_\nu)_{\nu \in \mathbb{I}}$ also belongs to $\mathbb{C}$ whenever the index set $\mathbb{I}$ is finite.

By proving that $\rho := \{(d, (d, \nu)) \mid d \in \Delta^{\mathcal{I}_\nu}, \nu \in \mathbb{I}\}$ is a Pr bisimulation, we obtain the following property for formulae that are $\mathbb{C}$-invariant under Pr bisimulation.

Proposition 1. *If the FOL formula $\phi(x)$ is $\mathbb{C}$-invariant under Pr bisimulation, then it is $\mathbb{C}$-invariant under finite disjoint unions.*

By Theorem 1, this implies that FOL formulae that are equivalent to $\mathcal{ALCSCC}$ concepts are $\mathbb{C}_{\mathsf{fb}}$- and $\mathbb{C}_{\mathsf{fin}}$-invariant under disjoint union. Before we can state the crucial lemma from [24], we must introduce one more notation. We call the class $\mathbb{C}$ of interpretations *localizable* if it is closed under both neighborhoods and finite disjoint unions.[5] Note that our classes $\mathbb{C}_{\mathsf{all}}$, $\mathbb{C}_{\mathsf{fb}}$ and $\mathbb{C}_{\mathsf{fin}}$ are localizable.

Lemma 1 ([24]). *If $\mathbb{C}$ is localizable, then any FOL formula $\phi(x)$ of quantifier depth q that is $\mathbb{C}$-invariant under finite disjoint unions is $(2^q - 1)$-local w.r.t. $\mathbb{C}$.*

Combining this lemma with Proposition 1, we can now link ℓ-locality with invariance under Pr bisimulation.

Corollary 1. *If $\mathbb{C}$ is localizable, then any FOL formula $\phi(x)$ of quantifier depth q that is $\mathbb{C}$-invariant under Pr bisimulation is ℓ-local w.r.t. $\mathbb{C}$ for $\ell := 2^q - 1$.*

Our next goal is now to show that, for FOL formulae, invariance under Pr bisimulation is equivalent to invariance under Pr (q,ℓ)-bisimulation for some $q, \ell \in \mathbb{N}$. Our first step in this direction is the following result for trees, whose proof can be found in [11].

---

[5] These conditions on $\mathbb{C}$ are not stated explicitly in [24], but are implicitly assumed.

Theorem 3. *If $\mathcal{I}$, $\mathcal{J}$ are trees of depth at most ℓ with roots d, e that are Pr (q,ℓ)-bisimilar, then these roots satisfy the same FOL formulae $\phi(x)$ of quantifier depth at most q.*

While not all interpretations in a class $\mathbb{C}$ need to be tree-shaped, we show that, for every interpretation in $\mathbb{C}_{all}$, $\mathbb{C}_{fb}$ or $\mathbb{C}_{fin}$, it is possible to find a Pr bisimilar interpretation in this class where the ℓ-neighborhood of a specific individual d is a tree with root d. Normally, this is achieved by unravelling [13], but this may yield an infinite interpretation, and is thus not suitable for our setting, where we are also interested in the class $\mathbb{C}_{fin}$. Instead, we introduce *partial unravelling* of $\mathcal{I}$, which preserves finiteness and (like unraveling) finite branching. Intuitively, the ℓ-*unravelling* of an interpretation $\mathcal{I}$ at an element $d \in \Delta^{\mathcal{I}}$ applies unraveling up to length ℓ, and then adds a copy of $\mathcal{I}$ at the end. The exact definition of this operation, which is an adaptation of the unravelling operation described in [13], can be found in [11]. Here, we only state two important properties of it.

Proposition 2. *Let $\mathcal{I}_\ell^d$ be the ℓ-unravelling of the interpretation $\mathcal{I}$ at $d \in \Delta^{\mathcal{I}}$, $\langle d \rangle$ the element corresponding to d in $\mathcal{I}_\ell^d$. Then,*

1. *The elements $d \in \Delta^{\mathcal{I}}$ and $\langle d \rangle \in \Delta^{\mathcal{I}_\ell^d}$ are Pr bisimilar.*
2. *The ℓ-neighborhood $\mathcal{N}_\ell^{\mathcal{I}_\ell^d}[\![\langle d \rangle]\!]$ of $\langle d \rangle$ in $\mathcal{I}_\ell^d$ is a tree of depth at most ℓ with root $\langle d \rangle$.*

The class $\mathbb{C}$ of interpretations is *closed under partial unravelling* if $\mathcal{I} \in \mathbb{C}$ implies $\mathcal{I}_\ell^d \in \mathbb{C}$ for all $\ell \in \mathbb{N}$. The following result links invariance under Pr bisimulation with invariance under Pr (q,ℓ)-bisimulation for FOL formulae.

Theorem 4. *Let $\mathbb{C}$ be localizable and closed under partial unravelling. For all FOL formulae $\phi(x)$, the following are equivalent:*

1. *$\phi(x)$ is $\mathbb{C}$-invariant under Pr bisimulation.*
2. *$\phi(x)$ is $\mathbb{C}$-invariant under Pr (q,ℓ)-bisimulation for some $q, \ell \in \mathbb{N}$.*

Proof. The implication "2. $\Rightarrow$ 1." is an immediate consequence of the fact that every Pr bisimulation is also a Pr (q,ℓ)-bisimulation for all $q, \ell \in \mathbb{N}$.

To prove the other direction, we assume 1. and that $\phi(x)$ has quantifier depth q. By assume 1 we deduce that $\phi(x)$ is ℓ-local w.r.t. $\mathbb{C}$ for $\ell := 2^q - 1$. Given $\mathcal{I}, \mathcal{J} \in \mathbb{C}$ and $d \in \Delta^{\mathcal{I}}$, $e \in \Delta^{\mathcal{J}}$, we know that the ℓ-unravellings $\mathcal{I}_\ell^d$ and $\mathcal{J}_\ell^e$ and the ℓ-neighborhoods $\mathcal{N}_d := \mathcal{N}_\ell^{\mathcal{I}_\ell^d}[\![\langle d \rangle]\!]$ and $\mathcal{N}_e := \mathcal{N}_\ell^{\mathcal{J}_\ell^e}[\![\langle e \rangle]\!]$ also belong to $\mathbb{C}$. Since $\phi(x)$ is $\mathbb{C}$-invariant under Pr bisimulation and ℓ-local w.r.t. $\mathbb{C}$ we obtain

$$\mathcal{I} \models \phi(d) \text{ iff } \mathcal{I}_\ell^d \models \phi(\langle d \rangle) \text{ iff } \mathcal{N}_d \models \phi(\langle d \rangle) \text{ and}$$
$$\mathcal{J} \models \phi(e) \text{ iff } \mathcal{J}_\ell^e \models \phi(\langle e \rangle) \text{ iff } \mathcal{N}_e \models \phi(\langle e \rangle). \qquad \text{(by Proposition 2)}$$

If ρ is a Pr (q,ℓ)-bisimulation with $(d,e) \in \rho$, then combining this relation with the Pr bisimulations linking d and $\langle d \rangle$ and e and $\langle e \rangle$ shows that there is a Pr (q,ℓ)-bisimulation ρ' between $\mathcal{I}_\ell^d$ and $\mathcal{I}_\ell^e$ with $(\langle d \rangle, \langle e \rangle) \in \rho'$. Since such a bisimulation looks only ℓ steps into the interpretation, the restriction of ρ' to the respective ℓ-neighborhoods $\mathcal{N}_d$ and $\mathcal{N}_e$ is also a Pr (q,ℓ)-bisimulation. Proposition 2 says that these neighborhoods are trees of depth at most ℓ, and thus we can apply Theorem 3 to obtain $\mathcal{N}_d \models \phi(\langle d \rangle)$ iff $\mathcal{N}_e \models \phi(\langle e \rangle)$.   □

Together with Theorem 2, this yields the desired non-definability results since the classes $\mathbb{C}_{\mathsf{all}}$, $\mathbb{C}_{\mathsf{fb}}$, and $\mathbb{C}_{\mathsf{fin}}$ are localizable and closed under partial unravelling.

Corollary 2. *Let $\mathbb{C}$ be localizable and closed under partial unravelling. Then there are $\mathcal{ALCSCC}$ concepts that are not FOL-definable w.r.t. $\mathbb{C}$.*

The first-order fragment of $\mathcal{ALCSCC}$. In [7], we have established that the FOL-definable subset of $\mathcal{ALCSCC}^\infty$ corresponds to the DL $\mathcal{ALCQt}$. This DL can be seen both as the extension of $\mathcal{ALCQ}$ where safe role types instead of just role names can be used in qualified number restrictions, and as the restriction of $\mathcal{ALCSCC}$ where only successor restrictions of the form $\mathsf{succ}(|\tau \cap C| \geqslant q)$ are available, where τ is a safe role type, $q \in \mathbb{N}$, and C is an $\mathcal{ALCQt}$ concept. To make the relationship to qualified number restrictions clear, we write such successor restrictions as $(\geqslant q\,\tau.C)$, and call them qualified number restrictions. Saying that this result was proved in [7] for $\mathcal{ALCSCC}^\infty$ means that it was shown w.r.t. the class $\mathbb{C}_{\mathsf{all}}$. In the following we prove that it also holds for the classes $\mathbb{C}_{\mathsf{fb}}$ and $\mathbb{C}_{\mathsf{fin}}$.

It is easy to see that every $\mathcal{ALCQt}$ concept can be translated into an equivalent FOL formula with one free variable, and thus $\mathcal{ALCQt}$ is a FOL-definable fragment of $\mathcal{ALCSCC}$. We will show that all FOL-definable concepts of $\mathcal{ALCSCC}$ are equivalent to one in $\mathcal{ALCQt}$. We define the *depth* of an $\mathcal{ALCQt}$ concept to be the maximal nesting of qualified number restrictions and the *breadth* to be the maximal number occurring in a qualified number restriction. With $\mathcal{ALCQt}_{q,\ell}$ we denote the set of $\mathcal{ALCQt}$ concepts of depth at most ℓ and breadth at most q. The following results for $\mathcal{ALCQt}_{q,\ell}$ are established in [11].

Proposition 3. *Let $\mathbb{C}$ be a class of interpretations, $q, \ell \in \mathbb{N}$, and assume that $\mathsf{N_C}$ and $\mathsf{N_R}$ are finite. Then the following holds:*

1. *Every $\mathcal{ALCQt}_{q,\ell}$ concept is $\mathbb{C}$-invariant under Pr (q,ℓ)-bisimulation.*
2. *Up to $\mathbb{C}$-equivalence, there are only finitely many $\mathcal{ALCQt}_{q,\ell}$ concepts.*
3. *For every $\mathcal{I} \in \mathbb{C}$ and $d \in \Delta^{\mathcal{I}}$ there is an $\mathcal{ALCQt}_{q,\ell}$ concept $\mathsf{Bisim}_\ell^q[d]$ such that $d \in \mathsf{Bisim}_\ell^q[d]^{\mathcal{I}}$ and $e \in \mathsf{Bisim}_\ell^q[d]^{\mathcal{J}}$ for an interpretation $\mathcal{J} \in \mathbb{C}$ and $d \in \Delta^{\mathcal{J}}$ implies that d and e are (q,ℓ)-bisimilar.*

Combining these results with Theorems 1 and 4, we obtain the following characterization of the FOL fragment on $\mathcal{ALCSCC}$.

Theorem 5. *Let $\mathbb{C}$ be localizable and closed under partial unravelling and $\mathsf{N_C}$, $\mathsf{N_R}$ be finite. For all FOL formulae $\phi(x)$, the following are equivalent:*

1. *$\phi(x)$ is $\mathbb{C}$-equivalent to some $\mathcal{ALCSCC}$ concept.*
2. *$\phi(x)$ is $\mathbb{C}$-invariant under Pr bisimulation.*
3. *$\phi(x)$ is $\mathbb{C}$-invariant under Pr (q,ℓ)-bisimulation for some $q, \ell \in \mathbb{N}$.*

4. $\phi(x)$ is $\mathbb{C}$-equivalent to some $\mathcal{ALCQt}$ concept.

Proof. That 1. implies 2. follows from Theorem 1 and the equivalence between 2. and 3. is stated in Theorem 4. In addition, 4. trivially implies 1.

Thus, it is sufficient to show that 3. implies 4. To this purpose, we define $C_\phi := \bigsqcup\{\mathsf{Bisim}_\ell^q[d] \mid \mathcal{I} \in \mathbb{C}, d \in \Delta^\mathcal{I} \text{ and } \mathcal{I} \models \phi(d)\}$. By 2. of Proposition 3, this disjunction is finite (up to equivalence), and thus C_ϕ is a well-formed $\mathcal{ALCQt}_{q,\ell}$ concept. First, assume that $\mathcal{I} \models \phi(d)$ with $\mathcal{I} \in \mathbb{C}$ and $d \in \Delta^\mathcal{I}$. Then, $d \in C_\phi^\mathcal{I}$ trivially follows from the fact that $\mathsf{Bisim}_\ell^q[d]$ occurs as a disjunct in C_ϕ.

Conversely, if $d \in C_\phi^\mathcal{I}$, then $d \in (\mathsf{Bisim}_\ell^q[e])^\mathcal{I}$ for some $\mathcal{J} \in \mathbb{C}$ and $e \in \Delta^\mathcal{J}$ such that $\mathcal{J} \models \phi(e)$. By 3. of Proposition 3, this implies that d and e are Pr (q,ℓ)-bisimilar. Hence, 3. of the present proposition implies that $\mathcal{I} \models \phi(d)$. Thus, we have shown that $\phi(x)$ and C_ϕ are $\mathbb{C}$-equivalent. $\square$

Recall that the classes $\mathbb{C}_{\mathsf{all}}$, $\mathbb{C}_{\mathsf{fb}}$ or $\mathbb{C}_{\mathsf{fin}}$ satisfy the assumptions of Theorem 5.

4 The Expressive Power of DLs with Concrete Domains

In [9,10] we have investigated the *abstract expressive power* of DLs with concrete domains, which only considers the abstract part of interpretations, i.e., ignores the values assigned to features. This allowed us to compare classical logics like $\mathcal{ALC}$ and FOL with DLs with concrete domains. Here, we want to compare extensions of $\mathcal{ALC}$ with different concrete domains using an appropriate notion of bisimulation, called $\mathfrak{D}$ bisimulation if $\mathfrak{D}$ is the concrete domain under consideration, and characterize $\mathcal{ALC}(\mathfrak{D})$ as the fragment of FOL($\mathfrak{D}$) that is invariant under $\mathfrak{D}$ bisimulation. The employed notion of bisimulation is the one for $\mathcal{ALC}$ (see, e.g., [13]) extended with an additional clause that deals with feature values. As in the previous section, we show our results not only for the class of all interpretations, but also for the restrictions to finitely branching and finite ones.

Definition 6. *Let $\mathfrak{D}$ be a concrete domain and $\mathcal{I}, \mathcal{J}$ interpretations of $\mathsf{N_C}$, $\mathsf{N_R}$ and $\mathsf{N_F}$ that assign elements of $\mathfrak{D}$ to features from $\mathsf{N_F}$. The relation $\rho \subseteq \Delta^\mathcal{I} \times \Delta^\mathcal{J}$ is a $\mathfrak{D}$ bisimulation between $\mathcal{I}$ and $\mathcal{J}$ if for all $A \in \mathsf{N_C}$, all $r \in \mathsf{N_R}$, all k-ary relations P of $\mathfrak{D}$, and all feature paths $p_1, \ldots, p_k$ over $\mathsf{N_R}$ and $\mathsf{N_F}$:*

atomic *if $(d, e) \in \rho$ then $d \in A^\mathcal{I}$ iff $e \in A^\mathcal{J}$;*
forth *if $(d, e) \in \rho$ and $d' \in r^\mathcal{I}(d)$, then there is $e' \in r^\mathcal{J}(e)$ such that $(d', e') \in \rho$;*
back *if $(d, e) \in \rho$ and $e' \in r^\mathcal{J}(e)$, then there is $d' \in r^\mathcal{I}(d)$ such that $(d', e') \in \rho$.*
features *if $(d, e) \in \rho$, then there is $(v_1, \ldots, v_k) \in P^D$ with $v_1 \in p_1^\mathcal{I}(d)$, $\ldots$, $v_k \in p_k^\mathcal{I}(d)$ iff there is $(w_1, \ldots, w_k) \in P^D$ with $w_1 \in p_1^\mathcal{J}(e)$, $\ldots$, $w_k \in p_k^\mathcal{J}(e)$.*

Bisimilarity between individuals and $\mathbb{C}$-invariance w.r.t. $\mathfrak{D}$ bisimulation are defined similarly to how it was done in Definition 2 w.r.t. Pr bisimulation.

A result analogous to Theorem 1 holds for $\mathcal{ALC}(\mathfrak{D})$ concepts if the concrete domain $\mathfrak{D}$ is weakly closed under negation.

Theorem 6. *If $\mathfrak{D}$ is WCUN and $\mathbb{C}$ is a class of interpretations of $\mathsf{N_C}$, $\mathsf{N_R}$ and $\mathsf{N_F}$ that assign elements of $\mathfrak{D}$ to features from $\mathsf{N_F}$, then every $\mathcal{ALC}(\mathfrak{D})$ concept is $\mathbb{C}$-invariant under $\mathfrak{D}$ bisimulation.*

Proof. The proof by structural induction on the concept C proceeds like the one for $\mathcal{ALC}$ in [13], except for the cases where C is a CD-restriction. We only consider these cases explicitly here. Thus, let ρ be a $\mathfrak{D}$ bisimulation between $\mathcal{I}$ and $\mathcal{J}$ with $(d, e) \in \rho$. We show that d and e satisfy the same CD-restrictions.

If $C := \exists p_1, \ldots, p_k.P$ then $d \in C^{\mathcal{I}}$ implies the existence of $v_1 \in p_1^{\mathcal{I}}(d), \ldots, v_k \in p_k^{\mathcal{I}}(d)$ such that $(v_1, \ldots, v_k) \in P^D$. Since ρ satisfies features, there must be $w_1 \in p_1^{\mathcal{J}}(e)$, $\ldots$, $w_k \in p_k^{\mathcal{J}}(e)$ such that $(w_1, \ldots, w_k) \in P^D$, hence $e \in C^{\mathcal{J}}$. Similarly, we can show that $e \in C^{\mathcal{J}}$ implies $d \in C^{\mathcal{I}}$.

If $C := \forall p_1, \ldots, p_k.P$, then $d \in C^{\mathcal{I}}$ implies that $(v_1, \ldots, v_k) \in P^D$ for all values $v_1 \in p_1^{\mathcal{I}}(d), \ldots, v_k \in p_k^{\mathcal{I}}(d)$. Since $\mathfrak{D}$ is WCUN, this is the case iff there are relations $P_1, \ldots, P_{n_P}$ of $\mathfrak{D}$ such that $(v_1, \ldots, v_k) \notin P_i^D$ for $i = 1, \ldots, n_P$. Using the features condition of ρ, we deduce that $(w_1, \ldots, w_k) \notin P_i^D$ for all $w_1 \in p_1^{\mathcal{J}}(e)$, $\ldots$, $w_k \in p_k^{\mathcal{J}}(e)$ and $i = 1, \ldots, n_P$. By WCUN it follows that $(w_1, \ldots, w_k) \in P^D$, and we conclude that $e \in C^{\mathcal{J}}$. The proof of the other direction is symmetric. $\square$

A Non-expressivity Result. We can use the notion of $\mathfrak{D}$ bisimulation to show that $\mathcal{ALC}(\mathfrak{D})$ cannot express certain concepts of the DL $\mathcal{ALC}(\mathfrak{D}')$, where $\mathfrak{D}'$ has the same domain set as $\mathfrak{D}$, but different relations. Coming back to the example in the introduction, we compare the expressive power of $\mathfrak{Q}_{+1}$ and $\mathfrak{Q}_{+2}$, both having domain set $\mathbb{Q}$, where the former has a binary relation $+_1$ relating $q \in \mathbb{Q}$ and $q + 1$ (and the complementary relation $\neq_{+_1}$) and the latter has a binary relation $+_2$ relating q and $q + 2$ (and the complementary relation $\neq_{+_2}$).

These two DLs have the same *abstract expressive power*. In fact, we can interchange CD-restrictions using relations $+_1$ and $\neq_{+_1}$ with restrictions of the same kind (existential or universal) using relations $+_2$ and $\neq_{+_2}$. Abstract models of a concept in one of these DLs are then the same as of the corresponding concept in the other DL: in one direction, we just double the feature values, and in the other we halve them. Nevertheless, we can show that their *concrete expressive power*, which takes the feature values into account, is incomparable.

Proposition 4. *Let $\mathbb{C}$ be $\mathbb{C}_{\mathsf{all}}$, $\mathbb{C}_{\mathsf{fb}}$, or $\mathbb{C}_{\mathsf{fin}}$. There are $\mathcal{ALC}(\mathfrak{Q}_{+_1})$ concepts that are not $\mathbb{C}$-equivalent to any $\mathcal{ALC}(\mathfrak{Q}_{+_2})$ concept (and vice versa).*

Proof. First, consider the $\mathcal{ALC}(\mathfrak{Q}_{+_1})$ concept $C := \exists rf, rf.+_1$ and assume by contradiction that it is $\mathbb{C}_{\mathsf{all}}$-equivalent to some $\mathcal{ALC}(\mathfrak{Q}_{+_2})$ concept D. Let us consider the interpretations $\mathcal{I}$ and $\mathcal{J}$ depicted in Fig. 1. Then, $a \in C^{\mathcal{I}}$ and by equivalence $a \in D^{\mathcal{I}}$, while $a_1 \notin C^{\mathcal{J}}$ and so $a_1 \notin D^{\mathcal{J}}$ by equivalence. This leads to a contradiction, since the relation ρ between $\mathcal{I}$ and $\mathcal{J}$ is a $\mathfrak{Q}_{+_2}$ bisimulation relating a and a_1, and by Theorem 6 this means that $a \in D^{\mathcal{I}}$ iff $a_1 \in D^{\mathcal{J}}$. Therefore, we conclude that C and D cannot be equivalent w.r.t. any class of interpretations that contains the two interpretations of Fig. 1. Vice versa, we can show with a similar argument that $\exists rf, rf.+_2$ cannot be expressed in $\mathcal{ALC}(\mathfrak{Q}_{+_1})$, but this requires slightly different interpretations. $\square$

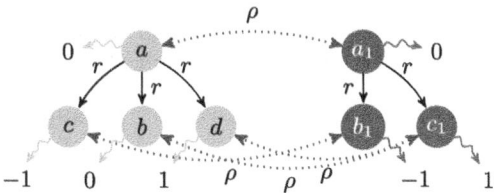

Fig. 1. A $\mathfrak{Q}_{+2}$ bisimulation ρ between $\mathcal{I}$ (left) and $\mathcal{J}$ (right).

FOL with concrete domains and $\mathcal{ALC}(\mathfrak{D})$. Since we are interested in charac-
terizing the concrete expressive power of $\mathcal{ALC}(\mathfrak{D})$, which takes the feature values
into account, we cannot compare $\mathcal{ALC}(\mathfrak{D})$ with FOL, where no such values are
available. Instead, we consider the extension $\mathrm{FOL}(\mathfrak{D})$ of FOL with the concrete
domain $\mathfrak{D}$ as introduced in [9,10]. The logic $\mathrm{FOL}(\mathfrak{D})$ is obtained from FOL by
adding *definedness predicates* $\mathrm{Def}(f)(t)$ with $f \in \mathsf{N_F}$ and t a first-order term, and
concrete domain predicates $P(f_1, \ldots, f_k)(t_1, \ldots, t_k)$ where P is a k-ary relation
of $\mathfrak{D}$, each t_i is a first-order term and $f_i \in \mathsf{N_F}$ for $i = 1, \ldots, k$.

The semantics of $\mathrm{FOL}(\mathfrak{D})$ formulae is defined in terms of first-order interpre-
tations $\mathcal{I} = (\Delta^{\mathcal{I}}, \cdot^{\mathcal{I}})$ that additionally assign partial functions $f^{\mathcal{I}} \colon \Delta^{\mathcal{I}} \rightharpoonup D$ to
$f \in \mathsf{N_F}$. The semantics of terms, Boolean connectives and first-order quantifiers
is defined as usual. Denoting the interpretation of a first-order term t w.r.t $\mathcal{I}$ and
a variable assignment w as $t^{\mathcal{I},w}$, the new predicates are interpreted as follows:

- $\mathcal{I} \models \mathrm{Def}(f)(t^{\mathcal{I},w})$ if $f^{\mathcal{I}}(t^{\mathcal{I},w})$ is defined, and
- $\mathcal{I} \models P(f_1, \ldots, f_k)(t_1^{\mathcal{I},w}, \ldots, t_k^{\mathcal{I},w})$ if $(f_1^{\mathcal{I}}(t_1^{\mathcal{I},w}), \ldots, f_k^{\mathcal{I}}(t_k^{\mathcal{I},w})) \in P^D$.

Note that if $(f_1^{\mathcal{I}}(t_1^{\mathcal{I},w}), \ldots, f_k^{\mathcal{I}}(t_k^{\mathcal{I},w})) \in P^D$ then each $f_i^{\mathcal{I}}(t_i^{\mathcal{I},w})$ must be defined.

It is easy to see (and explicitly shown in [9,10]) that $\mathcal{ALC}(\mathfrak{D})$ is a fragment of
$\mathrm{FOL}(\mathfrak{D})$. Our goal is to prove that it is the fragment of $\mathrm{FOL}(\mathfrak{D})$ that is invariant
under $\mathfrak{D}$ bisimulation, not just for the class of all interpretations, but also for
finite and finitely branching interpretations. For this, we use an approach that is
very similar to the one employed in Sect. 3. Recall that Lemma 1 turned out to
be an important model-theoretic tool in that approach since it provided us with
locality results for FOL formulae expressing $\mathcal{ALCSCC}$ concepts. The corresponding result also holds for $\mathrm{FOL}(\mathfrak{D})$. Note that the notions of *finite disjoint union*
and the corresponding $\mathbb{C}$-invariance w.r.t. classes $\mathbb{C}$ of interpretations of $\mathsf{N_C}$, $\mathsf{N_R}$
and $\mathsf{N_F}$ are obtained by extending Definition 5 to account for feature names in
the obvious way. For interpretations of $\mathsf{N_C}$, $\mathsf{N_R}$ and $\mathsf{N_F}$ we define ℓ-neighborhoods
by using the same notion of distance employed in Definition 4. This means that
the distance of two individuals is not determined by concrete domain predicates,
but only by role names. The notions of ℓ-locality of a $\mathrm{FOL}(\mathfrak{D})$ formula and of
$\mathbb{C}$-invariance w.r.t. classes $\mathbb{C}$ of interpretations of $\mathsf{N_C}$, $\mathsf{N_R}$ and $\mathsf{N_F}$ are obtained by
extending Definition 4 using this notion of neighborhood. In particular, the
extension of the classes $\mathbb{C}_{\mathsf{all}}$, $\mathbb{C}_{\mathsf{fb}}$, and $\mathbb{C}_{\mathsf{fin}}$ to interpretations taking feature names
into account are defined in the obvious way, and these classes are localizable.

Lemma 2. *If* $\mathbb{C}$ *is localizable, then a* $\mathsf{FOL}(\mathfrak{D})$ *formula* $\phi(x)$ *of quantifier depth* q *that is* $\mathbb{C}$-*invariant under disjoint unions is* ℓ-*local w.r.t.* $\mathbb{C}$ *for* $\ell := 2^q - 1$.

This result can be proved similarly to Lemma 1, by employing the translation of $\mathsf{FOL}(\mathfrak{D})$ formulae and $\mathsf{FOL}(\mathfrak{D})$ interpretations into FOL formulae and FOL interpretations introduced in [9,10] (see [11] for details).

In the following, we assume that the concrete domain $\mathfrak{D}$ is WCUN and has finitely many relations; both conditions are always satisfied by ω-admissible concrete domains [14,21]. Following the approach employed in the previous section, we introduce a bounded version of $\mathfrak{D}$ bisimulation, where now only the depth is bounded since there are no cardinality constraints.

Definition 7. *Let* $\mathcal{I}$, $\mathcal{J}$ *be interpretations of* $\mathsf{N_C}$, $\mathsf{N_R}$ *and* $\mathsf{N_F}$ *and* $\ell \in \mathbb{N}$. *The relation* $\rho \subseteq \Delta^{\mathcal{I}} \times \Delta^{\mathcal{J}}$ *is a* $\mathfrak{D}0$-*bisimulation if* ρ *satisfies the* **atomic condition** *of Definition 6 and for all* k-*ary relations* P *of* $\mathfrak{D}$ *and* $f_1, \ldots, f_k \in \mathsf{N_F}$:

values *if* $(d, e) \in \rho$ *then* $(f_1^{\mathcal{I}}(d), \ldots, f_k^{\mathcal{I}}(d)) \in P^D$ *iff* $(f_1^{\mathcal{J}}(e), \ldots, f_k^{\mathcal{J}}(e)) \in P^D$.

The relation ρ *is a* $\mathfrak{D}$ $(\ell + 1)$-*bisimulation if it is a* $\mathfrak{D}\ell$-*bisimulation that additionally satisfies the* **features** *conditions of Definition 6, and for all* $r \in \mathsf{N_R}$ *the following are satisfied:*

ℓ-**forth** *if* $(d, e) \in \rho$ *and* d' *is an* r-*successor of* d, *then there exist an* r-*successor* e' *of* e *and a* $\mathfrak{D}\ell$-*bisimulation* ρ' *such that* $(d', e') \in \rho'$;

ℓ-**back** *if* $(d, e) \in \rho$ *and* e' *is an* r-*successor of* e, *then there exist an* r-*successor* d' *of* d *and a* $\mathfrak{D}\ell$-*bisimulation* ρ' *such that* $(d', e') \in \rho'$.

The notions of bisimilarity and $\mathbb{C}$-*invariance w.r.t.* $\mathfrak{D}\ell$-*bisimulation are defined similarly to how it was done in Definition 2.*

In [11] we show that, under the assumption that the concrete domain $\mathfrak{D}$ is WCUN and has finitely many relations, results analogous to Proposition 1, Corollary 1, Theorem 3, Proposition 2, Theorem 4, and Proposition 3 also hold for $\mathsf{FOL}(\mathfrak{D})$ and $\mathcal{ALC}(\mathfrak{D})$, where $\mathcal{ALC}(\mathfrak{D})$ plays both the role of $\mathcal{ALCSCC}$ and of $\mathcal{ALCQt}$. Similarly to the proof of Theorem 4, these results can be combined to show the following characterization of $\mathcal{ALC}(\mathfrak{D})$ as the fragment of $\mathsf{FOL}(\mathfrak{D})$ that is invariant under $\mathfrak{D}$ bisimulation.

Theorem 7. *Let* $\mathbb{C}$ *be localizable and closed under partial unravelling,* $\mathfrak{D}$ *be WCUN and have finitely many relations, and* $\mathsf{N_C}$, $\mathsf{N_R}$, $\mathsf{N_F}$ *be finite. Then the following are equivalent for all* $\mathsf{FOL}(\mathfrak{D})$ *formulae* $\phi(x)$:

1. $\phi(x)$ *is* $\mathbb{C}$-*invariant under* $\mathfrak{D}$ *bisimulation.*
2. $\phi(x)$ *is* $\mathbb{C}$-*invariant under* $\mathfrak{D}\ell$-*bisimulation for some* $\ell \in \mathbb{N}$.
3. $\phi(x)$ *is equivalent to an* $\mathcal{ALC}(\mathfrak{D})$ *concept.*

Recall that the classes $\mathbb{C}_{\mathsf{all}}$, $\mathbb{C}_{\mathsf{fb}}$ and $\mathbb{C}_{\mathsf{fin}}$ satisfy the assumptions of Theorem 7. We further remark that, in contrast to the case of $\mathcal{ALCSCC}$, where there are concepts that are not FOL-definable, every $\mathcal{ALC}(\mathfrak{D})$ concept is $\mathsf{FOL}(\mathfrak{D})$-definable.

5   Conclusion

We have investigated the expressive power of concept description languages that allow their users to employ numerical constraints when defining concepts in two orthogonal ways. In contrast to our previous results on the expressive power of such languages [7–10], the approach employed here also works for restricted classes of interpretations such as finitely branching or finite ones. In [8], we have characterized the expressive power of TBoxes and cardinality boxes of $\mathcal{ALCSCC}^\infty$ (where arbitrary interpretations are considered) using global Pr bisimulations. It is at the moment not clear to us whether the results obtained there can be extended to the restricted classes of interpretations considered in the present paper. Another interesting topic for future research is to study the expressive power of $\mathcal{ALCOSCC}(\mathfrak{D})$, a joint extension of both $\mathcal{ALCSCC}$ and $\mathcal{ALC}(\mathfrak{D})$, whose complexity has recently been analyzed in [5]. The DLs $\mathcal{ALCSCC}$ and $\mathcal{ALC}(\mathfrak{D})$ are closed under all Boolean operations, whereas Kurtonina and de Rijke [20] characterize the expressive power of sub-Boolean fragments of $\mathcal{ALC}$. It would be interesting to see whether their results can be extended to the corresponding fragments of $\mathcal{ALCSCC}$ and $\mathcal{ALC}(\mathfrak{D})$. Like most bisimulation-based characterizations of the expressive power of logics, we assume here that the concept D in the DL $\mathcal{L}_2$ expressing the concept C in the DL $\mathcal{L}_1$ must be built over the same signature as C, i.e., no auxiliary symbols may be used. It would again be interesting to see whether inexpressivity results such as the one in Proposition 4 still hold if the use of auxiliary symbols is allowed, as for instance in [1,2]. In this context, work on conservative extensions could become relevant [16].

Acknowledgments. This work was partially supported by DFG grant 389792660 as part of TRR 248 – CPEC, by the German Federal Ministry of Education and Research (BMBF, SCADS22B) and the Saxon State Ministry for Science, Culture and Tourism (SMWK) by funding the competence center for Big Data and AI "ScaDS.AI Dresden/Leipzig".

References

1. Baader, F.: A formal definition for the expressive power of knowledge representation languages. In: Proceedings of the 9th European Conference on Artificial Intelligence, ECAI 1990, pp. 53–58 (1990)
2. Baader, F.: A formal definition for the expressive power of terminological knowledge representation languages. J. Log. Comput. **6**(1), 33–54 (1996). https://doi.org/10.1093/LOGCOM/6.1.33
3. Baader, F.: A new description logic with set constraints and cardinality constraints on role successors. In: Dixon, C., Finger, M. (eds.) FroCoS 2017. LNCS (LNAI), vol. 10483, pp. 43–59. Springer, Cham (2017). https://doi.org/10.1007/978-3-319-66167-4_3
4. Baader, F., Bednarczyk, B., Rudolph, S.: Satisfiability and query answering in description logics with global and local cardinality constraints. In: ECAI 2020 – 24th European Conference on Artificial Intelligence, pp. 616–623. IOS Press (2020). https://doi.org/10.3233/FAIA200146

5. Baader, F., Borgwardt, S., De Bortoli, F., Koopmann, P.: Concrete domains meet expressive cardinality restrictions in description logics. In: Barrett, C., Waldmann, U. (eds.) CADE-30: 30th International Conference on Automated Deduction, Proceedings. Lecture Notes in Computer Science, vol. 15943, pp.676–695. Springer (2025). https://doi.org/10.1007/978-3-031-99984-0_35

6. Baader, F., Calvanese, D., McGuinness, D.L., Nardi, D., Patel-Schneider, P.F. (eds.): The Description Logic Handbook: Theory, Implementation, and Applications. Cambridge University Press (2003). https://doi.org/10.1017/CBO9780511711787

7. Baader, F., De Bortoli, F.: On the expressive power of description logics with cardinality constraints on finite and infinite sets. In: Herzig, A., Popescu, A. (eds.) FroCoS 2019. LNCS (LNAI), vol. 11715, pp. 203–219. Springer, Cham (2019). https://doi.org/10.1007/978-3-030-29007-8_12

8. Baader, F., De Bortoli, F.: Description logics that count, and what they can and cannot count. In: Kovacs, L., Korovin, K., Reger, G. (eds.) ANDREI-60. Automated New-era Deductive Reasoning Event in Iberia. EPiC Series in Computing, vol. 68, pp. 1–25. EasyChair (2020). https://doi.org/10.29007/ltzn

9. Baader, F., De Bortoli, F.: The abstract expressive power of first-order and description logics with concrete domains. In: Proceedings of the 39th ACM/SIGAPP Symposium on Applied Computing, SAC 2024, pp. 754–761. Association for Computing Machinery, New York (2024). https://doi.org/10.1145/3605098.3635984

10. Baader, F., De Bortoli, F.: Logics with concrete domains: first-order properties, abstract expressive power, and (un)decidability. SIGAPP Appl. Comput. Rev. 24(3), 5–17 (2024). https://doi.org/10.1145/3699839.3699840

11. Baader, F., De Bortoli, F.: The Expressive Power of Description Logics with Numerical Constraints over Restricted Classes of Models (Extended Version). LTCS-Report 25-03, Chair of Automata Theory, Institute of Theoretical Computer Science, Technische Universität Dresden, Dresden, Germany (2025). https://doi.org/10.25368/2025.126

12. Baader, F., Hanschke, P.: A scheme for integrating concrete domains into concept languages. In: Mylopoulos, J., Reiter, R. (eds.) Proceedings of the 12th International Joint Conference on Artificial Intelligence, IJCAI 1991, pp. 452–457. Morgan Kaufmann (1991). http://ijcai.org/Proceedings/91-1/Papers/070.pdf

13. Baader, F., Horrocks, I., Lutz, C., Sattler, U.: An Introduction to Description Logic. Cambridge University Press (2017). https://doi.org/10.1017/9781139025355

14. Baader, F., Rydval, J.: Using model theory to find decidable and tractable description logics with concrete domains. J. Autom. Reason. 66(3), 357–407 (2022). https://doi.org/10.1007/s10817-022-09626-2

15. Borgida, A.: On the relative expressiveness of description logics and predicate logics. Artif. Intell. 82(1–2), 353–367 (1996). https://doi.org/10.1016/0004-3702(96)00004-5

16. Botoeva, E., Konev, B., Lutz, C., Ryzhikov, V., Wolter, F., Zakharyaschev, M.: Inseparability and conservative extensions of description logic ontologies: a survey. In: Pan, J.Z., et al. (eds.) Reasoning Web 2016. LNCS, vol. 9885, pp. 27–89. Springer, Cham (2017). https://doi.org/10.1007/978-3-319-49493-7_2

17. Calvanese, D.: Finite model reasoning in description logics. In: Aiello, L.C., Doyle, J., Shapiro, S.C. (eds.) Proceedings of the Fifth International Conference on Principles of Knowledge Representation and Reasoning (KR 1996), pp. 292–303. Morgan Kaufmann (1996)

18. Hollunder, B., Baader, F.: Qualifying number restrictions in concept languages. In: Allen, J.F., Fikes, R., Sandewall, E. (eds.) Proceedings of the 2nd International Conference on Principles of Knowledge Representation and Reasoning (KR 1991), pp. 335–346. Morgan Kaufmann (1991)

19. Kuncak, V., Rinard, M.: Towards efficient satisfiability checking for Boolean algebra with presburger arithmetic. In: Pfenning, F. (ed.) CADE 2007. LNCS (LNAI), vol. 4603, pp. 215–230. Springer, Heidelberg (2007). https://doi.org/10.1007/978-3-540-73595-3_15

20. Kurtonina, N., de Rijke, M.: Expressiveness of concept expressions in first-order description logics. Artif. Intell. **107**(2), 303–333 (1999). https://doi.org/10.1016/S0004-3702(98)00109-X

21. Lutz, C., Miličić, M.: A tableau algorithm for description logics with concrete domains and general TBoxes. J. Autom. Reason. **38**(1), 227–259 (2007). https://doi.org/10.1007/s10817-006-9049-7

22. Lutz, C., Piro, R., Wolter, F.: Description logic TBoxes: model-theoretic characterizations and rewritability. In: Proceedings of the 22nd International Joint Conference on Artificial Intelligence (IJCAI 2011), pp. 983–988. IJCAI/AAAI (2011). https://doi.org/10.5591/978-1-57735-516-8/IJCAI11-169

23. Lutz, C., Sattler, U., Tendera, L.: The complexity of finite model reasoning in description logics. Inf. Comput. **199**(1–2), 132–171 (2005). https://doi.org/10.1016/J.IC.2004.11.002

24. Otto, M.: Model theoretic methods for fragments of FO and special classes of (finite) structures. In: Esparza, J., Michaux, C., Steinhorn, C. (eds.) Finite and Algorithmic Model Theory, pp. 271–338. Cambridge University Press, Cambridge (2011). https://doi.org/10.1017/CBO9780511974960.007

25. Otto, M.: Graded modal logic and counting bisimulation (2023). http://arxiv.org/abs/1910.00039

26. de Rijke, M.: A note on graded modal logic. Stud. Logica. **64**(2), 271–283 (2000). https://doi.org/10.1023/A:1005245900406

27. Rosen, E.: Modal logic over finite structures. J. Logic Lang. Inf. **6**(4), 427–439 (1997). https://www.jstor.org/stable/40181601

28. van Benthem, J.: Modal correspondence theory. Ph.D. thesis, Mathematical Institute, University of Amsterdam, The Netherlands (1976)

Reasoning in OWL 2 EL with Hierarchical Concrete Domains

Francesco Kriegel[1,2]($^{\boxtimes}$) (iD)

[1] Theoretical Computer Science, Technische Universität Dresden, Dresden, Germany
francesco.kriegel@tu-dresden.de
[2] Center for Scalable Data Analytics and Artificial Intelligence (ScaDS.AI),
Dresden/Leipzig, Germany

Abstract. The $\mathcal{EL}$ family of description logics facilitates efficient polynomial-time reasoning and has been standardized as the profile OWL 2 EL of the Web Ontology Language. $\mathcal{EL}$ can represent and reason not only with symbolic knowledge but also with concrete knowledge expressed by numbers, strings, and other concrete datatypes. Such concrete domains must be convex to avoid introducing disjunctions "through the backdoor." However, existing concrete domains provide only limited utility. In order to overcome this issue, we introduce a novel form of concrete domains based on semi-lattices. They are convex by design and can thus be integrated into Horn-DLs such as $\mathcal{EL}$. Moreover, they allow for FBoxes to express dependencies between concrete features. We describe four instantiations concerned with real intervals, 2D-polygons, regular languages, and graphs.

1 Introduction

Concrete domains can be integrated in description logics (DLs) in order to refer to concrete knowledge expressed by numbers, strings, and other concrete datatypes [7]. They have mainly been investigated with DLs that are not Horn, such as $\mathcal{ALC}$ and its extensions, regarding decidability and complexity [14,18,20,49–51], reasoning procedures [26,27,50–52,58], an algebraic characterization [12,59], and their expressive power [3,6].

For computationally tractable description logics, other conditions on the concrete domains than above must be imposed. Suitable for the $\mathcal{EL}$ family are p-admissible concrete domains [4]: through them it is not possible to introduce disjunction into the logical domain so that the DL part retains its Horn character and, moreover, they guarantee that reasoning involving both the logical and the concrete domain remains tractable. Concrete domains have also been integrated with DL-Lite [2].

Existing p-admissible concrete domains for $\mathcal{EL}$ provide only limited utility. Using the concrete domain $\mathcal{D}_{\mathbb{Q},\text{diff}}$ [4], we could express with the concept inclusions (sys ≥ 140) $\sqsubseteq$ Hypertension and (dia ≥ 90) $\sqsubseteq$ Hypertension that a systolic blood pressure of 140 or higher indicates hypertension, as does a diastolic blood pressure of at least 90. Since the opposite relations $\leq$ are not available to ensure convexity, neither non-elevated blood pressure (dia. < 120 and sys. < 70) nor

© The Author(s) 2026
R. Thiemann and C. Weidenbach (Eds.): FroCoS 2025, LNAI 15979, pp. 40–60, 2026.
https://doi.org/10.1007/978-3-032-04167-8_3

elevated blood pressure (dia. between 120 and 140, and sys. between 70 and 90) are expressible. Mixed inequalities $<$, $\leq$, $>$, and $\geq$ may be used under certain limitations which of them may occur in left-hand sides and, respectively, in right-hand sides of concept inclusions [53]. While this retains convexity of the concrete domain, reasoning is then rather impaired since the usual completion procedure is only complete for consistency and classification, but not for subsumption.

An algebraic characterization of p-admissible concrete domains has put forth a further concrete domain $\mathcal{D}_{\mathbb{Q},\mathsf{lin}}$, which supports linear combinations of numerical features [11,13]. For instance, the concept inclusion $\top \sqsubseteq (\mathsf{sys} - \mathsf{dia} - \mathsf{pp} = 0)$, where $-$ is the difference operation in real arithmetic, expresses that the pulse pressure is the difference between the systolic and the diastolic blood pressure. In the medical domain, the combined expressivity of $\mathcal{D}_{\mathbb{Q},\mathsf{diff}}$ and $\mathcal{D}_{\mathbb{Q},\mathsf{lin}}$ would be useful since then with the concept inclusion $\mathsf{ICUPatient} \sqcap (\mathsf{pp} > 50) \sqsubseteq \mathsf{NeedsAttention}$ it could be expressed that intensive-care patients with a pulse pressure exceeding 50 need attention—but this combination is not convex anymore [1].

We introduce a novel form of concrete domains based on semi-lattices. A semi-lattice $(L, \leq, \wedge)$ consists of a set L, a partial order $\leq$, and a binary meet operation $\wedge$. The elements of L are taken as concrete values, and $\leq$ is understood as an "information order," i.e. $p \leq q$ means that p is more specific than q, like a subsumption order between concepts. The meet operation $\wedge$ is used to combine two values p and q to their meet value $p \wedge q$, which is the most general value that is more specific than both p and q. For instance, real intervals form a semi-lattice with subset inclusion $\subseteq$ as partial order and intersection $\cap$ as meet operation. With that, the statement $\mathsf{NonElevatedBP} \equiv (\mathsf{sys} \subseteq [0, 120)) \sqcap (\mathsf{dia} \subseteq [0, 70))$ defines non-elevated blood pressure, where $[0, 120)$ and $[0, 70)$ are real intervals.

Our new *hierarchical concrete domains* are convex by design, simply because a general value of a feature (such as $\mathsf{sys} \subseteq [0, 120)$) does not imply the disjunction of all more specific feature values (such as $\mathsf{sys} \subseteq [0, 0]$, $\mathsf{sys} \subseteq [1, 1]$, ..., $\mathsf{sys} \subseteq [119, 119]$). Atomic feature values are supported nonetheless when these are available as atoms in the semi-lattice. For instance, a specific numerical value p is represented by the singleton interval $[p, p]$ (which equals the one-element set $\{p\}$).

In addition, we introduce *FBoxes* consisting of *feature inclusions* that describe dependencies between features as well as aggregations of features. For instance, through the feature inclusion $\mathsf{pp} \subseteq \mathsf{sys} - \mathsf{dia}$, where $-$ is the difference operation in real interval arithmetic, we can obtain an interval value of the pulse pressure given intervals of the systolic and the diastolic blood pressure. With the concept inclusion $\mathsf{ICUPatient} \sqcap (\mathsf{pp} \subseteq (50, \infty)) \sqsubseteq \mathsf{NeedsAttention}$ we can now express that intensive-care patients having a pulse pressure above 50 need attention and, unlike in the combination of $\mathcal{D}_{\mathbb{Q},\mathsf{diff}}$ and $\mathcal{D}_{\mathbb{Q},\mathsf{lin}}$, computationally reason with that in polynomial time.

We provide four instantiations of hierarchical concrete domains based on real intervals, 2D-polygons, regular languages, and graphs. The former two are not only convex, but indeed p-admissible, i.e. equipping a DL from the $\mathcal{EL}$ family with them facilitates polynomial-time reasoning. In particular, we can employ linear programming for reasoning in the interval domain when the FBox is affine.

The regular-language domain is also convex (again, by design) but requires exponential time for reasoning. However, this only affects the concrete-domain reasoning itself so that reasoning in the logical $\mathcal{EL}$ part still runs in polynomial time. This holds similarly for the graph domain.

Of practical relevance is that our hierarchical concrete domains can be seamlessly integrated into the completion procedure and the ELK reasoner [4,5,40,42]. We demonstrate this for the case where nominals must be used safely, i.e. nominals must not occur in conjunctions and right-hand sides of concept inclusions must not be single nominals. We conjecture that full support for nominals can be achieved in the same way as without concrete domains [41].

Proofs and more technical details can be found in the extended version [46].

2   Preliminaries

We work with the description logic $\mathcal{EL}^{++}[\mathcal{D}]$ (OWL 2 EL) where $\mathcal{D}$ is a P-admissible concrete domain (as defined below). Consider a set $\mathbf{C}$ of *atomic concepts*, a set $\mathbf{R}$ of *roles*, a set $\mathbf{I}$ of *individuals*, a set $\mathbf{F}$ of *features*, and a set $\mathbf{P}$ of *predicates* where each $P \in \mathbf{P}$ has an arity $\mathsf{ar}(P) \in \mathbb{N}$. There are two special concepts $\bot$ and $\top$ with fixed meaning. A *constraint* has the form $\exists f_1, \ldots, f_k. P$ where P is a k-ary predicate and $f_1, \ldots, f_k$ are features. *Compound concepts* are built by

$$C ::= \bot \mid \top \mid \{i\} \mid A \mid \exists f_1, \ldots, f_k. P \mid C \sqcap C \mid \exists r. C$$

where A ranges over all atomic concepts, r over all roles, i over all individuals, and $\exists f_1, \ldots, f_k. P$ over all constraints. A *knowledge base (KB)* is a finite set of *concept inclusions (CIs)* $C \sqsubseteq D$ concerning concepts C and D, *role inclusions (RIs)* $R \sqsubseteq s$ involving *role chains* generated by $R ::= \varepsilon \mid R_1,\ R_1 ::= r \mid R_1 \circ R_1$ and roles s, and *range inclusions* $\mathsf{Ran}(r) \sqsubseteq C$ referring to roles r and concepts C—but every $\mathcal{EL}^{++}[\mathcal{D}]$ KB must satisfy an additional condition as explained in Sect. 4.

As syntactic sugar, we have *concept assertions* $\{i\} \sqsubseteq C$ (also written $i : C$), *role assertions* $\{i\} \sqsubseteq \exists r. \{j\}$ (also written $(i, j) : r$), *domain inclusions* $\exists r. \top \sqsubseteq C$ (also written $\mathsf{Dom}(r) \sqsubseteq C$), and *role exclusions* $\exists r_1. \ldots. \exists r_n. \top \sqsubseteq \bot$ (also written $r_1 \circ \cdots \circ r_n \sqsubseteq \bot$). Statements $C \sqsubseteq \bot$ are also called *concept exclusions*, and $C \equiv D$ is a *concept equivalence* that stands for the two CIs $C \sqsubseteq D$ and $D \sqsubseteq C$. Each KB $\mathcal{K}$ can be subdivided into an *ABox* $\mathcal{A}$ consisting of all concept and role assertions, an *RBox* $\mathcal{R}$ consisting of all role inclusions and exclusions, and a *TBox* $\mathcal{T}$ consisting of the remaining statements. The TBox together with the RBox is also called an *ontology* $\mathcal{O}$.

The semantics are defined through the fixed concrete domain $\mathcal{D}$ and all interpretations $\mathcal{I}$. The *concrete domain* $\mathcal{D} := (\mathsf{Dom}(\mathcal{D}), \cdot^{\mathcal{D}})$ consists of a set $\mathsf{Dom}(\mathcal{D})$ of *values* and an interpretation function $\cdot^{\mathcal{D}}$ that sends each predicate $P \in \mathbf{P}$ to a relation over $\mathsf{Dom}(\mathcal{D})$ with arity $\mathsf{ar}(P)$, i.e. $P^{\mathcal{D}} \subseteq \mathsf{Dom}(\mathcal{D})^{\mathsf{ar}(P)}$.

If the predicate P in a constraint $\exists f_1, \ldots, f_k. P$ is defined through a mathematical expression or a logical formula with k free variables, then we may represent the constraint also through this expression/formula but with the free variables replaced by the features $f_1, \ldots, f_k$. For instance, the constraint $\mathsf{sys} - \mathsf{dia} - \mathsf{pp} = 0$ from the introduction represents $\exists \mathsf{sys}, \mathsf{dia}, \mathsf{pp}. P_{(1,-1,-1),0}$ where $(P_{(1,-1,-1),0})^{\mathcal{D}} := \{(x,y,z) \mid x - y - z = 0\}$.

An interpretation $\mathcal{I} := (\mathsf{Dom}(\mathcal{I}), \cdot^{\mathcal{I}})$ consists of a non-empty set $\mathsf{Dom}(\mathcal{I})$, called *domain*, and an interpretation function $\cdot^{\mathcal{I}}$ that maps each atomic concept $A \in \mathbf{C}$ to a subset $A^{\mathcal{I}}$ of $\mathsf{Dom}(\mathcal{I})$, each role $r \in \mathbf{R}$ to a binary relation $r^{\mathcal{I}}$ over $\mathsf{Dom}(\mathcal{I})$, each individual $i \in \mathbf{I}$ to an element $i^{\mathcal{I}}$ of $\mathsf{Dom}(\mathcal{I})$, and each feature $f \in \mathbf{F}$ to a partial function $f^{\mathcal{I}}$ from $\mathsf{Dom}(\mathcal{I})$ to $\mathsf{Dom}(\mathcal{D})$. The interpretation function $\cdot^{\mathcal{I}}$ is extended to compound concepts as follows: $\perp^{\mathcal{I}} := \emptyset$, $\top^{\mathcal{I}} := \mathsf{Dom}(\mathcal{I})$, $\{i\}^{\mathcal{I}} := \{i^{\mathcal{I}}\}$, $(\exists f_1, \ldots, f_k. P)^{\mathcal{I}} := \{x \mid x \in \mathsf{Dom}(f_1^{\mathcal{I}}) \cap \cdots \cap \mathsf{Dom}(f_k^{\mathcal{I}}) \text{ and } (f_1^{\mathcal{I}}(x), \ldots, f_k^{\mathcal{I}}(x)) \in P^{\mathcal{D}}\}$, $(C \sqcap D)^{\mathcal{I}} := C^{\mathcal{I}} \cap D^{\mathcal{I}}$, and $(\exists r.C)^{\mathcal{I}} := \{x \mid \text{there is } y \text{ s.t. } (x,y) \in r^{\mathcal{I}} \text{ and } y \in C^{\mathcal{I}}\}$. Role chains are interpreted by $\varepsilon^{\mathcal{I}} := \{(x,x) \mid x \in \mathsf{Dom}(\mathcal{I})\}$ and $(R \circ S)^{\mathcal{I}} := \{(x,z) \mid \text{there is } y \text{ s.t. } (x,y) \in R^{\mathcal{I}} \text{ and } (y,z) \in S^{\mathcal{I}}\}$, and role ranges are interpreted as $\mathsf{Ran}(r)^{\mathcal{I}} := \{y \mid \text{there is } x \text{ s.t. } (x,y) \in r^{\mathcal{I}}\}$.

$\mathcal{I}$ *satisfies* a concept/role/range inclusion $X \sqsubseteq Y$, written $\mathcal{I} \models X \sqsubseteq Y$, if $X^{\mathcal{I}} \subseteq Y^{\mathcal{I}}$. If $\mathcal{I}$ satisfies all inclusions in a KB $\mathcal{K}$, then $\mathcal{I}$ is a *model* of $\mathcal{K}$, written $\mathcal{I} \models \mathcal{K}$. If $\mathcal{K}$ has a model, then it is *consistent*, and otherwise *inconsistent*. $\mathcal{K}$ *entails* an inclusion $X \sqsubseteq Y$ if $X \sqsubseteq Y$ is satisfied by all models of $\mathcal{K}$, written $\mathcal{K} \models X \sqsubseteq Y$ or $X \sqsubseteq^{\mathcal{K}} Y$, and we then say that X is *subsumed by* Y w.r.t. $\mathcal{K}$. Furthermore, $\mathcal{K}$ *entails* a KB $\mathcal{L}$ if $\mathcal{K}$ entails all inclusions in $\mathcal{L}$, written $\mathcal{K} \models \mathcal{L}$.

A *constraint inclusion* is of the form $\bigsqcap \Gamma \sqsubseteq \bigsqcup \Delta$ where Γ and Δ are finite sets of constraints. $\mathcal{I}$ *satisfies* $\bigsqcap \Gamma \sqsubseteq \bigsqcup \Delta$, written $\mathcal{I} \models \bigsqcap \Gamma \sqsubseteq \bigsqcup \Delta$, if $\bigcap \{\alpha^{\mathcal{I}} \mid \alpha \in \Gamma\} \subseteq \bigcup \{\beta^{\mathcal{I}} \mid \beta \in \Delta\}$. Moreover, $\bigsqcap \Gamma \sqsubseteq \bigsqcup \Delta$ is *valid*, written $\mathcal{D} \models \bigsqcap \Gamma \sqsubseteq \bigsqcup \Delta$, if it is satisfied in all interpretations. It is easy to see that validity is independent of the concepts, roles, and individuals and that it suffices to consider only one domain element. To this end, a *valuation* is a partial function v from $\mathbf{F}$ to $\mathsf{Dom}(\mathcal{D})$, and it *satisfies* $\exists f_1, \ldots, f_k. P$ if $(v(f_1), \ldots, v(f_k)) \in P^{\mathcal{D}}$. Now, $\bigsqcap \Gamma \sqsubseteq \bigsqcup \Delta$ is *valid* iff., for each valuation v, if v satisfies all $\alpha \in \Gamma$, then v satisfies some $\beta \in \Delta$.

We say that $\mathcal{D}$ is P-*admissible* if satisfiability of constraint conjunctions as well as validity of constraint inclusions are decidable in polynomial time and, moreover, $\mathcal{D}$ is *convex*, i.e. for each valid constraint inclusion $\bigsqcap \Gamma \sqsubseteq \bigsqcup \Delta$, there is a constraint $\beta \in \Delta$ such that $\bigsqcap \Gamma \sqsubseteq \beta$ is valid. We can use multiple P-admissible concrete domains by forming their disjoint union, which is P-admissible too.

3   Hierarchical Concrete Domains

A *semi-lattice* $\mathbf{L} := (L, \leq, \wedge)$ consists of a set L, a partial order $\leq$ on L, and a binary meet operation $\wedge$ on L, i.e. the following hold for all $p, q, p_1, p_2, p_3 \in L$:

(SL1) $p \leq p$ for each $p \in L$ (reflexive)

(SL2) if $p \leq q$ and $q \leq p$, then $p = q$ (anti-symmetric)

(SL3) if $p_1 \leq p_2$ and $p_2 \leq p_3$, then $p_1 \leq p_3$ (transitive)

(SL4) $p_1 \wedge p_2 \leq p_1$ and $p_1 \wedge p_2 \leq p_2$

(SL5) if $q \leq p_1$ and $q \leq p_2$, then $q \leq p_1 \wedge p_2$.

The strict part $<$ is defined by $p < q$ if $p \leq q$ but $q \not\leq p$, and we then say that p is *more specific than* q. Thus $p \leq q$ iff. $p < q$ or $p = q$, in which case we say that p is *more specific than or equal to* q. And $p \wedge q$ is the *meet* of p and q. It follows from the above conditions that $\wedge$ is associative, commutative, and idempotent. The finitary meet operation $\bigwedge$ is obtained from the binary one by setting $\bigwedge\{p\} := p$, $\bigwedge\{p, q\} := p \wedge q$, and $\bigwedge\{p_1, \ldots, p_n\} := p_1 \wedge \bigwedge\{p_2, \ldots, p_n\}$ whenever $n \geq 3$.

We say that $\mathbf{L}$ is *computable* if L and $\leq$ are decidable and $\wedge$ is computable. If all this is possible in polynomial time, then $\mathbf{L}$ is *polynomial-time computable*. $\mathbf{L}$ is *bounded* if it has a greatest element $\top$, i.e. $p \leq \top$ for every $p \in L$. Then we can also define a nullary meet as $\bigwedge \emptyset := \top$. In order to express impossible combinations of values, it might be convenient to add an artificial smallest element $\bot$ to the semi-lattice, i.e. $\bot \leq p$ for each $p \in L$. We then use $\bot$ to represent contradictory or ill-defined values. More specifically, $p \wedge q = \bot$ if it is impossible to combine the values p and q.

Example 1. A semi-lattice representing grades could have the values Attended, Passed, Failed, 1, 2, 3, 4, 5, 6, 1.0, 1.3, 1.7, 2.0, and so on. Its partial order $\leq$ is defined by Passed $\leq$ Attended, Failed $\leq$ Attended, 1 $\leq$ Passed, 2 $\leq$ Passed, 3 $\leq$ Passed, 4 $\leq$ Passed, 5 $\leq$ Failed, 6 $\leq$ Failed, $1.0 \leq 1$, $1.3 \leq 1$, $1.7 \leq 2$, $2.0 \leq 2$, etc. Here we need to add a smallest element $\bot$ since e.g. the meet of grades 1.0 and 5.0 cannot be reasonably defined.

For every KB $\mathcal{K}$ expressed in a decidable DL, the set of all concepts ordered by subsumption $\sqsubseteq^{\mathcal{K}}$ and with conjunction $\sqcap$ as meet operation is a computable, bounded semi-lattice. For each set M, $(\wp(M), \subseteq, \cap, M)$ and $(\wp(M), \supseteq, \cup, \emptyset)$ are bounded semi-lattices (where $\wp(M)$ is the powerset of M). They are only computable if restricted to finite or finitely representable subsets of M. In the following subsections we will introduce four application-relevant semi-lattices based on intervals, polygons, regular languages, and graphs.

Definition 2. *Given a bounded semi-lattice* $\mathbf{L} := (L, \leq, \wedge, \top)$, *the hierarchical concrete domain* $\mathcal{D}_{\mathbf{L}}$ *has values in* $\mathsf{Dom}(\mathcal{D}_{\mathbf{L}}) := L$ *and supports only constraints of the form* $\exists f. P_{\leq p}$, *written as* $f \leq p$, *involving a feature* f *and a value* p. *The semantics are* $(P_{\leq p})^{\mathcal{D}_{\mathbf{L}}} := \{q \mid q \in L \text{ and } q < p\}$ *and thus* $(f \leq p)^{\mathcal{I}} = \{x \mid f^{\mathcal{I}}(x) \leq p\}$. *Recall: this means that* f's *value is* p *or more specific, not smaller. We assume that* $\top$ *stands for an undefined value and thus all valuations are total, i.e.* $v(f) = \top$ *means that* f *has no value under* v. *In order to represent a most general value,* $\mathbf{L}$ *contains a second-largest element* $\square$, *i.e.* $\square < \top$ *and* $p \leq \square$ *for each* $p \in L \setminus \{\top\}$. *Since* $\bot$ *represents contradictory, ill-defined values, no valuation* v *assigns* $\bot$ *to any feature* f, *i.e.* $v(f) \neq \bot$.

Definition 3. *A feature inclusion (FI)* $f \leq H(g_1, \ldots, g_n)$ *consists of features* $f, g_1, \ldots, g_n$ *and a computable n-ary operation* $H \colon L^n \to L$ *that is monotonic in the sense that* $H(p_1, \ldots, p_n) \leq H(q_1, \ldots, q_n)$ *whenever* $p_1 \leq q_1, \ldots,$ *and* $p_n \leq q_n$ *(i.e. applying* H *to more specific values yields more specific values). A valuation* v *satisfies this FI if* $v(f) \leq H(v(g_1), \ldots, v(g_n))$, *denoted as* $v \models f \leq H(g_1, \ldots, g_n)$. *An FBox* $\mathcal{F}$ *is a finite set of FIs, and a valuation* v *satisfies*

$\mathcal{F}$, written $v \models \mathcal{F}$, if v satisfies every FI in $\mathcal{F}$. We call $\mathcal{F}$ acylic if the graph $(\mathbf{F}, \{(f, g_1), \ldots, (f, g_n) \mid f \leq H(g_1, \ldots, g_n) \in \mathcal{F}\})$ is, and cyclic otherwise.

The following example illustrates that FIs are "directed specifications" in the sense that values of the right-hand side features $g_1, \ldots, g_n$ yield, through the operation H, an upper bound for the value of the left-hand side feature f. However, this does not work in the other direction unless specified by other FIs.

Example 4. We use three features with interval values over the non-negative integers: sys for the systolic and dia for the diastolic blood pressure, and pp for the pulse pressure, which is the difference between the systolic and the diastolic pressure. The FI pp $\subseteq$ sys $-$ dia allows us to infer a value for pp when values for both sys and dia are given. The monotonic operator H in the right-hand side is $H([p_1, q_1], [p_2, q_2]) := [p_1, q_1] - [p_2, q_2]$, and the latter value is the difference in interval arithmetic ($= [p_1 - q_2, q_1 - p_2]$ but with negative subtraction results replaced by 0). According to the semantics, an interval value of the feature pp must be a subset of sys $-$ dia, i.e. if the latter two features are defined for an object x in a model $\mathcal{I}$ of the FI, then also $\mathsf{pp}^{\mathcal{I}}(x)$ is defined and is equal to or more specific than $H(\mathsf{sys}^{\mathcal{I}}(x), \mathsf{dia}^{\mathcal{I}}(x))$.

For instance, under the above FI the constraint inclusion (sys $\subseteq [110, 120]$) $\sqcap$ (dia $\subseteq [60, 70]$) $\sqsubseteq$ (pp $\subseteq [40, 60]$) is valid since $H([110, 120], [60, 70]) = [40, 60] \subseteq [40, 60]$. Without syntactic sugar, the first constraint is $\exists$sys.$P_{\subseteq[110,120]}$ involving the predicate $P_{\subseteq[110,120]} := \{[p, q], (p, q), [p, q), (p, q] \mid 110 \leq p \leq q \leq 120\}$.

In contrast, the constraint inclusion (sys $\subseteq [110, 120]$) $\sqcap$ (pp $\subseteq [40, 60]$) $\sqsubseteq$ (dia $\subseteq [60, 70]$) is not valid w.r.t. the above FI. A countervaluation is v with $v(\mathsf{sys}) = [110, 120]$, $v(\mathsf{dia}) = [0, \infty)$, $v(\mathsf{pp}) = [40, 60]$. This is because $[110, 120] - [0, \infty) = [0, 120]$ and $[40, 60] \subseteq [0, 120]$, i.e. v satisfies the FI, but v does not satisfy the latter constraint inclusion.

Definition 5. *The semantics of the concrete domain $\mathcal{D}_{\mathbf{L}}$ can be restricted w.r.t. an FBox $\mathcal{F}$ by considering only valuations satisfying $\mathcal{F}$. That is, a constraint inclusion $\sqcap \Gamma \sqsubseteq \bigsqcup \Delta$ is valid in $\mathcal{D}_{\mathbf{L}}$ w.r.t. $\mathcal{F}$, written $\mathcal{D}_{\mathbf{L}}, \mathcal{F} \models \sqcap \Gamma \sqsubseteq \bigsqcup \Delta$, if this inclusion is satisfied in all valuations that satisfy $\mathcal{F}$. Whenever we write "w.r.t. $\mathcal{F}$" in the following, only valuations satisfying $\mathcal{F}$ are considered.*

Using this semantics restricted by an FBox, convexity and P-admissibility are defined as before but the latter additionally takes the FBox $\mathcal{F}$ as part of the input. The underlying semi-lattice $\mathbf{L}$ is taken into account through the computational complexity of its value set L, its partial order $\leq$, and its meet operation $\wedge$.

Definition 6. *$\mathcal{D}_{\mathbf{L}}$ is admissible w.r.t. $\mathcal{F}$ if $\mathcal{D}_{\mathbf{L}}$ is convex and satisfiability of constraint conjunctions as well as validity of constraint inclusions are decidable, all w.r.t. $\mathcal{F}$. For a complexity class C, we say that $\mathcal{D}_{\mathbf{L}}$ is C-admissible w.r.t. $\mathcal{F}$ if, all w.r.t. $\mathcal{F}$, $\mathcal{D}_{\mathbf{L}}$ is convex and satisfiability of constraint conjunctions as well as validity of constraint inclusions are in C when $\mathcal{F}$ is part of the input.*

Next, we show that a hierarchical concrete domain $\mathcal{D}_{\mathbf{L}}$ is convex w.r.t. $\mathcal{F}$ if the semi-lattice $\mathbf{L}$ is complete or well-founded or the FBox $\mathcal{F}$ is acyclic. There might be further sufficient conditions for convexity; we leave this for future research.

Definition 7. *Let* **L** *be a bounded semi-lattice and* $\mathcal{F}$ *be an FBox. Given a finite set* Γ *of constraints over the concrete domain* $\mathcal{D}_{\mathbf{L}}$, *a* canonical valuation *of* Γ *w.r.t.* $\mathcal{F}$ *is a valuation* $v_{\Gamma,\mathcal{F}}$ *such that*

1. $v_{\Gamma,\mathcal{F}} \models \mathcal{F}$ *and*
2. $v_{\Gamma,\mathcal{F}} \models \alpha$ *iff.* $\mathcal{D}_{\mathbf{L}}, \mathcal{F} \models \bigsqcap \Gamma \sqsubseteq \alpha$ *for each constraint* α.

Moreover, we say that $\mathcal{D}_{\mathbf{L}}$ *has canonical valuations w.r.t.* $\mathcal{F}$ *if such a valuation* $v_{\Gamma,\mathcal{F}}$ *exists for every finite, w.r.t.* $\mathcal{F}$ *satisfiable* Γ.

Since for each constraint α in Γ, the inclusion $\bigsqcap \Gamma \sqsubseteq \alpha$ is valid, we infer with the second condition that $v_{\Gamma,\mathcal{F}}$ satisfies Γ.

A semi-lattice **L** is *complete* if every subset $P \subseteq L$ has a meet $\bigwedge P \in L$, i.e. such that $\bigwedge P \leq p$ for each $p \in P$ and, if $q \leq p$ for each $p \in P$, then $q \leq \bigwedge P$. Note that these two conditions generalize (SL4) and (SL5).

Theorem 8. *For each complete semi-lattice* **L** *and for every FBox* $\mathcal{F}$, *the concrete domain* $\mathcal{D}_{\mathbf{L}}$ *has canonical valuations and so is convex w.r.t.* $\mathcal{F}$.

Theorem 9. *Let* **L** *be a computable, bounded semi-lattice and* $\mathcal{F}$ *be an FBox. If* **L** *is well-founded or* $\mathcal{F}$ *is acyclic, then the concrete domain* $\mathcal{D}_{\mathbf{L}}$ *has computable canonical valuations and is admissible w.r.t.* $\mathcal{F}$.

Now, we want to determine the time requirement for computing a canonical valuation $v_{\Gamma,\mathcal{F}}$, which is measured w.r.t. the constraint set Γ and the FBox $\mathcal{F}$.

An operation $H : L^n \to L$ is *non-duplicating* if, for all $(p_1, \ldots, p_n) \in L^n$, the size of $H(p_1, \ldots, p_n)$ is no larger than the size of $(p_1, \ldots, p_n)$. An FBox is *non-duplicating* if all operations in it are non-duplicating and each feature occurs at most once in any right-hand side.

Proposition 10. *Consider a polynomial-time computable, bounded semi-lattice* **L** *such that its meet operation is non-duplicating. Further consider an acyclic, non-duplicating FBox* $\mathcal{F}$ *in which all occurring operations are polynomial-time computable. W.r.t.* $\mathcal{F}$, *the concrete domain* $\mathcal{D}_{\mathbf{L}}$ *has polynomial-time computable canonical valuations and is* P-*admissible.*

We obtain exponential complexity if $\wedge$ and $\mathcal{F}$ are not non-duplicating.

Proposition 11. *For every polynomial-time computable, bounded semi-lattice* **L** *and for every acyclic FBox* $\mathcal{F}$ *in which all occurring operations are polynomial-time computable, the concrete domain* $\mathcal{D}_{\mathbf{L}}$ *has exponential-time computable canonical valuations and is* EXP-*admissible w.r.t.* $\mathcal{F}$.

3.1   Intervals

Let N be a non-empty set of real numbers. The semi-lattice $\mathbf{Int}(N)$ consists of all intervals over N, is partially ordered by set inclusion $\subseteq$ and has set intersection $\cap$ as its meet operation. $\mathbf{Int}(N)$ is already bounded since its greatest element is $N = (-\infty, \infty)$, but we rather identify it with $\square$ and add an artificial greatest element $\top$. It also has a smallest element $\emptyset = (p, p)$ where $p \in N$ is arbitrary, and we identify this smallest element with the contradictory value $\bot$. The inclusion satisfies $[p_1, q_1] \subseteq [p_2, q_2]$ iff. $p_2 \leq p_1$ and $q_1 \leq q_2$, and the intersection satisfies $[p_1, q_1] \cap [p_2, q_2] = [\max(p_1, p_2), \min(q_1, q_2)]$, and similarly for the other interval types. It follows that $\mathbf{Int}(N)$ is polynomial-time computable since $\leq$ is decidable in polynomial time [30], and its meet operation is non-duplicating.

The hierarchical concrete domain $\mathcal{D}_{\mathbf{Int}(N)}$ is called the *interval domain* over N. Since for every number $p \in N$, the singleton $\{p\}$ equals the interval $[p, p]$, we can specify the precise numerical value of a feature with the constraint $f \subseteq \{p\}$, also written $f = p$. Moreover, instead of $f \subseteq [p, q]$ we may also write $p \leq f \leq q$.

Example 12. Through the interval domain over the non-negative 8-bit integers $N := \mathbb{N} \cap [0, 2^8 - 1]$ we could express non-elevated blood pressure by NonElevatedBP $\equiv$ (sys $\subseteq [0, 120)$) $\sqcap$ (dia $\subseteq [0, 70)$), elevated blood pressure by ElevatedBP $\equiv$ (sys $\subseteq [120, 140)$) $\sqcap$ (dia $\subseteq [70, 90)$), and hypertension by (sys $\subseteq [140, \infty)$) $\sqsubseteq$ Hypertension and (dia $\subseteq [90, \infty)$) $\sqsubseteq$ Hypertension. With the above syntactic sugar, the first statement can also be written as NonElevatedBP $\equiv$ ($0 \leq$ sys < 120) $\sqcap$ ($0 \leq$ dia < 70), and similarly for the other two. The concrete values of patient bob can be represented by the assertions bob : (sys $= 114$) and bob : (dia $\subseteq [69, 69]$). The KB consisting of all these aforementioned statements entails bob : NonElevatedBP.

Example 13. Continuing Example 4, we can additionally consider the two FIs dia $\subseteq$ sys $-$ pp and sys $\subseteq$ dia $+$ pp, which allow us to also infer interval values of dia and sys given interval values of the respective other two. Importantly, this does not destroy convexity.

This is in stark contrast to the concrete domain extending $\mathcal{D}_{\mathbb{Q}, \text{diff}}$ with constraints $f \geq b$, $f < b$, $f \leq b$, which allows to express interval values as well (in a different way though). There, the constraint inclusion (sys $-$ dia $= 40$) $\sqsubseteq$ (sys ≤ 120) $\sqcup$ (dia > 80) is valid, violating convexity. Additionally using the expressivity of $\mathcal{D}_{\mathbb{Q}, \text{lin}}$, we could express that pp $=$ sys $-$ dia by the CI $\top \sqsubseteq$ (sys $-$ dia $-$ pp $= 0$) as in Example 3 in [1]. Under this CI, the constraint inclusion (pp $= 40$) $\sqsubseteq$ (sys ≤ 120) $\sqcup$ (dia > 80) would be valid, also violating convexity.

In our interval domain over the non-negative integers and with the cyclic FBox $\{$pp $\subseteq$ sys $-$ dia, dia $\subseteq$ sys $-$ pp, sys $\subseteq$ dia $+$ pp$\}$, the similar constraint inclusion (pp $\subseteq [40, 40]$) $\sqsubseteq$ (sys $\subseteq [0, 120]$) $\sqcup$ (dia $\subseteq (80, \infty)$) is not valid. A countervaluation is v where $v(\text{sys}) = [40, \infty)$, $v(\text{dia}) = [0, \infty)$, $v(\text{pp}) = [40, 40]$. It satisfies the first FI since $[40, \infty) - [0, \infty) = [0, \infty) \supseteq [40, 40]$, the second FI since $[40, \infty) - [40, 40] = [0, \infty) \supseteq [0, \infty)$, and the third FI since $[0, \infty) + [40, 40] = [40, \infty) \supseteq [40, \infty)$.

Recall that the interval semi-lattice $\mathbf{Int}(N)$ is defined for every non-empty set N of real numbers. The set N is partially ordered by the usual ordering $\leq$ and has the meet operation min, i.e. $(N, \leq, \min)$ is itself a semi-lattice. It thus makes sense to say that N is complete. The real numbers $\mathbb{R}$, the non-negative real numbers $\mathbb{R}_+$, the integers $\mathbb{Z}$, the natural numbers $\mathbb{N}$, the n-bit integers, the n-bit floating-point numbers, the n-bit fixed-point numbers, and all finite subsets of $\mathbb{R}$ are complete, but the rational numbers $\mathbb{Q}$ is not—for instance, the infimum of $\{(1 + 1/n)^{n+1} \mid n \geq 0\}$ is Euler's number e, an irrational number. It is easy to see that the semi-lattice $\mathbf{Int}(N)$ is complete if the number set N is complete, and so we obtain the below corollary to Theorem 8.

Corollary 14. *If the semi-lattice $(N, \leq, \min)$ is complete, then the interval domain $\mathcal{D}_{\mathbf{Int}(N)}$ has canonical valuations and is convex w.r.t. every FBox $\mathcal{F}$.*

An immediate consequence of Theorem 9 is that the interval domain $\mathcal{D}_{\mathbf{Int}(\mathbb{R})}$ over all real numbers is admissible w.r.t. every acyclic FBox. Moreover, an obvious corollary to Proposition 10 is as follows.

Corollary 15. *W.r.t. each acyclic, non-duplicating FBox $\mathcal{F}$ in which all operations are polynomial-time computable, the interval domain $\mathcal{D}_{\mathbf{Int}(\mathbb{R})}$ has polynomial-time-computable canonical valuations and is P-admissible.*

Next, we employ linear programming to handle affine FBoxes, which might be cyclic. We call an FBox $\mathcal{F}$ *affine* if all operations in FIs in $\mathcal{F}$ are affine, i.e. all FIs are of the form $f \subseteq \sum_{i=1}^{n} P_i \cdot g_i + Q_i$ where the P_i and Q_i are intervals. For instance, the FI pp $\subseteq$ sys $-$ dia is affine, but bmi $\subseteq$ bodyMass/bodyHeight^2 is not. Since each affine FI represents two linear inequalities (one for the lower bound of the interval value of f, and another one for the upper bound), we can transform affine FBoxes into linear programs, which can be solved in polynomial time [33]. We thus obtain the following result.

Proposition 16. *Let $\underline{c}, \overline{c} \in \mathbb{R}_+$ be non-negative real numbers such that $\underline{c} \leq \overline{c}$. Restricted to closed intervals only, the interval domain $\mathcal{D}_{\mathbf{Int}([\underline{c}, \overline{c}])}$ over the non-negative real numbers between $\underline{c}$ and $\overline{c}$ is P-admissible w.r.t. each affine FBox $\mathcal{F}$, i.e. all FIs are of the form $f \subseteq \sum_{i=1}^{n} [\underline{a}_i, \overline{a}_i] \cdot g_i + [\underline{b}, \overline{b}]$.*

It remains an open problem, whether the interval domains $\mathcal{D}_{\mathbf{Int}([\underline{c}, \overline{c}])}$ remain P-admissible w.r.t. affine FBoxes when all interval types would be considered. We conjecture that the interval bounds can be computed using the same linear program, but determining the correct interval types (closed or open at the lower bound, closed or open at the upper bound) could possibly lead to a combinatorial explosion. It is further unclear whether, without the bounding interval $[\underline{c}, \overline{c}]$, the interval domain $\mathcal{D}_{\mathbf{Int}(\mathbb{R}_+)}$ would still be P-admissible w.r.t. affine FBoxes. The canonical valuation could then send features to intervals with upper bound $+\infty$, in which case the polytope described by the inequations would be unbounded. This requires an LP-solver with support for unbounded solution polytopes.

We can also handle affine FBoxes together with negative numbers, but then need to restrict the coefficient intervals $[\underline{a}_i, \overline{a}_i]$ to singletons—as otherwise the non-linear functions min and max would be required to compute a product $[\underline{a}_i, \overline{a}_i] \cdot g_i$, i.e. the system of inequalities would not be linear anymore and could therefore not be solved by linear-programming methods.

Proposition 17. *Let $\underline{c}, \overline{c} \in \mathbb{R}$ be real numbers such that $\underline{c} \leq \overline{c}$. Restricted to closed intervals, the interval domain $\mathcal{D}_{\mathbf{Int}([\underline{c}, \overline{c}])}$ over the real numbers in $[\underline{c}, \overline{c}]$ is P-admissible w.r.t. each affine FBox $\mathcal{F}$ involving only singleton coefficients, i.e. all FIs are of the form $f \subseteq \sum_{i=1}^{n} \{a_i\} \cdot g_i + [\underline{b}, \overline{b}]$.*

Linear programming becomes NP-hard when restricted to integers only [38]. Unless P = NP, the integer interval domains $\mathcal{D}_{\mathbf{Int}(\mathbb{Z})}$, $\mathcal{D}_{\mathbf{Int}(\mathbb{N})}$, and $\mathcal{D}_{\mathbf{Int}(\{0,1\})}$ are thus not P-admissible w.r.t. affine FBoxes. These domains are rather suitable for integration into Horn logics [55] that do not allow for polynomial-time reasoning, such as $\mathcal{ELI}$ [4], Horn-$\mathcal{ALC}$ [47], Horn-$\mathcal{SROIQ}$ [57], and existential rules [15].

Example 18. Example 3 in [1] shows that the combination of the concrete domains $\mathcal{D}_{\mathbb{Q},\mathsf{diff}}$ and $\mathcal{D}_{\mathbb{Q},\mathsf{lin}}$ is not enough to express that intensive-care patients need attention if their pulse pressure is larger than 50 or their current heart rate exceeds their maximal heart rate. Moreover, this combination is not even convex.

With our interval domain these statements can be expressed through the affine FIs $\mathsf{pp} \sqsubseteq \mathsf{sys} - \mathsf{dia}$, and $\mathsf{maxHR} \sqsubseteq 220 - \mathsf{age}$, and $\mathsf{exceedHR} \sqsubseteq \mathsf{hr} - \mathsf{maxHR}$, as well as the CIs $\mathsf{ICUPatient} \sqsubseteq (\mathsf{hr} \sqsubseteq \Box) \sqcap (\mathsf{sys} \sqsubseteq \Box) \sqcap (\mathsf{dia} \sqsubseteq \Box)$, and $\mathsf{ICUPatient} \sqcap (\mathsf{pp} \sqsubseteq (50, \infty)) \sqsubseteq \mathsf{NeedsAttention}$, and $\mathsf{ICUPatient} \sqcap (\mathsf{exceedHR} \sqsubseteq (0, \infty)) \sqsubseteq \mathsf{NeedsAttention}$.

3.2 2D-Polygons

A *2D-polygon* is a finite sequence of successively connected finite line segments in the real plane $\mathbb{R}^2$ such that the end vertex of the last segment equals the start vertex of the first. These line segments form a simple closed curve in $\mathbb{R}^2$, and by the Jordan Curve Theorem [28,36] each 2D-polygon has an *interior region* (bounded by the curve) and an *exterior region*. In the following we identify each 2D-polygon with the subset of $\mathbb{R}^2$ consisting of its boundary and the interior region. 2D-polygons are thoroughly studied in Computational Geometry and frequently used in geographic information systems (GIS).

Every 2D-polygon can be represented as a finite sequence of vertex coordinates in $\mathbb{R}^2$—its line segments then connect each two subsequent coordinates and, respectively, the first and last coordinate—and thus deciding the set of all 2D-polygons is trivial. Clipping algorithms allow for deciding in polynomial time if a polygon is a subset of another (i.e. polygon containment without moving or scaling operations) as well as for computing any Boolean operation involving two polygons (union, intersection, difference, xor) in polynomial time [24,54,63]. However, intersections can be of quadratic size and might consist of unions of disjoint 2D-polygons. In order to obtain a semi-lattice, which must be closed under its meet operation, it would therefore be necessary to take the set of all finite unions of separated 2D-polygons: we denote it by $\mathbf{UGon}(\mathbb{R}^2)$, its partial order is containment $\subseteq$, and its meet is intersection $\cap$. According to the above references, $\mathbf{UGon}(\mathbb{R}^2)$ is polynomial-time computable (w.r.t. arithmetic complexity). The hierarchical concrete domain $\mathcal{D}_{\mathbf{UGon}(\mathbb{R}^2)}$ is called *polygon domain* over $\mathbb{R}^2$. A corollary to Proposition 11 is as follows.

Corollary 19. *W.r.t. arithmetic complexity, the polygon domain $\mathcal{D}_{\mathbf{UGon}(\mathbb{R}^2)}$ has exponential-time computable canonical valuations and is EXP-admissible w.r.t. each acyclic FBox $\mathcal{F}$ in which all operations are polynomial-time computable.*

To the best of the author's knowledge, it is unclear whether the intersection of n polygons might reach an exponential size. If this worst case would not be possible and, moreover, all operations in $\mathcal{F}$ are non-duplicating, then $\mathcal{D}_{\mathbf{UGon}(\mathbb{R}^2)}$ would even be P-admissible w.r.t. $\mathcal{F}$ (w.r.t. arithmetic complexity).

Example 20. Locations can be represented as polygons in the real plane $\mathbb{R}^2$. For instance, we have "Nöthnitzer Straße 46, 01187 Dresden" $\subseteq$ "01187 Dresden" $\subseteq$ "Dresden" $\subseteq$ "Saxony" $\subseteq$ "Germany" $\subseteq$ "Europe" $\subseteq$ "Earth".

The situation is computationally easier with *convex* 2D-polygons, which contain all line segments between each two of their points. One can think of convex 2D-polygons as two-dimensional generalizations of closed intervals. Both in linear time, we can decide the subset relation $\subseteq$ and compute the intersection operation $\cap$ for convex 2D-polygons [56,60,62]. Intersection is non-duplicating [60]. However, deciding the set of all convex 2D-polygons is not trivial anymore but needs linear time [60]. We denote the semi-lattice of all convex 2D-polygons by $\mathbf{CGon}(\mathbb{R}^2)$, and it is linear-time computable (w.r.t. arithmetic complexity). The hierarchical concrete domain $\mathcal{D}_{\mathbf{CGon}(\mathbb{R}^2)}$ is called *convex-polygon domain* over $\mathbb{R}^2$.

Obviously, convex polygons are closed under intersection but not under union, difference, and xor. Since union is monotonic, it can be used in FBoxes when followed by the convex-hull operation (which computes the smallest enclosing polygon that is convex). This is, however, not possible for difference and xor since they are not monotonic. Suitable monotonic operations besides intersection and convex union are translation, rotation, and scaling, and these can be computed in linear time as well. Below is a corollary to Proposition 10.

Corollary 21. *W.r.t. each acyclic, non-duplicating FBox $\mathcal{F}$ in which all occurring operations are polynomial-time computable, the convex-polygon domain $\mathcal{D}_{\mathbf{CGon}(\mathbb{R}^2)}$ has polynomial-time computable canonical valuations and is P-admissible (w.r.t. arithmetic complexity).*

Contrary to $\mathbf{Int}(\mathbb{R})$, neither $\mathbf{UGon}(\mathbb{R}^2)$ nor $\mathbf{CGon}(\mathbb{R}^2)$ are complete. One reason is that the unit circle can be obtained as the intersection of regular polygons (for each $n \in \mathbb{N}$ with $n \geq 3$, take a smallest regular n-sided polygon that encloses the unit circle). The polygon semi-lattices are also not well-founded, and thus we cannot obtain corollaries to Theorems 8 and 9 w.r.t. cyclic FBoxes.

3.3   Regular Languages

Given a finite alphabet Σ, the semi-lattice $\mathbf{Reg}(\Sigma)$ consists of all regular languages over Σ, is partially ordered by set inclusion $\subseteq$, and its meet operation is set intersection $\cap$. It is not complete since regular languages are not closed under arbitrary intersections (only under finite ones). More specifically, $L = \bigcap\{\Sigma^* \setminus \{w\} \mid w \notin L\}$ for each language L, and thus for two symbols $a, b \in \Sigma$ the non-regular language $\{a^n b^n \mid n \in \mathbb{N}\}$ is an intersection of regular languages. Thus, convexity does not follow from Theorem 8.

In order to obtain a computable semi-lattice, we need to work with finite representations of regular languages. With regular expressions, binary intersections of regular languages can have exponential size even over a binary alphabet [25], i.e. the meet would not be computable in polynomial time. It is no alternative to instead use one-unambiguous/deterministic regular expressions since they cannot describe all regular languages and are not even closed under intersection, even though their inclusion problem is in polynomial time [19, 32, 48].

Using finite automata as representations is preferred, on the one hand since to obtain the meet/intersection of two regular languages we can compute the product of the respective finite automata in polynomial time [37]. On the other hand, a language inclusion $L_1 \subseteq L_2$ holds iff. the language equivalence $L_1 \cap L_2 = L_2$ holds, and thus it suffices to check if the product of both finite automata is equivalent to the second automaton. For deterministic automata this is possible in polynomial time [16, 31], but otherwise needs polynomial space [61].

The semi-lattice $\mathbf{DFA}(\Sigma)$ consists of all deterministic finite automata over Σ, is partially ordered by automata inclusion $\preceq$ where $\mathfrak{A} \preceq \mathfrak{B}$ if $L(\mathfrak{A}) \subseteq L(\mathfrak{B})$, and its meet operation is the product $\times$, which satisfies $L(\mathfrak{A} \times \mathfrak{B}) = L(\mathfrak{A}) \cap L(\mathfrak{B})$. It is thus polynomial-time computable. Furthermore, $\mathbf{FA}(\Sigma)$ comprises all finite automata and is polynomial-space computable. Since finite automata and deterministic ones have equal power in the sense that they both describe all regular languages, both semi-lattices can serve as representations of $\mathbf{Reg}(\Sigma)$.

The hierarchical concrete domains $\mathcal{D}_{\mathbf{DFA}(\Sigma)}$ and $\mathcal{D}_{\mathbf{FA}(\Sigma)}$ are called the *regular-language domains* over Σ. Since single words are regular languages, precise string values are supported: we may write $(f = w)$ instead of $(f \preceq \mathfrak{A})$ when $L(\mathfrak{A}) = \{w\}$. Further note that $\square$ is the automaton that accepts every string, $\perp$ accepts no string at all, and $\top$ is an artificial greatest element.

Example 22. Let Σ be an alphabet containing all Latin letters, e.g. The Unicode Standard. We use a feature hasTitle to represent the title string of a research paper. Further take a DFA $\mathfrak{A}$ such that $L(\mathfrak{A}) = \Sigma^* \circ \{\text{description logic}\} \circ \Sigma^*$. With that, the CI ScientificArticle $\sqcap$ (hasTitle $\preceq \mathfrak{A}$) $\sqsubseteq$ DLPaper expresses that the concept of all DL papers subsumes the concept of all scientific articles with a title containing "description logic" as substring.

Even without an FBox, the regular-language domains $\mathcal{D}_{\mathbf{DFA}(\Sigma)}$ and $\mathcal{D}_{\mathbf{FA}(\Sigma)}$ are in general not P-admissible. In a nutshell, meets need not be non-duplicating, and thus accumulating all upper bounds of the same feature could yield an exponentially large automaton. More specifically, if a constraint set Γ contains several constraints $f \preceq \mathfrak{A}$ for the same feature f, then computing the value $v_{\Gamma, \mathcal{F}}(f)$ boils down to computing the intersection of all these automata $\mathfrak{A}$. Since emptiness of intersections of finite automata is P Space-hard [43] and graph reachability is NL-complete [35], $v_{\Gamma, \mathcal{F}}(f)$ cannot be computed in polynomial time, unless P = P Space. We obtain, however, the following corollary to Proposition 11.

Corollary 23. *W.r.t. each acyclic FBox $\mathcal{F}$ in which all occurring operations are polynomial-time computable, the regular-language domain $\mathcal{D}_{\mathbf{DFA}(\Sigma)}$ has exponential-time computable canonical valuations and is* EXP-*admissible.*

The DFA operations corresponding to the language operations union $\cup$, intersection $\cap$, and complement $^-$ are polynomial-time computable. $\mathcal{D}_{\mathbf{DFA}(\Sigma)}$ is thus EXP-admissible w.r.t. each acyclic FBox involving these operations only. In contrast, concatenation $\circ$, Kleene-star *, mirror/reversal $^\frown$, left-quotients $\backslash$, and right-quotients $/$ on DFAs are exponential-time computable but not polynomial-time computable [65]. However on FAs, all operations but complement are polynomial-time computable, and mirror/reversal is even non-duplicating. $\mathcal{D}_{\mathbf{FA}(\Sigma)}$ is EXPSpace-admissible w.r.t. acyclic FBoxes using these polynomial-time operations.

It is worth mentioning that, if we have at most one inclusion (i.e. constraint or FI) per feature, then in the procedure in the proof of Theorem 9 neither the automata product operation nor the automata inclusion relation needs to be used, and so we have the following corollary.

Corollary 24. *Let $\mathcal{F}$ be an acyclic, non-duplicating FBox in which all occurring operations are polynomial-time computable. Further let Γ be a constraint set. If $\mathcal{F} \cup \Gamma$ contains, for each feature f, at most one inclusion with f on the left, then the canonical valuation of Γ w.r.t. $\mathcal{F}$ can be computed in polynomial time.*

Example 25. Assume the features givenName, familyName, and name are used to represent persons' names. Then for instance, the concept Male $\sqcap$ (givenName $\preceq \mathfrak{A}$) where $L(\mathfrak{A}) = \{\mathrm{F}\} \circ \Sigma^*$ describes all males whose given name starts with 'F'.

Moreover, the FI name $\preceq$ givenName $\circ$ {_} $\circ$ familyName allows to infer a regular language value of name when values of givenName and familyName are available (i.e. both are not $\top$). If the latter two are precise values (languages consisting of a single word), then also name gets a precise value through the FI. Note that '_' stands for a white space. The FI shortName $\preceq$ initial(givenName) $\circ$ {._} $\circ$ familyName generates a shortened form of a name that only contains the initial of the given name followed by a dot, where the function initial is defined by $L(\mathrm{initial}(\mathfrak{A})) := \{s \mid s \in \Sigma \text{ and there is } w \in \Sigma^* \text{ such that } s \circ w \in L(\mathfrak{A})\}$.

The semi-lattices $\mathbf{Reg}(\Sigma)$, $\mathbf{DFA}(\Sigma)$, and $\mathbf{FA}(\Sigma)$ are not well-founded since, already over the unary alphabet $\{a\}$, the regular languages $L_i := \{a^j \mid i \le j\}$ where $i \in \mathbb{N}$ form an infinite descending chain $L_0 \supset L_1 \supset L_2 \supset \cdots$. These semi-lattices are also not complete (see above). W.r.t. cyclic FBoxes, we can thus not conclude convexity by Theorems 8 and 9.

For a restricted class of FBoxes, however, we obtain systems of language inclusions known to be solvable in exponential time [10]. An n-ary operation H on $\mathbf{DFA}(\Sigma)$ is *left-linear* if $H(\mathfrak{X}_1, \ldots, \mathfrak{X}_n) = \mathfrak{X}_1 \circ \mathfrak{A}_1 \cup \cdots \cup \mathfrak{X}_n \circ \mathfrak{A}_n \cup \mathfrak{B}$ and *right-linear* if $H(\mathfrak{X}_1, \ldots, \mathfrak{X}_n) = \mathfrak{A}_1 \circ \mathfrak{X}_1 \cup \cdots \cup \mathfrak{A}_n \circ \mathfrak{X}_n \cup \mathfrak{B}$, where $\mathfrak{A}_1, \ldots, \mathfrak{A}_n, \mathfrak{B}$ are DFAs. An FBox $\mathcal{F}$ is *linear* if the operations in its FIs are either all left-linear or all right-linear.

Proposition 26. *The regular-language domain $\mathcal{D}_{\mathbf{DFA}(\Sigma)}$ has exponential-time computable canonical valuations and is EXP-admissible w.r.t. each linear FBox.*

If precise values (single words) are sufficient for the application, we could also use the semi-lattice $(\Sigma^* \cup \{\bot, \top\}, \le, \wedge)$ where $\le$ is the smallest partial order such

(a) $\mathcal{G}_{\text{carboxylic acid group}}$ (b) $\mathcal{G}_{\text{amino group}}$ (c) $\mathcal{G}_{\text{L-leucine}}$

Fig. 1. Three graphs representing chemical compounds

that $\bot < w < \top$ for each $w \in \Sigma^*$. The meet operation $\wedge$ thus satisfies $\top \wedge w = w$, $w \wedge w = w$, and $w \wedge \bot = \bot$ for each $w \in \Sigma^* \cup \{\bot, \top\}$, and $w_1 \wedge w_2 = \bot$ whenever $w_1, w_2 \in \Sigma^*$ with $w_1 \neq w_2$. This semi-lattice is complete and, by Theorem 8, its hierarchical concrete domain is convex w.r.t. every FBox. Since during the computation of a canonical valuation each feature value can be refined at most two times (from $\top$ to some w, and then possibly to $\bot$), this concrete domain is P-admissible w.r.t. each FBox in which all operations are polynomial-time computable. The disadvantage is, however, that string search like in Example 22 is not possible anymore. On the other hand, this suggests that in $\mathcal{D}_{\mathbf{DFA}(\Sigma)}$ and $\mathcal{D}_{\mathbf{FA}(\Sigma)}$ everything involving only precise values is possible in polynomial time.

3.4 Graphs

All finite, labeled graphs constitute a semi-lattice **Graph**, where the partial order $\leq$ is defined by $\mathcal{G} \leq \mathcal{H}$ if there is a homomorphism from $\mathcal{H}$ to $\mathcal{G}$. It is well-known that $\leq$ is NP-complete [21], but in P for acyclic graphs [22]. The meet of two graphs is their disjoint union, thus a non-duplicating operation, and the greatest element in this semi-lattice is the empty graph. Obviously, **Graph** is neither complete nor well-founded, and so we cannot apply Theorems 8 and 9. It thus remains unclear whether the *graph domain* $\mathcal{D}_{\mathbf{Graph}}$ is convex w.r.t. cyclic FBoxes.

Corollary 27. *The graph domain $\mathcal{D}_{\mathbf{Graph}}$ has computable canonical valuations w.r.t. acylic FBoxes. Moreover, it is NP-admissible w.r.t. every acyclic, non-duplicating FBox in which all operations are polynomial-time computable, and it is EXP-admissible w.r.t. every acyclic FBox in which all operations are polynomial-time computable.*

Example 28. Structural formulas of molecules can be represented as labeled graphs. Each node is labeled with the atom it represents, and the edges are labeled with the binding type (e.g. single bond, double bond, etc.). Figure 1 shows three exemplary graphs. Graph (c) represents L-leucine, and we can integrate it into a KB with the statement L-Leucine $\equiv$ (hasMolecularStructure $\leq$ $\mathcal{G}_{\text{L-leucine}}$). Moreover, the statement AminoAcid $\equiv$ (hasMolecularStructure $\leq$ $\mathcal{G}_{\text{carboxylic acid group}}$) $\sqcap$ (hasMolecularStructure $\leq \mathcal{G}_{\text{amino group}}$) expresses that amino acids are organic compounds that contain both amino and carboxylic acid functional groups. If $\mathcal{K}$ is the KB consisting of the aforementioned statements, then $\mathcal{K} \models$ L-Leucine $\sqsubseteq$ AminoAcid since $\mathcal{G}_{\text{L-leucine}} \leq \mathcal{G}_{\text{carboxylic acid group}} \wedge \mathcal{G}_{\text{amino group}}$.

4   Reasoning in $\mathcal{EL}^{++}$ with Hierarchical Concrete Domains

Like other convex concrete domains, a hierarchical concrete domain $\mathcal{D}_{\mathbf{L}}$ can be integrated into $\mathcal{EL}^{++}$ but, in addition to Sect. 2, every $\mathcal{EL}^{++}[\mathcal{D}_{\mathbf{L}}]$ KB may contain finitely many FIs. Of course, a model of such a KB must also satisfy all FIs in it. In order to guarantee that reasoning is decidable, a restriction on the interplay of RIs and range inclusions must be fulfilled by every $\mathcal{EL}^{++}[\mathcal{D}]$ KB [5], see Condition 1 below. To this end, we define the *range set* of a role r in $\mathcal{K}$ by $\mathsf{Range}(r, \mathcal{K}) := \{C \mid \text{there is a role } s \text{ s.t. } \mathcal{R} \models r \sqsubseteq s \text{ and } \mathsf{Ran}(s) \sqsubseteq C \in \mathcal{K}\}$, where $\mathcal{R}$ is the subset of all RIs in $\mathcal{K}$. All such range sets can be computed in polynomial time by first transforming each RI $r_1 \circ \cdots \circ r_n \sqsubseteq s$ into a context-free grammar rule $s \to r_1 \ldots r_n$ (see Lemma IV in [9] for details) and then deciding the word problem for this grammar (e.g. with the CYK algorithm [23,39,64]).

Definition 29. *Consider a bounded semi-lattice* $\mathbf{L}$. *An* $\mathcal{EL}^{++}[\mathcal{D}_{\mathbf{L}}]$ *knowledge base (KB)* $\mathcal{K}$ *is a finite set of CIs, RIs, range inclusions, and FIs such that*

1. $\mathsf{Range}(s, \mathcal{K}) \subseteq \mathsf{Range}(r_n, \mathcal{K})$ *for every RI* $r_1 \circ \cdots \circ r_n \sqsubseteq s$ *in* $\mathcal{K}$ *with* $n \geq 2$,
2. *and the hierarchical concrete domain* $\mathcal{D}_{\mathbf{L}}$ *is convex w.r.t. all FIs in* $\mathcal{K}$.

For a complexity class C *we say that* $\mathcal{D}_{\mathbf{L}}$ *is* C*-admissible w.r.t.* $\mathcal{K}$ *if* $\mathcal{D}_{\mathbf{L}}$ *is* C*-admissible w.r.t. the FBox consisting of all FIs in* $\mathcal{K}$.

For Condition 1 range inclusions on s must not imply further concept memberships than already implied by the range inclusions on r_n; otherwise emptiness of intersections of two context-free grammars could be reduced to subsumption [5].

Reasoning in $\mathcal{EL}^{++}[\mathcal{D}]$ can be done by means of a rule-based calculus [4,5, 40,42], and a hierarchical concrete domain $\mathcal{D}_{\mathbf{L}}$ can be seamlessly integrated into this calculus. Compared to the primal calculus [4,5], it is only necessary to take the FIs into account. For integration into the improved calculus [40,42] we only need to add the following two rules responsible for interaction between concrete and logical reasoning (where $\mathcal{F}$ consists of all FIs in the KB), see [46] for details.

$$\mathsf{R}_{\mathcal{D}}: \quad \frac{C \sqsubseteq (f_1 \leq p_1) \quad \cdots \quad C \sqsubseteq (f_m \leq p_m)}{C \sqsubseteq (g \leq q)} : \mathcal{D}_{\mathbf{L}}, \mathcal{F} \models \prod_{i=1}^{m}(f_i \leq p_i) \sqsubseteq (g \leq q)$$

$$\mathsf{R}_{\mathcal{D},\perp}: \quad \frac{C \sqsubseteq (f_1 \leq p_1) \quad \cdots \quad C \sqsubseteq (f_m \leq p_m)}{C \sqsubseteq \perp} : \prod_{i=1}^{m}(f_i \leq p_i) \text{ unsatisfiable in } \mathcal{D}_{\mathbf{L}}, \mathcal{F}$$

However, we restrict attention to nominal-safe KBs, i.e. nominals $\{i\}$ must not occur in conjunctions and each right-hand side of a concept or range inclusion must not be a single nominal $\{i\}$. Full support for nominals in $\mathcal{EL}^{++}[\mathcal{D}]$ is technically quite involved and makes reasoning more expensive: the degree of the polynomial describing the worst-case reasoning time would then be larger by 1 [41]. We conjecture the same for $\mathcal{EL}^{++}[\mathcal{D}_{\mathbf{L}}]$ KBs that are not nominal-safe.

Range inclusions are not natively supported by the rule-based calculus, but they must rather be eliminated [5]. This transformation was originally described for KBs in normal form only, but can now be done without prior transformation to normal form, see [46] for details.

Theorem 30. *Let* **L** *be a bounded semi-lattice. For all nominal-safe* $\mathcal{EL}^{++}[\mathcal{D}_{\mathbf{L}}]$ *KBs w.r.t. which the hierarchical concrete domain* $\mathcal{D}_{\mathbf{L}}$ *is* P-*admissible, the following reasoning tasks can be done in polynomial time: consistency, classification, subsumption checking, instance checking, and concept satisfiability.*

In the proof of the above result, we build a canonical model of the KB iff. it is consistent. Now with the hierarchical concrete domains we can use the canonical valuations for this. The benefit is that the canonical model is universal w.r.t. all nominal-safe assertions $\{i\} \sqsubseteq C$, before it was only universal w.r.t. such assertions without concrete constraints. Our canonical models are thus appropriate for computing optimal repairs [8,9,44,45] of KBs involving concrete domains.

We can also use NP- or EXP-admissible concrete domains in $\mathcal{EL}^{++}$. Reasoning works in the very same way, i.e. the logical reasoning can still be done in polynomial time, but the concrete reasoning is more expensive.

Theorem 31. *Fix a bounded semi-lattice* **L**. *For all nominal-safe* $\mathcal{EL}^{++}[\mathcal{D}_{\mathbf{L}}]$ *KBs w.r.t. which the hierarchical concrete domain* $\mathcal{D}_{\mathbf{L}}$ *is* NP-*admissible, the following reasoning problems are in* NP: *consistency, concept satisfiability, subsumption checking, and instance checking. They are in* EXP *if* $\mathcal{D}_{\mathbf{L}}$ *is* EXP-*admissible. In both cases, the classification can be computed in exponential time.*

5 Future Prospects

An interesting question for future research is whether non-local feature inclusions $f \leq H(R_1 \circ g_1, \ldots, R_n \circ g_n)$ would lead to undecidability or could be reasoned with, where the R_i are role chains. The operator must then be defined for lists of values, like in the non-local feature inclusion combinedWealth $\subseteq \sum$ (hasAccount∘balance)$+$ $\sum$ (holdsAsset ∘ value) over the interval domain, which computes the aggregated wealth of a person or company. At first sight, it seems that the undecidability proof for $\mathcal{EL}(\mathcal{D}_{\mathbb{Q}^2, \text{aff}})$ [13] cannot be adapted to this setting. (Mind the braces: $(\mathcal{D})$ instead of $[\mathcal{D}]$ allows for role chains in front of features.) The computation of canonical valuations must then take into account the graph structure induced by the role assertions entailed by the knowledge base.

In general, it is unclear whether a hierarchical concrete domain is admissible w.r.t. cyclic FBoxes. According to our results for interval domains and regular-language domains, admissibility can be ensured by approaches to solving systems of equations or inequations involving elements of the underlying semi-lattice. This is still open for the polygon domains and the graph domains.

Since hierarchical concrete domains are convex by design, they are also appropriate for other Horn logics and existential rules—extending the chase procedure with support for them would be practically relevant.

Acknowledgments. This work has been supported by Deutsche Forschungsgemeinschaft (DFG) in Projects 389792660 (CPEC) and 558917076 as well as by the Saxon State Ministry for Science, Culture, and Tourism (SMWK) by funding the Center for Scalable Data Analytics and Artificial Intelligence (ScaDS.AI).

References

1. Alrabbaa, C., Baader, F., Borgwardt, S., Koopmann, P., Kovtunova, A.: Combining proofs for description logic and concrete domain reasoning. In: Fensel, A., Ozaki, A., Roman, D., Soylu, A. (eds.) RuleML+RR 2023. LNCS, vol. 14244, pp. 54–69. Springer, Cham (2023). https://doi.org/10.1007/978-3-031-45072-3_4

2. Baader, F., Borgwardt, S., Lippmann, M.: Query rewriting for DL-lite with n-ary concrete domains. In: Proceedings of the 26th International Joint Conference on Artificial Intelligence (IJCAI), pp. 786–792 (2017). https://doi.org/10.24963/IJCAI.2017/109

3. Baader, F., Bortoli, F.D.: The abstract expressive power of first-order and description logics with concrete domains. In: Proceedings of the 39th ACM/SIGAPP Symposium on Applied Computing (SAC), pp. 754–761 (2024). https://doi.org/10.1145/3605098.3635984

4. Baader, F., Brandt, S., Lutz, C.: Pushing the $\mathcal{EL}$ envelope. In: Proceedings of the 19th International Joint Conference on Artificial Intelligence (IJCAI), pp. 364–369 (2005). http://ijcai.org/Proceedings/05/Papers/0372.pdf

5. Baader, F., Brandt, S., Lutz, C.: Pushing the $\mathcal{EL}$ envelope further. In: Proceedings of the 4th OWLED Workshop on OWL: Experiences and Directions. CEUR Workshop Proceedings (2008). https://ceur-ws.org/Vol-496/owled2008dc%5C_paper%5C_3.pdf

6. Baader, F., De Bortoli, F.: Logics with concrete domains: first-order properties, abstract expressive power, and (un)decidability. SIGAPP Appl. Comput. Rev. **24**(3), 5–17 (2024). https://doi.org/10.1145/3699839.3699840

7. Baader, F., Hanschke, P.: A scheme for integrating concrete domains into concept languages. In: Proceedings of the 12th International Joint Conference on Artificial Intelligence (IJCAI), pp. 452–457 (1991). http://ijcai.org/Proceedings/91-1/Papers/070.pdf

8. Baader, F., Koopmann, P., Kriegel, F., Nuradiansyah, A.: Computing optimal repairs of quantified ABoxes w.r.t. static $\mathcal{EL}$ TBoxes. In: Platzer, A., Sutcliffe, G. (eds.) CADE 2021. LNCS (LNAI), vol. 12699, pp. 309–326. Springer, Cham (2021). https://doi.org/10.1007/978-3-030-79876-5_18

9. Baader, F., Kriegel, F.: Pushing optimal ABox repair from $\mathcal{EL}$ towards more expressive Horn-DLs. In: Proceedings of the 19th International Conference on Principles of Knowledge Representation and Reasoning (KR), pp. 22–32 (2022). https://doi.org/10.24963/kr.2022/3

10. Baader, F., Küsters, R.: Unification in a description logic with transitive closure of roles. In: Nieuwenhuis, R., Voronkov, A. (eds.) LPAR 2001. LNCS (LNAI), vol. 2250, pp. 217–232. Springer, Heidelberg (2001). https://doi.org/10.1007/3-540-45653-8_15

11. Baader, F., Rydval, J.: An algebraic view on p-admissible concrete domains for lightweight description logics. In: Faber, W., Friedrich, G., Gebser, M., Morak, M. (eds.) JELIA 2021. LNCS (LNAI), vol. 12678, pp. 194–209. Springer, Cham (2021). https://doi.org/10.1007/978-3-030-75775-5_14

12. Baader, F., Rydval, J.: Description logics with concrete domains and general concept inclusions revisited. In: Peltier, N., Sofronie-Stokkermans, V. (eds.) IJCAR 2020. LNCS (LNAI), vol. 12166, pp. 413–431. Springer, Cham (2020). https://doi.org/10.1007/978-3-030-51074-9_24

13. Baader, F., Rydval, J.: Using model theory to find decidable and tractable description logics with concrete domains. J. Autom. Reason. **66**(3), 357–407 (2022). https://doi.org/10.1007/S10817-022-09626-2

14. Baader, F., Sattler, U.: Description logics with aggregates and concrete domains. Inf. Syst. **28**(8), 979–1004 (2003). https://doi.org/10.1016/S0306-4379(03)00003-6

15. Baget, J., Leclère, M., Mugnier, M., Salvat, E.: Extending decidable cases for rules with existential variables. In: Proceedings of the 21st International Joint Conference on Artificial Intelligence (IJCAI), pp. 677–682 (2009). http://ijcai.org/Proceedings/09/Papers/118.pdf

16. Bonchi, F., Pous, D.: Checking NFA equivalence with bisimulations up to congruence. In: Proceedings of the 40th Annual ACM SIGPLAN-SIGACT Symposium on Principles of Programming Languages (POPL), pp. 457–468 (2013). See also [29] and [17]. https://doi.org/10.1145/2429069.2429124

17. Bonchi, F., Pous, D.: Hacking nondeterminism with induction and coinduction. Commun. ACM **58**(2), 87–95 (2015). https://doi.org/10.1145/2713167

18. Borgwardt, S., Bortoli, F.D., Koopmann, P.: The precise complexity of reasoning in $\mathcal{ALC}$ with ω-admissible concrete domains. In: Proceedings of the 37th International Workshop on Description Logics (DL). CEUR Workshop Proceedings (2024). https://ceur-ws.org/Vol-3739/paper-1.pdf

19. Brüggemann-Klein, A., Wood, D.: One-unambiguous regular languages. Inf. Comput. **140**(2), 229–253 (1998). https://doi.org/10.1006/INCO.1997.2688

20. Carapelle, C., Turhan, A.: Description logics reasoning w.r.t. general TBoxes is decidable for concrete domains with the EHD-property. In: Proceedings of the 22nd European Conference on Artificial Intelligence (ECAI). Frontiers in Artificial Intelligence and Applications, pp. 1440–1448 (2016). https://doi.org/10.3233/978-1-61499-672-9-1440

21. Chandra, A.K., Merlin, P.M.: Optimal implementation of conjunctive queries in relational data bases. In: Proceedings of the 9th Annual ACM Symposium on Theory of Computing (STOC), pp. 77–90 (1977). https://doi.org/10.1145/800105.803397

22. Chekuri, C., Rajaraman, A.: Conjunctive query containment revisited. In: Afrati, F., Kolaitis, P. (eds.) ICDT 1997. LNCS, vol. 1186, pp. 56–70. Springer, Heidelberg (1997). https://doi.org/10.1007/3-540-62222-5_36

23. Cocke, J.: Programming languages and their compilers: preliminary notes, USA (1969)

24. Greiner, G., Hormann, K.: Efficient clipping of arbitrary polygons. ACM Trans. Graph. **17**(2), 71–83 (1998). https://doi.org/10.1145/274363.274364

25. Gruber, H., Holzer, M.: Finite automata, digraph connectivity, and regular expression size. In: Aceto, L., Damgård, I., Goldberg, L.A., Halldórsson, M.M., Ingólfsdóttir, A., Walukiewicz, I. (eds.) ICALP 2008. LNCS, vol. 5126, pp. 39–50. Springer, Heidelberg (2008). https://doi.org/10.1007/978-3-540-70583-3_4

26. Haarslev, V., Lutz, C., Möller, R.: A description logic with concrete domains and a role-forming predicate operator. J. Log. Comput. **9**(3), 351–384 (1999). https://doi.org/10.1093/LOGCOM/9.3.351

27. Haarslev, V., Möller, R., Wessel, M.: The description logic $\mathcal{ALCNH}_{R+}$ extended with concrete domains: a practically motivated approach. In: Goré, R., Leitsch, A., Nipkow, T. (eds.) IJCAR 2001. LNCS, vol. 2083, pp. 29–44. Springer, Heidelberg (2001). https://doi.org/10.1007/3-540-45744-5_4

28. Hales, T.C.: The Jordan curve theorem, formally and informally. Am. Math. Mon. **114**(10), 882–894 (2007). http://www.jstor.org/stable/27642361

29. Henzinger, T.A., Raskin, J.: The equivalence problem for finite automata: technical perspective. Commun. ACM **58**(2), 86 (2015). https://doi.org/10.1145/2701001

30. Hickey, T.J., Ju, Q., van Emden, M.H.: Interval arithmetic: from principles to implementation. **48**(5), 1038–1068 (2001). https://doi.org/10.1145/502102.502106
31. Hopcroft, J.E., Karp, R.M.: A linear algorithm for testing equivalence of finite automata. Technical report, TR71-114, Cornell University (1971). https://hdl.handle.net/1813/5958
32. Hovland, D.: The inclusion problem for regular expressions. J. Comput. Syst. Sci. **78**(6), 1795–1813 (2012). https://doi.org/10.1016/J.JCSS.2011.12.003
33. Jiang, S., Song, Z., Weinstein, O., Zhang, H.: A faster algorithm for solving general LPs. In: Proceedings of the 53rd Annual ACM SIGACT Symposium on Theory of Computing (STOC), pp. 823–832 (2021). https://doi.org/10.1145/3406325.3451058
34. Jones, N.D.: Space-bounded reducibility among combinatorial problems. J. Comput. Syst. Sci. **11**(1), 68–85 (1975). See also [34]. https://doi.org/10.1016/S0022-0000(77)80009-3
35. Jones, N.D.: Space-Bounded Reducibility among Combinatorial Problems. J. Comput. Syst. Sci. **11**(1), 68–85 (1975). See also [34]. https://doi.org/10.1016/S0022-0000(75)80050-X
36. Jordan, C.: Cours d'analyse de l'École Polytechnique—Volume 3: Calcul intégral, équations différentielles, Paris (1887). https://doi.org/10.1017/CBO9781107300064
37. Karakostas, G., Lipton, R.J., Viglas, A.: On the complexity of intersecting finite state automata and NL versus NP. Theoret. Comput. Sci. **302**(1–3), 257–274 (2003). https://doi.org/10.1016/S0304-3975(02)00830-7
38. Karp, R.M.: Reducibility among combinatorial problems. In: Miller, R.E., Thatcher, J.W., Bohlinger, J.D. (eds.) Complexity of Computer Computations. The IBM Research Symposia Series, pp. 85–103. Springer, Boston (1972). https://doi.org/10.1007/978-1-4684-2001-2_9
39. Kasami, T.: An Efficient Recognition and Syntax-Analysis Algorithm for Context-Free Languages. Report R-257, Coordinated Science Laboratory, University of Illinois, Urbana, Illinois (1966). https://doi.org/10.1007/978-1-4684-2001-2_9
40. Kazakov, Y., Klinov, P.: Advancing ELK: not only performance matters. In: Proceedings of the 28th International Workshop on Description Logics (DL). CEUR Workshop Proceedings (2015). http://hdl.handle.net/2142/74304
41. Kazakov, Y., Krötzsch, M., Simančík, F.: Practical reasoning with nominals in the $\mathcal{EL}$ family of description logics. In: Proceedings of the 13th International Conference on Principles of Knowledge Representation and Reasoning (KR) (2012). https://ceur-ws.org/Vol-1350/paper-27.pdf
42. Kazakov, Y., Krötzsch, M., Simančík, F.: The incredible ELK - from polynomial procedures to efficient reasoning with $\mathcal{EL}$ ontologies. J. Autom. Reason. **53**(1), 1–61 (2014). https://doi.org/10.1007/S10817-013-9296-3
43. Kozen, D.: Lower bounds for natural proof systems. In: Proceedings of the 18th Annual Symposium on Foundations of Computer Science (FOCS), pp. 254–266 (1977). https://doi.org/10.1109/SFCS.1977.16
44. Kriegel, F.: Beyond optimal: interactive identification of better-than-optimal repairs. In: Proceedings of the 40th ACM/SIGAPP Symposium on Applied Computing (SAC), pp. 1019–1026 (2025). https://doi.org/10.1145/3672608.3707750
45. Kriegel, F.: Optimal fixed-premise repairs of $\mathcal{EL}$ TBoxes. In: Bergmann, R., Malburg, L., Rodermund, S.C., Timm, I.J. (eds.) KI 2022. LNCS, vol. 13404, pp. 115–130. Springer, Cham (2022). https://doi.org/10.1007/978-3-031-15791-2_11

46. Kriegel, F.: Reasoning in OWL 2 EL with Hierarchical Concrete Domains (Extended Version). LTCS-Report 25-04, Chair of Automata Theory, Institute of Theoretical Computer Science, Technische Universität Dresden (2025). https://doi.org/10.25368/2025.127

47. Krötzsch, M., Rudolph, S., Hitzler, P.: Complexities of Horn description logics. ACM Trans. Comput. Logic **14**(1), 2:1–2:36 (2013). https://doi.org/10.1145/2422085.2422087

48. Losemann, K., Martens, W., Niewerth, M.: Closure properties and descriptional complexity of deterministic regular expressions. Theoret. Comput. Sci. **627**, 54–70 (2016). https://doi.org/10.1016/J.TCS.2016.02.027

49. Lutz, C.: NEXPTIME-complete description logics with concrete domains. ACM Trans. Comput. Log. **5**(4), 669–705 (2004). https://doi.org/10.1145/1024922.1024925

50. Lutz, C.: The complexity of description logics with concrete domains. Doctoral thesis, RWTH Aachen University, Germany (2002). https://doi.org/10.1145/1024922.1024925

51. Lutz, C., Areces, C., Horrocks, I., Sattler, U.: Keys, nominals, and concrete domains. J. Artif. Intell. Res. **23**, 667–726 (2005). https://doi.org/10.1613/JAIR.1542

52. Lutz, C., Miličić, M.: A tableau algorithm for description logics with concrete domains and general TBoxes. J. Autom. Reason. **38**(1–3), 227–259 (2007). https://doi.org/10.1007/S10817-006-9049-7

53. Magka, D., Kazakov, Y., Horrocks, I.: Tractable extensions of the description logic $\mathcal{EL}$ with numerical datatypes. J. Autom. Reason. **47**(4), 427–450 (2011). https://doi.org/10.1007/S10817-011-9235-0

54. Martınez, F., Ogáyar, C.J., Jiménez, J., Ruiz, A.J.R.: A simple algorithm for Boolean operations on polygons. Adv. Eng. Softw. **64**, 11–19 (2013). https://doi.org/10.1016/J.ADVENGSOFT.2013.04.004

55. McNulty, G.F.: Fragments of first order logic, I: universal Horn logic. J. Symb. Log. **42**(2), 221–237 (1977). https://doi.org/10.2307/2272123

56. O'Rourke, J., Chien, C., Olson, T., Naddor, D.: A new linear algorithm for intersecting convex polygons. Comput. Graph. Image Process. **19**(4), 384–391 (1982). https://doi.org/10.1016/0146-664X(82)90023-5

57. Ortiz, M., Rudolph, S., Šimkus, M.: Worst-case optimal reasoning for the Horn-DL fragments of OWL 1 and 2. In: Proceedings of the 12th International Conference on Principles of Knowledge Representation and Reasoning (KR) (2010). http://aaai.org/ocs/index.php/KR/KR2010/paper/view/1296

58. Pan, J.Z., Horrocks, I.: Reasoning in the $\mathcal{SHOQ}(\mathbf{D_n})$ description logic. In: Proceedings of the 15th International Workshop on Description Logics (DL). CEUR Workshop Proceedings (2002). https://ceur-ws.org/Vol-53/Pan-Horrocks-shoqdn-2002.ps

59. Rydval, J.: Using model theory to find decidable and tractable description logics with concrete domains. Doctoral thesis, Dresden University of Technology, Germany (2022). https://nbn-resolving.org/urn:nbn:de:bsz:14-qucosa2-799074

60. Shamos, M.I.: Computational geometry. Ph.D. thesis, Yale University, United States (1978). http://euro.ecom.cmu.edu/people/faculty/mshamos/1978ShamosThesis.pdf

61. Stockmeyer, L.J., Meyer, A.R.: Word problems requiring exponential time: preliminary report. In: Proceedings of the 5th Annual ACM Symposium on Theory of Computing (STOC), pp. 1–9 (1973). https://doi.org/10.1145/800125.804029

62. Toussaint, G.T.: A simple linear algorithm for intersecting convex polygons. Vis. Comput. **1**(2), 118–123 (1985). https://doi.org/10.1007/BF01898355
63. Vatti, B.R.: A generic solution to polygon clipping. Commun. ACM **35**(7), 56–63 (1992). https://doi.org/10.1145/129902.129906
64. Younger, D.H.: Recognition and parsing of context-free languages in time n^3. Inf. Control **10**(2), 189–208 (1967). https://doi.org/10.1016/S0019-9958(67)80007-X
65. Yu, S., Zhuang, Q., Salomaa, K.: The state complexities of some basic operations on regular languages. Theoret. Comput. Sci. **125**(2), 315–328 (1994). https://doi.org/10.1016/0304-3975(92)00011-F

Beyond Classical Logic

An Analytic Representation
of the Semantics of First-Order S5

Matthias Baaz[1], Mariami Gamsakhurdia[1], and Anela Lolić[2]

[1] Institute of Discrete Mathematics and Geometry, TU Wien, Vienna, Austria
{baaz,mariami}@logic.at
[2] Institute of Logic and Computation, TU Wien, Vienna, Austria
anela@logic.at

Abstract. One of the most fascinating examples of the failure of Beth's definability theorem and, consequently, of Craig's interpolation theorem, is quantified S5. In this paper, we intend to establish the interpolation property for fragments of quantified S5 using a formulation of the semantics of quantified S5 as an analytic calculus in its own right. This is especially straightforward for S5, because necessity (possibility) in S5 means for all worlds (there exists a world), and we have simply to extend every predicate by a world position (worlds and objects are to be considered as separate entities).

Keywords: Modal S5 · Interpolation · Two-sorted logic · Herbrand's theorem · Cut elimination · Prenex fragment

1 Introduction

Since Craig's seminal result on interpolation [6], interpolation has been recognized as a fundamental property of logical systems. Craig interpolation has wide-ranging applications across mathematics and computer science, including consistency proofs, model checking [21], and reasoning within modular specifications and ontologies. A logic L has interpolation if whenever $A \supset B$ holds in L there exists a formula I in the common language of A and B such that $A \supset I$ and $I \supset B$ both hold in L.

In propositional logic, interpolation properties can often be determined and classified using the foundational work of Maksimova cf. [15–17], which relies on algebraic methods. However, establishing interpolation in first-order logics is

M. Baaz—This research was funded in part by the Austrian Science Fund (FWF) 10.55776/P36571.

M. Gamsakhurdia—This research was funded in part by the Austrian Science Fund (FWF) 10.55776/P36571.

A. Lolić—Recipient of an APART-MINT Fellowship of the Austrian Academy of Sciences at the Institute of Logic and Computation of TU Wien. This research was funded in part by the Austrian Science Fund (FWF) 10.55776/I5848.

R. Thiemann and C. Weidenbach (Eds.): FroCoS 2025, LNAI 15979, pp. 63–79, 2026.
https://doi.org/10.1007/978-3-032-04167-8_4

significantly more challenging, even in systems where the propositional case is well understood.

A particularly intriguing example of the failure of interpolation (and of Beth's definability theorem) arises in quantified modal logic, especially quantified S5. In this paper, we explore the interpolation property for certain fragments of quantified S5. Our approach is based on a formulation of its semantics as an analytic calculus. This is particularly straightforward in the case of S5, where necessity and possibility are interpreted as quantification over all worlds or the existence of some world, respectively. We have simply to extend every predicate by a world position.

2   Quantified S5

In this section we will introduce the quantified version of the modal system S5. We will not use the equality symbol [2,3]. The syntax for the basic first-order modal logic is obtained simply by taking the syntax of classical first-order logic and adding the modal operator $\Box$. Just as in classical logic, a set of predicate symbols is given which we will denote using the metavariables $P, Q, R, \ldots$. For simplicity, we will not consider functions or individual constants. From a model-theoretic perspective, constants are just variables that are not being quantified. Function symbols can be modeled using predicate symbols. Thus, all terms in our modal language will be variables. We will refer to the language of quantified modal logic described here as $\mathcal{QML}$. Now we will proceed to define formulas, models, and the satisfaction relation for first-order modal formulas.

Definition 1. *We define formulas in quantified modal logic in the following way:*

1. *Any propositional symbol is a formula.*
2. *For any predicate symbol P of arity n, the expression $P(x_1, \ldots, x_n)$ is a formula.*
3. *The logical symbols $\top$ and $\bot$ are formulas.*
4. *If A and B are formulas, then $\neg A$, $A \wedge B$, $A \vee B$, and $A \supset B$ are formulas.*
5. *If A is a formula, $\forall x A(x)$ and $\Box A$ are formulas. We write $\exists x A(x)$ as an abbreviation for $\neg \forall x \neg A(x)$, and $\Diamond A$ as an abbreviation for $\neg \Box \neg A$.*

In the semantic framework for quantified modal logic adopted in this paper, variables are interpreted rigidly. That is, each variable designates the same object across all possible worlds. As a result, it is unnecessary to specify a separate domain of individuals for each world when defining a model. However, while terms refer rigidly, predicate interpretations may vary from world to world, their extensions are world-dependent.

Another important semantic choice concerns the domains over which quantifiers range. In this paper, we adopt *constant domain* quantified modal logic (see [1,8]), meaning that a single domain of quantification D is fixed and shared across all possible worlds in the model.

Definition 2. *A constant domain model M based on a Kripke frame $F = (W, R)$ is a tuple (W, R, D, V), where*

1. *W is a non-empty set of possible worlds,*
2. *$R \subseteq W \times W$ is a binary accessibility relation on W that is an equivalence relation (reflexive, symmetric, transitive).*
3. *D is a non-empty set of individuals referred to as a domain of quantification. For each $w \in W$, $D_w = D$ (so D_w is the same at each world—constant domains).*
4. *V is a valuation function mapping each n-place predicate symbol P to a subset $V(P) \subset W \times D^n$ depending on the world $w \in W$.*

Definition 3. *A variable assignment is a function usually referred to as a or b that assigns an element of the domain D to each variable for a constant domain model $M = (W, R, D, V)$.*

The modal logic thus models truth at a specific world. The satisfaction relation is defined as usual with the following definitions for the predicates and quantifiers, where a is a variable assignment:

$$
\begin{aligned}
(\mathfrak{M}, w) &\models p & \text{iff} \quad & w \in V(p) \\
(\mathfrak{M}, w) &\models \top & & \text{always} \\
(\mathfrak{M}, w) &\models \bot & & \text{never} \\
(\mathfrak{M}, w) &\models \neg\varphi & \text{iff} \quad & (\mathfrak{M}, w) \not\models \varphi \\
(\mathfrak{M}, w) &\models \varphi \wedge \psi & \text{iff} \quad & (\mathfrak{M}, w) \models \varphi \text{ and } (\mathfrak{M}, w) \models \psi \\
(\mathfrak{M}, w) &\models \Box\varphi & \text{iff} \quad & \text{for all } v \in W \text{ with } R(w, v) \text{ we have } \mathfrak{M}, v \models \varphi \\
(\mathfrak{M}, w) &\models \Diamond\varphi & \text{iff} \quad & \text{there is some } v \in W \text{ such that } R(w, v) \text{ holds} \\
& & & \text{and } \mathfrak{M}, v \models \varphi \\
(\mathfrak{M}, w) &\models P(x_1, \ldots, x_n)[a] & \text{iff} \quad & (w, a(x_1), \ldots, a(x_n)) \in V(P) \\
(\mathfrak{M}, w) &\models \forall x\varphi[a] & \text{iff} \quad & (\mathfrak{M}, w) \models \varphi[b] \text{ for every assignment } b \text{ that} \\
& & & \text{differs from } a \text{ at most on } x \\
(\mathfrak{M}, w) &\models \exists x\varphi[a] & \text{iff} \quad & (\mathfrak{M}, w) \models \varphi[b] \text{ for some assignment } b \text{ that} \\
& & & \text{differs from } a \text{ at most on } x
\end{aligned}
$$

Furthermore, we can already observe from the satisfaction definition that the modal operators, $\Box$ and $\Diamond$, can be seen as an encoding of quantification over the worlds that are accessible via R in a variable-free notation. This will become more apparent with the standard translation that we will present later, which transforms modal formulas to formulas in two-sorted classical first-order logic.

Note that models satisfying the equivalence of $\Box\forall x\phi$ and $\forall x\Box\phi$ are constant domain models (see [1]). The following results are well-known (see [8,13]).

Theorem 1. *The given semantics is sound and complete for the calculus for quantified S5 for the accessibility relation being symmetric $(A \supset \Box\Diamond A)$, reflexive $(\Box A \supset A)$, and transitive $(\Box A \supset \Box\Box A)$.*

Corollary 1. *As the accessibility relation is symmetric, reflexive, and transitive, $\Box$ can be interpreted as universal quantifier over the worlds, and $\Diamond$ can be interpreted as existential quantifier over the worlds.*

Thus, models in S5 are exactly those which have an equivalence relation as world relation R. We assume without loss of generality that there only is one equivalence class of worlds. Consequently, we have that $R = W \times W$. In light of this relationship, we refer to these kinds of models as S5-models.

The following formulas are valid in S5 (see [18], p. 113):

$$\Box\Box A = \Box A \qquad\qquad \Diamond\Box A = \Box A$$
$$\Diamond\Diamond A = \Diamond A \qquad\qquad \Box\Diamond A = \Diamond A$$

and can also be deduced semantically, as they follow from the simple fact that in S5-models all worlds are connected to another. From this we can see that if we have several modal operators at the beginning of a propositional S5-formula, only the innermost operator is relevant for the formula's meaning.

One of the most important consequences of the cut-elimination theorem is the interpolation theorem. Recall that

Definition 4. *A logic L admits interpolation if whenever $A \supset B$ holds in L, there is a formula I (called the interpolant) in the common language[1] of A and B such that $A \supset I$ and $I \supset B$ both hold in L.*

Craig proved interpolation as a lemma in order to prove *Beth's definability theorem*, which states that every implicitly definable symbol is also explicitly definable. In our setting, we consider a version of Beth's definability theorem specifically for *individual constants*, like in [7].

Proposition 1. *Craig's interpolation theorem implies Beth's definability theorem for constants.*

However, both, Craig's interpolation theorem and Beth's definability theorem fail for quantified S5, as was shown in Kit Fine's famous counterexample [7].

Fine's counterexample is constructed semantically via varying-domain Kripke models, but the failure persists even in constant domain models. The implicit definability fails to yield an explicit definition, and the induced failure of interpolation follows. We do not reproduce the full proof here due to its complexity. A semantic version can be found in [7], and syntactic reformulations have been discussed in later literature (e.g., [9,11]).

Theorem 2. *Beth's definability theorem and consequently the Craig interpolation lemma fail for quantified S5 with constant domain.*

Proof (Sketch). Let T be the theory that we get if we add the following two axioms to S5:

---

[1] Note that the language considered in this paper is function-free.

1. $p \supset \Diamond \forall x(F(x) \supset \Box(p \supset \neg F(x)))$,
2. $\neg p \supset \Box \exists (F(x) \wedge \Box(\neg p \supset F(x)))$.

It is shown in [7] that p is implicitly definable in T, but not explicitly definable.

For sequent calculi, usually Craig's interpolation theorem follows by proving Maehara's lemma [20]. There are propositional sequent calculi for S5 [5], but none of them can be extended analytically to a first-order calculus such that Craig's interpolation theorem, or Maehara's lemma holds. Although analytic sequent calculi exist for propositional S5 (see, e.g., [4,5]), no comparable system is currently known for quantified modal S5 that supports both full cut-elimination and the interpolation property as captured by Maehara's lemma. In many proof-theoretic frameworks, certain sequents - such as $A \rightarrow \Box \Diamond A$ - cannot be derived without the use of the cut rule. Moreover, Kit Fine's well-known counterexample demonstrates that both Craig's interpolation theorem and Beth's definability theorem fails in quantified S5. Any proof system validating Maehara's lemma in this setting would therefore contradict these established results.

For this reason, we adopt a purely semantic approach based on a two-sorted logic. This motivates the development of alternative proof-theoretic tools, such as the two-sorted translation and the mid-sequent interpolation techniques introduced in this paper.

3   Two-Sorted Logic $\mathcal{SL}$

The use of a two-sorted logic framework means that the language distinguishes between two types of variables and individual constants: those of the world sort and those of the domain sort (for individuals). Two-sorted logic can be viewed as a fragment of classical first-order logic. Formulas in this framework can be embedded into standard first-order logic by introducing additional predicates to indicate whether a variable should be of the sort world or the sort domain. In this paper, we follow the definition of two-sorted logic and the standard translation as presented in [19].

We begin by defining the language $\mathcal{SL}$ for two-sorted logic. Variables such as $x, y, z, \ldots$ are used for the domain sort, while $u, v, w, \ldots$ are used for the world sort. These two sets of variables are countably infinite and disjoint. Predicate symbols $P', Q', R', \ldots$ correspond to those in modal first-order logic. Specifically, if P is an n-ary predicate in the modal language, then P' is an $(n+1)$-ary predicate in two-sorted logic, with the additional argument indicating the world. Thus, P' is interpreted as a relation of type $world \times domain^n$. Again, the language contains no function symbols or constants. The syntax of formulas in $\mathcal{SL}$ is defined as follows:

Definition 5. *We define formulas in two-sorted modal logic as:*

1. *Atomic formulas $P'(v, x_1, \ldots, x_n)$ for a predicate symbol P' of sort $world \times domain^n$, and the atomic formula $\top$ and $\bot$ are formulas.*[2]

---

[2] No propositional constants (i.e., no atoms without world-variable arguments) are allowed, because otherwise their truth would not be world-dependent.

2. *If φ and ψ are formulas, then $\neg\varphi$, $\varphi \wedge \psi$, $\varphi \vee \psi$ and $\varphi \supset \psi$ are formulas.*
3. *If φ is a formula, a a free variable of domain sort and x a domain variable not occurring in φ, then the expressions $\forall x \varphi'$ and $\exists x \varphi'$ are formulas, where φ' is obtained from φ by replacing each occurrence of a in φ by x.*
4. *If φ is a formula, b a free variable of world sort and v a world variable not occurring in φ, then the expressions $\forall v \varphi'$ and $\exists v \varphi'$ are formulas, where φ' is obtained from φ by replacing each occurrence of b in φ by v.*

Now we are ready to give the definition of a model in $\mathcal{SL}$.

Definition 6. *An $\mathcal{SL}$-model is a triple $M = (W, D, V)$, where*

1. *W and D are non-empty disjoint sets,*
2. *V is a function mapping each $(n + 1)$-place predicate symbol P' to a subset $V(P') \subset W \times D^n$.*

Definition 7. *An assignment in an $\mathcal{SL}$-model M is a function $\mathfrak{a} = \mathfrak{a}_1 \cup \mathfrak{a}_2$, where $\mathfrak{a}_1$ maps every domain variable x to an element $\mathfrak{a}_1(x) \in D$ and $\mathfrak{a}_2$ maps every world variable u to an element $\mathfrak{a}_2(u) \in W$.*

The satisfaction relation $M \models \varphi[\mathfrak{a}]$ for two-sorted logic is defined in the usual way:

- $M \models P'(u, x_1, \ldots, x_n)[\mathfrak{a}]$ iff $(\mathfrak{a}_2(u), \mathfrak{a}_1(x_1), \ldots, \mathfrak{a}_1(x_n)) \in V(P')$,
- $M \models \forall u \varphi[\mathfrak{a}]$ iff $M \models \varphi[\mathfrak{b}]$ for every assignment $\mathfrak{b}$ that differs from $\mathfrak{a}$ at most on v,
- $M \models \forall x \varphi[\mathfrak{a}]$ iff $M \models \varphi[\mathfrak{b}]$ for every assignment $\mathfrak{b}$ that differs from $\mathfrak{a}$ at most on x,
- $M \models \top(v)[\mathfrak{a}]$ always holds,
- $M \models \bot(v)[\mathfrak{a}]$ never holds,

and the standard satisfaction definitions apply to the booleans.

This completes the definition of the two-sorted logic $\mathcal{SL}$. In the next section, we define a translation from formulas of quantified modal logic S5 into $\mathcal{SL}$.

4   The Standard Translation to $\mathcal{SL}$

We now define a standard translation of formulas from quantified modal logic S5 into the two-sorted logic $\mathcal{SL}$. This translation preserves validity and serves as the semantic foundation for our analysis of interpolation.

The central idea is to translate modal formulas into $\mathcal{SL}$, where their logical properties can be analyzed. In particular, key results, such as the cut-elimination theorem, Maehara's lemma, and Craig's interpolation theorem hold within $\mathcal{SL}$. As a result, interpolation properties in $\mathcal{SL}$ can be leveraged to study interpolation in the original modal framework, making the translation a powerful tool.

The standard translation shows that first-order and propositional modal logic are a fragment of classical first-order logic. When reduced to propositional modal logic, we can see that this logic is simply a variable-free notation for a fragment of first-order logic [2].

Embedding the language of quantified modal logic $\mathcal{QML}$ into the two-sorted language $\mathcal{SL}$ is straightforward. As previously discussed, each modal predicate symbol P is associated with a corresponding two-sorted predicate symbol P', where P' adds a world argument to reflect the modal structure.

Definition 8. *Given a world variable v, we define the standard translation ST_v from $\mathcal{QML}$ into $\mathcal{SL}$ as:*

$$ST_v(P(x_1,\ldots,x_n)) = P'(v,x_1,\ldots,x_n)$$
$$ST_v(\top) = \top$$
$$ST_v(\bot) = \bot$$
$$ST_v(\varphi \wedge \psi) = ST_v(\varphi) \wedge ST_v(\psi)$$
$$ST_v(\neg\varphi) = \neg ST_v(\varphi)$$
$$ST_v(\forall x\varphi) = \forall x ST_v(\varphi)$$
$$ST_v(\Box\varphi) = \forall w ST_w(\varphi)$$

where w is some fresh world variable.

Usually the two-sorted language and the standard translation also include and consider a predicate symbol R for the accessibility relation R on the worlds W. Since we will only translate formulas in the logic S5 in this work, where we have that $R = W \times W$ for every model, we can omit R. As all worlds are connected to all worlds and we work with constant domains, it consequently does not matter from which world variable v we start the translation ST_v if every subformula is in the scope of some modal operator.

It is important to note that the significance of the standard translation lies not in the syntactic form of the resulting formula, but in its *equivalence class*. Many formulas arising in proof constructions (such as interpolants) may not be direct translations of modal formulas but are nevertheless *equivalent* to such translations. This equivalence ensures that the modal meaning is preserved.

Definition 9. *Let $M = (W, D, V)$ be some $\mathcal{SL}$-model and $\mathfrak{a} = \mathfrak{a}_1 \cup \mathfrak{a}_2$ an assignment in M. Further, let $N = (W', R, D', V')$ be an S5-model and $\mathfrak{b}$ be an assignment in N such that $W = W'$, $D = D'$, $\mathfrak{b} = \mathfrak{a}_1$ and such that for any modal predicate symbol P and counterpart P' in the two-sorted language we have that $V(P) = V'(P')$. Then we call $(M, \mathfrak{a})$ and $(N, \mathfrak{b})$ equivalent, writing $(M, \mathfrak{a}) \sim (N, \mathfrak{b})$.*

Note that for each tuple $(M, \mathfrak{a})$ we can find a unique equivalent tuple $(N, \mathfrak{b})$. Now that we have defined the standard translation, the question arises whether the translation of a formula that is valid in constant-domain S5 is still valid in $\mathcal{SL}$.

Lemma 1. *Suppose that we have two equivalent models $(M, \mathfrak{a}) \sim (N, \mathfrak{b})$. For every formula φ in quantified modal logic and a world variable v we have that*

$$(N, \mathfrak{a}(v)) \models \varphi[\mathfrak{b}] \text{ iff } M \models ST_v(\varphi)[\mathfrak{a}].$$

Proof. Straightforward by induction on the structure of the formula φ.

Thus, the standard translation is validity preserving. We can also map the S5-models to models in two-sorted logic bijectively such that we can use them interchangeably: $M = (W, R, D, V) \mapsto N = (W, D, V)$.

We can further argue that valid S5 sentences remain valid under translation to $\mathcal{SL}$ by demonstrating that the translations of all axioms and inference rules of constant domain S5 can be derived within $\mathcal{SL}$ using Gentzen's sequent calculus. For example, we can derive the translation of the axiom $\Box A \supset \Box \Box A$, which is $\forall v A'(v) \supset \forall v \forall w A'(w)$, in the following way:

$$
\cfrac{\cfrac{\cfrac{A'(t) \to A'(t)}{\forall v A'(v) \to A'(t)} \forall_l}{\forall v A'(v) \to \forall w A'(w)} \forall_r}{\forall v A'(v) \to \forall v \forall w A'(w)} \forall_r
$$

A useful feature of the standard translation is that we can easily recognize whether a formula in $\mathcal{SL}$ originates from a modal formula by examining the structure of its world quantifiers.

In translations of modal formulas, each subformula is always bound by the innermost world quantifier that it is in the scope of.

For example, consider the modal formula $\Box \Diamond P$ which translates to $\forall w \exists u P'(u)$. Here, the variable u in the predicate $P'(u)$ is bound by the innermost world quantifier $\exists u$. That is, we will not get a formula from the translation in which different world-quantifiers bind the same subformula "cross-wise". The subformula $Q'(v) \wedge P'(w)$ in the formula $\forall w \forall v (Q'(v) \wedge P'(w))$, for example, is in the scope of both world quantifiers $\forall w$ and $\forall v$, even though the subformulas $Q'(v)$ and $P'(w)$ are only bound by one of them respectively, and the innermost wold quantifier that the subformula $P'(w)$ is in the scope of does not bind it. In this case, we say that the world-quantifiers *cross-bind*. In contrast, the world quantifiers in the translation $(\forall v (Q'(v) \wedge \exists w P'(w))) \wedge T'(u)$ of the formula $(\Box (Q \wedge \Diamond P)) \wedge T$ do not cross-bind as the subformulas that are being bound are bound by the innermost world-quantifier that they are in the scope of. Thus, formulas in $\mathcal{SL}$ in which world-quantifiers cross-bind express relations between worlds which cannot be expressed in modal logic. These observations motivate the definition of the *one-world-variable fragment*.

Definition 10. *Let v be some world variable. Then the one-world-variable fragment $\mathcal{SL}^v$ contains the formulas in the two-sorted logic $\mathcal{SL}$ in which every subformula is only bound by the innermost world quantifier. The only free world variable that might appear in a subformula is v, in which case the subformula is not in the scope of any other world-quantifier.*

Lemma 2. *For every quantified modal S5-formula φ, its translation $ST_v(\varphi)$ belongs to $\mathcal{SL}^v$ that can be expressed with a single bound world variable. In contrast, every formula in $\mathcal{SL}^v$ is the translation $ST_v(\varphi)$ of some formula φ in $\mathcal{QML}$.*

Proof. The first implication of the lemma can be easily derived from the definition of the translation ST_v. Conversely, we can construct a "re-translation" of formulas in one-world-variable fragment $\mathcal{SL}_v$ to quantified modal formulas:

$$Re_v : \mathcal{SL}^v \longrightarrow \mathcal{QML}$$
$$P(v, x_1, \ldots, x_n) \mapsto P(x_1, \ldots, x_n)$$
$$\bot \mapsto \bot$$
$$\varphi \wedge \psi \mapsto Re_v(\varphi) \wedge Re_v(\psi)$$
$$\neg\varphi \mapsto \neg Re_v(\varphi)$$
$$\forall x \varphi \mapsto \forall x\, Re_v(\varphi)$$
$$\forall v \varphi \mapsto \Box Re_v(\varphi)$$

It is easily checked that for every formula φ in $\mathcal{SL}^v$, we have that $\varphi = ST_v(Re_v(\varphi))$ and thus it is the translation of the formula $Re_v(\varphi)$ in $\mathcal{QML}$.

The fragment $\mathcal{SL}^v$ captures exactly those formulas in the two-sorted logic that correspond to modal S5 formulas with a single bound world variable per scope. This fragment provides a syntactic criterion for deciding retranslatability, and separates formulas with true modal structure from those which are only expressible in the extended two-sorted language. Its role is central in distinguishing genuine modal interpolants from purely logical ones.

Proposition 2. *A modal formula φ is valid in (constant domain) S5 if and only if its translation φ' is valid in the two-sorted first-order logic.*

Proof. The modalities are replaced inside-out by first-order quantifiers, binding all world positions which are free, and thus not bound yet.

Example 1. Consider the formula $\Box(\forall x A(x) \supset \Diamond \exists y A(y))$. This formula can be translated first to $\Box(\forall x A(x) \supset \exists w \exists y A'(w, y))$, and then to $\forall v(\forall x A'(v, x) \supset \exists w \exists y A'(w, y))$.

5   Proof-Theoretic Properties of $\mathcal{SL}$

The tools available in two-sorted logic are those familiar from classical first-order logic. In particular, it is possible to define a Gentzen style sequent calculus for $\mathcal{SL}$. The main adjustment lies in the treatment of quantifiers: when applying quantifier introduction rules, we must ensure that variables replace terms of the appropriate sort - either world or object. Aside from this consideration, the inference rules remain essentially unchanged. As a result, standard results such as the cut-elimination theorem, Maehara's lemma, and Craig's interpolation theorem all hold in $\mathcal{SL}$.

Theorem 3. $\mathcal{SL}$ *admits cut-elimination.*

Proof (Sketch). The structure of proof transformations mirrors the usual Gentzen system. The proof is similar to Gentzen's proof, with the difference that we consider a combined rank $r(\varphi)$ for two-sorted formulas to be the sum of the complexity from the object part and the world part of a formula φ.

We have the following consequence.

Corollary 2. $\mathcal{SL}$ *admits the Maehara's lemma for cut-free proofs.*

We briefly sketch the proof strategy for the extended mid-sequent theorem in the two-sorted sequent calculus for $\mathcal{SL}$. This mirrors the Gentzen-style mid-sequent constructions, adapted for a two-sorted system.

Theorem 4 (Extended mid-sequent theorem). *Let $\Gamma \vdash \Delta$ be a sequent in the two-sorted cut-free calculus $\mathcal{SL}$, such that all world quantifiers in $\Gamma \vdash \Delta$ are prenex. Then there exists a mid-sequent $\Sigma \vdash \Pi$ such that above the mid-sequent there are only inferences involving world quantifiers and propositional rules, and below the mid-sequent are only inferences involving object quantifiers and structural rules.*

Proof (Sketch). The proof proceeds by structural induction on the cut-free proof. We start with a cut-free proof of the given sequent. Identify object quantifier inferences ($\forall x$, $\exists x$) that are above propositional or world quantifier rules. Push these quantifier inferences down through the derivation by permuting them with:

 - Propositional rules (e.g., $\wedge, \vee, \supset$) - which do not interfere with quantifier bindings;
 - World/modal quantifiers - since $\mathcal{SL}$ uses sorted variables, these don't interfere.

Repeat until all object quantifier inferences are strictly below a chosen sequent (the mid-sequent), and the rest (world, propositional) are above. This reordering is sound because world and object quantifiers operate over disjoint classes of variables, so eigenvariable conditions remain preserved. At each step, structural rules (such as weakening and contraction) are permuted as needed. This allows us to stratify the derivation with a mid-sequent separating object quantifier reasoning from world quantifier reasoning.

The extended mid-sequent theorem yields several important consequences:

Corollary 3. *For every valid prenex formula in $S5$ of the form $\exists x_1 \ldots \exists x_n\, \varphi$, where φ is quantifier-free and may contain modalities, there exists a Herbrand disjunction:*
$$\varphi(t_1^1, \ldots, t_n^1) \vee \cdots \vee \varphi(t_1^k, \ldots, t_n^k)$$
which is equivalent (in $\mathcal{SL}$) to the original formula.

Proof. By the extended mid-sequent theorem, any derivation of a valid prenex formula in S5 admits a mid-sequent in which all object quantifier inferences are pushed below the propositional modal inferences. The resulting mid-sequent consists of a disjunction of quantifier-free instances, each of which corresponds to a formula in $\mathcal{SL}^V$ and represents a possible Herbrand expansion. The derivability of the disjunction follows by standard arguments from the cut-free calculus and modal interpretation of the two-sorted logic.

Remark 1. Unlike in classical logic, we do not require quantifier rules for both sorts to occur in the same fragment: the modal quantifiers may appear throughout the derivation. This is crucial for applications in modal logic, where the modal structure reflects the Kripke semantics and propositional S5 already lacks a standard analytic calculus.

The main novelty is that we only reorganize the proof with respect to object quantifier rules, leaving modal ones untouched.

Corollary 4. *The prenex fragment of quantified modal logic S5 admits Skolemization. That is, existential quantifiers may be replaced by Skolem functions without loss of validity in this fragment. The extended mid-sequent theorem ensures that Skolem terms do not need to depend on world variables.*

The Skolemization described above directly corresponds to the second epsilon theorem [12]. Skolemization fails in full quantified S5:

Proposition 3. *The implication $\Box A(c) \supset \exists x \Box A(x)$ is valid in constant domain S5. However, the converse $\exists x \Box A(x) \supset \Box \exists x A(x)$ fails.*

Proof (Sketch). This is a standard failure of modal quantifier shifts in constant domain semantics. While
$$\Box A(c) \supset \exists x \Box A(x)$$
holds due to domain constancy,
$$\exists x \Box A(x) \supset \Box \exists x A(x)$$
does not, because the witness for the existential quantifier in the accessible world may not be fixed across all worlds. A countermodel can be given with two worlds where the existential is satisfied in one, but the boxed existential fails globally.

Note that therefore Craig's interpolation theorem holds for all valid implications, however the interpolant is not always re-translatable in the language of quantified S5.

6   Interpolation

Interestingly, in our two-sorted logic $\mathcal{SL}$ (with full cut-elimination and the mid-sequent theorem), we can still extract an interpolant I - the system is expressive enough. However:

Proposition 4. *Any interpolant obtained in $\mathcal{SL}$ for Kit Fine's counterexample is not equivalent to any formula in the syntax of quantified S5.*

Proof. From the cut-free proof in $\mathcal{SL}$, Maehara's lemma yields an interpolant I. But this formula contains quantifier structures or term dependencies (from the two-sorted framework) that cannot be translated back into any formula of quantified S5. Thus, while I exists in $\mathcal{SL}$, there is no I' in the syntax of S5 such that $I = I'$.

6.1   Propositional Interpolation for S5

Propositional interpolation for S5 is known, but our new proof uses Maehara's lemma. Even in Fine's counterexample, interpolants exist but are not expressible in S5.

Proposition 5. *Propositional S5 interpolates.*

Proof. The propositional implication $A \supset B$ corresponds in the language of S5 to the monadic sequent $A' \rightarrow B'$. The Maehara interpolant is therefore a monadic expression. We consider an innermost $\forall$ on the right. We use a conjunctive normal form, a distribution and a confinement of the universal quantifiers to the negated and unnegated atoms where it actually binds the worlds (dual for $\exists$). By this procedure any of these world quantifiers binds all worlds in its scope, and the formula can be therefore understood as S5 formula. (Note that this procedure increases the size of interpolants.)

Example 2. Let C, D, P and Q be 0-place predicate symbols in constant domain S5 (so we are talking about formulas in propositional logic). We will try to find the interpolant of the following valid sequent consisting of non-prenex formulas:

$$\Diamond((P \vee P) \wedge C), \ \Diamond((Q \vee Q) \wedge C) \rightarrow \Diamond(P \vee D) \wedge \Diamond(Q \vee D), \ \Diamond P, \ \Diamond Q$$

As can be easily checked, a suitable interpolant in constant domain S5 would be the formula $\Diamond P \wedge \Diamond Q$. Let us see what kind of interpolant we get from applying Maehara's lemma.

1. Translate to $\mathcal{SL}$:

$$\forall v\big((P'(v) \vee P'(v)) \wedge C'(v)\big), \ \forall v\big((Q'(v) \vee Q'(v)) \wedge C'(v)\big) \rightarrow$$
$$\forall v(P'(v) \vee D'(v)) \wedge \forall v(Q'(v) \vee D'(v)), \ \forall v P'(v), \ \forall v Q'(v)$$

2. Use Maehara's Lemma to construct the interpolant from the proof of the translated formula: $\varphi_1 =$

$$\cfrac{\cfrac{\cfrac{\cfrac{\cfrac{\cfrac{\cfrac{\cfrac{P'(u) \to P'(u) \qquad P'(u) \to P'(u)}{P'(u) \vee P'(u) \to P'(u)}\lor_l}{P'(u) \vee P'(u) \to P'(u),\ P'(u)}w_r}{P'(u) \vee P'(u) \to P'(u) \vee D'(u),\ P'(u)}\lor_r}{(P'(u) \vee P'(u)) \wedge C'(u) \to P'(u) \vee D'(u),\ P'(u)}\land_l}{(P'(u) \vee P'(u)) \wedge C'(u) \to \exists v(P'(v) \vee D'(v)),\ P'(u)}\exists_r}{(P'(u) \vee P'(u)) \wedge C'(u),\ (Q'(b) \vee Q'(b)) \wedge C'(b) \to \exists v(P'(v) \vee D'(v)),\ P'(u)}w_l}{S_1 : (P'(u) \vee P'(u)) \wedge C'(u),\ (Q'(b) \vee Q'(b)) \wedge C'(b) \to \exists v(P'(v) \vee D'(v)),\ P'(u),\ Q'(b)}w_r$$

and $\varphi_2 =$

$$\cfrac{\cfrac{\cfrac{\cfrac{\cfrac{\cfrac{\cfrac{\cfrac{Q'(b) \to Q'(b) \qquad Q'(b) \to Q'(b)}{Q'(b) \vee Q'(b) \to Q'(b)}\lor_l}{Q'(b) \vee Q'(b) \to Q'(b),\ Q'(b)}w_r}{Q'(b) \vee Q'(b) \to Q'(b) \vee D'(b),\ Q'(b)}\lor_r}{(Q'(b) \vee Q'(b)) \wedge C'(b) \to Q'(b) \vee D'(b),\ Q'(b)}\land_l}{(Q'(b) \vee Q'(b)) \wedge C'(b) \to \exists v(Q'(v) \vee D'(v)),\ Q'(b)}\exists_r}{(P'(u) \vee P'(u)) \wedge C'(u),\ (Q'(b) \vee Q'(b)) \wedge C'(b) \to \exists v(Q'(v) \vee D'(v)),\ Q'(b)}w_l}{S_2 : (P'(u) \vee P'(u)) \wedge C'(u),\ (Q'(b) \vee Q'(b)) \wedge C'(b) \to \exists v(Q'(v) \vee D'(v)),\ P'(u),\ Q'(b)}w_r$$

We then obtain

$$\cfrac{\cfrac{\cfrac{\cfrac{\cfrac{\cfrac{(\varphi_1) \qquad (\varphi_2)}{S_1 \qquad S_2}}{F_1,\ (Q'(b) \vee Q'(b)) \wedge C'(b) \to \exists v(P'(v) \vee D'(v)) \wedge \exists v(Q'(v) \vee D'(v)),\ P'(u),\ Q'(b)}\land_r}{F_1,\ (Q'(b) \vee Q'(b)) \wedge C'(b) \to \exists v(P'(v) \vee D'(v)) \wedge \exists v(Q'(v) \vee D'(v)),\ \exists v P'(v),\ Q'(b)}\exists_r}{F_1,\ (Q'(b) \vee Q'(b)) \wedge C'(b) \to \exists v(P'(v) \vee D'(v)) \wedge \exists v(Q'(v) \vee D'(v)),\ \exists v P'(v),\ \exists v Q'(v)}\exists_r}{F_2,\ (Q'(b) \vee Q'(b)) \wedge C'(b) \to \exists v(P'(v) \vee D'(v)) \wedge \exists v(Q'(v) \vee D'(v)),\ \exists v P'(v),\ \exists v Q'(v)}\exists_l}{F_2,\ \exists v((Q'(v) \vee Q'(v)) \wedge C'(v)) \to \exists v(P'(v) \vee D'(v)) \wedge \exists v(Q'(v) \vee D'(v)),\ \exists v P'(v),\ \exists v Q'(v)}\exists_l$$

where

$$F_1 = (P'(u) \vee P'(u)) \wedge C'(u),$$

and

$$F_2 = \exists v\big((P'(v) \vee P'(v)) \wedge C'(v)\big).$$

By inductively reconstructing the interpolant using Maehara's lemma, we get the interpolant

$$I' = \exists w \exists v P'(v) \wedge Q'(w).$$

By shifting quantifiers we obtain $\exists v P'(v) \wedge \exists w Q'(w)$, a retranslation of what corresponds to the formula $\Diamond P \wedge \Diamond Q$.

6.2 Interpolation for Weak Fragments

We now consider a fragment of quantified modal S5 in which the object quantifiers and/or the modal operators are weak. Recall that a quantifier occurrence is said to be *strong* if it occurs positively as $\forall x$ or negatively as $\exists x$, *weak* if it occurs negatively as $\forall x$ or positively as $\exists x$. This syntactic condition ensures that quantifiers occur only in positions where they may be expanded into finite conjunctions or disjunctions during cut-free derivations, without violating the eigenvariable condition. As a result, the quantifiers can be eliminated and reintroduced purely propositionally. Modalities are analogously defined: $\square$ is strong in positive and $\lozenge$ is strong in negative positions; otherwise, they are weak.

Theorem 5. *Let $A \supset B$ be a valid implication in S5, where both the antecedent and succedent contain arbitrary quantifiers but only weak modalities. Then there is a formula I in the common language of A and B such that $A \supset I$ and $I \supset B$ are valid in S5.*

Proof. Let $A' \supset B'$ be the translation of $A \supset B$ to $\mathcal{SL}$ and I' its interpolant according to Craig's interpolation theorem. Note that all terms in worlds quantifier inferences can be restricted to one free-world variable a. Do not infer the world quantifiers, construct a first-order interpolant, and reintroduce the world quantifiers.

Corollary 5. *If both quantifiers and modalities are weak, the inteprolant is a propositional modal-free formula.*

Proof. We neither infer the weak world quantifiers nor the weak object quantifiers. Instead, we construct a propositional interpolant and then we reintroduce the quantifiers to restore the full logical context. The result is a modal-free propositional interpolant.

6.3   Interpolation for the Prenex Fragment

Here we show that interpolation holds in the prenex fragment of S5 by leveraging the extended mid-sequent theorem and a variant of Maehara's lemma. The key idea is that the quantifier prefix can be treated uniformly, and the modal-propositional matrix admits interpolation. The quantifier prefix can then be reintroduced, yielding an interpolant that also belongs to the prenex fragment.

Theorem 6. *Let $A' \supset B'$ be a valid implication in S5, where both the antecedent and succedent are prenex formulas of the form $QxA(x)$ and $QyB(y)$, where A and B contain no object quantifiers and Qx and Qy are object quantifiers only. Then there is a formula I in the common language of $QxA(x)$ and $QyB(y)$ such that $QxA(x) \supset I$ and $I \supset QyB(y)$ are valid in S5.*

Proof. By the extended mid-sequent theorem we have the Herbrand disjunction

$$A(\bar{t}_1) \ldots A(\bar{t}_m) \to A(\bar{s}_1) \ldots A(\bar{s}_n)$$

which has an interpolation I' which is the picture of a propositional modal interpolant I. Then, we infer the quantifiers accordingly.

7   Conclusion and Future Works

This work presents a syntactic proof-theoretic account of interpolation for first-order modal logic S5 via a two-sorted sequent calculus $\mathcal{SL}$, emphasizing mid-sequent theorems and cut-elimination. Unlike in the propositional setting, interpolation in first-order modal logic cannot, in general, be treated purely semantically. As Harvey Friedman showed [10], no recursive bound exists on the size of interpolants in classical logic, making semantic existence results non-constructive. Our calculus offers an explicit framework for extracting interpolants (and bounding their size syntactically). All results of this paper are simple consequences of the analytic sequent calculus for the semantics of S5. In this respect, many further results can be obtained, for example a classification of Skolemizing fragments according to an investigation in which cases the world positions can be removed from Skolem functions.

Interpolants derived via Maehara's lemma in $\mathcal{SL}$ may not always be retranslatable into the modal syntax. However, when quantifier scopes obey a one-variable discipline, such interpolants correspond to standard modal translations. Retranslation, when possible, often requires exponential unfolding, raising an open complexity question:

Are interpolants in $\mathcal{SL}$ significantly smaller than their modal counterparts?

We leave a detailed comparison for future work. However, the process of retranslating such an interpolant into an equivalent S5 formula - when possible - typically requires a nontrivial transformation. This transformation corresponds to a form of "unwinding", which resembles a decision procedure over the monadic fragment of first-order logic.

Given that monadic first-order logic is decidable but nontrivial in complexity (cf. the Bernays–Schönfinkel class), this suggests that:

- Interpolants in $\mathcal{SL}$ may be computationally or structurally more efficient;
- Their S5-translations may be longer or less optimal;
- This asymmetry emphasizes again the expressive strength of the two-sorted framework.

Aknowledgement. We thank Charlotte Jergitsch, as this paper extends her Master's thesis [14]. We also acknowledge helpful discussions and suggestions from colleagues throughout the development of this work.

References

1. Barkan, H.: On the interpretation of modal logic. Theoria **30**(2), 146–153 (1964)
2. Blackburn, P., van Benthem, J.: Modal logic: a semantic perspective. In: Handbook of Modal Logic, vol. 3, chap. 1. Elsevier (2007)
3. Braüner, T., Ghilardi, S.: Modal logic: a semantic perspective. In: Handbook of Modal Logic, vol. 3, chap. 9. Elsevier (2007)

4. Ciabattoni, A., Galatos, N., Terui, K.: From axioms to analytic rules in nonclassical logics. In: Proceedings of the Twenty-Third Annual IEEE Symposium on Logic in Computer Science, LICS 2008, Pittsburgh, PA, USA, 24–27 June 2008. pp. 229–240. IEEE Computer Society (2008). https://doi.org/10.1109/LICS.2008.39

5. Ciabattoni, A., Galatos, N., Terui, K.: Algebraic proof theory for substructural logics: cut-elimination and analyticity. Ann. Pure Appl. Logic **163**(3), 266–290 (2009)

6. Craig, W.: Three uses of the Herbrand-Gentzen theorem in relating model theory and proof theory. J. Symb. Logic **22**(03), 269–285 (1957)

7. Fine, K.: Failures of the interpolation lemma in quantified modal logic. J. Symb. Logic **44**(2), 201–206 (1979)

8. Fitting, M., Mendelsohn, R.L.: First-Order Modal Logic, Synthese Library, vol. 277. Springer, Cham (1998)

9. Flum, J., Ziegler, M.: Interpolation theorems for fragments of first-order modal logic. Math. Log. Q. **36**(1), 95–104 (1990)

10. Friedman, H.: The complexity of explicit definitions. Adv. Math. **20**(1), 18–29 (1976). https://doi.org/10.1016/0001-8708(76)90167-5. https://www.sciencedirect.com/science/article/pii/0001870876901675

11. Gabbay, D.M.: Semantical investigations in heyting's intuitionistic logic. In: Synthese Library. Springer, Cham (1981), chapter on interpolation failures

12. Hilbert, D., Bernays, P.: Grundlagen der mathematik. Springer, Cham (1934)

13. Hughes, G.E., Cresswell, M.J.: A New Introduction to Modal Logic. Routledge (1996)

14. Jergitsch, C.: Interpolation by translation. Master's thesis, TU Wien, Vienna, Austria (2023). http://hdl.handle.net/20.500.12708/176748

15. Maksimova, L.: Intuitionistic logic and implicit definability. Ann. Pure Appl. Logic **105**(1–3), 83–102 (2000)

16. Maksimova, L.L.: Craig's theorem in superintuitionistic logics and amalgamable varieties of pseudo-Boolean algebras. Algebra Logic **16**(6), 427–455 (1977)

17. Maksimova, L.L.: Interpolation properties of superintuitionistic logics. Stud. Logica. **38**(4), 419–428 (1979)

18. Steinacker, P.: Modallogik. In: Nichtklassische Logik - eine Einführung, chap. 3. Akademie-Verlag, Berlin (1988)

19. Sturm, H., Wolter, F.: First-order expressivity for s5-models: modal vs. two-sorted languages. J. Philos. Logic **44**(2), 201–206 (2000)

20. Takeuti, G.: Proof theory. Studies in Logic and the Foundations of Mathematics, 2nd edn. North-Holland (1987). https://doi.org/10.1016/S0049-237X(08)70603-7. https://www.sciencedirect.com/science/article/pii/S0049237X08706037

21. Vizel, Y., Weissenbacher, G., Malik, S.: Boolean satisfiability solvers and their applications in model checking. Proc. IEEE **103**(11), 2021–2035 (2015)

Deciding Satisfiability for Overlaid Symbolic Heaps

Nicolas Peltier[1] 📷, Quentin Petitjean[2(✉)] 📷, and Mihaela Sighireanu[2] 📷

[1] Univ. Grenoble Alpes, CNRS, LIG, 38000 Grenoble, France
[2] Univ. Paris-Saclay, ENS Paris-Saclay, CNRS, LMF, 91190 Gif-sur-Yvette, France
quentin.petitjean@ens-paris-saclay.fr

Abstract. Separation logic (SL) is a widely used formalism for verifying programs that manipulate dynamically allocated memory, relying on the separating conjunction $\star$ to combine disjoint heap structures. The standard approach in SL lacks the expressive power to handle overlaid data structures where multiple structures share some locations. We consider a logic that extends SL with a new separating conjunction operator $\circledast$, enabling the composition of heaps with shared locations that allocate distinct fields. Our fragment supports generic inductive definitions and introduces set variables to constrain the locations shared by overlapping structures. We prove that the satisfiability problem for this fragment is in NEXPTIME, by reducing it to the satisfiability problem in BAPA [11], a decidable logic combining Boolean algebra of sets and Presburger arithmetic.

Keywords: Separation logic · Satisfiability problem · Overlaid structures · BAPA

1 Introduction

Separation logic (SL) [9,21] is widely employed in program verification. It extends Hoare logic to enable reasoning about programs that manipulate dynamically allocated memory. In SL, formulæ are constructed using two types of atoms: the first, denoted $x \rightarrow (y_1, \ldots, y_k)$, indicates that a memory block containing the tuple formed by the values of $y_1, \ldots, y_k$ is allocated at (and only at) location x; the second, emp, represents the empty heap, i.e., a heap with no allocated locations. These atoms are combined into formulæ using logical connectives, including a distinctive operator known as the *separating conjunction* written $\star$. The formula $\varphi_1 \star \varphi_2$ asserts that φ_1 and φ_2 hold on disjoint portions of the heap. This connective enables *local reasoning*, which enhances the scalability by allowing program properties to be asserted and verified solely with reference to the heap regions it affects. Additionally, to support the specification of recursive data structures, SL incorporates predicate atoms defined by inductive rules with fixpoint semantics. For example, list segments from x to y may be defined by the

This work has been partially funded by the French National Research Agency project ANR-21-CE48-0011.

R. Thiemann and C. Weidenbach (Eds.): FroCoS 2025, LNAI 15979, pp. 80–97, 2026.
https://doi.org/10.1007/978-3-032-04167-8_5

following rules[1]:

$$\texttt{lseg}(x, y) \Leftarrow \texttt{emp} \star x \approx y, \quad \texttt{lseg}(x, y) \Leftarrow x \to (z) \star \texttt{lseg}(z, y). \tag{1}$$

The satisfiability and entailment problems have been extensively studied for various fragments of SL, particularly the so-called symbolic heaps fragment, which can be defined as (disjunctions of) existentially quantified separating conjunctions of atoms. It has been established that satisfiability in this fragment is ExpTime-complete [2], while entailment is undecidable. For the latter problem, decidability can be achieved by restricting the form of the inductive rules defining predicate symbols (see, e.g., [4, 8, 17]).

However, this standard fragment of SL has limited expressive power. The connective $\star$ only permits the combination of disjoint structures, which precludes reasoning about structures that share elements—a common scenario in practical applications. For instance, consider a collection of pairwise disjoint sublists alongside an additional list containing all elements from these sublists in some arbitrary order; here, the sublists share nodes with the encompassing list. Another example is a tree structure whose leaves are linked in a list in an arbitrary order. Modelling an operation such as tree expansion would require removing a node α from the list of leaves and adding new nodes both to the list and as successors of α in the tree. In this case, the order of leaves in the list is arbitrary, so encoding the structure with a single inductive predicate (e.g., defining a tree with leaves chained from left to right) would not capture the intended class of structures, as the described operation would not preserve this invariant. Notably, in this example, only some nodes (the leaves) are shared, while inner nodes remain distinct. Such data structures, where locations may be shared across multiple structures, are termed "overlaid".

To address this limitation, various fragments of SL have been explored. Some offer sound decision procedures for program analysis [3, 6, 15, 16], while others eschew inductive definitions in favour of an indexed separation conjunction combined with flow equations [10, 18]. Notably, the logic NOLL [6] can describe nested linked lists with shared nodes, with satisfiability and entailment being NP-complete and co-NP-complete, respectively. To our knowledge, however, no fragment of SL fully addresses generic overlaid data structures while providing decidability results.

Building on prior work investigating decidable fragments of SL [2, 4, 7, 14, 17, 20], we propose the logic OSL, inspired by [6, 8], that supports overlaid data structures. Specifically, we model the heaps as partial finite functions from pairs (ℓ, f) (where ℓ is a location and f is a field) to tuples of locations. One field is thus allowed to make one location point to a tuple of locations. The use of different fields allows associating several tuples of locations with the same location. As a result, a single field is sufficient to support standard data structures of SL. Heaps are combined using the weak separating conjunction operator $\circledast$ (introduced in [6]), which allows shared locations to allocate distinct record fields. OSL extends the simple inductive definitions of [6] to more

---

[1] We distinguish the equality in formula $\approx$ from the mathematical equality $=$. Moreover, in this paper, we adopt the convention that equations $x \approx y$ are satisfied only if the heap is empty. This entails no loss of generality in our context and simplifies the input language, as standard conjunction becomes dispensable.

general inductive definitions of [8], with the restriction that each inductive predicate allocates only one field. However, the value referenced by a field is a tuple of locations, enabling straightforward descriptions of tree-shaped structures; the key constraint is that a predicate cannot allocate multiple distinct fields. Additionally, the fragment incorporates set variables within inductive predicates to collect subsets of allocated locations. We use these variables in set constraints to impose conditions on the overlap between inductive structures.

To summarize, the classical conjunction $\wedge$ asserts that a heap satisfies two properties; the standard separating conjunction $\star$ asserts that a heap can be divided into two sub-heaps, each satisfying one side of the separating conjunction; and lastly, the overlaid separating conjunction $\circledast$ allows the two sub-heaps to overlap, provided that overlapping locations are allocated using distinct fields.

Example 1. The tree-and-list example can be encoded in OSL as the formula $\text{tree}(x, Y) \circledast \text{ls}(y, Y)$, where the predicate atoms are defined by the following rules:

$$\text{tree}(x, Y) \Leftarrow x.t \rightarrow () \star Y \approx \{x\}, \tag{2}$$

$$\text{tree}(x, Y) \Leftarrow x.t \rightarrow (x_1, x_2) \star \text{tree}(x_1, Y_1) \star \text{tree}(x_2, Y_2) \star Y \approx Y_1 \sqcup Y_2, \tag{3}$$

$$\text{ls}(y, Y) \Leftarrow y.l \rightarrow () \star Y \approx \{y\}, \tag{4}$$

$$\text{ls}(y, Y) \Leftarrow y.l \rightarrow (y') \star \text{ls}(y', Y') \star Y \approx \{y\} \sqcup Y', \tag{5}$$

where the rules employ two distinct fields, t and l, to encode trees and lists respectively[2]. The symbols x, y, y', x_1, x_2 denote location variables, while Y, Y', Y_1, Y_2 represent sets of locations. The symbol $\sqcup$ stands for set union.

In this paper, we investigate the satisfiability problem for OSL and we demonstrate that it is in NEXPTIME. Reasoning about OSL formulæ requires combining standard spatial reasoning in SL (to handle predicate definitions, equalities, and constraints ensuring that a given field is allocated only once) with cardinality constraints arising from shared set variables. For instance, the formula $\text{ls}_{\text{even}}(x, Y) \circledast \text{ls}_{\text{odd}}(x, Y)$ is unsatisfiable if ls_{even} and ls_{odd} describe lists of even and odd lengths with set variables collecting all locations, respectively. The formula $\text{ls}_1(x, X) \circledast \text{ls}_2(x, X)$ is satisfiable if ls_1 and ls_2 both denote non-empty lists, provided these lists are chained using distinct fields, while $\text{ls}_1(x, X) \star \text{ls}_2(x, X)$ is always unsatisfiable (as the lists are non-empty each structure must allocate x). We thus reduce the satisfiability problem for OSL to a satisfiability problem in the logic BAPA [12], which combines the Boolean algebra of sets of uninterpreted elements with Presburger arithmetic to capture cardinality constraints on sets.

All proofs are given in the appendix of the full version of the paper[3].

2   Separation Logic with Overlaid Inductive Definitions

We introduce OSL, the variant of SL we propose for the specification of overlaid data structures. After presenting its syntax and semantics, we illustrate its specification power and introduce some of its fragments that will be used in the following sections.

---

[2] Both the lists and trees end at the empty tuple ().

[3] The full version is available here: hal-05143101.

2.1 Syntax

In the definition below, the (possibly indexed) symbols φ, L, A, t, B and T denote *formulæ*, *equational atoms*, *arithmetic atoms*, *arithmetic terms*, *set atoms* and *set terms*, respectively (the symbol $\approx$ is overloaded). The symbols Φ, $\mathfrak{L}$, $\mathfrak{A}$, $\mathfrak{t}$, $\mathfrak{B}$ and $\mathfrak{T}$ denote the corresponding sets of objects of each sort.

Definition 1 (OSL formulæ). *Let $\mathcal{F}$ be a finite set of* field *symbols. Let $\mathcal{V}$ be a countably infinite set of* location *variables; let S be a countably infinite set of* set *variables, and let $\mathcal{P}$ be a set of* spatial predicate *symbols, where each symbol $p \in \mathcal{P}$ is associated with a unique arity $\#(p)$ (with countably infinite sets of predicate symbols of each arity). The set of* OSL *formulæ (or simply formulæ) φ is inductively defined as follows:*

$$\Phi \ni \varphi := \mathsf{emp} \mid x.f \to (y_1, \ldots, y_d) \mid L \mid B \mid A \mid \varphi_1 \vee \varphi_2$$
$$\mid \varphi_1 \star \varphi_2 \mid \varphi_1 \circledast \varphi_2 \mid p(x_1, \ldots, x_{\#(p)-1}, X)$$

with:

$$\mathfrak{L} \ni L := x \approx y \mid x \not\approx y \qquad \mathfrak{t} \ni t := K \mid t_1 \oplus t_2 \mid K \odot t \mid |T|$$
$$\mathfrak{A} \ni A := t_1 \approx t_2 \mid t_1 \not\approx t_2 \mid t_1 < t_2 \mid t_1 \not< t_2 \mid K \operatorname{div} t \mid K \operatorname{ndiv} t$$
$$\mathfrak{B} \ni B := T_1 \approx T_2 \mid T_1 \not\approx T_2 \mid T_1 \sqsubseteq T_2 \mid T_1 \not\sqsubseteq T_2$$
$$\mathfrak{T} \ni T := \{x\} \mid X \mid \emptyset \mid T_1 \sqcup T_2 \mid T_1 \sqcap T_2$$

where $\varphi_1, \varphi_2 \in \Phi$ are formulæ, $p \in \mathcal{P}, d \in \mathbb{N}, K \in \mathbb{Z}, x, y, x_1, \ldots, x_{\#(p)-1}, y_1, \ldots, y_d \in \mathcal{V}, f \in \mathcal{F}$ and $X \in S$.

The definition above adheres to the standard SL fragment known as (disjunctive) *symbolic heap*, while incorporating additional features to enable the specification of overlaid data structures. Note that negations are not supported; thus, negated versions of some operators are added. To allow for overlaid data structures, the points-to atom $x.f \to (y_1, \ldots, y_d)$ identifies a portion of the memory block allocated at location x by a field f (for convenience, the arity of fields (d) is not fixed). Another OSL-specific feature is the inclusion of set variables (in S), denoting finite sets of locations, and set constraints in formulæ. We write set variables in capital letters to distinguish them from location variables in $\mathcal{V}$. Set terms are composed from set variables and basic term $\emptyset$ and $\{x\}$ using union and intersection of sets. The set constraints $\mathfrak{B}$ and the arithmetic constraints $\mathfrak{A}$ are a subset of those in the logic BAPA [12]. The integer terms $\mathfrak{t}$ include arithmetic operations (addition $\oplus$ and multiplication $\odot$) and set cardinality denoted by $|T|$. For simplicity, we do not consider arithmetic variables (this is not restrictive, as they can be encoded by terms $|X|$ where X is a fresh set variable). The link between set variables and the heap is established using predicate atoms. Thus, a predicate atom $p(x_1, \ldots, x_{\#(p)-1}, X)$ has *exactly one* set argument, in addition to other arguments denoting locations. Intuitively, the set argument is intended to denote *a subset of the locations allocated in the data structure* specified by the predicate; it is defined in the predicate's definition. For readability, we assume that the set argument always occurs at the last position in the argument list. The last feature of OSL is the composition of formulæ using the "overlaid" separating conjunction operator $\circledast$, in addition to the classic separating conjunction $\star$. Intuitively, $\circledast$ composes formulæ specifying portions of memory defined by different fields inside the allocated memory regions.

To introduce predicate definitions and the OSL semantics, we use the following notations. The cardinality of a set X is denoted by $\mathrm{card}(X)$. The set $\{x \in \mathbb{Z} \mid i \le x \le j\}$ is denoted by $[\![i, j]\!]$. The domain of a function f is written $\mathrm{dom}(f)$. The powerset of a set S is written $\mathscr{P}(S)$. The set of free (location and set) variables occurring in φ is denoted by $fv(\varphi)$. A *substitution* σ is a function from $\mathcal{V}$ to $\mathcal{V}$, and from $\mathcal{S}$ to $\mathfrak{T}$. Its domain, $\mathrm{dom}(\sigma)$, is the set of variables x such that $\sigma(x) \ne x$, and its image is $\mathrm{img}(\sigma) = \sigma(\mathrm{dom}(\sigma))$. For any expression e (a variable, tuple, term or formula), we denote by $e\sigma$ the expression obtained from e by replacing each free occurrence of a variable x with $\sigma(x)$. We denote by $\{x_i \mapsto t_i \mid 1 \le i \le n\}$ the substitution that maps each variable x_i to t_i, where $x_i \in \mathcal{V} \cup \mathcal{S}$ and t_i is either a variable or a set term.

An *inductive rule associated with the predicate* $p \in \mathcal{P}$ has the following form in OSL (up to associativity and commutativity of $\star$):

$$p(x_1, \ldots, x_n, X) \Leftarrow x_r.f \rightarrow (\vec{z}) \star \bigstar_{i=1}^{m} q_i(\vec{y}_i, Y_i) \star \varphi \star \left(X \approx E \sqcup \bigsqcup_{u \in U} Y_u\right), \qquad (6)$$

where $r \in [\![1, n]\!]$ and the following syntactic restrictions are satisfied:

- the set variables Y_i are pairwise distinct set variables and distinct from X;
- the set term E is either the constant $\emptyset$ or the term $\{x_r\}$;
- $U \subseteq [\![1, m]\!]$ (the set U may be $\emptyset$, in which case $\bigsqcup_{u \in U} Y_u$ is $\emptyset$);
- the formula φ is a $\star$-conjunction of pure equational atoms $L \in \mathfrak{L}$.

The variables $x_1, \ldots, x_n, X$ are called *parameters* of p. We refer to the variables that appear in the right-hand side of the rule but are not among the predicate's parameters as the rule's *auxiliary variables*. These auxiliary variables include, in particular, the set variables Y_i. Formally, they are defined as $fv(x_r.f \rightarrow (\vec{z}) \star \bigstar_{i=1}^{m} q_i(\vec{y}_i, Y_i) \star \varphi \star (X \approx E \sqcup \bigsqcup_{u \in U} Y_u)) \setminus \{x_1, \ldots, x_n, X\}$. Our form of predicate rule extends classical inductive definitions of SL—such as those in [8]—by incorporating set parameters and set constraints. In the following, we shall assume that $U = [\![1, m]\!]$. This assumption simplifies the presentation, but does not affect the expressive power of the predicate definitions.

Remark 1. The conditions provided are less restrictive than those imposed in [8] to ensure the decidability of the entailment problem. No constraint is imposed on the spatial part of the formula, except that exactly one location x_r must be allocated in every rule[4]. However, the use of set constraints and arithmetic terms inside the rules is strictly limited: the only allowed constraint (besides equational atoms) is the equation $X \approx E \sqcup \bigsqcup_{u \in U} Y_u$, which relates the value of the set parameter X to the sets computed by recursive calls. It is essential that E contains only locations allocated by the rule, as this guarantees that the same location is added at most once to the computed set (this

---

[4] This condition is imposed for technical convenience only and does not limit the expressive power of predicate definitions.

ensures that E contains only allocated locations and facilitates the computation of the cardinality of X in Sect. 3.2). Note also that the rules do not contain the connective ⊛: as we will restrict the set of rules defining a predicate to use only one field (see Sect. 2.3), using this connective inside of a rule is pointless.

A *set of inductive definitions* (SID) $\mathcal{R}$ contains finitely many rules associated with predicate symbols in $\mathcal{P}$. We write $p(y_1, \ldots, y_n, Y) \Leftarrow_{\mathcal{R}} \psi$ if the SID $\mathcal{R}$ contains a rule $p(x_1, \ldots, x_n, X) \Leftarrow \varphi$, with $\psi = \varphi\{X \mapsto Y, x_i \mapsto y_i \mid i \in [\![1, n]\!]\}$.

Example 2. The following OSL formula specifies a heap where a (non-empty) binary tree $\texttt{treel}(r, h, N)$ and a list segment $\texttt{ls}(h, l, S)$ are overlaid such that the list starts in the left-most leaf of the tree h and contains some of this leaf's ancestors ($S \subseteq N$); the list ends into an empty memory block (l):

$$(\texttt{treel}(r, h, N) \circledast \texttt{ls}(h, l, S)) \star S \sqsubseteq N \star l.next \rightarrow () \tag{7}$$

The two predicates $\texttt{treel}$ and $\texttt{ls}$ are defined by the following rules:

$$\texttt{treel}(x_r, x_l, X) \Leftarrow x_r.sons \rightarrow () \star x_l \approx x_r \star X \approx \{x_r\}, \tag{8}$$

$$\texttt{treel}(x_r, x_l, X) \Leftarrow x_r.sons \rightarrow (y_l, y_r) \star x_l \not\approx x_r \star \texttt{treel}(y_l, x_l, Y_l) \star \texttt{tree}(y_r, Y_r) \tag{9}$$
$$\star X \approx \{x_r\} \sqcup Y_l \sqcup Y_r,$$

$$\texttt{tree}(x_r, X) \Leftarrow x_r.sons \rightarrow () \star X \approx \emptyset, \tag{10}$$

$$\texttt{tree}(x_r, X) \Leftarrow x_r.sons \rightarrow (y_l, y_r) \star \texttt{tree}(y_l, Y_l) \star \texttt{tree}(y_r, Y_r) \tag{11}$$
$$\star X \approx Y_l \sqcup Y_r,$$

$$\texttt{ls}(x, y, X) \Leftarrow x.next \rightarrow (y) \star x \not\approx y \star X \approx \{x\}, \tag{12}$$

$$\texttt{ls}(x, y, X) \Leftarrow x.next \rightarrow (z) \star x \not\approx y \star \texttt{ls}(z, y, Y) \star X \approx \{x\} \sqcup Y. \tag{13}$$

The auxiliary variables in rule 9 are y_l, y_r, Y_l and Y_r.

2.2   Semantics

Definition 2 (OSL structure). *Let $\mathcal{L}$ be a countably infinite set of so-called* locations. *An OSL structure is a tuple $(\mathfrak{s}, \mathfrak{h}, \Sigma)$ where $\mathfrak{s}$ is a* store, *i.e., a partial function from $\mathcal{V}$ to $\mathcal{L}$, $\mathfrak{h}$ is a* heap, *i.e., a partial finite function mapping pairs (ℓ, f) (where $\ell \in \mathcal{L}$ and $f \in \mathcal{F}$) to tuples of locations in $\mathcal{L}^*$ and Σ is a* set interpretation, *i.e., a partial function mapping set variables in S to finite subsets of $\mathcal{L}$.*

Thus $\text{dom}(\mathfrak{h}) \subseteq \mathcal{L} \times \mathcal{F}$ for all heaps $\mathfrak{h}$. We denote by $\text{dom}_f(\mathfrak{h})$ the set $\{\ell \mid (\ell, f) \in \text{dom}(\mathfrak{h})\}$ and by $\text{allocated}(\mathfrak{h})$ the set $\{\ell \mid \exists f \in \mathcal{F}. (\ell, f) \in \text{dom}(\mathfrak{h})\}$. For conciseness, we omit in the following the semantics of arithmetic terms t and arithmetic constraints A; their semantics is the expected one.

Definition 3 (Semantics of set terms). *Let T be a set term, $\mathfrak{s}$ be a store, and Σ be a set interpretation. The interpretation of set term denoted by $[\![T]\!]_{(\mathfrak{s}, \Sigma)}$ is a set of locations in $\mathcal{L}$ and it is inductively defined by the following rules:*

- $[\![0]\!]_{(s,\Sigma)} = \emptyset$;
- $[\![\{x\}]\!]_{(s,\Sigma)} = \{s(x)\}$;
- $[\![X]\!]_{(s,\Sigma)} = \Sigma(X)$;

- $[\![T_1 \sqcup T_2]\!]_{(s,\Sigma)} = [\![T_1]\!]_{(s,\Sigma)} \cup [\![T_2]\!]_{(s,\Sigma)}$;
- $[\![T_1 \sqcap T_2]\!]_{(s,\Sigma)} = [\![T_1]\!]_{(s,\Sigma)} \cap [\![T_2]\!]_{(s,\Sigma)}$.

Definition 4 (OSL semantics). *Given a formula φ, an SIDR and a structure $(s, \mathfrak{h}, \Sigma)$ with $fv(\varphi) \subseteq \mathrm{dom}(s) \cup \mathrm{dom}(\Sigma)$, the satisfaction relation $\models_R$ is inductively defined as the least relation such that $(s, \mathfrak{h}, \Sigma) \models_R \varphi$ iff one of the following conditions holds:*

- *$\varphi = \mathsf{emp}$ and $\mathfrak{h} = \emptyset$;*
- *$\varphi = (x.f \to (y_1, \ldots, y_d))$ and $\mathfrak{h} = [(s(x), f) \mapsto (s(y_1), \ldots, s(y_d))]$;*
- *$\varphi = (x \approx y)$, $s(x) = s(y)$ and $\mathfrak{h} = \emptyset$; or $\varphi = (x \not\approx y)$, $s(x) \neq s(y)$ and $\mathfrak{h} = \emptyset$;*
- *$\varphi = \varphi_1 \vee \varphi_2$ and $(s, \mathfrak{h}, \Sigma) \models_R \varphi_i$, for some $i \in \{1, 2\}$;*
- *$\varphi = \varphi_1 \star \varphi_2$ and there exist heaps $\mathfrak{h}_1, \mathfrak{h}_2$ such that $\mathfrak{h} = \mathfrak{h}_1 \cup \mathfrak{h}_2$, $\mathrm{allocated}(\mathfrak{h}_1) \cap \mathrm{allocated}(\mathfrak{h}_2) = \emptyset$ and $(s, \mathfrak{h}_i, \Sigma) \models_R \varphi_i$, for all $i \in \{1, 2\}$;*
- *$\varphi = \varphi_1 \circledast \varphi_2$ and there exist heaps $\mathfrak{h}_1, \mathfrak{h}_2$ such that $\mathfrak{h} = \mathfrak{h}_1 \cup \mathfrak{h}_2$, $\mathrm{dom}(\mathfrak{h}_1) \cap \mathrm{dom}(\mathfrak{h}_2) = \emptyset$ and $(s, \mathfrak{h}_i, \Sigma) \models_R \varphi_i$, for all $i \in \{1, 2\}$;*
- *$\varphi = p(x_1, \ldots, x_{\#(p)-1}, X)$, $p \in \mathcal{P}$ and $(s', \mathfrak{h}, \Sigma') \models_R \psi$, for some s' matching s on $x_1, \ldots, x_{\#(p)-1}$, some Σ' matching Σ on X and for some ψ such that $\varphi \Leftarrow_R \psi$;*
- *$\varphi = (T_1 \approx T_2)$, $[\![T_1]\!]_{(s,\Sigma)} = [\![T_2]\!]_{(s,\Sigma)}$ and $\mathfrak{h} = \emptyset$; the definition is similar for $\not\approx$, $\sqsubseteq$, $\not\sqsubseteq$.*

We write $\varphi \models_R \psi$ if for every structure $(s, \mathfrak{h}, \Sigma)$ we have $(s, \mathfrak{h}, \Sigma) \models_R \varphi \implies (s, \mathfrak{h}, \Sigma) \models_R \psi$. If both $\varphi \models_R \psi$ and $\psi \models_R \varphi$ hold, then we write $\varphi \equiv_R \psi$.

We emphasize that the atoms $x \approx y$ or $x \not\approx y$ only hold for empty heaps (this convention simplifies notations as it avoids the use of standard conjunction). The same convention applies to arithmetic and set constraints. Formulæ are taken modulo the usual properties of SL connectives: associativity and commutativity of $\star, \circledast$ and $\vee$, neutrality of emp for $\star$ and $\circledast$, and commutativity of $\approx, \not\approx$. Intuitively, the interpretation of $\varphi_1 \star \varphi_2$ is stronger than that of $\varphi_1 \circledast \varphi_2$, as the latter allows for the allocation of the block at the same (starting) location in both φ_1 and φ_2, provided the considered offsets (represented by fields) are different. For instance, $x.f \to (y) \circledast x.g \to (y)$ is satisfiable, but not $x.f \to (y) \star x.g \to (y)$ or $x.f \to (y) \circledast x.f \to (y)$. Note that $\mathfrak{h}_1 \cup \mathfrak{h}_2$ is well defined if $\mathrm{dom}(\mathfrak{h}_1) \cap \mathrm{dom}(\mathfrak{h}_2) = \emptyset$ and that $\mathrm{allocated}(\mathfrak{h}_1) \cap \mathrm{allocated}(\mathfrak{h}_2) = \emptyset \implies \mathrm{dom}(\mathfrak{h}_1) \cap \mathrm{dom}(\mathfrak{h}_2) = \emptyset$. Thus $\varphi_1 \circledast \varphi_2$ is a logical consequence of $\varphi_1 \star \varphi_2$.

Definition 5 (OSL model). *An R-model of a formula φ is a structure $(s, \mathfrak{h}, \Sigma)$ such that $(s, \mathfrak{h}, \Sigma) \models_R \varphi$. A formula ψ admitting an R-model is R-satisfiable (or simply satisfiable if R is clear from the context).*

2.3 1-Predicates

In the remainder of the paper, we assume that each predicate allocates a single field, in the sense that for every predicate $p \in \mathcal{P}$, there exists a unique field $f \in \mathcal{F}$ such that every points-to atom appearing in any unfolding of any atom $p(\vec{x}, X)$ is of the form $y.f \to (\vec{z})$, where $\vec{z}$ is a tuple of arbitrary length. More formally:

Definition 6 (*F*-formulæ). *Let* $F \subseteq \mathcal{F}$. *The set of F-formulæ and F-predicates are defined co-inductively as the biggest sets satisfying the following conditions:*

- *if $x.f \rightarrow (\vec{y})$ is an F-formula then $f \in F$;*
- *if $\varphi_1 \bullet \varphi_2$ is an F-formula (for some binary connective $\bullet$) then φ_1, φ_2 are F-formulæ;*
- *if $p(\vec{x}, X)$ is an F-formula then p is an F-predicate;*
- *if p is an F-predicate and $p(\vec{x}, X) \Leftarrow \varphi \in \mathcal{R}$ then φ is an F-formula.*

A 1-predicate *is a $\{f\}$-predicate, for some $f \in \mathcal{F}$.*

In particular, pure formulæ are always *F*-formulæ for all *F*. If φ is an $\{f\}$-formulæ, then it is clear that allocated($\mathfrak{h}$) $\subseteq \text{dom}_f(\mathfrak{h})$ holds for all models $(\mathfrak{s}, \mathfrak{h}, \Sigma)$ of φ. Consequently, $\varphi_1 \star \varphi_2$ and $\varphi_1 \circledast \varphi_2$ are equivalent if φ_1 and φ_2 are both $\{f\}$-formulæ (with the same field f). Notice also that, due to the form of the rule in Eq. 6, we also have $\Sigma(X) \subseteq \text{dom}_f(\mathfrak{h})$.

2.4 Normal Form

The decision procedure proposed in Sect. 3 applies to a pair $(\varphi, \mathcal{R})$ in which both components are in *normal form*. This form can be obtained from general OSL formulæ and SID through a syntactic translation, which may cause an exponential increase in their respective sizes. We define this normal form below by gradually introducing its components.

Symbolic Heap Formula. As in classical SL, a *symbolic heap formula* [1] is a (separating) conjunction of atoms. This fragment is especially interesting for program analysis. A symbolic heap formula does not contain the $\lor$ connective. By distributivity of $\star$ and $\circledast$ over $\lor$, any OSL formula φ can be transformed into an equivalent formula, denoted $dnf(\varphi)$, which is a disjunction of symbolic heap formulæ. Then, the satisfiability of $dnf(\varphi)$ can be tested by checking whether at least one of its disjuncts is satisfiable.

Injective Store Models. For proof's readability, we focus on models $(\mathfrak{s}, \mathfrak{h}, \Sigma)$ where $\mathfrak{s}$ is injective on location variables. This is enforced by adding a disequation $x \not\approx y$ for every pair of distinct location variables x, y.

Definition 7 (**Normal form**). *A pair $(\varphi, \mathcal{R})$ where V is the set of location variables in φ is in* normal form *if:*

1. *φ is a symbolic heap and contains a disequation $x \not\approx y$ for every pair of distinct variables in V.*
2. *If $p(\vec{x}, X) \Leftarrow \psi$ is a rule in $\mathcal{R}$, $y, z \in \mathcal{V}$, y is an auxiliary variable in ψ (i.e., a variable occurring in ψ but not in $\vec{x}$) and z is a variable distinct from y occurring in $\vec{x}$ or ψ, then ψ contains the atom $y \not\approx z$.*
3. *Each predicate p of arity $n + 1$ is associated with a subset $I_p \subseteq [\![1, n]\!]$ (called the* main parameters *of p), which satisfies the following properties:*
   - *For every atom $p(x_1, \dots, x_n, X)$ occurring in φ and every location variable y in V, there exists $i \in I_p$ such that $x_i = y$;*

- For every rule $p(x_1, \ldots, x_n, X) \Leftarrow \psi$ and every atom $q(y_1, \ldots, y_m, Y)$ in ψ, if $i \in I_p$, then there exists $j \in I_q$ such that $y_j = x_i$.

  These conditions are designed to ensure that all location variables in φ are passed as parameters to every predicate invoked during the evaluation of φ.

Condition 1 is not restrictive. Indeed, it is possible to enumerate all the equality relations on V and test satisfiability of φ for each of these relations, by replacing in φ all the variables in the same equivalence class by the same representative and by adding disequations between distinct representatives. Condition 2 is easy to enforce: a rule of the form $p(\vec{x}, X) \Leftarrow \psi$ that includes an auxiliary variable y and another (arbitrary) variable z can be replaced by two rules: $p(\vec{x}, X) \Leftarrow \psi\{y \mapsto z\}$ and $p(\vec{x}, X) \Leftarrow \psi \star y \not\approx z$, thus distinguishing the cases where y is equal to or different from z. Condition 3 is enforced by adding $|V|$ parameters to each predicate atom, corresponding to the variables in the set V. These additional parameters are simply propagated unchanged through recursive calls in predicate's rules.

Remark 2. As stated for all the components of the normal form, a general OSL formula and a SID can always be translated in normal form at the cost of a potential exponential increase in their respective sizes.

3   Satisfiability Problem

The satisfiability problem for OSL is defined as: "Given a formula $\varphi \in \Phi$ and a SID $\mathcal{R}$, does a structure $(\mathfrak{s}, \mathfrak{h}, \Sigma)$ exist such that $(\mathfrak{s}, \mathfrak{h}, \Sigma) \models_{\mathcal{R}} \varphi$?" Our main contribution is stated by the following theorem, which identifies a sufficient condition to decide this problem.

Theorem 1. *The satisfiability problem for OSL is decidable in exponential space if the predicates defined by the SID are 1-predicates.*

The result is obtained in two main steps summarised in the remainder of this section. We assume that the pair $(\varphi, \mathcal{R})$ is in normal form. As show in Sect. 2.4, this does not affect the expressive power of OSL.

The *first step* of the proof, presented in Sect. 3.1, introduces *decorations* of OSL formulæ. A decoration of a formula φ partitions the models of φ in such a way that each partition is characterized by (i) some aliasing and non-aliasing relations between the location variables, (ii) an assignment of location variables to the set variables, and (iii) an assignment of location variables to the allocated heap. Decorations are used to decorate predicate atoms and their defining rules in $\mathcal{R}$.

This results in a decorated SID $\mathcal{R}_{dec}$, in which only *consistent* rules are retained, namely, those where the partition induced by the decoration of the defining formula (i.e., the rule's right-hand side) is identical to the partition associated with the predicate being defined (i.e., the rule's left-hand side). This condition may be checked syntactically. Therefore, the initial question is split into N questions for the pairs $(\varphi_d, \mathcal{R}_d)$ obtained by decorating $(\varphi, \mathcal{R})$, where N is exponential in the size of the initial pair. Intuitively, this exponential blow-up is due to enumerating all decorations, which involves enumerating equivalence relations between free location variables, etc. The soundness and completeness of this step are stated by Theorem 2. Thus, if a formula φ has a model m, then there exists a decoration d such that the corresponding decorated formula φ_d also has m as a model. Conversely, if φ_d has m as a model, then m is also a model of φ.

This first step serves two purposes: (i) it ensures that all constraints induced by unfolding a predicate atom can be identified solely by inspecting predicate's decoration; and (ii) it enables the description of the cardinality of set variables as a context-free grammar (which in turn can be transformed into a Presburger formula). To illustrate the second point, consider the rules $p(x, y, X) \Leftarrow x.f \to () \star X \approx \emptyset$ and $p(x, y, X) \Leftarrow x.f \to () \star x \not\approx y \star X \approx \{x\}$. If $(\mathfrak{s}, \mathfrak{h}, \Sigma) \models p(x, y, X)$, then $\text{card}(\Sigma(X)) = 0$ when $\mathfrak{s}(x) = \mathfrak{s}(y)$ (i.e., x and y alias), and $\text{card}(\Sigma(X)) \in \{0, 1\}$ otherwise. In contrast, if $(\mathfrak{s}, \mathfrak{h}, \Sigma) \models p_d(x, y, X)$ with d a decoration, then the set of possible cardinalities of $\Sigma(X)$ depends only on the aliasing and non-aliasing relations in d: if d imposes a non-aliasing of x and y, then only the second rule can be unfolded and thus $\text{card}(\Sigma(X)) = 1$; if d does not impose any condition on x and y, then the first rule must be unfolded and $\text{card}(\Sigma(X)) = 0$; finally a decoration cannot impose an aliasing of x and y as there is no rule that requires such a condition. The second decoration admits models where $\mathfrak{s}(x) = \mathfrak{s}(y)$, but the cardinality of X does not depend on $\mathfrak{s}$.

The *second step*, presented in Sects. 3.2 and 3.3, translates a decorated pair $(\varphi_d, \mathcal{R}_d)$ into an equi-satisfiable formula in the logic BAPA [11]. The translation preserves all the set constraints of φ_d and it adds to them (a) Presburger formulæ that characterize the possible cardinalities of all set variables in φ_d; and (b) some set constraints encoding decorations, i.e., aliasing, non-aliasing, or membership constraints. Theorem 3 states that this translation is correct, i.e., it preserves satisfiability.

3.1 Decorations

Definition 8 (Decorated predicate symbol). *Let $p \in \mathcal{P}$ be a predicate symbol of arity $n + 1$. A decoration of p is a symbol $p_{I,J,\sim,\neq}$ such that I, J are subsets of $[\![1, n]\!]$ with $I \subseteq J$, $\sim$ is an equivalence relation over (i.e., partition of) $[\![1, n]\!]$ and $\neq$ is a symmetric binary relation on $[\![1, n]\!]$. The set of all decorations for symbols in $\mathcal{P}$ is denoted by $\mathcal{P}_{dec}$.*

Intuitively, the decoration of a predicate symbol fixes certain aspects of the model of an atom $p(x_1, \dots, x_n, X)$. For instance, $p_{I,J,\sim,\neq}$ specifies that I is the set of indices i (i.e., parameter positions) such that x_i occurs in X, and that J is the set of indices j such that x_j is allocated. The relations $\sim$ and $\neq$ encode aliasing and non-aliasing constraints, respectively: if $i \sim j$, then the store must map x_i and x_j to the same location; if $i \neq j$, then the locations of x_i and x_j must differ. Note that $i \neq j$ is *not* the negation of $i \sim j$, as both relations may be false in cases where no constraint is imposed on x_i and x_j. If $i(\neq \cap \sim) \neq \emptyset$, i.e., both $i \neq j$ and $i \sim j$ hold in a decoration, then the constraints resulting from the decoration are inconsistent; such decorations will be detected and eliminated in a later step (see Definition 14).

Definition 9 (Decorated formula). *A formula ψ is a decoration of a formula φ if it is obtained from φ by replacing every occurrence of a predicate symbol by a decoration of this symbol. A formula ψ is a decoration if there exists a formula φ such that ψ is a decoration of φ.*

Note that a predicate p symbol may appear in a formula with different decorations.

Definition 10 (Aliasing of a decorated formula). *Let ψ be a decoration of a symbolic heap formula with location variables V. The aliasing of ψ, denoted by $\equiv_\psi$, is the least reflexive, symmetric and transitive relation in V^2 such that $x \equiv_\psi y$ if one of the following conditions holds:*

(a) ψ contains an atom $x' \approx y'$ with $x \equiv_\psi x'$ and $y \equiv_\psi y'$;
(b) ψ contains an atom $p_{I,J,\sim,\neq}(x_1, \ldots, x_n, X)$ with $x_i \equiv_\psi x$, $x_j \equiv_\psi y$ and $i \sim j$.

Intuitively, $\equiv_\psi$ is the aliasing relation between the location variables of ψ induced by the equality atoms and the decorations of predicate symbols.

Definition 11 (Allocated variables). *Let ψ be a decoration of a symbolic heap formula with location variables V. The set of variables allocated by ψ, denoted by $alloc(\psi)$, is a subset of V inductively defined as the set of location variables y such that one of the following conditions holds:*

(a) ψ contains an atom of the form $y.f \to (\vec{z})$;
(b) ψ contains an atom $p_{I,J,\sim,\neq}(x_1, \ldots, x_n, X)$ such that $y = x_j$ with $j \in J$;
(c) $y \equiv_\psi y'$ with $y' \in alloc(\psi)$.

Intuitively, $alloc(\psi)$ denotes the set of variables in V that must be allocated in every model of ψ, given the decoration of predicates in ψ and the aliasing constraints.

Definition 12 (Distinguishing of a decorated formula). *Let ψ be a decoration of a symbolic heap formula with location variables V. The distinguishing of ψ, denoted $\not\equiv_\psi$, is the least symmetric relation in V^2 such that $x \not\equiv_\psi y$ if one of the following conditions holds:*

(a) ψ contains the atom $x \not\approx y$;
(b) ψ contains the atom $p_{I,J,\sim,\neq}(x_1, \ldots, x_n, X)$ with $x_i = x$, $x_j = y$ and $i \neq j$;
(c) ψ contains $\psi_1 \star \psi_2$, $x \in alloc(\psi_1)$ and $y \in alloc(\psi_2)$;
(d) $x \equiv_\psi x'$, $y \equiv_\psi y'$ and $x' \not\equiv_\psi y'$.

Intuitively, $\not\equiv_\psi$ is the disequality relation between the location variables of ψ induced by the disequality atoms, the decorations of predicate symbols and the separating conjunctions. The notion $\not\equiv_\psi$ is only used in (and thus defined for) decorated formulæ that appear in a right hand side of a predicate rule. Note that if ψ is in normal form, then $x \not\equiv_\psi y$ holds for all distinct variables x and y occurring in ψ. However, this property does not necessarily hold for formulæ obtained through unfolding, as parameter instantiation may introduce aliasing.

Definition 13 (Decorated set variable). *Let ψ be a decoration of a symbolic heap formula with location variables V and let Y be a set variable. The set of location variables attached to Y by ψ, denoted by $[Y]_\psi$, is inductively defined as the set of location variables $y \in V$ such that one of the following conditions holds:*

(a) ψ contains a set constraint $Y \approx E \sqcup \bigsqcup_{u \in U} Z_u$ (see Eq. 6) with $y \in E$ or $y \in [Z_u]_\psi$ for some $u \in U$;

(b) ψ contains an atom $p_{I,J,\sim,\neq}(x_1,\ldots,x_n,X)$ such that $X=Y$ and $y=x_i$ for some $i\in I$;
(c) $y\equiv_\psi y'$ with $y'\in[Y]_\psi$.

Intuitively, $[Y]_\psi$ is the subset of V, the location variables of ψ, that must be contained within the set variable Y given the decoration of predicates in ψ and the aliasing and set constraints.

Definition 14 (Consistent decoration). *The decoration ψ is consistent if the following condition holds: if $x\not\approx_\psi y$ then $x\not\equiv_\psi y$.*

Definition 15 (Decorated rule). *Let p be a predicate symbol, $p_{I,J,\sim,\neq}$ one of its decorations, and $p(x_1,\ldots,x_n,X)\Leftarrow\varphi$ a rule defining p in $\mathcal{R}$. A decorated rule for $p_{I,J,\sim,\neq}$ is a rule $p_{I,J,\sim,\neq}(x_1,\ldots,x_n,X)\Leftarrow\psi$ satisfying all the conditions below:*

- *ψ is a consistent decoration of φ;*
- *$i\sim j$ iff $x_i\equiv_\psi x_j$ for all $i,j\in[\![1,n]\!]$; and $i\neq j$ iff $x_i\not\equiv_\psi x_j$ for all $i,j\in[\![1,n]\!]$;*
- *$I=\{i\in[\![1,n]\!]\mid x_i\in[X]_\psi\}$; and $J=\{j\in[\![1,n]\!]\mid x_j\in alloc(\psi)\}$.*

The set of decorated rules obtained from $\mathcal{R}$ and the decorated predicate symbols is called a decorated SID *and it is denoted by $\mathcal{R}_{dec}$. The decoration of a pair $(\varphi,\mathcal{R})$ is a pair $(\psi,\mathcal{R}_{dec})$, where ψ is a decoration of φ and $\mathcal{R}_{dec}$ is the set of decorated rules obtained from $\mathcal{R}$.*

Example 3. Consider the following predicate p defined by the following rules in $\mathcal{R}$:

$$p(x,y,z,X)\Leftarrow x.f\to(y)\star x\not\approx y\star X\approx\emptyset,\quad p(x,y,z,X)\Leftarrow y.f\to(x)\star X\approx\{y\},$$
$$p(x,y,z,X)\Leftarrow z.f\to()\star X\approx\emptyset.$$

Let $\varphi=p(x,y,z,X)\star y\not\approx z\star z.f\to(x,y)$. The formula $\psi=p_{I,J,\sim,\neq}(x,y,z,X)\star y\not\approx z\star z.f\to(x,y)$ is a decoration of φ with $y\not\equiv_\psi z$. If $\sim$ is the identity, then $\equiv_\psi$ is the identity. Moreover:

- If $I=\emptyset$, $J=\{1\}$ and $1\neq2$ then $x\not\equiv_\psi y$, $alloc(\psi)=\{x,z\}$ and $[X]_\psi=\emptyset$. The only rule associated with $p_{I,J,\sim,\neq}$ is: $p_{I,J,\sim,\neq}(x,y,z,X)\Leftarrow x.f\to(y)\star x\not\approx y\star X\approx\emptyset$.
- If $I=\{2\}$, $J=\{2\}$ and $\neq$ is empty then $alloc(\psi)=\{y,z\}$ and $[X]_\psi=\{y\}$. The only rule associated with $p_{I,J,\sim,\neq}$ is $p_{I,J,\sim,\neq}(x,y,z,X)\Leftarrow y.f\to(x)\star X\approx\{y\}$.
- If $I=\emptyset$, $J=\{3\}$ then the decoration is inconsistent because we obtain $z\not\equiv_\psi z$. Indeed, the only rule associated with $p_{I,J,\sim,\neq}$ is: $p_{I,J,\sim,\neq}(x,y,z,X)\Leftarrow z\to()\star X\approx\emptyset$; this rule allocates z yielding a contradiction with the fact that z is already allocated by $z.f\to(x,y)$ in ψ.
- If $I=J=\emptyset$ then $p_{I,J,\sim,\neq}$ has no rule, hence $p_{I,J,\sim,\neq}(x,y,z,X)$ (hence also ψ) is (trivially) unsatisfiable.

Theorem 2. *Let $(\varphi,\mathcal{R})$ be a pair in normal form. For each structure $(\mathfrak{s},\mathfrak{h},\Sigma)$, we have $(\mathfrak{s},\mathfrak{h},\Sigma)\models_\mathcal{R}\varphi$ if and only if there exists a decoration $(\psi,\mathcal{R}_{dec})$ of $(\varphi,\mathcal{R})$ such that $(\mathfrak{s},\mathfrak{h},\Sigma)\models_{\mathcal{R}_{dec}}\psi$.*

3.2 Cardinality Constraints

We now begin the second step of the proof, which translates a decorated pair $(\varphi_d, \mathcal{R}_d)$ in normal form into a Presburger formula. We first consider the cardinality constraints on the sets of locations $[\![X]\!]_{(\mathfrak{s},\Sigma)}$ that appear in decorated predicate atoms $p_{I,J,\sim,\neq}(\vec{x}, X)$. The cardinalities of these sets are constrained by the (decorated) predicate's rules. These constraints are essential for satisfiability checking. For instance, as observed in the introduction, the formula $1\mathtt{s}_{even}(x, Y) \circledast 1\mathtt{s}_{odd}(x, Y)$ is unsatisfiable if $1\mathtt{s}_{even}$ and $1\mathtt{s}_{odd}$ describe lists of even and odd lengths respectively, and Y is defined in both cases to collect the set of locations allocated by each list. We show that the cardinality constraints induced by each decorated predicate atom can be encoded, in linear time, as an existential Presburger formula. To achieve this, we rely on known results [23] about the Presburger encoding of Parikh images of context-free languages.

Definition 16 (Cardinality of a decorated atom). *Let $p_{I,J,\sim,\neq}(\vec{x}, X)$ be a decorated predicate atom of $(\psi, \mathcal{R}_{dec})$. The* cardinality set *of $p_{I,J,\sim,\neq}(\vec{x}, X)$, which is denoted by $Sp(p_{I,J,\sim,\neq}(\vec{x}, X))$, is defined by:*

$$Sp(p_{I,J,\sim,\neq}(\vec{x}, X)) = \{\mathrm{card}\,(\Sigma(X)) \mid \exists (\mathfrak{s}, \mathfrak{h}, \Sigma).\,(\mathfrak{s}, \mathfrak{h}, \Sigma) \models_{\mathcal{R}_{dec}} p_{I,J,\sim,\neq}(\vec{x}, X)\}, \qquad (14)$$

i.e., it is a (possible unbounded) subset of $\mathbb{N}$, which collects the cardinalities of X for each structure satisfying $p_{I,J,\sim,\neq}(\vec{x}, X)$.

It is straightforward to show that $Sp(p_{I,J,\sim,\neq}(\vec{x}, X)) = Sp(p_{I,J,\sim,\neq}(\vec{x}, X)\sigma)$, for every renaming σ. In the following, we show that $Sp(p_{I,J,\sim,\neq}(\vec{x}, X))$ is a semi-linear set that can be encoded using an existential Presburger formula with one free variable. To this end, we define a context-free grammar for the predicate atom $p_{I,J,\sim,\neq}(\vec{x}, X)$ using the rules of $\mathcal{R}_{dec}$, such that the language of this grammar encodes the elements of $Sp(p_{I,J,\sim,\neq}(\vec{x}, X))$ in unary. The idea is to associate each predicate atom with a non-terminal of the grammar, and to associate each rule used in the unfolding with a production rule of the grammar. The set of non-terminals is finite because the set of predicate atoms is finite up to a renaming of parameters. The context-free grammar for $p_{I,J,\sim,\neq}(\vec{x}, X)$ is defined as follows.

Definition 17 (Grammar of cardinalities). *Let $\mathcal{R}_{dec}$ be a decorated SID. Let $a \mapsto N_a$ be any mapping from decorated atoms to symbols, such that $N_a = N_b$ iff a and b are identical up to a renaming. The* grammar of cardinalities *for the decorated atom $p_{I,J,\sim,\neq}(\vec{x}, X)$ is a context-free grammar $\mathcal{G}_{p_{I,J,\sim,\neq}(\vec{x},X)} = (N, \mathcal{T}, \mathcal{R}, N_0)$ where*

- *the set of terminals $\mathcal{T}$ is the singleton set $\{1\}$;*
- *the set of non-terminals N contains a non-terminal $N_{q_{K,L,\sim,\neq}(\vec{y},Y)}$ for each decorated predicate atom $q_{K,L,\sim,\neq}(\vec{y}, Y)$ (up to a renaming);*
- *the start symbol N_0 is $N_{p_{I,J,\sim,\neq}(\vec{x},X)}$;*
- *the set of derivation rules $\mathcal{R}$ contains a rule of the form*

$$N_{q_{K,L,\sim,\neq}(\vec{y},Y)} \rightarrow \omega\, N_{r^1_{K_1,L_1,\sim_1,\neq_1}(\vec{y}_1,Y_1)} \cdots N_{r^m_{K_m,L_m,\sim_m,\neq_m}(\vec{y}_m,Y_m)}, \qquad (15)$$

for all formulæ ψ such that $q_{K,L,\sim,\neq}(\vec{y}, Y) \Leftarrow_{\mathcal{R}_{dec}} \psi$ where:

- ψ is of the form $y_j.f \to (\vec{z}) \star \bigstar_{i=1}^{m} r^i_{K_i, L_i, \sim_i, \neq_i}(\vec{y}_i, Y_i) \star \varphi \star Y \approx E \sqcup \bigsqcup_{i=1}^{m} Y_i$;
- $\omega = 1$ if $E = \{y_j\}$, otherwise (i.e., if $E = \emptyset$) ω is the empty word ε.

We denote by $L(G)$ the language of words generated by the grammar G.

The Parikh image [19] of a word $\omega = \omega_1 \cdots \omega_k \in \mathcal{T}^*$ is the assignment $\sigma \in \mathbb{N}^{\mathcal{T}}$ that maps each symbol $a \in \mathcal{T}$ to the number of its occurrences in ω, i.e., $\sigma(a) =$ card$(j \mid a = \omega_j)$. The Parikh image of a set $L \subseteq \mathcal{T}^*$ is the set of Parikh images of all $\omega \in L$. If a language L is generated by a context-free grammar G, then the Parikh image of L can be represented by an existential Presburger formula ξ_G, which can be computed in linear time, by [23, Th. 4]. The formula ξ_G contains one free variable for each terminal symbol of G. We shall prove later that the Parikh image of the language defined by $G_{p_{I,J,\sim,\neq}(\vec{x},X)}$ is *exactly* the cardinality set $Sp(p_{I,J,\sim,\neq}(\vec{x},X))$. Since the grammar of cardinalities $G = G_{p_{I,J,\sim,\neq}(\vec{x},X)}$ has only one terminal, the formula ξ_G contains exactly one free variable and its size is in $O(|\mathcal{N}| + |\mathcal{N}| \cdot |\mathcal{R}|)$ where $\mathcal{N}$ and $\mathcal{R}$ are (respectively) the set of non-terminals and productions of $G_{p_{I,J,\sim,\neq}(\vec{x},X)}$. To simplify notations, we shall denote by $\xi_{p_{I,J,\sim,\neq}(\vec{x},X)}$ the formula ξ_G with $G = G_{p_{I,J,\sim,\neq}(\vec{x},X)}$, and by $\xi_{p_{I,J,\sim,\neq}(\vec{x},X)}(y)$ the formula obtained by replacing the unique free variable in ξ_G by y.

Remark 3. A smaller Presburger formula for $Sp(p_{I,J,\sim,\neq}(\vec{x},X))$ may be obtained by translating $\mathcal{R}_{dec}$ into a NFA over a singleton alphabet and by using the result of [22]. The resulting formula, obtained in polynomial time, does not contain universal quantifiers and its size is linear in the size of the NFA. We choose to use context-free grammars and the result in [23] in order to simplify the proof of correctness.

3.3 Translation from SL to BAPA

The syntax of BAPA formulæ is recalled below, with definitions slightly adapted for consistency with those of OSL[5].

Definition 18 (BAPA formulæ [11]). *The set of* BAPA*-formulæ φ^{BP} is inductively defined as follows:*

$$\varphi^{BP} := A^{BP} \mid B^{BP} \mid \varphi_1^{BP} \wedge \varphi_2^{BP} \mid \varphi_1^{BP} \vee \varphi_2^{BP} \mid \neg\varphi^{BP} \mid \exists X.\varphi^{BP} \mid \forall X.\varphi^{BP} \mid \exists k.\varphi^{BP} \mid \forall k.\varphi^{BP}$$

$$A^{BP} := t_1^{BP} \approx_{BP} t_2^{BP} \mid t_1^{BP} <_{BP} t_2^{BP} \mid K \operatorname{div} t^{BP} \quad t^{BP} := k \mid K \mid t_1^{BP} \oplus_{BP} t_2^{BP} \mid K \odot_{BP} t^{BP} \mid |T^{BP}|$$

$$B^{BP} := T_1^{BP} \approx_{BP} T_2^{BP} \mid T_1^{BP} \sqsubseteq_{BP} T_2^{BP} \quad T^{BP} := X \mid \emptyset \mid T_1^{BP} \sqcup_{BP} T_2^{BP} \mid T_1^{BP} \sqcap_{BP} T_2^{BP}$$

$$\tag{16}$$

where X is a set variable, K is an integer constant, and k is an integer variable.

Definition 19 (BAPA structure). *A BAPA structure is a tuple $(\mathbb{S}, \mathbb{I})$ where $\mathbb{S}$ is an interpretation of the set variables, i.e., a partial function from set variables to finite subsets $\mathcal{L}$, and $\mathbb{I}$ is an interpretation of the integer variables, i.e., a partial function from integer variables to $\mathbb{Z}$.*

The semantics of BAPA terms and formulæ are the expected ones.

---

[5] Specifically, instead of assuming a finite universe, we interpret set variables as finite subsets of $\mathcal{L}$, and omit all BAPA terms that depend on the universe, such as the complement operation.

Definition 20. *The function $\mathcal{T}^f$ maps a decorated symbolic heap formula in OSL to a BAPA term containing all (named) locations allocated by a field $f \in \mathcal{F}$. It is defined inductively as follows (where L, A and B denote pure atoms, defined as in Definition 1):*

- $\mathcal{T}^f(\mathrm{emp}) = \mathcal{T}^f(L) = \mathcal{T}^f(A) = \mathcal{T}^f(B) = \emptyset;$

- $\mathcal{T}^f(x.g \to (y_1, \ldots, y_d)) = \begin{cases} V_x & \text{if } g = f \\ \emptyset & \text{otherwise} \end{cases};$

- $\mathcal{T}^f(p_{I,J,\sim,\neq}(x_1, \ldots, x_n, X)) = \begin{cases} X \sqcup_{BP} \left(\bigsqcup_{j \in J}^{BP} V_{x_j} \right) & \text{if } p \text{ is a } \{f\}\text{-predicate} \\ \emptyset & \text{otherwise} \end{cases};$

- $\mathcal{T}^f(\psi_1 \bullet \psi_2) = \mathcal{T}^f(\psi_1) \cup \mathcal{T}^f(\psi_2)$ *for* $\bullet \in \{\star, \circledast\}.$

Definition 21 (BAPA translation function). *Let $X \mapsto i_X$ be an injective function mapping every set variable to an integer variable (which is intended to denote the cardinality of the set). The function $\mathcal{T}$ translates a set term in $\mathfrak{T}$ into a BAPA set term and a decorated symbolic heap formula into a BAPA formula, given a decorated SID $\mathcal{R}_{dec}$ (which, to simplify notations, is considered fixed in the context):*

- $\mathcal{T}(\{x\}) = V_x;\ \mathcal{T}(X) = X$ *if* $X \in \mathcal{S};\ \mathcal{T}(\emptyset) = \emptyset;\ \mathcal{T}(t) = t$ *if t is an arithmetic term;*
- $\mathcal{T}(\mathrm{emp}) = \mathbf{true};\ \mathcal{T}(x.f \to (y_1, \ldots, y_d)) = \mathbf{true};$
- $\mathcal{T}(x \approx y) = (V_x \approx_{BP} V_y);\ \mathcal{T}(x \not\approx y) = (V_x \sqcap_{BP} V_y \approx_{BP} \emptyset);$
- $\mathcal{T}(T_1 \approx T_2) = (\mathcal{T}(T_1) \approx_{BP} \mathcal{T}(T_2));$ *the definition is similar for $\sqcup, \sqcap, \sqsubseteq$ or $<;$*
- $\mathcal{T}(T_1 \not\approx T_2) = \neg(\mathcal{T}(T_1) \approx_{BP} \mathcal{T}(T_2));$ *the definition is similar for $\not\sqsubseteq$ or $\not<;$*
- $\mathcal{T}(K \operatorname{div} t) = (K \operatorname{div} \mathcal{T}(t));\ \mathcal{T}(K \operatorname{ndiv} t) = \neg(K \operatorname{div} \mathcal{T}(t));$
- $\mathcal{T}(p_{I,J,\sim,\neq}(x_1, \ldots, x_n, X)) = |X| \approx_{BP} i_X \wedge \xi_{p_{I,J,\sim,\neq}(x_1,\ldots,x_n,X)}(i_X)$
$$\wedge \left(\bigsqcup_{i \in I}^{BP} V_{x_i} \right) \sqsubseteq_{BP} X$$
$$\wedge \left(\bigsqcup_{x \in \{x_1,\ldots,x_n\} \setminus \{x_j \mid j \in I\}}^{BP} V_x \right) \sqcap_{BP} X \approx_{BP} \emptyset;$$
where the formula $\xi_{p_{I,J,\sim,\neq}(x_1,\ldots,x_n,X)}$ is defined as in Sect. 3.2.
- $\mathcal{T}(\psi_1 \star \psi_2) = \mathcal{T}(\psi_1) \wedge \mathcal{T}(\psi_2) \wedge \left(\bigsqcup_{f \in \mathcal{F}}^{BP} \mathcal{T}^f(\psi_1) \right) \sqcap_{BP} \left(\bigsqcup_{f \in \mathcal{F}}^{BP} \mathcal{T}^f(\psi_2) \right) \approx_{BP} \emptyset;$
- $\mathcal{T}(\psi_1 \circledast \psi_2) = \mathcal{T}(\psi_1) \wedge \mathcal{T}(\psi_2) \wedge \bigwedge_{f \in \mathcal{F}} \left(\mathcal{T}^f(\psi_1) \sqcap_{BP} \mathcal{T}^f(\psi_2) \approx_{BP} \emptyset \right).$

Proposition 1. *Let $T \in \mathfrak{T} \cup t$ be a set term or an arithmetic term. Let $(\mathfrak{s}, \mathfrak{h}, \Sigma)$ be an OSL structure. Let $\mathbb{S}$ be defined by $\mathbb{S}(V_x) = \{\mathfrak{s}(x)\}$ for all location variables x, and $\mathbb{S}(X) = \Sigma(X)$ for all set variables X. Then, for every interpretation $\mathbb{I}$, $[\![T]\!]_{(\mathfrak{s},\Sigma)} = [\![\mathcal{T}(T)]\!]_{(\mathbb{S},\mathbb{I})}.$*

Proof. The proof is by induction on T and t.

For each decorated symbolic heap ψ in normal form containing location variables $x_1, \ldots, x_n$, we associate the following BAPA formula called $C(\psi)$:

$$C(\psi) = |V_{x_1}| \approx_{BP} 1 \wedge \cdots \wedge |V_{x_n}| \approx_{BP} 1 \wedge \mathcal{T}(\psi). \tag{17}$$

Example 4. Let us consider the decorated formula $\psi = p_{I,J,\sim,\neq}(x,y,z,X) \star y \not\approx z \star z.f \rightarrow (x,y)$ taken from Example 3 with $I = \{2\}$, $J = \{2\}$, $\sim = \mathrm{Id}$, and $\neq = \emptyset$.

Then the BAPA formula obtained is:

$$C(\psi) = |V_x| \approx_{BP} 1 \wedge |V_y| \approx_{BP} 1 \wedge |V_z| \approx_{BP} 1 \wedge |X| \approx_{BP} i_X \wedge \xi_{p_{I,J,\sim,\neq}(x,y,z,X)}(i_X)$$
$$\wedge\; V_y \sqsubseteq_{BP} X \wedge (V_x \sqcup_{BP} V_z) \sqcap_{BP} X \approx_{BP} \emptyset \wedge V_y \sqcap_{BP} V_z \approx_{BP} \emptyset \wedge \mathrm{true} \tag{18}$$
$$\wedge\; \left(X \sqcup_{BP} V_y\right) \sqcap_{BP} V_Z \approx_{BP} \emptyset .$$

It is straightforward to verify that, for all decorations ψ of a formula φ, $C(\psi)$ is an existentially quantified BAPA formula. This translation allows us to establish the decidability of the satisfiability problem for a decorated symbolic heap:

Theorem 3. *Let $(\varphi, \mathcal{R})$ an OSL-formula and a SID in normal form. For all decorations $(\psi, \mathcal{R}_{dec})$ of $(\varphi, \mathcal{R})$, ψ has an $\mathcal{R}_{dec}$-model iff $C(\psi)$ is satisfiable (in BAPA).*

Theorem 1 then follows directly from Theorems 2 and 3. The NEXPTIME upper bound is obtained by observing that the size of the decorated, normalized set of rules is exponential in the size of the original SID, since the number of possible decorations and instantiations is exponential. Moreover, it is shown in [13] that satisfiability for existentially quantified BAPA formulæ is in NP.

4   Conclusion

We have developed a decision procedure to test the satisfiability of formulæ in a variant of separation logic (SL) that integrates inductively defined predicate symbols, overlaid data structures, set constraints, and Presburger arithmetic constraints on set cardinalities. This fragment, designed to address the limitations of standard SL in reasoning about overlaid data structures, uses a weaker form of separating conjunction and supports single-field inductive predicates augmented with set variables. Our procedure operates in exponential space, leveraging established results on the computation of the Parikh image of context-free languages over a unary alphabet and the satisfiability problem in the logic BAPA. This reduction yields a robust framework for handling complex memory models occurring in concurrent systems and advanced algorithmic designs, where locations may be shared across multiple data structures.

A natural extension of this work is to explore the entailment problem. Given the undecidability of entailment in many expressive SL variants (see for instance [5,20]), additional restrictions will be required to ensure decidability. Several questions also remain unresolved regarding satisfiability. First, the optimality of our procedure is uncertain: while satisfiability is clearly EXPTIME-hard[6], it is not clear whether NEXPTIME represents a tight upper bound. Second, it would be valuable to investigate whether the systematic enumeration of all decorations could be circumvented. This process currently incurs an exponential computational overhead, which does not affect the theoretical complexity analysis but poses practical challenges. Finally, it would be interesting to determine whether the conditions on the inductive rules could be relaxed. For instance, is satisfiability still decidable if a single predicate is permitted to allocate distinct fields?

---

[6] This follows from the lower bound given in [20], since that result does not use permissions and imposes strictly more restrictive conditions on the rules.

References

1. Berdine, J., Calcagno, C., O'Hearn, P.W.: Symbolic execution with separation logic. In: Yi, K. (ed.) APLAS 2005. LNCS, vol. 3780, pp. 52–68. Springer, Heidelberg (2005). https://doi.org/10.1007/11575467_5

2. Brotherston, J., Fuhs, C., Pérez, J.A.N., Gorogiannis, N.: A decision procedure for satisfiability in separation logic with inductive predicates. In: Proceedings of the Joint Meeting of the Twenty-Third EACSL Annual Conference on Computer Science Logic (CSL) and the Twenty-Ninth Annual ACM/IEEE Symposium on Logic in Computer Science (LICS), CSL-LICS 2014, pp. 1–10. Association for Computing Machinery, New York (2014). https://doi.org/10.1145/2603088.2603091

3. Drăgoi, C., Enea, C., Sighireanu, M.: Local shape analysis for overlaid data structures. In: Logozzo, F., Fähndrich, M. (eds.) SAS 2013. LNCS, vol. 7935, pp. 150–171. Springer, Heidelberg (2013). https://doi.org/10.1007/978-3-642-38856-9_10

4. Echenim, M., Iosif, R., Peltier, N.: Decidable entailments in separation logic with inductive definitions: beyond establishment. In: Baier, C., Goubault-Larrecq, J. (eds.) 29th EACSL Annual Conference on Computer Science Logic (CSL 2021). Leibniz International Proceedings in Informatics (LIPIcs), Dagstuhl, Germany, vol. 183, pp. 20:1–20:18. Schloss Dagstuhl – Leibniz-Zentrum für Informatik (2021). https://doi.org/10.4230/LIPIcs.CSL.2021.20

5. Echenim, M., Iosif, R., Peltier, N.: Entailment is undecidable for symbolic heap separation logic formulæ with non-established inductive rules. Inf. Process. Lett. **173**, 106169 (2022). https://doi.org/10.1016/j.ipl.2021.106169

6. Enea, C., Saveluc, V., Sighireanu, M.: Compositional invariant checking for overlaid and nested linked lists. In: Felleisen, M., Gardner, P. (eds.) ESOP 2013. LNCS, vol. 7792, pp. 129–148. Springer, Heidelberg (2013). https://doi.org/10.1007/978-3-642-37036-6_9

7. Gu, X., Chen, T., Wu, Z.: A complete decision procedure for linearly compositional separation logic with data constraints. In: Olivetti, N., Tiwari, A. (eds.) IJCAR 2016. LNCS (LNAI), vol. 9706, pp. 532–549. Springer, Cham (2016). https://doi.org/10.1007/978-3-319-40229-1_36

8. Iosif, R., Rogalewicz, A., Simacek, J.: The tree width of separation logic with recursive definitions. In: Bonacina, M.P. (ed.) CADE 2013. LNCS (LNAI), vol. 7898, pp. 21–38. Springer, Heidelberg (2013). https://doi.org/10.1007/978-3-642-38574-2_2

9. Ishtiaq, S.S., O'Hearn, P.W.: BI as an assertion language for mutable data structures. In: Proceedings of the 28th ACM SIGPLAN-SIGACT Symposium on Principles of Programming Languages, POPL 2001, pp. 14–26. Association for Computing Machinery, New York (2001). https://doi.org/10.1145/360204.375719

10. Krishna, S., Shasha, D., Wies, T.: Go with the flow: compositional abstractions for concurrent data structures. Proc. ACM Program. Lang. **2**(POPL), 37:1–37:31 (2017). https://doi.org/10.1145/3158125

11. Kuncak, V., Nguyen, H.H., Rinard, M.: An algorithm for deciding BAPA: Boolean algebra with presburger arithmetic. In: Nieuwenhuis, R. (ed.) CADE 2005. LNCS (LNAI), vol. 3632, pp. 260–277. Springer, Heidelberg (2005). https://doi.org/10.1007/11532231_20

12. Kuncak, V., Nguyen, H.H., Rinard, M.: Deciding Boolean algebra with presburger arithmetic. J. Autom. Reason. **36**(3), 213–239 (2006). https://doi.org/10.1007/s10817-006-9042-1

13. Kuncak, V., Rinard, M.: Towards efficient satisfiability checking for Boolean algebra with presburger arithmetic. In: Pfenning, F. (ed.) CADE 2007. LNCS (LNAI), vol. 4603, pp. 215–230. Springer, Heidelberg (2007). https://doi.org/10.1007/978-3-540-73595-3_15

14. Le, Q.L., Le, X.B.D.: An efficient cyclic entailment procedure in a fragment of separation logic. In: Kupferman, O., Sobocinski, P. (eds.) FoSSaCS 2023. LNCS, vol. 13992, pp. 477–497. Springer, Cham (2023). https://doi.org/10.1007/978-3-031-30829-1_23

15. Lee, O., Yang, H., Petersen, R.: Program analysis for overlaid data structures. In: Gopalakrishnan, G., Qadeer, S. (eds.) CAV 2011. LNCS, vol. 6806, pp. 592–608. Springer, Heidelberg (2011). https://doi.org/10.1007/978-3-642-22110-1_48

16. Lee, O., Yang, H., Petersen, R.: A divide-and-conquer approach for analysing overlaid data structures. Formal Methods Syst. Des. **41**(1), 4–24 (2012). https://doi.org/10.1007/s10703-012-0151-7

17. Matheja, C., Pagel, J., Zuleger, F.: A decision procedure for guarded separation logic complete entailment checking for separation logic with inductive definitions. ACM Trans. Comput. Logic **24**(1), 1:1–1:76 (2023). https://doi.org/10.1145/3534927

18. Meyer, R., Wies, T., Wolff, S.: Make flows small again: revisiting the flow framework. In: Sankaranarayanan, S., Sharygina, N. (eds.) TACAS 2023. LNCS, vol. 13993, pp. 628–646. Springer, Cham (2023). https://doi.org/10.1007/978-3-031-30823-9_32

19. Parikh, R.J.: On context-free languages. J. ACM **13**(4), 570–581 (1966). https://doi.org/10.1145/321356.321364

20. Peltier, N.: Testing the satisfiability of formulas in separation logic with permissions. In: Ramanayake, R., Urban, J. (eds.) TABLEAUX 2023. LNCS, vol. 14278, pp. 427–445. Springer, Cham (2023). https://doi.org/10.1007/978-3-031-43513-3_23

21. Reynolds, J.C.: Separation logic: a logic for shared mutable data structures. In: Proceedings 17th Annual IEEE Symposium on Logic in Computer Science, Copenhagen, Denmark, pp. 55–74 (2002). https://doi.org/10.1109/LICS.2002.1029817. ISSN 1043-6871

22. Sawa, Z.: Efficient construction of semilinear representations of languages accepted by unary nondeterministic finite automata. Fundamenta Informaticae **123**(1), 97–106 (2013). https://doi.org/10.3233/FI-2013-802

23. Verma, K.N., Seidl, H., Schwentick, T.: On the complexity of equational horn clauses. In: Nieuwenhuis, R. (ed.) CADE 2005. LNCS (LNAI), vol. 3632, pp. 337–352. Springer, Heidelberg (2005). https://doi.org/10.1007/11532231_25

Subtyping in Dependently-Typed Higher-Order Logic

Colin Rothgang[1,2](✉) [iD] and Florian Rabe[3] [iD]

[1] Imdea Software Institute, Madrid, Spain
colin.rothgang@posteo.net
[2] Universidad Politécnica de Madrid, Madrid, Spain
[3] Computer Science, FAU Erlangen-Nürnberg, Erlangen, Germany

Abstract. The recently introduced dependent typed higher-order logic (DHOL) offers an interesting compromise between expressiveness and automation support. It sacrifices the decidability of its type system in order to significantly extend its expressiveness over standard HOL. Yet it retains strong automated theorem proving support via a sound and complete translation to HOL.

We leverage this design to extend DHOL with refinement and quotient types. Both of these are commonly requested by practitioners but rarely provided by automated theorem provers. This is because they inherently require undecidable typing and thus are very difficult to retrofit to decidable type systems. But with DHOL already doing the heavy lifting, adding them is not only possible but elegant and simple.

Concretely, we add refinement and quotient types as special cases of subtyping. This turns the associated canonical inclusion resp. projection maps into identity maps and thus avoids costly changes in representation. We present the syntax, semantics, and translation to HOL for the extended language, including the proofs of soundness and completeness.

1 Introduction and Related Work

Motivation. Recently dependently typed higher-order logic (DHOL) was introduced [22]. It is a variant of HOL [2,6] that uses dependent function types $\Pi x{:}A.\ B$ instead of simple function types $A \rightarrow B$. It is designed to remain as simple and as close to HOL and ATPs as possible while meeting the frequent user demand of dependent types. Notably, contrary to typical formulations of dependent type theory, DHOL features a straightforward equality and classical Booleans at the cost of making typing undecidable.

Concretely, DHOL uses a type bool of propositions in the style of HOL, and equality $s =_A t{:}\,\mathsf{bool}$ of typed terms is a proposition, whose truth may depend on axioms in the theory or assumptions in the context. Equality $A \equiv B$ of types (which is not a proposition but a meta-level judgment) uses a straightforward congruence rule: if a dependent type constructor is applied to equal arguments, it produces equal types. Thus, equality of types and typing are undecidable. To yield practical tool support, DHOL reduces typing judgments to a series of proof

© The Author(s) 2026
R. Thiemann and C. Weidenbach (Eds.): FroCoS 2025, LNAI 15979, pp. 98–114, 2026.
https://doi.org/10.1007/978-3-032-04167-8_6

obligations, and [22] gives a sound and complete translation to HOL that allows using existing automated theorem provers for HOL to discharge these.

While undecidable typing is not used by most current ATPs or ITPs, it is justified by the pragmatic consideration that the ultimate task of theorem proving is undecidable anyway, and the difficulty of typing-related proof obligations is often small in comparison. Follow-up work on DHOL includes a native ATP for DHOL [17] and extensions with a choice operator [20] and polymorphism [21].

Contribution. The present paper leverages this key design choice and extends DHOL's expressivity at low cost by adding refinement and quotient types. Both work elegantly in languages with undecidable typing so that DHOL, for which the necessary meta-theory and infrastructure already exist, is a good base to support them. Indeed, the necessary changes to DHOL's syntax and semantics turned out to be few and simple—only the extension of the proof was difficult. We see DHOL as an intermediate between the automation support of HOL and the more expressive type theories of interactive provers such as those based on richer dependent type theories. In this sense, the present paper pushes the boundary of ATP-near languages a little further.

Refinement types $A|_p$ is the subtype of A consisting of the terms satisfying the predicate $p{:}A \to \mathsf{bool}$. They correspond to comprehension in set theory. They were already proposed in [22] (with ad-hoc subtyping rules), and here we give a systematic treatment. Critically, our refinement types avoid a change in representation: the injection $A|_p \to A$ is always a no-op, i.e., an identity map. This is in contrast to encodings of refinement types in decidable type theories, such as using the type $\Sigma x{:}A.p\,x$, or in set-theory, where, e.g., the injection $(A \to B) \to (A|_p \to B)$ is not a no-op.

Quotient types A/r, intuitively, consist of all equivalence classes of the equivalence relation $r{:}A \to A \to \mathsf{bool}$. Again we avoid representation changes: We use all terms of type A as terms of type A/r and adjust the equality $=_{A/r}$ to obtain the quotient semantics. Thus, the projection $A \to A/r$ is a no-op and we have the subtyping relation $A \prec: A/r$. In contrast, the usual definitions in set theory (via equivalence classes) or in decidable type theories (via setoids) require explicit changes in representation.

The statement $A \prec: A/r$ may look odd. It is sound because we use a different equality relation at the two types: $x =_A y$ implies $x =_{A/r} y$ but not the other way round. This approach captures the mathematical practice of using elements of A as elements of the quotient, often to the point that readers do not even notice anymore they are technically working with equivalence classes.

Together, this yields a subtype hierarchy of refinements and quotients of A:
$$A|_{\lambda x:A.\ \mathsf{false}} \prec: .\, . \prec: A|_p \prec: .\, . \prec: A|_{\lambda x:A.\ \mathsf{true}} \equiv A \equiv A/{=_A} \prec: .\, . \prec: A/r \prec: .\, . \prec: A/\lambda x, y{:}A.\ \mathsf{true}$$
from initial (empty) type to terminal (singleton) type.

Related Work. Systems based on HOL [11] use the subtype definition principle to introduce definitional refinement types. General refinement types in HOL were considered in [15]. But neither solution has a general notion of subtyping. Definitional quotient types for HOL were considered in [12] and [13] and, combined with refinement types, in [19]. Definitional solutions differ from ours in that they introduce new types that are isomorphic to the refinement/quotient types and then require explicit representation-changing injection/projections. [19] uses PERs to relativize type-based to set-based theorems.

In formal systems, the approach of quotients as supertypes has been adopted occasionally, e.g., in NuPRL's quotients [7] or in Quotient Haskell [3]. NuPRL's type theory in particular features refinement and quotient types similar to ours and uses essentially the same PER semantics [1]. The main difference to our approach is that DHOL tries to be as close to HOL (and thus HOL ATPs) as possible whereas NuPRL uses a very rich type theory.

PVS [18] subsumes DHOL and refinement types with polymorphism. It does not support quotients, but its horizontal subtyping between records resembles our quotient subtyping. Notably, it treats refinement subtyping and record subtyping as two separate judgments with slightly different rules.

In soft type systems, all types are refinements of a fixed universe of objects. For example, Mizar's [4] type system is inherently undecidable and supports dependent types and refinement types. It supports quotient types but only with a change in representation and not as supertypes.

Most ITPs allow users to construct refinement and quotient types at the cost of representation changes. Systems based on decidable dependent type theory like Coq [8] or Lean [9] typically use Σ-types for refinement and setoids for quotients. Lean provides some kernel support for quotients.

[21] adds polymorphism to DHOL, and in future work we want to combine both features. The key challenge will be to support *subtype-bounded* polymorphism.

Overview. We give a self-contained definition of DHOL in Sect. 2. Then we add subtyping in Sect. 3, refinements in Sect. 4, and quotients in Sect. 5. We develop the meta-theory in Sect. 6 (type normalization) and Sect. 7 (soundness/completeness). We present an application to typed set theory in Sect. 8.

2 Preliminaries: Dependently Typed Higher-Order Logic

The DHOL [22] **grammar** uses terms and types. A theory T declares typed constants $c{:}A$, axioms $\triangleright F$, and dependent type symbols $a{:}\Pi x_1{:}A_1. \ldots \Pi x_n{:}A_n. \mathsf{tp}$, which are applied to terms to obtain base types $a\ t_1 \ldots t_n$. Contexts declare typed variables $x{:}A$ and local assumptions $\triangleright F$ (but no new types). Dependent functions $\lambda x{:}A.\ t$ of type $\Pi x{:}A.\ B$ (written $A \to B$ if x does not occur free in B) map terms $x{:}A$ to terms of type $B(x)$. We recover HOL as the fragment in which all base types a have arity 0, in which case all function types are simple.

T	$::=$	$\circ \mid T, \mathsf{a}{:}(\Pi x{:}A.)^* \mathsf{tp} \mid T, \mathsf{c}{:}A \mid T, \triangleright F$	theories
Γ	$::=$	$. \mid \Gamma, x{:}A \mid \Gamma, \triangleright F$	contexts
A, B	$::=$	$\mathsf{a}\ t^* \mid \Pi x{:}A.\ B \mid \mathsf{bool}$	types
s, t, F, G	$::=$	$\mathsf{c} \mid x \mid \lambda x{:}A.\ t \mid s\ t \mid s =_A t \mid F \Rightarrow G$	terms (incl. propositions)

Following typical HOL-style [2], DHOL defines all connectives and quantifiers from the equality connective $s =_A t$. For example, forall is defined as $\forall x{:}A.\ F :=\lambda x{:}A.\ F =_{\Pi x:A.\ \text{bool}} \lambda x{:}A.\ \text{true}$. In particular, we can define the usual connectives and quantifiers and derive their usual proof rules. The only subtlety is that, DHOL needs *dependent* binary connectives: in an implication $F \Rightarrow G$, the well-formedness of G may depend on the truth of F, and accordingly for conjunction $F \wedge G$ which is defined as $\neg(F \Rightarrow \neg G)$. Because we see no way to define these from equality, we make dependent implication an additional primitive.

DHOL uses axiomatic equality $s =_A t$ in the style of FOL and HOL with a straightforward congruence rule for base types: type equality $a\ s_1\ \dots\ s_n \equiv a\ t_1\ \dots\ t_n$ holds if each s_i is equal to t_i. This makes type equality and thus typing undecidable. In line with HOL's simplicity and unlike dependent type theories based on Martin-Löf type theory [16], there is no support for type-valued computation like large elimination.

Example 1 (Lists). As an accessible running example, we show a formalization of lists over some type obj, both plain lists list and lists llist n with fixed length. Notably, the well-typedness of the statement of associativity of lconc now requires the associativity of plus.

nat: tp,   zero: nat,   succ: nat → nat,   plus: nat → nat → nat,
obj: tp,   list: tp,   nil: list,   cons: obj → list → list,   conc: list → list → list,
llist: nat → tp,   lnil: llist zero,
lcons: Πn:nat. obj → llist n → llist (succ n),
lconc: $\Pi m, n$:nat. llist m → llist n → llist (plus $m\ n$)

Name	Judgment	Intuition
theories	$\vdash T$ Thy	T is a well-formed theory
contexts	$\vdash_T \Gamma$ Ctx	Γ is a well-formed context
types	$\Gamma \vdash_T A$ tp	A is a well-formed type
typing	$\Gamma \vdash_T t{:}A$	t is a well-formed term of well-formed type A
validity	$\Gamma \vdash_T F$	well-formed Boolean F is derivable
equality of types	$\Gamma \vdash_T A \equiv B$	well-formed types A and B are equal

Fig. 1. DHOL Judgments

DHOL uses the **judgments** given in Fig. 1 and the **rules** listed in Fig. 2. Note that equality of terms is a special case of validity, whereas equality of types is not a Boolean but a separate judgment. Thus, users cannot state axioms equating types, and type equality is defined only by congruence. The rules are straightforward. In particular, type equality is checked structurally and reduced to a set of term equalities, which must then be discharged by an ATP.

Theories and contexts:

$$\frac{}{\vdash \circ \text{ Thy}} \qquad \frac{\vdash_T x_1{:}A_1, \ldots, x_n{:}A_n \text{ Ctx}}{\vdash T, a{:}\Pi x_1{:}A_1. \ldots \Pi x_n{:}A_n. \text{ tp Thy}} \qquad \frac{\vdash_T A \text{ tp}}{\vdash T, c{:}A \text{ Thy}} \qquad \frac{\vdash_T F{:}\text{bool}}{\vdash T, \triangleright F \text{ Thy}}$$

$$\frac{\vdash T \text{ Thy}}{\vdash_T . \text{ Ctx}} \qquad \frac{\Gamma \vdash_T A \text{ tp}}{\vdash_T \Gamma, x{:}A \text{ Ctx}} \qquad \frac{\Gamma \vdash_T F{:}\text{bool}}{\vdash_T \Gamma, \triangleright F \text{ Ctx}}$$

Well-formedness and equality of types:

$$\frac{a{:}\Pi x_1{:}A_1. \ldots \Pi x_n{:}A_n. \text{ tp in } T \quad \Gamma \vdash_T t_1{:}A_1 \quad \ldots \quad \Gamma \vdash_T t_n{:}A_n[x_1/t_1]\ldots[x_{n-1}/t_{n-1}]}{\Gamma \vdash_T a \, t_1 \, \ldots \, t_n \text{ tp}} \qquad \frac{\vdash_T \Gamma \text{ Ctx}}{\Gamma \vdash_T \text{bool tp}} \qquad \frac{\Gamma \vdash_T A \text{ tp} \quad \Gamma, x{:}A \vdash_T B \text{ tp}}{\Gamma \vdash_T \Pi x{:}A. B \text{ tp}}$$

$$\frac{a{:}\Pi x_1{:}A_1. \ldots \Pi x_n{:}A_n. \text{ tp in } T \quad \Gamma \vdash_T s_1 =_{A_1} t_1 \ldots \Gamma \vdash_T s_n =_{A_n[x_1/t_1]\ldots[x_{n-1}/t_{n-1}]} t_n}{\Gamma \vdash_T a \, s_1 \, \ldots \, s_n \equiv a \, t_1 \, \ldots t_n} \qquad \frac{\vdash_T \Gamma \text{ Ctx}}{\Gamma \vdash_T \text{bool} \equiv \text{bool}} \qquad \frac{\Gamma \vdash_T A \equiv A' \quad \Gamma, x{:}A \vdash_T B \equiv B'}{\Gamma \vdash_T \Pi x{:}A. B \equiv \Pi x{:}A'. B'}$$

Typing:

$$\frac{c{:}A' \text{ in } T \quad \Gamma \vdash_T A' \equiv A}{\Gamma \vdash_T c{:}A} \qquad \frac{\Gamma, x{:}A \vdash_T t{:}B \quad A' \equiv A}{\Gamma \vdash_T (\lambda x{:}A. t){:}\Pi x{:}A'. B} \qquad \frac{\Gamma \vdash_T F{:}\text{bool} \quad \Gamma, \triangleright F \vdash_T G{:}\text{bool}}{\Gamma \vdash_T F \Rightarrow G{:}\text{bool}}$$

$$\frac{x{:}A' \text{ in } \Gamma \quad \Gamma \vdash_T A' \equiv A}{\Gamma \vdash_T x{:}A} \qquad \frac{\Gamma \vdash_T f{:}\Pi x{:}A. B \quad \Gamma \vdash_T t{:}A}{\Gamma \vdash_T f \, t{:}B[x/t]} \qquad \frac{\Gamma \vdash_T s{:}A \quad \Gamma \vdash_T t{:}A}{\Gamma \vdash_T s =_A t{:}\text{bool}}$$

Equality: congruence, reflexivity, symmetry, β, η (transitivity and extensionality are derivable):

$$\frac{\Gamma \vdash_T A \equiv A' \quad \Gamma, x{:}A \vdash_T t =_B t'}{\Gamma \vdash_T \lambda x{:}A. t =_{\Pi x:A. B} \lambda x{:}A'. t'} \qquad \frac{\Gamma \vdash_T t =_A t' \quad \Gamma \vdash_T f =_{\Pi x:A. B} f'}{\Gamma \vdash_T f \, t =_B f' \, t'}$$

$$\frac{\Gamma \vdash_T t{:}A}{\Gamma \vdash_T t =_A t} \qquad \frac{\Gamma \vdash_T t =_A s}{\Gamma \vdash_T s =_A t} \qquad \frac{\Gamma \vdash_T (\lambda x{:}A. s){:}B}{\Gamma \vdash_T (\lambda x{:}A. s) \, t =_B s[x/t]} \qquad \frac{\Gamma \vdash_T t{:}\Pi x{:}A. B}{\Gamma \vdash_T t =_{\Pi x:A. B} \lambda x{:}A. t \, x}$$

Rules for validity: lookup, implication, Boolean equality and Boolean extensionality

$$\frac{\triangleright F \text{ in } T \quad \vdash_T \Gamma \text{ Ctx}}{\Gamma \vdash_T F} \qquad \frac{\Gamma, \triangleright F \vdash_T G}{\Gamma \vdash_T F \Rightarrow G} \qquad \frac{\Gamma \vdash_T F =_{\text{bool}} F' \quad \Gamma \vdash_T F'}{\Gamma \vdash_T F}$$

$$\frac{\triangleright F \text{ in } \Gamma \quad \vdash_T \Gamma \text{ Ctx}}{\Gamma \vdash_T F} \qquad \frac{\Gamma \vdash_T F \Rightarrow G \quad \Gamma \vdash_T F}{\Gamma \vdash_T G} \qquad \frac{\Gamma \vdash_T p \text{ true} \quad \Gamma \vdash_T p \text{ false}}{\Gamma, x{:}\text{bool} \vdash_T p \, x}$$

Fig. 2. DHOL Rules

Theories and contexts: $\quad \overline{\circ} := \circ \qquad \overline{T, D} := \overline{T}, \overline{D} \qquad \overline{.} := . \qquad \overline{\Gamma, D} := \overline{\Gamma}, \overline{D}$

$$\overline{a{:}\Pi x_1{:}A_1. \ldots \Pi x_n{:}A_n. \text{ tp}} := a{:}\text{tp}, \; a^*{:}\overline{A_1} \to \ldots \to \overline{A_n} \to a \to a \to \text{bool},$$
$$\triangleright \forall x_1{:}\overline{A_1}. \ldots \forall x_n{:}\overline{A_n}. \; \forall u, v{:}a. \; a^* \, x_1 \, \ldots \, x_n \, u \, v \Rightarrow u =_a v$$

$$\overline{c{:}A} := c{:}\overline{A}, \triangleright A^* \, c \, c \qquad \overline{x{:}A} := x{:}\overline{A}, \triangleright A^* \, x \, x$$

$$\overline{\triangleright F} := \triangleright \overline{F} \qquad \overline{\triangleright F} := \triangleright \overline{F}$$

Types: $\quad \overline{a \, t_1 \, \ldots \, t_n} := a \qquad (a \, t_1 \, \ldots \, t_n)^* \, s \, t := a^* \, \overline{t_1} \, \ldots \, \overline{t_n} \, s \, t$

$$\overline{\Pi x{:}A. B} := \overline{A} \to \overline{B} \qquad (\Pi x{:}A. B)^* \, f \, g := \forall x, y{:}\overline{A}. \; A^* \, x \, y \Rightarrow B^* \, (f \, x) \, (g \, y)$$

$$\overline{\text{bool}} := \text{bool} \qquad \text{bool}^* \, s \, t := s =_{\text{bool}} t$$

Terms: $\quad \overline{c} := c \qquad \overline{x} := x \qquad \overline{\lambda x{:}A. t} := \lambda x{:}\overline{A}. \overline{t} \qquad \overline{f \, t} := \overline{f} \, \overline{t}$

$$\overline{s =_A t} := A^* \, \overline{s} \, \overline{t} \qquad \overline{F \Rightarrow G} := \overline{F} \Rightarrow \overline{G}$$

if in DHOL	then in HOL
type A	type $\overline{A}$ and PER $A^*{:}\overline{A} \to \overline{A} \to \text{bool}$
term $t{:}A$	term $\overline{t}{:}\overline{A}$ satisfying $A^* \, \overline{t} \, \overline{t}$

Fig. 3. Definition of the Translation DHOL→HOL

Furthermore many well-known admissible HOL rules are also admissible in DHOL, see the extended preprint [5].

The **semantics** for DHOL and a **practical ATP workflow** are given by a sound and complete translation to HOL. The translation is dependency erasure, e.g., translating dependent types a $t_1 \ldots t_n$ to simple types a, effectively "'merging"' all instances of a dependent type into a large simple type. Figure 3 shows the details.

Typing and equality at A are recovered by generating a partial equivalence relation (PER) A^* for every HOL-type $\overline{A}$. A PER is a symmetric-transitive relation and the same as an equivalence relation on a subtype of $\overline{A}$. Thus, A corresponds in HOL to the quotient of the appropriate subtype of $\overline{A}$ by A^*.

DHOL terms are translated to their HOL analogues except that equality is translated to the respective PER: $\overline{s =_A t} := A^* \, \overline{s} \, \overline{t}$. In particular, the predicate $A^* \, \overline{t} \, \overline{t}$ captures whether t is a term of type A. For n-ary type symbols a, the translation generates an $n+2$-ary predicate a^* such that $a^* \, \overline{t_1} \ldots \overline{t_n}$ is the PER for a $t_1 \ldots t_n$. For function types, the PER is the usual condition for logical relations: functions are related if they map related inputs to related outputs.

3 Subtyping

The treatment of quotients as supertypes and the use of different equality relations at different types are subtly difficult. Thus, we first introduce subtyping by its defining extensional property, from which we will derive all subtyping rules:

Definition 1 (Subtyping). $\Gamma \vdash_T A \prec: B$ *abbreviates* $\Gamma, x{:}A \vdash_T x{:}B$.

Lemma 1. *In any extension of DHOL,* $\Gamma \vdash_T A \prec: B$ *iff* $\dfrac{\Gamma \vdash_T t{:}A}{\Gamma \vdash_T t{:}B}$ *is derivable.*

Proof. Left-to-right: We construct the function $(\lambda x{:}A.\ x){:}A \to B$ and derive the desired rule using the typing rule for function application.
Right-to-left: We start with $\Gamma, x{:}A \vdash_T x{:}A$ and apply the derivable rule.

This subtyping relation prevents *incidental* subtype instances, for which the rule from Lemma 1 is admissible but not derivable. For example, $A|_{\lambda x{:}A.\ \text{false}}$ is a subtype of all refinements of A, but not of all types. More generally, this definition precludes using induction on the terms of A to conclude $A \prec: B$. This restriction ensures that subtyping is preserved under, e.g., theory extensions, substitution, or language extensions. Importantly, subtyping preserves equality:

Lemma 2. *Consider some extension of DHOL with productions and rules. Assume (∗) that* $\Gamma \vdash_T x =_B x$ *implies* $\Gamma \vdash_T x : B$. *Let* $F := \forall x{:}A.\ \forall y{:}A.\ x =_A y \Rightarrow x =_B y$. *Then* $\Gamma \vdash_T A \prec: B$ *iff* $\Gamma \vdash_T F : \text{bool}$; *and if these hold, then also* $\Gamma \vdash_T F$.

(∗) is a very mild assumption and satisfied by all extensions given in this paper.

Proof.
Left-to-right: The assumption yields $\Gamma, x{:}A,\ y{:}A,\ \rhd\, x =_A y \vdash_T (\lambda x{:}A.\ x){:}A \to B$. We get $\Gamma, x{:}A,\ y{:}A,\ \rhd\, x =_A y \vdash_T (\lambda x{:}A.\ x)\ x =_B (\lambda x{:}A.\ x)\ y$ from congruence of function application and reflexivity and $x =_B y$ by β-reduction.
Right-to-left: Assume $x : A$. Instantiating F twice with x and applying modus ponens with $x =_A x$ yields $x =_B x$, from which we get $x : B$.

Lemma 3 (Preorder of Types). *In any extension of DHOL, subtyping is reflexive (in the sense that $\Gamma \vdash_T A \equiv B$ implies $\Gamma \vdash_T A \prec: B$) and transitive.*

Proof. Reflexivity: The assumption yields $\Gamma \vdash_T (\lambda x{:}A.\ x){:}A \to B$. Applying both to a term t of type A and β-reducing yields the rule from Lemma 1. Transitivity follows immediately from Lemma 1.

We also want to make subtyping an order. Anti-symmetry with respect to $\equiv$ is not derivable directly, i.e., we might have $\Gamma \vdash_T A \prec: B$ and $\Gamma \vdash_T B \prec: A$, in which case A and B would have the same terms, without being equal. Therefore, we *add* the anti-symmetry rule

$$\frac{\Gamma \vdash_T A \prec: B \qquad \Gamma \vdash_T B \prec: A}{\Gamma \vdash_T A \equiv B}\text{STantisym}$$

Notably, this is the only *change* made to DHOL so far—everything before has just been abbreviations. This change is conservative in the following sense:

Theorem 1 (Conservativity). *For DHOL as defined so far (without the extension we introduce below), we have $A \prec: B$ iff $A \equiv B$.*

Proof. We show by induction on derivations that each term has a unique type up to type equality and that all term equality axioms preserve typing.

Theorem 2 (Variance and Congruence for Function Types). *The usual rules for function types are derivable:*

$$\frac{\Gamma \vdash_T A' \prec: A \qquad \Gamma, x{:}A' \vdash_T B \prec: B'}{\Gamma \vdash_T \Pi x{:}A.\ B \prec: \Pi x{:}A'.\ B'} \qquad \frac{\Gamma \vdash_T A' \equiv A \qquad \Gamma, x{:}A' \vdash_T B \equiv B'}{\Gamma \vdash_T \Pi x{:}A.\ B \equiv \Pi x{:}A'.\ B'}$$

The second rule is primitive in DHOL but derivable in DHOL with subtyping.

Proof. The first rule follows from the definition of subtyping and η-expansion. The second rule is derived by (STantisym), establishing the hypotheses using the variance rule and reflexivity of subtyping.

4 Refinement Types

To add refinement types, we add only one production for types. We do not add productions for terms—refinement types only provide new typing properties for the existing terms. Then we add rules for, respectively, formation, introduction, elimination (two rules), and equality:

$$A ::= \quad A|_p \quad \text{type } A \text{ refined by predicate } p \text{ on } A$$

$$\frac{\Gamma \vdash_T p : A \to \mathsf{bool}}{\Gamma \vdash_T A|_p \ \mathsf{tp}} \qquad \frac{\Gamma \vdash_T t : A \quad \Gamma \vdash_T p \ t}{\Gamma \vdash_T t : A|_p}$$

$$\frac{\Gamma \vdash_T t : A|_p}{\Gamma \vdash_T t : A} \qquad \frac{\Gamma \vdash_T t : A|_p}{\Gamma \vdash_T p \ t} \qquad \frac{\Gamma \vdash_T s =_A t \quad \Gamma \vdash_T p \ s}{\Gamma \vdash_T s =_{A|_p} t}$$

Example 2 (Refining Lists by Length). We extend Example 1 by defining fixed-length lists as a refinement of lists. First, we axiomatize a predicate length on lists:

$$\text{length: list} \to \text{nat} \qquad \rhd \ \text{length nil} =_{\text{nat}} \text{zero}$$
$$\rhd \ \forall x{:}\mathsf{obj}. \ \forall l{:}\mathsf{list}. \ \text{length (cons } x \ l) =_{\text{nat}} \text{succ (length } l)$$

Then we define llist $n := \text{list}|_{\lambda l:\text{list. length } l =_{\text{nat}} n}$, and we can derive

$$\vdash \text{nil:llist zero} \qquad n{:}\mathsf{nat}\vdash \text{cons} : \Pi x{:}\mathsf{obj}. \ \Pi l{:}\text{llist } n. \ \text{llist (succ } n)$$

Theorem 3 (Congruence and Variance). *The following rules are derivable if the involved types are well-formed:*

$$\frac{\Gamma \vdash_T A \prec: A' \quad \Gamma, \ x{:}A, \ \rhd p \ x \vdash_T p' \ x}{\Gamma \vdash_T A|_p \ \prec: A'|_{p'}} \qquad \frac{\Gamma \vdash_T A \ \mathsf{tp}}{\Gamma \vdash_T A \equiv A|_{\lambda x:A. \ \text{true}}}$$

$$\frac{\Gamma \vdash_T A \equiv A' \quad \Gamma \vdash_T p =_{A \to \mathsf{bool}} p'}{\Gamma \vdash_T A|_p \equiv A'|_{p'}} \qquad \frac{\Gamma \vdash_T A|_p \ \mathsf{tp}}{\Gamma \vdash_T A|_p \ \prec: A}$$

Proof. To derive the first rule, we assume the hypotheses and $x{:}A|_p$. The elimination rules yield $x{:}A$ and $p \ x$, then the hypotheses yield $x{:}A'$ resp. $p' \ x$, finally the introduction rule yields $x{:}A'|_{p'}$.

To derive the second rule, we apply (STantisym) and use the introduction/elimination rules to show the two subtype relationships.

These then imply the other rules.

5   Quotient Types

To add quotient types we also extend the grammar with only one production for the type and rules for formation, introduction, elimination, and equality, where EqRel(r) abbreviates that r is an equivalence relation:

$$A ::= \quad A/r \quad \text{quotient of } A \text{ by equivalence relation } r$$

$$\frac{\Gamma \vdash_T A \text{ tp} \quad \Gamma \vdash_T r{:}A \to A \to \text{bool} \quad \Gamma \vdash_T \text{EqRel}(r)}{\Gamma \vdash_T A/r \text{ tp}} \qquad \frac{\Gamma \vdash_T t{:}A \quad \Gamma \vdash_T A/r \text{ tp}}{\Gamma \vdash_T t{:}A/r}$$

$$\frac{\Gamma \vdash_T s{:}A/r \quad \Gamma,\, x{:}A,\, \triangleright x =_{A/r} s \vdash_T t{:}B \quad \Gamma,\, x{:}A,\, x'{:}A,\, \triangleright x =_{A/r} s,\, \triangleright x' =_{A/r} s \vdash_T t =_B t[x/x']}{\Gamma \vdash_T t[x/s]{:}B[x/s]}$$

$$\frac{\Gamma \vdash_T s{:}A \quad \Gamma \vdash_T t{:}A \quad \Gamma \vdash_T r{:}A \to A \to \text{bool} \quad \Gamma \vdash_T \text{EqRel}(r)}{\Gamma \vdash_T (s =_{A/r} t) =_{\text{bool}} (r\ s\ t)}$$

Example 3 (Sets). We extend Example 1 by obtaining sets as a quotient of lists. First, we axiomatize a predicate for containing an element:

contains: list $\to$ obj $\to$ bool $\qquad \triangleright\ \forall x{:}\text{obj}.\ \neg(\text{contains nil } x)$
$\triangleright\ \forall x{:}\text{obj}.\ \forall y{:}\text{obj}.\ \forall l{:}\text{list}.\ (\text{contains } (\text{cons } y\ l)\ x) =_{\text{bool}} (x =_{\text{obj}} y \lor \text{contains } l\ x)$

Now we can define set := list$/\lambda l{:}\text{list}.\ \lambda m{:}\text{list}.\ \forall x{:}\text{obj}.\ \text{contains } l\ x =_{\text{bool}} \text{contains } m\ x$ as the type of lists containing the same elements. The equality at set immediately yields extensionality $\vdash \forall x, y{:}\text{set}.\ x =_{\text{set}} y \Leftrightarrow (\forall z{:}\text{obj}.\ \text{contains } x\ z =_{\text{bool}} \text{contains } y\ z)$.

Any l:list can be used as a representative of the respective equivalence class in set, and operations on sets can be defined via operations on lists, e.g., we can establish $\vdash$ conc : set $\to$ set $\to$ set. To derive this, we assume u:set and apply the elimination rule twice. First we apply it with $B = $ list $\to$ set and $t = $ conc u; we have to show conc $x =_{\text{list}\to\text{set}}$ conc x' under the assumption that x and x' are equal as sets. That yields a term conc u : list $\to$ set. We assume v:set and apply the elimination rule again with $B = $ set to obtain conc $u\ v$:set, and then conclude via λ-abstraction and η-reduction.

The elimination rule above looks overly complex. It can be understood best by comparing it to the following, simpler and more intuitive rule

$$\frac{\Gamma,\, x{:}A \vdash_T t{:}B \quad \Gamma,\, x{:}A,\, x'{:}A,\, \triangleright r\ x\ x' \vdash_T t =_B t[x/x']}{\Gamma,\, x{:}A/r \vdash_T t{:}B} (*)$$

This rule captures the well-known condition that a function t on A may be used as a function on A/r if t maps equivalent representatives x, x' equally. It follows from our elimination rule by putting $s = x$, but is subtly weaker:

Example 4. Continuing Example 3, assume a total order on obj and a function g:list$|_{\text{nonEmpty}} \to$ obj picking the maximum from a non-empty list. We should be able to apply g to some s:set that we know to be non-empty. But if we try to apply (∗) to obtain $g\ s$: obj, we get stuck trying to prove $g\ x =_{\text{obj}} g\ x'$ for any x, x' that are representatives of an *arbitrary* equivalence class of lists. We cannot use the condition that s is non-empty and thus only non-empty lists need to be considered. Thus, we cannot derive the well-formedness of $g\ x$.

Our elimination rule remedies that: here we need to show $g\ x =_{\text{obj}} g\ x'$ for any x, x' that are representatives of *the class of* s. Thus, we can use that x and x' are non-empty and that thus $g\ x$ is well-formed.

In dependent type theory, the two elimination rules are equivalent because we have a type $s = x$ and can use $\Pi s{:}A/r.\ s = x \to B$ as the return type. This is not possible in DHOL where $s = x$ is not a type but a Boolean.

Theorem 4 (Congruence and Variance). *The following rules are derivable if the involved types are well-formed and r, r' are equivalence relations:*

$$\frac{\Gamma \vdash_T A \prec: A' \quad \Gamma,\ x{:}A,\ y{:}A,\ \rhd r\ x\ y \vdash_T r'\ x\ y}{\Gamma \vdash_T \quad A/r \prec: A'/r'} \qquad \frac{\Gamma \vdash_T A\ \mathsf{tp}}{\Gamma \vdash_T A \equiv A/\lambda x{:}A.\ \lambda y{:}A.\ x =_A y}$$

$$\frac{\Gamma \vdash_T A/r\ \mathsf{tp}}{\Gamma \vdash_T A \prec: A/r} \qquad \frac{\Gamma \vdash_T A \equiv A' \quad \Gamma \vdash_T r =_{A \to A \to \mathsf{bool}} r'}{\Gamma \vdash_T A/r \equiv A'/r'}$$

Proof. For the first rule: Assume the hypotheses and $s{:}A/r$. Apply the elimination rule with $B = A'/r'$ and $t = x$. $x{:}A$, $y{:}A$, $\rhd x =_{A/r} s$, $\rhd x' =_{A/r} s \vdash_T x =_{A'/r'} x'$ by the equality rule (using $A \prec: A'$ and the second assumption). For the second rule, apply (STantisym) and use the introduction/elimination rules to show the two subtype relationships. The other rules follow from those two.

6   Normalizing Types

To build a type-checker, we derive normalization rules that reduce subtyping conditions to validity conditions that can then be discharged via an ATP. We prove rules for merging consecutive refinements and quotients and for the 4 possible combinations of a function type with a refinement or quotient:

Theorem 5 (Repeated Refinement/Quotient). *The following are derivable whenever the LHS is well-formed*

$$\vdash_T (A|_p)|_{p'} \equiv A|_{\lambda x{:}A.\ p\ x \wedge p'\ x} \tag{RR}$$

$$\vdash_T (A/r)/r' \equiv A/\lambda x{:}A.\ \lambda y{:}A.\ r'\ x\ y \tag{QQ}$$

$$\vdash_T (A/r)|_p \equiv (A|_p)/r \tag{RQ}$$

Proof. (RR): well-formedness of the LHS yields $p{:}A \to$ bool and $p'{:}A|_p \to$ bool, so p' x is well-formed as $\wedge$ is a *dependent* conjunction and $p\ x$ can be assumed while checking p' x. The well-formedness of the right-hand side (RHS) follows. Verifying the equality is straightforward by showing subtyping in both directions. (QQ): well-formedness of the LHS yields $r{:}A \to A \to$ bool and $r'{:}A/r \to A/r \to$ bool, so $A \prec: A/r$ implies r' x y (and thus the RHS) is well-formed. The relation on the RHS is an equivalence relation since r' is. To verify the type equality, we use Lemma 2 and show that both types induce the same equality. In particular, the type of r' already guarantees that it subsumes r.
(RQ): well-formedness of the LHS yields $r{:}A \to A \to$ bool and $p{:}A/r \to$ bool, implying $r{:}A|_p \to A|_p \to$ bool and $p{:}A \to$ bool. The well-formedness of the RHS follows. (Note the other direction does not hold in general.) To show the equality, we show both subtyping directions. For LHS$\prec$:RHS, we assume $x{:}A/r$ and $p\ x$ and apply the elimination rule for quotients using $t = x$ and $B = (A|_p)/r$. (Critically, this step would not go through if we had only used the weaker rule $*$ in Sect. 5.) For RHS$\prec$:LHS, we assume $x{:}(A|_p)/r$ and apply the elimination rule for quotients using $t = x$.

Theorem 6 (Refinement/Quotient in a Function Type). *The following are derivable if either side is well-formed:*

$$\vdash_T \Pi x{:}A.\ (B|_p) \equiv (\Pi x{:}A.\ B)|_{\lambda f{:}(\Pi x{:}A.\ B).\ \forall x{:}A.\ p\ (f\ x)} \qquad \text{(RCod)}$$

$$\vdash_T \Pi x{:}A/r.\ B \equiv (\Pi x{:}A.\ B)|_{\lambda f{:}\Pi x{:}A.\ B.\ \forall x,y{:}A.\ r\ x\ y \Rightarrow (f\ x) =_B (f\ y)} \qquad \text{(QDom)}$$

$$\vdash_T \Pi x{:}A.\ B/r :\succ (\Pi x{:}A.\ B)/\lambda f, g{:}\Pi x{:}A.\ B.\ \forall x{:}A.\ r\ (f\ x)\,(g\ x) \qquad \text{(QCod)}$$

The following is derivable if the RHS is well-formed:

$$\vdash_T \Pi x{:}A|_p.B :\succ (\Pi x{:}A.B)/\lambda f, g{:}\Pi x{:}A.B.\forall x{:}A.\ p\ x \Rightarrow (f\ x) =_B (g\ x)\ \text{(RDom)}$$

Proof. (RCod): Both subtyping directions are straightforward, as terms on either side are given by $\lambda x{:}A.\ t$ where t has type B and satisfies p.
(QDom): Both subtyping directions are straightforward, as both sides are subtypes of $\Pi x{:}A.\ B$ so their elements must preserve r.
(QCod): Assume a term f of RHS-type and show $x{:}A \vdash f\ x{:}B/r$ using the rules for quotients.
(RDom): Assume a term f of RHS-type and show $x{:}A|_p \vdash f\ x{:}B$ using the quotient elimination rule. The well-formedness of the LHS does not imply the well-formedness of the RHS since the well-formedness of B can rely on $p\ x$.

Maybe surprisingly, two of the subtyping laws in Theorem 6 are not equalities. The law for the refined domain *must not* be an equality:

Example 5 (Refined Domain (RDom)). The assumption $p\ x$ makes more terms well-typed, thus there may be functions $\Pi x{:}A|_p.\ B$ that are not a restriction of a function $\Pi x{:}A.\ B$. Consider the theory a:bool $\to$ tp, c:a true. Then a false is empty and so are $\Pi x{:}$bool. a x and its quotients. But with $p = \lambda x{:}$bool. x, we have $\vdash \lambda x{:}$bool$|_p$. c : $\Pi x{:}$bool$|_p$. a x.

The law for the quotiented codomain *may or may not* be an equality. This is related to the axiom of choice. Consider the two statements

$$\vdash_T \exists\, repr{:}B/r \to B.\ repr =_{B/r \to B/r} \lambda x{:}B/r.\ x$$

$$f{:}\Pi x{:}A.\ B/r \vdash_T \exists\, g{:}\Pi x{:}A.\ B.\ f =_{\Pi x{:}A.\ B/r}\ g$$

(Note that the first one is well-typed because $B \prec: B/r$.) Both have a claim to be called the axiom of choice: The first one expresses that every equivalence relation has a system of representatives. The second generalizes this to a family of equivalence relations. The latter implies the former (put $A := B/r$ and $f := \lambda x{:}B/r.\ x$). In the simply-typed case the former also implies the latter (pick $repr \circ f$ for g); but in the dependently-typed case, B and r may depend on x and the implication might not hold.

Both statements construct a new term from an existing one (*repr* behaves like the identity, and g like f) that has a different type but behaves the same up to quotienting. If the direction $\prec:$ were to hold in the law for the refined codomain, it would not only imply the existence of g from f but also allow using f as a representative of the equivalence class of possible values for g. That is in keeping with our goal of avoiding changes of representation. Therefore:

Definition 2 (Quotiented Codomain). *We adopt the rule below (which is an equality with Theorem 6) as an axiom whenever either side is well-formed:*

$$\vdash_T \Pi x{:}A.\ B/r \prec: (\Pi x{:}A.\ B)/\lambda f, g{:}\Pi x{:}A.\ B.\ \forall\, x{:}A.\ r\ (f\ x)(g\ x) \qquad (**)$$

Aggregating the above laws, we obtain a normalization algorithm for types:

Theorem 7 (Normalizing Types). *Every type is equal to a type of the form* $(A|_p)/r$ *where* $A, B ::= \mathsf{bool} \mid \mathsf{a}\ t^* \mid \Pi x{:}A|_p.\ B$. *In particular, if a type does not use refined domains, it is equal to a quotient of a refinement of a DHOL type.*

Proof. Using Theorem 6 with the axiom from Definition 2, all refinements and quotients can be pushed out of all function types except for a single refinement of the domain; if there is no such refinement, we can use $p := \lambda x{:}A.\ \mathsf{true}$. And using Theorem 5, those can be collected into a single quotient+refinement.

Together with the equality and variance rules from Theorems 2, 3, 4, this induces a **subtype-checking algorithm** that reduces subtyping to validity without ever expanding Definition 1. The latter is important because expanding Definition 1 would recurse into a computationally expensive problem. This algorithm is obviously sound as it only chains derived rules. We are confident, but have not proved yet, that it is also complete in the sense that subtyping can always be derived by using only our derived rules (i.e., without Definition 1) and a sound and complete theorem prover (which we obtain in Sect. 7).

It may be surprising and certainly complicates subtype-checking that we need to allow for refined domains in the normal forms. This limitation echoes an observation first made in [14] about combining dependent types and refinements. Effectively, the culprits are partial dependent functions that cannot be extended to total functions because the return type is well-defined and non-empty only for the refined domain. For future work, it would be interesting to use a higher-order logic with partial functions as a translation target, like the one of [10]. But we have not considered that option due to the lack of ATP support for such logics.

7   Soundness and Completeness

We extend the translation from Fig. 3 with cases for our two new productions:

$$\overline{A|_p} := \overline{A} \qquad (A|_p)^* \ s \ t := A^* \ s \ t \wedge \overline{p} \ s \wedge \overline{p} \ t$$
$$\overline{A/r} := \overline{A} \qquad (A/r)^* \ s \ t := \overline{r} \ s \ t \wedge A^* \ s \ s \wedge A^* \ t \ t$$

These definitions are not surprising as PERs in HOL are known to be closed under refinements and quotients.

Example 6 (PERs for a Quotiented Codomain). We calculate the PERs for both sides of the law for quotiented codomains in Theorem 6:

$$(\Pi x{:}A. \ B/r)^* \ f \ g$$
$$= \forall x, y{:}\overline{A}. \ A^* \ x \ y \Rightarrow (\overline{r} \ (f \ x) \ (g \ y) \wedge B^* \ (f \ x) \ (f \ x) \wedge B^* \ (g \ y) \ (g \ y))$$

Both this and $((\Pi x{:}A. \ B)/\lambda f, g{:}\Pi x{:}A. \ B. \ \forall x{:}A. \ r \ (f \ x) \ (g \ x))^* \ f \ g$ simplify to $\forall x{:}\overline{A}. \ A^* \ x \ x \Rightarrow \overline{r} \ (f \ x) \ (g \ x) \wedge B^* \ (f \ x) \ (f \ x) \wedge B^* \ (g \ x) \ (g \ x)$. This justifies adopting axiom (**). The simplification uses the substitution lemma from the extended preprint [5], the well-definedness of r, and the transitivity of $\overline{r}$.

Example 7 (PERs for a Refined Domain). We calculate the PERs for both sides of the law for refined domains in Theorem 6:

$$(\Pi x{:}A|_p. \ B)^* \ f \ g = \forall x, y{:}\overline{A}. \ A^* \ x \ y \wedge \overline{p} \ x \wedge \overline{p} \ y \Rightarrow B^* \ (f \ x) \ (g \ y)$$

$$((\Pi x{:}A. \ B)/\lambda f, g{:}\Pi x{:}A. \ B. \ \forall x{:}A. \ p \ x \Rightarrow (f \ x) =_B (g \ x))^* \ f \ g =$$
$$\forall x{:}\overline{A}. \ (A^* \ x \ x \Rightarrow \overline{p} \ x \Rightarrow B^* \ (f \ x) \ (g \ x)) \wedge$$
$$\left(\forall x, y{:}\overline{A}. \ A^* \ x \ y \Rightarrow B^* \ (f \ x) \ (f \ y)\right) \wedge$$
$$\left(\forall x, y{:}\overline{A}. \ A^* \ x \ y \Rightarrow B^* \ (g \ x) \ (g \ y)\right)$$

These are indeed not equivalent in line with our observation from Example 5.

Like in [22], this translation yields a sound (defined as in the previous paper) and complete theorem prover:

Theorem 8 (Completeness). *We have the invariants from Fig. 4.*

Proof. The subtyping claim is a slightly strengthened version of the claim obtained by expanding the definition of $\prec:$. The proof, given in the extended preprint [5], adapts the proof from [22] with additional cases for new productions and rules.

if in DHOL	then in HOL		
$\vdash T$ Thy	$\vdash \overline{T}$ Thy		
$\vdash_T \Gamma$ Ctx	$\vdash_{\overline{T}} \overline{\Gamma}$ Ctx		
$\Gamma \vdash_T A$ tp	$\overline{\Gamma} \vdash_{\overline{T}} \overline{A}$ tp	and	$\overline{\Gamma} \vdash_{\overline{T}} A^* : \overline{A} \to \overline{A} \to$ bool and A^* is a PER
$\Gamma \vdash_T A \equiv B$	$\overline{\Gamma} \vdash_{\overline{T}} \overline{A} \equiv \overline{B}$	and	$\overline{\Gamma}, x,y{:}\overline{A} \vdash_{\overline{T}} A^* \, x \, y =_{\text{bool}} B^* \, x \, y$
$\Gamma \vdash_T A \prec\colon B$	$\overline{\Gamma} \vdash_{\overline{T}} \overline{A} \equiv \overline{B}$	and	$\overline{\Gamma}, x,y{:}\overline{B} \vdash_{\overline{T}} A^* \, x \, y \Rightarrow B^* \, x \, y$
$\Gamma \vdash_T t{:}A$	$\overline{\Gamma} \vdash_{\overline{T}} \overline{t}{:}\overline{A}$	and	$\overline{\Gamma} \vdash_{\overline{T}} A^* \, \overline{t} \, \overline{t}$
$\Gamma \vdash_T F$	$\overline{\Gamma} \vdash_{\overline{T}} \overline{F}$		

Fig. 4. Invariants of the Translation

As in [22], the converse of Theorem 8 is much harder to state and prove. First we need a technical assumption: We call a type symbol a *inhabited* if at least one of its instances is provably non-empty.

Theorem 9 (Soundness). *In a well-formed DHOL-theory* $\vdash T$ Thy *in which every type symbol is inhabited:*

$$\text{If } \Gamma \vdash_T^{DHOL} F : \text{bool and } \overline{\Gamma} \vdash_{\overline{T}}^{HOL} \overline{F}, \text{ then } \Gamma \vdash_T^{DHOL} F$$

Proof. The key idea is to transform a HOL-proof of $\overline{F}$ into one that is in the image of the translation, at which point we can read off a DHOL-proof of F. The full proof is given in the extended preprint [5]. We expect the inhabitation requirement to be redundant, but have not been able to complete the proof without it yet. In any case, it is harmless because it is satisfied by all practical examples.

It is now straightforward to extend the DHOL implementation we gave in [22]: First run a bidirectional type-checker for DHOL, using the subtyping-checker sketched in Sect. 6, to establish well-typedness of theory and conjecture. Then translate conjecture and generated proof obligations and apply a HOL ATP.

8   Application to Typed Set Theory

DHOL with subtyping enables a novel formalization of typed set-theory:

$$\text{set: tp}, \quad \in \, : \text{set} \to \text{set} \to \text{bool}, \quad elem \, s := \text{set}|_{\lambda x:\text{set}. \ x \in s}$$

The key idea is that *elem s* is the DHOL *type* of set-theoretical elements of the *set s*. Leveraging that refinements and quotients do not require change of representation, we obtain a powerful combination of elegant high-level typed formalization and efficient low-level reasoning. All the routine constructions of untyped set theory can be lifted to their typed counterparts. For example, for products, we use $\times$:set $\to$ set $\to$ set and *pair*:set $\to$ set $\to$ set and the property

▷ $\forall x, y, s, t$:set. $(x \in s) \wedge (y \in t) \Rightarrow pair\ x\ y \in s \times t$, from which we can show that $pair : elem\ s \to elem\ t \to elem\ (s \times t)$.

We can also use DHOL-functions set $\to$ set as set-theoretical functions between sets s and t without a change in representation as the type $Functions\ s\ t := (\text{set} \to \text{set})|_p / r$ where $p\ f = \forall x$:set. $x \in s \Rightarrow (f\ x) \in t$ and $r\ f\ g = \forall x$:set. $x \in s \Rightarrow (f\ x) =_{\text{set}} (g\ x)$. This allows us to represent set-theoretical function application and composition $\circ$ directly as DHOL application/composition.

Consequently, theorem proving in typed set theory becomes very strong because a large share of the proving workload can be outsourced into typing-obligations. For example, the property that the composition of functions $f : Functions\ s\ t$ and $g : Functions\ t\ u$ has type $Functions\ s\ u$ becomes

▷ $\forall s, t, u$:set. $\forall f$:$Functions\ s\ t.\ \forall g$:$Functions\ t\ u.\ \forall x$:set. $x \in s \Rightarrow ((g \circ f)\ x) \in u$

which yields in HOL the conjecture below that current HOL ATPs solve easily.

▷ $\forall s$:set. $set\_rel\ s\ s \Rightarrow \forall t$:set. $set\_rel\ t\ t \Rightarrow \forall u$:set. $set\_rel\ u\ u \Rightarrow$
$\forall f$:set $\to$ set. $\forall x$:set. $x \in s \Rightarrow set\_rel(f\ x)(f\ x) \wedge (\forall x$:set. $x \in s \Rightarrow (f\ x) \in t) \Rightarrow$
$\forall g$:set $\to$ set. $\forall x$:set. $x \in t \Rightarrow set\_rel(g\ x)(g\ x) \wedge (\forall x$:set. $x \in t \Rightarrow (g\ x) \in u) \Rightarrow$
$\forall x$:set. $set\_rel\ u \Rightarrow x \in s \Rightarrow ((g\ (f\ x)) \in u)$

Below is the HOL translation of the conjecture that function composition is associative. It is similarly easily proved by current ATPs:

▷ $\forall s$:set. $set\_rel\ s\ s \Rightarrow \forall t$:set. $set\_rel\ t\ t \Rightarrow \forall u$:set. $set\_rel\ u\ u \Rightarrow \forall v$:set. $set\_rel\ v\ v \Rightarrow$
$\forall f$:set $\to$ set. $\forall x$:set. $x \in s \Rightarrow set\_rel(f\ x)(f\ x) \wedge (\forall x$:set. $x \in s \Rightarrow (f\ x) \in t) \Rightarrow$
$\forall g$:set $\to$ set. $\forall x$:set. $x \in t \Rightarrow set\_rel(g\ x)(g\ x) \wedge (\forall x$:set. $x \in t \Rightarrow (g\ x) \in u) \Rightarrow$
$\forall h$:set $\to$ set. $\forall x$:set. $x \in u \Rightarrow set\_rel(h\ x)(h\ x) \wedge (\forall x$:set. $x \in t \Rightarrow (h\ x) \in v) \Rightarrow$
$\forall x$:set. $set\_rel\ x\ x \Rightarrow x \in s \Rightarrow (set\_rel\ (h\ (g\ (f\ x)))\ (h\ (g\ (f\ x))))$

The corresponding TPTP files are available at https://gl.mathhub.info/MMT/LATIN2/-/tree/master/source/casestudies/2025-FroCos.

9   Conclusion and Future Work

DHOL combines higher-order logic with dependent types, obtaining an intuitive and expressive language, albeit with undecidable typing. We double down on this design by elegantly extending DHOL with two practically important type constructors that thrive in that setting: refinement and quotient types. Like dependent function types, these two require terms occurring in types. Both are near-impossible to add as an afterthought to a type theory with decidable typing.

We translate the resulting logic to HOL, obtaining a practical automated theorem proving workflow for DHOL with refinement and quotient types. Our main result is the proof of soundness and completeness of this translation.

We used an extensional subtyping approach, where $A \prec: B$ holds iff all A-terms also have type B. This allows combining typed representations and efficient reasoning. We established all the expected variance and normalization laws except for function types with refined domains. Future work must investigate how to improve on this to make normalizing types and thus subtype-checking simpler.

We also want to carry our results for DHOL over to existing refinement/quotient type systems for programming languages like Quotient Haskell, where DHOL-like axioms are used as lightweight specifications.

References

1. Allen, S.: A non-type-theoretic semantics for type-theoretic language. Ph.D. thesis, Cornell University (1987)
2. Andrews, P.: An Introduction to Mathematical Logic and Type Theory: To Truth Through Proof. Academic Press (1986)
3. Hewer, B., Hutton, G.: Quotient Haskell: lightweight quotient types for all. Proc. ACM Program. Lang. **8**(POPL) (2024). https://doi.org/10.1145/3632869
4. Bancerek, G., et al.: Mizar: state-of-the-art and beyond. In: Kerber, M., Carette, J., Kaliszyk, C., Rabe, F., Sorge, V. (eds.) CICM 2015. LNCS (LNAI), vol. 9150, pp. 261–279. Springer, Cham (2015). https://doi.org/10.1007/978-3-319-20615-8_17
5. Rothgang, C., Rabe, F.: Subtyping in DHOL – Extended preprint (2025). https://arxiv.org/abs/2507.02855
6. Church, A.: A formulation of the simple theory of types. J. Symb. Log. **5**(1), 56–68 (1940)
7. Constable, R., et al.: Implementing Mathematics with the Nuprl Development System. Prentice-Hall (1986)
8. Coq Development Team: The Coq Proof Assistant: Reference Manual. Technical report, INRIA (2015)
9. de Moura, L., Kong, S., Avigad, J., van Doorn, F., von Raumer, J.: The lean theorem prover (system description). In: Felty, A.P., Middeldorp, A. (eds.) CADE 2015. LNCS (LNAI), vol. 9195, pp. 378–388. Springer, Cham (2015). https://doi.org/10.1007/978-3-319-21401-6_26
10. Farmer, W.: A simple type theory with partial functions and subtypes. Ann. Pure Appl. Logic **64**(3), 211–240 (1993)
11. Gordon, M.: HOL: a proof generating system for higher-order logic. In: Birtwistle, G., Subrahmanyam, P. (eds.) VLSI Specification, Verification and Synthesis, pp. 73–128. Kluwer-Academic Publishers (1988)
12. Homeier, P.V.: A design structure for higher order quotients. In: Hurd, J., Melham, T. (eds.) TPHOLs 2005. LNCS, vol. 3603, pp. 130–146. Springer, Heidelberg (2005). https://doi.org/10.1007/11541868_9
13. Huffman, B., Kunčar, O.: Lifting and transfer: a modular design for quotients in Isabelle/HOL. In: Gonthier, G., Norrish, M. (eds.) CPP 2013. LNCS, vol. 8307, pp. 131–146. Springer, Cham (2013). https://doi.org/10.1007/978-3-319-03545-1_9
14. Hurd, J.: Predicate subtyping with predicate sets. In: Boulton, R., Jackson, P. (eds.) Theorem Proving in Higher Order Logics, pp. 265–280 (2001)
15. Kunčar, O., Popescu, A.: Comprehending Isabelle/HOL's consistency. In: Yang, H. (ed.) ESOP 2017. LNCS, vol. 10201, pp. 724–749. Springer, Heidelberg (2017). https://doi.org/10.1007/978-3-662-54434-1_27

16. Martin-Löf, P.: An intuitionistic theory of types: predicative part. In: Proceedings of the 1973 Logic Colloquium, pp. 73–118. North-Holland (1974)
17. Niederhauser, J., Brown, C., Kaliszyk, C.: Tableaux for automated reasoning in dependently-typed higher-order logic. In: Benzmüller, C., Heule, M., Schmidt, R. (eds.) Automated Reasoning, pp. 86–104. Springer, Cham (2024). https://doi.org/10.1007/978-3-031-63498-7_6
18. Owre, S., Rushby, J.M., Shankar, N.: PVS: a prototype verification system. In: Kapur, D. (ed.) CADE 1992. LNCS, vol. 607, pp. 748–752. Springer, Heidelberg (1992). https://doi.org/10.1007/3-540-55602-8_217
19. Popescu, A., Traytel, D.: Admissible types-to-pers relativization in higher-order logic. Proc. ACM Program. Lang. **7**(POPL) (2023). https://doi.org/10.1145/3571235
20. Ranalter, D., Brown, C., Kaliszyk, C.: Experiments with choice in dependently-typed higher-order logic. In: Bjørner, N., Heule, M., Voronkov, A. (eds.) Logic for Programming, Artificial Intelligence and Reasoning, pp. 311–320 (2024)
21. Ranalter, D., Rabe, F., Kaliszyk, C.: Polymorphic theorem proving for DHOL
22. Rothgang, C., Rabe, F., Benzmüller, C.: Theorem proving in dependently typed higher-order logic. In: Pientka, B., Tinelli, C. (eds.) Automated Deduction, pp. 438–455. Springer, Cham (2023). https://doi.org/10.1007/978-3-031-38499-8_25

Satisfiability Modulo Theories

Exploiting Partial-Assignment Enumeration in Optimization Modulo Theories

Gabriele Masina[✉][iD] and Roberto Sebastiani[✉][iD]

DISI, University of Trento, Trento, Italy
{gabriele.masina,roberto.sebastiani}@unitn.it

Abstract. Optimization Modulo Theories (OMT) extends Satisfiability Modulo Theories (SMT) with the task of optimizing some objective function(s). In OMT solvers, a CDCL-based SMT solver enumerates theory-satisfiable total truth assignments, and a theory-specific procedure finds an optimum model for each of them; the current optimum is then used to tighten the search space for the next assignments, until no better solution is found.

In this paper, we analyze the role of truth-assignment enumeration in OMT. First, we spotlight that the enumeration of *total* truth assignments is suboptimal, since they may over-restrict the search space for the optimization procedure, whereas using *partial* truth assignments instead can improve the effectiveness of the optimization. Second, we propose some assignment-reduction techniques for exploiting *partial-assignment enumeration* within the OMT context. We implemented these techniques in the OPTIMATHSAT solver, and we conducted an experimental evaluation on OMT benchmarks. The results confirm the improvement in both the efficiency of optimal solving and the quality of the obtained solutions for anytime solving.

Keywords: Optimization Modulo Theories · Enumeration · Partial Assignments

1 Introduction

Satisfiability Modulo Theories (SMT) is the problem of deciding the satisfiability of a logical formula w.r.t. some background theory, such as linear and nonlinear arithmetic, bit-vectors, arrays, or uninterpreted functions [2]. Many SMT-encodable problems also require the capability of finding models that are optimal w.r.t. some objective functions. These problems are grouped under the term Optimization Modulo Theories (OMT) [6,25,31]. OMT has been successfully applied to a wide range of problems, such as verification of timed and hybrid systems [14,31], numeric [16] and temporal planning [26,27], optimal scheduling [7], constrained goal modelling [24], hybrid machine learning [37], GAS optimization for smart contracts [1], and optimum encodings for quantum annealing [3,10], establishing OMT solvers as powerful tools for solving complex constraint optimization problems in various domains.

OMT Solving. A general OMT-solving strategy [25,31,32] consists in performing a sequence of incremental SMT calls, progressively tightening the range of values for the

© The Author(s) 2026
R. Thiemann and C. Weidenbach (Eds.): FroCoS 2025, LNAI 15979, pp. 117–134, 2026.
https://doi.org/10.1007/978-3-032-04167-8_7

objective function. Specifically, an SMT solver is used to enumerate $\mathcal{T}$-satisfiable truth assignments that propositionally satisfy the problem formula φ. For each such truth assignment, a $\mathcal{T}$-optimizer finds a $\mathcal{T}$-model of optimum cost within it. A constraint is then added to the formula to tighten the upper bound for the cost of the optimum model, and the search continues until the formula is found unsatisfiable. Besides optimal solving, an important feature of OMT solvers is the ability to provide the user with a good-enough solution within a given time budget. This capability, known as *anytime* OMT solving, is especially valuable in industrial applications where finding the optimum solution may be computationally impractical, and it is rather more important to obtain high-quality solutions quickly.

OMT techniques have been developed for $\mathcal{LRA}$ [6,32], $\mathcal{LIRA}$ [6,33], $\mathcal{NRA}$ [4], $\mathcal{NIA}$ [4], $\mathcal{BV}$ [23,39], and $\mathcal{FP}$ [39]. Also, OMT has been extended to deal with multiple objectives including lexicographic OMT [6,33], boxed OMT [6,17,33], min-max OMT [34], and Pareto OMT [6]. Recently, a Generalized OMT calculus has been proposed, extending the definition to objectives over partially ordered sets [41].

Partial Assignments Enumeration in SMT. The problem of truth assignment enumeration has been studied in recent years, mainly in the context of SAT and SMT enumeration (AllSAT and AllSMT). Typically, enumeration algorithms [12,13,15,35,36] rely their efficiency on the enumeration of partial assignments to reduce both the number of enumerated assignments and the computational time by up to an exponential factor. Several techniques have been proposed to find short satisfying partial assignments starting from a total assignment, trading off efficiency for effectiveness (e.g., [22,29,38]). Also, the impact of CNF-ization on the effectiveness of partial assignment reduction has been recently studied in [20,21].

Contributions. In this paper, we study the applicability of enumeration-based techniques to OMT solving, and, in particular, the usage of partial truth assignment reduction to improve the effectiveness and efficiency of OMT solving. First, we notice that OMT solvers typically invoke the $\mathcal{T}$-optimizer on total truth assignments, and we spotlight how this can be suboptimal in many cases. Second, we propose some ways to exploit partial truth assignments in OMT solving, tailoring existing techniques to the OMT context. We discuss the general idea for an arbitrary theory, and describe an implementation for the specific case of linear arithmetic over $\mathcal{LRA}$ and $\mathcal{LIRA}$, possibly combined with other theories. We implemented these strategies in the OMT solver OPTIMATHSAT [34], and we show through an empirical evaluation over OMT($\mathcal{LRA}$), OMT($\mathcal{LIRA}$), and OMT($\mathcal{LRA} \cup \mathcal{AR}$) benchmarks that they improve both the efficiency of optimal solving and the quality of obtained solutions for anytime solving.

Related Work. The idea of using partial assignments in OMT($\mathcal{LIRA}$) has been previously considered in [5,18]. In [5], the authors mention that in lazy OMT-solving, the truth assignments should preferably be prime implicants. This approach, however, is theory-blind; our reduction techniques, instead, specifically target theory-literals involved in optimization, which proves crucial for the solver efficiency. A similar idea was proposed in [18], where the truth assignments are reduced to prime implicants before invoking the $\mathcal{T}$-solver and $\mathcal{T}$-minimizer. Though our work is similar in flavour to theirs, there are some key differences: (a) their enumeration algorithm only adds clauses blocking the minimized truth assignment, whereas modern OMT solvers add cost bounds (cost $<$ ub) to prune the search space, which has been shown to be much more effective; (b) we also propose a cost-guided technique, which we show to perform much better in practice.

Organization. The rest of the paper is organized as follows. In Sect. 2, we provide the necessary background on SMT and OMT solving. In Sect. 3, we analyze the role of total and partial truth assignments in OMT solving. In Sect. 4, we propose two strategies to exploit partial truth assignments in OMT solving. In Sect. 5, we present an experimental evaluation of the proposed strategies over OMT($\mathcal{LRA}$), OMT($\mathcal{LIRA}$), and OMT($\mathcal{LRA} \cup \mathcal{AR}$) benchmarks. Finally, in Sect. 6, we conclude the paper and discuss future work.

2 Background

Notation and Terminology. We assume the standard setting with quantifier-free first-order formulas, and the standard notions of theory, satisfiability, logical consequence. We assume the reader is familiar with these notions and with the lazy CDCL-based SMT-solving approach, and refer to [2] for a comprehensive introduction to SMT.

In this paper, we denote SMT formulas by φ, theories by $\mathcal{T}$, variables by x, y, atoms by α, truth assignments by μ, η, and models by $\mathcal{M}$; all symbols possibly with subscripts or superscripts. We denote by $Atoms(\varphi)$ the set of atoms occurring in a formula φ.

2.1 Satisfiability Modulo Theories

Given a first-order theory $\mathcal{T}$, a $\mathcal{T}$-atom is any atomic formula built over the signature of $\mathcal{T}$. A $\mathcal{T}$-literal is a $\mathcal{T}$-atom or its negation. A $\mathcal{T}$-formula is either a $\mathcal{T}$-literal or a combination of formulas by means of standard Boolean operators. From now on, we assume every formula is in Conjunctive Normal Form (CNF), i.e., it is a conjunction ($\wedge$) of clauses, where each clause is a disjunction ($\vee$) of literals. (If it is not, then it can be easily converted into CNF by applying the standard transformations [28,40]).

Satisfiability Modulo Theories (SMT) is the problem of deciding the satisfiability of a first-order formula w.r.t some first-order theory $\mathcal{T}$, or combination of first-order theories $\mathcal{T} \cup \mathcal{T}'$. A formula is $\mathcal{T}$-satisfiable if it is satisfiable in a model of $\mathcal{T}$ (a $\mathcal{T}$-model). Popular theories include linear and nonlinear arithmetic over the reals or integers ($\mathcal{LRA}$, $\mathcal{NRA}$, $\mathcal{LIRA}$, and $\mathcal{NIRA}$), bit-vectors ($\mathcal{BV}$), and floating-point ($\mathcal{FP}$).

Lazy SMT-Solving. Given a formula φ with $Atoms(\varphi) = \{\alpha_1, \ldots, \alpha_n\}$, a truth assignment $\mu : Atoms(\varphi) \rightarrow \{\top, \bot\}$ maps atoms in φ to truth values. A partial truth assignment is a partial mapping, and a total truth assignment is a total mapping. We represent a truth assignment μ also as a conjunction of literals $\bigwedge_{\mu(\alpha_i)=\top} \alpha_i \wedge \bigwedge_{\mu(\alpha_i)=\bot} \neg \alpha_i$. We say that μ *propositionally satisfies* φ iff μ satisfies all clauses in φ.

The CDCL($\mathcal{T}$) algorithm [19] is based on the so-called lazy approach to SMT (see e.g., [2,30]), which exploits the fact that a $\mathcal{T}$-formula φ is $\mathcal{T}$-satisfiable iff there exists a truth assignment μ that propositionally satisfies φ and μ is $\mathcal{T}$-satisfiable. It combines a CDCL-based SAT-solver with a $\mathcal{T}$-specialized decision procedure called $\mathcal{T}$-solver to decide the consistency of a set of $\mathcal{T}$-literals. Whenever the SAT-solver finds a truth assignment μ propositionally satisfying φ, it invokes the $\mathcal{T}$-solver to check the $\mathcal{T}$-satisfiability of μ. If μ is $\mathcal{T}$-satisfiable, then the $\mathcal{T}$-solver returns a model $\mathcal{M}$, that is also a model of φ. Otherwise, the $\mathcal{T}$-solver returns a subset of μ that causes the $\mathcal{T}$-unsatisfiability, which is learned by the SAT-solver and used in subsequent iterations to prune the search space.

To maximize efficiency, most $\mathcal{T}$-solvers can be called incrementally via a stack-based interface, keeping the status of the search between calls. E.g., an efficient, incremental $\mathcal{LRA}$-solver, can be built on a variant of the Simplex algorithm designed to be integrated within a lazy SMT framework [11]. The combination of theories can be handled efficiently by delayed theory combination [8].

Another important feature of CDCL-based SMT solvers is that they provide a stack-based incremental interface, allowing to push and pop clauses and incrementally check the satisfiability of the formula conjoined with the pushed clauses, maintaining most of the learned information between calls.

2.2 Optimization Modulo Theories

Let $\mathcal{T}$ be a theory admitting some total order relation "$\leq$" over its domain, let φ be a $\mathcal{T}$-formula, and let cost be a $\mathcal{T}$-term which we call *objective function*. *Optimization Modulo Theories* (OMT($\mathcal{T}$)) is the problem of finding a model for φ that makes the value of cost minimum according to the order given by $\leq$ (maximization is dual) [4,31]. To simplify the presentation, we focus on minimization, but the same concepts apply to maximization as well. Notice that, in general, φ can be built on a combination of $\mathcal{T}$ with other theories (OMT($\mathcal{T} \cup \mathcal{T}'$)), and the same concepts apply to such cases [31,32].

Example 1. Consider the $\mathcal{LRA}$-formula on the rational variables x, y:

$$\varphi \stackrel{\text{def}}{=} ((2x - 3y \leq 6) \vee (x \leq 4)) \wedge \\ ((y \leq 2) \vee (y \leq -3x + 9) \vee (x < -2)). \tag{1}$$

φ is $\mathcal{LRA}$-satisfiable, e.g., the $\mathcal{LRA}$-model $\mathcal{M} \stackrel{\text{def}}{=} \{x \mapsto 3, y \mapsto 0\}$ satisfies φ.

Consider the OMT($\mathcal{LRA}$) problem $\langle \varphi, \text{cost} \rangle$ where φ is the $\mathcal{LRA}$-formula in (1), and cost $\stackrel{\text{def}}{=} -2x$. Then the model $\mathcal{M} \stackrel{\text{def}}{=} \{x \mapsto 3, y \mapsto 0\}$ has cost $= -6$. A better model of φ is, e.g., $\mathcal{M}' \stackrel{\text{def}}{=} \{x \mapsto 6, y \mapsto 2\}$, that has cost $= -12$. This model is also the model of φ with minimum cost.

Lazy OMT Solving. A general optimization strategy implemented by state-of-the-art OMT solvers, and typically used for OMT($\mathcal{LRA}$) and OMT($\mathcal{LIRA}$), is the so-called *linear-search* strategy [25,31,32]. It consists in solving a sequence of SMT problems where the space of feasible solutions is progressively tightened by learning unit clauses in the form (cost $<$ ub), ub being the currently-known upper bound for cost. At each iteration, the solver can either find a model $\mathcal{M}$ whose value of cost is smaller than ub, or detect the unsatisfiability of the current formula. In the first case, the solver invokes a $\mathcal{T}$-specific procedure, called $\mathcal{T}$-*minimizer*, to find an optimum model $\mathcal{M}'$ within the truth assignment induced by $\mathcal{M}$. Then, ub is set to $\mathcal{M}'$(cost), and the search continues. In the second case, the formula has no models with cost lower than ub, and the search terminates as the last model found is optimum.

Alternatively, the solver could also follow a *binary-search* strategy [31]. In this case, a lower and upper bound lb and ub are kept s.t. the optimum model lies in the interval (lb, ub]. At each iteration, an intermediate value pivot $\in$ (lb, ub] is chosen, and the solver checks if there exists a model with cost lower than pivot. If so, pivot becomes the new upper bound, otherwise, it becomes the new lower bound. The search terminates when lb and ub are equal, and the last model found is optimum. (In continuous domains, e.g., OMT($\mathcal{LRA}$), to guarantee termination, it is necessary to interleave binary-search steps with a linear-search step [31]). In this paper, we focus on the linear-search strategy, but the analysis applies to the binary-search strategy as well.

If φ is built on a combination of theories, then the $\mathcal{T}$-minimizer is invoked on $\mu_{\mathcal{T}} \cup \mu_{ed}$—i.e., the subset of μ containing only the atoms in $\mathcal{T}$ and the interface (dis-)equalities [31,32] The implementation of $\mathcal{T}$-minimizers for $\mathcal{LRA}$ and $\mathcal{LIRA}$ is briefly described in the next paragraph.

T-minimizers. A $\mathcal{LRA}$-minimizer [31,32] can be implemented as a simple extension of the Simplex-based $\mathcal{LRA}$-solver [11]. For $\mathcal{LIRA}$, a minimizer can be built on top of a branch-and-bound $\mathcal{LIRA}$-solver [5,6,33], by replacing the $\mathcal{LRA}$-solver with a $\mathcal{LRA}$-solver&minimizer to solve each relaxed subproblem. To find an optimum model within the truth assignment, once a $\mathcal{LIRA}$-model $\mathcal{M}$ is found, a constraint (cost < $\mathcal{M}$(cost)) is pushed onto the $\mathcal{LIRA}$-solver, and the search is iteratively refined until no better model exists. An alternative strategy, implemented, e.g., in OPTIMATHSAT, is the so-called *truncated* optimization [33], where the $\mathcal{LIRA}$-minimizer stops after finding the first model $\mathcal{M}$. Although this model may be sub-optimal for the current truth assignment—allowing the same assignment to be found again by the CDCL($\mathcal{T}$) procedure—this approach is typically much faster and remains effective in practice.

Remark 1. Importantly, the lazy OMT solving approach allows for an *anytime* behavior, i.e., we can interrupt the search at any time and return the best model found so far.

2.3 SAT and SMT Enumeration

SAT enumeration (AllSAT) is the problem of finding all the truth assignments that propositionally satisfy a propositional formula. SMT enumeration (AllSMT) is the problem of finding all $\mathcal{T}$-satisfiable truth assignments that propositionally satisfy a $\mathcal{T}$-formula. Since a partial assignment can be extended to 2^k total truth assignments, k being the number of unassigned atoms, finding short partial truth assignments is a key point in reducing both the number of enumerated truth assignments and the computational time by up to an exponential factor.

Many enumeration algorithms find total truth assignments, and then extract partial truth assignments from them by some reduction procedure. A basic reduction procedure is illustrated in Algorithm 1. It consists in iteratively dropping literals one-by-one from the truth assignment, checking if it still satisfies the formula. The resulting partial

---

Algorithm 1. REDUCE-ASSIGNMENT(φ, η)

Input: CNF formula φ, $\mathcal{T}$-satisfiable total truth assignment η satisfying φ

Output: Reduced (minimal) partial truth assignment $\mu \subseteq \eta$ satisfying φ

1: $\mu \leftarrow \eta$
2: **for** $\ell \in \mu$ **do**
3:   **if** $\mu \setminus \{\ell\}$ satisfies all clauses in φ **then**
4:     $\mu \leftarrow \mu \setminus \{\ell\}$
5: **return** μ

---

assignment is minimal, i.e., it cannot be further reduced without violating the satisfaction of the formula. Notice that the order in which literals are dropped can have a significant impact on the effectiveness of the reduction procedure.

3 An Analysis of Enumeration in OMT

In the following, to simplify the notation and the presentation, we refer to one single theory $\mathcal{T}$, but the results can be straightforwardly extended to combinations of theories.

As described in Sect. 2.2, a basic OMT solving schema involves the interaction of a combinatorial and a theory-specific optimization components. In the combinatorial component, an SMT solver enumerates $\mathcal{T}$-satisfiable truth assignments that propositionally satisfy the problem formula φ conjoined with increasingly tighter bounds on the cost of the optimum solution. In the theory-specific component, a $\mathcal{T}$-minimizer finds a $\mathcal{T}$-model of minimum cost within the constraints imposed by the given truth assignment. This model is then used to tighten the upper bound for the cost of the optimum model and continue the search, until the formula is found unsatisfiable.

Since the enumeration is based on the CDCL($\mathcal{T}$) schema [19], these truth assignments are typically *total*, i.e., they assign a truth value to each atom of the formula. However, we point out that total truth assignments can often over-constrain the search space for the optimum model, whereas relying on *partial* truth assignments can be much more effective. Intuitively, *by removing from the current satisfying truth assignment $\mathcal{T}$-constraints that are not strictly necessary for the propositional satisfaction of the formula, we enlarge the area within which the optimum model is searched, thus increasing the chances of finding a better optimum model.* This means that the solver can add a tighter upper bound to the cost of the global optimum, potentially reducing the number of search iterations needed to find it, and consequently the overall solving time. Moreover, this improvement can be crucial for anytime OMT solving, as it allows the solver to converge faster to better solutions within the given time limit.

We illustrate this idea in the following example.

Example 2. Consider the OMT($\mathcal{LRA}$) problem $\langle \varphi, \text{cost} \rangle$ where φ is the formula in (1) in Example 1, and cost $\overset{\text{def}}{=} -2x$. Consider the following scenario, which is graphically represented in Fig. 1. Consider the $\mathcal{LRA}$-satisfiable total truth assignment that propositionally satisfies φ:

$$\mu \overset{\text{def}}{=} \{(2x - 3y \leq 6), (y \leq 2), \neg(x < -2), (y \leq -3x + 9), (x \leq 4)\}. \tag{2}$$

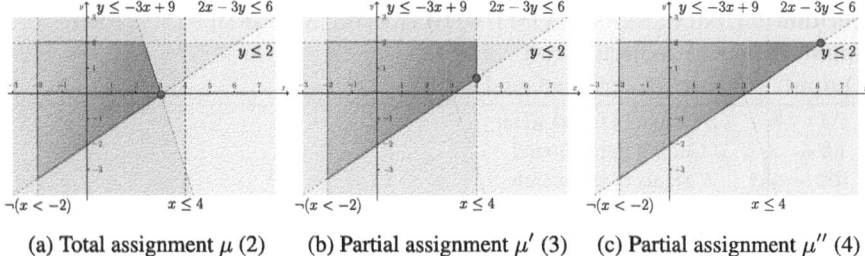

(a) Total assignment μ (2)   (b) Partial assignment μ' (3)   (c) Partial assignment μ'' (4)

Fig. 1. Graphical representation of Example 2. For each step, the half-planes representing the constraints in the truth assignment are delimited by dashed lines and colored in grey. The intersection of these constraints is colored in blue, with a gradient that follows the value of cost (the lower the value of cost, the more intense the color), and the red dot represents the optimum model found within this region. (Color figure online)

The optimum model of μ is $\{x \mapsto 3, y \mapsto 0\}$ with cost $= -6$ (Fig. 1a). We notice that some literals in μ are not strictly necessary for propositionally satisfying φ. In fact, we only need one true literal in each clause to propositionally satisfying the formula. Not every drop is equally effective, though. For instance, if we drop $(x \leq 4)$, $(y \leq 2)$, or $\neg(x < 2)$, then we get a truth assignment with the same optimum as μ, since these literals don't "oppose" to the optimization of cost in μ. Dropping at least one of the other two literals, instead, leads to a truth assignment with a better optimum model. For instance, if we drop $(y \leq -3x + 9)$, we get:

$$\mu' \stackrel{\text{def}}{=} \mu \setminus \{(y \leq -3x + 9)\} = \{(2x - 3y \leq 6), (y \leq 2), \neg(x < -2), (x \leq 4)\}. \quad (3)$$

The optimum model of μ' is $\{x \mapsto 4, y \mapsto 2/3\}$ with cost $= -8$ (Fig. 1b). At this point, two constraints, $(x \leq 4)$ and $(2x - 3y \leq 6)$, oppose to the optimization of cost, and either of them can be safely dropped. Assume that we drop $(x \leq 4)$, then we get:

$$\mu'' \stackrel{\text{def}}{=} \mu' \setminus \{(x \leq 4)\} = \{(2x - 3y \leq 6), (y \leq 2), \neg(x < -2)\} \quad (4)$$

with optimum model $\{x \mapsto 6, y \mapsto 2\}$ and cost $= -12$ (Fig. 1c). Now, the only literals opposing to the optimization of cost are $(2x - 3y \leq 6)$ and $(y \leq 2)$, but none of them can be dropped. Hence, no further improvement can be obtained.

In general, partial truth assignments have an optimum model that is necessarily better or equal to that of the total truth assignments extending them. Since multiple partial truth assignments can be obtained from a total one, the choice of which constraints to drop can be crucial to improve the quality of the optimum model found.

4   Exploiting Partial Truth Assignments in OMT

The general schema of our approach is presented in Algorithm 2. This algorithm is a variant of the basic OMT linear-search schema [31,32] described in Sect. 2.2. The main

---

Algorithm 2. LINEAR-SEARCH OMT WITH PARTIAL ASSIGNMENTS(φ, cost)

Input: Formula φ, objective cost

Output: SAT/UNSAT, optimum model $\mathcal{M}$

1: $\mathcal{M} \leftarrow \emptyset$ // Best model found so far
2: ub $\leftarrow \infty$ // Current upper bound
3: res $\leftarrow$ SAT   // Status of the search
4: **while** res = SAT **do**
5:     $\langle$res$, \eta\rangle \leftarrow$ SMT.IncrementalSolve($\varphi \wedge$ (cost $<$ ub))
6:     **if** res = SAT **then**
7:        $\mu \leftarrow$ OMT-REDUCE-ASSIGNMENT(φ, η, cost)
8:        $\mathcal{M} \leftarrow$ T-Solver.Minimize(μ, cost)
9:        ub $\leftarrow \mathcal{M}$(cost)
10: **if** $\mathcal{M} = \emptyset$ **then**
11:    **return** $\langle$UNSAT$, \emptyset\rangle$
12: **else**
13:    **return** $\langle$SAT$, \mathcal{M}\rangle$

---

difference is the call to the OMT-REDUCE-ASSIGNMENT procedure (line 7), which is responsible for reducing the truth assignment to be fed to the $\mathcal{T}$-minimizer, provided that the resulting partial truth assignment still propositionally satisfies the formula. Depending on the implementation of this procedure, the assignment-reduction strategy can be more or less effective in improving the search for the global optimum.

In Sect. 4.1 and Sect. 4.2, we describe two possible implementations of this procedure.

4.1 Basic Assignment Reduction

The first approach is to reduce the truth assignment using Algorithm 1 in Sect. 2.3, i.e., iterating over all the literals in the current truth assignment η, and dropping them one by one, if possible. A straightforward improvement is to only try to drop $\mathcal{T}$-literals, since they are the ones that, if dropped, can potentially enlarge the area within which the optimum $\mathcal{T}$-model is searched. In the case of theory combination, we drop only literals from the theory $\mathcal{T}$ of the "$\leq$" symbol w.r.t. which we minimize. Possibly, heuristics can be used to choose an appropriate dropping order; in our implementation, we used the default strategy that follows the appearance order of the atoms in the formula. This procedure is simple and general, and comes with a limited overhead, as each truth assignment is scanned only once to find the literals to drop, and the $\mathcal{T}$-minimizer is called only once for each candidate assignment.

This approach, however, might not be very effective in practice, as it "blindly" removes literals from the truth assignment without taking into account the properties of the OMT search strategy. In particular, the search space may be enlarged in a direction that does not improve the objective, bringing no benefit to the search. Accurately choosing which literals to drop is crucial because the removal of a literal may prevent the removal of other literals that could potentially be more relevant for the optimization.

Algorithm 3. OMT-REDUCE-ASSIGNMENT-GUIDED $(\varphi, \eta, \text{cost})$
    Input: Formula φ, $\mathcal{T}$-satisfiable total truth assignment η satisfying φ, objective cost
    Output: Reduced truth assignment $\mu \subseteq \eta$ satisfying φ

1:   $\mu \leftarrow \eta$
2:   $\mathcal{M} \leftarrow$ T-Solver.MinimizeApprox(μ, cost)
3:   $\ell \leftarrow$ T-Solver.ProposeLiteralToDrop$()$
4:   **while** $\ell \neq \perp$ **do**
5:     **if** $\mu \setminus \{\ell\}$ satisfies all clauses in φ **then**
6:       $\mu \leftarrow \mu \setminus \{\ell\}$
7:       $\mathcal{M} \leftarrow$ T-Solver.MinimizeApprox(μ, cost)
8:       $\ell \leftarrow$ T-Solver.ProposeLiteralToDrop$()$
9:   **return** μ

4.2 Guided Assignment Reduction

We propose an ad-hoc assignment-reduction technique for OMT solving, which is outlined in Algorithm 3. Suppose that, after the $\mathcal{T}$-minimizer has found a minimum model within the current truth assignment μ (line 2), it returns also one (or more) literal(s) that limit the current minimum (line 3). These literals are part of some (possibly minimal) $\mu' \subseteq \mu$ such that $\mu' \cup \{\text{cost} < \mathcal{M}(\text{cost})\}$ is $\mathcal{T}$-unsatisfiable. Intuitively, the removal of any literal $\ell \in \mu'$ is very likely to lead to a better optimum model, provided that $\mu \setminus \{\ell\}$ still propositionally satisfies φ (line 5).

We can then iteratively drop these literals and re-run the $\mathcal{T}$-minimizer, until no more literals can be dropped (lines 4–8). Notice that instead of T-Solver.Minimize, here we call T-Solver.MinimizeApprox, suggesting that also a relaxed optimization algorithm could be used. In the next paragraph, we describe how this can be exploited for $\mathcal{LIRA}$.

Notice that, in Algorithm 3, we only drop one literal before every optimization call; nevertheless, in principle, more literals could be dropped. Experimentally, we found that dropping more than one literal was not beneficial. The reason is that, generally, when a literal is removed, most of the other literals in μ' do not limit the current minimum anymore. Hence, their removal not only does not lead to a better optimum model, but also can prevent the removal of other more-relevant literals.

On Proposing Literals to Drop. For an arbitrary theory $\mathcal{T}$, a generic implementation for T-Solver.ProposeLiteralToDrop (Algorithm 3, lines 3, 8) could be as follows. Once a minimum model $\mathcal{M}$ for μ is found, invoke the $\mathcal{T}$-solver on $\mu \wedge (\text{cost} < \mathcal{M}(\text{cost}))$ and return a (possibly-minimal) conflict set. For some theories, ad-hoc (possibly heuristic) procedures can be employed. We describe two such techniques for $\mathcal{LRA}$ and $\mathcal{LIRA}$.

As we recalled in Sect. 2.2, a $\mathcal{LRA}$-minimizer can be implemented as a variant of the Simplex method [11,31], by which an optimum model is always found on a vertex of the polytope defined by the conjunction of $\mathcal{LRA}$-constraints on which it is invoked. Thus, in this case, the candidate constraints to be dropped are those that form such a vertex. This information can be easily obtained from the Simplex tableau [11].

For $\mathcal{LIRA}$, directly using a $\mathcal{LIRA}$-minimizer and then identifying the limiting constraints presents some challenges: (a) a single call to the branch-and-bound-based

$\mathcal{LIRA}$-minimizer is worst-case exponential, hence calling it multiple times (as in Algorithm 3) is not feasible; (b) extracting the limiting constraints from a $\mathcal{LIRA}$-minimizer is not straightforward. We thus propose proceeding as follows. First, for the procedure T-Solver.MinimizeApprox a $\mathcal{LRA}$-minimizer is invoked on the relaxation of μ. Then, the procedure T-Solver.ProposeLiteralToDrop can be implemented as for $\mathcal{LRA}$. The intuition here is that reasoning on the relaxation of μ is much easier and cheaper—especially if incremental calls are used—and still allows for enlarging the search area in a favourable direction for the $\mathcal{LIRA}$-minimizer. We remark that, after the assignment reduction, in Algorithm 2 (line 8), the complete $\mathcal{LIRA}$-minimizer is called.

As a last aspect, we suggest that, if the $\mathcal{T}$-minimizer is able to find an optimum model μ, then we can use these limiting literals $l_1, \ldots, l_n$ also to learn a theory lemma $(\neg(\mathsf{cost} < \mathsf{ub}) \vee \neg l_1 \vee \ldots \vee \neg l_n)$ that blocks truth assignments that we know are not better than the current upper bound ub—thus preventing useless calls to the $\mathcal{T}$-solver. The idea is that, in order to find a model with cost $< \mathsf{ub}$, we need to assign at least one of these literals to false. This is the case of $\mathcal{LRA}$, but not of $\mathcal{LIRA}$ if the truncated minimization method is used (see Sect. 2.2).

5   Experimental Evaluation

We implemented the above algorithms in the OMT solver OPTIMATHSAT [34], which is built on top of the MATHSAT5 SMT solver [9]. We evaluated the proposed strategies on a set of OMT($\mathcal{LRA}$), OMT($\mathcal{LIRA}$), and OMT($\mathcal{LRA} \cup \mathcal{AR}$) benchmarks coming from different sources, evaluating both solving time for optimum solving, and the quality of the solutions found within the given timeout for anytime solving. All the experiments were run on an Intel Xeon Gold 6238R @ 2.20GHz 28 Core machine with 128 GB of RAM, running Ubuntu Linux 22.04. The timeout was set at 1200 s. The tool, benchmarks and results are available at https://optimathsat.disi.unitn.it/resources/optimathsat-partial-assignments.tar.gz.

5.1   Benchmarks

We evaluated the proposed strategies on two classes of OMT($\mathcal{LRA}$) benchmarks: OMT-encoded optimal temporal planning [26, 27] and strip-packing problems [31, 32]. We also modified the strip-packing benchmarks to use OMT($\mathcal{LIRA}$) and OMT($\mathcal{LRA} \cup \mathcal{AR}$) encodings, to evaluate the effectiveness of our strategies in these theories.

Optimal Temporal Planning. In [26, 27], the authors proposed a way to encode optimal temporal planning problems into a sequence of OMT($\mathcal{LRA}$) problems. Each problem encodes a bounded version of the problem up to a fixed horizon, with additional abstract actions representing an over-approximation of the plans beyond the bound, minimizing the makespan, i.e., the total time taken to reach the goal. If the optimal plan is found without using the abstract actions, then the plan is optimum for the original problem. Otherwise, the horizon is increased, and the process is repeated. We generated problems using the industrial problems Majsp (80 instances), MajspSimplified (80 instances), and Painter (30 instances) [27], with increasing horizon $h \in \{5, 10, 15, 20, 25, 30, 35, 40\}$, for a total of 1520 instances.

Strip-Packing. The strip-packing problem (SP) requires arranging N rectangles with widths W_i and heights H_i into a strip of fixed height H and unlimited length. The goal is to minimize the length of the used part of the strip, ensuring all rectangles are placed without overlap or rotation. An OMT($\mathcal{LRA}$) encoding for SP was proposed in [32]. Following [32], we sampled H_i uniformly in $(0, 1]$, W_i in $(1, 2]$, and set $H = \sqrt{N}/2$.

We also generated OMT($\mathcal{LIRA}$) SP problems, by randomly choosing with equal probability whether encoding the coordinates of each rectangle with integer or rational variables. Finally, we generated OMT($\mathcal{LRA} \cup \mathcal{AR}$) encodings for SP, by simply replacing the variables x_i in the OMT($\mathcal{LRA}$) encoding with a $\mathcal{LRA} \cup \mathcal{AR}$ term $read(x, i + offset)$, where x is an array mapping from rationals to rationals, i is a constant indicating the index of the rectangle, and *offset* is a fresh rational variable.

For each of these encodings, we generated 25 random SP problems for each value of $N \in \{25, 50, 75, 100\}$, for a total of 100 instances per encoding.

5.2   Results

Figures 2, 3, 4 and 5 show the results on temporal planning and SP benchmarks for the different theories, respectively. For each benchmark set, we report a set of scatter plots.

On the rows, we have different metrics, namely the solving time in seconds (time(s)), the upper bound (u.b.)—i.e., the optimum value when the solver terminated within the time limit, or the value of the best solution found within the timeout otherwise—and the number of iterations (# iter) taken to reach the upper bound (see Algorithm 2).

On the columns, we compare the results obtained with the different truth-assignment-reduction strategies: in the left and center columns, we respectively compare the basic and the guided reductions with the plain algorithm without reductions. In the right column, we compare the two reduction strategies.

OMT($\mathcal{LRA}$) Benchmarks. The results are summarized in Figs. 2 and 3.

Optimal Temporal Planning (Fig. 2). In these benchmarks, with no truth-assignment reduction, OPTIMATHSAT reported 246 timeouts out of 1520 problems, 211 with the basic reduction, and 212 with the guided reduction.

From the plots (first row, left and center columns), we can see that applying either reduction almost uniformly improves the solving time with few exceptions, making optimal solving up to twice as fast as with no reduction.

Moreover, we observe that reducing truth assignments is very effective also for anytime solving (second row, left and center columns). Notice that when the solver terminated within the timeout with both strategies, then the corresponding points lie on the bisector, whereas when at least one strategy times out, the points are generally below the bisector. Indeed, this shows that, for anytime solving, both the basic and the guided reductions allow finding a much better upper bound than with no reduction.

Finally, we can see that both strategies are particularly effective in reducing the number of iterations needed to either find the optimum or to reach the best upper bound within the timeout (third row, left and center). Reducing the number of iterations is not

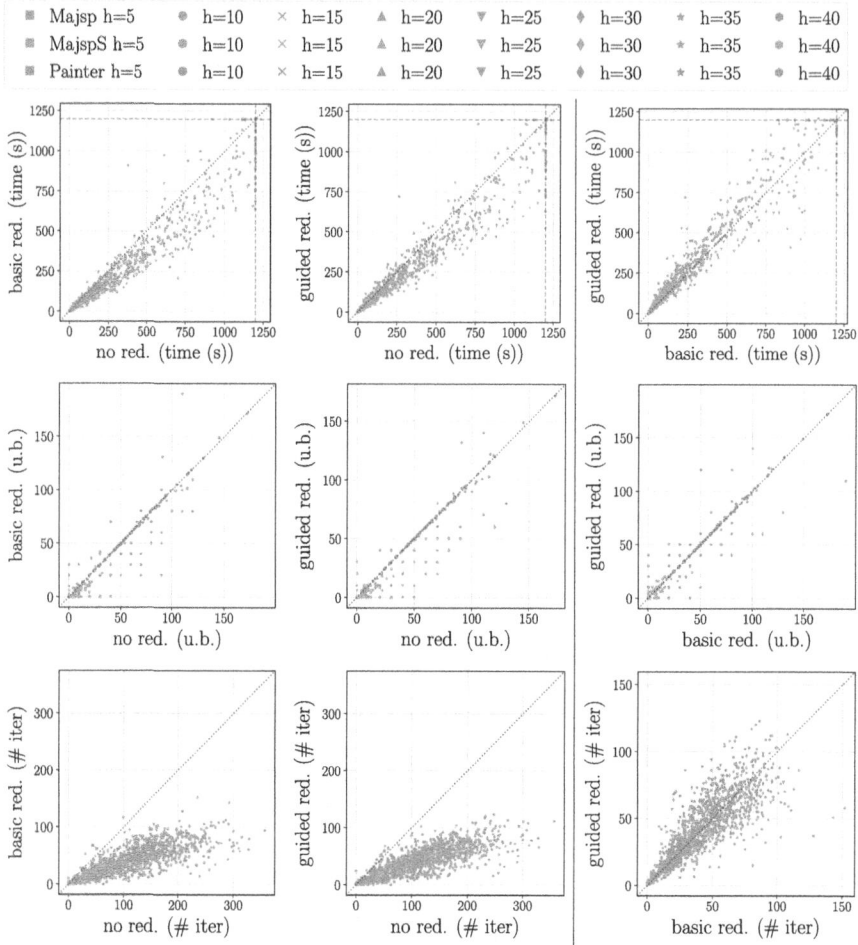

Fig. 2. Results on OMT($\mathcal{LRA}$)-encoded optimal temporal planning problems.

an advantage in itself, but it is a good indicator of the effectiveness of truth-assignment reduction strategies in OMT.

Overall, in these benchmarks there is no clear winner between the two reduction strategies (right column), but it is evident that applying either form of truth-assignment reduction can be beneficial in OMT, both for optimal and anytime solving.

Strip-Packing (Fig. 3). Since no instance in this set of benchmarks terminated within the timeout, for these benchmarks we omit the time plots. We can see that here the basic reduction strategy is not really effective, since the value of the upper bound is not improved compared to the no-reduction strategy (first row, left column). Also, the number of iterations only slightly decreases (second row, left column), suggesting that here blindly removing atoms from the truth assignment does not help much in finding

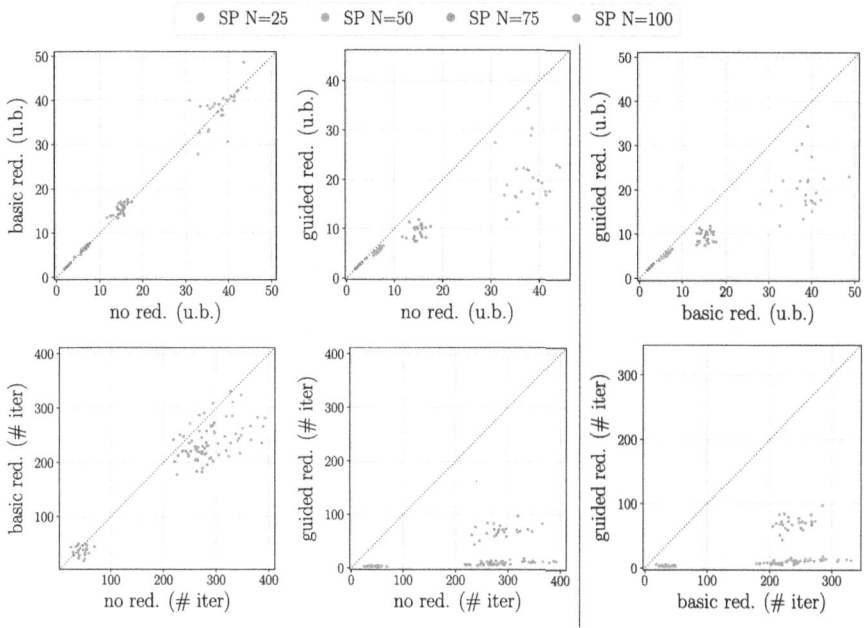

Fig. 3. Results on OMT($\mathcal{LRA}$)-encoded strip-packing problems.

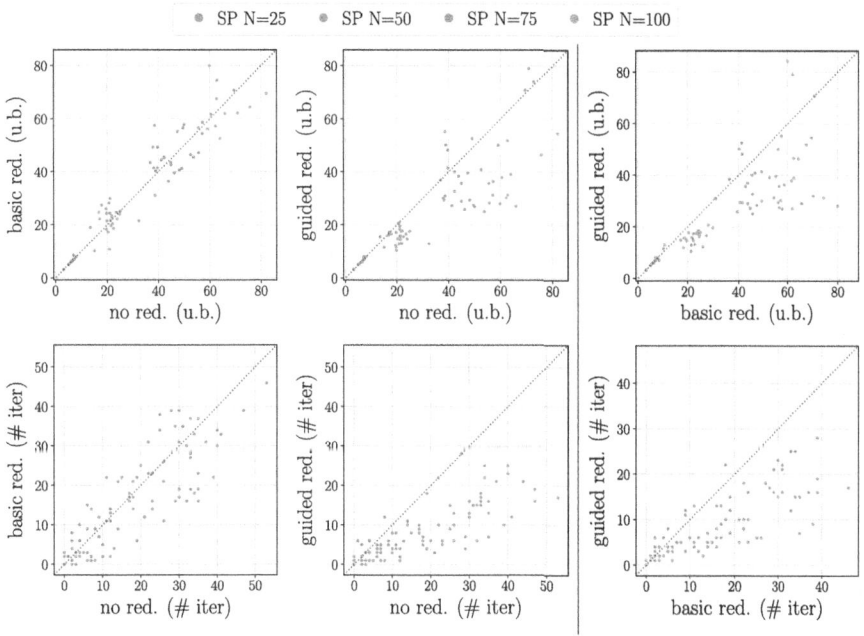

Fig. 4. Results on OMT($\mathcal{LIRA}$)-encoded strip-packing problems

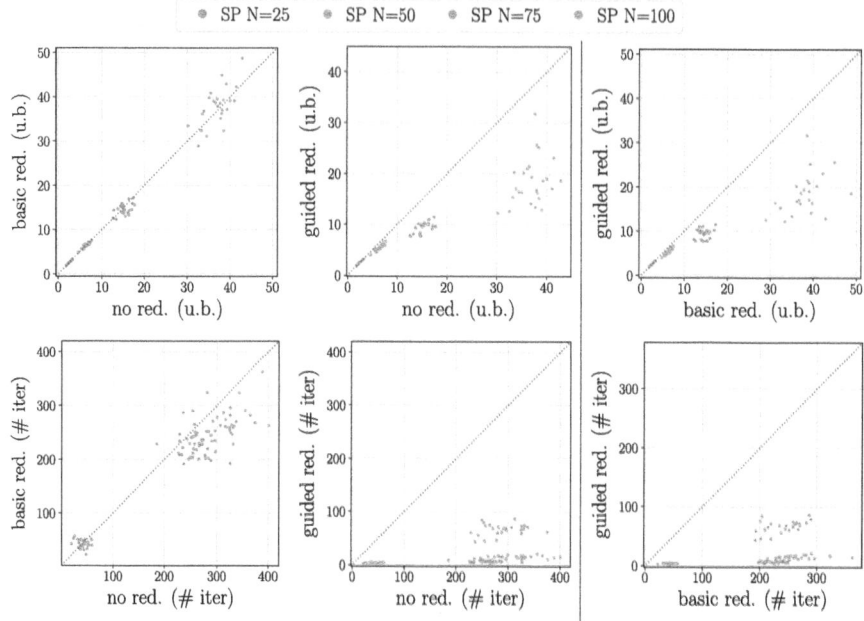

Fig. 5. Results on OMT($\mathcal{LRA} \cup \mathcal{AR}$)-encoded strip-packing problems.

better solutions. On the other hand, the guided reduction strategy is much more effective, since it allows finding a much better upper bound within the timeout (first row, center and right columns), and the number of iterations is drastically reduced (second row, center and right columns).

OMT($\mathcal{LIRA}$) Benchmarks. The results are summarized in Fig. 4.

Strip-Packing (Fig. 4). The plots show that also for $\mathcal{LIRA}$, the trend is similar to the one for $\mathcal{LRA}$. In fact, the basic reduction strategy is not very effective for improving the upper bound (first row, left column), and the number of iterations is only slightly reduced (second row, left column). On the other hand, the guided reduction allows finding a much better upper bound within the timeout (first row, center and right columns). Notice that, since these problems are much harder than the OMT($\mathcal{LRA}$) ones, the number of iterations completed within the timeout is much smaller, so that the upper bounds found are also bigger.

OMT($\mathcal{LRA} \cup \mathcal{AR}$) Benchmarks. The results are summarized in Fig. 5.

Strip-Packing (Fig. 5). Similarly, here we can see that the technique works also for combination of theories, such as $\mathcal{LRA} \cup \mathcal{AR}$. The results are similar to the ones for $\mathcal{LRA}$, and the advantage of the guided reduction is even more evident.

Discussion. The results show that applying either form of truth-assignment reduction can be beneficial in OMT, both for optimal and anytime solving, and that accurately selecting which atoms to remove from the truth assignment can make a significant difference in finding better solutions in fewer iterations.

We observe, however, that a much smaller number of iterations, i.e. of truth assignments enumerated, not always correlates linearly with the solving time. This can be due to several reasons.

First, we remark that global efficiency of OMT depends on several factors, including the enumeration order of truth assignments, and different literal selections may alter this order. Also, the removal of some literals from the assignments can prevent the removal of others in subsequent iterations. The effects of these factors are quite unpredictable.

Second, we notice that in these problems, the number of truth assignments enumerated is typically contained to a few hundred. In fact, in OMT the bounds on the objective function already allow performing a very effective pruning of the search space.

Moreover, this pruning is typically done by theory reasoning, and most of it has to be done anyway, regardless of the number of truth assignments enumerated. Making it in a single iteration or in many iterations may not reflect as much on the solving time, because of the efficient incrementality of SMT solvers, which can reduce a lot the cost of consecutive iterations.

6   Conclusions and Future Work

In this paper, we have investigated the role of truth assignment enumeration in OMT solving, and proposed some ways for exploiting partial truth assignments for improving the efficiency and effectiveness of the search. In particular, we have proposed a truth assignment reduction strategy that takes advantage of the properties of the optimization problem to accurately choose the atoms to remove from the truth assignment.

We have implemented the proposed strategies in the OPTIMATHSAT solver, and evaluated them on a set of OMT($\mathcal{LRA}$), OMT($\mathcal{LIRA}$), and OMT($\mathcal{LRA} \cup \mathcal{AR}$) benchmarks. Our experimental results show that the proposed strategies can significantly improve the performance of the solver, uniformly reducing the overall solving time for optimal solving, and finding much better solutions for anytime solving for all the analyzed theories.

Other truth assignment reduction strategies, such as entailment-based methods [12], have shown significant benefits for SAT enumeration. Their extension to OMT problems could be a promising direction for future work.

Acknowledgements. RS was partially supported by the project "AI@TN" funded by the Autonomous Province of Trento. RS was partially supported by the MUR PNRR project FAIR - Future AI Research (PE00000013) funded by the NextGenerationEU. RS was partially funded under the NRRP, Mission 4 Component 2 Investment 1.4, by the European Union—NextGenerationEU (proj. nr. CN 00000013). RS was supported in part by the TANGO project funded by the EU Horizon Europe research and innovation program under GA No 101120763, funded by the European Union. Views and opinions expressed are however those of the author(s) only and do not necessarily reflect those of the European Union, the European Health and Digital Executive Agency (HaDEA) or The European Research Council. Neither the European Union nor the granting authority can be held responsible for them.

References

1. Albert, E., Correas, J., Gordillo, P., Román-Díez, G., Rubio, A.: GASOL: gas analysis and optimization for Ethereum smart contracts. In: TACAS 2020. LNCS, vol. 12079, pp. 118–125. Springer, Cham (2020). https://doi.org/10.1007/978-3-030-45237-7_7

2. Barrett, C., Sebastiani, R., Seshia, S.A., Tinelli, C.: Satisfiability modulo theories. In: Handbook of Satisfiability, FAIA, vol. 336, pp. 1267–1329, 2 edn. IOS Press (2021). https://doi.org/10.3233/FAIA201017

3. Bian, Z., Chudak, F., Macready, W., Roy, A., Sebastiani, R., Varotti, S.: Solving SAT (and MaxSAT) with a quantum annealer: foundations, encodings, and preliminary results. Inf. Comput. **275**, 104609 (2020). https://doi.org/10.1016/j.ic.2020.104609

4. Bigarella, F., et al.: Optimization modulo non-linear arithmetic via incremental linearization. In: Konev, B., Reger, G. (eds.) FroCoS 2021. LNCS (LNAI), vol. 12941, pp. 213–231. Springer, Cham (2021). https://doi.org/10.1007/978-3-030-86205-3_12

5. Bjørner, N., Phan, A.D.: νZ - maximal satisfaction with Z3. In: Proceedings of the International Symposium on Symbolic Computation in Software Science, pp. 1–9 (2014). https://doi.org/10.29007/jmxj

6. Bjørner, N., Phan, A.-D., Fleckenstein, L.: νZ - an optimizing SMT solver. In: Baier, C., Tinelli, C. (eds.) TACAS 2015. LNCS, vol. 9035, pp. 194–199. Springer, Heidelberg (2015). https://doi.org/10.1007/978-3-662-46681-0_14

7. Bofill, M., Coll, J., Suy, J., Villaret, M.: An efficient SMT approach to solve MRCPSP/max instances with tight constraints on resources. In: Beck, J.C. (ed.) CP 2017. LNCS, vol. 10416, pp. 71–79. Springer, Cham (2017). https://doi.org/10.1007/978-3-319-66158-2_5

8. Bozzano, M., et al.: Efficient Theory Combination via Boolean Search. Inf. Comput. **204**(10), 1493–1525 (2006). https://doi.org/10.1016/j.ic.2005.05.011

9. Cimatti, A., Griggio, A., Schaafsma, B.J., Sebastiani, R.: The MathSAT5 SMT solver. In: Piterman, N., Smolka, S.A. (eds.) TACAS 2013. LNCS, vol. 7795, pp. 93–107. Springer, Heidelberg (2013). https://doi.org/10.1007/978-3-642-36742-7_7

10. Ding, J., Spallitta, G., Sebastiani, R.: Effective prime factorization via quantum annealing by modular locally-structured embedding. Sci. Rep. **14**(1), 3518 (2024). https://doi.org/10.1038/s41598-024-53708-7

11. Dutertre, B., de Moura, L.: A fast linear-arithmetic solver for DPLL(T). In: Ball, T., Jones, R.B. (eds.) CAV 2006. LNCS, vol. 4144, pp. 81–94. Springer, Heidelberg (2006). https://doi.org/10.1007/11817963_11

12. Fried, D., Nadel, A., Sebastiani, R., Shalmon, Y.: Entailing generalization boosts enumeration. In: SAT 2024. LIPIcs, vol. 305, pp. 13:1–13:14. LZI (2024). https://doi.org/10.4230/LIPIcs.SAT.2024.13

13. Fried, D., Nadel, A., Shalmon, Y.: AllSAT for combinational circuits. In: SAT 2023. LIPIcs, vol. 271, pp. 9:1–9:18. LZI (2023). https://doi.org/10.4230/LIPIcs.SAT.2023.9

14. Henry, J., Asavoae, M., Monniaux, D., Maïza, C.: How to compute worst-case execution time by optimization modulo theory and a clever encoding of program semantics. In: LCTES 2014, pp. 43–52. ACM (2014). https://doi.org/10.1145/2597809.2597817

15. Lahiri, S.K., Nieuwenhuis, R., Oliveras, A.: SMT techniques for fast predicate abstraction. In: Ball, T., Jones, R.B. (eds.) CAV 2006. LNCS, vol. 4144, pp. 424–437. Springer, Heidelberg (2006). https://doi.org/10.1007/11817963_39

16. Leofante, F., Giunchiglia, E., Ábrahám, E., Tacchella, A.: Optimal planning modulo theories. In: IJCAI 2020, vol. 4, pp. 4128–4134 (2020). https://doi.org/10.24963/ijcai.2020/571

17. Li, Y., Albarghouthi, A., Kincaid, Z., Gurfinkel, A., Chechik, M.: Symbolic optimization with SMT solvers. In: POPL 2014, pp. 607–618. ACM (2014). https://doi.org/10.1145/2535838.2535857

18. Ma, F., Yan, J., Zhang, J.: Solving generalized optimization problems subject to SMT constraints. In: Snoeyink, J., Lu, P., Su, K., Wang, L. (eds.) AAIM/FAW -2012. LNCS, vol. 7285, pp. 247–258. Springer, Heidelberg (2012). https://doi.org/10.1007/978-3-642-29700-7_23
19. Marques-Silva, J., Lynce, I., Malik, S.: Conflict-driven clause learning SAT solvers. In: Handbook of Satisfiability, FAIA, vol. 336. IOS Press (2021). https://doi.org/10.3233/FAIA200987
20. Masina, G., Spallitta, G., Sebastiani, R.: On CNF conversion for disjoint SAT enumeration. In: SAT 2023. LIPIcs, vol. 271, pp. 15:1–15:16. LZI (2023). https://doi.org/10.4230/LIPIcs.SAT.2023.15
21. Masina, G., Spallitta, G., Sebastiani, R.: On CNF conversion for SAT and SMT enumeration. J. Artif. Intell. Res. **83** (2025). https://doi.org/10.1613/jair.1.16870, to appear, preprint arXiv:2303.14971
22. Morgado, A., Marques-Silva, J.: Good learning and implicit model enumeration. In: ICTAI 2005, pp. 131–136. IEEE Computer Society (2005). https://doi.org/10.1109/ICTAI.2005.69
23. Nadel, A., Ryvchin, V.: Bit-vector optimization. In: Chechik, M., Raskin, J.-F. (eds.) TACAS 2016. LNCS, vol. 9636, pp. 851–867. Springer, Heidelberg (2016). https://doi.org/10.1007/978-3-662-49674-9_53
24. Nguyen, C.M., Sebastiani, R., Giorgini, P., Mylopoulos, J.: Multi-objective reasoning with constrained goal models. Requirements Eng. **23**(2), 189–225 (2016). https://doi.org/10.1007/s00766-016-0263-5
25. Nieuwenhuis, R., Oliveras, A.: On SAT modulo theories and optimization problems. In: Biere, A., Gomes, C.P. (eds.) SAT 2006. LNCS, vol. 4121, pp. 156–169. Springer, Heidelberg (2006). https://doi.org/10.1007/11814948_18
26. Panjkovic, S., Micheli, A.: Expressive optimal temporal planning via optimization modulo theory. In: AAAI 2023, vol. 37, no. 10, pp. 12095–12102 (2023). https://doi.org/10.1609/aaai.v37i10.26426
27. Panjkovic, S., Micheli, A.: Abstract action scheduling for optimal temporal planning via OMT. In: AAAI 2024, vol. 38, no. 18, pp. 20222–20229 (2024). https://doi.org/10.1609/aaai.v38i18.30002
28. Plaisted, D.A., Greenbaum, S.: A Structure-preserving clause form translation. J. Symb. Comput. **2**(3), 293–304 (1986). https://doi.org/10.1016/S0747-7171(86)80028-1
29. Ravi, K., Somenzi, F.: Minimal assignments for bounded model checking. In: Jensen, K., Podelski, A. (eds.) TACAS 2004. LNCS, vol. 2988, pp. 31–45. Springer, Heidelberg (2004). https://doi.org/10.1007/978-3-540-24730-2_3
30. Sebastiani, R.: Lazy satisfiability modulo theories. JSAT **3**(3–4), 141–224 (2007). https://doi.org/10.3233/SAT190034
31. Sebastiani, R., Tomasi, S.: Optimization in SMT with LA(Q) cost functions. In: Gramlich, B., Miller, D., Sattler, U. (eds.) IJCAR 2012. LNCS (LNAI), vol. 7364, pp. 484–498. Springer, Heidelberg (2012). https://doi.org/10.1007/978-3-642-31365-3_38
32. Sebastiani, R., Tomasi, S.: Optimization modulo theories with linear rational costs. ACM Trans. Comput. Logic **16**(2), 12:1–12:43 (2015). https://doi.org/10.1145/2699915
33. Sebastiani, R., Trentin, P.: Pushing the envelope of optimization modulo theories with linear-arithmetic cost functions. In: Baier, C., Tinelli, C. (eds.) TACAS 2015. LNCS, vol. 9035, pp. 335–349. Springer, Heidelberg (2015). https://doi.org/10.1007/978-3-662-46681-0_27
34. Sebastiani, R., Trentin, P.: OPTIMATHSAT: a tool for optimization modulo theories. J. Autom. Reason. **64**(3), 423–460 (2018). https://doi.org/10.1007/s10817-018-09508-6
35. Spallitta, G., Sebastiani, R., Biere, A.: Disjoint partial enumeration without blocking clauses. In: AAAI 2024, vol. 38, pp. 8126–8135 (2024). https://doi.org/10.1609/aaai.v38i8.28652

36. Spallitta, G., Sebastiani, R., Biere, A.: Disjoint projected enumeration for SAT and SMT without blocking clauses. Artif. Intell. **345**, 104346 (2025). https://doi.org/10.1016/j.artint.2025.104346

37. Teso, S., Sebastiani, R., Passerini, A.: Structured learning modulo theories. Artif. Intell. **244**, 166–187 (2017). https://doi.org/10.1016/j.artint.2015.04.002

38. Toda, T., Soh, T.: Implementing efficient all solutions SAT solvers. ACM J. Exp. Algorithmics **21**, 1–44 (2016). https://doi.org/10.1145/2975585

39. Trentin, P., Sebastiani, R.: Optimization modulo the theories of signed bit-vectors and floating-point numbers. J. Autom. Reason. **65**(7), 1071–1096 (2021). https://doi.org/10.1007/s10817-021-09600-4

40. Tseitin, G.S.: On the complexity of derivation in propositional calculus. In: Siekmann, J.H., Wrightson, G. (eds.) Automation of Reasoning. Symbolic Computation, pp. 466–483. Springer, Heidelberg (1983). https://doi.org/10.1007/978-3-642-81955-1_28

41. Tsiskaridze, N., Barrett, C., Tinelli, C.: Generalized optimization modulo theories. In: Benzmüller, C., Heule, M.J., Schmidt, R.A. (eds.) IJCAR 2024. LNCS, vol. 14739, pp. 458–479. Springer, Cham (2024). https://doi.org/10.1007/978-3-031-63498-7_27

Shininess, Strong Politeness, and Unicorns

Benjamin Przybocki[1]([✉]), Guilherme V. Toledo[2], and Yoni Zohar[2]

[1] University of Cambridge, Cambridge, UK
benjamin.przybocki@gmail.com
[2] Bar-Ilan University, Ramat Gan, Israel

Abstract. Shininess and strong politeness are properties related to theory combination procedures. In a paper titled "Many-sorted equivalence of shiny and strongly polite theories", Casal and Rasga proved that for decidable theories, these properties are equivalent. We refine their result by showing that: (i) shiny theories are always decidable, and therefore strongly polite; and (ii) there are (undecidable) strongly polite theories that are not shiny. This line of research is tightly related to a recent series of papers that have sought to classify all the relations between theory combination properties. We finally complete this project, resolving all of the remaining problems that were previously left open.

1 Introduction

In 2005, the shiny combination method was introduced [19], and was able to handle theories that were left out of the Nelson–Oppen method [11]. Unlike the Nelson–Oppen method, which requires both combined theories to be stably infinite, shiny combination requires a stronger property (*shininess*), but only from one of the theories. This allowed for theories that are not stably infinite, like the theory of bit-vectors [2], to be combined with other theories.

Shininess requires the ability to compute cardinalities of minimal models, which is computationally expensive. This was one of the reasons that led to the introduction of the polite combination method [15], replacing the computation of cardinalities by a computation of formulas called *witnesses*. The resulting property is called *politeness*. Later, in 2010, it was clarified that actually a stronger property is required for polite combination, called *strong politeness* [8]. While the definitions of shininess and strong politeness are different, in 2018, Casal and Rasga proved that they are equivalent for decidable theories [4].

In this paper, we investigate the equivalence between shininess and strong politeness, without assuming decidability. Our main result is that shiny theories are always strongly polite, while the converse does not hold. For the former, we show that shiny theories are always decidable, and then strong politeness follows. For the latter, we construct examples. Our examples are theories that are non-trivial, and build on a graph-theoretical interpretation of models.

We also study the relationship between strong politeness and additive politeness, a notion that was introduced in [16] to simplify strong politeness proofs,

© The Author(s) 2026
R. Thiemann and C. Weidenbach (Eds.): FroCoS 2025, LNAI 15979, pp. 135–152, 2026.
https://doi.org/10.1007/978-3-032-04167-8_8

and was shown to imply strong politeness. We prove that the converse does not hold in general, but it does hold in the absence of predicates (except equality).

Our results have several implications. First, they provide a deeper understanding of shininess and strong politeness. Second, since SMT solvers often deal with undecidable theories, combination methods for such theories can be useful for those cases in which the underlying solvers of both theories return a result. Third, our results entail that there are theories for which it is possible to compute witnesses but impossible to compute minimal models. This affirms the aforementioned motivation from [15] for the introduction of politeness, namely that the minimal model function is harder to compute in general than a witness.[1]

There is a completely different way to tell this story, leading to a fourth implication. The papers [21–23] analyzed connections between various properties, including (strong) politeness and shininess. For almost every combination of properties, they either found an example or proved that there are none. For three particular combinations, however, this was left open: Unicorn 1.0,[2] Unicorn 2.0, and Unicorn 3.0 theories. In [14], it was proved that Unicorn 1.0 theories do not exist. Here, we prove that Unicorn 2.0 theories exist, while Unicorn 3.0 theories do not. We also resolve a related question from [14] regarding uncountable signatures. This closes all questions regarding unicorn theories, thus completing the project of analyzing the connections between theory combination properties.

The two narratives are inter-related: the nonexistence of Unicorn 3.0 theories directly follows from the implication from shininess to strong politeness; And every theory that is strongly polite but not shiny is a Unicorn 2.0 theory.

Figure 1a shows the connections between shininess, strong politeness and additive politeness. Blue connections are known, black are new. Figure 1b lists the results on unicorns, referring each problem to the section where it is solved.

To summarize: Sect. 3 proves that all shiny theories are decidable (and therefore strongly polite), and concludes that there are no Unicorn 3.0 theories. Section 4 constructs strongly polite theories that are not shiny. All of them are Unicorn 2.0 theories. Section 5 proves that strong politeness does not imply additive politeness, except over algebraic signatures. Section 6 solves a related problem from [14]. Section 7 concludes with directions for future work.[3]

2   Preliminaries

In what follows, $\mathbb{N}$ denotes the set of non-negative integers, $\mathbb{N}^+ = \mathbb{N} \setminus \{0\}$, $|X|$ is the cardinality of the set X, $\aleph_0 = |\mathbb{N}|$, and $\mathbb{N}_\omega = \mathbb{N} \cup \{\aleph_0\}$.

2.1   Many-Sorted Logic

A *signature* Σ is a triple $(\mathcal{S}_\Sigma, \mathcal{F}_\Sigma, \mathcal{P}_\Sigma)$ where $\mathcal{S}_\Sigma$ is a non-empty set (of sorts), $\mathcal{F}_\Sigma$ is a set of function symbols, each equipped with an arity $\sigma_1 \times \cdots \times \sigma_n \to \sigma$,

---

[1] The adoption of polite combination in cvc5 [1] provides an empirical affirmation.

[2] In [14,21], these were simply called *Unicorn* theories. We rename them here to Unicorn 1.0, in order to be consistent with the other types of unicorns from [23].

[3] Some proofs are omitted and can be found in the arXiv version of this paper [13].

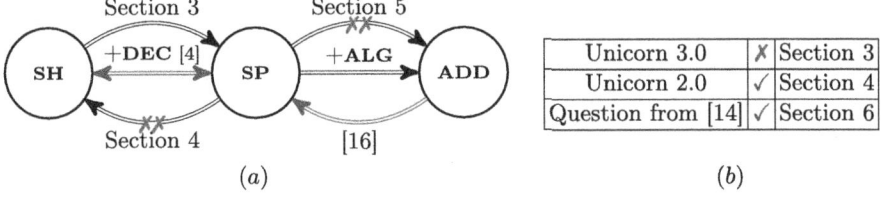

Unicorn 3.0	✗	Section 3
Unicorn 2.0	✓	Section 4
Question from [14]	✓	Section 6

(a)   (b)

Fig. 1. A summary of the contributions of this paper.

for $\sigma_1, \ldots, \sigma_n, \sigma \in \mathcal{S}_\Sigma$, and $\mathcal{P}_\Sigma$ is a set of predicate symbols, each with an arity $\sigma_1 \times \cdots \times \sigma_n$, for $\sigma_1, \ldots, \sigma_n \in \mathcal{S}_\Sigma$, that includes the equality symbol $=_\sigma$ of arity $\sigma \times \sigma$, for every $\sigma \in \mathcal{S}_\Sigma$, usually denoted simply as $=$. A signature is called *empty* if it contains no function and predicate symbols other than the equalities. The cardinality of a signature is the cardinality of $\mathcal{S}_\Sigma \cup \mathcal{F}_\Sigma \cup \mathcal{P}_\Sigma$.

We define terms, formulas, literals, clauses (disjunctions of literals), and sentences in the usual way; the set of free variables of sort σ in φ is denoted by $vars_\sigma(\varphi)$, the set of free variables whose sort σ lies in $S \subseteq \mathcal{S}_\Sigma$ is denoted by $vars_S(\varphi)$, and the set of all of its variables is simply $vars(\varphi)$. If s is a function symbol of arity $\sigma \to \sigma$ and x a variable of sort σ, we define recursively the terms $s^0(x) = x$ and $s^{n+1}(x) = s(s^n(x))$. A *Horn clause* is a formula of the form $\forall x_1, \ldots, x_n.\ \varphi$ such that φ is quantifier-free and has the form $\ell_1 \vee \cdots \vee \ell_m$ for literals $\ell_1, \ldots, \ell_m$, such that there is at most one $1 \leq i \leq m$ such that ℓ_i is an atomic formula (and all the other ℓ_is are negations of atomic formulas).

A Σ-*structure* $\mathbb{A}$ maps: each $\sigma \in \mathbb{A}$ to a non-empty set $\sigma^\mathbb{A}$, called the *domain of* σ *in* $\mathbb{A}$; each $f \in \mathcal{F}_\Sigma$ to a function $f^\mathbb{A} : \sigma_1^\mathbb{A} \times \cdots \times \sigma_n^\mathbb{A} \to \sigma^\mathbb{A}$, where $\sigma_1 \times \cdots \times \sigma_n \to \sigma$ is the arity of f; and each predicate $P \in \mathcal{P}_\Sigma$ to a subset $P^\mathbb{A}$ of $\sigma_1^\mathbb{A} \times \cdots \times \sigma_n^\mathbb{A}$, where $\sigma_1 \times \cdots \times \sigma_n$ is the arity of P. A Σ-*interpretation* $\mathcal{A}$ is a Σ-structure further equipped with a mapping of variables x to elements $x^\mathcal{A}$, such that if x has sort σ, then $x^\mathcal{A} \in \sigma^\mathcal{A}$. The value $\tau^\mathcal{A}$ of a term τ is defined as usual. If Γ is a set of terms, $\Gamma^\mathcal{A} = \{\tau^\mathcal{A} : \tau \in \Gamma\}$. Satisfaction is defined as usual, and denoted $\vDash$. Formulas we will make use of are given in Fig. 2, and an interpretation $\mathcal{A}$ that satisfies $\psi_{\geq n}^\sigma$ (or $\neq^\sigma (x_1, \ldots, x_n)$), $\psi_{\leq n}^\sigma$ or $\psi_{=n}^\sigma$ has, respectively, at least, at most, or exactly n elements in $\sigma^\mathcal{A}$. When $\mathcal{S}_\Sigma = \{\sigma\}$, we omit σ from these formulas.

$$\neq^\sigma (x_1, \ldots, x_n) = \bigwedge_{i=1}^{n-1} \bigwedge_{j=i+1}^{n} \neg(x_i = x_j) \qquad \psi_{\geq n}^\sigma = \exists x_1, \ldots, x_n.\ \neq^\sigma (x_1, \ldots, x_n)$$

$$\psi_{\leq n}^\sigma = \exists x_1, \ldots, x_n. \forall y.\ \bigvee_{i=1}^{n} y = x_i \qquad\qquad \psi_{=n}^\sigma = \psi_{\geq n}^\sigma \wedge \psi_{\leq n}^\sigma$$

Fig. 2. Cardinality formulas, all variables are of sort σ.

A Σ-*theory* $\mathcal{T}$ is the class of all Σ-interpretations that satisfy a set of sentences $Ax(\mathcal{T})$ called the axiomatization of $\mathcal{T}$. We call them $\mathcal{T}$-*interpretations*. A formula satisfied by a $\mathcal{T}$-interpretation is said to be $\mathcal{T}$-*satisfiable* (or simply satisfiable if $\mathcal{T}$ includes all Σ-interpretations), and if φ is satisfied by all $\mathcal{T}$-interpretations it is said to be $\mathcal{T}$-*valid*, and we write $\vDash_{\mathcal{T}} \varphi$. Two formulas are said to be $\mathcal{T}$-*equivalent* if they are satisfied by precisely the same $\mathcal{T}$-interpretations. A standard result that we will use is the Löwenheim–Skolem theorem.

Theorem 1 ([10]). *If Σ is countable and Γ is a satisfiable set of Σ-formulas, there is a Σ-interpretation $\mathcal{B}$ with $\mathcal{B} \vDash \Gamma$ and $|\sigma^{\mathcal{B}}| \leq \aleph_0$ for all $\sigma \in S_{\Sigma}$.*

2.2 Theory Combination Properties

In what follows, Σ is a signature and $\mathcal{T}$ is a Σ-theory. $\mathcal{T}$ is *decidable* if the set $\{\varphi \in QF(\Sigma) \mid \varphi \text{ is } \mathcal{T}\text{-satisfiable}\}$ is decidable, where $QF(\Sigma)$ is the set of quantifier-free formulas over Σ. $\mathcal{T}$ is *convex* [11] *w.r.t.* S if $\vDash_{\mathcal{T}} \varphi \rightarrow \bigvee_{i=1}^{n} x_i = y_i$ implies $\vDash_{\mathcal{T}} \varphi \rightarrow x_i = y_i$ for some $1 \leq i \leq n$, where φ is a conjunction of literals and x_i and y_i have sorts in S.

$\mathcal{T}$ is *stably infinite* [12] (respectively, has the *finite model property*) *w.r.t.* $S \subseteq S_{\Sigma}$ if for every $\mathcal{T}$-satisfiable $\varphi \in QF(\Sigma)$, there is a $\mathcal{T}$-interpretation $\mathcal{A}$ with $\mathcal{A} \vDash \varphi$ such that for every $\sigma \in S$, $|\sigma^{\mathcal{A}}| \geq \aleph_0$ (respectively, $|\sigma^{\mathcal{A}}| < \aleph_0$). $\mathcal{T}$ is *smooth* [15] *w.r.t.* S if for every quantifier-free formula φ, $\mathcal{T}$-interpretation $\mathcal{A}$ with $\mathcal{A} \vDash \varphi$, and function κ from S to the class of all cardinals such that $\kappa(\sigma) \geq |\sigma^{\mathcal{A}}|$ for every $\sigma \in S$, there is a $\mathcal{T}$-interpretation $\mathcal{B}$ with $\mathcal{B} \vDash \varphi$ and $|\sigma^{\mathcal{B}}| = \kappa(\sigma)$ for all $\sigma \in S$. If we add the assumption that $\kappa(\sigma) < \aleph_0$ for every $\sigma \in S_{\Sigma}$, the resulting property is called *finite smoothness* [14]. $\mathcal{T}$ is *stably finite* [15] if for every quantifier-free formula φ and $\mathcal{T}$-interpretation $\mathcal{A}$ with $\mathcal{A} \vDash \varphi$ there is a $\mathcal{T}$-interpretation $\mathcal{B}$ with $\mathcal{B} \vDash \varphi$, and $|\sigma^{\mathcal{B}}| < \aleph_0$ and $|\sigma^{\mathcal{B}}| \leq |\sigma^{\mathcal{A}}|$ for all $\sigma \in S$.

Take a finite set of variables V and an equivalence relation E on V such that, if x and y are of different sorts, then $x\cancel{E}y$ (where $\cancel{E}$ is the complement of E). We define the *arrangement* induced by E on V, denoted by δ_V^E or δ_V if explicitly mentioning E is not necessary, as the conjunction of the literals $x = y$ if xEy, and $\neg(x = y)$ if $x\cancel{E}y$.

$\mathcal{T}$ is *finitely witnessable* [15] *w.r.t.* S if it has a *witness* $wit : QF(\Sigma) \rightarrow QF(\Sigma)$, which is a computable function such that for any quantifier-free formula φ: φ and $\exists \overrightarrow{x}.\, wit(\varphi)$ are $\mathcal{T}$-equivalent, where $\overrightarrow{x} = vars(wit(\varphi)) \setminus vars(\varphi)$; and, if $wit(\varphi)$ is $\mathcal{T}$-satisfiable, there is a $\mathcal{T}$-interpretation $\mathcal{A}$ with $\mathcal{A} \vDash \varphi$ and $\sigma^{\mathcal{A}} = vars_{\sigma}(wit(\varphi))^{\mathcal{A}}$ for each $\sigma \in S$. $\mathcal{T}$ is *strongly finitely witnessable* [3] *w.r.t.* S if it has a *strong witness*, which is a witness that satisfies, for every quantifier-free formula φ, finite set of variables V whose sorts are in S, and arrangement δ_V in V, if $wit(\varphi) \wedge \delta_V$ is $\mathcal{T}$-satisfiable, then there exists a $\mathcal{T}$-interpretation $\mathcal{A}$ with $\mathcal{A} \vDash wit(\varphi) \wedge \delta_V$ and $\sigma^{\mathcal{A}} = vars_{\sigma}(wit(\varphi) \wedge \delta_V)^{\mathcal{A}}$ for each $\sigma \in S$. $\mathcal{T}$ is *polite*, respectively *strongly polite*, *w.r.t.* S if it is smooth and finitely witnessable *w.r.t.* S, respectively smooth and strongly finitely witnessable.

A *minimal model function* [19,23] *w.r.t.* $S \subseteq \mathcal{S}_\Sigma$ for $\mathcal{T}$ is a function that takes $\varphi \in QF(\Sigma)$ and returns a set $\mathsf{MM}_\mathcal{T}(\varphi)$ of functions $\mathbf{n}$ from S to the class of all cardinals such that, if φ is $\mathcal{T}$-satisfiable: for every $\mathbf{n}$ in $\mathsf{MM}_\mathcal{T}(\varphi)$, there exists a $\mathcal{T}$-interpretation $\mathcal{A}$ with $\mathcal{A} \vDash \varphi$ and $\mathbf{n}(\sigma) = |\sigma^\mathcal{A}|$ for all $\sigma \in S$; if $\mathbf{m}, \mathbf{n} \in \mathsf{MM}_\mathcal{T}(\varphi)$ and $\mathbf{m} \neq \mathbf{n}$, there exists $\sigma \in S$ such that $\mathbf{m}(\sigma) < \mathbf{n}(\sigma)$; and for every $\mathcal{T}$-interpretation $\mathcal{A}$ that satisfies φ, there exists $\mathbf{n} \in \mathsf{MM}_\mathcal{T}(\varphi)$ such that $\mathbf{n}(\sigma) \leq |\sigma^\mathcal{A}|$ for all $\sigma \in S$. $\mathcal{T}$ is called *shiny w.r.t.* S if it is smooth, stably finite, and has a computable minimal model function, all *w.r.t.* S.

$\mathcal{T}$ is a *Unicorn* 1.0 *theory w.r.t.* S if it is stably infinite, strongly finitely witnessable but not smooth, all *w.r.t.* S. It is a *Unicorn* 2.0 *theory w.r.t.* S if it is strongly finitely witnessable but does not have a computable minimal model function, both *w.r.t.* S [23]. It is a *Unicorn* 3.0 *theory w.r.t.* S if it is polite and shiny, but is not strongly polite, all *w.r.t.* S [23].

We have the following theorem:

Theorem 2 ([6,18]). *If $Ax(\mathcal{T})$ consists solely of Horn clauses, then $\mathcal{T}$ is convex.*

3   Shiny Theories Are Always Decidable (and Strongly Polite)

In [4], it was proven that for decidable theories, strong politeness and shininess are equivalent:

Theorem 3 ([4, Theorem 3.10]). *A decidable theory is strongly polite w.r.t. a finite set S of sorts if and only if it is shiny w.r.t. S.*

In this section, we show that the right-to-left direction holds without assuming decidability. Moreover, the reason for this is that shiny theories are in fact always decidable.

Now, it is important to clarify that the definition of shininess in [4] is slightly different from ours (which comes from [23]): in [4], the minimal model function of a Σ-theory $\mathcal{T}$ is only defined over $\mathcal{T}$-satisfiable Σ-formulas. With this definition, we cannot ask whether the minimal model function is computable for undecidable theories, since its domain is an undecidable set. In [23], a more general definition was found, that would apply also to undecidable theories. Thus, the domain of the minimal model function is all quantifier-free formulas, although the function can return anything for unsatisfiable formulas. This is natural: without knowing that a formula is $\mathcal{T}$-satisfiable, we may still be able to determine the size of its minimal model in case it is $\mathcal{T}$-satisfiable. However, this is not the only way one could have generalized the definition to undecidable theories; one could have instead allowed the minimal model function to be *partial*, so that the algorithm computing it may not terminate for unsatisfiable formulas. That said, we follow [23] in requiring the minimal model function to be total, an assumption we make essential use of.

With our definition, it makes sense to ask whether an undecidable theory is shiny. We show that the answer is always no: every shiny theory is decidable. In fact, we show something stronger, namely, that smoothness does not need to be assumed, but can be replaced by stable infiniteness.

Theorem 4. *If a theory T is stably infinite, stably finite, and has a computable minimal model function, all with respect to a non-empty set of sorts S, then T is decidable.*

Note that all the assumptions of the theorem are necessary: decidability does not follow from stable infiniteness and stable finiteness alone, and also not from either of them combined with the computability of the minimal model function. For more details on this, see Remark 1 of Sect. 4.4 below, where concrete examples are given.

Theorem 4 implies that shiny theories are decidable, since smoothness is a stronger property than stable infiniteness. As a corollary, we see that shininess implies strong politeness:

Corollary 1. *If a theory is shiny with respect to a finite set of sorts S, then it is strongly polite with respect to S.*

The fact that shininess implies politeness solves a problem that was left open in [23]. In that paper, it was left undetermined whether there exist Unicorn 3.0 theories, that is, theories that are polite and shiny, but not strongly polite. In particular, such theories, if exist, must be shiny without being strongly polite. But Corollary 1 tells us that such theories do not exist.

Corollary 2. *There are no Unicorn 3.0 theories.*

4   Some Strongly Polite Theories Are Not Shiny

In this section, we study the following question, which is the converse of the question from Sect. 3.

(∗) Does strong politeness imply shininess?

By Theorems 3 and 4, this is equivalent to asking whether strong politeness implies decidability. Similarly to Sect. 3, this is also related to a question left open in [23]: the existence of strongly finitely witnessable theories that do not have a computable minimal model function, a.k.a. Unicorn 2.0 theories. If such theories do not exist, then the answer to (∗) would be positive. In contrast, if such theories exist, this is still not enough to provide a negative answer: Unicorn 2.0 theories are definitely not shiny, since they do not have a computable minimal model function. But, they are only required to be strongly finitely witnessable, and not necessarily smooth. Thus, if a Unicorn 2.0 theory is found that is not smooth, this does not help us with determining the answer for (∗). In fact, thanks to [14, Theorem 2], we know that every strongly finitely witnessable theory that is also stably infinite is strongly polite (over countable signatures). Thus, a negative answer to $(*)$ can be obtained by finding a Unicorn 2.0 theory that is also stably infinite.

As part of our strategy to resolve $(*)$, we make a detour into the land of Unicorn 2.0 theories. One of the goals of [23] was to determine the feasibility of all Boolean combinations of model-theoretic properties studied there. After Sect. 3, we are closer to the end of that project, as it determined the feasibility of Unicorn 3.0 theories. To fully complete that project, we need to determine the feasibility of 10 different kinds of Unicorn 2.0 theories. Two of them, over empty signatures, will be shown to be impossible in Sect. 4.1. The remaining eight cases, all over non-empty signatures, are in fact possible, which we demonstrate in Sect. 4.2. Specifically, we prove that in non-empty signatures there are Unicorn 2.0 theories with all the possible combinations of the following properties: (1) being defined over a one-sorted (or many-sorted) signature; (2) being stably infinite (or not stably infinite); and (3) being convex (or not convex). In total, we present 8 Unicorn 2.0 theories. Since they include stably infinite ones, we obtain in Sect. 4.3 a positive answer to $(*)$. We conclude this section by completing the picture of strong politeness, shininess, and decidability, by showing which combinations of these properties are possible in Sect. 4.4.

4.1   Unicorns 2.0 over Empty Signatures

We prove that there are no Unicorn 2.0 theories over empty signatures with finitely many sorts.

We start by proving that all theories that are based on empty signatures with finitely many sorts are decidable.

Lemma 1. *If Σ is an empty signature with finitely many sorts and $\mathcal{T}$ is a Σ-theory, then $\mathcal{T}$ is decidable.*

Proof Sketch. Let $\{\sigma_1, \ldots, \sigma_n\}$ be the sorts of Σ. Using a result very similar to Dickson's lemma [5], which states a subset of $\mathbb{N}^n$ has only finitely many minimal elements, we obtain $\mathcal{T}$ has only finitely many interpretations $\mathcal{A}$ such that $(|\sigma_1^{\mathcal{A}}|, \ldots, |\sigma_n^{\mathcal{A}}|)$ is maximal. Because the signature is empty, to check whether φ is $\mathcal{T}$-satisfiable it is then enough to test whether φ has an interpretation $\mathcal{B}$ in equational logic such that $|\sigma_i^{\mathcal{B}}| \leq |\sigma_i^{\mathcal{A}}|$ for all $1 \leq i \leq n$.   □

Now, let us go back to Theorem 3. The proof of the left-to-right direction assumes decidability, strong finite witnessability and smoothness, and proves stable finiteness and the computability of the minimal model function. A closer look at the proof reveals that when proving computability of the minimal model function, smoothness is not used. We can therefore obtain the following lemma, that was nevertheless not mentioned explicitly in [4]:

Lemma 2. *If $\mathcal{T}$ is decidable and strongly finitely witnessable with respect to S, then it has a computable minimal model function with respect to S.*

Combining these two lemmas, we obtain that there are no Unicorn 2.0 theories over an empty signature with finitely many sorts.

Corollary 3. *If Σ is an empty signature with finitely many sorts, and $\mathcal{T}$ is a Σ-theory strongly finitely witnessable with respect to $S \subseteq \mathcal{S}_\Sigma$, then it has a computable minimal model function with respect to S.*

4.2 Unicorns 2.0 over Non-empty Signatures

Table 1. Signatures. All function symbols of Σ_* and f have arity $\sigma_1 \to \sigma_1$. N, T, and P have arity σ_1. Each P_i is a nullary predicate. $<$ has arity $\sigma_1 \times \sigma_1$.

Section	Signature	Sorts	Function Symbols	Predicate Symbols
Section 4.2	Σ_f	$\{\sigma_1\}$	$\{f\}$	$\emptyset$
	Σ_f^2	$\{\sigma_1, \sigma_2\}$	$\{f\}$	$\emptyset$
Section 4.4	Σ_1	$\{\sigma_1\}$	$\emptyset$	$\emptyset$
	Σ_P^n	$\{\sigma_1\}$	$\emptyset$	$\{P_1, P_2, \ldots\}$
Section 5	Σ_P	$\{\sigma_1\}$	$\emptyset$	$\{P\}$
Section 6	Σ_*	$\{\sigma_1\}$	$\{f_\rho \mid \rho \in 2^\omega\}$	$\{N, T, <\}$

We now prove that there are Unicorn 2.0 theories over non-empty signatures. We start with the one-sorted case. The many-sorted case will be dealt with in the end of this section. We work within a single-sorted signature Σ_f with only a unary function symbol f and sort σ_1, as described in Table 1.

Our theories will make use of the following formula:

Definition 1. *Given a number n and a variable x, we denote by $cycle_n(x)$ the formula $f^n(x) = x \wedge \bigwedge_{\substack{m|n \\ m \neq n}} f^m(x) \neq x$, where $m \mid n$ means that m divides n.*

In any Σ_f-interpretation $\mathcal{A}$, $f^\mathcal{A}$ is, of course, a unary function. As such, it gives rise to a directed graph in which the vertices are the elements of $\sigma_1^\mathcal{A}$, and each vertex has out-degree 1. For each $n \in \mathbb{N}^+$, and Σ_f-interpretation $\mathcal{A}$, $\mathcal{A} \models cycle_n(x)$ if $x^\mathcal{A}$ is a part of a cycle of length n. Notice that this is stronger than just having $\mathcal{A} \models f^n(x) = x$, as in the latter case we might also have $\mathcal{A} \models f^m(x) = x$ for some m that properly divides n.[4]

We define four Unicorn 2.0 Σ_f-theories: $\mathcal{T}_1, \mathcal{T}_2, \mathcal{T}_3, \mathcal{T}_4$. Their axiomatizations appear in Table 2. We will prove that $\mathcal{T}_1$, in addition to being Unicorn 2.0, is also stably infinite and convex; $\mathcal{T}_2$ is stably infinite but not convex; $\mathcal{T}_3$ is not stably infinite but convex; and $\mathcal{T}_4$ is neither stably infinite nor convex.

---

[4] In $cycle_n(x)$, the requirements $m|n$ and $m \neq n$ can be replaced by the requirement $m < n$. However, we chose an encoding that skips redundant cases.

Table 2. Theories. $cycle_n(x)$ is defined in Definition 1. S is an undecidable set of prime numbers. In $T\langle h \rangle$, $h : \mathbb{N} \to \{0,1\}$ is a non-computable function. ψ_n^P abbreviates the formula $(\exists x_1, \dots, x_n. \neq (x_1, \dots, x_n) \land \bigwedge_{i=1}^{n} P(x_i))$.

Section	Theory	Signature	Axiomatization	Source
Section 4.2	T_1	Σ_f	$\{(\exists x. cycle_n(x)) \to \forall x. f^2(x) \neq x \mid n \in S\}$	new
	T_2	Σ_f	$Ax(T_1) \cup \{\neg \exists x. cycle_6(x)\}$	new
	T_3	Σ_f	$Ax(T_1) \cup \{(\exists x. f(x) = x) \to \forall x. \forall y. x = y\}$	new
	T_4	Σ_f	$Ax(T_2) \cup Ax(T_3)$	new
Section 4.4	T_{EQ}	Σ_1	$\emptyset$	everywhere
	$T_{=1}$	Σ_1	$\{\psi_{=1}\}$	[21]
	$T\langle h \rangle$	Σ_P^n	$\{P_n : h(n) = 1\} \cup \{\neg P_n : h(n) = 0\} \cup \{\psi_{=1}\}$	new
Section 5	T_{2n}	Σ_P	$\{\psi_n^P \to \psi_{\geq 2n} \mid n \in \mathbb{N}^+\}$	new
Section 6	T_*	Σ_*	See Definition 4	new

Let us provide some intuition for their definitions. We assume an arbitrary but fixed undecidable set S of prime numbers that are greater than or equal to 7.[5] Let $\mathcal{A}$ be a Σ_f-interpretation, and let $G_\mathcal{A}$ be the graph induced by $f^\mathcal{A}$. Then: $\mathcal{A}$ is a T_1-interpretation if $G_\mathcal{A}$ either has no cycles whose lengths are in S, or it has no cycles of length 1 and 2. $\mathcal{A}$ is a T_2-interpretation if it is a T_1-interpretation, and, in addition, $G_\mathcal{A}$ has no cycles of length 6. $\mathcal{A}$ is a T_3-interpretation if it is a T_1-interpretation, and, in addition, if $G_\mathcal{A}$ has a loop (i.e., a cycle of length 1), then $\sigma_1^\mathcal{A}$ has a single element. Finally, $\mathcal{A}$ is a T_4-interpretation if it is both a T_2-interpretation and a T_3-interpretation.

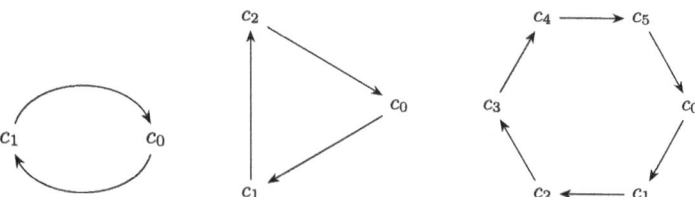

Fig. 3. The interpretations $\mathcal{A}_2$, $\mathcal{A}_3$ and $\mathcal{A}_6$, from left-to-right, all satisfy $f^6(x) = x$, but only $\mathcal{A}_6$ satisfies $cycle_6(x)$.

We prove that all theories $T_1, \dots, T_4$ are Unicorn 2.0 theories; that is, they are strongly finitely witnessable (Lemma 3) but do not have a computable minimal

---

[5] Such sets exist: consider any undecidable set S_0, and let S_1 be the image of the function p that takes a natural number i from S_0 and returns the ith prime number. Then, S_1 is also undecidable. Finally, define $S := S_1 \setminus \{1, \dots, 6\}$. Then S is an undecidable set of prime numbers greater than or equal to 7.

model function (Lemma 4). For the latter, it can be shown that a computable minimal model function can be used to decide S, contradicting its undecidability.

Lemma 3. *For each $i \in [4]$, T_i is strongly finitely witnessable.*

Lemma 4. *For each $i \in [4]$, T_i has no computable minimal model function.*

Now that we have found four Unicorn 2.0 theories, we prove which properties each of them admit: the first two are stably infinite while the last two are not, and T_1 and T_3 are convex while T_2 and T_4 are not.

For the first two theories, it is possible to add arbitrarily many elements to their interpretations without creating new cycles, and thus the resulting interpretations belong to the theories.

Lemma 5. *For each $i \in \{1,2\}$, the theory T_i is stably infinite.*

In contrast, theories T_3 and T_4 are not stably infinite, as they restrict the size of the domain.

Lemma 6. *For each $i \in \{3,4\}$, the theory T_i is not stably infinite.*

Proof. $f(x) = x$ is only T_3- and T_4-satisfiable by interpretations of size 1. □

Next, we show that T_1 and T_3 can be re-axiomatized using Horn clauses, and then from Theorem 2 we get that they are convex.

Lemma 7. *For each $i \in \{1,3\}$, the theory T_i is convex.*

Proof. If n is prime, we have that $cycle_n(x)$ is equivalent to $f^n(x) = x \wedge f(x) \neq x$, and therefore $(\exists x. cycle_n(x)) \to \forall x. f^2(x) \neq x$ is equivalent to $\forall x. \forall y. f^n(x) \neq x \vee f(x) = x \vee f^2(y) \neq y$. Also, $(\exists x. f(x) = x) \to \forall x. \forall y. x = y$ is equivalent to $\forall x. \forall y. \forall z. f(x) \neq x \vee y = z$. Therefore, T_i can be axiomatized by Horn clauses, which implies that T_i is convex by Theorem 2. □

Finally, we show that T_2 and T_4 are not convex.

Lemma 8. *For each $i \in \{2,4\}$, the theory T_i is not convex.*

Proof. We have $\models_{T_i} f^6(x) = x \to (f^2(x) = x \vee f^3(x) = x)$. Indeed, let $\mathcal{A}$ be a T_i-interpretation. Then clearly, $\mathcal{A} \not\models cycle_6(x)$. Now suppose $\mathcal{A} \models f^6(x) = x$. Then $\mathcal{A} \models f(x) = x$, or $\mathcal{A} \models f^2(x) = x$, or $\mathcal{A} \models f^3(x) = x$. If the first case holds, then so do the second and the third. Hence we get $\mathcal{A} \models f^2(x) = x$, or $\mathcal{A} \models f^3(x) = x$.

However, $\not\models_{T_i} f^6(x) = x \to f^2(x) = x$ and $\not\models_{T_i} f^6(x) = x \to f^3(x) = x$. Indeed, consider a T_i-interpretation $\mathcal{A}$ that satisfies $cycle_2(x) \wedge \neg cycle_3(x)$ (such as $\mathcal{A}_2$ from Fig. 3). Then $\mathcal{A} \models f^6(x) = x$ but $\mathcal{A} \not\models f^3(x) = x$. Similarly, Consider a T_i-interpretation $\mathcal{B}$ that satisfies $cycle_3(x) \wedge \neg cycle_2(x)$ (see $\mathcal{A}_3$ in Fig. 3). Then $\mathcal{A} \models f^6(x) = x$ but $\mathcal{A} \not\models f^2(x) = x$. □

With this, we have proven all necessary requirements for theories $\mathcal{T}_1, \ldots, \mathcal{T}_4$.

Now, we turn to theories over a many-sorted signature. For that, we utilize the signature Σ_f^2 from Table 1, that simply adds a sort (σ_2) to Σ_f. Rather than introducing completely new theories for this signature, we use the following result from [21], according to which a sort can be added while preserving all relevant properties.

Definition 2 ([21], **Definition 4**). *If $\mathcal{T}$ is a Σ_f-theory then $(\mathcal{T})^2$ is the Σ_f^2-theory axiomatized by $Ax(\mathcal{T})$.*

Lemma 9 ([21,23]). *Let $\mathcal{T}$ be a Σ_f-theory and X be either strong finite witnessability, computability of the minimal model function, stable infiniteness or convexity. Then: $\mathcal{T}$ admits property X with respect to $\{\sigma_1\}$ iff $(\mathcal{T})^2$ admits property X with respect to $\{\sigma_1, \sigma_2\}$.*

Thus, for the many-sorted case, we simply use the theories $(\mathcal{T}_1)^2$, $(\mathcal{T}_2)^2$, $(\mathcal{T}_3)^2$, and $(\mathcal{T}_4)^2$. For example, $(\mathcal{T}_1)^2$ has the exact same axiomatization as $\mathcal{T}_1$. It just has the additional sort σ_2 in its signature. Thus, every $\mathcal{T}_1$-interpretation can be turned into a $(\mathcal{T}_1)^2$-interpretation by simply assigning any non-empty domain to sort σ_2.

Corollary 4. *For each $i \in [4]$, $(\mathcal{T}_i)^2$ is strongly finitely witnessable and does not have a computable minimal model function. Further, $(\mathcal{T}_i)^2$ is stably infinite iff $i \in \{1, 2\}$ and is convex iff $i \in \{1, 3\}$.*

The results regarding Unicorn 2.0 theories over non-empty signatures are summarized in Table 3. For each theory, we list whether it is defined over a one-sorted signature, whether it is stably infinite, and whether it is convex.

Table 3. Unicorn 2.0 Theories in Non-empty Signatures.

Theory	One Sorted	Stably Infinite	Convex
$\mathcal{T}_1$	✓	✓	✓
$\mathcal{T}_2$	✓	✓	✗
$\mathcal{T}_3$	✓	✗	✓
$\mathcal{T}_4$	✓	✗	✗
$(\mathcal{T}_1)^2$	✗	✓	✓
$(\mathcal{T}_2)^2$	✗	✓	✗
$(\mathcal{T}_3)^2$	✗	✗	✓
$(\mathcal{T}_4)^2$	✗	✗	✗

4.3 Back to Theorem 3

We have now finished the detour to Unicorn 2.0 theories, and are able to come back to our original question (∗) from the beginning of the section, and provide a negative answer: decidability is required for the second direction of Theorem 3, or in other words, the converse of Corollary 1 does not hold without further assuming decidability.

Corollary 5. *There are theories that are strongly polite but are not shiny.*

Proof. For example, stably infinite Unicorn 2.0 theories T_1 and T_2 are such. Indeed, no Unicorn 2.0 theory can be shiny. Further, every such theory that is stably infinite must be strongly polite, as [14] has shown that stable infiniteness and strong finite witnessability imply smoothness.   □

By Theorem 3, this also means there are undecidable strongly polite theories.

Corollary 6. *There are theories that are strongly polite but are not decidable.*

4.4 Completing the Picture

From [4], we know that there are no decidable theories that are strongly polite but not shiny (or vice versa). From Theorem 4, we also know that there are no theories that are shiny but undecidable. From Corollary 5, we know that there are undecidable theories that are strongly polite but not shiny. What about the other possible combinations of decidability, shininess, and strong politeness?

We conclude this section by constructing theories for all the other combinations. The signatures for our theories are given in Table 1. The theories themselves are axiomatized in Table 2.

We start with a decidable, strongly polite and shiny theory. For that, we simply take the empty theory $T_{\mathbf{EQ}}$ over the empty one-sorted signature Σ_1. This is the theory that is axiomatized by the empty set of axioms. The congruence closure algorithm (see, e.g., [9]) decides it; and it was proven to be strongly polite in [8,15]. From Theorem 3 it is also shiny.

To obtain a theory that is decidable but neither shiny nor strongly polite, consider $T_{=1}$ (originally introduced in [21]), of structures with a single element. It is decidable, as it satisfies all equalities and no disequalities. It is clearly not smooth, and so it is neither strongly polite nor shiny.

Finally, for an undecidable theory that is neither shiny nor strongly polite, we use $T\langle h\rangle$, defined over signature Σ_P^n. It has nullary predicates $P_1, P_2, \ldots$, such that P_n holds iff $h(n) = 1$, for some non-computable function h, and all its models are singletons. $T\langle h\rangle$ is undecidable, otherwise we could compute h. Also, it is not smooth, so it is neither strongly polite nor shiny.

These results are summarized as a Venn diagram in Fig. 4. The left circle corresponds to strongly polite theories, the right circle to shiny theories, and the middle circle to decidable theories. Notice that the regions that correspond to decidable theories that are strongly polite but not shiny or vice versa are hatched, marking that they are empty, citing [4]. Similarly, the region that corresponds to shiny theories that are not decidable is also hatched, citing Theorem 4. All other regions are feasible, and have a white background. Each such region lists the evidence for its inhabitance. Notice that $\mathcal{T}\langle h \rangle$ is outside all the circles.

Remark 1. The examples of this section are useful in order to show that in Theorem 4 all three properties that are assumed are needed to ensure decidability. Indeed, The theory $\mathcal{T}\langle h \rangle$ is stably finite and has a computable minimal model function (every model has size 1), but it is not decidable. Further, the theories $\mathcal{T}_1$ and $\mathcal{T}_2$ from Sect. 4.2 are stably infinite and stably finite but not decidable. Finally, Peano arithmetic is stably infinite and has a computable minimal model function (every model is infinite), but it is not decidable. These examples make Theorem 4 more surprising than it may at first seem.

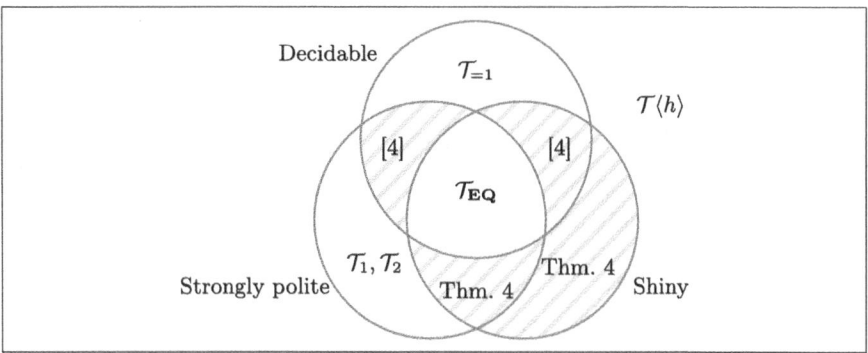

Fig. 4. A Venn diagram summarizing the feasible combinations of strong politeness, shininess and decidability.

5   Additive Politeness

In [16], the SMT-LIB theory of datatypes was proven to be strongly polite. It was observed there, however, that one of the challenges in proving strong politeness lies in the need to consider all possible arrangements, which is not needed when proving (weak) politeness. In order to make the proof of strong politeness more feasible, that paper introduced the notion of *additive witnesses*.

Definition 3 ([16], Definition 10). *Let $f : QF(\Sigma) \to QF(\Sigma)$. Let $S \subseteq \mathcal{S}_\Sigma$. We say that f is S-additive for $\mathcal{T}$ if $f(f(\varphi) \wedge \psi)$ and $f(\varphi) \wedge \psi$ are $\mathcal{T}$-equivalent and have the same set of S-sorted variables for every $\varphi, \psi \in QF(\Sigma)$, provided that ψ is a conjunction of flat literals such that every term in ψ is a variable whose sort is in S. When $\mathcal{T}$ is clear from the context, we say that f is S-additive. We say that $\mathcal{T}$ is additively finitely witnessable w.r.t. S if there exists a witness for $\mathcal{T}$ w.r.t. S which is S-additive. $\mathcal{T}$ is said to be additively polite w.r.t. S if it is smooth and additively finitely witnessable w.r.t. S.*

It has been proven in [16] that additively polite theories are strongly polite. The converse, however, does not hold. To show this, we define a theory that is strongly polite but not additively polite, over signature Σ_P from Table 1. It has a single sort σ_1, and one unary predicate symbol P. The theory, called $\mathcal{T}_{2n}$ and axiomatized in Table 2, admits those Σ_P-interpretations $\mathcal{A}$ where for each n, if there are at least n elements in $P^{\mathcal{A}}$, then there are at least $2n$ elements in $\sigma_1^{\mathcal{A}}$.

We prove that $\mathcal{T}_{2n}$ is strongly polite but not additively polite. We do the former by proving shininess and then using Corollary 1, and the latter by reasoning about cardinalities of models of $\mathcal{T}_{2n}$ that satisfy formulas in which P occurs.

Lemma 10. *The theory $\mathcal{T}_{2n}$ is strongly polite.*

Lemma 11. *The theory $\mathcal{T}_{2n}$ is not additively polite.*

Although strong politeness does not imply additive politeness in general, this implication holds for theories over *algebraic signatures*, which are signatures containing no predicate symbols (except equality) [7].

Theorem 5. *Let $\mathcal{T}$ be a theory over a countable algebraic signature, and let S be a set of sorts. If $\mathcal{T}$ is strongly polite with respect to S, then it is additively polite with respect to S.*

Note that the strongly polite theories $\mathcal{T}_1$ and $\mathcal{T}_2$ from Sect. 4.2 are over algebraic signatures, so they are additively polite.

6   Finite Smoothness Versus Smoothness

As the current paper started with Unicorn 3.0 theories (Sect. 3) and continued with Unicorn 2.0 theories (Sect. 4), we end it with Unicorn 1.0 theories.

In [14], Unicorn 1.0 theories were proven not to exist. The main step in the proof was the following theorem:

Theorem 6 ([14, Theorem 3]). *Let $\mathcal{T}$ be a theory over a countable signature. If $\mathcal{T}$ is stably finite and finitely smooth, both with respect to a set of sorts S, then $\mathcal{T}$ is smooth with respect to S.*

Since stably infinite and strongly finitely witnessable theories are both stably finite and finitely smooth [14, Lemmas 3 and 4], Theorem 6 implies that, over countable signatures, such theories are smooth. This is equivalent to the claim that Unicorn 1.0 theories do not exist.

Notice that in Theorem 6 the signature is assumed to be countable. In [14], the necessity of this assumption was left open. We show that the assumption is necessary, by constructing a theory that is stably finite and finitely smooth, but not smooth, over an uncountable signature.

We define in Table 1 a single-sorted signature Σ_* with unary predicates N and T, and a binary predicate $<$ (written infix).[6] The signature Σ_* also has

---

[6] Think of N as being short for "number" and T as being short for "tree".

function symbols $\{f_\rho \mid \rho \in 2^\omega\}$, where 2^ω is the set of infinite binary sequences. Next, we define the theory $\mathcal{T}_*$, which we will use to show that Theorem 6 fails for uncountable signatures. We do so by first defining a class of interpretations, and then closing it to make it a theory.[7]

Definition 4. *For each $n \in \mathbb{N}$, let $\{0,1\}^{\leq n}$ be the set of sequences over $\{0,1\}$ of length at most n. A Σ_*-interpretation $\mathcal{A}$ is called $*$-interpretation if there is $n \geq 2$ and $S \subseteq \{0,1\}^{n-1}$ such that: $\sigma_1^{\mathcal{A}} = [0, n-1] \cup \{0,1\}^{\leq n-2} \cup S$; $N^{\mathcal{A}} = [0, n-1]$; $T^{\mathcal{A}} = \{0,1\}^{\leq n-2} \cup S$; $a <^{\mathcal{A}} b$ if and only if $a, b \in N^{\mathcal{A}}$ and a is less than b as natural numbers; and for every $\rho \in 2^\omega$, we have that if $0 \leq m \leq n-2$ then $f_\rho^{\mathcal{A}}(m)$ is the sequence that consists of the first m elements of ρ, if $m = n-1$ then $f_\rho^{\mathcal{A}}(m) \in T^{\mathcal{A}}$, and if $m \in T^{\mathcal{A}}$ then $f_\rho^{\mathcal{A}}(m) = m$.*

Let $\mathcal{T}_*^-$ be the class of all $*$-interpretations, and let Ax be the set of Σ_*-sentences that are satisfied by all $*$-interpretations. Then, $\mathcal{T}_*$ is the theory axiomatized by Ax, that is, $Ax(\mathcal{T}_*) = Ax$.

We give some intuition for the definition of a $*$-interpretation $\mathcal{A}$. Given $S \subseteq \{0,1\}^{n-1}$, we can think of $T^{\mathcal{A}} = \{0,1\}^{\leq n-2} \cup S$ as representing a binary tree of height n in which the first $n-1$ layers are full (each binary sequence of length m is a node in the $(m+1)$th layer of the tree). We can think of $N^{\mathcal{A}} = [0, n-1]$ as representing numbers corresponding to each layer of the tree. Then, $\rho \in 2^\omega$ is a path through an infinite binary tree, and $f_\rho(m)$ picks out the $(m+1)$th element along that path, unless $m = n-1$, in which case $f_\rho(m)$ can be any element of the tree. See Fig. 5 for an illustrated example.

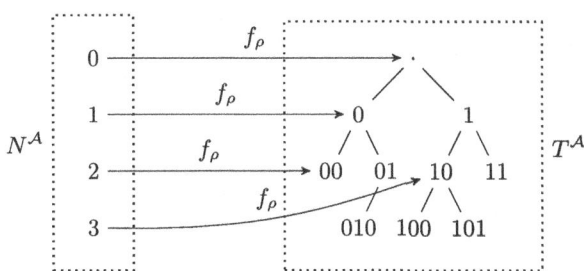

Fig. 5. Example of a $*$-interpretation $\mathcal{A}$, including values of the function f_ρ on $N^{\mathcal{A}}$, where $\rho = 0000\cdots$. Notice that $f_\rho(3)$ can be any element of the tree.

Indeed, $\mathcal{T}_*$ admits the required properties in order to refute Theorem 6 over uncountable signatures:

Theorem 7. *The theory $\mathcal{T}_*$ is stably finite and finitely smooth but not smooth.*

---

[7] The idea underlying the construction is inspired by [17, Exercise 2.3.1 (2)].

6.1   The Existence of Unicorns?

Theorem 7 gives a counterexample to Theorem 6 for theories over uncountable signatures, but Theorem 7 was used in [14] as a stepping stone to the following, showing that Unicorn 1.0 theories do not exist:

Theorem 8 ([14, **Theorem 2**]). *Let T be a theory over a countable signature. If T is stably infinite and strongly finitely witnessable, both with respect to a set of sorts S, then T is smooth with respect to S.*

Does this theorem generalize to uncountable signatures? The question is actually ill-posed. A strong witness is a *computable* function. If the signature is uncountable, the domain of this (computable) function is uncountable, which is impossible in the standard notion of computability. The question becomes well-posed if we consider a weaker version of strong finite witnessability, where the strong witness may be non-computable: Define a *strong pre-witness* to be a strong witness without the computability requirement. We have the following:

Theorem 9. *Let T be a theory and S be a finite set of sorts. Then, the following are equivalent: (1) T is stably finite and finitely smooth with respect to S; and (2) T is stably infinite and has a strong pre-witness with respect to S.*

In particular, this equivalence implies that T_* is stably infinite and has a strong pre-witness despite not being smooth. Thus, T_* is a Unicorn 1.0 theory, except for the requirement that its strong witness be computable. Unicorns may not exist, but T_* is pretty close to one.

7   Conclusion

We have refined the main result of [4], according to which strong politeness is the same as shininess for decidable theories, by showing that shininess implies strong politeness (since shiny theories are always decidable), while the converse does not hold in general. While doing so, we were able to close all open problems raised in a series of papers [14, 21–23], by proving that Unicorn 2.0 theories exist, Unicorn 3.0 theories do not, and even though Unicorn 1.0 theories do not exist, there are theories that admit a similar property.

This completes the classification of which Boolean combinations of eight properties relevant to theory combination are possible (namely: stable infiniteness and finiteness, smoothness, weak and strong finite witnessability, the finite model property, computability of the minimal model function, and convexity). The menagerie of theories we have constructed has already been useful for an ongoing research program that studies impossibility results in theory combination [20]. In the future, we hope to make further use of these theories to discover more about when theory combination is possible.

Acknowledgments. Toledo and Zohar were funded by the NSF-BSF grant 2020704, the ISF grant 619/21, and the Colman-Soref fellowship. Przybocki was supported by the NSF Graduate Research Fellowship Program under Grant No. DGE-2140739.

References

1. Barbosa, H., et al.: cvc5: a versatile and industrial-strength SMT solver. In: Fisman, D., Rosu, G. (eds) TACAS 2022. LNCS, vol. 13243, pp. 415–442. Springer, Cham (2022). https://doi.org/10.1007/978-3-030-99524-9_24
2. Barrett, C., Fontaine, P., Tinelli, C.: The satisfiability modulo theories library (SMT-LIB) (2016). www.SMT-LIB.org
3. Barrett, C.W., Dill, D.L., Stump, A.: A generalization of Shostak's method for combining decision procedures. In: Armando, A. (ed.) FroCoS 2002. LNCS (LNAI), vol. 2309, pp. 132–146. Springer, Heidelberg (2002). https://doi.org/10.1007/3-540-45988-X_11
4. Casal, F., Rasga, J.: Many-sorted equivalence of shiny and strongly polite theories. J. Autom. Reason. **60**(2), 221–236 (2017). https://doi.org/10.1007/s10817-017-9411-y
5. Dickson, L.E.: Finiteness of the odd perfect and primitive abundant numbers with n distinct prime factors. Amer. J. Math. **35**(4), 413 (1913)
6. Harrison, J.: Handbook of Practical Logic and Automated Reasoning, pp. xx+681. Cambridge University Press, Cambridge (2009). https://doi.org/10.1017/CBO9780511576430. ISBN 978-0-521- 89957-4
7. Hodges, W.: Model Theory. Encyclopedia of Mathematics and its Applications. Cambridge University Press (1993). https://doi.org/10.1017/CBO9780511551574
8. Jovanović, D., Barrett, C.: Polite theories revisited. In: Fermüller, C.G., Voronkov, A. (eds.) LPAR 2010. LNCS, vol. 6397, pp. 402–416. Springer, Heidelberg (2010). https://doi.org/10.1007/978-3-642-16242-8_29
9. Kroening, D., Strichman, O.: Decision Procedures - An Algorithmic Point of View. Texts in Theoretical Computer Science. An EATCS Series, 2nd edn. Springer (2016)
10. Monzano, M.: Introduction to many-sorted logic. In: Meinke, K., Tucker, J.V. (eds.) Many-sorted Logic and its Applications. Wiley Professional Computing. Wiley (1993)
11. Nelson, Greg, Oppen, Derek C.: Simplification by cooperating decision procedures. ACM Trans. Program. Lang. Syst. **1**(2), 245–257 (1979). https://doi.org/10.1145/357073.357079. ISSN 0164-0925
12. Oppen, D.C.: Complexity, convexity and combinations of theories. Theor. Comput. Sci. **12**(3), 291–302 (1980). https://doi.org/10.1016/0304-3975(80)90059-6. ISSN 0304-3975
13. Przybocki, B., Toledo, G.V., Zohar, Y.: Shininess, strong politeness, and unicorns. arXiv: 2507.04445 [cs.LO] (2025)
14. Przybocki, B., et al.: The nonexistence of unicorns and many- sorted Löwenheim-Skolem theorems. In: Platzer, A., et al. (eds.) FM 2024, Part I. LNCS, vol. 14933, pp. 658–675. Springer, Cham (2024). https://doi.org/10.1007/978-3-031-71162-6_34
15. Ranise, S., Ringeissen, C., Zarba, C.G.: Combining data structures with nonstably infinite theories using many-sorted logic. In: Gramlich, B. (ed.) FroCoS 2005. LNCS (LNAI), vol. 3717, pp. 48–64. Springer, Heidelberg (2005). https://doi.org/10.1007/11559306_3, https://hal.inria.fr/inria-00000570
16. Sheng, Y., et al.: Polite combination of algebraic datatypes. J. Autom. Reason. **66**(3), 331–355 (2022)
17. Tent, K., Ziegle, M.:. A Course in Model Theory. Lecture Notes in Logic, vol. 40, pp. x+248. Association for Symbolic Logic/Cambridge University Press, La

Jolla/Cambridge (2012). https://doi.org/10.1017/CBO9781139015417. ISBN 978-0-521-76324-0

18. Tinelli, C.: Cooperation of background reasoners in theory reasoning by residue sharing. J. Autom. Reason. **30**(1), 1–31 (2003)
19. Tinelli, C., Zarba, C.G.: Combining Nonstably Infinite Theories. J. Autom. Reason. **34**(3), 209–238 (2005)
20. Toledo, G.V., Przybocki, B., Zohar, Y.: Being polite is not enough (and other limits of theory combination). Accepted to CADE- 30 (2025)
21. Toledo, G.V., Zohar, Y., Barrett, C.: Combining combination properties: an analysis of stable infiniteness, convexity, and politeness. In: Pientka, B., Tinelli, C. (eds.) CADE 2023. LNCS, vol. 14132, pp. 522–541. Springer, Cham (2023). https://doi.org/10.1007/978-3-031-38499-8_30
22. Toledo, G.V., Zohar, Y., Barrett, C.: Combining finite combination properties: finite models and busy beavers. In: Sattler, U., Suda, M. (eds.) FroCoS 2023. LNCS, vol. 14279, pp. 159–175. Springer, Cham (2023). https://doi.org/10.1007/978-3-031-43369-6_9
23. de Toledo, G.V., Zohar, Y.: Combining combination properties: minimal models. In: Proceedings of LPAR 2024 (2024)

Polite Combination in Parametric Array Theories

Rodrigo Raya[1]([⊠])[iD] and Christophe Ringeissen[2][iD]

[1] École Polytechnique Fédérale de Lausanne, Lausanne, Switzerland
rodrigo.raya@epfl.ch
[2] Université de Lorraine, CNRS, Inria, LORIA, 54000 Nancy, France
christophe.ringeissen@loria.fr

Abstract. Parametric array theories are extensions of the quantifier-free theory of arrays with relations that hold componentwise. We observe that decision procedures for the satisfiability of these theories rely on a kind of finite witnessability property. We use this insight to show the politeness of these theories with respect to the index and element sorts. Our results clarify the politeness of the theory of sets with the cardinality operator, which was left open in the literature.

1 Introduction

Satisfiability procedures form the core of SMT solvers. Their goal is to increase the automation of the theorem-proving process, reducing the interaction with the solver operators. Program verification particularly benefits from theories representing data structures; therefore, state-of-the-art SMT solvers include efficient decision procedures for them. Automatic combination methods, such as Nelson-Oppen's [12], derive decision procedures for formulas in the combination of data structure theories with specific theories of indices and contents. Unfortunately, Nelson-Oppen's method does not work for non-stably infinite theories, such as those referring to finite domains. Polite theory combination [7,14] addresses this problem.

This paper shows the politeness of data structure theories that generalise the extensionality axiom [20] to functions and relation symbols. This extension is useful in the verification of parametrised systems, where it is important to specify properties in subsets of system components. Supporting such generalisation incurs only a mild overhead with respect to the extensional fragment [10] and recent work shows that the theory combines with cardinality, regular, and aggregation constraints while preserving decidability [5,17]. Here, we develop the observation that the decision procedures in [5,17] reduce the satisfiability of the theory to satisfiability over a finite model, a small model property analogous to finite witnessability in the polite theory combination framework. We illustrate this observation in three paradigmatic examples with component-wise operations [10], cardinality constraints [22], and set interpretations [1]. These theories

Research supported by the Swiss NSF Project P500PT_222338.

R. Thiemann and C. Weidenbach (Eds.): FroCoS 2025, LNAI 15979, pp. 153–168, 2026.
https://doi.org/10.1007/978-3-032-04167-8_9

extend the quantifier-free theory of power structures [4,9] with read and write operations.

Related Work. The literature on quantifier-free data structure theories is very broad. These include theories of sets [8], multisets [13], theories of sequences [18] and their combinations [5]. These combinations often include expressive theories such as theories with cardinality or aggregation constraints. These fragments can be used to encode further theories such as regular constraints [17,21]. The results regarding the modular combination of theories are comparatively under-developed. The main work, which also originated the research line on polite theory combination, is that of [14]. Logically, open problems in the area have arisen. In [2], it is left for future work to determine the politeness of a theory of sets with cardinality constraints. We solve this open problem and offer initial steps towards full modular combination of decision procedures for more modern data structure theories.

Contributions. We identify a family of data structure theories for which the polite theory combination method applies. In particular, we observe that the decision procedures for extensions of the theory of powers work by reducing satisfiability in the data structure to a finite number of satisfiability queries on witnesses on the indices or contents theory and show

- the politeness for theories of powers with component-wise operations (e.g. combinatory array logic) with respect to the index and element sorts,
- the politeness of theories of set abstractions with cardinality constraints (e.g. Zarba's theory of sets with cardinality constraints, which was left open in [2]) with respect to the index sort, and
- the politeness of theories with set interpretations (e.g. the simple flat array fragment with fixed set interpretations) with respect to the element sort and, when fixing formulas under set interpretations, also with respect to the index sort.

Paper Organisation. Section 2 introduces the polite combination framework. Section 3 introduces the data structure theories treated. Section 4 shows politeness of combinatory array logic. Section 5 shows the politeness of theories of sets with cardinality constraints. Section 6 shows the politeness of theories of interpreted sets with cardinalities. Section 7 concludes the paper.

2   Polite Combination

The polite combination method [7] provides a $T \cup T'$-satisfiability procedure when T and T' are signature-disjoint theories such that T and T' share only a set of sorts S, T is **strongly** polite w.r.t S, T' is an arbitrary theory, and satisfiability procedures are known for T and T'. Let us start with the definition of politeness [14]. Let Σ be a signature, let $S \subseteq \Sigma^S$ be a set of sorts, and let T be a Σ-theory. We say that T is *polite* with respect to S if it is both smooth and finitely witnessable with respect to S.

Definition 1 (Smoothness). *Let Σ be a signature, let $S = \{\sigma_1, \ldots, \sigma_n\}$ be a set of sorts in Σ, and let T be a Σ-theory. We say that T is smooth with respect to S if:*

- *for every T-satisfiable quantifier-free Σ-formula φ,*
- *for every T-interpretation $\mathcal{A}$ satisfying φ,*
- *for every cardinal numbers $\kappa_1, \ldots, \kappa_n$ such that $\kappa_i \geq |A_{\sigma_i}|$, for $i = 1, \ldots, n$,*

there exists a T-interpretation $\mathcal{B}$ satisfying φ such that

$$|B_{\sigma_i}| = \kappa_i, \quad \text{for } i = 1, \ldots, n$$

Definition 2 (Finite witnessability). *Let Σ be a signature, let S be a set of sorts in Σ, and let T be a Σ-theory. We say that T is finitely witnessable with respect to S if there exists a computable function witness that for every quantifier-free Σ-formula φ returns a quantifier-free Σ-formula $\psi = \text{witness}(\varphi)$ such that (i) φ and $(\exists \bar{v})\psi$ are T-equivalent, where $\bar{v} = \text{vars}(\psi) \setminus \text{vars}(\varphi)$; (ii) if ψ is T-satisfiable then there exists a T-interpretation $\mathcal{A}$ satisfying ψ such that $A_\sigma = [\text{vars}_\sigma(\psi)]^{\mathcal{A}}$, for each $\sigma \in S$.*

The next two propositions establish sufficient conditions to get smoothness and finite witnessability, considering only conjunctions of flat literals. A literal is *flat* if it is of the form, $x = f(y_1, \ldots, y_n)$, $p(y_1, \ldots, y_n)$, or $\neg p(y_1, \ldots, y_n)$, where $x, y_1, \ldots, y_n$ are variables, f is a function symbol, and p is a predicate symbol.

Proposition 1 (Smoothness). *Let Σ be a signature, let $S = \{\sigma_1, \ldots, \sigma_n\}$ be a set of sorts in Σ, and let T be a Σ-theory. Assume that for every conjunction Γ of flat Σ-literals, for every T-interpretation $\mathcal{A}$ satisfying Γ, for every sort $\tau \in S$, and for every cardinal number $\kappa > |A_\tau|$, there exists a T-interpretation $\mathcal{B}$ satisfying Γ such that $|B_\tau| = \kappa$, and $|B_\sigma| = |A_\sigma|$ for $\sigma \in S \setminus \{\tau\}$. Then T is smooth with respect to S.*

Proof. See [15, Proposition 11].

Proposition 2 (Finite Witnessability). *Let Σ be a signature, let S be a set of sorts in Σ and let T be a Σ-theory. Assume that there exists a computable function witness that for every conjunction Γ of flat Σ-literals such that $\text{vars}_\sigma(\Gamma) \neq \emptyset$, for each sort $\sigma \in S$, returns a quantifier-free Σ-formula $\psi = \text{witness}(\Gamma)$ such that (i) Γ and $(\exists \bar{v})\psi$ are T-equivalent, where $\bar{v} = \text{vars}(\psi) \setminus \text{vars}(\Gamma)$; (ii) if ψ is T-satisfiable then there exists a T-interpretation $\mathcal{A}$ satisfying ψ such that $A_\sigma = [\text{vars}_\sigma(\psi)]^{\mathcal{A}}$, for each $\sigma \in S$. Then T is finitely witnessable w.r.t. to S.*

Proof. See [15, Proposition 12].

Politeness implies strong politeness whenever the finite witness associated to T is S-additive [19]. A mapping w from conjunctions of literals to conjunctions of literals is said to be S-*additive* for T if $w(w(\phi) \wedge \varphi)$ and $w(\phi) \wedge \varphi$ are T-equivalent and have the same set of S-sorted variables for every conjunctions of literals ϕ and φ such that φ is a conjunction of flat literals where every term is a variable whose sort is in S. It is important to notice that all the finite witnesses constructed in this paper are actually S-additive, and in this context politeness is sufficient to achieve strong politeness.

3   Extensions of the Theory of Powers

The first-order theory of powers [9] is the first-order theory of the structure $\mathcal{M}^I$, where $\mathcal{M}$ is a given structure and I is a given set, whose carrier set is the set of all functions from I to the carrier set of $\mathcal{M}$, and the interpretation of functions and relations is defined component-wise in terms of the functions and relations in $\mathcal{M}$. For instance, in linear algebra one often considers the structure $\langle \mathbb{R}^N, + \rangle$, where we have the definition $a + b = c \leftrightarrow \forall i.a[i] + b[i] = c[i]$, that is, the relation $a + b = c$ holds for vectors if and only if it holds homogeneously at every component. We study three theories that extend this construction. The first fragment is combinatory array logic [10] which extends the quantifier-free theory of arrays with functions and relations defined componentwise. The second fragment is the theory of sets with cardinalities of Zarba [22] (we view sets as functions from an index sort to Boole's algebra $\langle \{0, 1\}, \wedge, \vee, \neg \rangle$). The last fragment is the simple flat array fragment [1, 16]. This fragment was also studied in [4, 6] to extend the results of [9] to more general structures and substructures.

3.1   Combinatory Array Logic

$$F ::= F_1 \wedge F_2 \,|\, F_1 \vee F_2 \,|\, \neg F \,|\, \mathrm{map}_R(\overline{A}) \,|\, A[i] = e$$
$$A ::= a \,|\, \mathrm{write}(A, i, E) \,|\, K(e) \,|\, \mathrm{map}_f(\overline{A})$$
$$E ::= A[i] \,|\, e$$

Fig. 1. T_{CAL}'s syntax.

Combinatory array logic [10], T_{CAL}, uses a quantifier-free many-sorted language, comprising a sort index for indices, a sort element for elements, and a sort array for arrays. In Fig. 1, we use instances of letter i to refer to variables of the index sort, letter e to refer to variables of sort element and letter a to refer to a variable of the array sort. Function symbol write takes as input an array, an index and an element and returns an array. Function read, $\_[\_]$, takes an array and an index and returns an element. Function K takes as input an element and returns an array which is constantly equal to that element. Function $\mathrm{map}_f(\overline{A})$

takes as input a tuple of arrays and returns an array where, for each index i, the i-th component is the result of applying the uninterpreted function f to the i-th component of the input arrays. Relation $\mathrm{map}_R(\overline{A})$ takes as input a tuple of arrays and returns true if and only if the uninterpreted relation R holds for each tuple of elements in the i-th component. Formally, the introduced symbols satisfy the following axioms.

$$\forall a, i, e. \, \mathrm{write}(a, i, e)[i] = e$$
$$\forall a, i, j, e. i = j \vee \mathrm{write}(a, i, e)[j] = a[j]$$
$$\forall e, i. K(e)[i] = e$$
$$\forall a_1, \ldots, a_k, i. \, \mathrm{map}_f \, (a_1, \ldots, a_k) \, [i] = f \, (a_1[i], \ldots, a_k[i])$$
$$\forall a_1, \ldots, a_k. \, \mathrm{map}_R(a_1, \ldots, a_k) \leftrightarrow \forall i. R(a_1[i], \ldots, a_k[i])$$

We use f for map_f and R for map_R when no ambiguity occurs.

3.2   Theories of Sets

$$F ::= A \,|\, F_1 \wedge F_2 \,|\, F_1 \vee F_2 \,|\, \neg F$$
$$A ::= i_1 = i_2 \,|\, i \in B \,|\, B_1 = B_2 \,|\, B_1 \subseteq B_2 \,|\, T_1 = T_2 \,|\, T_1 < T_2$$
$$B ::= x \,|\, \emptyset \,|\, B_1 \cup B_2 \,|\, B_1 \cap B_2 \,|\, B_1 \setminus B_2$$
$$T ::= k \,|\, K \,|\, T_1 + T_2 \,|\, K \cdot T \,|\, |B|$$
$$K ::= \ldots \,|\, -2 \,|\, -1 \,|\, 0 \,|\, 1 \,|\, 2 \,|\, \ldots$$

Fig. 2. T_Z's syntax.

We will use Zarba's theory of sets [22] for technical reasons (see Sect. 5). Zarba's theory uses a quantifier-free many-sorted language, comprising a sort index for indices, a sort int for integers, and a sort set for sets of indices. In Fig. 2, we use (indexed) instances of letter i to refer to variables of the index sort, letter x to refer to variables of sort set and letter k to refer to a variable of the integer sort. The language includes a first-order signature Σ_{index} to express constraints over the indices. It also includes constants $0, 1$, function $+$, and predicate $<$. Regarding sets, the language contains constant $\emptyset$, functions $\{\cdot\}$ (of sort index $\rightarrow$ set), $\cup, \cap, \setminus$ and predicates $\in, \subseteq$. Finally, there is the cardinality function $|\cdot|$ (of sort set $\rightarrow$ int). The semantics of these symbols is the standard.

Given a formula in T_Σ with set variables $S_1, \ldots, S_n$, a Venn region is the semantics of a Boolean algebra expression on $S_1, \ldots, S_n$. An elementary Venn region is the semantics of a Venn region of the form $S_1^{b_1} \cap \ldots S_n^{b_n}$ where $b \in \{0, 1\}$ and $S^0 := S$ and $S^1 := S^c$ (i.e. the absolute complement of S). We usually abbreviate such elementary Venn regions as E^β where $\beta = (b_1, \ldots, b_n)$. We often decompose Venn regions V into their elementary components as $V = \cup_{\{\beta | E_\beta \subseteq V\}} E_\beta$. This decomposition allows to transform a T_Z formula into an equivalent Presburger arithmetic formula with an analogous procedure to that of [8].

3.3   Interpreted Theories

The simple flat array fragment [1,5,16], T_F, uses a quantifier-free many-sorted language, comprising a sort index for indices, a sort elem for elements, a sort int for integers, a sort set for sets of indices, and a sort array for arrays. In Fig. 3, we use (indexed) instances of letter i to refer to variables of the index sort, letter e to refer to variables of the element sort, letter x to refer to variables of sort set, letter k to refer to a variable of the integer sort and letter a to refer to a variable of the array sort. The logic has as atoms set interpretations of the form $\{i \mid \varphi(\bar{a}[i], \bar{e})\}$ where $\bar{a}$ is a set of array variables, $\bar{a}[i]$ denotes the set of elements in the i-th component of the array variables, $\bar{e}$ is a set of constants of the element sort and φ is an uninterpreted first-order formula over the element sort. These set interpretations are combined with Boolean algebra expressions and cardinality constraints. The semantics of these symbols is the standard.

$$F ::= A \mid F_1 \wedge F_2 \mid F_1 \vee F_2 \mid \neg F$$
$$A ::= a[i] = e \mid i_1 = i_2 \mid i \in B \mid B_1 = B_2 \mid B_1 \subseteq B_2 \mid T_1 = T_2 \mid T_1 < T_2$$
$$B ::= x \mid \emptyset \mid B_1 \cup B_2 \mid B_1 \cap B_2 \mid B_1 \setminus B_2 \mid \{i \mid \varphi(\bar{a}[i], \bar{e})\}$$
$$T ::= k \mid K \mid T_1 + T_2 \mid K \cdot T \mid |B|$$
$$K ::= \ldots \mid -2 \mid -1 \mid 0 \mid 1 \mid 2 \mid \ldots$$

Fig. 3. T_F's syntax

4   Politeness of Combinatory Array Logic

4.1   Smoothness

Proposition 3. *Let $\mathcal{A}$ be a T_{CAL}-interpretation satisfying a conjunction Γ of flat Σ_{CAL}-literals. Then there exists a T_{CAL}-interpretation $\mathcal{B}$ satisfying Γ such that $|B_{elem}| = |A_{elem}|$ and $|B_{index}| = \kappa$, for each cardinal number $\kappa > |A_{index}|$.*

Proof. Let $V_\sigma = \mathrm{vars}_\sigma(\Gamma)$, for $\sigma \in \{\text{elem, index, array}\}$. We construct a T_{CAL}-interpretation $\mathcal{B}$ over $V_{\text{elem}} \cup V_{\text{index}} \cup V_{\text{array}}$ as follows. Fix a set A' (disjoint from A_{index}) such that $\mid A_{\text{index}} \cup A' \mid = \kappa$, and let $B_{\text{index}} = A_{\text{index}} \cup A'$, $B_{\text{elem}} = A_{\text{elem}}$ and $i^{\mathcal{B}} = i^{\mathcal{A}}$ for each index-variable $i \in V_{\text{index}}$ and $e^{\mathcal{B}} = e^{\mathcal{A}}$ for each elem-variable $e \in V_{\text{elem}}$. In order to define $\mathcal{B}$ over the array-variables, observe that by definition of the semantics the index set is non-empty. Thus, we may fix some index $i_0 \in A_{\text{index}}$, and for each array-variable $a \in V_{\text{array}}$, we let

$$a^{\mathcal{B}}(i) = \begin{cases} a^{\mathcal{A}}(i), & \text{if } i \in A_{\text{index}} \\ a^{\mathcal{A}}(i_0), & \text{otherwise} \end{cases}$$

By construction, $\mathcal{B}$ is a T_{CAL}-interpretation such that $|B_{\text{elem}}| = |A_{\text{elem}}|$ and $|B_{\text{index}}| = \kappa$. Next, we show that $\mathcal{B}$ satisfies all literals in Γ.

- Literals of the form $R(a_1, \ldots, a_n)$: Let $i \in B_{\text{index}}$.
  If $i \in A_{\text{index}}$ then $R(a_1^{\mathcal{B}}(i), \ldots, a_n^{\mathcal{B}}(i)) = R(a_1^{\mathcal{A}}(i), \ldots, a_n^{\mathcal{A}}(i))$.
  If $i \notin A_{\text{index}}$ then $R(a_1^{\mathcal{B}}(i), \ldots, a_1^{\mathcal{B}}(i)) = R(a_1^{\mathcal{A}}(i_0), \ldots, a_n^{\mathcal{A}}(i_0))$.
  Since we assume that $\mathcal{A} \models R(a_1, \ldots, a_n)$, it follows that $\mathcal{B} \models R(a_1, \ldots, a_n)$.
- Literals of the form $\neg R(a_1, \ldots, a_n)$:
  Since $\neg R(a_1^{\mathcal{A}}, \ldots, a_n^{\mathcal{A}})$, there exists $i \in A_{\text{index}}$ such that $\neg R(a_1^{\mathcal{A}}(i), \ldots, a_n^{\mathcal{A}}(i))$.
  It follows that $\neg R(a_1^{\mathcal{B}}(i), \ldots, a_n^{\mathcal{B}}(i))$, which implies $\neg R(a_1^{\mathcal{B}}, \ldots, a_n^{\mathcal{B}})$.
- Literals of the form $e = a[i]$:

$$e^{\mathcal{B}} = e^{\mathcal{A}} = [a[i]]^{\mathcal{A}} = a^{\mathcal{A}}\left(i^{\mathcal{A}}\right) = a^{\mathcal{B}}\left(i^{\mathcal{B}}\right) \quad \text{since } i^{\mathcal{A}} \in A_{\text{index}}$$

- Literals of the form $a = \text{write}(b, i, e)$:
  Let $j \in B_{\text{index}}$.
  If $j = i^{\mathcal{B}}$ then $a^{\mathcal{B}}\left(i^{\mathcal{B}}\right) = a^{\mathcal{A}}\left(i^{\mathcal{A}}\right) = e^{\mathcal{A}} = e^{\mathcal{B}}$.
  If $j \in A_{\text{index}}$ then $a^{\mathcal{B}}(j) = a^{\mathcal{A}}(j) = b^{\mathcal{A}}(j) = b^{\mathcal{B}}(j)$.
  If $j \notin A_{\text{index}}$ and $i_0 \neq i^{\mathcal{B}}$ then $a^{\mathcal{B}}(j) = a^{\mathcal{A}}(i_0) = b^{\mathcal{B}}(j)$.
  If $j \notin A_{\text{index}}$ and $i_0 = i^{\mathcal{B}}$ then $a^{\mathcal{B}}(j) = a^{\mathcal{A}}(i_0) = e^{\mathcal{A}} = b^{\mathcal{A}}(i_0) = b^{\mathcal{B}}(j)$.

Proposition 4. *Let $\mathcal{A}$ be a T_{CAL}-interpretation satisfying a conjunction Γ of flat Σ_{CAL}-literals. Then there exists a T_{CAL}-interpretation $\mathcal{B}$ satisfying Γ such that $|B_{index}| = |A_{index}|$ and $|B_{elem}| = \kappa$, for each $\kappa > |A_{elem}|$.*

Proof. Similar to the proof of Proposition 3, we construct an interpretation on the variables by adding new points to the elements' carrier. In this case, the interpretation of the array variables is as in the original model. The new structure satisfies all the literals since the new values do not occur in the interpretation of the literals.

Corollary 1 (Smoothness). *The theory T_{CAL} is smooth w.r.t. $\{elem, index\}$.*

4.2 Finite Witnessability

A witness function $\text{witness}_{\text{CAL}}$ for the theory T_{CAL} can be defined as follows. Without loss of generality, let Γ be a conjunction of flat Σ_{CAL}-literals such that $\text{vars}_{\text{index}}(\Gamma) \neq \emptyset$ and $\text{vars}_{\text{elem}}(\Gamma) \neq \emptyset$. We let $\text{witness}_{\text{CAL}}(\Gamma)$ be the result of applying to Γ the following transformation:

1. Replace each literal of the form $\neg R(a_1, \ldots, a_n)$ in Γ with a literal of the form $\neg R(a_1[i], \ldots, a_n[i])$, where i is a fresh index-variable.
2. For each array index i and each array variable a used in the formula, add formulas $a[i] = e_i$ where e_i is a fresh element variable.
3. Substitute other occurrences of the terms $a[i]$ by the element variable e_i introduced in Step 2 (to ensure that the shape of the literals is as in Proposition 5).

Remark 1. Let Γ be a conjunction of flat Σ_{CAL}-literals, let $\Delta = \text{witness}_{\text{CAL}}(\Gamma)$, and let $\bar{v} = \text{vars}(\Delta) \setminus \text{vars}(\Gamma)$. Then Γ and $(\exists \bar{v})\Delta$ are T_{CAL}-equivalent.

Proposition 5. *Let Γ be a conjunction of flat Σ_{CAL}-literals such that*

- $\text{vars}_{index}(\Gamma) \neq \emptyset$ and $\text{vars}_{elem}(\Gamma) \neq \emptyset$, and
- not containing any literal of the form $\neg R(a_1, \ldots, a_n)$.
- where each array read occurs in an equality with an element variable.

Then the following are equivalent:

1. Γ is T_{CAL}-satisfiable.
2. There exists a T_{CAL}- interpretation $\mathcal{A}$ satisfying Γ such that

$$A_{index} = [\text{vars}_{index}(\Gamma)]^{\mathcal{A}} \text{ and } A_{elem} = [\text{vars}_{elem}(\Gamma)]^{\mathcal{A}}$$

Proof. $(2 \Rightarrow 1)$. Immediate.

$(1 \Rightarrow 2)$. Let $V_\sigma = \text{vars}_\sigma(\Gamma)$, for $\sigma \in \{elem, index, array\}$. Since Γ is T_{CAL}-satisfiable, there exists a T_{CAL}-interpretation $\mathcal{B}$ satisfying Γ. Let $\mathcal{A}$ be the T_{CAL}-interpretation over $V_{elem} \cup V_{index} \cup V_{array}$ constructed as follows.

Let $A_{index} = V_{index}^{\mathcal{B}}$, $A_{elem} = V_{elem}^{\mathcal{B}}$, $i^{\mathcal{A}} = i^{\mathcal{B}}$, for each index-variable $i \in V_{index}$, $e^{\mathcal{A}} = e^{\mathcal{B}}$ for each element variable $e \in V_{elem}$ and $k^{\mathcal{A}} = k^{\mathcal{B}}$ for each integer variable $k \in V_{int}$. For each $a \in V_{array}$ and $i \in V_{index}$, let $a^{\mathcal{A}}(i^{\mathcal{A}}) = a^{\mathcal{B}}(i^{\mathcal{B}}) \in A_{elem}$.

Note that $\mathcal{A}$ is a well-defined T_{CAL}-interpretation, and that $A_\sigma = [\text{vars}_\sigma(\Gamma)]^{\mathcal{A}}$, for $\sigma \in \{index, elem\}$. Next, we show that $\mathcal{A}$ satisfies all literals in Γ.

- Literals of the form $R(a_1, \ldots, a_n)$: for $i \in A_{index}$,

$$R(a_1^{\mathcal{A}}(i^{\mathcal{A}}), \ldots, a_n^{\mathcal{A}}(i^{\mathcal{A}})) = R(a_1^{\mathcal{B}}(i^{\mathcal{B}}), \ldots, a_n^{\mathcal{B}}(i^{\mathcal{B}}))$$

- Literals of the form $e = a[i]$: $e^{\mathcal{A}} = e^{\mathcal{B}} = [a[i]]^{\mathcal{B}} = a^{\mathcal{B}}(i^{\mathcal{B}}) = a^{\mathcal{A}}(i^{\mathcal{A}})$
- Literals of the form $a = write(b, i, e)$:
  - If $j = i^{\mathcal{A}}$ then $a^{\mathcal{A}}(i^{\mathcal{A}}) = b^{\mathcal{B}}(i^{\mathcal{B}}) = e^{\mathcal{B}} = e^{\mathcal{A}}$.
  - If $j \in A_{index} \setminus \{i^{\mathcal{A}}\}$ then $a^{\mathcal{A}}(j^{\mathcal{A}}) = a^{\mathcal{B}}(j^{\mathcal{B}}) = b^{\mathcal{B}}(j^{\mathcal{B}}) = b^{\mathcal{A}}(j^{\mathcal{A}})$.

Proposition 6 (Additivity). T_{CAL} is additively finitely witnessable w.r.t. any nonempty set of sorts $S \subseteq \{elem, index\}$.

Proof. It follows directly from the definition of additivity. We show that $f = \text{witness}_{CAL}(\Gamma)$ is S-additive. To this end, let ϕ, φ be two quantifier-free formulas over CAL's signature such that φ is a conjunction of flat literals where every term is a variable whose sort is in S. Then $f(f(\phi) \wedge \varphi)$ and $f(\phi) \wedge \varphi$

- are T_{CAL}- equivalent: $f(f(\phi) \wedge \varphi) = f(f(\phi)) \wedge f(\varphi) = f(\phi) \wedge \varphi$.
- have the same set of S-sorted variables.

Proposition 7 (Finite witnessability). The theory T_{CAL} is additively finite witnessable with respect to $\{elem, index\}$.

Proof. By Proposition 2 , Remark 1, and the additivity of witness_{CAL}.

By Corollary 1 and Proposition 7, we get:

Theorem 1 (Politeness). The theory T_{CAL} is strongly polite with respect to $\{elem, index\}$.

5 Politeness of Sets with Cardinalities

We will now discuss the politeness of theories of sets that use cardinality constraints. Several such theories exist in the literature, including Zarba's fragment [22], Kunčak-Rinard's fragment [8] and Bansal et al.'s fragment [2,3].

The fragment of [8] is not polite with respect to the index sort. This fragment includes syntax to denote the universe set $\mathcal{U}$, to denote the absolute complement of a set S, i.e. the set $\mathcal{U} \setminus S$ and an integer constant denoting the cardinality of $\mathcal{U}$. A formula of the form $|\mathcal{U}| = 3$ immediately shows that this theory is not smooth with respect to the index sort.

We will show that the theories [2,3,22] are polite with respect to the index sort. For smoothness, observe that the complement of the set variables in a formula cannot be used [2,3,22] (thus the definition of a "place" in [22] requiring at least one output equal to one). For finite witnessability, observe that one needs to introduce as many index variables as indicated by the minimal size of the universe. [2,3] left the politeness of this theory for future work.

5.1 Smoothness

Proposition 8. *Let $\mathcal{A}$ be a T_Z-interpretation satisfying a conjunction Γ of flat Σ_Z-literals. Then there exists a T_Z-interpretation $\mathcal{B}$ satisfying Γ such that $|\mathcal{B}_{index}| = \kappa$, for each $\kappa > |\mathcal{A}_{index}|$.*

Proof. Let $V_\sigma = \text{vars}_\sigma(\Gamma)$, for $\sigma \in \{\text{index, set, int}\}$. Construct a T_Z-interpretation $\mathcal{B}$ over $V_{\text{index}} \cup V_{\text{set}} \cup V_{\text{int}}$ as follows. Fix a set A' such that $|A_{\text{index}} \cup A'| = \kappa$, let $B_{\text{index}} = A_{\text{index}} \cup A'$, $i^\mathcal{B} = i^\mathcal{A}$, for each index-variable $i \in V_{\text{index}}$, $x^\mathcal{B} = x^\mathcal{A}$, for each set-variable $x \in V_{\text{set}}$ and $s^\mathcal{B} = s^\mathcal{A}$, for each integer variable $s \in V_{\text{int}}$. By construction $\mathcal{B}$ is a T_Z-interpretation such that $|B_{\text{index}}| = \kappa$. Moreover, $\mathcal{B}$ satisfies all literals in Γ, since the newly introduced indices in A' belong to the complement of the union of all the interpretations of the set variables of the formula, which is unconstrained as we are using the relative complement of sets. ∎

Corollary 2 (Smoothness). *The theory T_Z is smooth with respect to index.*

5.2 Finite Witnessability

Witness Function. A witness function witness_Z for the theory T_Z can be defined as follows. Without loss of generality, let Γ be a conjunction of flat Σ_Z-literals such that $\text{vars}_{index}(\Gamma) \neq \emptyset$. $\text{witness}_Z(\Gamma)$ outputs the conjunction of Γ and the result of the following transformation.

1. Replace index variables i with singleton sets $\{i\}$ and impose $|\{i\}| = 1$.
2. Replace formulas $i \in x$ by $\{i\} \cap x = \{i\}$ and $i \notin x$ by $\{i\} \cap x = \emptyset$.
3. Replace $i_1 = i_2$ by $\{i_1\} = \{i_2\}$ and $i_1 \neq i_2$ by $\{i_1\} \neq \{i_2\}$.
4. Replace $x = y$ by $x \subseteq y \wedge y \subseteq x$ and $x \subseteq y$ by $|x \setminus y| = 0$.
5. Replace $x \neq y$ by $|x \setminus y \cup y \setminus x| > 0$ and $x \not\subseteq y$ by $|x \setminus y| > 0$.

6. We set up a linear integer programming problem obtained from applying the Venn region decomposition for each Boolean algebra expression B_i appearing in an equation of the form $|B_i| = k$. Doing this for every such equation, we get a formula

$$G \wedge \bigwedge_{j=1}^{2^n} l_{\beta_j} \geq 0 \wedge \bigwedge_{i=0}^{p} \sum_{j=1}^{2^n} [\![B_i]\!]_{\beta_j} \cdot l_{\beta_j} = k_i$$

where G is the quantifier-free Presburger arithmetic formula resulting from the original by substituting each occurrence of an expression $|B_i|$ by k_i, each bit-number β_j viewed as a bit-string in $\{0,1\}^n$ represents the *elementary* Venn region $E_{\beta_j} = S_1^{\beta_j(1)} \cap \ldots \cap S_n^{\beta_j(n)}$ over the set variables $S_1, \ldots, S_n$ occurring in the formula (where $S^0 := S^c$ and $S^1 := S$), l_{β_j} represents the cardinality of E_{β_j} and $[\![B_i]\!]_{\beta_j}$ equals one when $E_{\beta_j} \subseteq B_i$ and zero otherwise.

7. The linear integer program minimises the linear function $\sum_{j=0}^{2^n-1} l_{\beta_j}$.

8. We solve the linear integer program. If there is no solution, we output the formula $\bot$. Otherwise, let s be the minimal solution for the linear integer program. For each family of cardinalities l_{β_j} of the elementary Venn regions such that $s = \sum_{j=0}^{2^n-1} l_{\beta_j}$, we check the system of cardinality constraints together with the requirement that the set E_{β_j} has cardinality at least l_{β_j} is satisfiable. For each such family, we build the following formula.

   – We introduce for each elementary Venn region E_{β_j}, l_{β_j} index variables g and require that they are mutually distinct with atoms of the form $g_1 \neq g_2$ and that they belong to E_{β_j}, with atoms of the form $g \in E_{\beta_j}$.
   – Rewrite the terms $g \in E_{(0,\ldots,0)}$ into $g \notin S_1 \cup \ldots \cup S_n$ and absolute complements S^c as relative complements $(S_1 \cup \ldots \cup S_n) \setminus S$, so that the resulting formula contains no absolute complements (not supported in the fragment of [22]).

9. We output the disjunction of the formulas constructed in the previous step.

Proposition 9. *Let Γ be a conjunction of flat Σ_Z-literals, let $\Delta = witness_Z(\Gamma)$, and let $\bar{v} = \text{vars}(\Delta) \setminus \text{vars}(\Gamma)$. Then Γ and $(\exists \bar{v}) \Delta$ are T_Z-equivalent.*

Proof. Indeed, if $\mathcal{A}$ is a model of Γ then it contains at least s elements. Moreover, any such collection of s elements satisfies the disjunction introduced in Step 9. Thus, $\mathcal{A}$ satisfies $(\exists \bar{v}) \Delta$. The converse direction is trivial since Γ is part of Δ. $\qquad \blacksquare$

Proposition 10. *Let Γ be a conjunction of flat Σ_Z-literals with $\text{vars}_{index}(\Gamma) \neq \emptyset$. If Δ is T_Z-satisfiable then there exists a T_Z-interpretation $\mathcal{A}$ satisfying Δ such that $\mathcal{A}_{index} = [\text{vars}_{index}(\Gamma)]^{\mathcal{A}}$.*

Proof. If Δ is T_Z-satisfiable then it is also satisfied by a structure $\mathcal{A}$ of minimal index-set size s. Since Δ requires the existence of s distinct indices, it follows that the interpretations of the indices of the formula yield the carrier set of the index sort in $\mathcal{A}$. $\qquad \blacksquare$

We next show that the witness function as given is not additive.

Example 1. On input $i_1 \in S \wedge i_2 \in S$, the witness procedure would output $i_1 \in S \wedge i_2 \in S \wedge g \in S$. Now, if we take $i_1 \neq i_2$ as a second formula in the definition of additivity. Then the output of the witness function applied to the formula $i_1 \in S \wedge i_2 \in S \wedge g \in S \wedge i_1 \neq i_2$ is $i_1 \in S \wedge i_2 \in S \wedge g_1 \in S \wedge g_2 \in S \wedge i_1 \neq i_2 \wedge g_1 \neq g_2$, which is not equivalent to $i_1 \in S \wedge i_2 \in S \wedge g \in S$.

We next give an additive modification of the witness function.

Proposition 11 (Additivity). *T_Z is additively finitely witnessable w.r.t. index.*

Proof. Consider the function f defined as follows for any input formula ϕ:

- if ϕ is not arranged then output the disjunction of applying f to $arr \wedge \phi$ for each arrangement arr of the index variables in ϕ.
- if ϕ is a T_Z-satisfiable formula of the form $\phi' \wedge \varphi$, where ϕ' is a witness formula of some arranged input and φ is a conjunction of literals between *index* variables such that $\mathrm{vars}_{index}(\varphi) \subseteq \mathrm{vars}_{index}(\phi')$, then $f(\phi) = \phi$;
- if ϕ is a T_Z-satisfiable formula of the form $\phi' \wedge \varphi'$, where φ' is a conjunction of literals between *index* variables x, y such that $x \notin \mathrm{vars}_{index}(\phi')$ or $y \notin \mathrm{vars}_{index}(\phi')$, then $f(\phi) = f(\phi') \wedge \varphi'$;
- otherwise, $f(\phi) = \mathrm{witness}_Z(\phi)$.

According to this definition of f and using φ and φ' as introduced above, we have

$$f(f(\phi) \wedge \varphi \wedge \varphi') = f(f(\phi) \wedge \varphi) \wedge \varphi' = f(\phi) \wedge \varphi \wedge \varphi'$$

Consequently, f is *index*-additive.

Proposition 12 (Finite witnessability). *The theory T_Z is additively finitely witnessable with respect to the sort index.*

Proof. By Propositions 2, 9, 10, and 11.

By Corollary 2 and Proposition 12, we get:

Theorem 2 (Politeness). *The theory T_Z is strongly polite with respect to the sort index.*

6   Politeness for Theories with Set Interpretations

We will now discuss the politeness of theories of sets that use cardinality constraints and set interpretations. A technical condition is required in order to show smoothness with respect to the sort index. This condition allows us to enlarge theories' models in the Venn region determined by the complement of all set variables. We focus on the satisfiability problem of a subtheory of T_F that fixes the formulas under set interpretations, is closed under propositional operations and satisfies the technical condition. The polite combination method is applicable to this subtheory.

Definition 3. *If $\varphi_1, \ldots, \varphi_n$ are the formulas under set interpretations in the T_F-formula φ, $cl(\varphi_1, \ldots, \varphi_n)$ denotes the sentence $\exists \overline{v}. \bigwedge_{i=1}^{n} \neg \varphi_i(\overline{v}, \overline{c})$. Assuming that $cl(\varphi_1, \ldots, \varphi_n)$ is T_F-satisfiable, the theory $T_F(\varphi_1, \ldots, \varphi_n)$ is the set of Σ_F-sentences φ such that the formulas under set interpretations in φ are in $\varphi_1, \ldots, \varphi_n$, and $T_F \cup \{cl(\varphi_1, \ldots, \varphi_n)\} \models \varphi$.*

6.1   Smoothness

Proposition 13. *Let $\mathcal{A}$ be a T_F-interpretation satisfying a conjunction Γ of flat Σ_F-literals in $T_F(\varphi_1, \ldots, \varphi_n)$. Then there exists a T_F-interpretation $\mathcal{B}$ satisfying Γ such that $|\mathcal{B}_{elem}| = |\mathcal{A}_{elem}|$ and $|\mathcal{B}_{index}| = \kappa$, for each cardinal number $\kappa > |\mathcal{A}_{index}|$.*

Proof. Let $V_\sigma = \text{vars}_\sigma(\Gamma)$, for $\sigma \in \{\text{elem}, \text{index}, \text{array}, \text{set}, \text{int}\}$. We construct a T_F-interpretation $\mathcal{B}$ over $V_{\text{elem}} \cup V_{\text{index}} \cup V_{\text{array}} \cup V_{\text{set}} \cup V_{\text{int}}$ as follows. Fix a set A' such that $| A_{\text{index}} \cup A' | = \kappa$, and let $B_{\text{index}} = A_{\text{index}} \cup A'$, $B_{\text{elem}} = A_{\text{elem}}$ and $i^{\mathcal{B}} = i^{\mathcal{A}}$ for each index-variable $i \in V_{\text{index}}$, $e^{\mathcal{B}} = e^{\mathcal{A}}$ for each elem-variable $e \in V_{\text{elem}}$, $s^{\mathcal{B}} = s^{\mathcal{A}}$ for each set-variable $s \in V_{\text{set}}$ and $k^{\mathcal{B}} = k^{\mathcal{A}}$ for each integer-variable $k \in V_{\text{int}}$.

In order to define $\mathcal{B}$ over the array-variables, observe that by Definition 3, if we list all the m formulas $\varphi_j(\bar{a}[i], \bar{c})$ occurring in set interpretations in Γ, then the formula $\exists \bar{v}. \bigwedge_{j=1}^n \neg\varphi_j(\bar{v}, \bar{c})$ is true. This gives us a value $\bar{v}_0$ such that the formula $\bigwedge_{j=1}^n \neg\varphi_j(\bar{v}_0, \bar{c})$ is true. Observe that we may define as $\bar{v}_0$ the set of values at the newly introduced indices. This is because the formula only restricts indices values on the union of set interpretations. Thus, for each array-variable $a \in V_{\text{array}}$, we let

$$a^{\mathcal{B}}(i) = \begin{cases} a^{\mathcal{A}}(i) & \text{if } i \in A_{\text{index}} \\ (\bar{v}_0)_j & \text{where } a = (\bar{a})_j \end{cases}$$

By construction, $\mathcal{B}$ is a T_F-interpretation such that $|B_{\text{elem}}| = |A_{\text{elem}}|$ and $|B_{\text{index}}| = \kappa$. Next, we show that $\mathcal{B}$ satisfies all literals in Γ.

- Literals of the form $R(e_1, \ldots, e_n)$, $R(i_1, \ldots, i_n)$ or $R(k_1, \ldots, k_n)$: immediate.
- Literals of the form $|S| = k$: immediate by definition of $\mathcal{B}$.
- Literals of the form $S = \{i \mid \varphi(\bar{a}[i], \bar{c})\}$: Let $i \in B_{\text{index}}$.
  If $i \in A_{\text{index}}$ then $\varphi(a_1^{\mathcal{B}}(i), \ldots, a_n^{\mathcal{B}}(i)) = \varphi(a_1^{\mathcal{A}}(i), \ldots, a_n^{\mathcal{A}}(i))$.
  If $i \notin A_{\text{index}}$ then $\varphi(a_1^{\mathcal{B}}(i), \ldots, a_n^{\mathcal{B}}(i)) = \varphi((\bar{v}_0)_1(i), \ldots, (\bar{v}_0)_n(i)) = \bot$.
  Since $\mathcal{A} \models S = \{i \mid \varphi(\bar{a}[i], \bar{c})\}$, $S^{\mathcal{A}} = S^{\mathcal{B}}$ and we have that $\{i \mid \varphi(\bar{a}[i], \bar{c})\}^{\mathcal{A}} = \{i \mid \varphi(\bar{a}[i], \bar{c})\}^{\mathcal{B}}$, it follows that $\mathcal{B} \models S = \{i \mid \varphi(\bar{a}[i], \bar{c})\}$.
- Literals of the form $e = a[i]$:

$$e^{\mathcal{B}} = e^{\mathcal{A}} = [a[i]]^{\mathcal{A}} = a^{\mathcal{A}}(i^{\mathcal{A}}) = a^{\mathcal{B}}(i^{\mathcal{B}}) \qquad \text{since } i^{\mathcal{A}} \in A_{\text{index}}$$

$\square$

Proposition 14. *Let $\mathcal{A}$ be a T_F-interpretation satisfying a conjunction Γ of flat Σ_F-literals. Then there exists a T_F-interpretation $\mathcal{B}$ satisfying Γ such that $|B_{index}| = |A_{index}|$ and $|B_{elem}| = \kappa$, for each $\kappa > |A_{elem}|$.*

Proof. Similar to the proof of Proposition 4, we construct an interpretation on the variables by adding new points to the elements' carrier. The interpretation of the array variables is as in the original model. The new structure satisfies all the literals since the new values do not occur in the interpretation of the literals.

Corollary 3 (Smoothness).

- T_F *is smooth w.r.t. elem.*
- $T_F(\varphi_1, \ldots, \varphi_n)$ *is smooth w.r.t.* $\{elem, index\}$.

Proof. By Propositions 1, 13, and 14.

6.2   Finite Witnessability

Witness Function. A witness function $witness_F$ for the theory T_F can be defined as follows. Without loss of generality, let Γ be a conjunction of flat Σ_F-literals such that $vars_{elem}(\Gamma) \neq \emptyset$ and $vars_{index}(\Gamma) \neq \emptyset$. $witness_F(\Gamma)$ outputs the conjunction of Γ and the result of the following transformation.

1–7. These steps are analogous to the ones for the theory of sets with cardinalities.
8. Each set variable S in Γ may be interpreted, i.e. Γ contains an equation of the form $S = \{i \mid \varphi(\bar{a}[i], \bar{c})\}$, or uninterpreted, if no such equation exists. To each elementary Venn region E_{β_j} we associate a formula $\varphi^{\beta_j} := \exists \bar{v}. \bigwedge_{i=1}^{n} \varphi^{\beta_j(i)}(\bar{v}, \bar{c})$, where $\varphi^{\beta_j(i)}$ is the formula in the set interpretation of S_i if $\beta_j(i) = 1$, its negation if $\beta_j(i) = 0$ or $\top$ if S_i is uninterpreted. For each $\beta_j \in \{0, 1\}^n$, we add the constraint $l_{\beta_j} = 0$ if φ^{β_j} is unsatisfiable.
9. We solve the linear integer program. If there is no solution, we output the formula $\bot$. Otherwise, let s be the minimal solution for the linear integer program. For each family of cardinalities l_{β_j} of the elementary Venn regions such that $s = \sum_{j=0}^{2^n-1} l_{\beta_j}$, we check the system of cardinality constraints together with the requirement that the set E_{β_j} has cardinality at least l_{β_j} is satisfiable. For each such family, we build the following formula.
   - We introduce for each elementary Venn region E_{β_j}, l_{β_j} index variables i and require that they are mutually distinct with atoms of the form $i_1 \neq i_2$ and that they belong to E_{β_j}, with atoms of the form $i \in E_{\beta_j}$.
   - Rewrite the terms $i \in E_{(0,\ldots,0)}$ into $i \notin S_1 \cup \ldots \cup S_n$ and absolute complements S^c as relative complements $(S_1 \cup \ldots \cup S_n) \setminus S$, so that the resulting formula contains no absolute complements.
10. We output the disjunction of the formulas constructed in the previous step.
11. For each array index i and each array variable a used in the constructed formulas, add formulas $a[i] = e_i$ where e_i is a fresh element variable.

Proposition 15. *Let* Γ *be a conjunction of flat* Σ_F-literals, let $\Delta = witness_F(\Gamma)$, and let $\bar{v} = vars(\Delta) \setminus vars(\Gamma)$. *Then* Γ *and* $(\exists \bar{v})\Delta$ *are* T_F-equivalent.

Proof. Indeed, if $\mathcal{A}$ is a model of Γ then it contains at least n elements. Moreover, there will be some distribution of these s elements over the Venn diagram satisfying the disjunction introduced in Step 10 Thus, $\mathcal{A}$ satisfies $(\exists \bar{v})\Delta$. The converse direction is trivial since Γ is part of Δ.

Proposition 16. *Let Γ be a conjunction of flat Σ_F-literals such that* $\text{vars}_{elem}(\Gamma) \neq \emptyset$ *and* $\text{vars}_{index}(\Gamma) \neq \emptyset$. *If Δ is T_F-satisfiable then there exists a T_F-interpretation $\mathcal{A}$ satisfying Δ such that $A_{index} = [\text{vars}_{index}(\Gamma)]^{\mathcal{A}}$ and $A_{elem} = [\text{vars}_{elem}(\Gamma)]^{\mathcal{A}}$*

Proof. If Δ is T_F-satisfiable then it is also satisfied by a structure $\mathcal{A}$ of minimal index-set size s. Since Δ requires the existence of s distinct indices, it follows that the interpretations of the index variables yield the carrier set of the index sort in $\mathcal{A}$. Since all the array elements referenced by the indices are also in the formula, it follows that the interpretations of the element variables in the formula yield the carrier set of the element sort in $\mathcal{A}$.

Proposition 17 (Additivity). *T_F is additively finitely witnessable w.r.t. $\{elem, index\}$.*

Proof The proof is analogous to the one given in Proposition 11.

Proposition 18 (Finite witnessability). *The theory T_F is additively finitely witnessable with respect to $\{elem, index\}$.*

Proof. By Proposition 2, 15, 16 and 17.

By Corollary 3, Proposition 18, we get:

Theorem 3 (Politeness).

- T_F is strongly polite with respect to elem.
- $T_F(\varphi_1, \ldots, \varphi_n)$ is strongly polite w.r.t. $\{elem, index\}$.

7   Conclusion

We investigated the politeness of several theories of data structures introduced after the original work on the subject [14]. We proved that extending the quantifier-free theory of arrays with component-wise relations preserves politeness with respect to the index and element sorts. We showed the politeness properties for a variant of the theory of sets with cardinalities [22], reusing the idea of computing the minimal size of the universe for the finite witness function. [2] left the politeness of this theory for future work. We finally showed the politeness with respect to the index and element sorts of the simple flat array fragment [5]. When fixing the formulas in the set interpretations. An interesting research direction would be to compare our politeness results with the handling of finite structures in [11].

References

1. Alberti, F., Ghilardi, S., Pagani, E.: Cardinality constraints for arrays (decidability results and applications). Formal Methods Syst. Design **51**(3), 545–574 (2017). https://doi.org/10.1007/s10703-017-0279-6
2. Bansal, K., Barrett, C., Reynolds, A., Tinelli, C.: Reasoning with finite sets and cardinality constraints in SMT. Log. Methods Comput. Sci. **14**(4) (2018). https://doi.org/10.23638/LMCS-14(4:12)2018
3. Bansal, K., Reynolds, A., Barrett, C., Tinelli, C.: A new decision procedure for finite sets and cardinality constraints in SMT. In: Olivetti, N., Tiwari, A. (eds.) IJCAR 2016. LNCS (LNAI), vol. 9706, pp. 82–98. Springer, Cham (2016). https://doi.org/10.1007/978-3-319-40229-1_7
4. Feferman, S., Vaught, R.: The first order properties of products of algebraic systems. Fundam. Math. **47**(1), 57–103 (1959)
5. Ghilardi, S., Pagani, E.: Higher-order quantifier elimination, counter simulations and fault-tolerant systems. J. Autom. Reason. **65**(3), 425–460 (2020). https://doi.org/10.1007/s10817-020-09578-5
6. Hodges, W.: Model Theory. Encyclopedia of Mathematics and its Applications. Cambridge University Press, Cambridge (1993)
7. Jovanović, D., Barrett, C.: Polite theories revisited. In: Fermüller, C.G., Voronkov, A. (eds.) LPAR 2010. LNCS, vol. 6397, pp. 402–416. Springer, Heidelberg (2010). https://doi.org/10.1007/978-3-642-16242-8_29
8. Kuncak, V., Rinard, M.: Towards efficient satisfiability checking for Boolean algebra with Presburger arithmetic. In: Pfenning, F. (ed.) CADE 2007. LNCS (LNAI), vol. 4603, pp. 215–230. Springer, Heidelberg (2007). https://doi.org/10.1007/978-3-540-73595-3_15
9. Mostowski, A.: On direct products of theories. J. Symb. Log. **17**(1), 1–31 (1952). https://doi.org/10.2307/2267454
10. de Moura, L., Bjorner, N.: Generalized, efficient array decision procedures. In: 2009 Formal Methods in Computer-Aided Design, pp. 45–52. IEEE, Austin (2009). https://doi.org/10.1109/FMCAD.2009.5351142
11. de Moura, L., Bjørner, N.: Model-based theory combination. Electron. Notes Theor. Comput. Sci. **198**(2), 37–49 (2008). https://doi.org/10.1016/j.entcs.2008.04.079
12. Nelson, G., Oppen, D.C.: Simplification by cooperating decision procedures. ACM Trans. Program. Lang. Syst. **1**(2), 245–257 (1979). https://doi.org/10.1145/357073.357079
13. Piskac, R., Kuncak, V.: Decision procedures for multisets with cardinality constraints. In: Logozzo, F., Peled, D.A., Zuck, L.D. (eds.) VMCAI 2008. LNCS, vol. 4905, pp. 218–232. Springer, Heidelberg (2008). https://doi.org/10.1007/978-3-540-78163-9_20
14. Ranise, S., Ringeissen, C., Zarba, C.G.: Combining data structures with nonstably infinite theories using many-sorted logic. In: Gramlich, B. (ed.) FroCoS 2005. LNCS (LNAI), vol. 3717, pp. 48–64. Springer, Heidelberg (2005). https://doi.org/10.1007/11559306_3
15. Ranise, S., Ringeissen, C., Zarba, C.G.: Combining data structures with nonstably infinite theories using many-sorted logic. Rapport de recherche 5678, INRIA (2005)
16. Raya, R., Kunčak, V.: NP satisfiability for arrays as powers. In: Finkbeiner, B., Wies, T. (eds.) VMCAI 2022. LNCS, vol. 13182, pp. 301–318. Springer, Cham (2022). https://doi.org/10.1007/978-3-030-94583-1_15

17. Raya, R., Kunčak, V.: Succinct ordering and aggregation constraints in algebraic array theories. J. Log. Algebraic Methods Program. **140**, 100978 (2024). https://doi.org/10.1016/j.jlamp.2024.100978
18. Sheng, Y., et al.: Reasoning about vectors using an SMT theory of sequences. In: Blanchette, J., Kovács, L., Pattinson, D. (eds.) IJCAR 2022. LNCS, vol. 13385, pp. 125–143. Springer, Cham (2022). https://doi.org/10.1007/978-3-031-10769-6_9
19. Sheng, Y., Zohar, Y., Ringeissen, C., Lange, J., Fontaine, P., Barrett, C.: Polite combination of algebraic datatypes. J. Autom. Reason. **66**(3), 331–355 (2022). https://doi.org/10.1007/s10817-022-09625-3
20. Stump, A., Barrett, C., Dill, D., Levitt, J.: A decision procedure for an extensional theory of arrays. In: Proceedings 16th Annual IEEE Symposium on Logic in Computer Science, pp. 29–37. IEEE Computer Society, Boston (2001). https://doi.org/10.1109/LICS.2001.932480
21. Wies, T., Piskac, R., Kuncak, V.: Combining theories with shared set operations. In: Ghilardi, S., Sebastiani, R. (eds.) FroCoS 2009. LNCS (LNAI), vol. 5749, pp. 366–382. Springer, Heidelberg (2009). https://doi.org/10.1007/978-3-642-04222-5_23
22. Zarba, C.G.: Combining sets with cardinals. J. Autom. Reason. **34**(1), 1–29 (2005). https://doi.org/10.1007/s10817-005-3075-8

Number Theory Combination: Natural Density and SMT

Guilherme V. Toledo[✉] and Yoni Zohar

Bar-Ilan University, Ramat Gan, Israel
guivtoledo@gmail.com

Abstract. The study of theory combination in Satisfiability Modulo Theories (SMT) involves various model theoretic properties (e.g., stable infiniteness, smoothness, etc.). We show that such properties can be partly captured by the natural density of the spectrum of the studied theories, which is the set of sizes of their finite models. This enriches the toolbox of the theory combination researcher, by providing new tools to determine the possibility of combining theories. It also reveals interesting and surprising connections between theory combination and number theory.

1 Introduction

Imagine this: you are a researcher in Satisfiability Modulo Theories (SMT) [2], studying a theory $\mathcal{T}$, which is the combination of theories $\mathcal{T}_1$ and $\mathcal{T}_2$ (in the same way that, say, the theory of lists of integers is the combination of the theories of lists and integers). Given algorithms for $\mathcal{T}_1$ and $\mathcal{T}_2$, you can plug them together using theory combination methods, such as Nelson and Oppen's method [12], polite combination [14], shiny combination [20], or gentle combination [8].

But, before you can produce a decision procedure for $\mathcal{T}$, you must test certain properties of $\mathcal{T}_1$ and $\mathcal{T}_2$, or their absence, to determine their applicability to the combination method. For example, using the Nelson-Oppen method requires that both theories are stably infinite, while using the polite combination method requires that one of them is strongly polite. The obvious way of doing so is by directly applying the definitions of these properties, what can be highly non-trivial (for example, to prove a theory is strongly polite, one needs to construct a computable function satisfying an involved set of conditions).

In this paper, we give you alternative tests, based on number theoretic *natural densities* [19], computed over the *spectrum* of the theory [10]. When testing whether a theory admits or lacks a theory combination property, you can now use these tests. We provide examples for cases where this is simpler to do, compared to the direct application of the definitions. Beyond the introduction of such tools, the results of this paper relate number theory and theory combination in surprising and insightful ways. We focus on one-sorted theories, leaving many-sorted ones for future work.

© The Author(s) 2026
R. Thiemann and C. Weidenbach (Eds.): FroCoS 2025, LNAI 15979, pp. 169–187, 2026.
https://doi.org/10.1007/978-3-032-04167-8_10

Section 2 surveys relevant notions. Section 3 contains our main results: sufficient and necessary conditions for theory combination properties, in terms of the natural density, our most involved (and perhaps more interesting) results being found in Sect. 3.2.4 and 3.2.5; we also have in Sect. 3.2.1 important results relating gentleness to politeness, shininess and stable infiniteness. In Sect. 4 we provide generalizations to non-empty signatures. Section 5 summarizes, and gives directions for future research.

Related Work

0-1-*Laws and Densities.* Studies on spectra and densities go back as far as [4,7,9]. While we consider only models of a theory, these results, including the famous 0-1 laws, concern *random models*, that is, any models. 0-1 laws remain powerful for theories with finite axiomatizations (as we can represent their axiomatizations using a conjunction), but here we consider also infinite axiomatizations. Later studies, such as [3,5], considered densities with respect to a theory, or even a (sufficiently well-behaved) class of models, but have not considered properties associated with theory combination. We focus on theories, and on the relationship between their combination properties and the behavior of their density.

Descriptive Complexity. Note that we use slightly different definitions for the spectrum of a theory than those found in descriptive complexity [10]: although our definition of $Spec(\mathcal{T}, \phi)$ is the usual one for the spectrum of a formula relative to a theory, the spectrum of a theory $\mathcal{T}$ is more commonly understood as the map from cardinals to cardinals which, given κ, returns the number of non-isomorphic models of $\mathcal{T}$ of cardinality κ. But for the case of finite cardinalities in the empty signature this map would return either 0 or 1. Then, our definition coincides with taking the pre-image of 1 in the more standard definition.

Theory Combination Properties. The current paper deals with, among other topics, Boolean combinations of theory combination properties (especially in Table 1), something comprehensively researched in [23,25,26]. While those papers study the combinations of properties per se, here we focus on establishing these properties (or lack of) through the analysis of their density.

2   Preliminaries

If X is a set, $|X|$ denotes its cardinality. We denote by $\aleph_0$ the cardinality of $\mathbb{N}$, which for us contains 0; the set $\mathbb{N} \smallsetminus \{0\}$ is denoted by $\mathbb{Z}^+$.

2.1   First-Order Logic

One can find a standard reference in first-order logic in [17]. A first-order *signature* Σ is a pair $(\mathcal{F}_\Sigma, \mathcal{P}_\Sigma)$, where: $\mathcal{F}_\Sigma$ is a countable set of function symbols, each with an arity $n \in \mathbb{N}$; and $\mathcal{P}_\Sigma$ is a countable set of predicate symbols, each with an arity $n \in \mathbb{N}$, containing at least the equality = of arity 2. We denote by Σ_1 the signature with no function or predicate symbols other than =, which is therefore called *empty*. Assuming countably many variables, we define by structural induction *terms*, *literals*, *formulas*, and *sentences* (formulas without free variables) in the usual way. The set of all quantifier-free Σ-formulas is denoted by $QF(\Sigma)$; the set of all variables in φ shall be written as $vars(\varphi)$.

A Σ-*interpretation* $\mathcal{A}$ consists of: a non-empty set $dom(\mathcal{A})$, called the *domain* of $\mathcal{A}$; for each function symbol f of arity n, a function $f^{\mathcal{A}} : dom(\mathcal{A})^n \to dom(\mathcal{A})$; for each predicate symbol P of arity n, a subset $P^{\mathcal{A}}$ of $dom(\mathcal{A})^n$, where $=^{\mathcal{A}}$ is the identity; and, for every variable x, an element $x^{\mathcal{A}}$ of $dom(\mathcal{A})$. The value of a term α in $\mathcal{A}$ is denoted by $\alpha^{\mathcal{A}}$, while for a set of terms Γ we make $\Gamma^{\mathcal{A}} = \{\alpha^{\mathcal{A}} : \alpha \in \Gamma\}$; if $\mathcal{A}$ satisfies the formula φ, we write $\mathcal{A} \vDash \varphi$. Recurrent formulas include those in Fig. 1, that are satisfied by an interpretation $\mathcal{A}$ iff: $dom(\mathcal{A})$ has at least n elements, in the case of $\psi_{\geq n}$; $dom(\mathcal{A})$ has at most n elements, in the case of $\psi_{\leq n}$; and $dom(\mathcal{A})$ has precisely n elements, in the case of $\psi_{=n}$. Notice that $\psi_{\geq n}$ can be defined in terms of $\psi_{\leq n}$, however we explicitly define both for greater clarity.

$$\neq (x_1, \ldots, x_n) = \bigwedge_{i=1}^{n-1} \bigwedge_{j=i+1}^{n} \neg(x_i = x_j) \qquad \psi_{\leq n} = \exists\, x_1, \ldots, x_n.\, \forall\, y.\, \bigvee_{i=1}^{n} y = x_i$$

$$\psi_{\geq n} = \exists\, x_1 \ldots x_n.\, \neq (x_1, \ldots, x_n) \qquad \psi_{=n} = \psi_{\geq n} \wedge \psi_{\leq n}$$

Fig. 1. Cardinality formulas.

A *theory* is the class of all interpretations (thus called $\mathcal{T}$-interpretations, or the models of $\mathcal{T}$) satisfying some set of sentences $Ax(\mathcal{T})$ (which does not need to be computably enumerable), called the *axiomatization* of $\mathcal{T}$. A formula φ is then: ($\mathcal{T}$-)*satisfiable* if there is a ($\mathcal{T}$-)interpretation that satisfies φ; ($\mathcal{T}$-)*equivalent* to a formula ψ if every ($\mathcal{T}$-)interpretation that satisfies one also satisfies the other; and ($\mathcal{T}$-)*valid* if every ($\mathcal{T}$-)interpretation satisfies φ, denoted $\vDash\varphi$ ($\vDash_{\mathcal{T}}\varphi$).

We denote, for $n \leq m$, the set $\{n, \ldots, m\}$ by $[n, m]$; if $n = 0$, we simplify it to $[m]$. Of course, $|[n, m]| = m - n + 1$, and $|[m]| = m + 1$. Furthermore, $A \cap [1, n]$ will be denoted by A_n; we denote $\{|dom(\mathcal{A})| : \mathcal{A}$ is a $\mathcal{T}$-interpretation$\} \cap \mathbb{N}$ by $Spec(\mathcal{T})$, and we define $Spec_n(\mathcal{T})$ as $Spec(\mathcal{T}) \cap [1, n]$. Analogously, $Spec(\mathcal{T}, \phi)$ is the set of finite cardinalities of $\mathcal{T}$-interpretations that satisfy ϕ. We can then also define $Spec_n(\mathcal{T}, \phi)$ as $Spec(\mathcal{T}, \phi) \cap [1, n]$.

2.2   Number Theory

The *natural density* [19] of a set $A \subseteq \mathbb{N}$ is the following real number, if the limit indeed exists (and then we say the density of A exists): $\mu(A) = \lim_{n \to \infty} |A \cap [n]|/|[n]|$.

Example 1. Consider the set A of even non-negative integers: we then have that $\mu(A)$ is the limit of the sequence a_n which equals $(n+2)/2(n+1)$ if n is even, and $1/2$ if it is odd, meaning that $\mu(A)$ exists and equals $1/2$.

It is easy to prove that μ satisfies, for all disjoint sets A and B for which it is defined: $0 \le \mu(A)$; $\mu(\mathbb{N}) = 1$; and $\mu(A \cup B) = \mu(A) + \mu(B)$. The subsets of the non-negative integers we shall calculate the natural density of are sets of finite cardinalities of interpretations in a theory: since they are never zero (as we assume $dom(\mathcal{A})$ is never empty), we can change $\mu(A)$ to be the limit of the ratio of $|A \cap \{1, \ldots, n\}|$ to $|\{1, \ldots, n\}| = n$.[1] With this, we can finally define the natural density of a theory (relative to a quantifier-free formula or not) as the natural density of its spectrum: $\mu(\mathcal{T}) = \lim_{n \to \infty} |Spec_n(\mathcal{T})|/|[1, n]|$, and $\mu(\mathcal{T}, \phi) = \lim_{n \to \infty} |Spec_n(\mathcal{T}, \phi)|/|[1, n]|$.

Definition 1. *Let $r \in \mathbb{R}$. r is computable [27] if there are computable sequences $\{a_n\}_{n \in \mathbb{N}}$ in $\mathbb{Z}$ and $\{b_n\}_{n \in \mathbb{N}}$ in $\mathbb{Z}^+$ with $\lim_{n \to \infty} a_n/b_n = r$.*

Example 2. Every rational number p/q is computable: just take $a_n = p$ and $b_n = q$. The number $\sum_{n=1}^{\infty} 2^{-\varsigma(n)} = 0.57824...$ is not computable, for ς the busy beaver function [13], which maps $n \in \mathbb{N}$ to the maximum number of 1's a Turing machine with at most n states can write when it halts, assuming the tape begins with only 0's. Now, $0.57824....$ is the limit of $5/10, 57/100, 578/1000, \ldots$ Consider then the theory $\mathcal{T}$ with models of size 1 through 5, 11 through $52 = 57 - 5$, 101 through $521 = 578 - 57$, and so on. Its density is the limit of the fractions $5/10$, $57/100$, $578/1000$ and so on, i.e. $0.57824...$, although this number is irrational. More generally, any $0 \le r \le 1$ is the density of some theory.

2.3   Theory Combination

In what follows, let Σ be an arbitrary signature and $\mathcal{T}$ be a Σ-theory.

$\mathcal{T}$ is **stably infinite** [12] if for every satisfiable quantifier-free formula ϕ, there is a $\mathcal{T}$-interpretation $\mathcal{A}$ that satisfies ϕ with $|dom(\mathcal{A})| \ge \aleph_0$. $\mathcal{T}$ is **smooth** when, for all quantifier-free formulas ϕ, $\mathcal{T}$-interpretations $\mathcal{A}$ that satisfy ϕ, and cardinals $\kappa > |dom(\mathcal{A})|$, there exists a $\mathcal{T}$-interpretation $\mathcal{B}$ that satisfies ϕ with $|dom(\mathcal{B})| = \kappa$. Notice that being smooth implies being stably infinite.

$\mathcal{T}$ is **finitely witnessable** [14] when there is a computable function wit (called a witness) from the quantifier-free formulas into themselves such that, for every quantifier-free formula ϕ: (*I*) ϕ and $\exists \vec{x}. wit(\phi)$ are $\mathcal{T}$-equivalent, where $\vec{x} = vars(wit(\phi)) \setminus vars(\phi)$; and (*II*) if $wit(\phi)$ is $\mathcal{T}$-satisfiable, then there is a $\mathcal{T}$-interpretation $\mathcal{A}$ that satisfies $wit(\phi)$ and, in addition, $dom(\mathcal{A}) = vars(wit(\phi))^{\mathcal{A}}$ (that is, every element of $dom(\mathcal{A})$ is the interpretation of a variable in $wit(\phi)$). Now, given a finite set of variables V on the signature Σ, and an equivalence E on V, the **arrangement** on V induced by E, written δ_V^E or δ_V if E is clear from context, is the formula $\bigwedge_{xEy}(x = y) \wedge \bigwedge_{x\overline{E}y} \neg(x = y)$, where $\overline{E}$ is the complement of E. Intuitively, an arrangement codifies the relationships between a finite set

---

[1] Of course, this does not change the value of $\mu(A)$.

of variables, that is, if they should be equal or different to one another. T is then **strongly finitely witnessable** [11] if it has a witness wit (that in this case will be called a strong witness) satisfying, in addition to (I) and (II), the stronger (II^*): for every finite set of variables V and arrangement δ_V on V, if $wit(\phi) \wedge \delta_V$ is T-satisfiable, then there exists a T-interpretation $\mathcal{A}$ that satisfies that formula and, in addition, $dom(\mathcal{A}) = vars(wit(\phi) \wedge \delta_V)^{\mathcal{A}}$.

Example 3. The theory axiomatized by $\{\psi_{\leq 3}\}$ has as strong witness $wit(\phi) = \phi \wedge \bigwedge_{i=1}^{3} x_i = x_i$, where x_1, x_2 and x_3 are fresh variables (i.e., not in ϕ).

T has the **finite model property (FMP)** if for every T-satisfiable quantifier-free formula ϕ, there is a T-interpretation $\mathcal{A}$ that satisfies ϕ with $|dom(\mathcal{A})| < \aleph_0$.[2] Consider $\mathbb{N}_\omega = \mathbb{N} \cup \{\aleph_0\}$. A **minimal model function** [21] for T is a function $\mathbf{minmod}_T : QF(\Sigma) \to \mathbb{N}_\omega$ such that, if ϕ is quantifier-free and T-satisfiable, then $\mathbf{minmod}_T(\phi) = n$ if, and only if: there exists a T-interpretation $\mathcal{A}$ that satisfies ϕ with $|dom(\mathcal{A})| = n$; and if $\mathcal{B}$ is another T-interpretation that satisfies ϕ, then $|dom(\mathcal{B})| \geq n$.

Example 4. The theory axiomatized by $\{\psi_{\geq 3}\}$ has a computable minimal model function. To calculate it on a quantifier-free formula ϕ, take the cardinality n of the smallest interpretation in equational logic that satisfies ϕ, which can easily be found algorithmically. If $n < 3$, $\mathbf{minmod}(\phi) = 3$; otherwise $\mathbf{minmod}(\phi) = n$.

T is **(strongly) polite** if it is smooth and (strongly) finitely witnessable. It is **shiny** if it is smooth, has the FMP and a computable minimal model function. T is **gentle** [8] if for every quantifier-free formula ϕ, $Spec(T, \phi)$ is *fully computable*, that is: (i) it is computable; (ii) it is either co-finite,[3] or a finite set of finite cardinalities, and there is an algorithm with ϕ as input that tells which one is the case; (iii) if $Spec(T, \phi)$ is finite, $\max(Spec(T, \phi))$ is computable, and if it is infinite $\max(\mathbb{N} \setminus Spec(T, \phi))$ is computable, both with ϕ as input.[4]

Example 5. Consider the Σ_1-theory T_{even}^∞ (see [25]), with axiomatization $\{\neg\psi_{=2n+1} : n \in \mathbb{N}\}$: it is not gentle, as $x = x$ has as spectrum the set of even positive numbers, which is neither finite nor cofinite.

3   Theory Combination and Natural Density

In this section we establish various connections between model-theoretic properties of a theory, and its natural density. We focus our investigation on the empty signature Σ_1, that has a single sort and no function and predicate symbols other than equality. Generalizations to non-empty signatures are given in Sect. 4.

---

[2] A common definition for the finite model property demands this condition holds for all formulas, but in theory combination quantifier-free formulas are typically used.

[3] *I.e.*, $\mathbb{N} \setminus Spec(T, \phi)$ is finite.

[4] If $Spec(T, \phi)$ or $\mathbb{N} \setminus Spec(T, \phi)$ are empty, their respective maxima are 0, as usual, so T must be decidable as $\max(Spec(T, \phi)) = 0$ iff ϕ is not T-satisfiable.

We start with the empty signature, because a theory on such a signature has essentially one natural density, while for the non-empty case we must consider the density with respect to both a formula and the theory (this can also be done on the empty case, but all $\mathcal{T}$-satisfiable formulas will give the same density). Furthermore, some results will not hold on the non-empty case, such as the third item in Theorem 1 below.

Section 3.1 deals with sufficient conditions: if the density satisfies them, then we can deduce some combination properties. Section 3.2 obtains necessary conditions: one would use the contrapositive and conclude that the theory does not have the properties at hand, and then at least one knows that a different combination method has to be used.

3.1   Sufficient Conditions

In Theorem 1 we identify sufficient conditions for stable infiniteness, the finite model property and finite witnessability, properties that are needed for Nelson-Oppen combination, shiny combination, and polite combination, respectively.

Theorem 1. *The positivity of the natural density $\mu(\mathcal{T})$ of a Σ_1-theory $\mathcal{T}$ is sufficient for $\mathcal{T}$ to: 1. be stably infinite; 2. have the finite model property; and 3. be finitely witnessable.*

Remark 1. [5] The proof of the third item in Theorem 1 is more involved than that of the first two, which are routine. Szemerédi's theorem [18], which settled a well-know conjecture by Erdös and Turán, showed that each set with positive natural density contains arbitrarily long finite subsequences in arithmetic progression (i.e., the difference between two consecutive elements is constant). Item 3 is a similarly flavored result, although with a much simpler proof than that of Erdös and Turán, that will guarantee that any theory $\mathcal{T}$ which is not finitely witnessable and has a natural density must satisfy $\mu(\mathcal{T}) = 0$.

The following example shows a simple application of Theorem 1.

Example 6. Fix some positive natural number n, and consider the theory $\mathcal{T}_{\geq n}$, with axiomatization $\{\psi_{\geq n}\}$. It obviously has positive density. By Theorem 1 it is stably infinite, has the finite model property, and is finitely witnessable.

The following example shows that all the reciprocals of Theorem 1 are false, a single counterexample being enough for all three.

Example 7. Take the Σ_1-theory $\mathcal{T}_{=2^i}$ with axiomatization $\{\psi_{\geq 2^n} \vee \bigvee_{i=0}^{n} \psi_{=2^i} : n \in \mathbb{N}\}$, which has interpretations $\mathcal{A}$ with domains whose cardinality is either infinite or a power of two. It is stably infinite, has the finite model property and is finitely witnessable,[6] but $\mu(\mathcal{T}_{=2^i}) = \lim_{n \to \infty} \frac{|Spec_n(\mathcal{T}_{=2^i})|}{n} = \lim_{n \to \infty} \frac{\lfloor \log_2(n) \rfloor + 1}{n} = 0$.

---

[5] Full proofs appear in [24].

[6] A witness being, if ϕ has n variables, $wit(\phi) = \phi \wedge \bigwedge_{i=1}^{2^n} x_i = x_i$, for fresh x_is.

The following example shows the sharpness of Theorem 1, in the sense that its assumption is really needed to reach its conclusions.

Example 8. The conclusion of Theorem 1 cannot hold under the assumption that $\mu(T) = 0$. The theory T_∞, with axiomatization $\{\psi_{\geq n} : n \in \mathbb{Z}^+\}$, has only infinite models. It has density 0 but does not have the finite model property. The theory T_1, with axiomatization $\{\psi_{=1}\}$, has a single model up to isomorphism, with a single element. It has density 0 but is not stably infinite. For item 3, a theory that is not finitely witnessable and has natural density 0 is T_ς, from [26], with axiomatization $\{\psi_{\geq\varsigma(n)} \vee \bigvee_{i=2}^{n} \psi_{=\varsigma(i)} : n \in \mathbb{N} \setminus \{0,1\}\}$ for $\varsigma : \mathbb{N} \to \mathbb{N}$ the busy beaver function (see Example 2). The cardinalities of its finite models are precisely the Busy Beaver numbers, that is, the elements of the image of ς. We can show that $\mu(T) = 0$. In a way, item 3 of Theorem 1 shows that every theory not finitely witnessable must, like ς, "escape" all computable functions, and thus have natural density 0.

3.2   Necessary Conditions

We now move on to the results establishing necessary conditions for gentleness (Sect. 3.2.1), smoothness and finite model property (Sect. 3.2.2), strong finite witnessability (Sect. 3.2.3), the computability of a minimal model function (Sect. 3.2.4), and finite witnessability (Sect. 3.2.5).

We consider, therefore, 7 properties related to theory combination in total. Were we to consider all Boolean combinations of them, we would need to analyze 128 cases; [23, Theorems 5,6,7] has shown, however, that for Σ_1 there are only 8 of these possibilities, excluding gentleness. It may look like we need to analyze 16 possibilities then, but we can cut them down to 9 by using Lemmas 1 and 2 below. This will allow us to easily write down all possible natural densities for every combination, what will be done in Sect. 3.2.6.

3.2.1   Gentleness

Theorem 2. *If T is a Σ_1-theory with a density, then $\mu(T)$ being equal to 0 or 1 is a necessary condition for T to be gentle.*

Proof (Sketch). By taking a tautology ϕ for a gentle Σ_1-theory T, we see that $Spec(T) = Spec(T, \phi)$ is either finite (and then its density is 0) or co-finite (and then its density is 1).

The following example provides a simple application of Theorem 2.

Example 9. Consider the theory T_{even}^∞ from Example 5: it's density is $1/2$, what implies by the theorem it is not gentle.

The reciprocal of Theorem 2 is false, as shown by the next example.

Example 10. Example 7 presents a theory $T_{=2^i}$ that has density 0 but is not gentle (since both $Spec(T_{=2^i})$ and $\mathbb{N} \setminus Spec(T_{=2^i})$ are infinite). On the other hand, take the Σ_1-theory $T_{\neq 2^i}$ with axiomatization $\{\neg\psi_{=2^n} : n \in \mathbb{N}\}$, which has interpretations $\mathcal{A}$ with either $|dom(\mathcal{A})|$ infinite, or $|dom(\mathcal{A})|$ finite but not a power of two. It is not gentle, yet $\mu(T_{\neq 2^i}) = \lim_{n \to \infty} \frac{|Spec_n(T_{\neq 2^i})|}{n} = \lim_{n \to \infty} \frac{n - \lfloor \log_2(n) \rfloor - 1}{n} = 1$.

Notice also that both cases of Theorem 2 are possible, namely: there are gentle theories with density 0 and gentle theories with density 1. Before showing them, let us present two useful lemmas, that relate gentleness to other properties: the first shows that the computability involved in gentleness is enough to guarantee the computability of a minimal model function, and that the forms of the possible spectra in a gentle theory lead to it having the finite model property.

Lemma 1. *If T is gentle, then T has a computable minimal model function and the finite model property, and therefore is finitely witnessable as well.*

Proof (Sketch). Because the spectra of any quantifier-free formula in a gentle theory is either a finite set of finite cardinalities or co-finite, it always contains an element of $\mathbb{N}$, implying the finite model property. To compute **minmod**$(\phi) =$ $\min(Spec(T, \phi))$ we use the facts that the spectrum is always computable, if it is finite we know $\max(Spec(T, \phi))$, and if it is co-finite we know $\max(\mathbb{N} \setminus Spec(T, \phi))$.

The second of our useful lemmas reveals two unexpected results involving gentleness: that a theory that is not stably infinite is gentle, and that a strongly finitely witnessable theory is also gentle; This lemma, however, is restricted to Σ_1, while the previous one is not. This extends to gentleness, in a way, the research found in [23, 25, 26] of combining combination properties, at least for the one-sorted, empty signature.

Lemma 2. *Let T be a Σ_1-theory: if T is not stably infinite, or if it is strongly finitely witnessable, then T is gentle.*

Proof (Sketch). If T is not stably infinite, its models must have a maximum cardinality, so all spectra are finite sets of finite cardinalities. If T is strongly finitely witnessable but not stably infinite we then have nothing to prove; if it is strongly finitely witnessable and stably infinite we have that, by [25], it is smooth and has the finite model property, so the spectra are co-finite.

Example 11.

1. The trivial Σ_1-theory $T_{\geq 1}$, with axiomatization $\{\psi_{\geq 1}\}$, consists of all Σ_1-interpretations. It is strongly finitely witnessable (given its axiomatization is given by an universal formula, this is proven in [15]), and of course $Spec_n(T_{\geq 1}) =$ $[1, n]$ so $\mu(T_{\geq 1}) = 1$.
2. The Σ_1-theory T_I from Example 8 is also strongly finitely witnessable and thus gentle (Lemma 2), but $Spec_n(T_I) = \{1\}$ so $\mu(T_I) = 0$.
3. An example of a Σ_1-theory that is gentle and has density 0, but is not strongly finitely witnessable, is denoted by $T_{\langle m,n \rangle}$, for any fixed $m, n \in \mathbb{Z}^+$. It has axiomatization $\{\psi_{=m} \vee \psi_{=n}\}$, and its models have cardinalities m or n.

3.2.2 Smoothness and Finite Model Property

The next result involves both smoothness and the finite model property.

Theorem 3. *If $\mathcal{T}$ is a Σ_1-theory with a density, $\mu(\mathcal{T})$ being equal to 1 is necessary for $\mathcal{T}$ to simultaneously admit smoothness and the finite model property.*

Proof (Sketch). The proof is dual to that of Theorem 1: if a theory is smooth and has the finite model property, it has all sufficiently large numbers as cardinalities of its models, and its density is therefore 1.

The following example not only allows one to visualize the use of Theorem 3, but will also help later in providing examples for each and all possible combination of the properties under consideration.

Example 12. Consider again $\mathcal{T}_{even}^\infty$ from Example 9, with density $1/2$. It was already shown in [16] that $\mathcal{T}_{even}^\infty$ has the finite model property without being smooth, but notice that Theorem 3 perfectly encapsulates an intuition for why that is: as the theory has the finite model property, it has a finite model; were it smooth, it would have models of all larger cardinalities, and thus density 1.

Example 13. The reciprocal of Theorem 3 is false, as we can see from the theory $\mathcal{T}_{\neq 2^i}$ defined in Example 10, which is not smooth.

Now, Example 12 shows an example of a theory that has the finite model property but is not smooth. But all three other Boolean combinations of these two properties are possible, as seen below.

Example 14.

1. The theory $\mathcal{T}_{\geq 1}$ from Example 11 is smooth and has the finite model property.
2. One example of a smooth theory without the finite model property is the Σ_1-theory $\mathcal{T}_\infty$ from Example 8. It has density 0, as it has no finite models.
3. To see one of a theory that is neither smooth nor has the finite model property, which by Theorem 1 must have density 0, fix an $n \in \mathbb{Z}^+$ and consider the Σ_1-theory $\mathcal{T}_{n,\infty}$, defined in [25] by the axiomatization $\{\psi_{=n} \vee \psi_{\geq m} : m \in \mathbb{Z}^+\}$. Its finite models must have cardinality n.

3.2.3 Strong Finite Witnessability

The following result, which is a corollary of earlier ones, is specially useful: proving a theory is not strongly finitely witnessable is quite challenging; it involves finding a quantifier-free formula, a set of variables, and an arrangement on that set which fail the conditions to be a strong witness, for every candidate for a strong witness. Checking whether the theory's density is 0 or 1 can be fairly easier.

Corollary 1. *If $\mathcal{T}$ is a Σ_1-theory with a density, then $\mu(\mathcal{T})$ being equal to 0 or 1 is a necessary condition for $\mathcal{T}$ to be strongly finitely witnessable.*

Proof. By Lemma 2 and Theorem 2.

Example 15. The theory T_{even}^∞ from Example 9 is not strongly finitely witnessable, as proven in [16], but the proof found there is quite involved, demanding careful use of arrangements. Here, we only need to point to the fact that T_{even}^∞ has natural density $1/2$.

Example 16. The reciprocal of Corollary 1 is false: the theories $T_{=2^i}$ and $T_{\neq 2^i}$ from Examples 7 and 10 have, respectively, densities 0 and 1, but neither is strongly finitely witnessable, which follows from the fact that both are stably infinite without being smooth, together with [25, Theorem 7], which shows stably infinite, one-sorted theories that are strongly finitely witnessable are smooth.

3.2.4   Computability of Minimal Model Functions

We move now to the question of computability of a minimal model function, one of the more complex topics in this paper. For this, we first establish in Proposition 1 a connection between this and the computability of the spectra.

Proposition 1. T *is a* Σ_1*-theory with a computable minimal model function if, and only if,* $Spec(T)$ *is computable.*

This proposition plays an important role in the proof of the theorem below:

Theorem 4. *If* T *is a* Σ_1*-theory with a density, the fact that* $\mu(T)$ *is a computable number is a necessary condition for* T *to have a computable minimal model function. Furthermore, for every computable number* $0 \leq r \leq 1$*, there exists a* Σ_1*-theory* T *with* $\mu(T) = r$ *that has a computable minimal model function and the finite model property, but is not smooth.*

The proof of the first part takes a theory T with a computable minimal model function, and from Proposition 1 one sees that $Spec(T)$ is computable; we then prove that this implies $\mu(T)$ is itself a computable real number, ruling out non-computable numbers. Indeed, if A is a computable set, the sequence $\{|A_n|\}_{n\in\mathbb{N}} = \{|\{k \in A : k \leq n\}|\}_{n\in\mathbb{N}}$ is computable (and so is $\{n\}_{n\in\mathbb{N}}$, but that is obvious); if $\mu(A) = r$, we have $r = \lim_{n\to\infty} |A_n|/n$, proving r is computable.

We prove the second part by constructing in Definition 2 below, from two sequences $\{a_n\}_{n\in\mathbb{N}}$ and $\{b_n\}_{n\in\mathbb{N}}$, a function f whose image (which will also equal the spectrum of the theory to be constructed) will be a computable set and have a density associated to the mediants of the ratios a_n/b_n, where the mediant of the fractions a/b and c/d is the fraction $(a+c)/(b+d)$. Although tedious to prove, it is true that the limit of the mediants of the ratios between two sequences equals the limit of the ratios, and this guarantees that the natural density of the image of f will be the limit of a_n/b_n.

Definition 2. *Given sequences* $\{a_n\}_{n\in\mathbb{N}}$ *and* $\{b_n\}_{n\in\mathbb{N}}$ *with* $0 < a_n < b_n$ *and* $a_n, b_n \in \mathbb{N}$*, for all* $n\in\mathbb{N}$*, we define an associated function* $f : \mathbb{Z}^+ \to \mathbb{Z}^+$ *inductively as follows:* $f(n) = n$ *for* $1 \leq n \leq a_0$*, and* $f(n) = a_0$ *for* $a_0 + 1 \leq n \leq b_0$*; and, assuming* $f(n)$ *defined for all* $1 \leq n \leq M = \sum_{i=0}^{m} b_i$*, for any* $m \geq 0$*, we make* $f(n) = n$ *for* $M+1 \leq n \leq M + a_{m+1}$*, and* $f(n) = M + a_{m+1}$ *for* $M + a_{m+1} + 1 \leq n \leq M + b_{m+1}$*.*

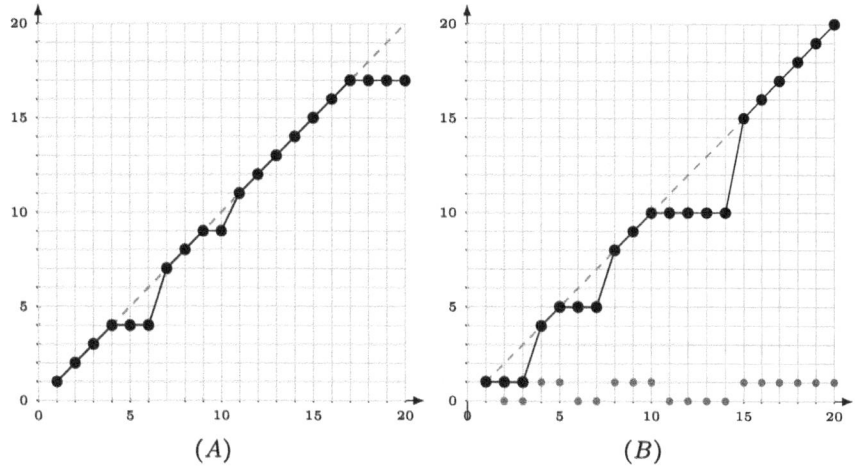

Fig. 2. (A) Initial values of the function f from Definition 2, for $a_0 = 4$, $a_1 = 3$, $a_2 = 7$, $b_0 = 6$, $b_1 = 4$ and $b_2 = 10$. (B) Initial values of the functions G (smaller, red bullet points) and f (larger, black bullet points) from the case with computable r of Theorem 5, for $a_0 = 1$, $a_1 = 2$, $a_2 = 3$, $b_0 = 2$, $b_1 = 3$, $b_2 = 5$, $g(1) = 1$, $g(2) = 1$ and $g(3) = 0$.

The construction defined in Definition 2 is outlined in Fig. 2 (A). Notice the step-shape of the function, that can be computed by induction on n.

We next show an application of Theorem 4, by identifying a theory that according to this theorem does not have a computable minimal model function, but this fact seems difficult to prove without using this theorem.

Example 17. Take $\Omega = 0.57824\ldots$ from Example 2. Take the sequence of fractions $5/10, 57/100, \ldots$ converging to Ω, and define a function f as in Definition 2: so $f(n) = n$ for $1 \le n \le 4$, and $f(n) = 5$ for $5 \le n \le 10$; $f(n) = n$ for $11 \le n \le 66$, and $f(n) = 67$ for $67 \le n \le 110$, and so on. Define then a theory $\mathcal{T}_\Omega$ with axiomatization $\{\psi_{\ge f(n+1)} \vee \bigvee_{i=1}^{n} \psi_{=f(n)} : n \in \mathbb{Z}^+\}$: it has models of size 1 through 5, 11 through 67, and so on.[7] We can prove that it has natural density Ω, and thus does not have a computable minimal model function. It is, however unclear how one would prove this without resorting to Theorem 4 and Proposition 1.

The reciprocal of Theorem 4 is false, in the sense that a theory without a computable minimal model function can still have a computable natural density.

Example 18. Consider again the theory $\mathcal{T}_\varsigma$ from Example 8, whose natural density we have shown to be the computable number 0, despite the fact it does not have a computable minimal model function (see [6, Lemma 128]), what by Proposition 1 means $Spec(\mathcal{T}_\varsigma)$ is not computable.

---

[7] Notice $\mathcal{T}_\Omega$ is not the same as the theory from Example 2: indeed, the construction from Definition 2 is more general.

Notice that, from [25, Lemma 7] and [23, Theorem 4], the theories in Theorem 4 are also finitely witnessable without being strongly finitely witnessable. They are also not gentle in the case that $0 < \mu(\mathcal{T}) < 1$. It is still possible to come up with gentle examples for $\mu(\mathcal{T}) = 1$ or $\mu(\mathcal{T}) = 0$, as the next example shows.

Example 19. To obtain Σ_1-theories $\mathcal{T}$, with $\mu(\mathcal{T}) = 1$ or $\mu(\mathcal{T}) = 0$, that have a computable minimal model function and are gentle but not strongly finitely witnessable it is enough to consider, for the first case, $\mathcal{T}$ with axiomatization $\{\psi_{=1} \vee \psi_{\geq 3}\}$; for the second, $\mathcal{T}$ with axiomatization $\{\psi_{=1} \vee \psi_{=3}\}$.

3.2.5   Finite Witnessability

The theorems so far have provided necessary conditions for a theory to be gentle, smooth, strongly finitely witnessable, or have a computable minimal model function. We now show that this is as far as this goes: namely, we cannot achieve necessary conditions using natural densities for finite witnessability alone.

In fact, any real number r is the natural density of a finitely witnessable theory. If r is computable then Theorem 4 already constructs a finitely witnessable theory $\mathcal{T}$ with $\mu(\mathcal{T}) = r$, as [23, Theorem 4] proved that a theory with a computable minimal model function is finitely witnessable. However, in the next theorem we construct such a theory also for non-computable numbers. In addition, the theorem shows that the generated theory does not need to have a computable minimal model function even if r is computable. These will constitute the most intricate results of this paper.

Theorem 5. *For every number $0 \leq r \leq 1$, there exists a Σ_1-theory $\mathcal{T}$ with $\mu(\mathcal{T}) = r$ that is finitely witnessable yet doesn't have a computable minimal model function.*

The proof of Theorem 5 is divided in two cases: when r is computable, and when it is not. When it is not, we write it in decimal notation, take the obvious series of decimal fractions converging to it, define the function f as in Definition 2 and take the theory whose spectrum is the image of f.

If r is computable, which is the difficult case, we take computable sequences $\{a_n\}_{n \in \mathbb{N}}$ and $\{b_n\}_{n \in \mathbb{N}}$ such that a_n/b_n converges to r, and a non-computable function $g : \mathbb{Z}^+ \to \{0, 1\}$. We then define an auxiliary function $G : \mathbb{Z}^+ \to \{0, 1\}$ by making, for $M = 2\sum_{i=0}^m b_i$: $G(M + 1) = g(m + 2)$; $G(n) = 0$ for $M + 2 \leq n \leq 2(b_{m+1} - a_{m+1}) + M$; $G(2(b_{m+1} - a_{m+1}) + M + 1) = 0$ if $g(m + 2) = 1$, and otherwise $G(2(b_{m+1} - a_{m+1}) + M + 1) = 1$; and $G(n) = 1$ for $2(b_{m+1} - a_{m+1}) + M + 2 \leq n \leq M + 2b_{m+1}$. We make $f(n) = \max\{m \leq n : G(m) = 1\}$, and take the theory whose spectrum is the image of f, axiomatized by $\{\psi_{\geq f(n+1)} \vee \bigvee_{i=1}^n \psi_{=f(i)} : n \in \mathbb{Z}^+\}$, which will have a density equal to whatever is the limit of a_n/b_n, i.e. r. An example of this construction appears in Fig. $2(B)$, where the smaller, red bullet points represent G, and the larger, black bullet points represent f: for the corresponding theory we will have $Spec_{20}(\mathcal{T}) = \{1, 4, 5, 8, 9, 10, 15, 16, 17, 18, 19, 20\}$.

3.2.6   Summary

We can now, as this section about necessary conditions for the empty signature comes to an end, summarize its overall arch: we have seen what are all possible values for the density of a theory given some of its theory combination properties, for all such combinations of properties.

In Table 1, **SI** stands for stably infinite; **SM** for smooth; **FW** for finitely witnessable; **SW** for strongly finitely witnessable; **FM** for the finite model property; **CF** for a computable minimal model function; and **G** for gentle. **REC** denotes the set of real computable numbers.

Each line in the table corresponds to a possible combination of properties (that remains possible after Lemmas 1 and 2). For example, the first line corresponds to theories that admit all properties, while the second line correspond to theories that are stably infinite, smooth, have a computable minimal model function, but do not admit any of the other properties.

For each possible combination of properties, we list in the table the possible natural densities of theories that admit the corresponding properties. For example, theories that admit all properties must have density one.[8]

The column titled "Reference" leads to the result in this paper proving the values are indeed restricted to the mentioned ones; and the column "Construction" refers to examples of theories having the possible natural densities shown.

Table 1. Classification of combinations *vis-à-vis* their natural densities.

SI	SM	FW	SW	FM	CF	G	Natural densities	Reference	Construction
T	T	T	T	T	T	T	1	Theorem 3	Example 11
		F	F	F	T	F	0	Theorem 1	Example 14
	F	T	F	T	T	T	$\{0,1\}$	Theorem 2	Example 19
						F	**REC** $\cap$ $[0,1]$	Theorem 4	Theorem 4
				T	F	F	$[0,1]$	Theorem 5	Theorem 5
		F	F	T	F	F	0	Theorem 1	Example 8
				F	T	F	0	Theorem 1	Example 14
F	F	T	T	F	T	T	0	Theorem 1	Example 11
			F	T	T	T	0	Theorem 1	Example 11

4 Non-empty Signatures

In this section we provide generalizations of the results of Sect. 3 to non-empty signatures. We are able to do so by considering $\mu(\mathcal{T}, \phi)$ for all formulas ϕ, rather than $\mu(\mathcal{T})$: this is due to the fact that in a non-empty signature we can have two quantifier-free satisfiable formulas with distinct densities.

---

[8] The theory found in this specific row, $\mathcal{T}_{\geq 1}$ from Example 11, is strongly finitely witnessable, and Lemma 2 then shows it is also gentle, as implied by the table.

Example 20. Take the theory $\mathcal{T}$ on the signature with a unary function s, axiomatized by $\{\psi_{=2} \lor \forall x.s(x){=}x\}$. In its models that do not have exactly two elements, s must be interpreted as the identity. For $\phi_1 = \neg(s(x) = x)$ and $\phi_2 = (s(x) = x)$ we have $\mu(\mathcal{T}, \phi_1) = 0$ and $\mu(\mathcal{T}, \phi_2) = 1$.

We start by generalizing items 1 and 2 in Theorem 1. As for the third item of Theorem 1, we show in Example 22 below that it cannot be generalized similarly.

Theorem 6. *The positivity of $\mu(\mathcal{T}, \phi)$ for every $\mathcal{T}$-satisfiable quantifier-free formula ϕ is sufficient for $\mathcal{T}$ to be stably infinite and have the finite model property.*

In the next example we show how to use Theorem 6.

Example 21. Consider a signature Σ with only function symbols, and the Σ-theory $\mathcal{T}$ of uninterpreted functions. For every quantifier-free formula ϕ and $\mathcal{T}$-interpretation $\mathcal{A}$ that satisfies it, we can add an element a to its domain, from that it follows that $\mu(\mathcal{T}, \phi) = 1$, and that $\mathcal{T}$ is stably infinite. But by using Theorem 6 we can also conclude that the theory of uninterpreted functions has the finite model property.

Next, we generalize the result concerning gentleness to non empty signatures. The proof of the following result is, *mutatis mutandis*, the same as Theorem 2.

Theorem 7. $\mu(\mathcal{T}, \phi)$ *being in $\{0, 1\}$ for all quantifier-free $\mathcal{T}$-satisfiable formulas ϕ is a necessary condition for $\mathcal{T}$ to be gentle.*

The following theorem generalizes Theorem 3, and provides a necessary condition for smoothness and the finite model property for non-empty signatures.

Theorem 8. *Let $\mathcal{T}$ be a theory. $\mu(\mathcal{T}, \phi)$ being equal to 1 for all $\mathcal{T}$-satisfiable quantifier-free formulas ϕ is then a necessary condition for $\mathcal{T}$ to simultaneously be smooth and have the finite model property.*

Theorem 8 can be used to show that the third item of Theorem 1 is not generalizable to non-empty signatures.

Example 22. Consider the function $\varsigma^{-1} : \mathbb{N} \to \mathbb{N}$ which is a left inverse of ς, and the theory $\mathcal{T}_\varsigma^s$ on the signature with only a single unary function s, both defined in [26]. Both ς^{-1} and $\mathcal{T}_\varsigma^s$ are given in Fig. 3. It is smooth, has the finite model property, but is not finitely witnessable (see [22, Lemmas 71,72,73]), meaning $\mu(\mathcal{T}_\varsigma^s, \phi) = 1$ for all quantifier-free $\mathcal{T}_\varsigma^s$-satisfiable formulas ϕ by Theorem 8. Thus, the obvious generalization of item 3 of Theorem 1 is not valid.

Theorem 8 is also useful to show, for example, that a variant of the SMT-LIB theory of bit-vectors is not smooth.

Example 23. Fix $n \in \mathbb{Z}^+$, and consider the one-sorted fragment of the SMT-LIB theory $\mathbf{BV}[n]$ of bit-vectors [1] of length n, with the usual operations (but without concatenation and extraction). The domain of its interpretations has cardinality 2^n, and so it has the finite model property. By Theorem 8 this theory is not smooth, as for any quantifier-free formula ϕ one has $\mu(\mathbf{BV}[n], \phi) = 0$.

$$\psi_{\geq n}^{=} = \exists x_1. \cdots \exists x_n. \left[\neq (x_1, \ldots, x_n) \wedge \bigwedge_{i=1}^{n} [s(x_i) = x_i] \right]$$

$$\psi_{=n}^{=} = \exists x_1. \cdots \exists x_n. \left[\neq (x_1, \ldots, x_n) \wedge \bigwedge_{i=1}^{n} [s(x_i) = x_i] \wedge \forall x. \left[[s(x) = x] \rightarrow \bigvee_{i=1}^{n} x = x_i \right] \right]$$

$$\varsigma^{-1}(k) = \min\{l : \varsigma(l+1) > \varsigma(k)\}$$

$$Ax(\mathcal{T}_{\varsigma}^s) = \left\{ (\psi_{\geq k+1} \wedge \psi_{\geq \varsigma^{-1}(k+1)}^{=}) \vee \bigvee_{i=1}^{k+1} (\psi_{=i} \wedge \psi_{=\varsigma^{-1}(i)}^{=}) : k \in \mathbb{N} \right\}$$

Fig. 3. The theory $\mathcal{T}_{\varsigma}^s$.

Next, we generalize Corollary 1 to non-empty signatures.

Theorem 9. $\mu(\mathcal{T}, \phi)$ *being equal to* 0 *or* 1 *for every quantifier-free* $\mathcal{T}$*-satisfiable* ϕ *is necessary for* $\mathcal{T}$ *to be strongly finitely witnessable.*

Example 20 shows tightness of Theorems 7 and 9: we can have a strongly finitely witnessable,[9] gentle[10] theory $\mathcal{T}$ with two quantifier-free $\mathcal{T}$-satisfiable formulas that have densities 0 and 1. It also shows that the positivity in Theorem 6 cannot hold for only some quantifier-free $\mathcal{T}$-satisfiable formulas ϕ, as the theory shown is not stably infinite.

The following two theorems generalize, respectively, Theorems 4 and 5. For Theorem 4, we need an alternative, non-empty version of Proposition 1. Indeed, it is not clear that if the sets $Spec(\mathcal{T}, \phi)$ are all computable, $\mathcal{T}$ should have a computable minimal model function; the reciprocal, however, is true.

Proposition 2. *If* $\mathcal{T}$ *is a theory with a computable minimal model function, then* $Spec(\mathcal{T}, \phi)$ *is computable for all quantifier-free* $\mathcal{T}$*-satisfiable formulas* ϕ.

Theorem 10. *If* $\mathcal{T}$ *is a theory with all densities* $\mu(\mathcal{T}, \phi)$, *for all quantifier-free* $\mathcal{T}$*-satisfiable formulas* ϕ, *the fact that all* $\mu(\mathcal{T}, \phi)$ *are computable is a necessary condition for* $\mathcal{T}$ *to have a computable minimal model function. Furthermore, for every computable number* $0 \leq r \leq 1$, *there is a theory* $\mathcal{T}$ *that has a computable minimal model function and a quantifier-free formula* ϕ *with* $\mu(\mathcal{T}, \phi) = r$.

Theorem 11. *If* $\mathcal{T}$ *is a theory, and* ϕ *a quantifier-free* $\mathcal{T}$*-satisfiable formula, nothing can be said about* $\mu(\mathcal{T}, \phi)$ *if* $\mathcal{T}$ *is only known to be finitely witnessable; that is, for every computable number* $0 \leq r \leq 1$, *there exists a theory* $\mathcal{T}$, *that is finitely witnessable, and a quantifier-free formula* ϕ *with* $\mu(\mathcal{T}, \phi) = r$.

Notice that Theorem 11 is a straightforward application of Theorem 5: indeed, for a Σ_1-theory $\mathcal{T}$ with $\mu(\mathcal{T}) = r$, any $\mathcal{T}$-satisfiable quantifier-free formula ϕ will give us $\mu(\mathcal{T}, \phi) = 1$.

---

[9] The strong witness is $wit(\phi) = \phi \wedge \neg(x = y)$, for fresh variables x and y.
[10] From the fact it is strongly finitely witnessable and Lemma 2.

5 Conclusion

We have studied connections between densities and model-theoretic properties. Table 2 summarizes our main results. For each property, we refer to the theorems that characterize its possible densities, both for empty and non-empty signatures.

Table 2. Summary of main results.

Property	Empty case	Non-empty case
Stable Infiniteness	Theorem 1	Theorem 6
Finite Model Property	Theorem 1	Theorem 6
Gentleness	Theorem 2	Theorem 7
Smoothness	Theorem 3	Theorem 8
Strong Finite Witnessability	Corollary 1	Theorem 9
Comp. of Min. Mod. Fun.	Theorem 4	Theorem 10
Finite Witnessability	Theorem 5	Theorem 11, Example 22

We conclude by sketching the next steps. In this paper we only considered one-sorted theories, even though many-sorted theories are commonly used in SMT. The main reason for that is that densities for many-sorted theories would be defined on tuples rather than on numbers (i.e. on the cardinalities of the domains rather than on that of the single domain), and it is unclear how this generalization would materialize. We leave this investigation for future work, and briefly describe concrete options for such a generalization.

What makes the natural density so natural is the fact that it calculates the ratio of the number of elements in a set A to the number of elements in $\mathbb{N}$ by doing that for numbers under a bound, and then letting said bound go to infinite. But there is no single way of doing that in $\mathbb{N}^m$, so we are forced to make a choice. Once fixed a bound n, do we, for example:

(i) bound all coordinates simultaneously by n (i.e., $\mu(A) = \lim_{n \to \infty} |A_n|/n^m$ for $A_n = A \cap [n]^m$)? (ii) bound the distance of a tuple to the origin by n (i.e., $A_n = A \cap B_d(n)$, where $B_d(n) = \{\mathbf{p} \in \mathbb{N}^m : d(\mathbf{0}, \mathbf{p}) \leq n\}$, for $\mathbf{0}$ the origin)? (iii) If so, what metric do we use to calculate the distance? Do we use the taxicab distance, where $d_1(\mathbf{p}, \mathbf{q}) = \sum_{i=1}^{n} |p_i - q_i|$, or the generalized euclidean distances $d_m(\mathbf{p}, \mathbf{q}) = (\sum_{i=1}^{n} (p_i - q_i)^m)^{1/m}$, or something entirely different?

There is a plurality of "natural densities" to explore. Even more, while some generalizations will characterize properties w.r.t. the entire set of sorts $\{\sigma_1, \ldots, \sigma_n\}$, others will characterize them with respect to some subset of sorts, while others will offer no characterization whatsoever.

All of this is left to a future work, but we expect that the results from the current paper will still be useful for many-sorted logic, as many of the potential many-sorted densities would rely on the separate projections to each sort.

Acknowledgments. This work was partially funded by the NSF-BSF grant 2020704, the ISF grant 619/21, and the Colman-Soref fellowship.

References

1. Barrett, C., Fontaine, P., Tinelli, C.: The SMT-LIB standard: version 2.6. Technical report, Department of Computer Science, The University of Iowa (2017). http:// smt-lib.org
2. Barrett, C., Sebastiani, R., Seshia, S., Tinelli, C.: Satisfiability modulo theories. In: Biere, A., Heule, M.J.H., van Maaren, H., Walsh, T. (eds.) Handbook of Satisfiability, Second Edition. Frontiers in Artificial Intelligence and Applications, vol. 336, chap. 33, pp. 825–885. IOS Press (2021). http://www.cs.stanford.edu/~barrett/ pubs/BSST21.pdf
3. Bell, J., Burris, S.: Compton's method for proving logical limit laws. Contemp. Math. **558**, 97–128 (2011)
4. Carnap, R.: Logical Foundations of Probability. Chicago University of Chicago Press, Chicago (1950)
5. Compton, K.J., Henson, C.W., Shelah, S.: Nonconvergence, undecidability, and intractability in asymptotic problems. Ann. Pure Appl. Log. **36**, 207–224 (1987). https://doi.org/10.1016/0168-0072(87)90017-0
6. de Toledo, G.V., Zohar, Y.: Combining combination properties: minimal models (2024). http://arxiv.org/abs/2405.01478
7. Fagin, R.: Probabilities on finite models. J. Symb. Log. **41**(1), 50–58 (1976)
8. Fontaine, P.: Combinations of theories for decidable fragments of first-order logic. In: Ghilardi, S., Sebastiani, R. (eds.) FroCoS 2009. LNCS (LNAI), vol. 5749, pp. 263–278. Springer, Heidelberg (2009). https://doi.org/10.1007/978-3-642-04222-5_16
9. Glebskii, Y.V., Kogan, D.I., Liogon'kii, M.I., Talanov, V.A.: Volume and fraction of satisfiability of formulas of the lower predicate calculus. Kibernetica (Kiev) **5**, 17–27 (1969)
10. Immerman, N.: Descriptive Complexity. Texts in Computer Science, 1999th edn. Springer, New York (1998)
11. Jovanović, D., Barrett, C.: Polite theories revisited. In: Fermüller, C.G., Voronkov, A. (eds.) LPAR 2010. LNCS, vol. 6397, pp. 402–416. Springer, Heidelberg (2010). https://doi.org/10.1007/978-3-642-16242-8_29
12. Nelson, G., Oppen, D.C.: Simplification by cooperating decision procedures. ACM Trans. Program. Lang. Syst. **1**(2), 245–257 (1979). https://doi.org/10.1145/357073.357079
13. Radó, T.: On non-computable functions. Bell Syst. Tech. J. **41**(3), 877–884 (1962). https://doi.org/10.1002/j.1538-7305.1962.tb00480.x
14. Ranise, S., Ringeissen, C., Zarba, C.G.: Combining data structures with nonstably infinite theories using many-sorted logic. In: Gramlich, B. (ed.) FroCoS 2005. LNCS, vol. 3717, pp. 48–64. Springer, Heidelberg (2005). https://doi.org/10.1007/11559306_3, https://hal.inria.fr/inria-00000570
15. Sheng, Y., Zohar, Y., Ringeissen, C., Lange, J., Fontaine, P., Barrett, C.: Polite combination of algebraic datatypes. J. Autom. Reason. **66**(3), 331–355 (2022). https://doi.org/10.1007/s10817-022-09625-3

16. Sheng, Y., Zohar, Y., Ringeissen, C., Reynolds, A., Barrett, C., Tinelli, C.: Politeness and stable infiniteness: stronger together. In: Platzer, A., Sutcliffe, G. (eds.) CADE 2021. LNCS (LNAI), vol. 12699, pp. 148–165. Springer, Cham (2021). https://doi.org/10.1007/978-3-030-79876-5_9

17. Smullyan, R.R.: First-Order Logic. Ergebnisse der Mathematik und ihrer Grenzgebiete. 2. Folge. Springer, Heidelberg (2012). https://books.google.com.br/books?id=ZyLyCAAAQBAJ

18. Szemerédi, E.: On sets of integers containing k elements in arithmetic progression. Acta Arith. **27**, 199–245 (1975). https://doi.org/10.4064/aa-27-1-199-245

19. Tenenbaum, G.: Introduction to Analytic and Probabilistic Number Theory. Cambridge Studies in Advanced Mathematics, vol. 46. Cambridge University Press, Cambridge (1995). Transl. from the 2nd French ed. by C.B. Thomas

20. Tinelli, C., Zarba, C.G.: Combining nonstably infinite theories. J. Autom. Reason. **34**(3), 209–238 (2005)

21. Tinelli, C., Zarba, C.G.: Combining nonstably infinite theories. J. Autom. Reason. **34**(3), 209–238 (2005). https://doi.org/10.1007/s10817-005-5204-9

22. Toledo, G., Zohar, Y., Barrett, C.: Combining finite combination properties: finite models and busy beavers (2023). http://arxiv.org/abs/2307.07885

23. Toledo, G.V., Zohar, Y.: Combining combination properties: minimal models. In: Bjorner, N., Heule, M., Voronkov, A. (eds.) Proceedings of 25th Conference on Logic for Programming, Artificial Intelligence and Reasoning. EPiC Series in Computing, vol. 100, pp. 19–35. EasyChair (2024). https://easychair.org/publications/paper/9KKC, https://doi.org/10.29007/6qkh

24. Toledo, G.V., Zohar, Y.: Number theory combination: natural density and SMT (2025). http://arxiv.org/abs/2505.16840

25. Toledo, G.V., Zohar, Y., Barrett, C.: Combining combination properties: an analysis of stable infiniteness, convexity, and politeness. In: Pientka, B., Tinelli, C. (eds.) CADE 2023. LNCS, vol. 14132, pp. 522–541. Springer, Cham (2023). https://doi.org/10.1007/978-3-031-38499-8_30

26. Toledo, G.V., Zohar, Y., Barrett, C.: Combining finite combination properties: finite models and busy beavers. In: Sattler, U., Suda, M. (eds.) FroCoS 2023. LNCS, vol. 14279, pp. 159–175. Springer, Cham (2023). https://doi.org/10.1007/978-3-031-43369-6_9

27. Turing, A.M.: On computable numbers, with an application to the entscheidungsproblem. Proc. London Math. Soc. **s2-42**(1)2, 30–265 (1937). https://londmathsoc.onlinelibrary.wiley.com/doi/abs/10.1112/plms/s2-42.1.230, http://arxiv.org/abs/https://londmathsoc.onlinelibrary.wiley.com/doi/pdf/10.1112/plms/s2-42.1.230, https://doi.org/https://doi.org/10.1112/plms/s2-42.1.230

Term Rewrite Systems

Weighted Rewriting

Martin Avanzini[1] and Akihisa Yamada[2]($\boxtimes$)

[1] Centre Inria d'Université Côte d'Azur, Sophia Antipolis, France
martin.avanzini@inria.fr
[2] AIST, Tokyo Waterfront, Tokyo, Japan
akihisa.yamada@aist.go.jp

Abstract. We introduce the notion of weighted abstract reduction systems (weighted ARSs), generalising standard and relative ARSs by allowing non-uniform weights on transition steps. Weighted ARSs give rise to a theory of rewriting where quantitative properties—noteworthy complexity related properties—can be more directly studied. Unlike these standard notions, weighted ARSs permit the study of quantitative properties of reduction systems of non-uniform weight, such as the analysis of expectation-based properties of probabilistic systems. We establish ranking functions as a means to analyse (strong) boundedness of weighted ARSs, i.e., the property that weights of reductions are bounded from above. We showcase their applicability by instantiating them to weighted term rewrite systems and probabilistic reduction systems, the latter generalising Lyapunov ranking functions to reason about expected derivation heights.

1 Introduction

Rewriting [7] provides a foundational theory of computing, with significant impact on both the theoretical aspects of computer science and the development of programming languages. Traditionally, rewriting primarily focuses on qualitative properties—such as whether a system is terminating or confluent. However, many applications in program analysis require a more fine-grained, *quantitative* perspective. Complexity analysis, cost-sensitive transformations, and resource-aware reasoning all demand a deeper understanding of the quantitative aspects of reduction processes. The study of such quantitative features is crucial for various quality assurance tasks, including guaranteed response time, smart contract deployment costs, resilience against side-channel attacks, security of cryptographic routines, and provable safety guarantees.

Abstract reduction systems (ARSs) provide a general model for a wide class of, possibly nondeterministic or probabilistic, systems. A key strength of ARSs is that they permit studying program properties independently of specific programming paradigms. Yet, they often fail to capture quantitative aspects effectively. A prototypical example is the complexity analysis of high-level, declarative languages, where a single reduction step is not an elementary operation. For

R. Thiemann and C. Weidenbach (Eds.): FroCoS 2025, LNAI 15979, pp. 191–208, 2026.
https://doi.org/10.1007/978-3-032-04167-8_11

instance, in the case of the λ-calculus, it is unrealistic to assume that a single β-reduction step incurs a uniform cost. To endow the λ-calculus with a reasonable cost model—one that relates to Turing machines—Dal Lago and Martini [10] for instance propose to measure the cost of a step in terms of the absolute difference between the size of the reduct and redex. Some approaches to complexity analysis (e.g., [2,8,11]) allow the specification of a program's resource consumption through annotations, the cost of a reduction step thereby becomes dependent on the annotation. A final example, where ARSs fail to model costs effectively, are stochastic, i.e., probabilistic systems.

The key observation of our work is that all these models can be effectively modeled by a *weighted* extension of ARSs, where reduction steps additionally carry *weight* information. Weights are taken from a general (ordered) monoid, whose structure is used to define reflexive and transitive closures, and thereby multi-step reductions. The monoid's unit serves as the basis for reflexivity, while its binary operation is used for sequential composition.

Weights are otherwise left abstract, and can thereby encompass a range of quantitative aspects.

– Using the ordered monoid $\langle \mathbb{N}, 0, +, \leq \rangle$, weighted ARSs encompass rewriting under a *unitary cost measure*, where each reduction step is attributed a unit cost 1. The cost measure of Dal Lago and Martini [10] falls also within this setting, attributing cost $\max(1, |M| - |N|)$ to each β-step $M \rightarrow_\beta N$.
– Taking the ordered monoid $\langle \mathbb{N}, 0, \mathsf{max}, \leq \rangle$, weighted ARSs endow computations with *"watermark"-like cost models*, such as (maximal) space usage.
– Products of monoids, with all operations extended pointwise, can be used to track simultaneously several cost metrics.
– Modelling stochastic reductions as an ARS over (multi)distributions [4], taking weights $\langle \mathbb{R}_{\geq 0}, 0, +, \leq \rangle$ facilitates the study of *expected* resource usage.
– The monoid $\langle \mathbb{N}^{\mathsf{Var} \rightarrow \mathbb{N}}, 0, + \rangle$, with all operations extended pointwise, can attribute non-ground rewrite steps with a *variable-size cost measure*.

Weighted ARSs provide a natural framework for studying quantitative aspects of computations directly. This encompasses quantitative variations of properties traditionally studied—such as strategies, confluence, and termination—taking for instance the length, or more generally cost, of reductions into account. In this work, we focus on termination-like properties, specifically *boundedness*, demanding that (cumulative) weights remain finite. We establish *ranking functions*, formalized as embeddings from weighted ARSs into a *canonical* weighted ARS over weights themselves, as a methodology for proving (strong) *boundedness*. Specifically, we show that this methodology is sound if the underlying monoid is *positive*, and is complete if the monoid is bounded-complete and continuous. Notably, all of the aforementioned instances fall within this setting.

A natural question then is how these abstract notions relate to concrete settings. First, we show that $\mathbb{N}$-weighted ARSs provide a conservative extension of classical and relative ARSs, serving as a sanity check of the proposed theory. We then introduce *weighted term rewrite systems (TRSs)* and *barycentric ARSs*. The former generalises first-order term rewrite systems, where each rule carries a weight. We show how monotone $\mathcal{F}$-algebras, a sound and complete method for proving termination of TRSs, generalize to a sound and complete method for proving (strong) boundedness of weighted TRSs. Barycentric ARSs allow us to model probabilistic reductions in a way that weights correspond to expected runtimes or costs. We establish *affine ranking functions* as a mean to reason about boundedness of barycentric ARSs.

Related Work. Attaching weights to rules is a natural idea that appears in various contexts throughout the literature. One of the most well-studied examples is the theory of weighted automata (cf. [12]). In the context of term rewriting, a form of weighted (integer) TRSs was employed in [17] in order to keep track of the original runtime cost during simplifying the systems. The idea has also been applied to endow imperative [6], functional probabilistic [1], and quantum programs [5] with *non-uniform* cost models, non-uniform in the sense that computation costs of different primitives are not necessarily equal. Our weighted ARSs extract the common essence and serve as a foundation of these works.

A closely related, but fundamentally different idea to incorporate quantitative information is to *map* reduction steps to weights. For instance, in their study of hyper-normalisation, van Oostrom and Toyama [18] introduce *monoid-measured* ARSs, where steps are assigned weights from a monoid, yielding a derivation measure that abstracts over reduction length. Gavazzo and Florio [15] define *quantitative ARSs*, where steps are mapped to elements of a *quantale*—a monoid endowed with a semilattice structure that satisfies certain distributivity laws. Their construction induces a notion of *distance* between terms in the ARS, conforming to the standard axioms of a metric space. In a similar fashion, weighted transition systems [19] generalize weighted automata with additional structures for metrical analysis. Laird et al. [16] endow a non-deterministic version of Plotkin's PCF with a quantitative semantics, where the denotation of a (non-deterministic) function is turned from a relation between inputs and outputs, to a function assigning weights to input/output pairs.

The fundamental difference of our work lies in the structure of the rewriting relation: rather than augmenting ARSs ($R \subseteq A \times A$) with mappings $A \times A \to W$, we extend ARSs to a ternary relation ($R \subseteq W \times A \times A$). As a result, our framework imposes no intrinsic constraints on the nature of weights—for instance, they need not represent distances or abstract measures of derivation length.

Finally, Faggian [13] introduces another orthogonal formalism, also dubbed *quantitative ARSs* (QARSs), particularly aimed for the study of quantitative behaviors of probabilistically evolving systems. QARSs assign quantities—the *observations*—to states ($A \to W$). This way, fundamental properties of QARSs can be studied through the sequence of observations. QARSs are mainly used to study so called *asymptotic* behaviors of infinite reduction sequences, e.g., uniqueness of "limits" of reductions.

Outline. In Sect. 2, we introduce weighted ARSs and their fundamental properties. In Sect. 3 we establish ranking functions as a means to reason about

bound on the weight an initial state can produce. In Sect. 4 we present the afore-mentioned instances of weighted ARSs: standard ARSs, weighted TRSs, and barycentric ARSs, and conclude in Sect. 5.

2   Weighted Abstract Rewriting

In this section we formally introduce *weighted ARSs*—a generalization of ARSs where transitions between states have (possibly different) *weights*. To model the concatenation of multiple weighted reduction steps, we will assume that weights have a monoidal structure. This enables us to model reflexivity and transitivity in the weighted setting. We will also demand that weights are (partially) ordered, so that we can argue about bounds on weights.

We quickly recap some basic notions. A *partially ordered set (poset)* is a set W equipped with a partial order $\leq$ on W. We say a subset $X \subseteq W$ of a poset has an *(upper) bound* $b \in W$ (written $X \leq b$), if $x \leq b$ for all $x \in X$. We say W is *bounded-complete* if every $X \subseteq W$ that has an upper bound in W has the least one, $\sup X$. A *monoid* is a set W equipped with an associative operator $+$ defined on W and its neutral element $0 \in W$, i.e., $(x + y) + z = x + (y + z)$ and $0 + x = x + 0 = x$ for all $x, y, z \in W$. A monoid W is *ordered* if it is also a poset where $x \leq y$ implies $x + z \leq y + z$ and $z + x \leq z + y$ for all $x, y, z \in W$. An ordered monoid W is *positive* if $0 \leq w$ for all $w \in W$. We say W is *continuous* if whenever $\sup X \in W$ is defined, $\sup \{x + w \mid x \in X\}$ is defined and is $\sup X + w$.

Example 1. The sets $\mathbb{N}$ and $\mathbb{R}_{\geq 0}$ of natural and non-negative real numbers form bounded-complete positive monoids with 0, $+$, and $\leq$ as usual. For any nonempty X, the function space $X \to W$ over a bounded-complete positive monoid W forms one with respect to the pointwise extensions, i.e., $0(x) := 0$, $(f + g)(x) := f(x) + g(x)$, and $f \leq g :\Longleftrightarrow \forall x \in X. \ f(x) \leq g(x)$.

Definition 1 (weighted ARS). *A W-weighted ARS over state space A and positive monoid W is a ternary relation[1] $\leadsto \ \subseteq W \times A \times A$. We write $\leadsto^{[w]}$ for $\{\langle a, b \rangle \mid \langle w, a, b \rangle \in \ \leadsto\}$, and hence $a \leadsto^{[w]} b$ means $\langle w, a, b \rangle \in \ \leadsto$. We say $\leadsto$ is a weighted order if it is*

- *reflexive: $a \leadsto^{[0]} a$ for all $a \in A$; and*
- *transitive: $a \leadsto^{[w]} b$ and $b \leadsto^{[v]} c$ implies $a \leadsto^{[w+v]} c$ for all $a, b, c \in A$.*

We denote by $\hat{\leadsto}$ the least weighted order containing $\leadsto$, and write $\leadsto^w$ for $\hat{\leadsto}^{[w]}$. When we know that $\leadsto$ is transitive, we may write $\leadsto^w$ instead of $\leadsto^{[w]}$. Alternatively, the ARS $\leadsto^w$ can be defined by the following inference rules:

$$\frac{}{a \leadsto^0 a} \qquad \frac{a \leadsto^{[w]} b}{a \leadsto^w b} \qquad \frac{a \leadsto^w b \quad b \leadsto^v c}{a \leadsto^{w+v} c}$$

---

[1]   In the literature a weighted relation is often given as $A \times W \times A$. In our context, $W \times A \times A$ turns out notationally more convenient.

Definition 2 (closures and normal forms). *Given a weighted ARS $\rightsquigarrow \subseteq \mathcal{W} \times A \times A$, we define transitive weighted ARSs $\rightsquigarrow^{\geq}$ and $\rightsquigarrow^{>}$ as follows:*

$$a \rightsquigarrow^{\geq w} b :\Longleftrightarrow \exists v \geq w.\ a \rightsquigarrow^v b \qquad a \rightsquigarrow^{> w} b :\Longleftrightarrow \exists v > w.\ a \rightsquigarrow^v b$$

We call $\rightsquigarrow^{\geq}$ the downward closure *as $w \geq v$ implies $\rightsquigarrow^{\geq w} \subseteq \rightsquigarrow^{\geq v}$. By convention, we write $\rightsquigarrow^* \subseteq A \times A$ for $\rightsquigarrow^{\geq 0}$ and $\rightsquigarrow^+$ for $\rightsquigarrow^{> 0}$. We say $a \in A$ is a* normal form *(or* terminal*) with respect to $\rightsquigarrow$ if no such $b \in A$ exists that $a \rightsquigarrow^+ b$. The set of normal forms with respect to $\rightsquigarrow$ is denoted by $\mathsf{NF}(\rightsquigarrow)$.*

Definition 3 (weighted reduction sequence). *A reduction sequence w.r.t. a weighted ARS $\rightsquigarrow$ is a (possibly infinite) sequence $a_0 \rightsquigarrow^{[w_1]} a_1 \rightsquigarrow^{[w_2]} a_2 \rightsquigarrow^{[w_3]} \dots$. The sequence is called*

- *terminating, if there exists $n \in \mathbb{N}$ such that $w_n = w_{n+1} = \dots = 0$;*
- *bounded (by $b \in \mathcal{W}$), if $w_1 + \dots + w_n \leq b$ for any $n = 1, 2, \dots$;*
- *Zeno, if it is bounded but not terminating.*

Example 2. Consider the $\mathbb{R}_{\geq 0}$-weighted ARS $\rightsquigarrow := \{\langle \frac{1}{2^n}, n, n+1 \rangle \mid n \in \mathbb{N}\} \cup \{\langle 0, n, n \rangle \mid n \in \mathbb{N}\}$ over states $\mathbb{N}$. Reduction sequences such as $0 \rightsquigarrow^{[1]} 1 \rightsquigarrow^{[1/2]} 2 \rightsquigarrow^{[0]} 2 \rightsquigarrow^{[0]} \dots$ are terminating, as after the third step only weight-0 steps occur. The sequence $0 \rightsquigarrow^{[1]} 1 \rightsquigarrow^{[1/2]} 2 \rightsquigarrow^{[1/4]} 3 \rightsquigarrow^{[1/8]} \dots$ is not terminating as $\frac{1}{2^n} \neq 0$ for any $n \in \mathbb{N}$, but is bounded by $1 + \frac{1}{2} + \frac{1}{4} + \frac{1}{8} + \dots = 2$; i.e., Zeno.

We now define the properties of weighted ARSs that are of interest in this work. The first two properties generalize the corresponding notions of standard ARSs, and the next two generalize the positive and strong almost-sure termination of probabilistic ARSs [4,9], respectively; the latter was (independently) called "bounded termination" by [14], which inspired the naming below.

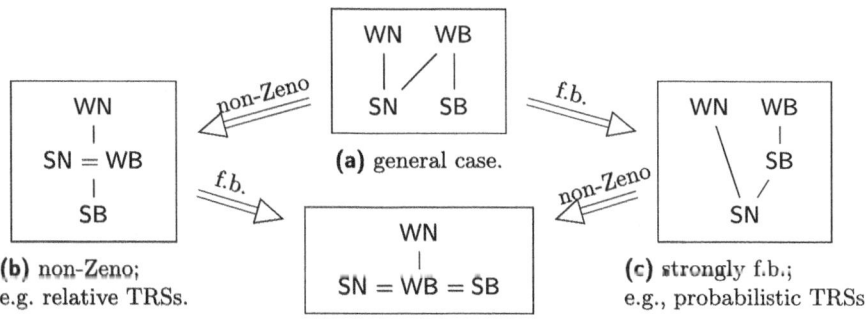

Fig. 1. Hasse diagrams illustrating the impact of non-Zeno and finite branching restrictions on the relationships among the properties from Definition 4. Here TRSs are supposed to be finite.

Definition 4 (properties of weighted ARSs). *A weighted ARS $\rightsquigarrow$ over A is*

1. $\mathsf{WN}_{\rightsquigarrow}(S)$*: (weakly) normalizing on $S \subseteq A$ if every $a \in S$ has $b \in \mathsf{NF}(\rightsquigarrow)$ such that $a \rightsquigarrow^* b$;*
2. $\mathsf{SN}_{\rightsquigarrow}(S)$*: terminating on $S \subseteq A$ if any reduction sequence from any $a \in S$ is terminating;*
3. $\mathsf{WB}_{\rightsquigarrow}(S)$*: weakly bounded on $S \subseteq A$ if any reduction sequence from any $a \in S$ is bounded;*
4. $\mathsf{SB}_{\rightsquigarrow}(S)$*: strongly bounded on $S \subseteq A$ if every $a \in S$ has $p \in \mathcal{W}$ such that any reduction sequence from a is bounded by p;*
5. *strongly finitely branching if for every $a \in A$, both $\{\langle w, b \rangle \mid a \rightsquigarrow^{[w]} b\}$ and $\{b \mid a \rightsquigarrow^0 b\}$ are finite;*
6. *non-Zeno if it admits no Zeno sequence.*

Figure 1 depicts the relationships between these properties, formally proven in Proposition 1 below. The various Hasse diagrams illustrate the following cases: (a) without restrictions; (b) non-Zeno systems; (c) strongly finitely branching systems; and (d) systems that are both strongly finitely branching and non-Zeno. These subclasses are of particular interest, as each corresponds to a distinct class of reduction systems, studied within this work.

Proposition 1. *Let $\rightsquigarrow \subseteq \mathcal{W} \times A \times A$ be a weighted ARS and let $S \subseteq A$. Then*

1. $\mathsf{SN}_{\rightsquigarrow}(S) \implies \mathsf{WN}_{\rightsquigarrow}(S)$;
2. $\mathsf{SB}_{\rightsquigarrow}(S) \implies \mathsf{WB}_{\rightsquigarrow}(S)$;
3. $\mathsf{SN}_{\rightsquigarrow}(S) \implies \mathsf{WB}_{\rightsquigarrow}(S)$;
4. $\mathsf{SN}_{\rightsquigarrow}(S) \iff \mathsf{WB}_{\rightsquigarrow}(S)$ *if $\rightsquigarrow$ is non-Zeno;*
5. $\mathsf{SN}_{\rightsquigarrow}(S) \implies \mathsf{SB}_{\rightsquigarrow}(S)$ *if $\rightsquigarrow$ is strongly finitely branching;*

Proof. We only present interesting ones: 3 and 5. For 3, consider $a_0 \rightsquigarrow^{[w_1]} a_1 \rightsquigarrow^{[w_2]} a_2 \rightsquigarrow^{[w_3]} \cdots$. By assumption $w_n = w_{n+1} = \cdots = 0$ for some $n \in \mathbb{N}$. Defining $p := w_1 + \cdots w_{n-1}$ proves that the considered sequence is bounded.

For 5, suppose that $\mathsf{SN}_{\rightsquigarrow}(S)$ and $\rightsquigarrow$ is strongly finitely branching. For an arbitrary $a \in S$, we prove the set $X := \{w \mid \exists b.\ a \rightsquigarrow^w b\}$ is bounded. Note that there is a surjection onto X from the paths of the graph over A where for each $w > 0$ with $a \rightsquigarrow^{[w]} \cdot \rightsquigarrow^0 b$ there is a corresponding arc from a to b. As this graph is finitely branching, König's Lemma tells that if there are infinitely many paths, then there exists an infinite path $a \rightsquigarrow^0 \cdot \rightsquigarrow^{[w_1]} a_1 \rightsquigarrow^0 \cdot \rightsquigarrow^{[w_2]} \cdots$ with $w_i > 0$. Such reduction does not exist, due to the termination condition. Therefore X is finite, and thus $\sum_{w \in X} w$ is an upper bound of X due to positiveness. $\square$

The implications in Proposition 1 are strict, as illustrated by examples in Fig. 2. As for classical ARSs, weak normalisation does not imply strong normalisation (Fig. 2(a)). The Zeno weighted ARS from Fig. 2(b) shows that in general boundedness does not imply normalisation. The non-Zeno, infinitely branching weighted ARS from Fig. 2(c) shows that weak boundedness and normalisation does not imply strong boundedness. Figure 2(d) is another counterexample of the claim, which is finitely branching as a graph but fails the finiteness of zero-weighted reductions required in Definition 4(5).

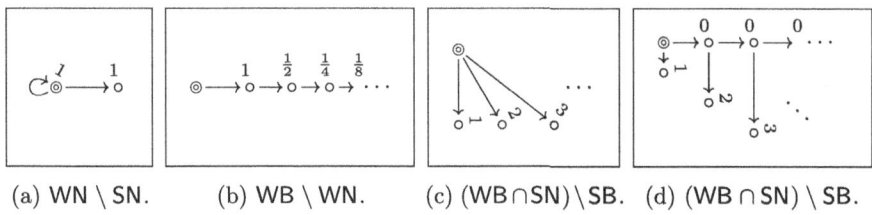

(a) WN \ SN.   (b) WB \ WN.   (c) (WB∩SN)\SB.   (d) (WB ∩ SN) \ SB.

Fig. 2. Examples demonstrating the strictness of the implications in Proposition 1.

3   Bound Analysis via Ranking Functions

Ranking functions are the prototypical way to prove termination, and also play a fundamental role in complexity analysis. For discrete programs over a state space A with transition relation $\mapsto \subseteq A \times A$, a ranking function is a function $\eta : A \to \mathbb{N} \cup \{\infty\}$ which is finite on initial states and decreases along state transitions: $a \mapsto b$ implies $\eta(a) > \eta(b)$ (i.e., η *embeds* $\mapsto$ into $>$). In this section, we adapt ranking functions to weighted ARSs, formalised as embeddings between weighted ARSs.

Definition 5 (embedding). *Let $\leadsto \subseteq W \times A \times A$ and $\succ \subseteq W \times X \times X$ be weighted ARSs. We say a mapping $\eta : A \to X$ is an* embedding *of $\leadsto$ into $\succ$ if $a \leadsto^{[w]} b$ implies $\eta(a) \succ^{[w]} \eta(b)$.*

An embedding is required to strictly preserve the weight of reduction steps. It is possible to relax the condition so that a step of weight w is embedded into a step of weight at least w; however, the same effect is achievable by embedding into the downward-closed weighted ARS $\succ^{\geq w}$.

An embedding witnesses that every $\leadsto$-reduction sequence can be associated with a corresponding $\succ$-reduction sequence of identical weight. Indeed, for any state $a \in A$, the maximal weight of $\leadsto$-reduction sequences is controlled in terms of $\eta(a)$ and $\succ$. To state the relationship precisely, we introduce the notion of *potential*: a function in the state space capturing possible reduction weights.

Definition 6 (potential). *Let $\leadsto \subseteq W \times A \times A$ be a weighted ARS. We define the* potential *of $a \in A$ as the set $\mathsf{Pot}_{\leadsto}(a) := \{w \mid \exists b.\ a \leadsto^w b\} \subseteq W$. We write $\mathsf{pot}_{\leadsto}(a)$ for $\sup \mathsf{Pot}_{\leadsto}(a)$.*

Note that a is a normal form of $\leadsto$ if its (only) potential is 0. Proving strong boundedness is equivalent to proving boundedness on potentials, by definition.

Proposition 2. $\mathsf{SB}_{\leadsto}(S)$ *iff for every $a \in S$, $\mathsf{Pot}_{\leadsto}(a)$ has a bound $b \in W$.*

Theorem 1 (embedding, soundness). *Let $\eta : A \to X$ be an embedding of $\leadsto \subseteq W \times A \times A$ into $\succ \subseteq W \times X \times X$. Then $\mathsf{Pot}_{\leadsto}(a) \subseteq \mathsf{Pot}_{\succ}(\eta(a))$ for every $a \in A$. In particular, for $S \subseteq A$, $\mathsf{SB}_{\succ}(\eta(S))$ implies $\mathsf{SB}_{\leadsto}(S)$.*

Proof. Fix $a \in A$ and $w \in \mathsf{Pot}_{\leadsto}(a)$, i.e., $a \leadsto^w b$ for some $b \in A$. Thus, there is a sequence

$$a = a_0 \leadsto^{[w_1]} a_1 \leadsto^{[w_2]} \ldots \leadsto^{[w_n]} a_n = b$$

such that $w = w_1 + \cdots + w_n$. By Definition 5,

$$\eta(a) = \eta(a_0) \succ^{[w_1]} \eta(a_1) \succ^{[w_2]} \ldots \succ^{[w_n]} \eta(a_n) = \eta(b)$$

i.e., $\eta(a) \succ^w \eta(b)$ and hence $w \in \mathsf{Pot}_{\succ}(\eta(a))$. This concludes $\mathsf{Pot}_{\leadsto}(a) \subseteq \mathsf{Pot}_{\succ}(\eta(a))$. Moreover, if $\mathsf{Pot}_{\succ}(\eta(a))$ has a bound $b \in W$ then so does $\mathsf{Pot}_{\leadsto}(a)$, trivially. Hence, $\mathsf{SB}_{\succ}(\eta(S))$ implies $\mathsf{SB}_{\leadsto}(S)$ by Proposition 2. $\qquad\square$

Ranking functions can now be seen as embeddings into a canonical order $\succ_W$ defined as follows. Note that $\succ_W$ is downward-closed by construction.

Definition 7 (ranking function). *Let $\infty \notin W$ be a fresh top element. We denote by W^∞ the ordered monoid extending W, where $w < \infty$ and $w + \infty := \infty$ for all $w \in W$. We define the weighted order $\succ_W \subseteq W \times W^\infty \times W^\infty$ by $x \succ_W^{[w]} y :\Longleftrightarrow x \geq w + y$. We call an embedding $\eta : A \to W^\infty$ of a weighted ARS $\leadsto \subseteq W \times A \times A$ into $\succ_W$ a (W-valued) ranking function for $\leadsto$.*

Lemma 1. *For a positive monoid W, $\mathsf{SB}_{\succ_W}(W)$ and $\mathsf{pot}_{\succ_W}(x) = x$.*

Proof. Fix $x \in W$. Note that $\mathsf{Pot}_{\succ_W}(x) = \{w \in W \mid \exists y \in W^\infty. \; x \geq w + y\}$. Because of positiveness, $x \geq w + y$ implies $w \leq x$ and thus x is a bound of $\mathsf{Pot}_{\succ_W}(x)$. Since $x = x + 0 \in \mathsf{Pot}_{\succ_W}(x)$, x is the maximum and thus supremum of $\mathsf{Pot}_{\succ_W}(x)$, i.e., $\mathsf{pot}_{\succ_W}(x) = \sup \mathsf{Pot}_{\succ_W}(x) = x$. $\qquad\square$

The following is an immediate consequence of Theorem 1 and Lemma 1:

Corollary 1 (ranking functions, soundness). *If a weighted ARS $\leadsto \subseteq W \times A \times A$ admits a ranking function $\eta : A \to W^\infty$ with $\eta(S) \subseteq W$ for $S \subseteq A$, then $\mathsf{SB}_{\leadsto}(S)$. In particular, $\mathsf{pot}_{\leadsto}(a) \leq \eta(a)$ for every $a \in S$.*

Completeness also holds, at least if the weights constitute a bounded-complete continuous monoid. Since $\mathbb{N}$ and $\mathbb{R}_{\geq 0}$ with usual 0, $+$ and $\leq$ are such instances, $\mathbb{N}$-valued ($\mathbb{R}_{\geq 0}$-valued) ranking functions yield both a sound and complete methodology for proving strong boundedness. We leave it for a future work to find a milder condition preserving completeness.

Theorem 2 (ranking functions, completeness). *If W is a bounded-complete continuous monoid and a weighted ARS $\leadsto \subseteq W \times A \times A$ is strongly bounded on S, then $\leadsto$ admits a ranking function $\eta : A \to W^\infty$ with $\eta(S) \subseteq W$.*

Proof. Observe that $\sup X \in W^\infty$ is defined for any $X \subseteq W$: if X has a bound in W then $\sup X \in W$ due to bounded-completeness, and $\sup X = \infty$ otherwise. Therefore, $\mathsf{pot}_{\leadsto} : A \to W^\infty$ is defined.

Now we show that pot is an embedding of $\leadsto$ into $\succ_W$. So we prove that $a \leadsto^{[w]} b$ implies $\mathsf{pot}_{\leadsto}(a) \succ_W^{[w]} \mathsf{pot}_{\leadsto}(b)$. If $\mathsf{pot}_{\leadsto}(a) = \infty$ the claim is trivial. Otherwise, using $a \leadsto^{[w]} b$, observe that

$$\mathsf{Pot}_{\leadsto}(a) = \{v \mid \exists c. \; a \leadsto^v c\} \supseteq \{w + u \mid \exists c. \; b \leadsto^u c\} =: X.$$

Since $\mathsf{pot}_{\leadsto}(a) \in \mathcal{W}$ is a bound of $\mathsf{Pot}(a)$, it is also a bound of X; thus, $\sup X \in \mathcal{W}$ is defined due to bounded-completeness. Now due to continuity

$$\mathsf{pot}_{\leadsto}(a) \geq \sup X = w + \sup\{u \mid b \leadsto^{u} c\} = w + \mathsf{pot}_{\leadsto}(b),$$

i.e., indeed $\mathsf{pot}_{\leadsto}(a) \succ_{\mathcal{W}}^{[w]} \mathsf{pot}_{\leadsto}(b)$ holds. Finally, since $\mathsf{SB}_{\leadsto}(S)$ means that $\mathsf{Pot}_{\leadsto}(a)$ has a bound in $\mathcal{W}$ for every $a \in S$, bounded-completeness gives $\mathsf{pot}_{\leadsto}(a) \in \mathcal{W}$. This concludes $\mathsf{pot}_{\leadsto}(S) \subseteq \mathcal{W}$. $\qquad\square$

4 Instances

Having defined weighted ARSs and a method to prove strong boundedness, the aim of this section is to demonstrate their versatility. We begin by formally stating the connection between (unitary) weighted ARSs and ARSs, ensuring that the notions we introduced align with standard concepts in abstract rewriting. Next, we generalize term rewrite systems (TRSs) to weighted TRSs, where rules carry weights, and show how the interpretation method can be used to prove strong boundedness. Finally, we introduce barycentric ARSs. One particular class of barycentric ARSs is given by probabilistic ARSs, with weights modelling expected runtime. Through ranking functions, we obtain a methodology for proving probabilistic termination properties.

4.1 Abstract Reduction System

We may identify an ARS $\mapsto \subseteq A \times A$ as the $\mathbb{N}$-weighted ARS $\{1\} \times \mapsto = \{\langle 1, a, b\rangle \mid a \mapsto b\}$. This is justified by the following correspondences. As usual, $\mapsto^{n}$, $\mapsto^{+}$, $\mapsto^{*}$, and $\mathsf{NF}(\mapsto)$ denote the standard n-th fold, transitive closure, reflexive-transitive closure, and the set *normal forms* of $\mapsto$, respectively. The *derivation height* $\mathsf{dh}_{\mapsto}(a) \in \mathbb{N}^{\infty}$ of $a \in A$ with respect to $\mapsto$ is defined by $\mathsf{dh}_{\mapsto}(a) := \sup\{n \in \mathbb{N} \mid \exists b.\ a \mapsto^{n} b\}$.

Proposition 3. *For any (unweighted) ARS $\mapsto \subseteq A \times A$:*

- *$(\{1\} \times \mapsto)^{\alpha} = \mapsto^{\alpha}$ where $\alpha \in \mathbb{N} \cup \{*, +\}$,*
- *$\mathsf{NF}(\{1\} \times \mapsto) = \mathsf{NF}(\mapsto)$, and $\mathsf{pot}_{\{1\} \times \mapsto}(s) = \mathsf{dh}_{\mapsto}(s)$.*

Clearly the $\mathbb{N}$-weighted ARS $\{1\} \times \mapsto$ is non-Zeno, so termination coincides with weak boundedness due to Proposition 1 (see also Fig. 1(b)). If $\mapsto$ is finitely branching, then $\{1\} \times \mapsto$ is strongly finitely branching, and termination coincides with weak and strong boundedness (see Fig. 1(d)).

The correspondence extends to relative reduction. The reduction of an ARS $\mapsto$ *relative* to another ARS $\sim$ is modeled by the ARS $\mapsto/\sim := \sim^{*} \circ \mapsto \circ \sim^{*}$. Attributing $\mapsto$ weight one and $\sim$ weight zero allows us to model relative reduction through $\mathbb{N}$-weighted ARS $\mapsto//\sim := (\{1\} \times \mapsto) \cup (\{0\} \times \sim)$.

Proposition 4. *For any ARSs $\mapsto, \sim \subseteq A \times A$:*

- $(\mapsto\!/\!\!/\!\sim)^0 = \sim^*$ and $(\mapsto\!/\!\!/\!\sim)^n = (\mapsto\!/\!\sim)^n$ where $n = 1, 2, \ldots,$
- $(\mapsto\!/\!\!/\!\sim)^* = (\mapsto \cup \sim)^* = \sim^* \cup (\mapsto\!/\!\sim)^*,$
- $(\mapsto\!/\!\!/\!\sim)^+ = (\mapsto\!/\!\sim)^+,$
- $\mathsf{NF}(\mapsto\!/\!\!/\!\sim) = \mathsf{NF}(\mapsto\!/\!\sim)$, and $\mathsf{pot}_{\mapsto\!/\!\!/\!\sim}(s) = \mathsf{dh}_{\mapsto\!/\!\sim}(s).$

4.2   Term Rewrite Systems

We now introduce weighted versions of *term rewrite systems* (*TRSs*), i.e., TRSs where each rule carries a weight. Usual TRSs correspond to $\{1\} \times \mathcal{R}$. The reduction relation attributed to a weighted TRS will be given as a weighted ARS over terms. We define monotone algebras (i.e., the interpretation method) as a sound and complete methodology for proving strong boundedness.

We quickly recap notations. For a signature $\mathcal{F}$ and variables $\mathcal{V}$, let us denote by $\mathcal{T}(\mathcal{F}, \mathcal{V})$ the set of terms. Terms are denoted by s, t, l, r below. For a substitution σ, we write $t\sigma$ for its application to a term t. For a context C, i.e., term with one special symbol $\square$, we denote by $C[t]$ the term obtained by replacing $\square$ in C by t. With $\mathsf{Var}(t)$ we denote the set of variables in t.

Definition 8 (weighted TRS). *A* $\mathcal{W}$-*weighted rule is a triple* $\langle w, l, r \rangle \in \mathcal{W} \times \mathcal{T}(\mathcal{F}, \mathcal{V}) \times \mathcal{T}(\mathcal{F}, \mathcal{V})$, *where* variable conditions $l \notin \mathcal{V}$ *and* $\mathsf{Var}(r) \subseteq \mathsf{Var}(l)$ *hold. A* $\mathcal{W}$-*weighted TRS is a set* $\mathcal{R}$ *of weighted rules.*

Definition 9 (weighted rewrite relation). *A* $\mathcal{W}$-*weighted rewrite relation is a* $\mathcal{W}$-*weighted ARS* $\rightsquigarrow$ *that is closed under substitutions and contexts; i.e.,* $C[l\sigma] \rightsquigarrow^{[w]} C[r\sigma]$ *for every context* C *and substitution* σ *whenever* $l \rightsquigarrow^{[w]} r$.

We define the weighted ARS $\rightsquigarrow_{\mathcal{R}}$ over $\mathcal{T}(\mathcal{F}, \mathcal{V})$ as the least weighted rewrite relation containing $\mathcal{R}$; more concretely $C[l\sigma] \rightsquigarrow_{\mathcal{R}}^{[w]} C[r\sigma]$ for every weighted rule $\langle w, l, r \rangle \in \mathcal{R}$, context C and substitution σ. It is well known that a TRS is terminating if and only if it is included in a well-founded rewrite relation. A similar correspondence holds for weighted TRSs:

Theorem 3. *Let* $\mathcal{R}$ *be a* $\mathcal{W}$-*weighted TRS. The rewrite relation* $\rightsquigarrow_{\mathcal{R}}$ *is strongly bounded if and only if* $\mathcal{R} \subseteq \succ$ *for a strongly bounded weighted rewrite relation* $\succ$.

Proof. For the "if" direction, suppose $\succ$ is a strongly bounded rewrite relation containing $\mathcal{R}$. Suppose $C[l\sigma] \rightsquigarrow_{\mathcal{R}}^{[w]} C[r\sigma]$ with $\langle w, l, r \rangle \in \mathcal{R}$. Since $\mathcal{R} \subseteq \succ$, we have $l \succ^{[w]} r$, as $\succ$ is a rewrite relation it follows that $C[l\sigma] \succ^{[w]} C[r\sigma]$. Consequently, the identity function embeds $\rightsquigarrow_{\mathcal{R}}$ into $\succ$. From this, it follows that $\rightsquigarrow_{\mathcal{R}}$ is strongly bounded by Theorem 1. The "only if" direction follows by taking $\rightsquigarrow_{\mathcal{R}}$ for $\succ$. $\square$

The interpretation method, which interprets terms through an algebra into a well-founded order $\succ$, is among the most fundamental methods for proving termination of standard TRSs. This method naturally adapts to weighted TRSs for proving strong boundedness: An $\mathcal{F}$-*algebra* is a set $\mathcal{A}$ equipped with the *interpretation* $f_{\mathcal{A}} : \mathcal{A}^n \to \mathcal{A}$ of every n-ary symbol $f \in \mathcal{F}$. The interpretation $[\![s]\!]_{\mathcal{A}}^{\alpha}$ of terms $s \in \mathcal{T}(\mathcal{F}, \mathcal{V})$ under *assignment* $\alpha : \mathcal{V} \to \mathcal{A}$ is defined as usual.

Definition 10 (weighted monotone $\mathcal{F}$-algebra). *A ($\mathcal{W}$-weighted) monotone $\mathcal{F}$-algebra $\langle \mathcal{A}, \succ \rangle$ consists of an $\mathcal{F}$-algebra $\mathcal{A}$ and a weighted ARS $\succ \subseteq \mathcal{W} \times A \times A$, such that every interpretation is monotone with respect to $\succ$, that is, $x \succ^{[w]} y$ implies $f_{\mathcal{A}}(\dots, x, \dots) \succ^{[w]} f_{\mathcal{A}}(\dots, y, \dots)$ for every $f \in \mathcal{F}$.*

Given a monotone $\mathcal{F}$-algebra $\langle \mathcal{A}, \succ \rangle$ we define the weighted ARS $\succ_{\mathcal{A}}$ over terms by $s \succ_{\mathcal{A}}^{[w]} t$ iff $[\![s]\!]_{\mathcal{A}}^{\alpha} \succ^{[w]} [\![t]\!]_{\mathcal{A}}^{\alpha}$ holds for every assignment $\alpha : \mathcal{V} \to X$.

Lemma 2. *For a monotone $\mathcal{F}$-algebra $\langle \mathcal{A}, \succ \rangle$, $\succ_{\mathcal{A}}$ is a weighted rewrite relation.*

Proof. Reasoning inductively, $[\![s\theta]\!]_{\mathcal{A}}^{\alpha} = [\![s]\!]_{\mathcal{A}}^{[\theta]^{\alpha}}$, where $[\![\cdot]\!]_{\mathcal{A}}^{\alpha}$ is extended homomorphically to the substitution θ. Closure under substitutions now follows from definition of $\succ_{\mathcal{A}}$, closure under contexts by monotonicity.   □

Let us call an $\mathcal{F}$-algebra $\langle \mathcal{A}, \succ \rangle$ strongly bounded if $\succ$ is.

Theorem 4. *A weighted TRS $\mathcal{R}$ is strongly bounded if and only if $\mathcal{R} \subseteq \succ_{\mathcal{A}}$ for a strongly bounded monotone $\mathcal{F}$-algebra $\langle \mathcal{A}, \succ \rangle$.*

Proof. The "if"-direction follows by Theorem 3 and Lemma 2. The "only if" direction holds taking for $\langle \mathcal{A}, \succ \rangle$ the $\mathcal{W}$-weighted $\mathcal{F}$-algebra $\langle \mathcal{T}, \leadsto_{\mathcal{R}} \rangle$, where $\mathcal{T}$ is the term algebra. Trivially, $\mathcal{R} \subseteq \leadsto_{\mathcal{R}} = (\leadsto_{\mathcal{R}})_{\mathcal{T}}$ and $\leadsto_{\mathcal{R}}$ is monotone.   □

One prototypical instance for the order $\succ$ is the canonical weighted ARS $\succ_{\mathbb{N}}$; this way, interpretations over naturals can be seen as a way to inductively define ranking functions on TRSs. Another noticeable instance is $\succ_{\mathbb{R}_{\geq 0}}$; using such real-valued interpretations one can prove strong boundedness, which is equivalent to termination as long as the set of rewrite rules is finite (compare Fig. 1(d)).

4.3 Barycentric ARSs

Probabilistic ARSs were introduced by Bournez and Garnier [9] as a means to study reduction systems with probabilistic behavior. In essence, probabilistic ARS (over objects A) allow sampling of reducts from a (probability) *distribution*, a function $d : A \to [0,1]$ with $\sum_{a \in A} d(a) = 1$, assigning to each $a \in A$ a *probability* $d(a)$. Rules in probabilistic ARSs take the form $a \to d$; the intended meaning of such a rule is that a reduces to b with probability $d(b)$. When a *policy* that resolves non-deterministic choices is fixed, reduction sequences can be defined in terms of stochastic processes. Equivalently, reduction can be defined directly through an ARS over *multidistributions* [3,4], a structure that generalises probability distributions and multisets, encapsulating the probabilistic and non-deterministic effects, respectively. We will generalize probabilistic ARSs into a class of weighted ARSs called *barycentric ARSs*. Before, we recap notions, following the presentation of [4].

We denote the set of distributions on A by $\mathcal{D}(A)$. The *convex combinations* of distributions are defined by $\left(\sum_{i \in I} p_i \cdot d_i \right)(a) := \sum_{i \in I} p_i \cdot d_i(a)$ for $\sum_{i \in I} p_i = 1$. We may view distributions as sets of pairs of $a \in A$ and $p > 0$ written $p : a$, i.e., $d = \{d(a) : a \mid a \in A, d(a) > 0\}$. A *(sub-)multidistribution* on A is a multiset μ of such pairs $p : a$, satisfying $|\mu| := \sum_{(p:a)\in\mu} p = 1 \ (\leq 1)$. We denote the set of (sub-)multidistributions on A by $\mathcal{M}(A)$ ($\mathcal{M}^{\leq 1}(A)$). The *(sub-)convex combination* of multidistributions $\langle\mu_i\rangle_{i\in I}$ along probabilities $p_i > 0$ with $\sum_{i\in I} p_i \leq 1$ is the (sub-)multidistribution defined by:

$$\biguplus_{i\in I} p_i \cdot \mu_i := \{\!\{ p_i \cdot q_j : a_j \mid i \in I, \ \mu_i = \{\!\{ q_j : a_j \}\!\}_{j\in J}, j \in J \}\!\}$$

A *probabilistic ARS* over A is a set $\mathcal{P} \subseteq A \times \mathcal{M}(A)$. The *probabilistic one-step reduction* is given in [4] by an ARS $\hookrightarrow_{\mathcal{P}} \subseteq \mathcal{M}^{\leq 1}(A) \times \mathcal{M}^{\leq 1}(A)$. Informally, $\mu \hookrightarrow_{\mathcal{P}} \nu$ if ν is obtained from μ by (i) removing terminal objects ($\nexists\mu. \ a \ \mathcal{P} \ \mu$), and by (ii) replacing every occurrence of a reducible object a by a corresponding reduct scaled by the associated probability. Formally, the ARS $\hookrightarrow_{\mathcal{P}}$ can be defined inductively, as follows:

$$\frac{\nexists\mu. \ a \ \mathcal{P} \ \mu}{\{\!\{1 : a\}\!\} \hookrightarrow_{\mathcal{P}} \varnothing} \qquad \frac{a \ \mathcal{P} \ \mu}{\{\!\{1 : a\}\!\} \hookrightarrow_{\mathcal{P}} \mu} \qquad \frac{\sum_{i\in I} p_i \leq 1 \quad \forall i \in I. \ \mu_i \hookrightarrow_{\mathcal{P}} \nu_i}{\biguplus_{i\in I} p_i \cdot \mu_i \hookrightarrow_{\mathcal{P}} \biguplus_{i\in I} p_i \cdot \nu_i}$$

A *probabilistic reduction sequence* is a sequence $\vec{\mu} = \langle \mu_0, \mu_1, \mu_2 \ldots \rangle$ such that

$$\mu_0 \hookrightarrow_{\mathcal{P}} \mu_1 \hookrightarrow_{\mathcal{P}} \mu_2 \hookrightarrow_{\mathcal{P}} \cdots \tag{1}$$

where μ_n represents the state distribution after n-step transitions from the initial state distribution μ_0. As terminal objects are removed along the way, $|\mu_n|$ quantifies the possibility of having state transitions of length at least n, following the reduction strategy implicit in (eq:red).

Let $\mathsf{red}_{\mathcal{P}}(\mu)$ denote the set of all probabilistic reduction sequences starting form μ. A probabilistic ARS $\mathcal{P}$ is said to be *almost surely terminating (AST)* if the probability of having infinite transitions is zero: $\lim_{n\to\infty} |\mu_n| = 0$ for any $\vec{\mu} \in \mathsf{red}_{\mathcal{P}}(\{\!\{1 : a\}\!\})$ of any $a \in A$; $\mathcal{P}$ is said to be *positively AST* if the *expected derivation length* $\mathsf{edl}(\vec{\mu}) := \sum_{n\geq 1} |\mu_n| \in \mathbb{R}_{\geq 0}^{\infty}$ is finite for any $\vec{\mu} \in \mathsf{red}_{\mathcal{P}}(\{\!\{1 : a\}\!\})$ of any $a \in A$;

and $\mathcal{P}$ is *strongly AST* if the *expected derivation height*

$$\mathsf{edh}_{\mathcal{P}}(\mu) := \sup\{\mathsf{edl}(\vec{\nu}) \mid \vec{\nu} \in \mathsf{red}_{\mathcal{P}}(\mu)\}$$

is finite for any $\mu = \{\!\{1 : a\}\!\}$ with $a \in A$.

Example 3. Let $\underline{\mathbb{N}} := \{\underline{n} \mid n \in \mathbb{N}\}$ be a fresh copy of $\mathbb{N}$, and consider the probabilistic ARS $\mathcal{G}$ over $\mathbb{N} \uplus \underline{\mathbb{N}}$, defined as

$$\mathcal{G} := \{\langle \underline{n}, \{\!\{ ^1/_2 : n, \, ^1/_2 : \underline{n+1} \}\!\} \rangle \mid n \in \mathbb{N}\} \ .$$

Then, for instance, there is an infinite reduction sequence

$$\{\!\{1 : \underline{0}\}\!\} \hookrightarrow_{\mathcal{G}} \{\!\{ ^1/_2 : 0, \, ^1/_2 : \underline{1} \}\!\} \hookrightarrow_{\mathcal{G}} \{\!\{ ^1/_4 : 1, \, ^1/_4 : \underline{2} \}\!\} \hookrightarrow_{\mathcal{G}} \{\!\{ ^1/_8 : 2, \, ^1/_8 : \underline{3} \}\!\} \hookrightarrow_{\mathcal{G}} \cdots$$

whose expected derivation length is $1 + \frac{1}{2} + \frac{1}{4} + \cdots = 2$.

Now we capture probabilistic ARS as a class of weighted ARSs, where the states and weights constitute *barycentric algebras*. A *barycentric algebra* (also called a *convex space*) is typically given as a set X equipped with a binary operation $+_p : X \times X \to X$ with $x +_p y$ giving the mean of x and y weighted by $p \in [0, 1]$, satisfying certain laws. The binary operator extends to finite sums $\sum_{i=0}^n p_i \cdot x_i$ for $\sum_{i=0}^n p_i = 1$, and partially to infinite sums $\sum_i p_i \cdot x_i$, which can then be used to define a partial expectation operator $\mathbb{E} : \mathcal{M}(X) \rightharpoonup X$. In this paper, we just assume the presence of such partial operator $\mathbb{E}$.

Definition 11 (multidistribution-algebra). *A partial $\mathcal{M}$-algebra is a set X equipped with a partial barycenter operator $\mathbb{E} : \mathcal{M}(X) \rightharpoonup X$. We say X is an $\mathcal{M}$-algebra if $\mathbb{E}(\mu) \in X$ for all $\mu \in \mathcal{M}(X)$. An $\mathcal{M}$-algebraic monoid is a monoid which is also an $\mathcal{M}$-algebra.*

The monoid $\mathbb{R}_{\geq 0}$ is a partial $\mathcal{M}$-algebra by defining $\mathbb{E}(\{\!\{p_i : x_i\}\!\}_{i \in I}) := \sum_{i \in I} p_i \cdot x_i$, and $\mathbb{R}_{\geq 0}^\infty$ is an $\mathcal{M}$-algebra. The sets $\mathcal{D}(X)$ and $\mathcal{M}(X)$ of distributions and multidistributions are $\mathcal{M}$-algebras with $\mathbb{E}(\{\!\{p_i : d_i\}\!\}_{i \in I}) := \sum_{i \in I} p_i \cdot d_i$ and $\mathbb{E}(\{\!\{p_i : \mu_i\}\!\}_{i \in I}) := \biguplus_{i \in I} p_i \cdot \mu_i,$[2] respectively. This, in turn, allows us to model ARSs with probabilistic behaviour as *barycentric ARSs*.

Definition 12 (barycentric ARS). *A barycentric ARS is a weighted ARS $\leadsto \subseteq W \times A \times A$ where W is a partial $\mathcal{M}$-algebra and A is an $\mathcal{M}$-algebra, such that if $\mathbb{E}\{\!\{p_i : w_i\}\!\}_{i \in I} \in W$ and $\forall i \in I.\ a_i \leadsto^{[w_i]} b_i$, then*

$$\mathbb{E}\{\!\{p_i : a_i\}\!\}_{i \in I} \leadsto^{[\mathbb{E}\{\!\{p_i : w_i\}\!\}_{i \in I}]} \mathbb{E}\{\!\{p_i : b_i\}\!\}_{i \in I} \,.$$

Given a weighted ARS $\leadsto \subseteq W \times A \times A$, we denote the least barycentric weighted order extending $\leadsto$ by $\tilde{\leadsto}$.

Example 4. The $\mathbb{R}_{\geq 0}$-weighted ARS $\leadsto_{\mathcal{R}}$ over distributions of molecules, defined by the single rule

$$\{1/2 : \text{HCl}, 1/2 : \text{NaOH}\} \leadsto_{\mathcal{R}}^{[56.5]} \{1/2 : \text{NaCl}, 1/2 : \text{H}_2\text{O}\} \,,$$

models the classical neutralization reaction, turning hydrogen chloride and sodium hydroxide into salt and water, at a unit weight of 56.5 (kJ/mol). Then, for instance, there is a derivation leading to a normal form:

$\{1/5 : \text{HCl}, 4/5 : \text{NaOH}\}$

$\quad = \quad 1/5\{1/2 : \text{HCl}, 1/2 : \text{NaOH}\} + 1/5\{1/2 : \text{HCl}, 1/2 : \text{NaOH}\} + 3/5\{1 : \text{NaOH}\}$

$\quad \tilde{\leadsto}_{\mathcal{R}}^{11.3}\ 1/5\{1/2 : \text{NaCl}, 1/2 : \text{H}_2\text{O}\} + 1/5\{1/2 : \text{HCl}, 1/2 : \text{NaOH}\} + 3/5\{1 : \text{NaOH}\}$

$\quad \tilde{\leadsto}_{\mathcal{R}}^{11.3}\ 1/5\{1/2 : \text{NaCl}, 1/2 : \text{H}_2\text{O}\} + 1/5\{1/2 : \text{NaCl}, 1/2 : \text{H}_2\text{O}\} + 3/5\{1 : \text{NaOH}\}$

$\quad = \quad \{1/5 : \text{NaCl}, 1/5 : \text{H}_2\text{O}, 3/5 : \text{NaOH}\} \,.$

---

[2] This instantiation is possible because we do not impose the usual idempotency law $x +_p x = x$, i.e., we do not require $\mathbb{E}\{\!\{p_i : \mu\}\!\}_{i \in I} = \mu$ for $\sum_i p_i = 1$ to hold.

Example 5. The $\mathbb{R}_{\geq 0}$-weighted ARS $\mathcal{G}$ from Example 3 is modeled as weighted ARS over multidistributions $\mathcal{M}(\mathbb{N} \cup \underline{\mathbb{N}})$ defined through the rules

$$\{\!\!\{1 : \underline{n}\}\!\!\} \leadsto_{\mathcal{G}}^{[1]} \{\!\!\{1/2 : n, 1/2 : \underline{n+1}\}\!\!\} \qquad \text{for all } n \in \mathbb{N}.$$

Then, for instance, the following infinite reduction, whose weight is bounded precisely by 2, corresponds to the reduction from Example 3:

$$\{\!\!\{1 : \underline{0}\}\!\!\} \tilde{\leadsto}_{\mathcal{G}}^{1} \{\!\!\{1/2 : 0, 1/2 : \underline{1}\}\!\!\} \tilde{\leadsto}_{\mathcal{G}}^{1/2} \{\!\!\{1/2 : 0, 1/4 : 1, 1/4 : \underline{2}\}\!\!\} \tilde{\leadsto}_{\mathcal{G}}^{1/4} \cdots .$$

The above construction generalises to arbitrary probabilistic ARSs: Given a probabilistic ARS $\mathcal{P}$ over A, we define the $\mathbb{R}_{\geq 0}$-weighted ARS over the state space $\mathcal{M}(A)$ by $\{\!\!\{1 : a\}\!\!\} \leadsto_{\mathcal{P}}^{[1]} \mu :\Longleftrightarrow a \mathcal{P} \mu$. The induced barycentric weighted order $\tilde{\leadsto}_{\mathcal{P}}$ can also be defined inductively:

$$\frac{}{\mu \tilde{\leadsto}_{\mathcal{P}}^{0} \mu} \qquad \frac{\mu \tilde{\leadsto}_{\mathcal{P}}^{w} \nu \quad \nu \tilde{\leadsto}_{\mathcal{P}}^{v} \xi}{\mu \tilde{\leadsto}_{\mathcal{P}}^{w+v} \xi} \qquad \frac{a \mathcal{P} \mu}{\{\!\!\{1 : a\}\!\!\} \tilde{\leadsto}_{\mathcal{P}}^{1} \mu} \qquad \frac{\forall i \in I. \; \mu_i \tilde{\leadsto}_{\mathcal{P}}^{w_i} \nu_i}{\biguplus_{i \in I} p_i \cdot \mu_i \tilde{\leadsto}_{\mathcal{P}}^{\Sigma_{i \in I} \, p_i \cdot w_i} \biguplus_{i \in I} p_i \cdot \nu_i}$$

where the last rule assumes $\sum_{i \in I} p_i \cdot w_i < \infty$. Unlike the one-step $\hookrightarrow_{\mathcal{P}}$, the weighted order $\tilde{\leadsto}_{\mathcal{P}}$ already covers multi-step reductions. As illustrated in Example 5, terminals remain persistent through reductions. The weight w in a step $\mu \tilde{\leadsto}_{\mathcal{P}}^{w} \nu$ gives the expected number of reduction steps carried out in the reduction from μ to ν. Precisely, the potentials reflect expected derivation heights:

Lemma 3. *Let $\mathcal{P} \subseteq A \times \mathcal{M}(A)$ be a probabilistic ARS over A. Then $\mathsf{edh}_{\mathcal{P}}(\mu) = \mathsf{pot}_{\tilde{\leadsto}_{\mathcal{P}}}(\mu)$ for every proper multidistribution $\mu \in \mathcal{M}(A)$.*

Proof. Observe that, for $\mu, \nu, \rho \in \mathcal{M}^{\leq 1}(A)$, if $\mu \hookrightarrow_{\mathcal{P}} \nu$, then $\mu \uplus \rho \tilde{\leadsto}_{\mathcal{P}}^{|\nu|} \nu \uplus \xi \uplus \rho$, where $\xi \subseteq \mu$ gives the sub-multidistribution of terminals in μ.

We first show

$$\mathsf{edh}_{\mathcal{P}}(\mu) = \sup \left\{ \sum_{i=1}^{\infty} |\mu_i| \; \middle| \; \mu \hookrightarrow_{\mathcal{P}} \mu_1 \hookrightarrow_{\mathcal{P}} \mu_2 \hookrightarrow_{\mathcal{P}} \dots \right\} \leq \mathsf{pot}_{\tilde{\leadsto}_{\mathcal{P}}}(\mu)$$

for every proper multidistribution μ. To this end, consider an infinite reduction of the form $\mu \hookrightarrow_{\mathcal{P}} \mu_1 \hookrightarrow_{\mathcal{P}} \mu_2 \hookrightarrow_{\mathcal{P}} \cdots$. The above observation inductively yields

$$\mu \tilde{\leadsto}_{\mathcal{P}}^{|\mu_1|} \mu_1 \uplus \xi_1 \tilde{\leadsto}_{\mathcal{P}}^{|\mu_2|} \mu_2 \uplus \xi_1 \uplus \xi_2 \tilde{\leadsto}_{\mathcal{P}}^{|\mu_3|} \dots \tilde{\leadsto}_{\mathcal{P}}^{|\mu_n|} \mu_n \uplus \xi_1 \uplus \dots \uplus \xi_n ,$$

and thus $\mu \tilde{\leadsto}_{\mathcal{P}}^{|\mu_1| + \dots + |\mu_n|} \mu_n \uplus \xi_1 \uplus \dots \uplus \xi_n$ for every $n \in \mathbb{N}$. By the definition of potentials, we have $|\mu_1| + \dots + |\mu_n| \leq \mathsf{pot}_{\tilde{\leadsto}_{\mathcal{P}}}(\mu)$ for every $n \in \mathbb{N}$, and thus $\sum_{i=1}^{\infty} |\mu_i| \leq \mathsf{pot}_{\tilde{\leadsto}_{\mathcal{P}}}(\mu)$. We conclude by showing

$$\mathsf{edh}_{\mathcal{P}}(\mu) \geq \sup \{ w \mid \mu \tilde{\leadsto}_{\mathcal{P}}^{w} \nu \} = \mathsf{pot}_{\tilde{\leadsto}_{\mathcal{P}}}(\mu) ,$$

that is, $w \leq \mathsf{edh}_{\mathcal{P}}(\mu)$ whenever $\mu \tilde{\leadsto}_{\mathcal{P}}^{w} \nu$. More precisely we prove $\mathsf{edh}_{\mathcal{P}}(\mu) \geq w + \mathsf{edh}_{\mathcal{P}}(\nu)$ by induction on the derivation of $\mu \tilde{\leadsto}_{\mathcal{P}}^{w} \nu$. The claim is trivial if $\mu = \nu$ and $w = 0$. If $\mu \tilde{\leadsto}_{\mathcal{P}}^{u} \xi \tilde{\leadsto}_{\mathcal{P}}^{v} \nu$ and $w = u + v$, then

$$\mathsf{edh}_{\mathcal{P}}(\mu) \geq u + \mathsf{edh}_{\mathcal{P}}(\xi) \geq u + v + \mathsf{edh}_{\mathcal{P}}(\nu) = w + \mathsf{edh}_{\mathcal{P}}(\nu)$$

by the induction hypotheses. If $\mu = \{\!\{1 : a\}\!\}$, $a \, \mathcal{P} \, \nu$, and $w = 1$, then we conclude as $\mathsf{edh}_\mathcal{P}(\{\!\{1 : a\}\!\}) \geq 1 + \mathsf{edh}_\mathcal{P}(\nu)$ by definition of $\mathsf{edh}_\mathcal{P}$. Finally, consider $\mu = \biguplus_{i \in I} p_i \cdot \mu_i$, $\nu = \biguplus_{i \in I} w_i \cdot \nu_i$, $w = \sum_{i \in I} p_i \cdot w_i$, and $\mu_i \leadsto_\mathcal{P}^{w_i} \nu_i$ for all $i \in I$. It is not difficult to show that $\mathsf{edh}_\mathcal{P}(\mu) = \sum_{i \in I} p_i \cdot \mathsf{edh}_\mathcal{P}(\mu_i)$ (cf. [4, Lemma 4]). By induction hypothesis, $\mathsf{edh}_\mathcal{P}(\mu_i) \geq w_i + \mathsf{edh}_\mathcal{P}(\nu_i)$, and consequently,

$$\mathsf{edh}_\mathcal{P}(\mu) = \sum_{i \in I} p_i \cdot \mathsf{edh}_\mathcal{P}(\mu_i) \geq \sum_{i \in I} p_i \cdot (w_i + \mathsf{edh}_\mathcal{P}(\nu_i)) = w + \mathsf{edh}_\mathcal{P}(\nu). \qquad \square$$

Proposition 5. *A probabilistic ARS $\mathcal{P} \subseteq A \times \mathcal{M}(A)$ is strongly AST iff $\tilde{\leadsto}_\mathcal{P}$ is strongly bounded on singleton multidistributions.*

As we have seen in Corollary 1 and Theorem 2, embeddings of $\tilde{\leadsto}$ into the canonical $\mathcal{W}$-weighted ARS $\succ_\mathcal{W}$ are also sound and complete for proving strong boundedness of barycentric ARSs. For soundness, one can use embeddings of $\leadsto$ instead of the barycentric extension $\tilde{\leadsto}$, if the embeddings are *affine*.

Definition 13 (affinity). *Let A and X be $\mathcal{M}$-algebras, with barycenter operators $\mathbb{E}_A$ and $\mathbb{E}_X$, respectively. We say a mapping $\eta : A \to X$ is affine if $\eta\left(\mathbb{E}_A\{\!\{p_i : a_i\}\!\}_{i \in I}\right) = \mathbb{E}_X\{\!\{p_i : \eta(a_i)\}\!\}_{i \in I}$.*

Theorem 5 (affine embedding, soundness). *Let $\mathcal{W}$ be a partial $\mathcal{M}$-algebra, A and X be $\mathcal{M}$-algebras, and $\eta : A \to X$ an affine embedding of $\leadsto \subseteq \mathcal{W} \times A \times A$ into a barycentric weighted order $\succ \subseteq \mathcal{W} \times X \times X$. Then $\mathsf{Pot}_{\tilde{\leadsto}}(a) \subseteq \mathsf{Pot}_\succ(\eta(a))$. In particular, $\mathsf{SB}_\succ(\eta(S))$ implies $\mathsf{SB}_{\tilde{\leadsto}}(S)$.*

Proof. We prove by induction on the derivation that $a \tilde{\leadsto}^w b$ implies $\eta(a) \succ^w \eta(b)$. Hence η is an embedding from $\tilde{\leadsto}$ to $\succ$, and we conclude the claim by Theorem 1. The interesting case is when $a = \mathbb{E}\{\!\{p_i : a_i\}\!\}_{i \in I} \tilde{\leadsto}^w \mathbb{E}\{\!\{p_i : b_i\}\!\}_{i \in I} = b$, $w = \mathbb{E}\{\!\{p_i : w_i\}\!\}_{i \in I} \in \mathcal{W}$, and $a_i \tilde{\leadsto}^{w_i} b_i$ for all $i \in I$. Then induction hypothesis gives $\eta(a_i) \succ^{w_i} \eta(b_i)$, and since η is affine and $\succ$ is barycentric, we conclude

$$\eta(a) = \eta\left(\mathbb{E}\{\!\{p_i : a_i\}\!\}_{i \in I}\right) = \mathbb{E}\{\!\{p_i : \eta(a_i)\}\!\}_{i \in I}$$
$$\succ^w \mathbb{E}\{\!\{p_i : \eta(b_i)\}\!\}_{i \in I} = \eta\left(\mathbb{E}\{\!\{p_i : b_i\}\!\}_{i \in I}\right) = \eta(b). \qquad \square$$

For any $\mathbb{R}_{\geq 0}$-valued function $h : A \to \mathbb{R}_{\geq 0}$, the expectation $\mathbb{E}h\left(\{p_i : a_i\}_{i \in I}\right) := \sum_{i \in I} p_i \cdot h(a_i)$ is affine on $\mathcal{D}(A)$ or $\mathcal{M}(A)$. Moreover, $\succ_{\mathbb{R}_{\geq 0}} \subseteq \mathbb{R}_{\geq 0} \times \mathbb{R}_{\geq 0}^\infty \times \mathbb{R}_{\geq 0}^\infty$ is a barycentric weighted order, as $\forall i \in I$. $x_i \geq w_i + y_i$ implies

$$\sum_{i \in I} p_i \cdot x_i \geq \sum_{i \in I} p_i \cdot (w_i + y_i) = \sum_{i \in I} p_i \cdot w_i + \sum_{i \in I} p_i \cdot y_i,$$

i.e., $\mathbb{E}\{\!\{p_i : x_i\}\!\}_{i \in I} \succ_{\mathbb{R}_{\geq 0}}^{\mathbb{E}\{\!\{p_i : w_i\}\!\}_{i \in I}} \mathbb{E}\{\!\{p_i : y_i\}\!\}_{i \in I}$. Therefore, $\mathbb{R}_{\geq 0}$-valued ranking functions are sound for proving strong boundedness of barycentric $\mathbb{R}_{\geq 0}$-weighted ARSs. This generalises to arbitrary partial $\mathcal{M}$-algebras $\mathcal{W}$, provided $\mathcal{W}^\infty$ forms an $\mathcal{M}$-algebra which is

- *monotone*: if $\forall i \in I.\ x_i \geq y_i$, then $\mathbb{E}\{\!\{p_i : x_i\}\!\}_{i \in I} \geq \mathbb{E}\{\!\{p_i : y_i\}\!\}_{i \in I}$; and
- *superadditive*: $\mathbb{E}\{\!\{p_i : x_i + y_i\}\!\}_{i \in I} \geq \mathbb{E}\{\!\{p_i : x_i\}\!\}_{i \in I} + \mathbb{E}\{\!\{p_i : y_i\}\!\}_{i \in I}$.

Theorem 6 (ranking functions, soundness). *Let $\mathcal{W}$ be an $\mathcal{M}$-algebraic positive monoid such that $\mathcal{W}^\infty$ is monotone and superadditive. If a weighted ARS $\rightsquigarrow\ \subseteq \mathcal{W} \times A \times A$ admits an affine ranking function $\eta : A \to \mathcal{W}^\infty$ with $\eta(S) \subseteq \mathcal{W}$, then $\mathsf{SB}_{\rightsquigarrow}(S)$. In particular, $\mathsf{pot}_{\rightsquigarrow}(a) \leq \eta(a)$ for every $a \in S$.*

Proof. To use Theorem 5 we show that the weighted order $\succ_{\mathcal{W}}\ \subseteq \mathcal{W} \times \mathcal{W}^\infty \times \mathcal{W}^\infty$ is barycentric. So consider $x_i, y_i \in \mathcal{W}^\infty$ such that $x_i \succ_{\mathcal{W}}^{w_i} y_i$, i.e., $x_i \geq w_i + y_i$ for all $i \in I$, and $\mathbb{E}(\{\!\{p_i : w_i\}\!\}_{i \in I}) \in \mathcal{W}$. We have, indeed,

$$\mathbb{E}\{\!\{p_i : x_i\}\!\}_{i \in I} \geq \mathbb{E}\{\!\{p_i : w_i + y_i\}\!\}_{i \in I} \geq \mathbb{E}\{\!\{p_i : w_i\}\!\}_{i \in I} + \mathbb{E}\{\!\{p_i : y_i\}\!\}_{i \in I},$$

by monotonicity and superadditivity. Now $\mathsf{Pot}_{\rightsquigarrow}(a) \subseteq \mathsf{Pot}_{\succ_{\mathcal{W}}}(\eta(a))$ by Theorem 5, so with Lemma 1 we conclude

$$\mathsf{pot}_{\rightsquigarrow}(a) = \sup \mathsf{Pot}_{\rightsquigarrow}(a) \leq \sup \mathsf{Pot}_{\succ_{\mathcal{W}}}(\eta(a)) = \mathsf{pot}_{\succ_{\mathcal{W}}}(\eta(a)) = \eta(a) \in \mathcal{W}. \qquad \square$$

Example 6. Theorem 6 proves that $\rightsquigarrow_{\mathcal{R}}$ from Example 4 is strongly bounded on all distributions using the affine ranking function $\mathbb{E}h$, where $h(\mathrm{HCl}) = h(\mathrm{NaOH}) = 56.5$, and $h(\mathrm{NaCl}) = h(\mathrm{H_2O}) = 0$; being a ranking function is exemplified by:

$$\mathbb{E}h(\{1/2 : \mathrm{HCl}, 1/2 : \mathrm{NaOH}\}) = 1/2 \cdot h(\mathrm{HCl}) + 1/2 \cdot h(\mathrm{NaOH}) = 56.5$$
$$= 56.5 + 1/2 \cdot h(\mathrm{NaCl}) + 1/2 \cdot h(\mathrm{H_2O}) = 56.5 + \mathbb{E}h(\{1/2 : \mathrm{HCl}, 1/2 : \mathrm{NaOH}\}).$$

Example 7. We can prove that $\rightsquigarrow_{\mathcal{G}}$ from Example 4 is strongly bounded, by defining $h(\underline{n}) = 2$ and $h(n) = 0$. Then, for any $n \in \mathbb{N}$,

$$\mathbb{E}h(\{\!\{1 : \underline{n}\}\!\}) = 2 \geq 1 + 1/2 \cdot h(n) + 1/2 \cdot h(\underline{n+1}) = 1 + \mathbb{E}h(\{\!\{1/2 : n, 1/2 : \underline{n+1}\}\!\}).$$

Theorem 6 encompasses the soundness of *probabilistic ranking functions* [4]. As illustrated in the above example, if there exists $h : A \to \mathbb{R}_{\geq 0}$ such that $h(a) \geq 1 + \mathbb{E}h(\mu)$ for all $a\ \mathcal{P}\ \mu$, then Theorem 6 ensures that $\rightsquigarrow_{\mathcal{P}}$ over $\mathcal{M}(A)$ is strongly bounded, i.e., $\mathcal{P}$ is strongly AST. They are also complete for proving strong AST of probabilistic ARSs [4], since pot serves as a ranking function. We conjecture that affine ranking functions are complete for a reasonably wide class of barycentric ARSs; however, pot is not necessarily affine in general: note that $\mathsf{pot}_{\rightsquigarrow_{\mathcal{R}}}(\{1 : \mathrm{HCl}\}) = \mathsf{pot}_{\rightsquigarrow_{\mathcal{R}}}(\{1 : \mathrm{NaOH}\}) = 0$ in Example 4.

5   Conclusion

In this work, we introduced weighted ARSs, providing a framework for studying rewriting systems with quantitative properties, particularly those related to complexity. By assigning uniform weights, weighted ARSs generalize standard and relative rewriting while enabling the analysis of reduction systems with non-uniform weights, such as expectation-based properties in probabilistic systems. To study (strong) boundedness in this setting, we established ranking functions as a central tool, and have seen how these adapt to weighted term rewrite systems and barycentric ARSs, encompassing probabilistic reduction systems.

As future work, it would for instance be interesting to enrich the theory with a study of confluence and related properties.

References

1. Avanzini, M., Barthe, G., Dal Lago, U.: On continuation-passing transformations and expected cost analysis. Proc. ACM Program. Lang. **5**(ICFP), 1–30 (2021). https://doi.org/10.1145/3473592
2. Avanzini, M., Dal Lago, U.: Automating sized-type inference for complexity analysis. Proc. ACM Program. Lang. **1**(ICFP), 43:1–43:29 (2017). https://doi.org/10.1145/3110287
3. Avanzini, M., Dal Lago, U., Yamada, A.: On probabilistic term rewriting. In: Gallagher, J.P., Sulzmann, M. (eds.) FLOPS 2018. LNCS, vol. 10818, pp. 132–148. Springer, Cham (2018). https://doi.org/10.1007/978-3-319-90686-7_9
4. Avanzini, M., Dal Lago, U., Yamada, A.: On probabilistic term rewriting. Sci. Comput. Program. **185** (2020). https://doi.org/10.1016/J.SCICO.2019.102338
5. Avanzini, M., Moser, G., Péchoux, R., Perdrix, S., Zamdzhiev, V.: Quantum expectation transformers for cost analysis. In: Baier, C., Fisman, D. (eds.) LICS 2022: 37th Annual ACM/IEEE Symposium on Logic in Computer Science, Haifa, Israel, 2–5 August 2022, pp. 10:1–10:13. ACM (2022). https://doi.org/10.1145/3531130.3533332
6. Avanzini, M., Moser, G., Schaper, M.: A modular cost analysis for probabilistic programs. Proc. ACM Program. Lang. **4**(OOPSLA), 172:1–172:30 (2020). https://doi.org/10.1145/3428240
7. Baader, F., Nipkow, T.: Term Rewriting and All That. Cambridge University Press, Cambridge (1998)
8. Baillot, P., Ghyselen, A., Kobayashi, N.: Sized types with usages for parallel complexity of pi-calculus processes. In: Haddad, S., Varacca, D. (eds.) 32nd International Conference on Concurrency Theory, CONCUR 2021, 24–27 August 2021, Virtual Conference. LIPIcs, vol. 203, pp. 34:1–34:22. Schloss Dagstuhl - Leibniz-Zentrum für Informatik (2021). https://doi.org/10.4230/LIPICS.CONCUR.2021.34
9. Bournez, O., Garnier, F.: Proving positive almost-sure termination. In: Giesl, J. (ed.) RTA 2005. LNCS, vol. 3467, pp. 323–337. Springer, Heidelberg (2005). https://doi.org/10.1007/978-3-540-32033-3_24
10. Dal Lago, U., Martini, S.: An invariant cost model for the lambda calculus. In: Beckmann, A., Berger, U., Löwe, B., Tucker, J.V. (eds.) CiE 2006. LNCS, vol. 3988, pp. 105–114. Springer, Heidelberg (2006). https://doi.org/10.1007/11780342_11

11. Danielsson, N.A.: Lightweight semiformal time complexity analysis for purely functional data structures. In: Necula, G.C., Wadler, P. (eds.) Proceedings of the 35th ACM SIGPLAN-SIGACT Symposium on Principles of Programming Languages, POPL 2008, San Francisco, California, USA, 7–12 January 2008, pp. 133–144. ACM (2008). https://doi.org/10.1145/1328438.1328457

12. Droste, M., Kuske, D.: Weighted automata. In: Pin, J. (ed.) Handbook of Automata Theory, pp. 113–150. European Mathematical Society Publishing House, Zürich, Switzerland (2021). https://doi.org/10.4171/AUTOMATA-1/4

13. Faggian, C.: Probabilistic rewriting and asymptotic behaviour: on termination and unique normal forms. Log. Methods Comput. Sci. **18**(2) (2022). https://doi.org/10.46298/LMCS-18(2:5)2022

14. Fu, H., Chatterjee, K.: Termination of nondeterministic probabilistic programs. In: Enea, C., Piskac, R. (eds.) VMCAI 2019. LNCS, vol. 11388, pp. 468–490. Springer, Cham (2019). https://doi.org/10.1007/978-3-030-11245-5_22

15. Gavazzo, F., Florio, C.D.: Elements of quantitative rewriting. Proc. ACM Program. Lang. **7**(POPL), 1832–1863 (2023). https://doi.org/10.1145/3571256

16. Laird, J., Manzonetto, G., McCusker, G., Pagani, M.: Weighted relational models of typed lambda-calculi. In: 28th Annual ACM/IEEE Symposium on Logic in Computer Science, LICS 2013, New Orleans, LA, USA, 25–28 June 2013, pp. 301–310. IEEE Computer Society (2013). https://doi.org/10.1109/LICS.2013.36

17. Naaf, M., Frohn, F., Brockschmidt, M., Fuhs, C., Giesl, J.: Complexity analysis for term rewriting by integer transition systems. In: Dixon, C., Finger, M. (eds.) FroCoS 2017. LNCS (LNAI), vol. 10483, pp. 132–150. Springer, Cham (2017). https://doi.org/10.1007/978-3-319-66167-4_8

18. van Oostrom, V., Toyama, Y.: Normalisation by random descent. In: Kesner, D., Pientka, B. (eds.) 1st International Conference on Formal Structures for Computation and Deduction, FSCD 2016, June 22-26, 2016, Porto, Portugal. LIPIcs, vol. 52, pp. 32:1–32:18. Schloss Dagstuhl - Leibniz-Zentrum für Informatik (2016). https://doi.org/10.4230/LIPICS.FSCD.2016.32

19. Thrane, C., Fahrenberg, U., Larsen, K.G.: Quantitative analysis of weighted transition systems. J. Logic Algebraic Program. **79**(7), 689–703 (2010). https://doi.org/10.1016/j.jlap.2010.07.010

Graph-Embedded Rewrite Systems: Combination and Undecidability Results

Serdar Erbatur[1] , Andrew M. Marshall[2]([envelope]) , Paliath Narendran[3] , and Christophe Ringeissen[4]

[1] University of Texas at Dallas, Richardson, TX, USA
serdar.erbatur@utdallas.edu
[2] University of Mary Washington, Fredericksburg, VA, USA
marshall@umw.edu
[3] University at Albany, SUNY, Albany, NY, USA
pnarendran@albany.edu
[4] Université de Lorraine, CNRS, Inria, LORIA, 54000 Nancy, France
christophe.ringeissen@loria.fr

Abstract. In this paper, we consider the knowledge problems of *deduction* and *static equivalence* in the formal analysis of security protocols. We extend a recent result that developed a decision procedure for these problems in the non-disjoint combination $R \cup E$, where R is a subterm E-convergent term rewrite system (TRS) and E is a restricted form of permutative theory. Here, we consider the same combination problem but replace the subterm E-convergent TRS with a superclass of subterm E-convergent, called *contracting* E-convergent. We show that the previous decision procedure can be extended to obtain a new algorithm for this larger class of combined theories.

We also explore the gap between the contracting TRSs, for which deduction and static-equivalence are decidable, and a larger superclass called *graph-embedded* for which these problems are undecidable. This gap is of interest since one would like to get closer to graph-embedded and still maintain decidability of the above "knowledge problems." We show that at least one way of weakening the restrictions of the contracting definition will not work, as it leads to undecidability results for deduction and static equivalence. We also show that a subset of the graph-embedded rules is still sufficient to obtain undecidability.

Keywords: Permutative Equational Theories · Term Rewriting · Combination

1 Introduction

In the formal analysis of security protocols, a number of tools have been developed that use constraint solving in term algebras [3,8,10,11,15,20,25,29,30]. These tools implement algorithms and procedures to reason about the knowledge an adversary could gain by observing a protocol in execution. Two key

© The Author(s) 2026
R. Thiemann and C. Weidenbach (Eds.): FroCoS 2025, LNAI 15979, pp. 209–227, 2026.
https://doi.org/10.1007/978-3-032-04167-8_12

measures of this knowledge are *(intruder) deduction* [24,28] and *static equiva-lence* [1], and there has been substantial work on developing decision procedures for these problems (e.g., [1,4,7,11,13,18]). These procedures typically model pro-tocols symbolically, using rewrite systems or equational theories, and are often proven sound and complete for specific classes of theories.

One of the most common such classes is that of subterm convergent term rewrite systems. These are systems where the right-hand side of each rule is a strict subterm of the left-hand side or a constant (see, e.g., [1,11]). In recent work [9,16], an extension of this class, called *graph-embedded*, was introduced. This class leverages the graph minor relation in term graphs to define a super-class of subterm convergent systems. However, deduction and static equivalence problems are undecidable for graph-embedded systems. To address this, a sub-class called *contracting* was identified in [9,16], for which both problems remain decidable.

In this paper, we begin to explore the gap between the contracting and graph-embedded classes. This is of interest because narrowing this gap could allow for broader classes of theories to be analyzed while preserving decidability. We show that at least one natural weakening of the contracting definition leads to undecidability for both deduction and static equivalence. Furthermore, we examine restrictions of the graph-embedded definition, demonstrating that even a single rule from this definition can lead to undecidability. While it is plausible that the gap between contracting and graph-embedded systems can be reduced without sacrificing decidability, the best approach to achieving this remains an open question.

Another important aspect of many decision procedures is the ability to handle combinations of theories, particularly when some components cannot be oriented into a term rewrite system—for example, theories involving Associativity and Commutativity (AC). In recent work [19], decision procedures were developed for deduction and static equivalence in combined theories of the form $R \cup E$, where R and E are non-disjoint. In [19] R is a subterm convergent term rewrite system, and E several types of permutative theories.

In this paper, we again consider the same combination scenario $R \cup E$ but go beyond the restriction that R is a subterm rewrite system. Rather, we investigate the case where R is a contracting rewrite system and R is convergent modulo a permutative theory E. We show that the procedure developed in [19] can be adapted to the larger class of theories where R is contracting. Thus, we obtain decision procedures for deductions and static equivalence in this larger class of theories.

Paper Outline: Section 2 contains the preliminaries and background information. Section 3 presents several new combination results. In particular, it introduces the main result presented in Theorem 5. Section 4 presents several new unde-cidable results. First, for a contracting systems without depth restrictions, The-orem 6. Then, showing two subsets of the graph-embedded systems still have undecidable knowledge problems, Theorem 7 and Theorem 8. Finally, Sect. 5 contains the conclusions and future work.

2   Preliminaries

We use the standard notation of equational unification [6] and term rewriting systems [5]. Given a first-order signature Σ and a (countable) set of variables V, the Σ-terms over variables V are built in the usual way by taking into account the arity of each function symbol in Σ. Each Σ-term is well-formed: if it is rooted by an n-ary function symbol in Σ, then it has necessarily n direct subterms. The set of Σ-terms over variables V is denoted by $T(\Sigma, V)$. The set of variables from V occurring in a term $t \in T(\Sigma, V)$ is denoted by $Var(t)$. A term t is *ground* if $Var(t) = \emptyset$. A term t is *linear* if each variable in $Var(t)$ occurs only once in t. For any position p in a term t (including the root position ε), $t(p)$ is the symbol at position p, $t|_p$ is the subterm of t at position p, and $t[u]_p$ is the term t in which $t|_p$ is replaced by u. A substitution is an endomorphism of $T(\Sigma, V)$ with only finitely many variables not mapped to themselves. A substitution is denoted by $\sigma = \{x_1 \mapsto t_1, \ldots, x_m \mapsto t_m\}$, where the domain of σ is $Dom(\sigma) = \{x_1, \ldots, x_m\}$ and the range of σ is $Ran(\sigma) = \{t_1, \ldots, t_m\}$. Application of a substitution σ to t is written $t\sigma$. A Σ-equation is a pair of Σ-terms denoted by $s =^? t$ or simply $s = t$ when it is clear from the context that we do not refer to an axiom. The size of a term t, denoted by $|t|$, is defined inductively as follows: $|f(t_1, \ldots, t_n)| = 1 + \sum_{i=1}^{n} |t_i|$ if f is an n-ary function symbol with $n \geq 1$, $|c| = 1$ if c is a constant, and $|x| = 1$ if x is a variable. The depth of a term t, denoted by $depth(t)$, is defined inductively as follows: $depth(f(t_1, \ldots, t_n)) = 1 + \max_{i=1, \ldots, n} depth(t_i)$ if f an n-ary function symbol with $n \geq 1$, $depth(c) = 1$ if c is a constant, and $depth(x) = 0$ if x is a variable.

2.1   Equational Theories

Given a set E of Σ-axioms (i.e., pairs of terms in $T(\Sigma, V)$, denoted by $l = r$), the *equational theory* $=_E$ is the congruence closure of E under the law of substitutivity (by a slight abuse of terminology, E is often called an equational theory). Equivalently, $=_E$ can be defined as the reflexive transitive closure $\leftrightarrow_E^*$ of an equational step $\leftrightarrow_E$ defined as follows: $s \leftrightarrow_E t$ if there exist a position p of s, $l = r$ (or $r = l$) in E, and substitution σ such that $s|_p = l\sigma$ and $t = s[r\sigma]_p$. An equational theory E is said to be *permutative* if for any $l = r$ in E, the number of occurrences of any (function or variable) symbol in l is equal to the number of occurrences of that symbol in r. Well-known theories such as Associativity $(A = \{(x + y) + z = x + (y + z)\})$, Commutativity $(C = \{x + y = y + x\})$, and Associativity-Commutativity $(AC = A \cup C)$ are permutative theories. A theory E is *syntactic* if it has finite *resolvent presentation* S, defined as a finite set of axioms S such that each equality $t =_E u$ has an equational proof $t \leftrightarrow_S^* u$ with at most one equational step $\leftrightarrow_S$ applied at the root position. The theories C and AC are syntactic [22].

2.2   Rewrite Relations

Given a signature Σ, an oriented Σ-axiom is called a rewrite rule of the form $l \rightarrow r$ such that $l, r \in T(\Sigma, V)$, l is not a variable and $Var(r) \subseteq Var(l)$. A finite set of rewrite rules is called a *term rewriting system* (TRS, for short). Let R be any TRS. For any Σ-terms s and t, s *R-rewrites* to t, denoted by $s \rightarrow_R t$, if there exist a position p of s, $l \rightarrow r \in R$, and substitution σ such that $s|_p = l\sigma$ and $t = s[r\sigma]_p$. The term s is said to be *R-reducible*, $s|_p$ is called a *redex*, and in the particular case where $s|_p = l\sigma$, s *R-rewrites* to t, denoted by $s \rightarrow_R t$. A term is an *innermost redex* if none of its proper subterms is a redex. The symmetric relation $\leftarrow_R \cup \rightarrow_R$ is denoted by $\longleftrightarrow_R$. The rewrite relation $\rightarrow_R$ is confluent if $\longleftrightarrow_R^*$ is included in $\rightarrow_R^* \circ \leftarrow_R^*$. The rewrite relation $\rightarrow_R$ is *convergent* if $\rightarrow_R$ is both terminating and confluent. When $\rightarrow_R$ is convergent, we have that for any terms t, t', $t \longleftrightarrow_R^* t'$ iff $t \downarrow_R = t' \downarrow_R$, where $t \downarrow_R$ (resp., $t' \downarrow_R$) denotes the unique normal form of t (resp., t') w.r.t $\rightarrow_R$. A convergent TRS R is said to be *subterm convergent* if for any $l \rightarrow r \in R$, r is either a strict subterm of l or a constant. We refer to [5] for the classical notions of overlap and critical pair. Hence, a trivial critical pair is obtained by an overlap at the root position of a rule with a renaming of the same rule. A TRS with no non-trivial critical pairs is *non-overlapping*.

Let us now introduce the notion of equational rewriting, also called class rewriting [21]. Given a TRS R and an equational theory E, the rewrite relation of R modulo E is defined as follows: $s \rightarrow_{R,E} t$ if there exist some position p in s, some rule $l \rightarrow r \in R$ and a substitution μ such that $s|_p =_E l\mu$ and $t = s[r\mu]_p$. The TRS R is said to be *E-convergent* if the relation $=_E \circ \rightarrow_R \circ =_E$ is terminating and $\longleftrightarrow_{R\cup E}^* \subseteq \rightarrow_{R,E}^* \circ =_E \circ \leftarrow_{R,E}^*$. In an E-convergent TRS R, any term t admits a unique R-normal form modulo E denoted by $t \downarrow_{R,E}$, and for any terms s and t, we have $s \longleftrightarrow_{R\cup E}^* t$ iff $(s \downarrow_{R,E}) =_E (t \downarrow_{R,E})$.

2.3   Knowledge Problems

The applied pi calculus and frames are used to model attacker knowledge [2]. In this model, the set of messages or terms which the attacker knows, and which could have been obtained from observing one or more protocol sessions, are the set of terms in $Ran(\sigma)$ of the frame $\phi = \nu\tilde{n}.\sigma$, where σ is a substitution ranging over ground terms. We also need to model cryptographic concepts such as nonces, keys, and publicly known values. We do this by using *names*, which are essentially free constants. Here also, we need to track the names which the attacker knows, such as public values, and the names which the attacker does not know a priori, such as freshly generated nonces. $\tilde{n}$ consists of a finite set of restricted names; these names represent freshly generated names which remain secret from the attacker. The set of names occurring in a term t is denoted by $fn(t)$. For any frame $\phi = \nu\tilde{n}.\sigma$, let $fn(\phi)$ be the set of names $fn(\sigma) \setminus \tilde{n}$ where $fn(\sigma) = \bigcup_{t \in Ran(\sigma)} fn(t)$; and for any term t, let $t\phi$ denote—by a slight abuse of notation—the term $t\sigma$. For any term t, we say that t satisfies the name restriction of ϕ if $fn(t) \cap \tilde{n} = \emptyset$.

Definition 1 (Deduction). *Let $\phi = \nu\tilde{n}.\sigma$ be a frame, and t a ground term. We say that t is deduced from ϕ modulo E, denoted by $\phi \vdash_E t$, if there exists a term ζ such that $\zeta\sigma =_E t$ and $fn(\zeta) \cap \tilde{n} = \emptyset$. The term ζ is called a recipe of t in ϕ modulo E.*

Another form of knowledge is the ability to tell if two frames are *statically equivalent* modulo E.

Definition 2 (Static Equivalence). *Two terms s and t are equal in a frame $\phi = \nu\tilde{n}.\sigma$ modulo an equational theory E, denoted $(s =_E t)\phi$, if $s\sigma =_E t\sigma$, and $\tilde{n} \cap (fn(s) \cup fn(t)) = \emptyset$. The set of all equalities $s = t$ such that $(s =_E t)\phi$ is denoted by $Eq(\phi)$. Given a set of equalities Eq, the fact that $(s =_E t)\phi$ for all $s = t \in Eq$ is denoted by $\phi \models Eq$. Two frames $\phi = \nu\tilde{n}.\sigma$ and $\psi = \nu\tilde{n}.\tau$ are statically equivalent modulo E, denoted as $\phi \approx_E \psi$, if $Dom(\sigma) = Dom(\tau)$, $\phi \models Eq(\psi)$ and $\psi \models Eq(\phi)$.*

Deduction and static equivalence are known to be decidable for subterm convergent rewrite systems [1].

2.4 Graph-Embedded Rewrite Systems

Let us know introduce the graph-embedded and contracting systems. These systems were introduced in [16] and then simplified in [9], where they are used to expand on the class of subterm convergent term rewrite systems. The idea behind the definitions was to capture the "near subterm" properties of many systems that model the properties of cryptographic protocols. Many systems were close but not fully subterm. That is, the right-hand side of some rules contain terms formed from the symbols and variable on the left but which are not strict subterms.

Example 1 (Blind Signatures). For example, the theory of blind signatures [11] is such a theory that is beyond subterm:

$$checksign(sign(x, y), pk(y)) \rightarrow x$$
$$unblind(blind(x, y), y) \rightarrow x$$
$$unblind(sign(blind(x, y), z), y) \rightarrow sign(x, z)$$

Consider the rule $unblind(sign(blind(x, y), z), y) \rightarrow sign(x, z)$. Notice that while $sign(x, z)$ is not a strict subterm of $unblind(sign(blind(x, y), z), y)$ it can be formed from the function symbols and variables contained in this term.

The expanded definitions allowed these systems to be captured under one single definition. To begin, we need to define the components that will be used in the two definitions, this includes a type of restricted permutation.

Definition 3 (Leaf and Subterm Permutations). *We define two types of permutations, $\approx_s$ and $\approx_l$:*

1. *For terms t and t', we say t is* subterm permutatively equal *to t', denoted $t \approx_s t'$, if one of the following is true:*
   (a) $t = t'$, where t and t' are constants or variables, or
   (b) $t = f(u_1, \ldots, u_n)$ and $t' = f(u_{\sigma(1)}, \ldots, u_{\sigma(n)})$ where f is an n-ary function symbol, $n \geq 1$, and σ is a permutation of the indexes $(1, \ldots, n)$.

2. *For terms t and t', we say t is* leaf permutatively *equal to t', denoted $t \approx_l t'$, if t' is obtained from t by applying a permutation on the set of leaves (variables and constants) occurring in t.*

The first type of permutation, $\approx_s$, allows for permutation inside the term but preserves the layer like structure of the function symbols in the term graph. The second type of permutation in the classical leaf permutability and is restricted to the leaf nodes, i.e., just the variables and constants of the term graph. Notice that the two types of permutations, $\approx_s$ and $\approx_l$, do not encompass all permutative theories since $\approx_s$ permutes subterms just below the root while $\approx_l$ permutes just the leaves. We will use a combination of the above two permutations in the definition employed for graph-embedded TRS.

Definition 4 (Permutatively Equal). *For terms t and t', we say t is permutatively equal to t', denoted $t \approx t'$, if $t \approx_s t'' \approx_l t'$, for some term t''.*

The class of contracting TRS first starts by modeling the graph minor relation in the TRS setting. This is done by a set of rewrite *schemas*. This set of rewrite schemata then induces a graph-embedded term rewrite system. Notice that this is very similar to what is often done when considering the homeomorphic embedding relation in TRSs.

Definition 5 (Graph-Embedding). *Consider the following reduction relation, $\rightarrow^*_{R_{gemb}}$, where R_{gemb} is the set of rules given by the instantiation of the following rule schema:*

$$\left\{ \begin{array}{l} \text{for any } f \in \Sigma \\ (1)\ f(x_1,\ldots,x_n) \rightarrow x_i \\ (2)\ f(x_1,\ldots,\ x_{i-1},\ x_i,\ x_{i+1}\ \ldots,\ x_n) \rightarrow f(x_1,\ldots,\ x_{i-1},\ x_{i+1},\ \ldots,\ x_n) \\ \quad \text{and for any } f,g \in \Sigma \\ (3)\ f(x_1,\ldots,x_{i-1},g(\bar{z}),x_{i+1},\ \ldots,x_m) \rightarrow g(x_1,\ldots,\ x_{i-1},\bar{z},x_{i+1},\ \ldots,x_m) \\ (4)\ f(x_1,\ldots,x_{i-1},g(\bar{z}),x_{i+1},\ \ldots,x_m) \rightarrow f(x_1,\ldots,\ x_{i-1},\bar{z},x_{i+1},\ \ldots,x_m) \end{array} \right\}$$

We say a term t' is graph-embedded *in a term t, denoted $t \succcurlyeq_{gemb} t'$, if t' is a well formed term such that $t \rightarrow^*_{R_{gemb}} t'$.*

A TRS R is graph-embedded *if for any $l \rightarrow r \in R$, $l \succcurlyeq_{gemb} r$ or r is a constant.*

The graph-embedded class is not sufficient to obtain decidability of static equivalence, so we next need to introduce a type of projection rule that ensure access to subterms and thus decidability of deduction and static equivalence.

Definition 6 (Projecting Rule). *Let R be a TRS, x a variable and t a term with a single occurrence of x. A projecting rule in R over t leading to x is a rule in R which is a variant of $t' \rightarrow x$ where t' is a superterm of t with no additional occurrences of x.*

Another way to view the projection rules of the above definition is that t' is a context, $t'[\ ]$, and there is a rule of the form $t'[t] \rightarrow x$. The way these projecting rules relate to the entire term rewrite system can now be defined.

Definition 7 (Projection-Closed Derivation). *Let R be a TRS. A non-empty R_{gemb}-derivation is said to be projection-closed with respect to R if it has the form*

$$s \to_{R_{gemb}}^{l \to r, \gamma} s' \to_{R_{gemb}}^* t$$

where

- *s is a linear term and t is a well formed term,*
- *$l \to r$ is a R_{gemb} rule among (1), (2) and (4),*
- *γ is a variable renaming s.t.:*
- *if $l \to r$ is rule (1), $f(x_1, \ldots, x_n) \to x_i$, then for any $x_i \gamma$ occurring in t there exists a projecting rule in R over $f(x_1, \ldots, x_n)\gamma$ leading to $x_i \gamma$,*
- *if $l \to r$ is rule (4),*

$$f(x_1, \ldots, x_{i-1}, g(\bar{z}), x_{i+1}, \ldots, x_m) \to f(x_1, \ldots, x_{i-1}, \bar{z}, x_{i+1}, \ldots, x_m)$$

  then for any $z_i \gamma$ occurring in t there exists a projecting rule in R over $g(\bar{z})\gamma$ leading to $z_i \gamma$,
- *$s' \to_{R_{gemb}}^* t$ is either projection-closed with respect to R or empty.*

Definition 8 (Projection-Closed Permutative Equality). *Let R be a TRS and $l = r$ a permutative equality obtained by one or zero applications of $\approx_s$ followed by one or zero applications of $\approx_l$. The equality $l = r$ is said to be projection-closed with respect to R if the following holds: for any variable x occurring in a strict subterm $l' \neq x$ of l and in a strict subterm r' of r such that $l' \neq r'$, there exists a projecting rule in R over l' leading to x.*

Based on Definitions 7 and 8, we can now introduce the subset of graph-embedded rules for which we can obtain decidability of the knowledge problems.

Definition 9 (Contracting TRS). *A TRS R is said to be contracting if for any non-subterm rule $l \to r$ in R one of the following holds:*

- *there exist a position p of l, a substitution σ ranging over variables, a projection-closed derivation $g \to_{R_{gemb}}^+ d$ with respect to R such that $l|_p = g\sigma$ and $r = d\sigma$ is of depth 1,*
- *$l = r$ is a permutative equality of depth 2 which is projection-closed with respect to R.*

A contracting TRS, R, is strictly contracting *if for any $l \to r \in R$, $depth(l) > depth(r)$.*

Example 2. Consider the theory of blind signatures from Example 1. This theory is contracting. Let's look at the rule: $unblind(sign(blind(x, y), z), y) \to sign(x, z)$. Let $l = unblind(sign(blind(x, y), z), y)$.
Then, $l = unblind(sign(blind(x, y), z), y) \to_{R_{gemb}}^{\epsilon, rule\ 1} sign(blind(x, y), z)$. We can start the projection-closed derivation at $l|_1 = sign(blind(x, y), z)$. This leads to $sign(blind(x, y), z) \to_{R_{gemb}}^{rule\ 4} sign(x, y, z) \to_{R_{gemb}}^{rule\ 2} sign(x, z)$. We also need the required projecting rule, given the above projection-closed derivation.
The step, $sign(blind(x, y), z) \to_{R_{gemb}}^{rule\ 4} sign(x, y, z)$, applied rule 4 below the root, to remove the $blind()$ function symbol. Thus, there must be a projecting rule, which is the rule $unblind(blind(x, y), y) \to x$.

2.5   Restricted Classes of Permutative Theories

Leaf permutative theories are a further restriction on permutative theories where for each axiom, $l = r$, r is a leaf permutation of l, i.e., $r = l\sigma$, where σ is a permutation of the leaf nodes of l. It has already been shown in [9] that deduction is decidable in permutative theories but static equivalence is not [17].

Definition 10 (Variable-Permuting Theory). *An axiom $l = r$ is said to be variable-permuting [26] if all the following conditions are satisfied:*

1. *the set of occurrences of l is identical to the set of occurrences of r,*
2. *for any non-variable occurrence p of l, $l(p) = r(p)$,*
3. *for any $x \in Var(l) \cup Var(r)$, the number of occurrences of x in l is identical to the number of occurrences of x in r.*

An equational theory E is said to be separate variable-permuting *(SVP, for short) if for any $l = r \in E$ we have:*

- *$l = r$ is a variable-permuting axiom,*
- *l and r are rooted by the same function symbol that does not occur elsewhere in E.*

An inner constructor *symbol of E is a function symbol from E that never occurs at the root of any equality in E.*

Example 3 (Intruder Theory with a Permutative Axiom). Let us consider a theory used in practice to model a group messaging protocol [12]. For this protocol, the theory modeling the intruder can be defined [27] as a combination $R \cup K$ where $K = \{keyexch(x, pk(x'), y, pk(y')) = keyexch(x', pk(x), y', pk(y))\}$ and

$$R = \left\{ \begin{array}{ll} adec(aenc(m, pk(sk)), sk) & \rightarrow m \quad getmsg(sign(m, sk)) \rightarrow m \\ checksign(sign(m, sk), m, pk(sk)) \rightarrow ok \quad sdec(senc(m, k), k) & \rightarrow m \end{array} \right\}.$$

R is a subterm convergent TRS and K is a *SVP* theory such that the shared symbol pk is an inner constructor of K and a constructor of R.

An equational theory E is *closed by paramodulation* if E is a finite set of equalities saturated with respect to the classical paramodulation rule [23]. Thus, an equational theory is saturated by paramodulation when, after exhaustive applications of the paramodulation rule, no further non-redundant equalities.

Lemma 1. *Any SVP theory is closed by paramodulation.*

Critical for the results in this paper is the following from [17].

Theorem 1 ([17]). *Static equivalence is undecidable in general for variable permuting theories.*

Theorem 2 ([17]). *Both deduction and static equivalence are decidable in any SVP theory.*

It has already been shown in [9] that it is possible to combine $\approx$-free contracting convergent TRS with permutative theories to obtain decidability results for deduction. However, since static equivalence is undecidable in general for even variable permuting theories [17], there was no equivalent result for static equivalence.

Theorem 3. *Let R be any contracting convergent TRS and E any SVP theory such that the function symbols shared by R and E are constructors for R and inner constructors for E. Then, both deduction and static equivalence are decidable in $R \cup E$.*

Proof. The combination result from [18] can be applied due to Theorem 2. $\square$

Next, we consider going beyond the restriction of only sharing constructors.

3   Equational Rewriting Modulo Permutative Theories

In this section we start investigating the possibility to consider E is syntactic permutative, e.g., E is a permutative theory closed by paramodulation, and R is E-convergent. In this case, an additional finiteness assumption is required, as shown below. The investigated approach relies on the possibility of computing a finite representation of all the terms that are matched modulo E by the left-hand sides of the TRS R.

Definition 11. *An E-variant of a term l is a pair (t, σ) such that $t =_E l\sigma$ and $Dom(\sigma)$ is included in $fv(l)$. Given two E-variants (u, θ) and (v, γ) of a term l, (u, θ) is more general than (v, γ), denoted by $(u, \theta) \leq_E (v, \gamma)$ if there exists a substitution τ such that $u\tau =_E v$ and $\theta\tau =_E \gamma$. A complete set of E-variants of l, denoted by $CV_E(l)$, is a set of E-variants of l such that for any E-variant (v, γ) of l, there exists $(u, \theta) \in CV_E(l)$ such that $(u, \theta) \leq_E (v, \gamma)$. The equational theory E is said to have the* Finite Equational Variant Property *(FEVP, for short) if any term admits a finite complete set of E-variants.*

Given a syntactic permutative theory E, we have developed in [19] a general procedure that, when terminating, computes a finite set of terms E-matched by l, denoted by $CMT_E(l)$ and such that $\{(t, \sigma) \mid t \in CMT_E(l), l\sigma =_E t\}$ is a finite $CV_E(l)$. This procedure, called MTG is defined as a rule-based system consisting of a matching procedure for syntactic permutative theories plus some additional rules to guide the instantiation of terms to be E-matched by l, in case the matching procedure fails when the terms are too small. The MTG procedure is not guaranteed to terminate for an arbitrary syntactic permutative theory E. However, the MTG procedure is guaranteed to terminate for permutative theories closed under paramodulation which are known to be syntactic [23], and so we have:

Theorem 4. *Any permutative theory closed by paramodulation has the FEVP.*

Definition 12. *Assume R is TRS such that for any $l \to r \in R$, $CMT_E(l)$ is finite. Under this assumption, the size of R modulo E, denoted by $|R|$, is defined as follows: $|R| = \max\{|t| \mid t \in CMT_E(l),\ l \to r \in R\}$.*

From now on, we assume that E is a syntactic permutative theory and R is a contracting E-convergent TRS such that $|R|$ is defined. We introduce below some notions defined with respect to $|R|$, such as the completion of a frame and a set of equalities generated by terms bounded by $|R|$.

Definition 13. *Given a term t, $gst_E(t)$ denotes the set of terms E-equal to some term in $\bigcup_{\{t' \mid t' =_E t\}} gst(t')$, where $gst(t')$ is the set of (well-typed) terms reachable by R_{gemb} from t'. For any normalized frame $\phi = \nu\tilde{n}.\sigma$, let $gst_E(\sigma)$ be the set of terms $\bigcup_{x \in Dom(\sigma)} gst_E(x\sigma)$. The set of terms $D_*(\phi)$ is the smallest set D such that:*

(1) $Ran(\sigma) \subseteq D$,
(2) if $t_1, \ldots, t_n \in D$ and $f(t_1, \ldots, t_n) \in gst_E(\sigma)$ then $f(t_1, \ldots, t_n) \in D$,
(3) if $t \in D$, $t' \in gst_E(\sigma)$, $t =_E t'$, then $t' \in D$,
(4) if there is a root reduction $s[\bar{d}] \to^\epsilon_{R,E} t$ where $|s| \leq |R|$, $fn(s) \cap \tilde{n} = \emptyset$, $\bar{d} \in D$ and $t \in gst_E(\sigma)$, then $t \in D$.

Let $\sigma_* = \sigma\{\chi_u \mapsto u \mid u \in D_*(\phi) \backslash Ran(\sigma)\}$ where χ_u is a fresh variable. The frame $\phi_* = \nu\tilde{n}.\sigma_*$ is called the completion of ϕ with respect to contexts bounded by $|R|$. Given a recipe ζ_u for each $u \in D_*(\phi) \backslash Ran(\sigma)$, the substitution $\{\chi_u \mapsto \zeta_u \mid u \in D_*(\phi) \backslash Ran(\sigma)\}$ is called a recipe substitution of ϕ and is denoted by ζ_ϕ. The set $Eq^B_\zeta(\phi)$ is the set of equalities $t\zeta_\phi = t'\zeta_\phi$ such that $(t\zeta_\phi =_{RE} t'\zeta_\phi)\phi$ and t, t' are terms such that $|t| \leq |R|$, $|t'| \leq |R|$ and $(fn(t) \cup fn(t')) \cap \tilde{n} = \emptyset$.

In the following, we present reduction methods from $RE = R \cup E$ to the combined theory $\emptyset \cup E$ where $\emptyset$ is the empty theory over the function symbols occurring in R but not in E. In the next subsections, this combined theory is simply denoted by E.

3.1 Deduction

The decision procedure for the deduction problem in RE is based on the following reduction lemma.

Lemma 2 (Deduction). *Let $RE = R \cup E$ where E is any syntactic permutative theory and R is any contracting E-convergent TRS such that $|R|$ is defined. For any normalized frame ϕ and any normalized term t, we have that $\phi \vdash_{RE} t$ if and only if $\phi_* \vdash_E t$.*

3.2 Static Equivalence

In a way similar to what is done for disjoint combinations [14], we extend the input frames with the instantiation of recipes of all deducible terms occurring in the completions.

Definition 14. *Let $\phi = \nu\tilde{n}.\sigma$ be a frame. Let Π be a set of terms t such that $t\sigma$ is ground and t satisfies the name restriction of ϕ. The Π-extension of ϕ is the frame $\Pi\phi = \nu\tilde{n}.\{\chi_t \mapsto t \mid t \in \Pi\}\sigma$.*

Given any normalized frames $\phi = \nu\tilde{n}.\sigma$ and $\psi = \nu\tilde{n}.\tau$ such that $Dom(\sigma) = Dom(\tau)$, let $\bar{\phi} = (\Pi\phi)\!\downarrow_{R,E}$, and $\bar{\psi} = (\Pi\psi)\!\downarrow_{R,E}$ where Π is the set of subterms in $Ran(\zeta_\phi) \cup Ran(\zeta_\psi)$.

Lemma 3. *We have $(\bar{\phi})_* = \bar{\phi}$, $(\bar{\psi})_* = \bar{\psi}$ and $\phi \approx_{RE} \psi$ if and only if $\bar{\phi} \approx_{RE} \bar{\psi}$.*

The decision procedure for static equivalence in RE is based on the following reduction lemma:

Lemma 4 (Static Equivalence). *Let $RE = R \cup E$ where E is any syntactic permutative theory and R is any contracting E-convergent TRS such that $|R|$ is defined. For any normalized frames $\bar{\phi}$ and $\bar{\psi}$, we have $\bar{\phi} \approx_{RE} \bar{\psi}$ iff $\bar{\psi} \models Eq^B(\bar{\phi})$ and $\bar{\phi} \models Eq^B(\bar{\psi})$ and $\bar{\phi} \approx_E \bar{\psi}$.*

3.3 Decidability Results and Correctness Proofs

According to the above reduction lemmas, we get the following result.

Theorem 5. *Let $RE = R \cup E$ where E is any syntactic permutative theory and R is any contracting E-convergent TRS such that $|R|$ is defined. If both deduction and static equivalence are decidable in E, then both deduction and static equivalence are decidable in RE.*

Corollary 1. *Let $RE = R \cup E$ where E is any SVP theory and R is any contracting E-convergent TRS. Then, both deduction and static equivalence are decidable in RE.*

The proofs of the reduction lemmas rely on the following technical lemma:

Lemma 5. *Let $RE = R \cup E$ where E is any syntactic permutative theory and R is any contracting E-convergent TRS such that $|R|$ is defined. Assume $\bar{\phi} \approx_E \bar{\psi}$ and $\bar{\psi} \models Eq^B(\bar{\phi})$. For any term s satisfying the name restriction and for any term t such that $s\bar{\phi} \to_{R,E} t$, there exists a term u satisfying the name restriction such that $t =_E u\bar{\phi}$ and $s\bar{\psi} =_{RE} u\bar{\psi}$.*

Proof. There are two possibilities.

(i) Let us first assume that the rewrite step occurs at the root position. Suppose $s\bar{\phi} =_E l\mu$ with $l \to r \in R$. For any $x \in fv(l)$, $x\mu$ is possibly a term of the form $t\bar{\phi}$ where t is a subterm of s. Consider a constant-abstraction mapping π defined as follows: for any maximal subterm $s|_p\bar{\phi}$ occurring in $x\mu$ where $x \in fv(l)$, let $\pi(s|_p\bar{\phi}) = c_p$ where c_p is a fresh free constant. For the term $s'\bar{\phi}$ obtained from $s\bar{\phi})$ by replacing each maximal subterm $s|_p\bar{\phi}$ by the constant $\pi(s|_p\bar{\phi})$, we have that s' is a small context such that $|s'| \leq |R|$ and $s'\bar{\phi} \to_{R,E} r\mu$ for $l \to r \in R$. By assumption, R is contracting and so we have $r\mu =_E u'\bar{\phi}$ for some term u'. By replacing back the constants introduced by the constant abstraction, we have $(s'\bar\phi)\pi^{-1} \to_{R,E} \circ =_E (u'\bar\phi)\pi^{-1}$, where $(s'\bar\phi)\pi^{-1} = s\bar\phi$ and $(u'\bar\phi)\pi^{-1} = u\bar\phi$ for some term u. Consequently, $s\bar\phi \to_{R,E} \circ =_E u\bar\phi$. By definition of Eq^B and by assumption on $\bar\psi$, we have that $s'\bar\psi =_{RE} u'\bar\psi$. By replacing each constant $\pi(s|_p\bar\phi)$ with $s|_p\bar\psi$, we get $s\bar\psi =_{RE} u\bar\psi$.

(ii) Let us now assume that the rewrite step occurs below the root position. There exists a position $p \neq \epsilon$ such that $s'\bar\phi = (s'\bar\phi)[s\bar\phi]_p$ with $s\bar\phi \to_{R,E}^\epsilon t$. By the case (i) above, there exists a term u such that $t =_E u\bar\phi$ and $s\bar\psi =_{RE} u\bar\psi$. Then, we have

$$s'\bar\phi \to_{R,E} (s'\bar\phi)[t]_p =_E (s'\bar\phi)[u\bar\phi]_p = (s'[u]_p)\bar\phi$$

and

$$s'\bar\psi = (s'\bar\psi)[s\bar\psi]_p =_{RE} (s'\bar\psi)[u\bar\psi]_p = (s'[u]_p)\bar\psi$$

$\square$

4   Undecidability Results

One approach that could be investigated to expand the above results would be to try to weaken the definition of projection-closed equality (Definition 8) so that more permutative theories could be considered in the framework of contracting TRS. However, we show that if we weaken the definition of contracting, Definition 9, by relaxing the type of permutations allowed, we quickly run into undecidability results.

It turns out that while the above restrictions detailed in Definition 9 may be able to be weakened slightly, one still requires restrictions on both the rule applications and the permutations allowed or undecidability results follow. Indeed, we next show that we can consider subsets of the rules from the graph-embedded definition and these subsets still lead to the undecidability of the knowledge problems.

4.1   A Weaker Contracting Definition

Let us first consider removing the depth restriction from the definition of contracting TRS (Definition 8). We show that by removing this restriction we run into undecidability. To prove this result we start with a construction developed in [17] showing that a Linear Bounded Automaton's (LBA) transition function can be simulated by a leaf permuting TRS. This in turn is used to show that static equivalence is undecidable in leaf permuting theories. However, the resulting TRS, simulating the LBA, from [17] is permutative but not contracting. The TRS is missing the required projection rules of Definition 8. These rule cannot just be added since they will have overlaps with the existing rules and thus interfere with the LBA simulation. We can however, modify slightly the construction from [17] to prevent these overlaps when adding the required projection rules.

To detail the modification, we first give a brief overview of the construction. Given a LBA $M = (Q, \Sigma, \Gamma, q_0, q_a, q_r, \delta)$, assume $\Sigma = \{a_1, a_2, \ldots, a_n\}$ and $\Gamma = \{<, >, \sqcup\} \cup \Sigma$, where $<, >$ are the left and right end caps respectively, and $\sqcup$ is the blank symbol. Terms can be constructed that simulate the state of the LBA by introducing three function symbols, f, g, h and three constants, a, b, and P. h is used to represent the state of the LBA. To represent state q_i, a constant b is placed at the ith position with the remaining positions containing a constants. There is an extra position in h, one more than $|Q|$ and it is used to represent a dummy or default state. g has arity $|\Gamma|$ and is used to encode the alphabet characters. A constant b at position i in g with a constants placed at all other positions to encode a_i. f is used to form terms which consist of an encoding of a state, an encoding of a single character, and an f-rooted subterm or the constant P. The subterm is used to encode the rest of the string. The constant P is used to stop the encoding. For example, suppose you have a state $<q_0 0>$ of the LBA, $|Q| = 2$, and $\Gamma = \{<, >, 0, \sqcup\}$. Then the term representation of this would be:

$$f(h(b, a, a), g(b, a, a, a), f(h(a, a, b), g(a, a, b, a), f(h(a, a, b), g(a, b, a, a), P)))$$

Then, the left and right moves of the LBA can be simulated by a permutative TRS. For example, if the LBA has a move $\delta(q_0, <) = (q_1, <, R)$ one of the rules for this transition would then be:

$$f(h(b, a, a), g(b, a, a, a), f(h(a, a, b), g(a, a, b, a), x)) \rightarrow$$
$$f(h(a, a, b), g(b, a, a, a), f(h(a, b, a), g(a, a, b, a), x))$$

Notice that there would be several versions of this rule, since this is the version with the 0 symbol encoded as the next symbol to read, right of $<$. Likewise for a LBA transition $\delta(q_0, >) = (q_1, >, L)$, one of the rules would be:

$$f(h(a, a, b), g(a, a, b, a), f(h(b, a, a), g(a, b, a, a), x)) \rightarrow$$
$$f(h(a, b, a), g(a, a, b, a), f(h(a, a, b), g(a, a, b, a), x))$$

Now, notice we can't just add projection rules to this TRS. The required projection rule for the above right-move example transition would be:

$$f(h(a, a, b), g(a, a, b, a), x) \rightarrow x$$

However, notice that this overlaps with the above left-move transition.

Theorem 6. *Static equivalence is undecidable in general for contracting TRSs without a depth restriction.*

Proof. We can fix the above issue with overlapping projection rules by introducing two dummy states instead of one, a left-dummy state, q_{ld}, and a right-dummy state, q_{rd}. This can be done by increasing the arity of h by one. The second to last position being the left-dummy state and the final position the right dummy-state. Thus if $|Q| = n$, h has arity of $n + 2$. For example, in the above case with $|Q| = 2$, the left dummy state $q_{ld} = h(a, a, b, a)$ and the right $q_{rd} = h(a, a, a, b)$.

The initial state of the LBA tape has just right-dummy states with the LBA tape head to the left of all the dummy states. Right moves by the LBA change the dummy states, that are now left of the LBA tape head, to left-dummy states. Likewise, left rule moves of the LBA change left-dummy states back to right-dummy states.

We illustrate these modifications with the two rule examples from above. The right moves are now modified as follows:

$$f(h(b, a, a, a), g(b, a, a, a), f(h(a, a, a, b), g(a, a, b, a), x)) \rightarrow$$
$$f(h(a, a, b, a), g(b, a, a, a), f(h(a, b, a, a), g(a, a, b, a), x))$$

The left moves are modified as follows:

$$f(h(a, a, b, a), g(a, a, b, a), f(h(b, a, a, a), g(a, b, a, a), x)) \rightarrow$$
$$f(h(a, b, a, a), g(a, a, b, a), f(h(a, a, a, b), g(a, a, b, a), x))$$

Now when we add the projection rules for right LBA moves we have rules of the form:

$$f(h(a, a, b, a), g(a, a, b, a), x) \rightarrow x$$

However, this now doesn't overlap the left move rules of the LBA since they include the subterm for the right-dummy state $h(a, a, a, b)$ instead of the left-dummy that is now included in the projection rules, $h(a, a, b, a)$. The same occurs for the left LBA moves.   □

4.2   Subset of Graph-Embedded

Next, let us consider subsets of the rules from the graph-embedded definition.

Definition 15. *A rule-4 graph-embedded term rewrite system is any TRS, R, such that for all $l \rightarrow r \in R$, $l \rightarrow^+_{R_{gemb}} r$, using only rules (4) and (2) of Definition 5. Denote this set of graph-embedded rules as R_4.*

Likewise, a rule-3 graph-embedded term rewrite system is any TRS, R, such that for all $l \rightarrow r \in R$, $l \rightarrow^+_{R_{gemb}} r$, using only rules (3) and (2) of Definition 5.

Rule-4 Graph-Embedded: First, we can consider the restricted rule-4 graph-embedded TRSs and use a result previously developed for homeomorphic embedded TRSs.

Theorem 7. *Deduction is undecidable in general for rule-4 graph-embedded TRS.*

Proof. Assume for each $l \rightarrow r \in R$, for some TRS R, that $l \rightarrow^*_{R_{emb}} r$, r is homeomorphically embedded in l, *and* the root symbol of l remains the root symbol for r, $l(\epsilon) = r(\epsilon)$. Then, $l \rightarrow^*_{R_4} r$. Notice that any homeomorphic rewrite step below the root can be emulated by several applications of rule (4) and (2). If $t = f(\bar{t}_1, g(x_1, \ldots, x_i, \ldots, x_n), \bar{t}_2) \rightarrow_{R_{gemb}} f(\bar{t}_1, x_i, \bar{t}_2)$ then,

$$t = f(\bar{t}_1, g(x_1, \ldots, x_i, \ldots, x_n), \bar{t}_2) \rightarrow_{(4)}$$
$$f(\bar{t}_1, x_1, \ldots, x_i, \ldots, x_n, \bar{t}_2) \rightarrow_{(4)}^{n-1} f(\bar{t}_1, x_i, \bar{t}_2).$$

In [9] it is shown that deduction is undecidable in general for homeomorphic embedded TRS. The proof uses a reduction from the Modified Post Correspondence Problem (MPCP). The TRS developed in that reduction was the following:

$$B = \bigcup_{i=1}^{n} \{f(\widetilde{\alpha}_i(x), g_i(y), \widetilde{\beta}_i(z), unlocked(z)) \rightarrow f(x, y, z, unlocked(z))\},$$

$$U = \{f(x, y, x, locked(unlocked(z))) \rightarrow f(x, y, x, unlocked(z))\}.$$

Notice that each of these rules is both homeomorphic embedded and root symbol preserving. Thus, each of these rules is also rule-4 graph-embedded. □

Rule-3 Graph-Embedded: Next, consider the rule-3 graph-embedded TRSs. For this reduction we will use the Modified Post Correspondence Problem (MPCP) an undecidable version of the well known undecidable Post Correspondence Problem (PCP). Let $\Gamma = \{a, b\}$ be the alphabet of the $MPCP$ problem. Then, an instance of the problem is a finite set of string pairs, $S = \{(\alpha_i, \beta_i)| i \in [1, n]\} \subseteq \Gamma^+ \times \Gamma^+$, and an input string $\alpha_0 \in \Gamma^*$. A solution is a sequence of indexes $i_1, \ldots i_k \in [1, n]$ such that $\alpha_{i_1} \alpha_{i_2} \ldots \alpha_{i_k} = \beta_{i_1} \beta_{i_2} \ldots \beta_{i_k}$, α_0 is a suffix of $\alpha_{i_1} \alpha_{i_2} \ldots \alpha_{i_k}$, and α_0 is a suffix of $\beta_{i_1} \beta_{i_2} \ldots \beta_{i_k}$. That is, there is a string $\alpha' \in \Gamma^*$ s.t. $\alpha_{i_1} \alpha_{i_2} \ldots \alpha_{i_k} = \alpha' \cdot \alpha_0 = \beta_{i_1} \beta_{i_2} \ldots \beta_{i_k}$. Notice that the standard PCP is easily reducible to this $MPCP$ by setting α_0 to the empty string.

Theorem 8. *Deduction is undecidable in general for rule-3 graph-embedded TRS.*

Proof. Let $P = \{(\alpha_i, \beta_i)| i \in [1, n]\}$ be an instance of MPCP over the alphabet $\Gamma = \{a, b\}$ with the input string $\alpha_0 \in \Gamma^*$. We can convert this MPCP problem into the TRS setting. First, let f be a binary function symbol and let a and b be constants, and let $d_1, \ldots, d_n$, be public constants, one for each string pair of the MPCP. We can convert a string over Γ into a term using f, a and b in a recursive fashion. For $\gamma \in \Gamma^+$ and $x \in V$, let $\widetilde{\gamma}(x)$ denote the term version defines as follows: If $\gamma = a$ (or b) then $\widetilde{\gamma}(x) = f(a, x)$ (likewise $\widetilde{\gamma}(y) = f(b, y)$). If $\gamma = a \cdot \gamma'$ then $\widetilde{\gamma}(x) = f(u, \widetilde{\gamma'}(x))$. Let lck (for locked), $ulck$ (for unlocked), and d, d_i $(0 \leq i \leq n)$ be *public* constants. Now, construct a TRS, R, as follows: for each pair $\{(\alpha_i, \beta_i)| i \in [1, n]\}$ we create the rule

$$f(f(f(ulck, v), f(d_i, x)), f(\widetilde{\alpha_i(y)}, \widetilde{\beta_i(z)})) \rightarrow f(f(f(ulck, v), x), f(y, z))$$

Add one final "unlocking" rule to R:

$$f(f(f(ulck, f(lck, v)), f(d_0, x)), f(y, y)) \rightarrow f(f(f(ulck, v), x), f(y, y)).$$

The d_i ensure there are no critical pairs between rules and thus we have a convergent TRS. In addition, note that each rule in R can be obtained by using just rule-3 (and rule-2 to remove extra terms). That is, $\forall\, l \to r \in R,\ l \to^+_{(3),(2)} r$.

Now for the $MPCP$ instance, construct the frame $\phi = \nu\tilde{n}.\sigma$ with $\tilde{n} = \{c, e\}$ and $\sigma = \{v \mapsto f(ulck, f(lck, e)),\ x \mapsto \widetilde{\alpha_0}(c)\}$. Likewise, construct a deduction problem with the target term $M = f(f(f(ulck, e), d),\ f(c, c))$.

First, suppose there exists a recipe term, t, such that $t\sigma \downarrow_R = M$. Then the first rule that must be applied is the unlocking rule, since it is required before any of the other rules can be applied. The unlocking rule also ensures that the two strings are equal. Next, each remaining rewrite step corresponds to a single string pair from the $MPCP$, ensuring the recipe corresponds to a solution. The solution can be extracted from the indexes of each of the d_i constants occurring in the rewrite derivation.

Second, it also easy to see that if there is a solution to the $MPCP$ we can from that solution construct a recipe to deduce M. For example, if the solution is $i_1, \ldots i_k \in [1, n]$. Then, a recipe would be:

$$t = f(f(v, f(d_0, f(d_{i_1}, f(\ldots, f(d_{i_k}, d)))))),\ f(\widetilde{\alpha'(x)}, \widetilde{\beta'(x)}))$$

where $\alpha_{i_1}\alpha_{i_2}\ldots\alpha_{i_k} = \alpha' \cdot \alpha_0 = \beta' \cdot \alpha_0 = \beta_{i_1}\beta_{i_2}\ldots\beta_{i_k}$ $\square$

5   Conclusions

In this paper, we have extended the combination result from [19], providing decision procedures for the problems of deduction and static equivalence in the combination $R \cup E$, where R is contracting and E-convergent. This improves upon the previous result, which required R to be subterm E-convergent.

We also examined the gap between two extensions of subterm TRSs, contracting and graph-embedded, with respect to the decidability of knowledge problems. We showed that several natural attempts to narrow this gap while preserving decidability fail, leading to TRSs with undecidable knowledge problems. Nevertheless, it remains plausible that a class of systems closer to graph-embedded than contracting could be defined in a way that maintains decidability. Identifying the best approach to achieve this remains an open question.

Regarding the undecidability proof for deduction in rule-3 TRSs, we note that since the terms involve a single non-constant function symbol, rule-3 behaves similarly to rule-4. It would be interesting to investigate whether this proof could be adapted to avoid relying on the presence of a single function symbol.

References

1. Abadi, M., Cortier, V.: Deciding knowledge in security protocols under equational theories. Theor. Comput. Sci. **367**(1–2), 2–32 (2006)

2. Abadi, M., Fournet, C.: Mobile values, new names, and secure communication. In: Hankin, C., Schmidt, D. (eds.) Conference Record of POPL 2001: The 28th ACM SIGPLAN-SIGACT Symposium on Principles of Programming Languages, London, UK, 17–19 January 2001, pp. 104–115. ACM (2001)
3. Armando, A., et al.: The AVISPA tool for the automated validation of internet security protocols and applications. In: Etessami, K., Rajamani, S.K. (eds.) CAV 2005. LNCS, vol. 3576, pp. 281–285. Springer, Heidelberg (2005). https://doi.org/10.1007/11513988_27
4. Ayala-Rincón, M., Fernández, M., Nantes-Sobrinho, D.: Intruder deduction problem for locally stable theories with normal forms and inverses. Theor. Comput. Sci. **672**, 64–100 (2017)
5. Baader, F., Nipkow, T.: Term Rewriting and All That. Cambridge University Press, New York (1998)
6. Baader, F., Snyder, W.: Unification theory. In: Robinson, J.A., Voronkov, A. (eds.) Handbook of Automated Reasoning, pp. 445–532. Elsevier and MIT Press (2001)
7. Baudet, M., Cortier, V., Delaune, S.: YAPA: a generic tool for computing intruder knowledge. ACM Trans. Comput. Log. **14**(1), 4 (2013)
8. Blanchet, B.: An efficient cryptographic protocol verifier based on Prolog rules. In: 14th IEEE Computer Security Foundations Workshop (CSFW-14 2001), Cape Breton, Nova Scotia, Canada, 11–13 June 2001, pp. 82–96. IEEE Computer Society (2001)
9. Bunch, C., Satterfield, S.D., Erbatur, S., Marshall, A.M., Ringeissen, C.: Knowledge problems in protocol analysis: extending the notion of subterm convergent (2025). https://arxiv.org/abs/2401.17226
10. Chadha, R., Cheval, V., Ciobâcă, S., Kremer, S.: Automated verification of equivalence properties of cryptographic protocols. ACM Trans. Comput. Log. **17**(4), 23:1–23:32 (2016)
11. Ciobâcă, S., Delaune, S., Kremer, S.: Computing knowledge in security protocols under convergent equational theories. J. Autom. Reasoning **48**(2), 219–262 (2012)
12. Cohn-Gordon, K., Cremers, C., Garratt, L., Millican, J., Milner, K.: On ends-to-ends encryption: asynchronous group messaging with strong security guarantees. In: Lie, D., Mannan, M., Backes, M., Wang, X. (eds.) Proceedings of the 2018 ACM SIGSAC Conference on Computer and Communications Security, CCS 2018, Toronto, ON, Canada, 15–19 October 2018, pp. 1802–1819. ACM (2018)
13. Conchinha, B., Basin, D.A., Caleiro, C.: FAST: an efficient decision procedure for deduction and static equivalence. In: Schmidt-Schauß, M. (ed.) Proceedings of RTA 2011, Novi Sad, Serbia. LIPIcs, vol. 10, pp. 11–20. Schloss Dagstuhl - Leibniz-Zentrum fuer Informatik (2011)
14. Cortier, V., Delaune, S.: Decidability and combination results for two notions of knowledge in security protocols. J. Autom. Reasoning **48**(4), 441–487 (2010). https://doi.org/10.1007/s10817-010-9208-8
15. Cremers, C.J.F.: The scyther tool: verification, falsification, and analysis of security protocols. In: Gupta, A., Malik, S. (eds.) CAV 2008. LNCS, vol. 5123, pp. 414–418. Springer, Heidelberg (2008). https://doi.org/10.1007/978-3-540-70545-1_38
16. Dwyer Satterfield, S., Erbatur, S., Marshall, A.M., Ringeissen, C.: Knowledge problems in security protocols: going beyond subterm convergent theories. In: Gaboardi, M., van Raamsdonk, F. (eds.) 8th International Conference on Formal Structures for Computation and Deduction (FSCD 2023). Leibniz International Proceedings in Informatics (LIPIcs), vol. 260, pp. 30:1–30:19. Schloss Dagstuhl – Leibniz-Zentrum für Informatik, Dagstuhl, Germany

(2023). https://doi.org/10.4230/LIPIcs.FSCD.2023.30. https://drops.dagstuhl.de/entities/document/10.4230/LIPIcs.FSCD.2023.30

17. Erbatur, S., Marshall, A.M., Narendran, P., Ringeissen, C.: Deciding knowledge problems modulo classes of permutative theories. In: Bowles, J., Søndergaard, H. (eds.) LOPSTR 2024. LNCS, vol. 14919, pp. 47–63. Springer, Cham (2024). https://doi.org/10.1007/978-3-031-71294-4_3

18. Erbatur, S., Marshall, A.M., Ringeissen, C.: Notions of knowledge in combinations of theories sharing constructors. In: de Moura, L. (ed.) CADE 2017. LNCS (LNAI), vol. 10395, pp. 60–76. Springer, Cham (2017). https://doi.org/10.1007/978-3-319-63046-5_5

19. Erbatur, S., Marshall, A.M., Ringeissen, C.: Computing knowledge in equational extensions of subterm convergent theories. Math. Struct. Comput. Sci. **30**(6), 683–709 (2020)

20. Escobar, S., Meadows, C., Meseguer, J.: Maude-NPA: cryptographic protocol analysis modulo equational properties. In: Aldini, A., Barthe, G., Gorrieri, R. (eds.) FOSAD 2007-2009. LNCS, vol. 5705, pp. 1–50. Springer, Heidelberg (2009). https://doi.org/10.1007/978-3-642-03829-7_1

21. Jouannaud, J., Kirchner, H.: Completion of a set of rules modulo a set of equations. SIAM J. Comput. **15**(4), 1155–1194 (1986). https://doi.org/10.1137/0215084

22. Kirchner, C., Klay, F.: Syntactic theories and unification. In: Logic in Computer Science, LICS 1990, Proceedings of the Fifth Annual IEEE Symposium on Logic in Computer Science, pp. 270–277 (1990). https://doi.org/10.1109/LICS.1990.113753

23. Lynch, C., Morawska, B.: Basic syntactic mutation. In: Voronkov, A. (ed.) CADE 2002. LNCS (LNAI), vol. 2392, pp. 471–485. Springer, Heidelberg (2002). https://doi.org/10.1007/3-540-45620-1_37

24. Millen, J., Shmatikov, V.: Constraint solving for bounded-process cryptographic protocol analysis. In: Proceedings of the 8th ACM Conference on Computer and Communications Security, CCS 2001, pp. 166–175. ACM, New York (2001). https://doi.org/10.1145/501983.502007

25. Mödersheim, S., Viganò, L.: The open-source fixed-point model checker for symbolic analysis of security protocols. In: Aldini, A., Barthe, G., Gorrieri, R. (eds.) FOSAD 2007-2009. LNCS, vol. 5705, pp. 166–194. Springer, Heidelberg (2009). https://doi.org/10.1007/978-3-642-03829-7_6

26. Narendran, P., Otto, F.: Single versus simultaneous equational unification and equational unification for variable-permuting theories. J. Autom. Reason. **19**(1), 87–115 (1997)

27. Nguyen, K.: Formal verification of a messaging protocol. Internship report (2019). Work done under the supervision of Vincent Cheval and Véronique Cortier

28. Paulson, L.C.: The inductive approach to verifying cryptographic protocols. Comput. Secur. **6**, 85–128 (1998)

29. Schmidt, B., Meier, S., Cremers, C.J.F., Basin, D.A.: Automated analysis of Diffie-Hellman protocols and advanced security properties. In: Chong, S. (ed.) 25th IEEE Computer Security Foundations Symposium, CSF 2012, Cambridge, MA, USA, 25–27 June 2012, pp. 78–94. IEEE Computer Society (2012)

30. Turuani, M.: The CL-Atse protocol analyser. In: Pfenning, F. (ed.) RTA 2006. LNCS, vol. 4098, pp. 277–286. Springer, Heidelberg (2006). https://doi.org/10.1007/11805618_21

Data-Driven Runtime Complexity Analysis

Samuel Frontull$^{(\boxtimes)}$ (ID), Manuel Meitinger$^{(\boxtimes)}$ (ID), and Georg Moser$^{(\boxtimes)}$ (ID)

Department of Computer Science, University of Innsbruck, Innsbruck, Austria
{samuel.frontull,georg.moser}@uibk.ac.at,
manuel.meitinger@student.uibk.ac.at

Abstract. We establish a data-driven method for the assessment of the runtime complexity of first-order term rewrite systems (TRSs for short). The fully automated complexity analysis of TRSs has a long tradition in rewriting and numerous sophisticated static analysis methods have been developed. The recent success in machine learning motivates the quest for data-driven analysis techniques, which, while unsound in principle, can potentially return insightful upper bounds on the runtime complexity where traditional (static) techniques fail. We present the first such technique based on bottom-up rule unfolding, akin to a variant of backward narrowing. Further, we employ a dedicated notion of data fitting that is fine-tuned to the estimation of asymptotic complexities. We provide ample experimental data indicating the viability of the approach.

Keywords: term rewriting · complexity analysis · automation · machine learning

1 Introduction

Term rewriting is a conceptually simple but powerful abstract model of computation that underlies much of declarative programming. In order to assess the complexity of a (terminating) term rewrite system it is natural to look at the maximal length of derivation sequences, as suggested by Hofbauer and Lautemann in [13]. Further, to stay true to the motivation via declarative programming one typically restricts the starting terms to so-called *basic terms*, while often also focusing on *innermost rewriting*. That is, the complexity of a TRS is captured by the notion of *(innermost) runtime complexity*, cf. [12] and recent years have shown significant advances in the area, cf. [3,10,12,16,18,20,23,25,31]. Here, we restrict ourselves to fully automated methods that focus on the worst-case upper bounds of the runtime complexity of rewrite systems and have given only a handful of references. Similarly, for the fully automated resource analysis of (functional) programs a plethora of techniques have been introduced, for examples see [15] for a comprehensive survey on techniques in the amortised analysis of functional programs alone.

All these analyses are *static* analyses that work fully automatically, that is, the analysis works without user intervention and is based on the "source code",

© The Author(s) 2026
R. Thiemann and C. Weidenbach (Eds.): FroCoS 2025, LNAI 15979, pp. 228–246, 2026.
https://doi.org/10.1007/978-3-032-04167-8_13

Table 1. Experimental validation of the data-driven analysis.

	#	unsound (%)	compl. (%)	no val.	unk.	new (%)	acc. (%)
innermost	663	81 (12.2)	486 (73.3)	75	21	215 (32.4)	138 (51.3)
poly	536	16 (3.0)	460 (85.8)	46	14	215 (40.1)	112 (62.9)
fp + term.	169	7 (4.1)	138 (81.7)	24	0	25 (14.8)	74 (74.7)
full	959	203 (21.2)	568 (59.2)	113	75	296 (30.9)	204 (40.3)
poly	653	31 (4.7)	519 (79.5)	74	29	296 (45.3)	155 (64.9)
fp + term.	111	7 (6.3)	80 (72.1)	24	0	27 (24.3)	39 (75.0)

The benchmark suite is taken from the complexity categories of the *Termination Problem Database* (*TPDB*); in particular it indicates the number of (i) *unsound*; (ii) *compliant*; (iii) *new*; and finally (iv) *accurately* predicted examples, respectively. Note that accuracy is defined w.r.t. known results on the (innermost) runtime complexity of TRSs. To indicate the effect of preprocessing of the data we have highlighted the effect of filtering on benchmarks of polynomial complexity ("*poly*") or those that encode (uniformly) terminating functional programs ("*fp + term.*").

the TRS in question. On the other hand, there has been immense progress in machine learning in recent years, motivating a renewed focus on *data-driven techniques*. By design, such an analysis can only be sound *in the limit*, cf. [27]. At most we can hope to prove a soundness result in relation to the number of dynamic samples we have taken from program evaluations that have been used to learn the runtime complexity of the TRS in question.

Based on the sophisticated machine learning methodologies now available, one may hope to quickly yield a powerful (and fast) tool, trading soundness for expressivity. This may be expected to be a simple exercise. Alas, a number of challenges had to be overcome to achieve this. This study is partly motivated by recent work by Pham et al. [26] on the use of data-driven methods in a hybrid amortised resource analysis of functional programs.

More precisely, we make the following contributions: 1) We develop a novel preprocessing method that synthesises *worst-case inputs*. That is, for a given TRS $\mathcal{R}$ we seek out input terms whose derivation height w.r.t. $\mathcal{R}$ is maximally large. These inputs are then used to generate a suitable number of data points for the learner. 2) We define a suitable learning method to predict the runtime complexity of $\mathcal{R}$ in the best possible way. The method is fine-tuned for *adequacy and compliance* of the prediction. 3) We prove a statistical soundness theorem, that is, sound "in the limit", cf. Corollary 1. 4) We provide ample experimental evidence for the viability of the method. The overview of the results is given in Table 1. The table details results on the full and innermost runtime complexity. The experimental results are also available online.[1] We validatedthe method on

---

[1] See https://www.uibk.ac.at/en/theoretical-computer-science/research/ddrca/, the site also provides an interface to analyse arbitrary TRSs.

a significantly sized benchmark suite and compared to earlier results obtained on this benchmark (see Sect. 6 for details). In line with standard terminology, we call our predictions for a TRS $\mathcal{R}$ *accurate*, if the correct runtime complexity of $\mathcal{R}$ is known and the prediction is optimal. We call the prediction *compliant*, if it does not violate known lower bounds on the runtime complexity of $\mathcal{R}$.

We emphasise that our method can provide novel results on the runtime complexity of hundreds of TRSs that so far could not be analysed by static techniques. This holds true for full or innermost rewriting, respectively. This is somewhat remarkable, as the benchmark suite represents over a decade of research on fully automated static runtime complexity analyses. As the employed benchmarks are of significant size, the "correct" complexity of the TRS in question is not necessarily known. Thus, our results also provide validation results on the expressivity of the bench-suite itself.

Related Work. To the best of our knowledge, this is the first data-driven runtime complexity analysis of rewrite systems. We clarify the connection of our research to related work. Our method of choosing a worst-case input to define suitable data points as prerequisite for the learner is related to techniques that analyse the (worst-case) lower bound of the runtime complexity (see e.g. [9]). The witness term obtained in this context ideally serves as worst-case input. However, in practice the corresponding certificates issued by AProVE [10] or TcT [4] are only partly available, at least in a machine-parse-able format. Unfortunately, these instances are far too rare among the tested dataset, as can also be seen in the full experimental results.[2] Similarly, *fuzzing* [8] is a related technique as well. Fuzzing is used to uncover software bugs, by changing the input over and over again in order to reach all possible control flows. However, the fact that the problem set contains arbitrary TRSs with neither a fixed start term nor checkable grammar (e.g. building an array with :: has meaning and rules in a programming language, in a TRS it is just another function symbol) meant that this method is infeasible, as every possible symbol combination would need to be checked, without any guarantee, that the replacement chain's result is a value and without taking the cost model into account. Pham et al. [26] establish a hybrid amortised resource analysis of functional programs. The methodology is only partly comparable, as we (i) focus on unrestricted term rewrite systems; (ii) we employ a static technique to single out *worst-case input terms*, rather than learning the program input distribution, as in [26]; and (iii) we target only asymptotic complexities. Further, we note that our method is more efficient.

Outline. In the next section, we provide a high-level overview of the methodology employed. In Sect. 3 we provide basic notions and definitions. Section 4 introduces our synthesis technique for worst-case inputs and also clarifies the challenges entailed by this endeavour for arbitrary (first-order) rewrite systems. Subsequently, in Sect. 5 we detail the learning algorithm and state our statisti-

---

[2] In principle, we could have tried to adapt the source code of these provers ourselves, but AProVE is not open source and TcT only partly supports lower bound analysis.

cal soundness theorem. The setup of the experiments is explained in Sect. 6. We conclude and sketch future work in Sect. 7.

Table 2. Motivating examples: Arithmetic functions represented as rewrite systems

1:	$x - 0 \to x$	
2:	$\mathsf{s}(x) - \mathsf{s}(y) \to x - y$	
3:	$0 \div \mathsf{s}(y) \to 0$	
4:	$\mathsf{s}(x) \div \mathsf{s}(y) \to \mathsf{s}((x-y) \div \mathsf{s}(y))$	

1:	$x \cdot 0 \to 0$	
2:	$x \cdot \mathsf{s}(y) \to (x \cdot y) + x$	
3:	$x + \mathsf{s}(y) \to \mathsf{s}(x+y)$	
4:	$x + 0 \to x$	
5:	$0 + x \to x$	
6:	$\mathsf{s}(x) + y \to \mathsf{s}(x+y)$	

2 Overview

In this section, we give a bird's eye view on the contribution, explaining the obtained statistical analysis in a step-by-step fashion on simple motivating examples, cf. Table 2.

Consider the TRS $\mathcal{R}_1$ given to the left of Table 2. Obviously the TRS computes division of two natural numbers, represented as numerals. Further it is not difficult to see that the runtime complexity of $\mathcal{R}_1$ is *linear*, more precisely the number of rewrite steps to normal-form, starting with term $\mathsf{s}^m(0) \div \mathsf{s}^n(0)$ can be bounded precisely as $m + m/n + 1$, for $m \geqslant n$ and $n > 0$. In the literature on automated complexity analysis of TRS, however, one typically focuses on *asymptotic* bounds. Thus, in the following we will only be concerned with asymptotic bounds. Our approach correctly identifies the optimal linear (asymptotic) bound.

Now, consider TRS $\mathcal{R}_2$ given to the right of Table 2, encoding multiplication and addition, respectively. This amounts to a seemingly natural, although redundant definition. However, the redundancy makes the example no longer orthogonal, while the impredicative nature of the definition of multiplication increases its complexity, cf. [6]. Nevertheless, static analysers like AProVE [10] or TcT [4] can pinpoint its cubic runtime complexity fully automatically. Our approach also derives this optimal runtime complexity in a matter of seconds.[3] The ambiguity of the examples provides some challenges for the correct preparation of the data points and synthesis of worst case inputs. (See Sects. 4 and 5 for further details.)

Example 1. Reconsider the TRS $\mathcal{R}_1$. The automated analysis of its linear complexity provides some challenges. This is mainly due to the (natural) definition

---

[3] Kindly note, however, that the "optimal" cubic upper bound is rather removed from the actual precise multivariate bound of $\mathrm{rc}_{\mathcal{R}_2}$. The derivation height of $\mathsf{s}^m(0) \cdot \mathsf{s}^n(0)$ is precisely bounded by $2n + 1 + \frac{1}{2}m(n^2 + n)$.

of division in Rule 4. First, the rule makes the system *duplicating* as the variable x appears twice on the right-hand side. Second, the structure of the recursive call in Rule 4 requires not too trivial techniques to upper-bound the runtime complexity fully automatically, cf. [1,10,25].

As the (precise) runtime complexity can be easily calculated by hand, it is natural to believe that a stochastic approach should be able to handle the example well. A prerequisite is to generate a sufficient amount of training data as basis for the learner. This data should represent rewrite sequences that are as close as possible to the actual runtime complexity of the TRS $\mathcal{R}$ in question. Thus, we seek to find a set $\{t_i \mid i \in I\}$ of input (basic) terms of size at most n, so that the maximum of $\mathsf{dh}(t_i)_{i \in I}$ is as close as possible to $\mathsf{rc}_{\mathcal{R}}(n)$. We call such terms *worst-case input terms*. Rather than randomly generating terms for that, we aim at a more principled approach, essentially applying a variant of *narrowing* [11] that allows for *backward reasoning*.

Example 2 (continued from Example 1). W.r.t. $\mathcal{R}_1$ observe that this TRS is (i) *orthogonal*, that is, there is no overlap between the defining rules of subtraction and division; and (ii) *completely defined*, that is, all evaluations eventually end up in a numeral $\mathsf{s}^n(0)$ for some $n \geq 0$ or more generally a *value*, that is built up from constructor symbols. Put differently, $\mathcal{R}_1$ can be conceived as the translation of a first-order functional program for division. Using our algorithm—detailed in Algorithm 1 below— and grouping terms by the size of the first input numeral, worst-case input terms $\mathsf{s}^m(0) \div \mathsf{s}(0)$ $(m \geq 0)$ are singled out.

This is achieved by differentiating simple rules, essentially the base cases of the definitions, from complex rules, that is, the recursive cases. Employing bottom-up rule unfolding from values and leading up to initial terms, one generates a look-up table of evaluation costs that is used to select the most likely candidates for worst-case inputs. To avoid overlooking costly evaluations this follows a breadth-first search strategy. The simplicity of our running examples obfuscates a number of challenges here. As emphasised, the example is a functional program, normal-forms are values and there is no ambiguity. Subsequently, the bottom-up approach correctly identifies the worst-case inputs. This also works best for an innermost strategy. In general, in particular for full rewriting, neither is a suitable input term easy to identify nor is it certain that the normal-forms of the rewrite system considered are actually values. Due to the inherent complexity of computing the worst-case inputs, the algorithm is computationally demanding and may simply time out. Still, its design principle is led by the assumption that the TRS in question is close to a functional program and ideally the result of a transformation step from a functional program, say in OCaml, cf. [2]. Based on the identification of the worst-case inputs, it is straightforward to generate data points that indicate the runtime complexity of the considered rewrite system.

Example 3 (continued from Example 2). In Fig. 1 we indicate the original (raw) estimation of the runtime complexity of the running TRS $\mathcal{R}_1$ (on the left-hand side). The raw data cannot be used directly. Rather, we preprocess the data. For

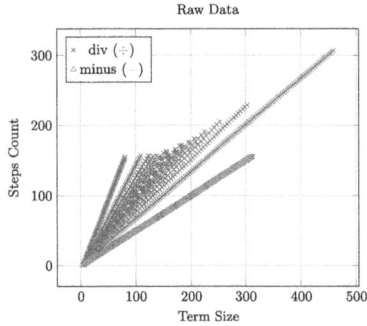 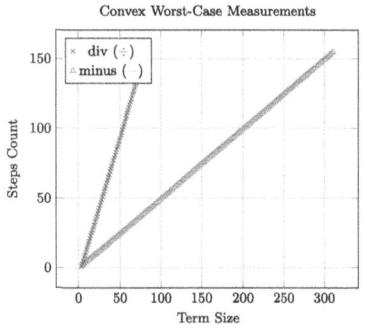

Fig. 1. Visualisation of the Runtime Complexity of $\mathcal{R}_1$.

the collection of worst-case inputs $s^m(0) \div s^n(0)$, only the maximum observed derivation heights are retained. Moreover, we apply an iterative filtering process that retains only those data points where the angle between two consecutive points is at least as large as the angle between the previous two points. We refer to the resulting points as the *convex worst-case measurements*. The right-hand side of Fig. 1 shows the convex worst-case measurements obtained from the data points illustrated on the left.

Based on the convex worst-case measurements, we employ empirical techniques to estimate the asymptotic runtime complexity of the TRS. A simple fitting model is not sufficient to achieve good results on adequacy and compliance. The fitting of models to data is usually guided by a loss function that has to be minimised. As any function on a closed interval $[a, b]$ can be approximated arbitrarily well by a polynomial of degree n for $n \to \infty$ (*Weierstrass Approximation Theorem*), attempting to fit the data as well as possible can lead to overly complex models that capture not only the underlying patterns but also the noise, which ultimately reduces the level of compliance. Instead, we follow the *difference rule* heuristic developed by McGeoch et al. [21]. This heuristic estimates the asymptotic complexity bounds by iteratively computing discrete derivatives to empirical data. It is guaranteed to be sound for the considered data points. That is, it provides sound upper bounds on the derivation height of the considered (worst-case) input terms. This implies that our methodology is *statistically sound*, that is sound "in the limit". The error rate of our prediction falls in relation to the size of test data explored, cf. Corollary 1 below.

Example 4 (continued from Example 3). W.r.t. the running example $\mathcal{R}_1$, the difference rule heuristic yields linear asymptotic complexity for the defined function symbols – and $\div$, respectively. Thus, we correctly (and optimally) conclude *linear* runtime complexity of $\mathcal{R}_1$.

3   Preliminaries

We briefly review standard notions in machine learning [7,22,24,28] and exemplify them in our context. Consider *binary classifications*. Then there are four basic combinations between ground truth and prediction: (i) *true positive* (TP), that is, a property has been classified correctly; (ii) *true negative* (TN), that is, the absence of a property has been classified correctly; (iii) *false positive* (FP), that is, an incorrect positive classification; and finally (iv) *false negative* (FN), that is, an incorrect negative classification. Then the quality of a learner can be succinctly expressed. For example, its *accuracy* is given as the fraction $TP/(TP+TN)$, while *precision* indicates the ratio $TP/(TP+FP)$, etc. [22,28]. These binary classifications are partly generalisable to multi-class classifications. In particular *accuracy* simply means the fraction of correct classifications over all classifications. For the examples in the TPDB concerned with (full) runtime complexity, the optimal runtime complexity is known for about 31% of the data suite, that is, 506 TRSs. Among these our method correctly predicts the runtime complexity for 204 TRSs. This gives an accuracy of $204/506 = 40.3\%$. *Compliance* in our context means that the classification of the runtime complexity is sound w.r.t. the known lower bounds in the test suites. Here the expected ground truth is derived from the accumulated knowledge about the TPDB, represented by the results of the so-called *Virtual Best Solver* in the corresponding competitions.[4] In order to guarantee comparability with positive results obtained by static solvers, we relate the compliant predictions to the full test suite, rather than—as in the case for adequacy—only to those that have been predicted at all.

Term Rewriting. We assume familiarity with term rewriting [5,30] but briefly review basic concepts and notations. Let $\mathcal{V}$ denote a countably infinite set of variables and $\mathcal{F}$ a signature, such that $\mathcal{F}$ contains at least one constant. We write $Var(t)$ to denote the set of variables occurring in term t. A term t is called *linear* if it does not contain multiple occurrences of the same variable. The *size* $|t|$ of a term is defined as the number of symbols in t. We suppose $\mathcal{F} = \mathcal{C} \uplus \mathcal{D}$, where $\mathcal{C}$ denotes a finite, non-empty set of *constructor symbols*, $\mathcal{D}$ is a finite set of *defined function symbols*, and $\uplus$ denotes disjoint union. Constructor terms, denoted as $\mathcal{T}(\mathcal{C}, \mathcal{V})$, are usually called *values*. A *context* is a term containing zero, or multiple occurrences of a hole $\square$. If C is a context that contains exactly n holes and $t_1, \ldots, t_n$ are terms, then $C[t_1, \ldots, t_n]$ denotes the result of replacing the holes in C from left to right by $t_1, \ldots, t_n$. If there is exactly one occurrence of $\square$ in C, then C is called a one-hole context, also denoted by $C[]$. A *substitution* σ is a mapping of variables to terms. Substitutions are conceived as sets of assignments: $\sigma = \{x_1 \mapsto t_1, \ldots, x_n \mapsto t_n\}$. We write $\mathsf{dom}(\sigma)$ ($\mathsf{rg}(\sigma)$) to denote the domain (range) of σ. Let σ, τ be substitutions such that $\mathsf{dom}(\sigma) \cap \mathsf{dom}(\tau) = \varnothing$. Then we denote the (disjoint) union of σ and τ as $\sigma \uplus \tau$. Nodes in (the term tree of) t are called *positions*. $\mathcal{P}os(t)$ denotes the set of positions in t and

---

[4] See https://termcomp.github.io/Y2024/.

$\mathcal{FP}os(t) = \{p \in \mathcal{P}os(t) \mid t(p) \in \mathcal{F}\}$ the set of function positions. A position in t determines both a prefix and a subterm of t namely the prefix with its (only) hole at position p, denoted by $t[]_p$, and (an occurrence of) the subterm occurring at position p, denoted by $t|_p$. If p is a position in t, then $t(p)$ denotes the symbol occurring in t at position p. If $s\sigma \equiv t\sigma$, then the substitution σ is called a unifier for t and s. If t and s are unifiable, then there is, again, a most general unifier (mgu), that is, a unifier that is minimal with respect to the ordering $\preceq$ on substitutions.

A *rewrite rule* is a pair $\ell \to r$ of terms such that (i) $\mathsf{root}(\ell)$ is defined, and (ii) $\mathcal{V}\mathrm{ar}(\ell) \supseteq \mathcal{V}\mathrm{ar}(r)$, where $\mathsf{root}(\ell)$ is the root symbol of ℓ. A rule $\ell \to r$ is called *left-linear*, if ℓ is linear. A (first-order) term rewrite system over $\mathcal{F}$ is a finite set of rewrite rules. In the sequel, $\mathcal{R}$ always denotes a TRS. The rewrite relation is denoted as $\to_\mathcal{R}$ and we use the standard notation for its transitive and reflexive closure. We simply write $\to$ for $\to_\mathcal{R}$ if $\mathcal{R}$ is clear from context. Let s and t be terms. If exactly n steps are performed to rewrite s to t, we write $s \to^n t$. A term that cannot be reduced further (w.r.t. some TRS $\mathcal{R}$) is called *normal-form*.

Runtime Complexity Analysis. We are sometimes only concerned with *innermost* rewriting, that is, an eager evaluation strategy. The *innermost rewrite relation* $\xrightarrow{i}_\mathcal{R}$ of a TRS $\mathcal{R}$ is defined on terms as follows: $s \xrightarrow{i}_\mathcal{R} t$ if there exists a rewrite rule $\ell \to r \in \mathcal{R}$, a context C, and a substitution σ such that $s = C[\ell\sigma], t = C[r\sigma]$, and all proper sub-terms of $\ell\sigma$ are normal-forms of $\mathcal{R}$.

A TRS is *left-linear* if all rules are left-linear, it is non-overlapping if there are no critical pairs, that is, no ambiguity exists in applying rules. A TRS is *orthogonal* if it is left-linear and non-overlapping. A TRS is *completely defined* if all ground normal-forms are values. Note that an orthogonal TRS is confluent. An orthogonal and completely-defined TRS, we may also simply call a *functional program*.[5] Let s and t be terms, such that t is in normal-form. Then a *derivation* $D: s \to^*_\mathcal{R} t$ with respect to a TRS $\mathcal{R}$ is a finite sequence of rewrite steps. The *derivation height* of a term s with respect to a well-founded, finitely branching relation $\to$ is defined as: $\mathsf{dh}(s, \to) = \max\{n \mid \exists t \; s \to^n t\}$. A term $t = f(t_1, \dots, t_k)$ is called *basic* if f is defined, and all $t_i \in \mathcal{T}(\mathcal{C}, \mathcal{V})$.

We define the *(innermost) runtime complexity* (of $\mathcal{R}$). Let $\mathcal{R}$ be a TRS. The *runtime complexity* and the *innermost runtime complexity* of $\mathcal{R}$ are defined as follows. (i) $\mathsf{rc}_\mathcal{R}(n) := \max\{\mathsf{dh}(t, \to_\mathcal{R}) \mid t \text{ is basic and } |t| \leqslant n\}$ and (ii) $\mathsf{irc}_\mathcal{R}(n) := \max\{\mathsf{dh}(t, \xrightarrow{i}_\mathcal{R}) \mid t \text{ is basic and } |t| \leqslant n\}$. In the following we may also refer to the (innermost) runtime complexity as *cost* thus alluding to the connection of rewrite systems and programs.

4 Worst-Case Input Generation

In this section, we delineate how to synthesise *worst-case input terms*, that is, those input terms $(t_i)_{i\in I}$ that maximise $\mathsf{dh}(t_i)_{i\in I}$, for some suitable defined index

---

[5] It is easy to automatically verify that a TRS is orthogonal. However, for verification of completely definedness we use approximations to define the corresponding benchmark suite.

Algorithm 1. Pseudo-code of work list algorithm.

Require: *initialRules*
  foundRules ← ∅
  pendingRules ← *initialRules*
  delayedRules ← ∅   ▷ Delayed rules are all recursive.
  loop
    while *pendingRules* ≠ ∅ **do**   ▷ Simplify all non-recursive rules.
      for all *rule* ∈ *pendingRules* **do**
        foundRules ← *foundRules* ∪ {*rule*}
        pendingRules ← *pendingRules* \ {*rule*}
        for all *derivableRule* ∈ computeDerivableRules(*rule*, *foundRules*) **do**
          if *derivedRule.isRecursive* **then**
            delayedRules ← *delayedRules* ∪ {*derivableRule*}
          else
            pendingRules ← *pendingRules* ∪ {*derivableRule*}
          end if
        end for
      end for
    end while
    if *delayedRules* = ∅ **or** *wallTime* > *maxTime* **then return**
    else
      steps ← 0   ▷ Find the longest recursive replacement chains...
      for all *rule* ∈ *delayedRules* **do**
        steps ← max(*steps*, *rule.recursiveSteps*)
      end for
      for all *rule* ∈ *delayedRules* **do**   ▷ ...and add them to the worklist.
        if *rule.recursiveSteps* = *steps* **then**
          pendingRules ← *pendingRules* ∪ {*rule*}
          delayedRules ← *delayedRules* \ {*rule*}
        end if
      end for
    end if
  end loop

---

set I. Our method singles out those initial terms that are most likely to yield the longest derivation heights, thus constitute good examples to learn the worst-case runtime complexity. For that we implemented a tool that can find the replacement chain(s) from an input basic term to a normal-form, yielding the highest derivation height (or cost). A replacement chain is a consecutive application of matching term replacement rules. Note that for arbitrary TRSs, there is no explicit *start* term—a main function, so to speak—every function occurring in the TRS must be considered an entry point.

We take inspiration from the realm of functional programs, where the normal-form is always a *value*, that is, consists only of constructors and variables, without any defined function symbols.[6] Replacement rules returning such a value will be referred to as *simple* rules, rules containing at least one function on the right-hand side as *complex* rules.

A rewrite rule $\ell \rightarrow^n r$ is called *simple* if r does not contain any defined function symbol. Otherwise, it is *complex*. *Simplifying* a complex rule is combining it with a simple rule into another simple rule, or a complex rule with fewer function invocations on the right-hand side. Suppose we have a complex rule $c : \ell_1 \rightarrow^a r_1$, a simple rule $s : \ell_2 \rightarrow^b r_2$ and a unifier $\mu = \mathrm{mgu}(r_1|_p, \ell_2)$ where $p \in \mathcal{FPos}(r_1)$. Then we define the *simplification* of c with s, denoted as $c \triangleleft s$, as $\ell_1\mu \rightarrow^{a+b} r_1[r_2]_p\mu$. To illustrate, consider a function that checks the equality of integers, represented as TRS.

$$1: \quad 0 = 0 \rightarrow^1 \top \qquad 3: \qquad \mathsf{s}(x) = 0 \rightarrow^1 \bot$$
$$2: \; 0 = \mathsf{s}(x) \rightarrow^1 \bot \qquad 4: \; \mathsf{s}(x_1) = \mathsf{s}(x_2) \rightarrow^1 x_1 = x_2 \; .$$

Rules 1 to 3 are simple rules, since their right-hand side is a constructor, $\top$ or $\bot$. Rule 4 is complex. Simplifying Rule 4 with, say, Rule 1, the left-hand side of the simple rule needs to match the right-hand side of the complex rule. This can be achieved with the unification $\sigma = \{x_1 \mapsto 0, x_2 \mapsto 0\}$. Thus, the rule resulting from $4 \triangleleft 1$ is $\mathsf{s}(0) = \mathsf{s}(0) \rightarrow^2 \top$. Performing this step over and over while keeping track of the number of simplifications, the resulting set of simple rules provides a *lookup table* of program input values (to the left) to their resulting output (to the right), and, more importantly, to the runtime cost (number of replacements). Essentially, this amounts to a *backward reasoning* variant of narrowing, that is, starting from values and leading up to initial terms.

Thus, for simple examples, finding the program's worst execution path for a given input becomes straightforward. (Since in general the lookup table grows exponentially, this method has its limits, though.) There is, however, another challenge that is not apparent in the simple example from before: What to do if there are multiple choices for simplification? Consider the following slightly more complex (but abstract) example.

$$1: \; \mathsf{main}([]) \rightarrow^1 0 \qquad 2: \mathsf{main}(x :: t) \rightarrow^1 \mathsf{costly}(x) + \mathsf{main}(t)$$
$$3: \mathsf{costly}(0) \rightarrow^1 0 \qquad 4: \mathsf{costly}(\mathsf{s}(x)) \rightarrow^1 \mathsf{costly}(x) + \mathsf{costly}(x) \; .$$

A naive strategy would be to first compute $2 \triangleleft 3$, yielding the complex rule $\mathsf{main}(0 :: t) \rightarrow^2 0 + \mathsf{main}(t)$, followed by $(2 \triangleleft 3) \triangleleft 1$ to get $\mathsf{main}(0 :: []) \rightarrow^3 0 + 0$. This simple rule can be applied arbitrarily often to simplify Rule 2 again and again, returning

$$\mathsf{main}(0 :: 0 :: []) \rightarrow^5 0 + 0 + 0 \; ,$$
$$\mathsf{main}(0 :: 0 :: 0 :: []) \rightarrow^7 0 + 0 + 0 + 0 \; , \; \ldots$$

---

[6] The special case of functions of arity 0—effectively *constants*—are handled in a preprocessing step that simply replaces any occurrence of the constant's function symbol (LHS) with its value (RHS).

never expanding the costly function. To mitigate this issue, the solver performs a *breadth-first search* strategy, that is, it keeps track of the replacement history of all used simple and complex functions, alongside the replacement cost. It employs a work-list algorithm, where all non-recursive replacements are handled first. New rules resulting in a recursion are placed in a separate secondary list. Once the primary list is finished, the replacement history of all recursive rules in the secondary list is used to compute the number of replacements (steps) since the last recursion. The rules with the largest of those numbers are then moved to the primary work list (cf. Algorithm 1). Using this heuristic prevents the stochastic analyser from being fed data of only one recursion. In other words, ordering recursive rules this way prevents the algorithm from being greedy and allows it to be complete.

Theorem 1. *For terminating, completely defined TRSs, Algorithm 1 will yield all possible replacement chains up to a fixed length that end in a value term.*

Proof. By induction on the length n of the replacement chains. (i) Base Case $n = 1$: the corresponding simple rule is already present in $\mathcal{R}$ and thus added to the foundRules set during the first iteration of the while loop. (ii) Step Case: We assume that we found all replacement chains up to length n, and show that all rules linking to those will be discovered by the algorithm as well. We split the not-yet-found rules into two categories: recursive and non-recursive. Non-recursive rules are added to the pendingRules set, which in turn is enumerated again and its rules are added to the foundRules set (first part of the algorithm). Recursive derivable rules—replacement chains invoking the same rule two or more times—are added to the delayedRules set, which is then processed in the second part of the algorithm once there are no more pendingRules (which must occur since $\mathcal{R}$ is finite). The second part of the algorithm guarantees that at least one rule in delayedRules will be moved to pendingRules, which in turn is moved to foundRules. So to prove that every delayed rule will eventually be placed in foundRules, we need to show that it's not possible for it to be skipped in the recursiveSteps-based selection indefinitely. This, however, follows by the definition (calculation) of recursiveSteps: If a rule is moved from delayedRules to pendingRules, any further recursive replacement chain found in the while loop will have a recursiveSteps of 1 regarding that rule. If the recursion is in a different rule, recursiveSteps might be higher, but since every further simplification removes at least one function symbol, this is only possible $\#(\mathcal{R})$ number of times, after which all new derivable rules will be queued after rules with the original recursiveSteps. Thus, no recursive rule is kept in the pendingRules set forever, and moved to foundRules eventually.   □

To clarify, the reason for choosing recursive rules with the most steps is not done because of any *cost* associated with steps—the algorithm is mostly cost-agnostic—its purpose is to find every possible recursive replacement chain. Think of replacement chains as paths through a directed graph, starting at some input term and resulting in a value. The latter is where the algorithm starts, i.e. with all simple rules that return a value. It then enters the aforementioned two-parted loop, where the first part extends all found paths as far as possible, without resulting in another cycle, but stores information about possible cycles. The second part then proceeds to find the largest cycles that can be formed and adds them to the known paths, repeating the first phase, and so on. This ensures that all replacement chains are found if the algorithm runs to its *natural* end, i.e. when no more simplifications can be performed or found. The run-time is, however, also limited by a user-defined timeout, since a TRS might be too complex or not fulfil the requirements as stated in Theorem 1.

Finally, to get the *worst-case* input, the analyser must group the input terms for each function by length and use the aforementioned lookup table to find the highest cost. This process can be refined by taking the syntactic meaning of constructors into account, grouping input terms by factors with more semantic meaning—like input array size or input tree height—but for arbitrary TRSs where terms have no semantic connotations, term length is the most general grouping method available, as far as term *costs* are concerned.

Table 3. Example output of Algorithm 1 for the TRS $\mathcal{R}_2$ from Table 2.

$$x{\cdot}0 \rightarrow^1 0$$

$$x{\cdot}s(y) \rightarrow^1 (x{\cdot}y)+x$$

$$x+0 \rightarrow^1 x$$

$$0+x \rightarrow^1 x$$

$$x+s(y) \rightarrow^1 s(x+y)$$

$$s(x)+y \rightarrow^1 s(x+y)$$

$$0{\cdot}s(@\mathrm{var}_2) \rightarrow^2 0{\cdot}@\mathrm{var}_2$$

$$0{\cdot}s(0) \rightarrow^3 0$$

$$s(0)+@\mathrm{var}_8 \rightarrow^2 s(@\mathrm{var}_8)$$

$$s(@\mathrm{var}_7)+0 \rightarrow^2 s(@\mathrm{var}_7)$$

$$0+s(@\mathrm{var}_6) \rightarrow^2 s(@\mathrm{var}_6)$$

$$@\mathrm{var}_5+s(0) \rightarrow^2 s(@\mathrm{var}_5)$$

$$s(0){\cdot}s(@\mathrm{var}_2) \rightarrow^3 s(s(0){\cdot}@\mathrm{var}_2)$$

$$\dots$$

$$s^4(0){\cdot}s^4(0) \rightarrow^{19} s^{12}(0)+s^4(0)$$

$$s^4(0){\cdot}s^4(0) \rightarrow^{24} s^{16}(0)$$

$$s^{16}(0)+s^{10}(@\mathrm{var}_{74}) \rightarrow^{27} s^{26}(@\mathrm{var}_{74})$$

$$\dots$$

For TRSs resulting from translating a functional program, this approach might not be targeted enough and also wastes time in recursions that generate less cost. Optimising the algorithm for TRS where there is a known main term is part of future work, which is covered in more detail later, when we discuss future work (see Sect. 7). Algorithm 1 shows the pseudocode of the work list algorithm. Figure 3 displays the rules synthesised by this algorithm for TRS $\mathcal{R}_2$. This output is the basis for the data-driven analysis.

5   Data-Driven Analysis

In this section we describe the approach we take when analysing the data collected in the worst-case input generation phase to determine the asymptotic complexity. To do this, we rely on the *difference rule* heuristic proposed in [21]. In contrast to conventional curve fitting methods, which focus on precise fitting to the observed data, this heuristic emphasises compliance by attempting to determine conservative upper bounds while taking into account the inherent limitations of finite data.

We define a *rule-induced measurement* as $\mathsf{meas}(\ell \to^n r) = (\mathsf{root}(\ell), |\ell|, n)$. For instance, consider the rule $\mathsf{s}^{16}(0)+\mathsf{s}^{10}(@\mathrm{var}_{74}) \to^{27} \mathsf{s}^{26}(@\mathrm{var}_{74})$ (the last rule listed in Fig. 3). For this rule, $\mathsf{root}(\ell) = +$ and $|\ell| = 29$. Thus, the rule-induced measurement is $(+, 29, 27)$. In Fig. 2, we visualise the rule-induced measurements obtained from the rules generated in the worst-case input generation phase of the TRS $\mathcal{R}_2$ from Table 2, where (i) the x-axis represents the term size $|\ell|$; (ii) the y-axis represents the number of steps n needed to rewrite ℓ to r; and (iii) the colour and marker style of each point distinguishes the different root symbols $\mathsf{root}(\ell)$. The first step in our analysis is to preprocess these measurements, where for each distinct root symbol $\mathsf{root}(\ell)$, we (a) retain only the maximum n-value for each distinct $|\ell|$; (b) sort the corresponding measurements in increasing order of $|\ell|$ (we call the resulting list the *worst-case measurements*); and (c) compute the *convex* worst-case measurements that includes the one with the smallest $|\ell|$-value. In (5), we start with the first two measurements in the sorted list and iteratively construct the convex and non-decreasing sequence by checking whether the angle[7] of to the next candidate point is at least as large as the angle between the last two points in the current subsequence. With this, we obtain for each function a list of (X, Y) data points, where X is a vector of k distinct non-negative values $|l|$ arranged in increasing order. The line segments connecting these consecutive points form a *polyline*.

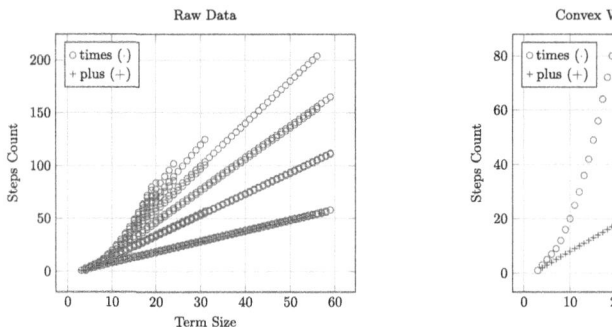
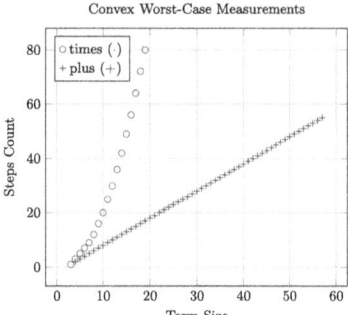

Fig. 2. Visualisation of the Runtime Complexity of $\mathcal{R}_2$.

Theorem 2. *There is no worst-case measurement above the polyline formed by the convex worst-case measurements.*

---

[7] we compute the angle between two-points $p_1 = (x_1, y_1)$ and $p_2 = (x_2, y_2)$ with $\mathsf{angle}(p_1, p_2) = atan2(y_2 - y_1, x_2 - x_1)$.

Proof. Let $s = ((x_0, y_0), (x_1, y_1), \ldots (x_n, y_n))$ be the convex worst-case measurements resulting from the filtering of a set of worst-case measurements W. Assume that there exists a measurement point $p_q = (x_q, y_q) \in W$, with $x_0 \leq x_q \leq x_n$, that is not included in s and above the curve formed by s. If $x_q = x_0$, then p_q would have to coincide with the first measurement point and would be included, contradicting our assumption. Therefore, we must have $x_i < x_q \leq x_{i+1}$ for some $0 \leq i < n$. Let x_k be the largest such x_i. Then, we have $x_q \leq x_{k+1}$. Let $a_k = \text{angle}(p_{k-1}, p_k)$ and $a_{k+1} = \text{angle}(p_k, p_{k+1})$. By assumption, we would have $a_{k+1} < \text{angle}(p_k, p_q) = a_q$. However, that would also imply $a_k \leq a_q$, violating the convexity condition required for exclusion. Hence, p_q would have been included, contradicting our assumption. □

Thus, by Theorem 2, we can guarantee statistical soundness of the data filtering process. We estimate the asymptotic complexity of each function with the *difference rule* heuristic presented in [21].

Difference Rule. This heuristic estimates the asymptotic complexity bounds by iterating numerical differentiation to the empirical data. The Newton form of a polynomial f of degree k is expressed as: $P_k(x) = \sum_{n=0}^{k} f[x_0, \ldots, x_n] \cdot \prod_{j=0}^{n-1}(x - x_j)$, where $\prod_{j=0}^{-1}(x - x_j) = 1$ and the coefficients $f[x_0, \ldots, x_n]$ are the so-called nth Newton divided differences, recusively defined as: $f[x_j, \ldots, x_n] := \frac{f[x_{j+1}, \ldots, x_n] - f[x_j, \ldots, x_{n-1}]}{x_n - x_j}$ with $f[x_i] := f(x_i)$. P_k is computed with k interpolation points $(x_0, y_0), \ldots, (x_k, y_k)$ and has the property that $P_k(x_i) = y_i = f(x_i)$ for $i \in \{0, \ldots, k\}$.

Theorem 3. *If f is a polynomial of degree d, then $f[x_0, \ldots, x_k] = 0$ for $k > d$.*

Proof. This theorem has been proven in [29]. Because of the unique solvability of the interpolating polynomial P_k (Theorem 2.1.1.1 [29]), where $P_k(x_i) = y_i = f(x_i)$ for $k \geq d$, the coefficients for x^k given by $f[x_0, \ldots, x_k]$ must vanish for $k > d$. □

This result provides a practical approach to determining the asymptotic complexity by identifying the iteration i at which $f[x_0, \ldots, x_i]$ vanishes. To mitigate the effects of noise in empirical data, the heuristic terminates when the correlation of the divided differences falls below a predefined threshold (which we set to 0.005). The number of iterations i directly determines the asymptotic complexity of the function, given by $\mathcal{O}(x^i)$.

Example 5. The first plot in Fig. 3 visualises the divided difference values computed for the *plus* function from $\mathcal{R}_2$ for $d = 1$, plotted against the corresponding x values. The points exhibit a non-increasing trend, suggesting a linear complexity. For the *times* function, we plot the computed points for $d = 1, 2, 3$, where a non-increasing trend is observed for $d = 3$. This suggests that the asymptotic complexity of the *times* function is cubic.

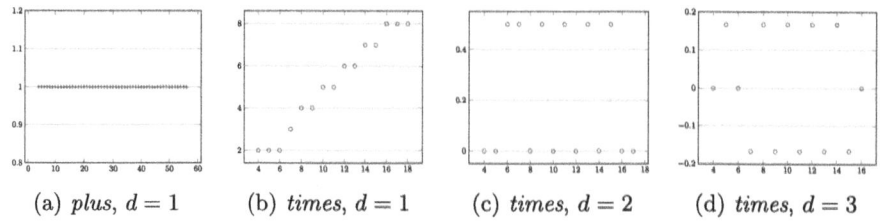

| (a) *plus, d = 1* | (b) *times, d = 1* | (c) *times, d = 2* | (d) *times, d = 3* |

Fig. 3. Divided difference values for the *plus* and the *times* function from $\mathcal{R}_2$ plotted against the corresponding x-values.

We determine the asymptotic complexity for all distinct functions in a TRS. The overall asymptotic complexity of the entire TRS is then based on the highest complexity determined for the individual functions.

Corollary 1. *For completely defined, terminated TRSs the method presented is sound in the limit.*

Proof. By Theorem 1, we know that for a completely defined, terminating TRS $\mathcal{R}$, Algorithm 1 will eventually find all (worst-case) evaluations for each defined function symbol f. If the runtime complexity of f is bounded by a polynomial of degree d, the filtering process allows the extraction of k convex worst-case measurements. Thus, by Theorem 3, we know that whenever $k > d$, the divided difference heuristic allows to determine the correct degree d on this set of measurements.

Note that the divided difference method can also be exploited to determine polynomials with their corresponding coefficients. However, in our approach, we only use it to determine the degree of the polynomial.

6   Experimental Evaluation

We have evaluated the method on a significantly sized benchmark suite from the *Termination Problem Database* (*TPDB* for short),[8] a comprehensive repository of problems related to the termination and complexity analysis of rewrite systems. We tested against the results in the corresponding *full* and *innermost* *runtime complexity* categories of last years' *Termination and Complexity Competition* (*TermComp*).[9] To verify the level of compliance of our approach, we benchmarked our results against the employed *Virtual Best Solvers* (*VBS*), summarising decades of results on static runtime complexity analysis. The results are summarised in Table 1; the full benchmarks and experimental results are available online.[10] Our experimental results demonstrate the potential of our data-driven approach by revealing 215 (innermost) and 296 (full) new upper bounds

---

[8] See https://github.com/TermCOMP/TPDB.
[9] See https://termcomp.github.io/Y2024/.
[10] See https://www.uibk.ac.at/en/theoretical-computer-science/research/ddrca/.

that were previously unknown. In particular, 166 (innermost) and 243 (full) of these upper bounds are below exponential complexity. An illustrative example is `raML/queue.raml`, whose observed data points are shown in Fig. 4. Static analysis tools have not yet been able to determine an upper bound for this TRS. Using our method, we were able to determine a quadratic upper bound for the runtime complexity by analysing the worst-case measurements of `startBreadth2`, a specialised instance of the main function. However, naturally there are also cases where our method is unable to identify worst-case measurements. As a result, the asymptotic complexity derived from the statistical analysis of this data is unsound.

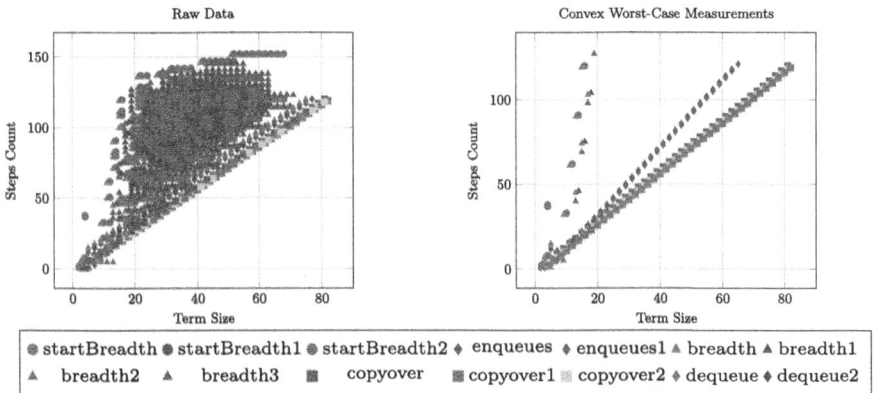

Fig. 4. Visualisation of the Runtime Complexity of *queue* (selected functions).

7   Conclusion and Future Work

In this paper, we have presented the first data-driven analysis of full and innermost runtime complexity of first-order rewrite systems. To make this method strong in practice, we have combined it with a novel worst-case input generation method. We have evaluated the method on a significantly sized benchmark suite from the TPDB and tested it against the *Virtual Best Solvers* for suitable complexity categories in TermComp. Our method provides new (and compliant) results for hundreds of tested TRSs.

In future work, we will compare these achievements directly with the data-driven method mentioned in [26], as well as compare to other analysis methods for functional programs (e.g. [2,14,17,19]). The idea is to transform a given functional program by defunctionalisation into a first-order rewrite system and subsequently employ the techniques studied here. Here we would also strive for precise upper bounds on the program cost—employing a monotonic cost model. This is based on a complexity preserving and reflecting transformation of (potentially) higher-order functional programs to TRSs, established by Avanzini et al. [2]. Knowing the underlying functional program of a TRS can also be used to improve the algorithm's performance of synthesising worst-case inputs (see Sect. 4). Having a specific and single entry point provides the ability of looking at all the terms occurring top-down to improve the choice of performed simplifications bottom-up. The hope here is to drastically decrease the amount of time spent following recursions that do not yield relevant information regarding said main function.

Acknowledgements. We would like to thank the anonymous reviewers for their work and invaluable suggestions, which greatly improved our presentation. This work is partly supported by the FWF Project AUTOSARD: "Automated Sublinear Amortised Resource Analysis of Data Structures".

References

1. Arts, T., Giesl, J.: Termination of term rewriting using dependency pairs. Theor. Comput. Sci. **236**(1–2), 133–178 (2000). https://doi.org/10.1016/S0304-3975(99)00207-8
2. Avanzini, M., Lago, U.D., Moser, G.: Analysing the complexity of functional programs: higher-order meets first-order. In: Proceedings of 20th ICFP, pp. 152–164. ACM (2015). https://doi.org/10.1145/2784731.2784753
3. Avanzini, M., Moser, G.: Complexity of Acyclic Term Graph Rewriting. In: Proceedings of 1st FSCD. LIPIcs, vol. 52, pp. 10:1–10:18. Schloss Dagstuhl - Leibniz-Zentrum für Informatik (2016). https://doi.org/10.4230/LIPICS.FSCD.2016.10
4. Avanzini, M., Moser, G., Schaper, M.: TcT: Tyrolean Complexity Tool. In: Chechik, M., Raskin, J.-F. (eds.) TACAS 2016. LNCS, vol. 9636, pp. 407–423. Springer, Heidelberg (2016). https://doi.org/10.1007/978-3-662-49674-9_24
5. Baader, F., Nipkow, T.: Term Rewriting and All That. Cambridge University Press, Cambridge (1998). https://doi.org/10.1017/CBO9781139172752
6. Bellantoni, S.J., Cook, S.A.: A new recursion-theoretic characterization of the polytime functions. Comput. Complex. **2**, 97–110 (1992). https://doi.org/10.1007/BF01201998
7. Bishop, C.: Pattern Recognition and Machine Learning. Information Science and Statistics, Springer, New York (2006). https://doi.org/10.5555/1162264
8. Boehme, M., Cadar, C., Roychoudhury, A.: Fuzzing: Challenges and Reflections. IEEE Softw. **38**(3), 79–86 (2021). https://doi.org/10.1109/MS.2020.3016773
9. Frohn, F., Giesl, J., Hensel, J., Aschermann, C., Ströder, T.: Lower bounds for runtime complexity of term rewriting. J. Autom. Reason. **59**(1), 121–163 (2017). https://doi.org/10.1007/S10817-016-9397-X
10. Giesl, J., et al.: Analyzing Program Termination and Complexity Automatically with AProVE. J. Autom. Reason. **58**(1), 3–31 (2017). https://doi.org/10.1007/S10817-016-9388-Y
11. Hanus, M.: The integration of functions into logic programming: From theory to practice. J. Log. Program. **19**(20), 583–628 (1994). https://doi.org/10.1016/0743-1066(94)90034-5

12. Hirokawa, N., Moser, G.: Automated Complexity Analysis Based on the Dependency Pair Method. In: Armando, A., Baumgartner, P., Dowek, G. (eds.) IJCAR 2008. LNCS (LNAI), vol. 5195, pp. 364–379. Springer, Heidelberg (2008). https://doi.org/10.1007/978-3-540-71070-7_32

13. Hofbauer, D., Lautemann, C.: Termination proofs and the length of derivations. In: Dershowitz, N. (ed.) RTA 1989. LNCS, vol. 355, pp. 167–177. Springer, Heidelberg (1989). https://doi.org/10.1007/3-540-51081-8_107

14. Hoffmann, J., Das, A., Weng, S.: Towards automatic resource bound analysis for OCaml. In: Proceedings of 44th POPL, pp. 359–373. ACM (2017). https://doi.org/10.1145/3009837.3009842

15. Hoffmann, J., Jost, S.: Two decades of automatic amortized resource analysis. Math. Struct. Comput. Sci. **32**(6), 729–759 (2022). https://doi.org/10.1017/S0960129521000487

16. Hofmann, M., Moser, G.: Amortised Resource Analysis and Typed Polynomial Interpretations. In: Dowek, G. (ed.) RTA 2014. LNCS, vol. 8560, pp. 272–286. Springer, Cham (2014). https://doi.org/10.1007/978-3-319-08918-8_19

17. Hofmann, M., Leutgeb, L., Obwaller, D., Moser, G., Zuleger, F.: Type-based analysis of logarithmic amortised complexity. Math. Struct. Comput. Sci. **32**(6), 794–826 (2022). https://doi.org/10.1017/S0960129521000232

18. Hofmann, M., Moser, G.: Multivariate amortised resource analysis for term rewrite systems. In: Proceedings of 13th TLCA. LIPIcs, vol. 38, pp. 241–256. Schloss Dagstuhl - Leibniz-Zentrum für Informatik (2015). https://doi.org/10.4230/LIPICS.TLCA.2015.241

19. Leutgeb, L., Moser, G., Zuleger, F.: ATLAS: Automated Amortised Complexity Analysis of Self-adjusting Data Structures. In: Silva, A., Leino, K.R.M. (eds.) CAV 2021. LNCS, vol. 12760, pp. 99–122. Springer, Cham (2021). https://doi.org/10.1007/978-3-030-81688-9_5

20. Lommen, N., Meyer, É., Giesl, J.: Control-Flow Refinement for Complexity Analysis of Probabilistic Programs in KoAT (Short Paper). In: Proceedings of 12th IJCAR. LNCS, vol. 14739, pp. 233–243 (2024). https://doi.org/10.1007/978-3-031-63498-7_14

21. McGeoch, C.C., Cohen, P.R.: How to find big-oh in your data set (and how not to). In: Madigan, D., Smyth, P. (eds.) Proceedings of the Sixth International Workshop on Artificial Intelligence and Statistics. Proceedings of Machine Learning Research, vol. R1, pp. 347–354. PMLR (1997). https://doi.org/10.1007/BFb0052828

22. Mohri, M., Rostamizadeh, A., Talwalkar, A.: Foundations of Machine Learning. Adaptive Computation and Machine Learning series, MIT Press, Cambridge (2012). https://dl.acm.org/doi/10.5555/3360093

23. Moser, G., Schneckenreither, M.: Automated amortised resource analysis for term rewrite systems. Sci. Comput. Program. **185** (2020). https://doi.org/10.1016/J.SCICO.2019.102306

24. Murphy, K.: Machine Learning: A Probabilistic Perspective. Adaptive Computation and Machine Learning series, MIT Press, Cambridge (2012). https://dl.acm.org/doi/book/10.5555/2380985

25. Noschinski, L., Emmes, F., Giesl, J.: Analyzing Innermost Runtime Complexity of Term Rewriting by Dependency Pairs. JAR **51**(1), 27–56 (2013). https://doi.org/10.1007/s10817-013-9277-6

26. Pham, L., Saad, F.A., Hoffmann, J.: Robust Resource Bounds with Static Analysis and Bayesian Inference. Proc. ACM Program. Lang. **8**(PLDI) (2024). https://doi.org/10.1145/3656380

27. Sanders, P., Fleischer, R.: Asymptotic Complexity from Experiments? A Case Study for Randomized Algorithms. In: Näher, S., Wagner, D. (eds.) WAE 2000. LNCS, vol. 1982, pp. 135–146. Springer, Heidelberg (2001). https://doi.org/10.1007/3-540-44691-5_12
28. Shalev-Shwartz, S., Ben-David, S.: Understanding Machine Learning: From Theory to Algorithms. Cambridge University Press, Cambridge (2014). https://doi.org/10.1017/CBO9781107298019
29. Stoer, J., Bulirsch, R., Bartels, R., Gautschi, W., Witzgall, C.: Introduction to Numerical Analysis, vol. 1993. Springer, Heidelberg (1980). https://doi.org/10.1007/978-0-387-21738-3
30. TeReSe: Term Rewriting Systems, Cambridge Tracks in Theoretical Computer Science, vol. 55. Cambridge University Press, Cambridge (2003). https://doi.org/10.1017/S095679680400526X
31. Winkler, S., Moser, G.: Runtime Complexity Analysis of Logically Constrained Rewriting. In: LOPSTR 2020. LNCS, vol. 12561, pp. 37–55. Springer, Cham (2021). https://doi.org/10.1007/978-3-030-68446-4_2

Difference of Constrained Patterns in Logically Constrained Term Rewrite Systems

Naoki Nishida$^{(\boxtimes)}$ [ID], Misaki Kojima$^{(\boxtimes)}$ [ID], and Yuto Nakamura

Graduate School of Informatics, Nagoya University, Furo-cho,
Chikusa-ku, Nagoya 4648601, Japan
{nishida,kojima}@i.nagoya-u.ac.jp

Abstract. Considering patterns as sets of their instances, a difference operator over patterns computes a finite set of two given patterns, which represents the difference between the dividend pattern and the divisor pattern. A complement of a pattern is a pattern set, the ground constructor instances of which comprise the complement of the ground constructor instances of the former pattern. Given finitely many unconstrained linear patterns, using a difference operator over linear patterns, a complement algorithm returns a finite set of linear patterns as a complement of the given patterns. In this paper, we extend the difference operator and complement algorithm to constrained linear patterns used in logically constrained term rewrite systems (LCTRSs, for short) that have no user-defined constructor term with a sort for built-in values. Then, as for left-linear term rewrite systems, using the complement algorithm, we show that quasi-reducibility is decidable for such LCTRSs with decidable built-in theories. For the single use of the difference operator over constrained patterns, only divisor patterns are required to be linear.

Keywords: Logically constrained rewriting · Complement · Unification · Quasi-reducibility

1 Introduction

Complements of *patterns*—terms rooted by defined symbols with constructor arguments—have been studied in the field of term rewriting due to their various usefulness [12,15,27,28,39]. A *complement* of a pattern $f(s_1, \ldots, s_n)$ is a set Q of patterns, the ground constructor instances of which comprise the complement set of the ground constructor instances of $f(s_1, \ldots, s_n)$: $\mathcal{G}_\mathcal{C}(Q) = \mathcal{G}_\mathcal{C}(f(x_1, \ldots, x_n)) \setminus \mathcal{G}_\mathcal{C}(f(s_1, \ldots, s_n))$, where $x_1, \ldots, x_n$ are pairwise distinct variables, $\mathcal{C}$ is a set of constructors, $T(\mathcal{C})$ is the set of ground constructor terms, $\mathcal{G}_\mathcal{C}(s)$ is the set of ground constructor instances of a term s, and $\mathcal{G}_\mathcal{C}(Q) = \bigcup_{s \in Q} \mathcal{G}_\mathcal{C}(s)$.

This work was partially supported by JSPS KAKENHI Grant Number JP24K02900, Grant-in-Aid for JSPS Fellows Grant Number JP24KJ1240, and the Kayamori Foundation of Informational Science Advancement.

R. Thiemann and C. Weidenbach (Eds.): FroCoS 2025, LNAI 15979, pp. 247–266, 2026.
https://doi.org/10.1007/978-3-032-04167-8_14

Given a finite set P of linear patterns, the *complement algorithm* in [15, 28] returns a finite set $\overline{P}$ of linear patterns as a complement of patterns in P: $\mathcal{G}_{\mathcal{C}}(\overline{P}) = \mathcal{G}_{\mathcal{C}}(\{f(x_1, \ldots, x_n) \mid f \in \mathcal{D}\}) \setminus \mathcal{G}_{\mathcal{C}}(P)$, where $\mathcal{D}$ is a set of considered defined symbols and $x_1, \ldots, x_n$ are pairwise distinct variables. Patterns in P are assumed to be pairwise non-overlapping. The algorithm is based on a *difference* operator $\ominus$ over linear patterns. The difference operator $\ominus$ takes two linear patterns s, t as input and returns a finite set of linear patterns, which represents the difference of the *dividend* s and the *divisor* t w.r.t. ground constructor instances: $\mathcal{G}_{\mathcal{C}}(s \ominus t) = \mathcal{G}_{\mathcal{C}}(s) \setminus \mathcal{G}_{\mathcal{C}}(t)$.

The operator $\ominus$ is extended for finite sets of linear patterns: Given finite sets P, Q of linear patterns, $P \ominus Q$ is a finite set of linear patterns such that $\mathcal{G}_{\mathcal{C}}(P \ominus Q) = \mathcal{G}_{\mathcal{C}}(P) \setminus \mathcal{G}_{\mathcal{C}}(Q)$. As an application, the complement algorithm implies decidability of *quasi-reducibility*[1]—non-existence of irreducible ground patterns—of left-linear TRSs: A left-linear TRS $\mathcal{R}$ is quasi-reducible if and only if $\{f(x_1, \ldots, x_n) \mid f \in \mathcal{D}\} \ominus \{\ell \mid \ell \to r \in \mathcal{R}\} = \emptyset$, where $x_1, \ldots, x_n$ are pairwise different variables. Quasi-reducibility is often assumed for target rewrite systems in equivalence checking based on *rewriting induction* [14, 34].

Many compilers and interpreters of practical programming languages check the exhaustiveness of function definitions and case-statements. As for left-linear TRSs, algorithms for the exhaustiveness checking have been developed in several formulations (see, e.g., [29]). For patterns without guard conditions, the exhaustiveness (i.e., quasi-reducibility) is decidable [18, 40]. On the other hand, to the best of our knowledge, there is no full exhaustiveness checker for languages that allows us to attach guard conditions, which may include user-defined predicates, to patterns. To decide it, we need decidable SMT solving for the combination of all built-in theories that the languages support, which are usually undecidable.

Recently, program verification by means of *logically constrained term rewrite systems* (LCTRSs, for short) [25] are well investigated [10, 14, 16, 17, 19, 20, 22, 23, 30, 32, 41]. LCTRSs are extensions of *term rewrite systems* (TRSs, for short) by allowing rewrite rules to have guard constraints which are evaluated under equipped built-in theories. LCTRSs combine classic *term rewriting* (see, e.g., [3, 33]) with built-in data types and constraints from user-specified first-order theories, specifically those supported by modern SMT solvers (cf. [4, 5]). This allows for a high expressivity that is useful for representing many programming language constructs directly, together with robust tool support, e.g., the tool Ctrl [26], for automated reasoning. For instance, equivalence checking by means of LCTRSs is useful to ensure the correctness of terminating functions (cf. [14]). Due to these features, LCTRSs are known to be useful computational models of not only functional but also imperative programs.

LCTRS tools [23, 26, 38] rely on SMT solvers and often consider decidable built-in theories for given LCTRSs. On the other hand, to the best of our knowledge, neither a difference operator nor a complement algorithm has been investigated for constrained patterns, while an SMT-based sufficient condition for

---

[1] Quasi-reducibility is called *quasi-reductivity* in some papers (e.g., [2, 14, 24]) and *pattern completeness* in the context of functional programming [40].

left-patternless constrained rewrite systems [23,37][2] and procedural sufficient conditions for quasi-reducibility of LCTRSs [24] and conditional constrained TRSs [6] have been shown.

Example 1.1. Let us consider the sort set $\mathcal{S}_1 = \{int, bool, list\}$, the $\mathcal{S}_1$-sorted signature $\Sigma_1 = \{n : int \mid n \in \mathbb{Z}\} \cup \{true, false : bool, nil : list, cons : int \times list \rightarrow list, f : list \times int \rightarrow int\}$, and the following artificial LCTRS:

$$
\mathcal{R}_1 = \begin{cases}
(1) & f(nil, y_1) \rightarrow 0 & [y_1 \leq 0], \\
(2) & f(cons(x_2, xs_2), y_2) \rightarrow f(xs_2, y_2 - 1) & [x_2 \leq 0 \wedge y_2 > 0], \\
(3) & f(cons(x_3, cons(z_3, zs_3)), y_3) \rightarrow x_3 + f(zs_3, y_3 - 2) & [x_3 > 0 \wedge y_3 > 1]
\end{cases}
$$

Complements of unconstrained patterns $f(nil, y_1)$ and $f(cons(x_1, nil), y_1)$ are, e.g., $\{f(cons(x_1, xs_1), y_1)\}$ and $\{f(nil, y_1), f(cons(x_1, cons(z_1, zs_1)), y_1)\}$, respectively. The LCTRS $\mathcal{R}_1$ is not quasi-reducible because none of the following constrained patterns is defined:

(a) $f(nil, y_a) \, [\neg(y_a \leq 0)]$
(b) $f(cons(x_b, nil), y_b) \, [\neg(x_b \leq 0 \wedge y_b > 0)]$
(c) $f(cons(x_c, cons(z_c, zs_c)), y_c) \, [\neg(x_c \leq 0 \wedge y_c > 0) \wedge \neg(x_c > 0 \wedge y_c > 1)]$

It would be easy to find the first undefined constrained pattern (a) above. On the other hand, the second and third ones (b), (c) above are not so trivial because we have to consider a unified form of the left-hand sides of the second and third rules (2), (3) to compute (b), (c). For this reason, it is not so easy to know that $\mathcal{R}_1$ is not quasi-reducible. Note that the following LCTRS obtained from $\mathcal{R}_1$ by adding rules for the above undefined constrained patterns is quasi-reducible:

$$
\mathcal{R}_1' = \mathcal{R}_1 \cup \begin{cases}
(a) & f(nil, y_a) \rightarrow 0 \, [\neg(y_a \leq 0)], \\
(b) & f(cons(x_b, nil), y_b) \rightarrow 0 \, [\neg(x_b \leq 0 \wedge y_b > 0)], \\
(c) & f(cons(x_c, cons(z_c, zs_c)), y_c) \rightarrow 0 \, [\neg(x_c \leq 0 \wedge y_c > 0) \\
& \wedge \neg(x_c > 0 \wedge y_c > 1)]
\end{cases}
$$

In this paper, we propose a difference operator and a complement algorithm for constrained patterns used in left-linear LCTRSs that have finitely many user-defined function symbols and have no user-defined constructor term with a theory sort for built-in values.[3] To this end, we extend the difference operator $\ominus$ and the complement algorithm $\overline{\cdot}$ mentioned above to constrained patterns. The extended difference operator and complement algorithm are still computable for constrained patterns over signatures with decidable built-in theories. Then, as an application of the complement algorithm, we show that quasi-reducibility is decidable for the aforementioned LCTRSs with decidable built-in theories. Complete proofs for correctness of the results can be seen in the full version [31].

---

[2] The sufficient condition for *reduction-completeness* is applicable to quasi-reducibility.
[3] The latter is equivalent to the condition that all theory sorts are *inextensible* [13].

Example 1.2 (our goal). Let us consider the LCTRSs $\mathcal{R}_1$ and $\mathcal{R}_1'$ in Example 1.1 again. Given the constrained patterns $f(x, ys)$ [true] and (1), the extended difference operator $\ominus$ returns $\{\, f(\text{nil}, y_a)\, [\,\neg(y_a \leq 0)\,],\, f(\text{cons}(x, xs), y)\, [\,\text{true}\,]\, \}$ as a complement of (1). Given $\{(1), (2), (3)\}$, the extended complement algorithm $\overline{\cdot}$ returns $\{(a), (b), (c)\}$ as a complement of $\{(1), (2), (3)\}$. This implies that $\mathcal{R}_1$ is not quasi-reducible. On the other hand, given $\{(1), (2), (3), (a), (b), (c)\}$, the complement algorithm $\overline{\cdot}$ returns the empty set, and thus $\mathcal{R}_1'$ is quasi-reducible.

In addition to the extension to constrained patterns, we relax the linearity assumption of dividends of $\ominus$ over constrained patterns, i.e., we no longer assume the linearity of dividends, while the linearity is assumed for the extended complement algorithm: For $s\,[\phi] \ominus t\,[\psi]$, only the divisor t is assumed to be linear; for $P \ominus Q$, both P, Q are assumed to be sets of constrained linear patterns. The extended operator and complement algorithm behave in the same way as those of unconstrained patterns. Thus, a side effect of the extension to constrained patterns, for the unconstrained case with $s \ominus t$, only t is assumed to be linear.

LCTRSs in this paper are assumed to have no user-defined constructor term with a theory sort. This is not a restriction for program verification by means of LCTRSs because LCTRSs obtained from practical programs by the existing transformations [14, 16, 17, 23] are left-linear systems satisfying the restriction.

The main contributions of this paper are (i) the extension of the difference operator and the complement algorithm to constrained patterns, (ii) the relaxation of the linearity assumption to dividends of $\ominus$ over (constrained) patterns, and (iii) decidability of quasi-reducibility of LCTRSs in the aforementioned class.

2   Preliminaries

In this section, we briefly recall LCTRSs [14, 25]. Familiarity with basic notions and notations on term rewriting [3, 33] is assumed.

This paper deals with a first-order $\mathcal{S}$-sorted signature Σ, where $\mathcal{S}$ is a set of sorts. Let $\Sigma' \subseteq \Sigma$. A term in $T(\Sigma', \mathcal{V})$ is called a Σ'-*term*, where $\mathcal{V}$ is a (countably infinite) set of $\mathcal{S}$-sorted variables. A term t is called an *instance* of a term t' (or t' is called *more general than* t), written as $t \gtrsim t'$, if there exists a substitution σ such that $t = t'\sigma$. We write $t > t'$ if $t \gtrsim t'$ but $t' \not\gtrsim t$. The *height* of a term t, written as $height(t)$, is recursively defined as follows: $height(t) = 0$ if $t \in \mathcal{V}$; $height(t) = 1 + \max\{height(t_1), \ldots, height(t_n)\}$ if $t = f(t_1, \ldots, t_n)$ for some n-ary function symbol f and terms $t_1, \ldots, t_n$ such that $n \geq 0$. Note that the height of t in this paper does not correspond to the height of the corresponding tree of t. A position p of a term t is called *above* (*strictly above*) a position q of t, written as $p \leq q$ ($p < q$), if there exists a position p' of $t|_p$ such that $pp' = q$ ($pp' = q$ and $p' \neq \epsilon$). Positions p, q of a term t are called *parallel*, written as $p \,\|\, q$, if $p \not\leq q$ and $q \not\leq p$. A substitution σ is called *more general than* a substitution θ, written as $\sigma \lesssim \theta$, if there exists a substitution δ such that $\theta = (\delta \circ \sigma)$. For a set X of variables, we call σ *ground* w.r.t. X (X-*ground*, for short) if $\mathcal{D}om(\sigma) \supseteq X$ and $\mathcal{VR}an(\sigma|_X) = \emptyset$, i.e., $x\sigma$ is ground for any variable $x \in X$. A substitution

σ which is a sort-preserving mapping from $\mathcal{V}$ to $T(\Sigma, \mathcal{V})$ is said to be a Σ'-*substitution* if $\mathcal{R}an(\sigma) \subseteq T(\Sigma', \mathcal{V})$. A term s is called an *instance of t w.r.t. Σ'* (Σ'-instance, for short) if there exists a Σ'-substitution σ such that $s = t\sigma$. For a substitution σ, we write $\sigma = mgu(s, t)$ if σ is an mgu of s, t.

To define an LCTRS [14,25] over an $\mathcal{S}$-sorted signature Σ, we consider the following sorts, signatures, mappings, and constants: *Theory sorts* in $\mathcal{S}_{theory}$ and *term sorts* in $\mathcal{S}_{term}$ such that $\mathcal{S} = \mathcal{S}_{theory} \uplus \mathcal{S}_{term}$; a *theory signature* Σ_{theory} and a *term signature* Σ_{terms} such that $\Sigma = \Sigma_{theory} \cup \Sigma_{terms}$ and $\iota_1, \ldots, \iota_n, \iota \in \mathcal{S}_{theory}$ for any symbol $f : \iota_1 \times \cdots \times \iota_n \to \iota \in \Sigma_{theory}$; a mapping $\mathcal{I}$ that assigns to each theory sort ι a (non-empty) set $\mathcal{A}_\iota$, called the universe of ι (i.e., $\mathcal{I}(\iota) = \mathcal{A}_\iota$); a mapping $\mathcal{J}$, called an *interpretation* for Σ_{theory}, that assigns to each function symbol $f : \iota_1 \times \cdots \times \iota_n \to \iota \in \Sigma_{theory}$ a function $f^{\mathcal{J}}$ in $\mathcal{I}(\iota_1) \times \cdots \times \mathcal{I}(\iota_n) \to \mathcal{I}(\iota)$ (i.e., $\mathcal{J}(f) = f^{\mathcal{J}}$); a set $\mathcal{V}al_\iota \subseteq \Sigma_{theory}$ of *value-constants* $a : \iota$ for each theory sort ι such that $\mathcal{J}$ gives a bijection from $\mathcal{V}al_\iota$ to $\mathcal{I}(\iota)$. We denote $\bigcup_{\iota \in \mathcal{S}_{theory}} \mathcal{V}al_\iota$ by $\mathcal{V}al$. Note that $\mathcal{V}al \subseteq \Sigma_{theory}$. For readability, we may not distinguish $\mathcal{V}al_\iota$ and $\mathcal{I}(\iota)$, i.e., for each $v \in \mathcal{V}al_\iota$, v and $\mathcal{J}(v)$ may be identified. We require that $\Sigma_{terms} \cap \Sigma_{theory} \subseteq \mathcal{V}al$. Symbols in $\Sigma_{theory} \setminus \mathcal{V}al$ are *calculation symbols*, for which we may use infix notation. A term in $T(\Sigma_{theory}, \mathcal{V})$ is called a *theory term*. We recursively define the *interpretation* $[\![\cdot]\!]_{\mathcal{J}}$ of ground theory terms as $[\![f(s_1, \ldots, s_n)]\!]_{\mathcal{J}} = \mathcal{J}(f)([\![s_1]\!]_{\mathcal{J}}, \ldots, [\![s_n]\!]_{\mathcal{J}})$.

We typically choose a theory signature $\mathcal{S}_{theory}$ such that $\mathcal{S}_{theory} \supseteq \mathcal{S}_{core} = \{bool\}$, $\mathcal{V}al_{bool} = \{\mathsf{true}, \mathsf{false} : bool\}$, $\Sigma_{theory} \supseteq \Sigma_{core} = \mathcal{V}al_{bool} \cup \{\wedge, \vee, \Rightarrow, \Leftrightarrow : bool \times bool \to bool, \neg : bool \to bool\} \cup \{=_\iota, \neq_\iota : \iota \times \iota \to bool \mid \iota \in \mathcal{S}_{theory}\}$, $\mathcal{I}(bool) = \{\top, \bot\}$, and $\mathcal{J}$ interprets these symbols as expected: $\mathcal{J}(\mathsf{true}) = \top$ and $\mathcal{J}(\mathsf{false}) = \bot$. We omit the sort subscripts ι from $=_\iota$ and $\neq_\iota$ if they are clear from the context. A theory term with sort *bool* is called a *constraint*. A substitution γ is said to *respect* a constraint ϕ if $x\gamma \in \mathcal{V}al$ for all $x \in \mathcal{V}ar(\phi)$ and $[\![\phi\gamma]\!]_{\mathcal{J}} = \top$, where $\mathcal{V}ar(\phi)$ denotes the set of variables appearing in ϕ. A constraint ϕ is said to be *satisfiable* if $[\![\phi\gamma]\!] = \top$ for some substitution γ respecting ϕ.

A *constrained rewrite rule* is a triple $\ell \to r \; [\varphi]$ such that ℓ and r are terms of the same sort, φ is a constraint, and ℓ is neither a theory term nor a variable. If $\varphi = \mathsf{true}$, then we may write $\ell \to r$. We define $\mathcal{L}\mathcal{V}ar(\ell \to r \; [\varphi])$ as $\mathcal{V}ar(\varphi) \cup (\mathcal{V}ar(r) \setminus \mathcal{V}ar(\ell))$, the set of *logical variables* in $\ell \to r \; [\varphi]$ which are variables instantiated with value-constants in rewriting terms. We say that a substitution γ *respects* $\ell \to r \; [\varphi]$ if $\gamma(x) \in \mathcal{V}al$ for all $x \in \mathcal{L}\mathcal{V}ar(\ell \to r \; [\varphi])$ and $[\![\varphi\gamma]\!]_{\mathcal{J}} = \top$. Regarding the signature of $\mathcal{R}$, we denote the set $\{f(x_1, \ldots, x_n) \to y \; [y = f(x_1, \ldots, x_n)] \mid f \in \Sigma_{theory} \setminus \mathcal{V}al, \; x_1, \ldots, x_n, y$ are pairwise distinct variables$\}$ by $\mathcal{R}_{calc}$. The elements of $\mathcal{R}_{calc}$ are called *calculation rules* and we often deal with them as constrained rewrite rules even though their left hand sides are theory terms. The *rewrite relation* $\to_{\mathcal{R}}$ is a binary relation over terms, defined as follows: For a term s, $s[\ell\gamma]_p \to_{\mathcal{R}} s[r\gamma]_p$ if and only if $\ell \to r \; [\varphi] \in \mathcal{R} \cup \mathcal{R}_{calc}$ and γ respects $\ell \to r \; [\varphi]$. A reduction step with $\mathcal{R}_{calc}$ is called a *calculation*. A *logically constrained term rewrite system* (LCTRS, for short) is defined as an abstract reduction system $(T(\Sigma, \mathcal{V}), \to_{\mathcal{R}})$, simply denoted by $\mathcal{R}$. An LCTRS is usually given by supplying Σ, $\mathcal{R}$, and an informal description of $\mathcal{I}$ and $\mathcal{J}$ if these are not clear from the context. The set of *normal forms* of $\mathcal{R}$ is denoted by $NF_{\mathcal{R}}$. An LCTRS $\mathcal{R}$ is said to be *left-linear* if for every rule in $\mathcal{R}$, the left-hand side is linear. Note that $\mathcal{R}_{calc}$ is left-linear.

The *integer signature* Σ_{int} is $\Sigma_{core} \cup \{+, -, \times, \exp, \operatorname{div}, \operatorname{mod} : int \times int \rightarrow int\} \cup \{\geq, > : int \times int \rightarrow bool\} \cup \mathcal{V}al_{int}$ where $\mathcal{S}_{theory} \supseteq \{int, bool\}$, $\mathcal{V}al_{int} = \{\mathsf{n} \mid n \in \mathbb{Z}\}$, $\mathcal{I}(int) = \mathbb{Z}$, and $\mathcal{J}(\mathsf{n}) = n$ for any $n \in \mathbb{Z}$—we use n (in sans-serif font) as the value-constant for $n \in \mathbb{Z}$ (in *math* font). We define $\mathcal{J}$ in a natural way. An LCTRS over a signature Σ with $\Sigma_{theory} = \Sigma_{int}$ is called an *integer LCTRS*.

Example 2.1. The term $\mathsf{f}(\mathsf{cons}(1, \mathsf{cons}(2, \mathsf{cons}(0, \mathsf{cons}(3, \mathsf{cons}(4, \mathsf{nil}))))), 5)$ is reduced by the LCTRS $\mathcal{R}_1$ in Example 1.1 to 4 as follows: $\mathsf{f}(\mathsf{cons}(1, \mathsf{cons}(2, \mathsf{cons}(0, \mathsf{cons}(3, \mathsf{cons}(4, \mathsf{nil}))))), 5) \rightarrow_{\mathcal{R}_1} 1 + \mathsf{f}(\mathsf{cons}(0, \mathsf{cons}(3, \mathsf{cons}(4, \mathsf{nil}))), 5 - 2) \rightarrow_{\mathcal{R}_1} 1 + \mathsf{f}(\mathsf{cons}(0, \mathsf{cons}(3, \mathsf{cons}(4, \mathsf{nil}))), 3) \rightarrow_{\mathcal{R}_1} 1 + \mathsf{f}(\mathsf{cons}(3, \mathsf{cons}(4, \mathsf{nil})), 3 - 1) \rightarrow_{\mathcal{R}_1}^* 4$.

A function symbol f is called a *defined symbol* of $\mathcal{R}$ if there exists a rule $f(\ell_1, \ldots, \ell_n) \rightarrow r\ [\varphi] \in \mathcal{R} \cup \mathcal{R}_{calc}$; non-defined elements of Σ are called *constructors* of $\mathcal{R}$. Note that all value-constants are constructors of $\mathcal{R}$. We denote the sets of defined symbols and constructors of $\mathcal{R}$ by $\mathcal{D}_{\mathcal{R}}$ and $\mathcal{C}_{\mathcal{R}}$, respectively: $\mathcal{D}_{\mathcal{R}} = \{f \mid f(\ldots) \rightarrow r\ [\varphi] \in \mathcal{R} \cup \mathcal{R}_{calc}\}$ and $\mathcal{C}_{\mathcal{R}} = \Sigma \setminus \mathcal{D}_{\mathcal{R}}$. A $\mathcal{C}_{\mathcal{R}}$-term is called a *constructor term* of $\mathcal{R}$. A term of the form $f(t_1, \ldots, t_n)$ with $f \in \mathcal{D}_{\mathcal{R}}$ and $t_1, \ldots, t_n \in T(\mathcal{C}_{\mathcal{R}}, \mathcal{V})$ is called a *pattern* (or *basic*) (of $\mathcal{R}$). We call $\mathcal{R}$ a *constructor system* if the left-hand side of each rule $\ell \rightarrow r\ [\varphi] \in \mathcal{R}$ is a pattern. An LCTRS $\mathcal{R}$ is called *quasi-reducible* if every ground pattern is a redex of $\mathcal{R}$.

Example 2.2. The LCTRSs $\mathcal{R}_1$ and $\mathcal{R}_1'$ in Example 1.1 are left-linear constructor integer LCTRSs, $\mathcal{R}_1$ is not quasi-reducible, and $\mathcal{R}_1'$ is quasi-reducible.

In the rest of the paper, for a signature Σ, we are interested in defined symbols and constructors without an LCTRS $\mathcal{R}$ which splits Σ to $\mathcal{D}_{\mathcal{R}}$ and $\mathcal{C}_{\mathcal{R}}$. For this reason, without specifying $\mathcal{R}$, we often split a signature Σ to the sets $\mathcal{D}, \mathcal{C}$ of defined symbols and constructors, respectively: $\Sigma = \mathcal{D} \uplus \mathcal{C}$.

Finally, we define constrained patterns and their instances.

Definition 2.3 (constrained term [14,24,25]). *A constrained term over Σ is a pair $t\ [\psi]$ of a term $t : \iota$ and a constraint ψ. The sort of $t\ [\psi]$ is ι. A constrained term $t\ [\psi]$ is called* linear *if t is linear; $t\ [\psi]$ is called* linear w.r.t. logical variables *(LV-linear, for short) if t is linear w.r.t. $\mathcal{V}ar(\psi)$; $t\ [\psi]$ is called* value-free *if $t \in T(\Sigma \setminus \mathcal{V}al, \mathcal{V})$; $t\ [\psi]$ is called a* constrained pattern *if t is a pattern.*

Definition 2.4 (ground instances $\mathcal{G}_{\mathcal{C}}(t\ [\psi])$). *Let $t\ [\psi]$ be a constrained term. We denote the set of all ground $\mathcal{C}$-instances of $t\ [\psi]$ by $\mathcal{G}_{\mathcal{C}}(t\ [\psi])$: $\mathcal{G}_{\mathcal{C}}(t\ [\psi]) = \{t\sigma \mid \sigma \text{ is a } \mathcal{V}ar(t)\text{-ground } \mathcal{C}\text{-substitution respecting } \psi\}$. We extend $\mathcal{G}_{\mathcal{C}}(\cdot)$ for sets of constrained terms: $\mathcal{G}_{\mathcal{C}}(P) = \bigcup_{t\ [\psi] \in P} \mathcal{G}_{\mathcal{C}}(t\ [\psi])$. The set of ground $\mathcal{C}$-instances of an unconstrained term s is denoted by $\mathcal{G}_{\mathcal{C}}(s)$: $\mathcal{G}_{\mathcal{C}}(s) = \mathcal{G}_{\mathcal{C}}(s\ [\mathsf{true}])$.*

Convention (Convention on Term Equivalence). From the perspective that a (constrained) pattern represents the set of its ground instances, we consider a renamed variant $t' [\psi']$ of a constrained term $t [\psi]$ to be identical with $t [\psi]$, while we require ψ' to be semantically equivalent to ψ. To distinguish such equivalence from the usual one, we write $t [\psi] \doteq t' [\psi']$: $t [\psi] \doteq t' [\psi']$ if and only if there exists a renaming δ such that $t = t'\delta$, $Var(t) \cap Var(\psi) = Var(t'\delta) \cap Var(\psi'\delta)$, and $((\exists \vec{x}.\ \psi) \Leftrightarrow (\exists \vec{y}.\ \psi'\delta))$ is valid, where $\{\vec{x}\} = Var(\psi) \setminus Var(t)$ and $\{\vec{y}\} = Var(\psi'\delta) \setminus Var(t'\delta)$. The equivalence is also used for unconstrained terms: $t \doteq t'$ if and only if $t [\mathsf{true}] \doteq t' [\mathsf{true}]$. Given a set P of constrained terms, $\dot{P}$ denote a minimal set that contains exactly one representative for each equivalence class of constrained terms in P. In computing the union of sets of constrained terms, we use the equivalence $\doteq$. To be more precise, we define the union of (constrained) term sets w.r.t. $\doteq$ as follows: $P \dot{\cup} Q := \dot{U}$, where $U = P \cup Q$. The disjoint union $\uplus$ w.r.t. $\doteq$ is defined as follows: Given sets P, Q, U of constrained terms, $P \dot{\uplus} Q = P \dot{\cup} Q$ if and only if both of the following statements hold: (i) for any constrained term $s [\phi] \in P$, there exists no constrained term $t [\psi]$ in Q such that $s [\phi] \doteq t [\psi]$, and (ii) for any constrained term $t [\psi] \in Q$, there exists no constrained term $s [\phi]$ in P such that $s [\phi] \doteq t [\psi]$. We analogously define $\dot{\cup}, \dot{\uplus}$ for unconstrained terms. We abuse $\cup$ and $\uplus$ for $\dot{\cup}$ and $\dot{\uplus}$, respectively.

3   Complements of Constructor Terms and Substitutions

In this section, we define complements of constructor terms and constructor substitutions and then recall the operations in [15, 27, 28] to compute finite complements of linear constructor terms and constructor substitutions. In the rest of the paper, we consider a signature $\Sigma = \mathcal{D} \uplus \mathcal{C}$ without notice. For examples in this section, we use a subsignature $\Sigma_1' = \mathcal{D}_1 \cup \mathcal{C}_1'$ of Σ_1, where $\mathcal{D}_1 = \{\mathsf{f}\}$ and $\mathcal{C}_1' = \{\mathsf{nil}, \mathsf{cons}, 0, 1\}$.

We first define complements of $\mathcal{C}$-terms, $\mathcal{C}$-substitutions, and patterns.

Definition 3.1 (complement). *A set P of $\mathcal{C}$-terms is called a* complement *of a $\mathcal{C}$-term $u : \iota$ if $\mathcal{G}_\mathcal{C}(P) = \{t \in T(\mathcal{C}) \mid t : \iota\} \setminus \mathcal{G}_\mathcal{C}(u)$. A set Θ of $\mathcal{C}$-substitutions is called a* complement *of a $\mathcal{C}$-substitution σ w.r.t. a term $t \in T(\Sigma, \mathcal{V})$ if $\mathcal{G}_\mathcal{C}(\{t\rho \mid \rho \in \Theta, t\sigma \neq t\rho\}) = \mathcal{G}_\mathcal{C}(t) \setminus \mathcal{G}_\mathcal{C}(t\sigma)$. A set P of patterns is called a* complement *of a pattern $f(s_1, \ldots, s_n)$ if $\mathcal{G}_\mathcal{C}(P) = \mathcal{G}_\mathcal{C}(f(x_1, \ldots, x_n)) \setminus \mathcal{G}_\mathcal{C}(f(s_1, \ldots, s_n))$, where $x_1, \ldots, x_n$ are pairwise distinct variables. A set P of patterns is called a* complement *of a set Q of patterns if $\mathcal{G}_\mathcal{C}(P) = \mathcal{G}_\mathcal{C}(\{f(x_1, \ldots, x_n) \mid f \in \mathcal{D}\}) \setminus \mathcal{G}_\mathcal{C}(Q)$, where $x_1, \ldots, x_n$ are pairwise distinct variables.*

Note that complements are not unique in general. Note also that complements of variables and the identity substitution are the empty set.

Example 3.2. The set $\{\mathsf{nil}, \mathsf{cons}(x, \mathsf{cons}(x', xs))\}$ is a complement of $\mathsf{cons}(y, \mathsf{nil})$. The set $\{\{xs \mapsto \mathsf{nil}, y \mapsto 1\}, \{xs \mapsto \mathsf{cons}(x', xs'), y \mapsto 0\}, \{xs \mapsto \mathsf{cons}(x', xs'), y \mapsto 1\}\}$ is a complement of $\{xs \mapsto \mathsf{nil}, y \mapsto 0\}$ w.r.t. $\mathsf{f}(xs, y)$. The set $\{\mathsf{f}(\mathsf{nil}, 1), \mathsf{f}(\mathsf{cons}(x', xs'), y)\}$ is a complement of $\mathsf{f}(\mathsf{nil}, 0)$.

Next, we recall the constructions of complements of linear $\mathcal{C}$-terms and $\mathcal{C}$-substitutions. We follow the formulation in [15].

For a term u, if $\mathcal{G}_\mathcal{C}(u)$ is infinite, then the linearity of u w.r.t. variables with sorts for inductively defined terms such as *list* in Example 1.1 is necessary for finiteness of a complement of u (cf. [27, Proposition 4.5]). For this reason, in computing complements of $\mathcal{C}$-terms, we only consider linear terms.

Definition 3.3 ($\overline{u}$ of linear $\mathcal{C}$-term u [15]). *For a linear $\mathcal{C}$-term u, we define a set $\overline{u}$ of terms recursively as follows: $\overline{x} = \emptyset$ for a variable $x \in \mathcal{V}$, and $\overline{c(u_1, \ldots, u_n)} = \{c'(x_1, \ldots, x_m) \mid c' \neq c, \ c' : \iota_1' \times \cdots \times \iota_m' \to \iota \in \mathcal{C}\} \cup \bigcup_{i=1}^n \{c(u_1, \ldots, u_{i-1}, u_i', y_{i+1}, \ldots, y_n) \mid u_i' \in \overline{u_i}\}$, where $c : \iota_1 \times \cdots \times \iota_n \to \iota \in \mathcal{C}$, $x_1, \ldots, x_m$ are pairwise distinct variables, and $y_{i+1}, \ldots, y_n$ are pairwise distinct fresh variables for any $i \in \{1, \ldots, n\}$.*

For a linear term $u : \iota$, $\overline{u}$ is a finite complement of u (i.e., $\mathcal{G}_\mathcal{C}(\overline{u}) = \{t \in T(\mathcal{C}) \mid t : \iota\} \setminus \mathcal{G}_\mathcal{C}(u)$), which is a set of linear $\mathcal{C}$-terms.

Example 3.4. For $\mathcal{C}_1' = \{\mathsf{nil}, \mathsf{cons}, 0, 1\}$, we have that $\overline{0} = \{1\}$, $\overline{1} = \{0\}$, $\overline{\mathsf{nil}} = \{\mathsf{cons}(x, xs)\}$, and $\overline{\mathsf{cons}(0, \mathsf{cons}(z_3, zs_3))} = \{\mathsf{nil}, \mathsf{cons}(1, ys), \mathsf{cons}(0, \mathsf{nil})\}$.

The construction below for $\mathcal{C}$-substitutions is based on the construction $\overline{\cdot}$ for linear $\mathcal{C}$-terms, and thus it works on *linear* substitutions. A substitution σ is called *linear w.r.t.* $X \subseteq \mathcal{V}$ (X-linear, for short) if $x\sigma$ is linear for any variable $x \in X$. A $\mathcal{V}$-linear substitution is simply called *linear*.

Definition 3.5 ($\overline{\sigma}$ of linear $\mathcal{C}$-substitution σ [15]). *Let σ be a linear $\mathcal{C}$-substitution. We define a set $\overline{\sigma}$ of substitutions as follows: $\overline{\sigma} = \{\rho \mid Dom(\rho) = Dom(\sigma), \ \rho \neq \sigma, \ \forall x \in Dom(\sigma). \ x\rho \in \overline{x\sigma} \cup \{x\sigma\}\}$.*

For a linear $\mathcal{C}$-substitution σ and a linear $\mathcal{C}$-term t, $\{\rho \mid \rho \in \overline{\sigma}, \ t\rho \neq t\sigma\}$ is a finite complement of σ w.r.t. t (i.e., $\mathcal{G}_\mathcal{C}(\{t\rho \mid \rho \in \overline{\sigma}, \ t\rho \neq t\sigma\}) = \mathcal{G}_\mathcal{C}(t) \setminus \mathcal{G}_\mathcal{C}(t\sigma)$), which is a finite set of linear $\mathcal{C}$-substitutions.

Example 3.6. For $\mathcal{C}_1' = \{\mathsf{nil}, \mathsf{cons}, 0, 1\}$, we have that $\overline{\{xs \mapsto \mathsf{nil}, \ y \mapsto 0\}} = \{\{xs \mapsto \mathsf{nil}, \ y \mapsto 1\}, \{xs \mapsto \mathsf{cons}(x', xs'), \ y \mapsto 0\}, \{xs \mapsto \mathsf{cons}(x', xs'), \ y \mapsto 1\}\}$.

4 Difference of Constrained Patterns

In this section, we extend the difference operator $\ominus$ over unconstrained linear patterns [15,27,28] to constrained ones. Unlike [15,27,28], we do not require dividend patterns to be linear, while we still require divisor ones to be linear.

4.1 Difference Operator for Unconstrained Linear Patterns

We briefly recall the difference operator $\ominus$ over unconstrained linear patterns.

For unifiable patterns s, t with their mgu σ and without any common variables, the idea of $\ominus$ is based on the following property:

$$\mathcal{G}_\mathcal{C}(s) = \mathcal{G}_\mathcal{C}(s\sigma) \uplus \mathcal{G}_\mathcal{C}(\{s\rho \mid \rho \in \overline{\sigma}, \ s\rho \neq s\sigma\})$$

Since $s\sigma = t\sigma$ and $\mathcal{G}_C(s) \cap \mathcal{G}_C(t) = \mathcal{G}_C(t\sigma)$, the above property implies that $\mathcal{G}_C(s) \setminus \mathcal{G}_C(t) = \mathcal{G}_C(\{s\rho \mid \rho \in \overline{\sigma}, s\rho \neq s\sigma\})$ and thus $\{s\rho \mid \rho \in \overline{\sigma}, s\rho \neq s\sigma\}$ is a complement of s. To compute $\overline{\sigma}$, the mgu σ has to be a C-substitution. By definition, it is clear that any mgu of patterns are C-substitutions. We define the difference operator $\ominus$ for linear patterns as follows.

Definition 4.1 ($\ominus$ over linear patterns [15]). *We define the difference operator $\ominus$ over linear patterns as follows: $s \ominus t = \{s\rho \mid \rho \in \overline{\sigma}, s\rho \neq s\sigma\}$ if s, t' are unifiable, where $t \doteq t'$, $Var(s) \cap Var(t') = \emptyset$, and $\sigma = mgu(s, t')$; otherwise, $s \ominus t = \{s\}$. Note that $s \ominus s = \emptyset$.*

To compute $s \ominus t$, s does not have to be linear, while $\sigma|_{Var(s)}$ must be linear. A sufficient condition for $\sigma|_{Var(s)}$ being linear is linearity of t' (i.e., t).

Proposition 4.2. *Let s, t be unifiable terms with $Var(s) \cap Var(t) = \emptyset$, and σ be an mgu of s, t. If t is linear, then $\sigma|_{Var(s)}$ is linear.*

Proof (Sketch). We generalize this claim to unification problems of the form $\{u_1 =^? u_1', \ldots, u_k =^? u_k'\}$ and use the unification procedure in [3, Section 4.6]. To distinguish variables in s and t, we do not swap both sides of $=^?$ and prepare the Eliminate rule for both sides of $=^?$. Then, we show that the initial unification problem $\{s =^? t\}$ can be transformed into an extended solved form $\{x_1 =^? t_1, \ldots, x_n =^? t_n, s_1 =^? y_1, \ldots, s_m =^? y_m\}$ such that $x_1, \ldots, x_n$ are pairwise distinct variables in s, $y_1, \ldots, y_m$ are pairwise distinct variables in t, none of $s_1, \ldots, s_m$ is a variable, $\{x_1, \ldots, x_n, y_1, \ldots, y_m\} \cap Var(t_1, \ldots, t_n, s_1, \ldots, s_m) = \emptyset$, and t_i is linear for all $1 \leq i \leq n$. A complete proof can be seen in [31]. □

For a pattern s and a linear pattern t, $s \ominus t$ is a finite complement of patterns with sort ι w.r.t. ground C-instances of s (i.e., $\mathcal{G}_C(s \ominus t) = \mathcal{G}_C(s) \setminus \mathcal{G}_C(t)$).

Example 4.3. For $\Sigma_1' = \{f, nil, cons, 0, 1\}$, we have that $f(xs, y) \ominus f(nil, 0) = \{f(nil, 1), f(cons(x', xs'), 0), f(cons(x', xs'), 1)\}$.

4.2   Extension of Difference Operator to Constrained Patterns

In the definition of $\ominus$ for unconstrained patterns, for $s \ominus t$, unifiability of s and t is used. Thus, for the extension, we define unifiability of constrained terms.

Definition 4.4. (unifiability of constrained terms). *Two constrained terms $s[\phi]$ and $t[\psi]$ are said to be unifiable if s and t are unifiable and their mgu θ with $Dom(\theta) \subseteq Var(s, t)$ satisfies both of the following: $x\theta \in Val \cup V$ for all variables $x \in Var(\phi, \psi)$, and $\phi\theta \land \psi\theta$ is satisfiable.*

Example 4.5. The constrained terms $f(nil, y_1)[y_1 \leq 0]$ and $f(nil, y_a)[y_a > 0]$ are not unifiable, but $f(nil, y_1)[y_1 \leq 0]$ and $f(xs, y)[true]$ are unifiable by means of an mgu $\{y_1 \mapsto y, xs \mapsto nil\}$ of $f(nil, y_1)$ and $f(xs, y)$; their instance by means of the mgu is $f(nil, y)[y \leq 0 \land true]$.

In considering ground constructor instances of a constrained term $s\,[\phi]$, logical variables—variables in ϕ—are instantiated by value-constants but others are instantiated by arbitrary ground terms. Under our assumption that there is no user-defined constructor term with a theory sort, any variable with a theory sort is instantiated by value-constants only, and no variable with a non-theory sort is instantiated by any value-constant. For this reason, unlike the usual discussion on the instantiation of variables in the LCTRS setting (e.g., [1]), we do not take care of whether a variable is logical or not.

To compute finite complements, the constructions of complements in Sect. 3 rely on finiteness of signatures, which is usually assumed for TRSs in practice. However, signatures of LCTRSs are infinite in general. For example, signatures of integer LCTRSs include the integers and are thus infinite. For this reason, complements are often infinite, e.g., a complement of the value-constant 0 is $\{\mathsf{n} \mid n \in \mathbb{Z} \setminus \{0\}\}$. On the other hand, user-defined constructors (i.e., $\mathcal{C} \setminus \mathcal{V}al$) are usually finite. Since we consider constrained patterns, we can move value-constants in terms to constraints. For example, we transform the constrained pattern $\mathsf{f}(\mathsf{nil}, 0)\,[\mathsf{true}]$ into $\mathsf{f}(\mathsf{nil}, x)\,[x = 0]$, where x is a fresh variable. In summary, we consider value-free constrained patterns. Since each constrained term has an equivalent value-free constrained term [21,24], in the rest of this paper, we assume w.l.o.g. that constrained patterns are value-free. For a constrained term $s\,[\phi]$, we denote its value-free variant by $\tilde{s}\,[\tilde{\phi}]$ [21]: $\tilde{s} = s[y_1, \ldots, y_n]_{p_1, \ldots, p_n}$ and $\tilde{\phi} = \phi \wedge \bigwedge_{i=1}^{n}(y_i = s|_{p_i})$, where $p_1, \ldots, p_n$ are the positions of values in s, and $y_1, \ldots, y_n$ are pairwise distinct variables such that $\{y_1, \ldots, y_n\} \cap \mathcal{V}ar(s, \phi) = \emptyset$. It is clear that $\mathcal{G}_{\mathcal{C}}(s\,[\phi]) = \mathcal{G}_{\mathcal{C}}(\tilde{s}\,[\tilde{\phi}])$.

For the extension of $\ominus$ to constrained patterns, the key property of $\ominus$—$\mathcal{G}_{\mathcal{C}}(s) = \mathcal{G}_{\mathcal{C}}(s\sigma) \uplus \mathcal{G}_{\mathcal{C}}(\{s\rho \mid \rho \in \overline{\sigma}, \, s\rho \neq s\sigma\})$—is adapted to unifiable constrained patterns $s\,[\phi], t\,[\psi]$ with $\sigma = mgu_{\mathcal{C}}(s, t)$ as follows:

$$\mathcal{G}_{\mathcal{C}}(s\,[\phi]) = \mathcal{G}_{\mathcal{C}}(s\sigma\,[\phi\sigma \wedge \psi\sigma]) \uplus \mathcal{G}_{\mathcal{C}}(s\sigma\,[\phi\sigma \wedge \neg\psi\sigma]) \uplus \mathcal{G}_{\mathcal{C}}(\{s\rho\,[\phi\sigma] \mid \rho \in \overline{\sigma}, \, s\rho \neq s\sigma\})$$

The first and second ones are obtained by the following division of $\mathcal{G}_{\mathcal{C}}(s\sigma\,[\phi\sigma])$: $\mathcal{G}_{\mathcal{C}}(s\sigma\,[\phi\sigma]) = \mathcal{G}_{\mathcal{C}}(s\sigma\,[\phi\sigma \wedge \psi\sigma]) \uplus \mathcal{G}_{\mathcal{C}}(s\sigma\,[\phi\sigma \wedge \neg\psi\sigma])$. The third one can be obtained similarly to the unconstrained case, but we restrict instances to those satisfying $\phi\sigma$. This is because all ground $\mathcal{C}$-instances in $s\,[\phi]$ satisfy ϕ, i.e., a substitution to obtain a ground $\mathcal{C}$-instance in $s\,[\phi]$ respects ϕ. Since $s\,[\phi]$ and $t\,[\psi]$ are assumed to be value-free, we have that $\mathcal{R}an(\sigma|_{\mathcal{V}ar(\phi,\psi)}) \subseteq \mathcal{V}$. Thus, by definition, for all substitutions $\rho \in \overline{\sigma}$, we have that $\rho|_{\mathcal{V}ar(\phi,\psi)} = \sigma|_{\mathcal{V}ar(\phi,\psi)}$, and hence $\phi\sigma = \phi\rho$.

Following the idea above, we extend the difference operator $\ominus$ to value-free constrained patterns.

Definition 4.6 ($\ominus$ over value-free constrained patterns). *We define a difference operator $\ominus$, which takes a value-free constrained pattern as a dividend and takes a value-free constrained linear pattern as a divisor, as follows:*

$$s\,[\phi] \ominus t\,[\psi] = \begin{cases} \begin{aligned} &\{s\rho\,[\phi\sigma] \mid \rho \in \overline{\sigma}, \, s\rho \neq s\sigma\} \\ &\cup \{s\sigma\,[\phi\sigma \wedge \neg\psi'\sigma] \mid (\phi\sigma \wedge \neg\psi'\sigma) \text{ is satisfiable}\} \\ &\hspace{5em} \text{if } s\,[\phi], t'\,[\psi'] \text{ are unifiable} \end{aligned} \\[1em] \{s\,[\phi]\} \hspace{8em} \text{otherwise} \end{cases}$$

where $t'[\psi'] \doteq t[\psi]$, $\mathcal{V}ar(s,\phi) \cap \mathcal{V}ar(t',\psi') = \emptyset$, *and* $\sigma = mgu(s,t')$.

By definition, it is clear that $s[\phi] \ominus s'[\phi'] = \emptyset$ for any value-free constrained pattern $s'[\phi']$ such that $s'[\phi'] \doteq s[\phi]$.

Example 4.7. For $\Sigma_1 = \{\mathsf{f}, \mathsf{nil}, \mathsf{cons}\} \cup \{\mathsf{n} \mid n \in \mathbb{Z}\}$, we have that $\mathsf{f}(xs, y)[\mathsf{true}] \ominus$ $\mathsf{f}(\mathsf{nil}, y_1)[y_1 \leq 0] = \{\mathsf{f}(\mathsf{nil}, y_\mathsf{a})[\neg(y_\mathsf{a} \leq 0)], \mathsf{f}(\mathsf{cons}(x', xs'), y')[\mathsf{true}]\}$. In addition to Σ_1, let us consider a defined symbol $\mathsf{g} : list \times list \to list$. A complement of the term $\mathsf{g}(x, x)[\mathsf{true}]$ is, e.g., $\{\mathsf{g}(t_1, t_2) \mid t_1 : list, t_2 : list \in T(\mathcal{C}'_1), t_1 \neq t_2\}$, and there is no finite complement of $\mathsf{g}(x, x)[\mathsf{true}]$ (cf. [27, Proposition 4.5]).

The following theorem shows correctness of $\ominus$ over constrained patterns.

Theorem 4.8 (correctness of $s[\phi] \ominus t[\psi]$). *For a value-free constrained pattern $s[\phi] : \iota$ and a value-free constrained linear pattern $t[\psi]$, $s[\phi] \ominus t[\psi]$ is a finite set of value-free constrained patterns with sort ι such that*

1. *$\mathcal{G}_\mathcal{C}(u[\varphi]) \cap \mathcal{G}_\mathcal{C}(u'[\varphi']) = \emptyset$ for any different constrained patterns $u[\varphi], u'[\varphi'] \in (s[\phi] \ominus t[\psi])$,*
2. *if $s[\phi]$ is linear, then $s[\phi] \ominus t[\psi]$ is a set of constrained linear patterns,*
3. *$s < u$ for any constrained term $u[\varphi] \in (s[\phi] \ominus t[\psi])$,*
4. *$\max\{height(s), height(t)\} \geq height(u)$ for any term $u[\varphi] \in (s[\phi] \ominus t[\psi])$, and*
5. *$\mathcal{G}_\mathcal{C}(s[\phi] \ominus t[\psi]) = \mathcal{G}_\mathcal{C}(s[\phi]) \setminus \mathcal{G}_\mathcal{C}(t[\psi])$.*

Proof (Sketch). This can be proved as a straightforward extension of the correctness proof for unconstrained patterns to constrained ones by means of the following properties: $\{s\rho \mid \rho \in \overline{\sigma}, s\rho \neq s\sigma\}$ is a set of value-free patterns; $\sigma|_{\mathcal{V}ar(\phi,\psi')} = \rho|_{\mathcal{V}ar(\phi,\psi')}$ for any $\rho \in \overline{\sigma}$; $\mathcal{G}_\mathcal{C}(s\sigma[\phi\sigma]) = \mathcal{G}_\mathcal{C}(s\sigma[\phi\sigma \wedge \psi'\sigma]) \uplus \mathcal{G}_\mathcal{C}(s\sigma[\phi\sigma \wedge \neg\psi'\sigma])$ for an arbitrary constraint ψ'. A complete proof can be seen in [31]. $\square$

5   Complements of Constrained Patterns

In this section, we first extend the complement algorithm for unconstrained linear patterns in [15,27,28] to constrained patterns. Then, using the extended complement algorithm, we show that quasi-reducibility is decidable for left-linear LCTRSs over a signature Σ with decidable built-in theories such that Σ_{terms} is finite and there is no constructor $c : \iota_1 \times \cdots \times \to \iota \in \mathcal{C}_\mathcal{R}$ with $\iota \in \mathcal{S}_{theory}$.

Complements of constrained patterns are defined as a straightforward extension of complements of unconstrained patterns.

Definition 5.1 (complement of constrained patterns). *A set P of constrained patterns is called a* complement *of a set P' of constrained patterns w.r.t. an n-ary defined symbol $f \in \mathcal{D}$ if $\mathcal{G}_\mathcal{C}(P) = \mathcal{G}_\mathcal{C}(\{f(x_1, \ldots, x_n)\}) \setminus \mathcal{G}_\mathcal{C}(P')$, where $x_1, \ldots, x_n$ are pairwise distinct variables. A set P of constrained patterns is called a* complement *of a constrained pattern $f(s_1, \ldots, s_n)[\phi]$ if P is a complement of $\{f(s_1, \ldots, s_n)[\phi]\}$ w.r.t. f. A set P of constrained patterns is called a* complement *of a set P' of constrained patterns if $\mathcal{G}_\mathcal{C}(P) = \mathcal{G}_\mathcal{C}(\{f(x_1, \ldots, x_n) \mid f \in \mathcal{D}\}) \setminus \mathcal{G}_\mathcal{C}(\Gamma')$, where $x_1, \ldots, x_n$ are pairwise distinct variables.*

Note that as for unconstrained patterns, complements of constrained patterns are not unique.

Example 5.2. Let us consider the $\mathcal{S}_1$-sorted signature Σ_1 in Example 1.1 again. The set $\{(a)\ \mathsf{f}(\mathsf{nil}, y_a)\,[\neg(y_a \leq 0]), (b)\ \mathsf{f}(\mathsf{cons}(x_b, \mathsf{nil}), y_b)\,[\mathsf{true}]\}$ is a complement of (1) $\mathsf{f}(\mathsf{nil}, y_1)\,[y \leq 0]$.

5.1 Difference Operator over Sets of Constrained Patterns

The complement algorithm in [15,27,28] is defined by the repetition of applying the difference operator $\ominus$ over patterns. Thus, as in [15,27,28], we extend $\ominus$ to finite sets of constrained patterns in order to have the results in Example 1.2.

In computing $P \ominus Q$, if there exist constrained patterns $s\,[\phi] \in P$ and $t\,[\psi] \in Q$ such that $s\,[\phi] \ominus t\,[\psi] \neq \{s\,[\phi]\}$, then we recursively compute $((P \setminus \{s\,[\phi]\}) \cup (s\,[\phi] \ominus t\,[\psi])) \ominus ((Q \setminus \{t\,[\psi]\}) \cup (t\,[\psi] \ominus s\,[\phi]))$. In Sect. 4.2, we required divisors of $\ominus$ to be linear, and thus $t\,[\psi]$ has to be linear. It is difficult to know which constrained terms are selected as a divisor for $\ominus$ over constrained patterns. For this reason, to ensure the linear of divisors for the application of $\ominus$ to constrained patterns, we assume that all constrained terms in Q are linear, while not all of them may be necessarily linear. Then, for the recursive call of $\ominus$ for sets of constrained patterns, we would like to ensure that all constrained patterns in $(Q \setminus \{t\,[\psi]\}) \cup (t\,[\psi] \ominus s\,[\phi])$ are linear. Since Q is assumed to be linear in advance, we need to ensure that all constrained patterns in $t\,[\psi] \ominus s\,[\phi]$ are linear. Therefore, for the extension of $\ominus$ to sets of constrained patterns, we assume that all constrained patterns in P are linear, as well as Q.

Definition 5.3 ($\ominus$ over sets of value-free constrained linear patterns). *We extend $\ominus$ for finite sets of value-free constrained linear patterns as follows: For finite sets P, Q of value-free constrained linear patterns,*

$$P \ominus Q = \begin{cases} (P' \cup (s\,[\phi] \ominus t\,[\psi])) \ominus (Q' \cup (t\,[\psi] \ominus s\,[\phi])) \\ \quad \textit{if } P = P' \uplus \{s\,[\phi]\}, Q = Q' \uplus \{t\,[\psi]\}, \textit{and} s\,[\phi] \ominus t\,[\psi] \neq \{s\,[\phi]\} \\ P \quad \textit{otherwise} \end{cases}$$

Since $\ominus$ over sets of value-free constrained linear patterns is non-deterministic, there may be two or more sets that can be results of $P \ominus Q$, while all the results are correct. In addition, a result of $P \ominus Q$ is not always minimal. Note that using $\overline{\sigma}$, $s\,[\phi] \ominus t\,[\psi]$ and $t\,[\psi] \ominus s\,[\phi]$ can be computed simultaneously.

Example 5.4. For $\Sigma_1 = \{f, \text{nil}, \text{cons}\} \cup \{n \mid n \in \mathbb{Z}\}$, we have that

$$
\{f(xs, y) \,[\text{true}]\} \ominus \left\{
\begin{array}{ll}
(1) & f(\text{nil}, y_1) \,[y_1 \le 0], \\
(2) & f(\text{cons}(x_2, xs_2), y_2) \,[x_2 \le 0 \land y_2 > 0], \\
(3) & f(\text{cons}(x_3, \text{cons}(z_3, zs_3)), y_3) \,[x_3 > 0 \land y_3 > 1]
\end{array}
\right\}
$$

$$
= \left\{
\begin{array}{ll}
(\text{a}) & f(\text{nil}, y_{\text{a}}) \,[\neg(y_{\text{a}} \le 0)], \\
(1') & f(\text{cons}(x', xs'), y') \,[\text{true}]
\end{array}
\right\} \ominus \{\,(2),\,(3)\,\}
$$

$$
= \left\{
\begin{array}{ll}
(\text{a}) & f(\text{nil}, y_{\text{a}}) \,[\neg(y_{\text{a}} \le 0)], \\
(2') & f(\text{cons}(x', xs'), y') \,[\neg(x' \le 0 \land y' > 0)]
\end{array}
\right\} \ominus \{\,(3)\,\}
$$

$$
= \left\{
\begin{array}{ll}
(\text{a}) & f(\text{nil}, y_{\text{a}}) \,[\neg(y_{\text{a}} \le 0)], \\
(\text{b}) & f(\text{cons}(x_{\text{b}}, \text{nil}), y_{\text{b}}) \,[\text{true}], \\
(\text{c}) & f(\text{cons}(x_{\text{c}}, \text{cons}(z_{\text{c}}, zs_{\text{c}})), y_{\text{c}}) \,[\neg(x_{\text{c}} \le 0 \land y_{\text{c}} > 0) \land \neg(x_{\text{c}} > 0 \land y_{\text{c}} > 1)]
\end{array}
\right\} \ominus \emptyset
$$

$$
= \{(\text{a}), (\text{b}), (\text{c})\}
$$

A key for correctness of $\ominus$ over sets of (constrained) linear patterns is non-overlappingness between (constrained) patterns in dividends sets of $\ominus$. We define a notion of non-overlappingness of constrained patterns and their sets.

Definition 5.5 (C-non-overlappingness of constrained terms). *Two constrained terms $s\,[\phi], t\,[\psi]$ are called* non-overlapping w.r.t. C *(C-non-overlapping, for short) if $\mathcal{G}_C(s\,[\phi]) \cap \mathcal{G}_C(t\,[\psi]) = \emptyset$. Two sets P, Q of constrained terms are said to be C-non-overlapping if $\mathcal{G}_C(P) \cap \mathcal{G}_C(Q) = \emptyset$. A set P of constrained terms is said to be* pairwise C-non-overlapping *if any two different constrained terms $s\,[\phi], t\,[\psi] \in P$ are C-non-overlapping.*

Example 5.6. The constrained terms $f(\text{nil}, y_1)\,[y_1 \le 0]$ and $f(\text{nil}, y_{\text{a}})\,[\neg(y_{\text{a}} \le 0)]$ are C_1-non-overlapping, but $f(\text{nil}, y_1)\,[y_1 \le 0]$ and $f(xs, y)\,[\text{true}]$ are not C_1-non-overlapping because, e.g., $f(\text{nil}, 0) \in \mathcal{G}_{C_1}(f(\text{nil}, y_1)\,[y_1 \le 0]) \cap \mathcal{G}_{C_1}(f(xs, y)\,[\text{true}])$.

Note that non-overlappingness and unifiability of constrained patterns are dual properties: $s\,[\phi], t\,[\psi]$ are C-non-overlapping if and only if $s\,[\phi]$ and $t'\,[\psi']$ are not unifiable, where $t'\,[\psi'] \doteq t\,[\psi]$ and $Var(s, \phi) \cap Var(t', \psi') = \emptyset$.

For correctness of $P \ominus Q$, we assume that P is pairwise C-non-overlappingness.

Example 5.7. For $\Sigma_1 = \{f, \text{nil}, \text{cons}\} \cup \{n \mid n \in \mathbb{Z}\}$, we have that a result of $\{f(\text{nil}, y)\,[\text{true}], f(xs, y)\,[\text{true}]\} \ominus \{f(xs', y')\,[\text{true}]\}$ is $\{f(\text{nil}, y)\,[\text{true}]\}$, which is not an expected one. Since $f(xs, y) \lesssim f(\text{nil}, y)$, the set $\{f(\text{nil}, y)\,[\text{true}], f(xs, y)\,[\text{true}]\}$ is redundant from the viewpoint of ground instances.

The following proposition shows the correctness of $\bigcirc$ over sets of value-free constrained linear patterns.

Theorem 5.8 (correctness of $P \ominus Q$). *Let P, Q be finite sets of value-free constrained linear patterns. If P is pairwise C-non-overlapping, then $P \ominus Q$ is a pairwise C-non-overlapping finite set of value-free constrained linear patterns such that $\mathcal{G}_C(P \ominus Q) = \mathcal{G}_C(P) \setminus \mathcal{G}_C(Q)$.*

Proof (Sketch). To prove this claim, we show that for finite sets P, Q of value-free constrained linear patterns, all of the following hold: (i) if P is pairwise $\mathcal{C}$-non-overlapping, $P = P' \uplus \{s\,[\phi]\}$, $Q = Q' \uplus \{t\,[\psi]\}$, and $s\,[\phi] \ominus t\,[\psi] \neq \{s\,[\phi]\}$, then P' and $\{s\,[\phi] \ominus t\,[\psi]\}$ are $\mathcal{C}$-non-overlapping, and (ii) if P is pairwise $\mathcal{C}$-non-overlapping, then $\mathcal{G}_{\mathcal{C}}(P \ominus Q) = \mathcal{G}_{\mathcal{C}}(P) \setminus \mathcal{G}_{\mathcal{C}}(Q)$.

The first statement (i) is a straightforward extension of the corresponding statement for unconstrained linear patterns to constrained ones. The difficulty of the second statement (ii) is the well-founded order for induction. Let h be the maximum height of terms in P, Q. Then, in computing $P \ominus Q$, the heights of all terms considered during the computation are less than or equal to h, and thus such terms are finitely many. We denote by $T(\Sigma, \mathcal{V})_{\leq h}$ the set of terms whose heights are less than or equal to h. Then, We define a quasi-order $\succsim_{\leq h}$ over terms in $T(\Sigma, \mathcal{V})_{\leq h}$ as follows: $s \succsim_{\leq h} t$ if and only if $s \precsim t$, $height(s) \leq h$, and $height(t) \leq h$. The strict part $\succ_{\leq h}$ of $\succsim_{\leq h}$ is defined as $\succ_{\leq h} = (\succsim_{\leq h} \setminus \precsim_{\leq h})$. Note that $s \succ_{\leq h} t$ if and only if $s < t$, $height(s) \leq h$, and $height(t) \leq h$. In computing $s\,[\phi] \ominus t\,[\psi]$, the resulting set may contain $s\sigma\,[\phi\sigma \wedge \neg\psi'\sigma]$ and we may have that $s = s\sigma$ (and thus $(\phi\sigma \wedge \neg\psi'\sigma) = (\phi \wedge \neg\psi')$. On the other hand, since $\phi \wedge \psi'$ and $\neg\psi'$ are satisfiable, we have that $\{\theta \mid [\![\phi\theta]\!] = \top\} \supset \{\theta \mid [\![(\phi \wedge \neg\psi')\theta]\!] = \top\}$. However, the sets may be infinite, and thus the relation $\supset$ for the sets is not well-founded in general. To overcome the problem, we consider the number of constrained terms $t\,[\psi]$ such that $s\,[\phi] \ominus t\,[\psi] \neq \{s\,[\phi]\}$. Let $\succsim_{\leq h, \mathbb{N}}$ be the order of lexicographic products of terms and natural numbers compared by $\succsim_{\leq h}$ and $\geq_{\mathbb{N}}$. Let $\succ_{\leq h, \mathbb{N}} = (\succsim_{\leq h, \mathbb{N}} \setminus \precsim_{\leq h, \mathbb{N}})$. Then, it is clear that $\succ_{\leq h, \mathbb{N}}$ is well-founded. We define the weight w for pairs of sets of constrained linear patterns as follows: $w(P, Q) = \{(s, n) \mid s\,[\phi] \in P, n = |\{t\,[\psi] \in Q \mid s\,[\phi] \ominus t\,[\phi] \neq \{s\,[\phi]\}\}|\,\}$. When $P \ominus Q$ calls $P' \ominus Q'$, we have that $w(P, Q) \succ_{\leq h, \mathbb{N}} w(P', Q')$. The second statement (ii) can be proved by induction on the well-founded order $\succ_{\leq h, \mathbb{N}}$ with the weight w. A complete proof can be seen in [31].   □

Note that for $P \ominus Q$, if there are no constrained terms $s\,[\phi] \in P$ and $t\,[\psi] \in Q$ such that $s\,[\phi] \in P$ and $t\,[\psi] \in Q$ are not unifiable, then neither P nor Q must be a set of constrained linear patterns and P must not be pairwise $\mathcal{C}$-non-overlapping.

5.2   Complement Algorithm for Constrained Linear Patterns

In this section, we first show a complement algorithm for sets of value-free constrained linear patterns, and then show that quasi-reducibility is decidable for some class of left-linear LCTRSs with decidable built-in theories.

Definition 5.9. *Let f be an n-ary defined symbol in $\mathcal{D}$, and Q be a finite set of value-free constrained linear patterns. Then, we define a finite set $\overline{(Q)}_f$ of constrained patterns as follows: $\overline{(Q)}_f = \{f(x_1, \ldots, x_n)\,[\text{true}]\} \ominus Q$, where $x_1, \ldots, x_n$ are pairwise distinct variables. We extend $\overline{(\cdot)}_f$ for $\mathcal{D}$ as follows: $\overline{Q} = \bigcup_{f \in \mathcal{D}} \overline{(Q)}_f$.*

Example 5.10. For $\Sigma_1 = \{f, \text{nil}, \text{cons}\} \cup \{n \mid n \in \mathbb{Z}\}$ in Example 1.1, we have that $\overline{\{(1), (2), (3)\}} = \overline{(\{(1), (2), (3)\})}_f = \{(a), (b), (c)\}$.

As a direct consequence of Theorem 5.8, the following claim holds for $\overline{(\cdot)}_f$.

Theorem 5.11. *Let Q be a pairwise C-non-overlapping finite set of value-free constrained linear patterns, and f an n-ary defined symbol in $\mathcal{D}$. Then, $\mathcal{G}_C(\overline{(Q)}_f)$ $= \mathcal{G}_C(f(x_1,\ldots,x_n)\,[\mathsf{true}]) \setminus \mathcal{G}_C(\{t\,[\psi] \in Q \mid root(t) = f\})$ and $\overline{(Q)}_f$ is a complement of Q w.r.t. f, where $x_1,\ldots,x_n$ are pairwise distinct variables.*

Proof (Sketch). By definition, during the computation of $\overline{(Q)}_f$, all constrained patterns in the left-hand sides of $\ominus$ are rooted by f. Thus, no constrained term $t\,[\psi]$ in Q such that $root(t) \neq f$ is not unifiable with any constrained pattern in the left-hand sides of $\ominus$, and hence $\{f(x_1,\ldots,x_n)\,[\mathsf{true}]\} \ominus Q =$ $\{f(x_1,\ldots,x_n)\,[\mathsf{true}]\} \ominus \{t\,[\psi] \in Q \mid root(t) = f\}$. Then, by Theorem 5.8, $\overline{(Q)}_f$ is a complement of Q w.r.t. f. A complete proof can be seen in [31].   □

The following corollary is a direct consequence of Theorem 5.11.

Corollary 5.12. *For a pairwise C-non-overlapping finite set Q of value-free constrained linear patterns, $\mathcal{G}_C(\overline{Q}) = \mathcal{G}_C(\{f(x_1,\ldots,x_n) \mid f \in \mathcal{D}\}) \setminus \mathcal{G}_C(Q)$, where $x_1,\ldots,x_n$ are pairwise distinct variables.*

Corollary 5.12 immediately implies decidability of quasi-reducibility for left-linear LCTRSs with decidable built-in theories.

Theorem 5.13. *Let $\mathcal{R}$ be a finite left-linear LCTRS such that Σ_{terms} is finite and there is no constructor $c : \iota_1 \times \cdots \times \iota_n \to \iota \in \mathcal{C}_\mathcal{R}$ with $\iota \in \mathcal{S}_{theory}$. Then, $\mathcal{R}$ is quasi-reducible if and only if $\{\tilde{\ell}\,[\tilde{\phi}] \mid \ell \to r\,[\phi] \in \mathcal{R},\ \ell$ is a pattern$\} = \emptyset$. Thus, quasi-reducibility is decidable for such LCTRSs with decidable built-in theories.*[4]

Proof (Sketch). Since the built-in theory is decidable, by the well-founded order in the proof of Theorem 5.8, the set $\{\tilde{\ell}\,[\tilde{\phi}] \mid \ell \to r\,[\phi] \in \mathcal{R},\ \ell$ is a pattern$\}$ is computable, and thus its emptiness is decidable. Therefore, quasi-reducibility of $\mathcal{R}$ is decidable. A complete proof can be seen in [31].   □

Example 5.14. The LCTRS $\mathcal{R}_1$ in Example 1.1 is not quasi-reducible because $\{\mathsf{f}(xs,y)\,[\mathsf{true}]\} \ominus \{(1),(2),(3)\} = \{(\mathrm{a}),(\mathrm{b}),(\mathrm{c})\}$. On the other hand, the LCTRS $\mathcal{R}_1'$ is quasi-reducible because $\{\mathsf{f}(xs,y)\,[\mathsf{true}]\} \ominus \{(1),(2),(3),(\mathrm{a}),(\mathrm{b}),(\mathrm{c})\} = \emptyset$.

6   Related Work

As mentioned before, to the best of our knowledge, there is no work for difference operators and complement algorithms for constrained patterns, and decidability of quasi-reducibility in the LCTRS setting, while some sufficient conditions have been investigated [24,37].

---

[4] It is sufficient that all constraints of constrained rewrite rules in $\mathcal{R}$ are in a class of a decidable theory. For example, the integer theory is not decidable, but the constraints of $\mathcal{R}_1$ and $\mathcal{R}_1'$ are formulas of Presburger arithmetic.

There are several works on quasi-reducibility and *sufficient completeness* of TRSs and constrained rewrite systems. Decidability of quasi-reducibility has been shown in [18] without yielding a practical algorithm. Then, complement algorithms have been proposed [15,27,28], which are used as decision procedures for quasi-reducibility of left-linear TRSs. *Negation elimination* from equational formulas [12,39] is a well-investigated application of complement algorithms. *Tree automata techniques* [11] can be used to obtain complements, and thus they also yield decision procedures for quasi-reducibility of left-linear TRSs. Recently, a well-designed decision procedure for quasi-reducibility of TRSs has been proposed [40]. However, to the best of our knowledge, the above procedures have not yet been extended to constrained rewrite systems, and the extension is not so trivial.

Sufficient completeness is equivalent to quasi-reducibility for terminating systems. A sufficient condition for sufficient completeness of constrained and conditional rewrite systems based on constrained tree automata techniques has been shown in [6]. In addition, as mentioned in Sect. 1, an SMT-based sufficient condition for left-patternless constrained rewrite systems [23,37] and a procedural sufficient condition for quasi-reducibility of LCTRSs [24] have been shown.

For programming languages, there are some works on the exhaustiveness checking. In [29], a method for examining pattern-matching anomalies of ML programming languages has been proposed. This method checks two points: there are no useless patterns, and it considers all patterns. This method is implemented on OCaml but is also useful for Haskell. However, guards are not considered: Standard ML of New Jersey does not allow us to write guards for pattern matching; a recent version of the GHC implementation of Haskell does not implement any form of exhaustiveness checking even without guards, while there is a check for redundancy of patterns, which does not work for guards. When compiling programs, OCaml compilers warn users about guard constraints attached to patterns so that they can take care of the exhaustiveness of constrained patterns, which is not checked by the compilers. As mentioned before, due to the SMT solving for supported built-in theories, the exhaustiveness checking for guarded patterns is not realistic.

Unification of constrained terms in Definition 4.4 is a bit different from *unification modulo built-ins* [9, Definition 11]. Unlike ours, the unification is defined for terms, and unifiers are pairs of substitutions and constraints.

Another related work on unification of constrained terms is unification with abstraction and theory instantiation for SMT solving [35]. The algorithm for such unification is very similar to the syntactic unification procedure [3, Section 4.6], while it considers underlying theories and disequalities as constraints. Unlike the algorithm, our unification of constrained terms $s\,[\phi], t\,[\psi]$ first uses syntactic unification to obtain an mgu σ of s and t, and then check satisfiability of $\phi\sigma \wedge \psi\sigma$.

Matching logic [7,8,36] (ML, for short) is a first-order logic variant to reason about structures by allowing formulas to represent terms, and is expressive enough and very powerful. For example, $s \ominus t$ with $Var(s) \cap Var(t) = \emptyset$ can be represented by the formula $s \wedge \neg t$. However, decidability of ML formulas is not clear due to its generality.

7 Conclusion

In this paper, we extended the difference operator and the complement algorithm in the unconstrained setting to constrained linear patterns, proposing a difference operator and a complement algorithm for constrained linear patterns used in LCTRSs that have finitely many user-defined function symbols and have no user-defined constructor term with a theory sort for built-in value-constants. Then, we showed that quasi-reducibility is decidable for such LCTRSs. Many LCTRSs obtained from practical programs by existing transformations belong to the class. We will implement the algorithm in our LCTRS tool as future work.

For brevity, we had some restrictions, e.g., non-existence of user-defined constructor terms with theory sorts. A future work is to drop such restrictions, proposing a difference operator and a complement algorithm for more general classes of LCTRSs.

The complexity of the complement algorithm for constrained linear patterns relies on that of SMT solving used in the computation. We are interested in complexity of the algorithm without the complexity of SMT solving. Analysis of such complexity is another future work.

References

1. Aoto, T., Nishida, N., Schöpf, J.: Equational theories and validity for logically constrained term rewriting. In: Rehof, J. (ed.) Proceedings of the 9th International Conference on Formal Structures for Computation and Deduction. Leibniz International Proceedings in Informatics, vol. 299, pp. 31:1–31:21. Schloss Dagstuhl – Leibniz-Zentrum für Informatik (2024). https://doi.org/10.4230/LIPICS.FSCD.2024.31
2. Aoto, T., Toyama, Y., Kimura, Y.: Improving rewriting induction approach for proving ground confluence. In: Miller, D. (ed.) Proceedings of the 2nd International Conference on Formal Structures for Computation and Deduction. LIPIcs, vol. 84, pp. 7:1–7:18. Schloss Dagstuhl – Leibniz-Zentrum für Informatik (2017). https://doi.org/10.4230/LIPICS.FSCD.2017.7
3. Baader, F., Nipkow, T.: Term Rewriting and All That. Cambridge University Press (1998). https://doi.org/10.1145/505863.505888
4. Barrett, C., Fontaine, P., Tinelli, C.: The Satisfiability Modulo Theories Library (SMT-LIB) (2016). https://www.SMT-LIB.org
5. Barrett, C.W., Sebastiani, R., Seshia, S.A., Tinelli, C.: Satisfiability modulo theories. In: Biere, A., Heule, M., van Maaren, H., Walsh, T. (eds.) Handbook of Satisfiability, Frontiers in Artificial Intelligence and Applications, vol. 336, pp. 1267–1329, 2nd edn. IOS Press (2021). https://doi.org/10.3233/FAIA201017
6. Bouhoula, A., Jacquemard, F.: Sufficient completeness verification for conditional and constrained TRS. J. Appl. Log. **10**(1), 127–143 (2012). https://doi.org/10.1016/J.JAL.2011.09.001

7. Chen, X., Roşu, G.: Matching μ-logic. In: Proceedings of the 34th Annual ACM/IEEE Symposium on Logic in Computer Science, pp. 1–13. IEEE (2019). https://doi.org/10.1109/LICS.2019.8785675

8. Chen, X., Roşu, G.: Matching mu-logic: foundation of K framework (invited paper). In: Roggenbach, M., Sokolova, A. (eds.) Proceedings of the 8th Conference on Algebra and Coalgebra in Computer Science. LIPIcs, vol. 139, pp. 1:1–1:4. Schloss Dagstuhl – Leibniz-Zentrum für Informatik (2019). https://doi.org/10.4230/LIPICS.CALCO.2019.1

9. Ciobâcă, Ş, Arusoaie, A., Lucanu, D.: Unification modulo builtins. In: Moss, L.S., de Queiroz, R., Martinez, M. (eds.) WoLLIC 2018. LNCS, vol. 10944, pp. 179–195. Springer, Heidelberg (2018). https://doi.org/10.1007/978-3-662-57669-4_10

10. Ciobâcă, Ş, Lucanu, D.: A coinductive approach to proving reachability properties in logically constrained term rewriting systems. In: Galmiche, D., Schulz, S., Sebastiani, R. (eds.) IJCAR 2018. LNCS (LNAI), vol. 10900, pp. 295–311. Springer, Cham (2018). https://doi.org/10.1007/978-3-319-94205-6_20

11. Comon, H., et al.: Tree automata techniques and applications (2007). http://www.grappa.univ-lille3.fr/tata

12. Fernández, M.: Negation elimination in empty or permutative theories. J. Symb. Comput. **26**(1), 97–133 (1998). https://doi.org/10.1006/JSCO.1998.0203

13. Fuhs, C., Guo, L., Kop, C.: An innermost DP framework for constrained higher-order rewriting. In: Fernández, M. (ed.) Proceedings of the 10th International Conference on Formal Structures for Computation and Deduction. LIPIcs, vol. 337, pp. 20:1–20:24. Schloss Dagstuhl – Leibniz-Zentrum für Informatik (2025). https://doi.org/10.4230/LIPIcs.FSCD.2025.20

14. Fuhs, C., Kop, C., Nishida, N.: Verifying procedural programs via constrained rewriting induction. ACM Trans. Comput. Logic **18**(2), 14:1–14:50 (2017). https://doi.org/10.1145/3060143

15. Higashiwada, N., Aoto, T.: Automatically proving sufficient completeness of conditional term rewriting systems. In: Manuscript for the presentation at the 124th Workshop of IPSJ Special Interest Group on Programming, pp. 1–6 (2019). (in Japanese)

16. Kanazawa, Y., Nishida, N.: On transforming functions accessing global variables into logically constrained term rewriting systems. In: Niehren, J., Sabel, D. (eds.) Proceedings of the 5th International Workshop on Rewriting Techniques for Program Transformations and Evaluation. Electronic Proceedings in Theoretical Computer Science, vol. 289, pp. 34–52. Open Publishing Association (2019)

17. Kanazawa, Y., Nishida, N., Sakai, M.: On representation of structures and unions in logically constrained rewriting. In: IEICE Technical Report SS2018-38, the Institute of Electronics, Information and Communication Engineers, vol. 118, no. 385, pp. 67–72 (2019). (in Japanese)

18. Kapur, D., Narendran, P., Zhang, H.: On sufficient-completeness and related properties of term rewriting systems. Acta Informatica **24**(4), 395–415 (1987). https://doi.org/10.1007/BF00292110

19. Kojima, M., Nishida, N.: From starvation freedom to all-path reachability problems in constrained rewriting. In: Hanus, M., Inclezan, D. (eds.) PADL 2023. LNCS, vol. 13880, pp. 161–179. Springer, Cham (2023). https://doi.org/10.1007/978-3-031-24841-2_11

20. Kojima, M., Nishida, N.: Reducing non-occurrence of specified runtime errors to all-path reachability problems of constrained rewriting. J. Logical Algebraic Methods Program. **135**, 1–19 (2023). https://doi.org/10.1016/j.jlamp.2023.100903

21. Kojima, M., Nishida, N.: A sufficient condition of logically constrained term rewrite systems for decidability of all-path reachability problems with constant destinations. J. Inf. Process. **32**, 417–435 (2024)
22. Kojima, M., Nishida, N., Matsubara, Y.: Transforming concurrent programs with semaphores into logically constrained term rewrite systems. In: Riesco, A., Nigam, V. (eds.) Informal Proceedings of the 7th International Workshop on Rewriting Techniques for Program Transformations and Evaluation, pp. 1–12 (2020)
23. Kojima, M., Nishida, N., Matsubara, Y.: Transforming concurrent programs with semaphores into logically constrained term rewrite systems. J. Logical Algebraic Methods Program. **143**, 1–23 (2025). https://doi.org/10.1016/j.jlamp.2024.101033
24. Kop, C.: Quasi-reductivity of logically constrained term rewriting systems. CoRR abs/1702.02397 (2017). http://arxiv.org/abs/1702.02397
25. Kop, C., Nishida, N.: Term rewriting with logical constraints. In: Fontaine, P., Ringeissen, C., Schmidt, R.A. (eds.) FroCoS 2013. LNCS (LNAI), vol. 8152, pp. 343–358. Springer, Heidelberg (2013). https://doi.org/10.1007/978-3-642-40885-4_24
26. Kop, C., Nishida, N.: Constrained term rewriting tool. In: Davis, M., Fehnker, A., McIver, A., Voronkov, A. (eds.) LPAR 2015. LNCS, vol. 9450, pp. 549–557. Springer, Heidelberg (2015). https://doi.org/10.1007/978-3-662-48899-7_38
27. Lassez, J.-L., Marriott, K.: Explicit representation of terms defined by counter examples. In: Nori, K.V. (ed.) FSTTCS 1986. LNCS, vol. 241, pp. 96–107. Springer, Heidelberg (1986). https://doi.org/10.1007/3-540-17179-7_6
28. Lazrek, A., Lescanne, P., Thiel, J.J.: Tools for proving inductive equalities, relative completeness, and ω-completeness. Inf. Comput. **84**(1), 47–70 (1990). https://doi.org/10.1016/0890-5401(90)90033-E
29. Maranget, L.: Warnings for pattern matching. J. Funct. Program. **17**(3), 387–421 (2007). https://doi.org/10.1017/s0956796807006223
30. Nishida, N., Kojima, M., Matsumi, A.: A nesting-preserving transformation of SIMP programs into logically constrained term rewrite systems. J. Logical Algebraic Methods Program. **144**, 1–15 (2025). https://doi.org/10.1016/j.jlamp.2025.101045
31. Nishida, N., Kojima, M., Nakamura, Y.: Difference of constrained patterns in logically constrained term rewrite systems (full version). CoRR abs/2505.04080 (2025). https://doi.org/10.48550/arXiv.2507.04080
32. Nishida, N., Winkler, S.: Loop detection by logically constrained term rewriting. In: Piskac, R., Rümmer, P. (eds.) VSTTE 2018. LNCS, vol. 11294, pp. 309–321. Springer, Cham (2018). https://doi.org/10.1007/978-3-030-03592-1_18
33. Ohlebusch, E.: Advanced Topics in Term Rewriting. Springer, Cham (2002). https://doi.org/10.1007/978-1-4757-3661-8
34. Reddy, U.S.: Term rewriting induction. In: Stickel, M.E. (ed.) CADE 1990. LNCS, vol. 449, pp. 162–177. Springer, Heidelberg (1990). https://doi.org/10.1007/3-540-52885-7_86
35. Reger, G., Suda, M., Voronkov, A.: Unification with abstraction and theory instantiation in saturation-based reasoning. In: Beyer, D., Huisman, M. (eds.) TACAS 2018. LNCS, vol. 10805, pp. 3–22. Springer, Cham (2018). https://doi.org/10.1007/978-3-319-89960-2_1
36. Rosu, G.: Matching logic. Logical Methods Comput. Sci. **13**(4) (2017). https://doi.org/10.23638/LMCS-13(4:28)2017
37. Sakata, T., Nishida, N., Sakabe, T., Sakai, M., Kusakari, K.: Rewriting induction for constrained term rewriting systems. IPSJ Trans. Program. **2**(2), 80–96

(2009). (in Japanese) (a translated summary is available from https://www.trs.css.i.nagoya-u.ac.jp/crisys/)

38. Schöpf, J., Mitterwallner, F., Middeldorp, A.: Confluence of logically constrained rewrite systems revisited. In: Benzmüller, C., Heule, M.J.H., Schmidt, R.A. (eds.) Automated Reasoning. LNCS, vol. 14740, pp. 298–316. Springer, Cham (2024). https://doi.org/10.1007/978-3-031-63501-4_16

39. Tajine, M.: The negation elimination from syntactic equational formula is decidable. In: Kirchner, C. (ed.) RTA 1993. LNCS, vol. 690, pp. 316–327. Springer, Heidelberg (1993). https://doi.org/10.1007/978-3-662-21551-7_24

40. Thiemann, R., Yamada, A.: A verified algorithm for deciding pattern completeness. In: Rehof, J. (ed.) Proceedings of the 9th International Conference on Formal Structures for Computation and Deduction. LIPIcs, vol. 299, pp. 27:1–27:17. Schloss Dagstuhl–Leibniz-Zentrum für Informatik (2024). https://doi.org/10.4230/LIPICS.FSCD.2024.27

41. Winkler, S., Middeldorp, A.: Completion for logically constrained rewriting. In: Kirchner, H. (ed.) Proceedings of the 3rd International Conference on Formal Structures for Computation and Deduction. Leibniz International Proceedings in Informatics, vol. 108, pp. 30:1–30:18. Schloss Dagstuhl–Leibniz-Zentrum für Informatik (2018). https://doi.org/10.4230/LIPIcs.FSCD.2018.30

Theorem Proving

Iterative Monomorphisation

Tanguy Bozec[1,2]([⊠])[ID] and Jasmin Blanchette[2][ID]

[1] ENS Paris-Saclay, Université Paris-Saclay, Gif-sur-Yvette, France
[2] Ludwig-Maximilians-Universität München, Munich, Germany
tanguy.bozec@ens-paris-saclay.fr

Abstract. Monomorphisation can be used to extend monomorphic provers to support polymorphic logics. We describe a pragmatic iterative approach. We implemented it in the Zipperposition prover, where it is used to translate away polymorphism before invoking the monomorphic prover E as a backend. Our evaluation shows that this approach increases Zipperposition's success rate. Moreover, we find that iterative monomorphisation outperforms some native implementations of polymorphism.

Keywords: Polymorphism · monomorphism · automated reasoning

1 Introduction

Automatic theorem provers provide automation for proof assistant users. Many proof assistants, such as HOL4 [16], HOL Light [9] and Isabelle/HOL [13], support rank 1 polymorphism, where type quantification is allowed at the top level of formulae. By contrast, many automatic provers only work with monomorphic logics. One way to close this gap is to extend automatic provers to natively support polymorphism, as has been done in Vampire [1]. However, this entails a lot of work that must be redone for every prover. The alternative is to translate polymorphic problems to monomorphic problems.

To achieve this, one approach [2] is to encode a complete polymorphic type system, but this increases the size of the input problem substantially and slows down provers [2]. Another approach to encode polymorphism is based on iterative monomorphisation, as described by Böhme [5, Section 2.2.1]. Iterative monomorphisation heuristically instantiates the formulae's type variables with concrete types. However, any translation relying on a finite number of instantiations is inevitably incomplete. By a typed version of the compactness theorem, for any first order polymorphic formula φ, there exists an equisatisfiable finite set of monomorphic instances of φ, but it cannot be computed in general [1, Theorem 1].

Böhme's approach is implemented as part of Isabelle/HOL's SMT (satisfiability modulo theories) integration [5, Chapter 2]. This implementation is also used by Sledgehammer [6,14] to interface with superposition based automatic theorem provers. However, it is documented only superficially [5, Section 2.2.1]. An iterative monomorphisation approach is also described in the context of SMT-LIB [7]. Moreover, a similar algorithm appears to be implemented in the MESON tactic [8] of HOL Light, but it is undocumented.

R. Thiemann and C. Weidenbach (Eds.): FroCoS 2025, LNAI 15979, pp. 269–286, 2026.
https://doi.org/10.1007/978-3-032-04167-8_15

In this paper, we present an algorithm based on our understanding of Böhme's description and implementation (Sect. 3). We also provide a more detailed description to help future implementers. In addition, we present some optimisations to curb the combinatorial explosions (Sect. 4).

The algorithm works as follows. The input problem is a set of formulae. All the problem's symbols are collected, and the polymorphic symbol instances are matched against the monomorphic ones. This yields new symbol instances, both polymorphic and monomorphic. The process is then iterated, making use of the newly generated instances. Consider the unary type constructor list. If a formula contains list(α), where α is a type variable, the types list(int), list(list(int)), etc., can be generated. However, because new types emerge through matching, list(list(int)) can be obtained only once the list(int) instance has been generated.

To keep the number of generated formulae finite, we limit the number of iterations. After the iterations are completed, the new monomorphic symbol instances are used to instantiate the polymorphic symbols in the problem's formulae, generating new monomorphic formulae. Finally, because monomorphic provers support only nullary type constructors, types must be 'mangled'; for example, the compound type list(int) might be mangled to list_int.

We implemented iterative monomorphisation in Zipperposition [18], a higher order prover written in OCaml. Although Zipperposition is polymorphic, it uses the monomorphic prover E [15] as a backend. Thanks to our work, E can now be used with polymorphic problems. Moreover, our implementation can be used as a preprocessor for other stand-alone provers. Our source code is available online.Our evaluation on the TPTP [17] tries to answer three questions (Sect. 6):

1. Is the new Zipperposition with the E backend more successful on polymorphic problems than Zipperposition without backend?
2. How competitive are monomorphic provers on monomorphised problems?
3. Is iterative monomorphisation more effective than the native polymorphism implemented in polymorphic provers?

2   Preliminaries

Our algorithm works independently of the structure of the problem's formulae. It relies exclusively on the formulae's monomorphic and polymorphic symbol instances. Type variables are assumed to be implicitly universally quantified at a formula's top level. The precise form of formulae is left unspecified. Due to this generality, iterative monomorphisation can be used with any standard variant of rank 1 polymorphic logic. In particular, it can work with the polymorphic first and higher order logics embodied by TPTP's TF1 and TH1 syntaxes [3,11].

Our abstract framework relies on the following basic definitions.

Definition 1. A (*polymorphic*) *type* τ is a type variable (e.g. α) or the application of an n-ary type constructor to n types (e.g. list(α), map(int, string)). If $n = 0$, we omit the parentheses (e.g. int). A type is *monomorphic* if it contains no type variables.

Definition 2. A (function or predicate) symbol f has a *type arity* that specifies the number of type arguments it takes. A *symbol instance* is a symbol applied to type arguments listed between angle brackets: $f\langle \tau_1, \ldots, \tau_n \rangle$, where each τ_i is a type. If $n = 0$, we omit the angle brackets (e.g. f).

Definition 3. A *(type) substitution* is a partial function mapping a finite number of type variables to corresponding types. Substitutions are written as $\sigma = \{\alpha_1 \mapsto \tau_1, \ldots, \alpha_n \mapsto \tau_n\}$. They are assumed to be lifted to formulae; thus, $\sigma(\varphi)$ yields the variant of φ in which each α_i is replaced by τ_i. Given two substitutions τ, υ, the successive application of τ and υ is denoted by $\upsilon \circ \tau$.

Definition 4. Two substitutions $\{\alpha_1 \mapsto \tau_1, \ldots, \alpha_m \mapsto \tau_m\}$ and $\{\beta_1 \mapsto \upsilon_1, \ldots, \beta_n \mapsto \upsilon_n\}$ are said to be *compatible* if $\alpha_i = \beta_j$ implies $\tau_i = \upsilon_j$ for all i, j.

Definition 5. Given two types τ, υ, *matching* υ against τ either fails or yields a substitution σ such that $\sigma(\upsilon) = \tau$.

3   High Level Algorithm

The iterative monomorphisation algorithm takes a polymorphic problem as input and returns a monomorphic problem. It applies a bounded number of iterations, each taking a polymorphic problem as argument and returning a problem with new partially instantiated formulae. Once the iterations are completed, a final step discards all non-monomorphic formulae.

The initial phase of each iteration computes two maps, M and N, from the input problem Φ.

- Given a symbol f occurring in Φ, the set $M(f)$ consists of all monomorphic type argument tuples to which f is applied in Φ. For example, if $\mathsf{foldl}\langle \mathsf{nat}, \mathsf{int} \rangle$ occurs in Φ, then $(\mathsf{nat}, \mathsf{int}) \in M(\mathsf{foldl})$.
- Given a formula $\varphi \in \Phi$ and a symbol f occurring in φ, the set $N(\varphi)(f)$ consists of all type argument tuples to which f is applied in φ and which contain a type variable. For example, if $\mathsf{foldl}\langle \mathsf{nat}, \mathsf{list}(\alpha) \rangle$ occurs in φ, then $(\mathsf{nat}, \mathsf{list}(\alpha)) \in N(\varphi)(\mathsf{foldl})$.

N is parametrised with φ because type variables are implicitly quantified at the formula level. The formula indicates the scope of type variables. This is not necessary for M since all the types it contains are monomorphic. To avoid copying the monomorphic types for each formula, M and N are kept separate.

Once the maps M and N are initialised, each iteration performs the following steps to create new instances of formulae:

1. Create an empty set of formulae Φ'.
2. For each formula $\varphi \in \Phi$ and for each symbol f occurring in φ:
   2.1. For each $(\tau_1, \ldots, \tau_n) \in M(f)$ and $(\upsilon_1, \ldots, \upsilon_n) \in N(\varphi)(f)$ and for each i, match υ_i against τ_i, yielding the substitution σ_i in case of success.
   2.2. If all n matchings are successful and the substitutions σ_i are pairwise compatible, add the formula $(\sigma_1 \circ \cdots \circ \sigma_n)(\varphi)$ to Φ'.
3. Return $\Phi \cup \Phi'$.

The algorithm is trivially sound because the newly generated formulae are instances of the initial problem's formulae. However, it is not complete.

Example 6. Consider the following problem:

$\langle 1 \rangle$ $\mathsf{p}\langle\mathsf{int}\rangle(0)$
$\langle 2 \rangle$ $\forall a : \alpha, as : \mathsf{list}(\alpha).\ \mathsf{p}\langle\alpha\rangle(a) \to \mathsf{p}\langle\mathsf{list}(\alpha)\rangle(as)$

The first iteration matches α against int for p, generating the formula

$\langle 3 \rangle$ $\forall a : \mathsf{int}, as : \mathsf{list}(\mathsf{int}).\ \mathsf{p}\langle\mathsf{int}\rangle(a) \to \mathsf{p}\langle\mathsf{list}(\mathsf{int})\rangle(as)$

The second iteration matches α against $\mathsf{list}(\mathsf{int})$, leading to the formula

$\langle 4 \rangle$ $\forall a : \mathsf{list}(\mathsf{int}), as : \mathsf{list}(\mathsf{list}(\mathsf{int})).\ \mathsf{p}\langle\mathsf{list}(\mathsf{int})\rangle(a) \to \mathsf{p}\langle\mathsf{list}(\mathsf{list}(\mathsf{int}))\rangle(as)$

Similarly the third iteration adds

$\langle 5 \rangle$ $\forall a{:}\mathsf{list}(\mathsf{list}(\mathsf{int})), as{:}\mathsf{list}(\mathsf{list}(\mathsf{int})).$
$\mathsf{p}\langle\mathsf{list}(\mathsf{list}(\mathsf{int}))\rangle(a) \to \mathsf{p}\langle\mathsf{list}(\mathsf{list}(\mathsf{list}(\mathsf{int})))\rangle(as)$

This example illustrates how an infinite number of new formulae can be generated from a simple initial problem. Any reasonable implementation must limit the number of new type arguments, substitutions and formulae.

4   Low Level Algorithm

The algorithm presented above is too naïve in practice. In this section, we present a lower level algorithm with the following features. First, numeric bounds are introduced to stop combinatorially explosive enumerations. Second, type argument tuples are separated into an old set and a new set to avoid re-computing some of the same matchings in successive iterations. Third, substitutions are directly applied to the type arguments instead of the formulae. This avoids having to re-extract the type arguments from the formulae at each iteration. New formulae are generated only once all iterations are completed, in a separate, final step.

The data structures used in the algorithm are based on the ones used in the high level description. Instead of a map M from symbols to monomorphic type argument tuples, we now have M_{old} and M_{new}, which play the same role whilst also distinguishing between those type argument tuples that have already been matched against and those that have not. Similarly, N_{old} and N_{new} replace the map N from formulae to symbols to non-monomorphic type argument tuples. Finally, we maintain a map S from formulae to the substitutions generated by the matchings. It is used to generate new formulae in the final phase.

All sets referenced in the algorithm are finite. Moreover, the algorithm relies on primitives whose implementation depends on the specifics of the grammar and logic used. Functions computing the following are assumed to be available:

- *initialisation*(Φ), where Φ is a set of (polymorphic) formulae, extracts the initial type argument maps M and N from Φ.

Function *iterative_monomorphisation*(Φ)
    Data: set Φ of polymorphic formulae
    Result: set of monomorphic formulae

    $(M_{\text{old}}, N_{\text{old}}) \leftarrow (\emptyset, \emptyset)$
    $(M_{\text{new}}, N_{\text{new}}) \leftarrow initialisation(\Phi)$
    $S \leftarrow \emptyset$

    for $i = 1$ **to** num_loops **do**
        $(M_{\text{next}}, N_{\text{next}}) \leftarrow (\emptyset, \emptyset)$
        foreach $\varphi \in \Phi$ **do**
            $(M_\Delta, N_\Delta, S_\Delta) \leftarrow$
                $formula\_mono\_step(\varphi, M_{\text{old}}, M_{\text{new}}, N_{\text{old}}(\varphi), N_{\text{new}}(\varphi))$
            $S(\varphi) \leftarrow S(\varphi) \cup S_\Delta$
            $M_{\text{next}} \leftarrow M_{\text{next}} \cup M_\Delta$
            $N_{\text{next}}(\varphi) \leftarrow N_{\text{next}}(\varphi) \cup N_\Delta$
        $(M_{\text{old}}, M_{\text{new}}) \leftarrow (M_{\text{old}} \cup M_{\text{new}}, M_{\text{next}})$
        $(N_{\text{old}}, N_{\text{new}}) \leftarrow (N_{\text{old}} \cup N_{\text{new}}, N_{\text{next}})$

    return $mangle(generate\_mono\_formulae(\Phi, S))$

Fig. 1. Algorithm for iterative monomorphisation.

- $type\_vars(\tau_1, \ldots, \tau_n)$, where $\tau_1, \ldots, \tau_n$ are types, gathers all the type variables from each type $\tau_1, \ldots, \tau_n$ into a set. This function is overloaded to accept a formula φ as input, in which case it returns the set of all type variables which occur in the formula.
- $match(\upsilon, \tau)$, where υ and τ are types, matches υ against τ and either fails or returns $Some(\sigma)$, where σ results from the matching. The algorithm matches only non-monomorphic types against monomorphic types.
- $domain(\sigma)$ returns the set of type variables α such that $\sigma(\alpha) \neq \alpha$.
- $compatible(\sigma_1, \sigma_2)$ tests the compatibility between σ_1 and σ_2.
- $mangle(\Phi)$, where Φ is a set of monomorphic formulae, returns the same set of formulae where all types have been mangled.

The iterative monomorphisation algorithm is given in Fig. 1. It has three phases. The first phase applies a *monomorphisation step* to each formula in Φ until the user-set limit, num_loops, is reached. This limit is the only bound necessary for the algorithm to terminate. We use the colour blue to identify bounds and code related to bounds. At the end of each of these iterations, the old and new type argument maps are updated with newly generated types. No new formulae are generated at this stage, only new type arguments and substitutions. Once these iterations are completed, the first phase is complete and the substitutions used to create new type argument tuples are passed to *generate_mono_formulae* for the second phase. This is when the new formulae are generated. The third phase mangles the composite types of the newly monomorphised formulae. This allows targeting a simply typed logic with no support for *n*-ary type constructors.

Function $formula\_mono\_step(\varphi, M_{old}, M_{new}, N_{old}(\varphi), N_{new}(\varphi))$

    Data: polymorphic formula φ

           old and new monomorphic type argument maps M_{old}, M_{new}

           old and new non-monomorphic type argument maps $N_{old}(\varphi), N_{new}(\varphi)$

    Result: monomorphic type argument map

           non-monomorphic type argument map

           set of substitutions

max_mono_args $\leftarrow$
  $min(max(\text{mono\_floor}, |M_{old} \cup M_{new}| \cdot \text{mono\_mult}), \text{mono\_cap})$

max_nonm_args $\leftarrow$
  $min(max(\text{nonm\_floor}, |N_{old}(\varphi) \cup N_{new}(\varphi)| \cdot \text{nonm\_mult}), \text{nonm\_cap})$

$S \leftarrow \emptyset$

$S' \leftarrow matches(M_{new}, N_{new}(\varphi)) \cup matches(M_{new}, N_{old}(\varphi)) \cup$
$matches(M_{old}, N_{new}(\varphi))$

$(M_{next}, N_{next}(\varphi)) \leftarrow (\emptyset, \emptyset)$

foreach $\sigma \in S'$ **do**

    foreach $(f \mapsto (v_1, \ldots, v_n)) \in N_{old}(\varphi) \cup N_{new}(\varphi)$ **do**

        if $type\_vars(v_1, \ldots, v_n) \subseteq subst\_dom(\sigma)$ **then**

            if $|M_{next}| <$ max_mono_args **then**

                $M_{next}(f) \leftarrow M_{next}(f) \cup \{(\sigma(v_1), \ldots, \sigma(v_n))$

                $S \leftarrow S \cup \{\sigma\}$

            else if $|N_{next}(\varphi)| \geq$ max_nonm_args **then**

                $M_{next} \leftarrow M_{next} \setminus (M_{old} \cup M_{new})$

                $N_{next}(\varphi) \leftarrow N_{next}(\varphi) \setminus (N_{old}(\varphi) \cup N_{new}(\varphi))$

                return $(M_{next}, N_{next}(\varphi), S)$

        else

            if $|N_{next}(\varphi)| <$ max_nonm_args **then**

                $N_{next}(\varphi)(f) \leftarrow N_{next}(\varphi)(f) \cup \{(\sigma(v_1), \ldots, \sigma(v_n))\}$

                $S \leftarrow S \cup \{\sigma\}$

return $(M_{next} \setminus (M_{old} \cup M_{new}), N_{next}(\varphi) \setminus (N_{old}(\varphi) \cup N_{new}(\varphi)), S)$

Fig. 2. Algorithm for formula monomorphisation step

The formula monomorphisation algorithm is given in Fig. 2. It forms the core of the process. Essentially, it computes new type argument tuples for a single formula. Type argument tuples are matched against each other to obtain a set of substitutions which is iterated over in the outermost loop. The separation of type argument tuples into old and new maps is used to ensure that only combinations involving at least one new map are considered. This avoids re-computing some matchings processed in previous iterations. New tuples are obtained by applying each substitution to each non-monomorphic type argument tuple such that at least one tuple component is instantiated by the substitution.

The total number of type argument tuples can increase cubically in the number of type argument tuples at each iteration and can therefore grow doubly exponentially in the number of iterations. We give a sketch of how such growth can occur for a single formula. If we assume that after k iterations, there are N_k

type argument tuples in total divided evenly between monomorphic and non-monomorphic type argument tuples, then there can be up to $\left(\frac{N_k}{2}\right)^2$ successful matches, yielding as many substitutions. Each substitution is then applied to each non-monomorphic type argument for a total of $\left(\frac{N_k}{2}\right)^3$ possible new type argument tuples. If half of these new type argument tuples are monomorphic and the other half are non-monomorphic, then the next iteration will begin with $N_{k+1} = N_k^3 \cdot 2^{-3}$ evenly split type argument tuples. Therefore, the total number of type argument tuples on the kth iteration can reach $N_k = N_0^{3^k} \cdot 2^{\frac{-3^{k+2}+3}{2}}$.

Depending on the shape and size of the input problem and the number of iterations performed, the doubly exponential growth may be problematic. Introducing bounds addresses this potential issue. The limit on the number of newly generated monomorphic type argument tuples is $\min(\max(\mathsf{mono\_mult} \cdot m, \mathsf{mono\_floor}), \mathsf{mono\_cap})$, where m is the total number of monomorphic type argument tuples. The components of this limit are

1. mono_cap, a limit on the total number of new type argument tuples;
2. mono_mult, which is used to allow the total number of (monomorphic) type argument tuples to grow by a certain proportion of the current number m of monomorphic type argument tuples;
3. mono_floor, which balances out mono_mult, preventing mono_mult from inhibiting new type argument tuple generation if m is too low.

Similar bounds are used for the non-monomorphic type argument tuples: The limit on the number of new non-monomorphic type argument tuples is $\min(\max(\mathsf{nonm\_mult} \cdot n, \mathsf{nonm\_floor}), \mathsf{nonm\_cap})$, where n is the number of non-monomorphic type argument tuples associated with the current formula. An important difference with the monomorphic case is that n depends on the current formula being processed whilst m does not. Both in the monomorphic and in the non-monomorphic case, the maximum number of newly generated type argument tuples is fixed per formula and per iteration.

The *matches* function, which computes the substitutions used for generating new type arguments, is given in Fig. 3. Each symbol instance from $N(\varphi)$ is matched against all corresponding symbol instances from M. For two such symbol instances, the types from the non-monomorphic type argument tuple are matched component-wise against the types from the monomorphic type argument tuple. The resulting substitutions are composed if they are compatible. In the algorithm, compatibility is checked by making sure the **foreach** loop has successfully iterated over all elements of the type argument tuple. If any substitutions are incompatible, the matchings are discarded. Since the composition of two compatible substitutions is commutative, the order of composition is irrelevant. The total number of substitutions generated is limited by substitution_cap.

The various bounds presented here overlap to some extent. For instance, having at most substitution_cap substitutions generated by *matches* may be sufficient to curb the number of new type argument tuples, making the mono_cap, mono_mult, mono_floor triplet superfluous. Nonetheless every bound has uses.

Function $matches(M, N(\varphi))$
   Data: monomorphic type argument map M
           non-monomorphic type argument map $N(\varphi)$
   Result: set of substitutions

$S \leftarrow \emptyset$

foreach $f \mapsto (v_1, \ldots, v_n) \in N(\varphi)$ **do**
   foreach $(\tau_1, \ldots, \tau_n) \in M(f)$ **do**
      if $|S| >$ substitution_cap **then**
         return S
      if for all $0 \leq i \leq n$, $match(v_i, \tau_i) = Some(\sigma_i)$ **then**
         if $\sigma_1, \ldots, \sigma_n$ are compatible **then**
            $\sigma \leftarrow \sigma_1 \circ \cdots \circ \sigma_n$
            $S \leftarrow S \cup \{\sigma\}$

return S

Fig. 3. Algorithm for match generation.

Function $generate\_mono\_formulae(\Phi, S)$
   Data: set Φ of polymorphic formulae
           substitution map S
   Result: set of monomorphic formulae

$\Psi \leftarrow \emptyset$

foreach $\varphi \in \Phi$ **s.t.** φ is non-monomorphic **do**
   foreach $\sigma \in mono\_substs(S(\varphi), type\_vars(\varphi), \emptyset, \{\})$ **do**
      if $|\Psi| <$ max_new_formulae **then**
         $\Psi \leftarrow \Psi \cup \{\sigma(\varphi)\}$
      else
         return Ψ
return Ψ

Fig. 4. Algorithm for monomorphic formula generation.

For example, problems that lead to few successful matches but many type argument tuples may benefit from a limit on the number of new type argument tuples whilst problems for which substitution generation is more combinatorially explosive may benefit from a limit on the number of generated substitutions.

Once all monomorphisation iterations have been completed, we are left with a set of the substitutions that have been used to generate new type arguments. The last phase uses this set to instantiate the type variables in the input problem's non-monomorphic formulae. In the presence of bounds, the order in which the elements of S are traversed affects the formulae resulting from the last phase.

The *generate_mono_formulae* function is given in Fig. 4. It generates monomorphising substitutions and applies them to the polymorphic formulae of the input problem that they instantiate. A substitution σ is *monomorphising* for a formula φ if $\sigma(\varphi)$ is monomorphic. Since the substitutions are monomorphising relative to the formula they are applied to, the resulting formulae will

Function $mono\_substs(S, V, S_{res}, \sigma)$

    Data: set S of substitutions
           set V of type variables
           set S_{res} of substitutions
           substitution σ
    Result: set of substitutions

    if $V = \emptyset$ **then**
        return $S_{res} \cup \{\sigma\}$
    else
        let α **s.t.** $\alpha \in V$
        foreach $\sigma_\Delta \in S$ **s.t.** $\alpha \in domain(\sigma_\Delta)$ **and** $compatible(\sigma, \sigma_\Delta)$
        do
            if $|S_{res}| <$ max_substs **then**
                $S_{res} \leftarrow$
                    $mono\_substs(S, V \setminus domain(\sigma_\Delta), S_{res}, \sigma_\Delta \circ \sigma)$
            else
                return S_{res}
        return S_{res}

Fig. 5. Algorithm for monomorphising substitution generation.

be monomorphic. The max_new_formulae bound is used to control the total number of new formulae. It overlaps with max_substs but can be useful to set an absolute limit on the size of the final problem.

To monomorphise a polymorphic formula, we first compute its monomorphising substitutions using the $mono\_substs$ function given in Fig. 5. Such substitutions are computed using a recursive function. Given a set V of type variables and a set $S(\varphi)$ of substitutions, it selects a substitution σ_Δ from $S(\varphi)$ that instantiates at least one of the type variables in V. It is important that σ_Δ be compatible with σ so that they can be composed and the function recursively called to instantiate the remaining type variables.

The Zipperposition implementation of the $mono\_substs$ function uses a map from type variables to substitutions instead of a set to filter the relevant substitutions from S efficiently. The max_substs bound exists for two main reasons:

1. The iterative monomorphisation algorithm can generate up to max_substs new monomorphic formulae per initial polymorphic formula. Generating an excessive number of new formulae can overwhelm the prover. The final number of output formulae is limited to at most $|\Phi| \cdot$ max_substs.
2. The $mono\_substs$ function is the algorithm's most combinatorially explosive part. For a formula φ, if $S(\varphi)$ contains n substitutions that each instantiate exactly one of v type variables, up to n^v monomorphising substitutions may be generated. Recall that the total number of type argument tuples used to generate $S(\varphi)$ can be doubly exponential in the number of loop iterations. The starting n may therefore already be very large.

5   Detailed Example

To illustrate the low level version of the iterative algorithm, we consider the following (admittedly contrived) initial problem:

⟨1⟩ $p\langle int, nat\rangle(-1, 3) \wedge p\langle int, int\rangle(-1, -2)$
⟨2⟩ $\forall x : \alpha, y : list(\alpha), z : \beta. \; p\langle list(\alpha), \alpha\rangle(y, x) \wedge p\langle \alpha, \alpha\rangle(x, x) \wedge p\langle \alpha, \beta\rangle(x, z)$

M_{new} is initialised with $\{p \mapsto \{(int, nat), (int, int)\}$ and N_{new} with $\{\langle 2\rangle \mapsto \{p \mapsto \{(list(\alpha), \alpha), (\alpha, \alpha), (\alpha, \beta)\}\}\}$. Then we enter the main loop (assuming num_loops is at least 1). We iterate over each formula and call *formula_mono_step* for each of them. Nothing happens for formula ⟨1⟩ because it contains no type variables. For formula ⟨2⟩, M_{new} and $N_{new}(\langle 2\rangle)$ are passed as arguments to *matches*.

The three non-monomorphic type argument tuples are matched against their monomorphic counterparts in M_{new}:

- $(list(\alpha), \alpha)$ fails in both cases because $list(\alpha)$ fails to match against int.
- (α, α) fails to match against (int, nat) because the substitutions resulting from the match of the first and second element of the tuple are incompatible. The second match is successful and yields the substitution $\sigma_1 = \{\alpha \mapsto int\}$
- (α, β) succeeds in both cases and generates the substitutions $\sigma_2 = \{\alpha \mapsto int, \beta \mapsto int\}$ and $\sigma_3 = \{\alpha \mapsto int, \beta \mapsto nat\}$.

Then *matches* returns, and the substitutions are used to generate new type argument tuples. Each substitution is applied to the type arguments of the function symbols of formula ⟨2⟩ because they are the only function symbols with non-monomorphic type arguments. The table below summarises the situation:

	σ_1	σ_2	σ_3
$(list(\alpha), \alpha)$	$(list(int), int)$	$(list(int), int)$	$(list(int), int)$
(α, α)	(int, int)	(int, int)	(int, int)
(α, β)	(int, β)	(int, int)	(int, nat)

With a simple two-formula initial problem, there are already up to nine new type arguments tuples generated at this step in the first iteration alone, although only four are unique. Once the new type argument tuples are added to their respective maps, a new iteration is begun. We only consider one iteration and continue to the next phase of the algorithm.

The next function to be called is *generate_formulae*. It iterates over all non-monomorphic formulae of the initial problem; in our case, this will only be ⟨2⟩. The set of type variable tuples of ⟨2⟩ is passed to *mono_substs* along with the set of all previously generated substitutions.

First, we instantiate α, the first type variable of ⟨2⟩. If σ_1 is selected to instantiate α, both σ_2 and σ_3 will in turn be selected to instantiate β. This will generate two monomorphising substitutions, $\sigma_1 \circ \sigma_2 = \sigma_2$ and $\sigma_1 \circ \sigma_3 = \sigma_3$, which are added to the set of monomorphising substitutions S_{res}. Now σ_2 is selected. It simultaneously instantiates α and β. Here, σ_2 is already in S_res and is therefore ignored, and σ_3 is treated similarly. No more than substitution_cap monomorphising substitutions can be generated in this way.

Now, the monomorphising substitutions have been generated. We only need to apply them to the formula they monomorphise. This is repeated for all non-monomorphic formulae or until max_new_formulae is reached. The order of formulae will impact the output problem in the latter case. For some larger input problems, *mono_substs* could be sufficiently explosive to only allow a handful of different formulae to be monomorphised. The ability to set substitution_cap independently can help avoid this issue.

Finally, if the target language supports only nullary type construtors, the types of all monomorphic formulae, both new and old, are mangled. Assuming that mangling is not necessary, the algorithm outputs

$\langle 1 \rangle$ $\mathsf{p}\langle\mathsf{int},\mathsf{nat}\rangle(-1,3) \wedge \mathsf{p}\langle\mathsf{int},\mathsf{int}\rangle(-1,-2)$

$\langle 3 \rangle$ $\forall x : \mathsf{int}, y : \mathsf{list}(\mathsf{int}), z : \mathsf{int}.\ \mathsf{p}\langle\mathsf{list}(\mathsf{int}),\mathsf{int}\rangle(y,x) \wedge \mathsf{p}\langle\mathsf{int},\mathsf{int}\rangle(x,x) \wedge$
$$\mathsf{p}\langle\mathsf{int},\mathsf{int}\rangle(x,z)$$

$\langle 4 \rangle$ $\forall x : \mathsf{int}, y : \mathsf{list}(\mathsf{int}), z : \mathsf{nat}.\ \mathsf{p}\langle\mathsf{list}(\mathsf{int}),\mathsf{int}\rangle(y,x) \wedge \mathsf{p}\langle\mathsf{int},\mathsf{int}\rangle(x,x) \wedge$
$$\mathsf{p}\langle\mathsf{int},\mathsf{nat}\rangle(x,z)$$

In this example, two new monomorphic formulae are generated.

6   Evaluation

The monomorphisation algorithm is parametrised by many bounds. The first part of the evaluation process seeks appropriate values for these bounds. The second part compares the performance of Zipperposition without E and with the new monormorphising E backend on polymorphic problems. The third part compares the performance of different provers on polymorphic problems and their monomorphised counterparts.

The benchmarks are taken from version 8.2.0 of the TPTP library [17]. The library contains 1765 problems in TF1 and TH1, corresponding respectively to first and higher order logic with rank 1 polymorphism. Because Zipperposition does not support reasoning with real numbers, we removed all problems that include them. In total, our benchmark suite contains 1534 polymorphic problems. We chose as a measure of success for a given prover (or prover configuration) the number of problems that could be solved by the prover in at most 30 s per problem with a single thread. Our raw evaluation data is available online.[1]

Parameter Optimisation
Each bound of the monomorphisation process represents a tradeoff: a higher bound allows for a more exhaustive instantiation of type variables but takes more time. Since we cannot test all possible combinations of values for all bounds to find the best compromise between completeness and speed, we group closely

---

[1] https://zenodo.org/records/14881532.

related bounds together and test combinations of values for the bounds in these groups. Once we find the best performing set of values for a group, we assign these values to the corresponding bounds as we begin the search for the next group. If several groups result in the same number of proved problems, we select the most constraining values. Winning entries are shown in bold in Tables 1 to 6.

To guard against overfitting took place, we carried out the part of the evaluation related to parameter optimisation and all preliminary evaluations on 500 randomly chosen problems out of the 1534 selected problems. We carried out the rest of the evaluations on the remaining 1034 problems.

Before finding values to assign to the bounds of the monomorphisation algorithm, we must choose which base options to run Zipperposition with. Because the space of possible base configurations is too large to evaluate exhaustively, we evaluated, in a preliminary experiment, all pre-existing portfolio configurations that called E against our benchmark suite of 500 problems. Since E could not treat these non-monomorphic problems, it was disabled. The preliminary evaluation found that the 40_b.comb configuration performed best by proving 131 problems. This configuration became the base configuration, which we used as a basis to evaluate the monomorphisation options.

We conducted additional informal evaluations on the 500 problems to find appropriate default values and test ranges for the monomorphisation bounds. We started the option evaluation process with the base configuration and the following default values for monomorphisation bounds and parameters for E:

- nonm_cap: ∞
- nonm_mult: 1
- nonm_floor: 50
- substitution order: separation
- substitution_cap: ∞
- max_substs: 10

- max_new_formulae: 2000
- new formulae limit multiplier: 0
- monomorphisation timeout: 20
- num_loops: 4
- E timeout: 30
- E call point: 0

The initial values for the mono_cap, mono_mult and mono_floor options are irrelevant because the options' values are set when computing Table 1.

Table 1 groups bounds that control the maximum number of newly generated monomorphic type arguments per formula and per iteration. The limit on newly generated type arguments is determined by three components that form a natural group of bounds.

The table shows that generating no new monomorphic type arguments seems to be the best approach. This result may seem counterintuitive, but it is possible to monomorphise formulae without generating monomorphic type arguments. This is because non-monomorphic type argument generation can produce substitutions that instantiate one or more type variables, and it is these substitutions that are used to monomorphise formulae.

Table 2 is similar to Table 1 except that it evaluates the bounds limiting the number of new *non*-monomorphic type arguments. The bound values are lower because we found non-monomorphic type arguments to be combinatorially explosive in preliminary evaluations. The table confirms that non-monomorphic

Table 1. Evaluation of bounds for monomorphic type argument generation

	cap										
	500				1000				∞		
	floor										
mult	0	50	100	200	0	50	100	200	0	50	100	200
0	**178**	161	161	156	178	160	160	156	178	161	160	156
1	155	155	155	158	153	154	154	156	154	154	155	155
2	154	154	153	154	153	153	154	152	154	153	154	154
∞	153	154	153	155	155	153	154	156	159	160	161	161

Table 2. Evaluation of bounds for non-monomorphic type argument generation

	cap										
	500				1000				∞		
	floor										
mult	0	10	50	100	0	10	50	100	0	10	50	100
0	125	**184**	182	177	125	184	182	177	125	184	182	177
0.5	176	184	182	177	176	184	182	177	176	184	182	177
1	182	181	178	177	182	181	178	177	182	181	178	177
∞	173	174	174	174	174	174	173	173	125	125	125	125

type argument generation drives the creation of useful non-monomorphic formulae. This is indicated by the very low number of problems solved when no new non-monomorphic type arguments are allowed. Performance of the monomorphisation algorithm seems to plateau for some ranges of values and drops off beyond.

The substitution generation phase occurs once all type arguments have been generated. The bound limiting the number of monomorphising substitutions per formula is directly related to the order which dictates how such monomorphising substitutions are generated. The heuristic greatly affects monomorphising substitution generation. The 'age' order of substitution orders substitutions generated in earlier iterations first. The 'random' order randomly shuffles substitutions. Finally, the 'separation' order separates the substitutions into groups of substitutions generated in the same iteration and generates monomorphising substitutions from each of these groups independently. Table 3 shows that the values of bounds limiting the number of monomorphising substitutions seem to affect performance only when the 'separation' heuristic is used.

Table 4 groups the bounds related to the size of the output problem to be passed to the E prover. The absolute limit is the maximum number of formulae passed to E. The multiplier limits the total number of newly generated formulae based on the problem's initial number of formulae. We find that the E prover tends to perform better when given a limited number of formulae.

Table 3. Evaluation of bounds for substitution generation

	substitution order		
mono subst	age	random	separation
2	161	178	175
5	161	178	180
7	161	178	182
10	161	178	**184**

Table 4. Evaluation of bounds directly related to the size of the output problem

	formula multiplier			
formula cap	1	2	3	∞
500	**184**	184	184	183
2000	184	184	184	184
∞	168	178	183	125

Table 5. Evaluation of parameters related to the depth of monomorphisation

	mono time			
num. loops	5	10	20	30
1	183	184	183	183
2	**186**	186	186	185
3	186	186	186	185
4	186	186	186	185
5	185	185	185	184

For larger problems, the monomorphisation algorithm may time out despite the bounds. In these cases, neither Zipperposition nor E will have had a chance to try to solve the problem. To avoid this, a timer can interrupt the monomorphisation algorithm, after which Zipperposition resumes normal operation. Table 5 tests the amount of time that is allocated to monomorphisation against the number of iterations of the monomorphisation algorithm. Neither parameter seems to substantially affect the algorithm's performance.

Table 6 shows the impact of the options with which we call the E prover. The point at which Zipperposition interrupts its normal operation and begins the monomorphisation process is determined by the 'E call point' parameter. It is expressed as a fraction of the total time allotted to Zipperposition. The E timeout (in seconds) limits how long E is run before being interrupted, at which point Zipperposition resumes normal operation. The longer Zipperposition runs before E is invoked, the more formulae are generated, and the more combina-

Table 6. Evaluation of parameters related to the E prover

	E call point			
E timeout	0	0.1	0.2	0.3
2	180	143	132	124
5	**185**	142	134	125
10	184	143	132	125
20	184	137	133	125
30	182	133	134	125

Table 7. Evaluation of Zipperposition without E vs. with E

	without E	with E	union
500 problem suite	160	198	207
1034 problem suite	337	410	434

torially explosive iterative monomorphisation is. This likely explains the poor performance for greater values of the E call point.

E as a Zipperposition backend

We compare the performance of two instances of Zipperposition. By default, Zipperposition may call E as a backend when given a monomorphic problem [18]. The first instance is run in the portfolio mode `portfolio.sequential.py`, which attempts to prove the problem with various configurations tried in succession. Since all given problems are non-monomorphic, these configurations can never invoke E as a backend, this instance is therefore labeled 'without E'. The second instance is a modification of the `portfolio.sequential.py` file where each configuration is modified analogously to `40_b.comb` with the options obtained in the previous evaluation phase. This instance can successfully call E as a backend because it is able to provide E with a monomorphised problem. Each of the two instances is evaluated on the set of the 500 previously used problems, and the set of the remaining 1034 problems is evaluated separately. The proportion of problems successfully solved on the 500 and 1034 problem suites are similar, suggesting that no overfitting took place during the option optimisation phase.

Table 7 shows that the use of E as a backend markedly improves the performance of Zipperposition. It is not a strict improvement, since some problems are solved without E and not with E.

Monomorphisation as a Preprocessor

To evaluate the usefulness of iterative monomorphisation as an alternative to native polymorphism, two competitive higher order polymorphic provers were run on the 1034 problem suite. We chose Leo-III and Zipperposition. Unfortunately we needed to exclude Vampire because of parsing issues. The fix for these issues was unavailable for Vampire's higher order branch at the time of the evaluation.

Table 8. Evaluation of native polymorphism vs. monomorphisation

	Native	Mono	Union
E	–	340	340
Leo-III with E	157	231	274
Zipperposition	339	351	404

Table 8 shows the results. The monomorphisation approach is evaluated in two steps. First, each problem is monomorphised using the options obtained from the first evaluation phase except for the monomorphisation timeout option, which is increased to 30 s. For 149 problems, monomorphisation times out. Second, each prover is run on the remaining monomorphised problems, and the results are tallied in the 'Mono' column. In addition to the polymorphic provers used in the 'Native' tests, the monomorphic prover E is run on the monomorphised problems to provide an additional point of comparison. Instead of running each prover for 30 s on the monomorphised problems, the monomorphisation time (rounded up to the nearest second) is subtracted to compare fairly against the 'Native' column, which does not have a similar preprocessing phase.

Despite the monomorphisation timeouts, monomorphisation is more effective than Leo-III's and Zipperposition's native polymorphism on the benchmarks.

7   Conclusion

We described a translation algorithm that iteratively instantiates polymorphic types to produce monomorphic problems. Our primary motivation was to improve the success rate of Zipperposition and its monomorphic E backend, and indeed our evaluation shows a clear improvement. We also saw that even with automatic provers that support polymorphism, iterative monomorphisation is a better alternative in practice.

We see the following avenues for future work. First, iterative monomorphisation blindly enumerates candidate instantiations, without exploiting any knowledge about the logical structure of the formulae in which symbols occur. For example, a lemma $p\langle\alpha\rangle$ cannot be used to prove the conjecture $\neg p\langle nat\rangle$ because of the incompatible polarities, but our algorithm instantiates α with nat regardless. Second, some automatic provers as well as tools such as Sledgehammer include relevance filters that heuristically select a subset of the available axioms; filters such as MePo [12] and SInE [10] are iterative and could be interleaved with monomorphisation. Third, although one would expect native implementations of polymorphism to outperform any preprocessor, currently this is not the case, suggesting that there is considerable room for improvement on the native front.

Acknowledgements. We thank Sascha Böhme for fruitful discussions. We thank Jannis Limperg, Mark Summerfield, and the peer reviewers for suggesting textual improvements. This research is co-funded by the European Union (ERC, Nekoka, 101083038).

Views and opinions expressed are however those of the authors only and do not necessarily reflect those of the European Union or the European Research Council. Neither the European Union nor the granting authority can be held responsible for them.

References

1. Bhayat, A., Reger, G.: A polymorphic Vampire. In: Peltier, N., Sofronie-Stokkermans, V. (eds.) IJCAR 2020. LNCS (LNAI), vol. 12167, pp. 361–368. Springer, Cham (2020). https://doi.org/10.1007/978-3-030-51054-1_21

2. Blanchette, J.C., Böhme, S., Popescu, A., Smallbone, N.: Encoding monomorphic and polymorphic types. In: Piterman, N., Smolka, S.A. (eds.) TACAS 2013. LNCS, vol. 7795, pp. 493–507. Springer, Heidelberg (2013). https://doi.org/10.1007/978-3-642-36742-7_34

3. Blanchette, J.C., Paskevich, A.: TFF1: the TPTP typed first-order form with rank-1 polymorphism. In: Bonacina, M.P. (ed.) CADE 2013. LNCS (LNAI), vol. 7898, pp. 414–420. Springer, Heidelberg (2013). https://doi.org/10.1007/978-3-642-38574-2_29

4. Bobot, F., Paskevich, A.: Expressing polymorphic types in a many-sorted language. In: Tinelli, C., Sofronie-Stokkermans, V. (eds.) FroCoS 2011. LNCS (LNAI), vol. 6989, pp. 87–102. Springer, Heidelberg (2011). https://doi.org/10.1007/978-3-642-24364-6_7

5. Böhme, S.: Proving Theorems of Higher-Order Logic with SMT Solvers. PhD thesis, Technische Universität München (2012)

6. Böhme, S., Nipkow, T.: Sledgehammer: Judgement Day. In: Giesl, J., Hähnle, R. (eds.) IJCAR 2010. LNCS (LNAI), vol. 6173, pp. 107–121. Springer, Heidelberg (2010). https://doi.org/10.1007/978-3-642-14203-1_9

7. Bonichon, R., Déharbe, D., Tavares, C.: Extending SMT-LIB v2 with λ-terms and polymorphism. In: Rümmer, P., Wintersteiger, C.M. (eds.) SMT 2014. CEUR Workshop Proceedings, vol. 1163, pp. 53–62. CEUR-WS.org (2014)

8. Harrison, J.: Optimizing proof search in model elimination. In: McRobbie, M.A., Slaney, J.K. (eds.) CADE 1996. LNCS, vol. 1104, pp. 313–327. Springer, Heidelberg (1996). https://doi.org/10.1007/3-540-61511-3_97

9. Harrison, J.: HOL Light: an overview. In: Berghofer, S., Nipkow, T., Urban, C., Wenzel, M. (eds.) TPHOLs 2009. LNCS, vol. 5674, pp. 60–66. Springer, Heidelberg (2009). https://doi.org/10.1007/978-3-642-03359-9_4

10. Hoder, K., Voronkov, A.: Sine qua non for large theory reasoning. In: Bjørner, N., Sofronie-Stokkermans, V. (eds.) CADE 2011. LNCS (LNAI), vol. 6803, pp. 299–314. Springer, Heidelberg (2011). https://doi.org/10.1007/978-3-642-22438-6_23

11. Kaliszyk, C., Sutcliffe, G., Rabe, F.: TH1: The TPTP typed higher-order form with rank-1 polymorphism. In: Fontaine, P., Schulz, S., Urban, J. (eds.) PAAR 2016. CEUR Workshop Proceedings, vol. 1635, pp. 41–55. CEUR-WS.org (2016)

12. Meng, J., Paulson, L.C.: Lightweight relevance filtering for machine-generated resolution problems. J. Appl. Log. **7**(1), 41–57 (2009)

13. Nipkow, T., Wenzel, M., Paulson, L.C. (eds.): Isabelle/HOL. LNCS, vol. 2283. Springer, Heidelberg (2002). https://doi.org/10.1007/3-540-45949-9

14. Paulson, L.C., Blanchette, J.C.: Three years of experience with Sledgehammer, a practical link between automatic and interactive theorem provers. In: Sutcliffe, G., Schulz, S., Ternovska, E. (eds.) IWIL-2010. EPiC, vol. 2, pp. 1–11. EasyChair (2012)

15. Schulz, S.: E – a brainiac theorem prover. AI Commun. **15**(2–3), 111–126 (2002)
16. Slind, K., Norrish, M.: A brief overview of HOL4. In: Mohamed, O.A., Muñoz, C., Tahar, S. (eds.) TPHOLs 2008. LNCS, vol. 5170, pp. 28–32. Springer, Heidelberg (2008). https://doi.org/10.1007/978-3-540-71067-7_6
17. Sutcliffe, G.: The TPTP problem library and associated infrastructure – from CNF to TH0, TPTP v8.2.0. J. Autom. Reason. **59**(4), 483–502 (2017)
18. Vukmirović, P., Bentkamp, A., Blanchette, J., Cruanes, S., Nummelin, V., Tourret, S.: Making higher-order superposition work. In: Platzer, A., Sutcliffe, G. (eds.) CADE 2021. LNCS (LNAI), vol. 12699, pp. 415–432. Springer, Cham (2021). https://doi.org/10.1007/978-3-030-79876-5_24

The Dependently Typed Higher-Order Form for the TPTP World

Daniel Ranalter[1]($\boxtimes$)(iD), Cezary Kaliszyk[1,2](iD), Florian Rabe[3](iD), and Geoff Sutcliffe[4](iD)

[1] Computational Logic, University of Innsbruck, Innsbruck, Austria
d.ranalter@gmail.com
[2] School of Computing, University of Melbourne, Melbourne, Australia
ckaliszyk@unimelb.edu.au
[3] Computer Science, University of Erlangen-Nuremberg, Erlangen, Germany
florian.rabe@fau.de
[4] Department of Computer Science, University of Miami, Coral Gables, USA
geoff@cs.miami.edu

Abstract. Much of the current research and development in the field of automated reasoning builds on the infrastructure provided by the TPTP World. The TPTP language for logical formulae is central to the far-reaching adoption of the TPTP World. This paper introduces the Dependently Typed higher-order Form (DHF) of the TPTP language. It takes advantage of already established binders in the syntax, and is thus a minimally intrusive extension to the Typed Higher-order Form (THF). A starting set of over 100 problems is provided to exhibit the usefulness and incite interest in DHF. Some tools that are already able to reason about problems in the DHF language are discussed.

Keywords: Automated Theorem Proving · Dependent Types · Higher-Order Logic

1 Introduction

The TPTP World [31] is a well-established infrastructure that supports research, development, and deployment of Automated Theorem Proving (ATP) systems. The TPTP language [27] is one of the keys to the success of the TPTP World. It has variants that support uniform expression of logical formulae across a wide range of logics. The TPTP language is used for writing both problems and solutions, which enables convenient communication between ATP systems and tools. The majority of modern ATP systems accept input in TPTP syntax. The TPTP language variants that form the basis for this work are the monomorphic and polymorphic typed higher-order forms (TH0 and TH1) [8,32] (see Sect. 2.1 for the background and further variants).

All the existing typed TPTP language variants are *simply* typed. However, there is a steady increase of interest in *dependently* typed systems, such as

© The Author(s) 2026
R. Thiemann and C. Weidenbach (Eds.): FroCoS 2025, LNAI 15979, pp. 287–305, 2026.
https://doi.org/10.1007/978-3-032-04167-8_16

Agda [3], Rocq [1,37], and Lean [9]. This interest extends to the SMT community, where the proposed version 3.0 of SMT-LIB is to include dependent types[1]. Dependent types allow for the elegant formulation of complex data structures, possibly even a direct encoding of correctness properties. This paper introduces the Dependently Typed higher-order Form (DHF) of the TPTP language.

While dependent types are frequently used in interactive theorem proving, Automated Theorem Proving (ATP) has yet to embrace dependent types. Rothgang et al. made first steps towards bringing ATP and dependent types together, by introducing dependently typed higher-order logic (DHOL) [17,18]. With only two minor extensions to the familiar syntax of Church-style HOL [6], DHOL makes dependent types easily accessible: HOL base types are extended into dependent base types that can take term arguments, and the function type $A \to B$ is changed into a dependent function type $\Pi x : A.B$. Originally DHOL did not allow quantifying over types or stating the equality of types, but a polymorphic version is in development.

As in FOL and HOL, DHOL allows arbitrary axioms that may constrain equality of terms in undecidable ways, and consequently DHOL's type checking is undecidable (see Sect. 3.2). To manage this complication Rothgang et al. provide an algorithm that reduces the well-formedness of a statement to a set of proof obligations. Thus theorem proving is needed to check the well-formedness of a problem's formulae, not just to prove the conjecture. Happily, typically that does not make it harder to prove the conjecture. To increase ATP support for DHOL, Rothgang et al. define a translation from well-typed DHOL to HOL that preserves provability in both directions, thereby making DHOL available for regular HOL ATP systems, albeit without leveraging DHOL's dependent types for more efficient proving. Furthermore, the translation introduces additional axioms capturing the constraints of the dependent types, thereby potentially complicating proof search. Several interactive theorem provers had previously employed the same idea, sacrificing decidable typing to gain the expressivity of dependent types, while keeping the general feel of the language simple. Most importantly, PVS [12] essentially contains DHOL as a fragment, but extends it beyond the capabilities of current *automated* provers. Mizar [38], using soft typing on top of first-order set theory, can also capture DHOL-like features.

A detail missing from the original formulation of DHOL was the choice operator. Ranalter et al. investigated the effects of losing the non-emptiness constraint in DHOL on Hilbert's choice in [16]. To this end, they extended the – to the authors knowledge – first native implementation of DHOL into the ATP system Lash, by Niederhauser et al. [11]. Their experiments strongly suggest that native reasoning in DHOL significantly outperforms reasoning on translated problems.

This work describes how DHOL is being integrated into the TPTP World, in a new TPTP language variant "Dependently Typed higher-order Form" (DHF), with monomorphic and polymorphic subvariants (DT0 and DT1). DHF requires only very minor changes to the familiar TPTP language syntax, mostly using existing notions for binders and application operators, thereby providing the

---

[1] smt-lib.org/version3.

ATP community with the necessary foundations on which research into dependently typed automated reasoning can thrive. A set of over 100 problems in DHF, taken from several different sources, has been curated as an initial contribution to the TPTP problem library. The problems provide a spread of interesting formulations focusing on a variety of difficulty levels in proving the conjecture as well as in type checking.

Section 2 reviews the TPTP World and establishes the necessary background for DHOL, slightly generalizing the original DHOL definition to make it more suitable for TPTP. Section 3 introduces the new DHF form. Section 4 gives a short overview of the starting set of problems, and Sect. 5 introduces tools that already support the new form. Finally, Sect. 6 concludes and gives an outlook over future work.

2   Preliminaries

2.1   The TPTP World and Infrastructure

The TPTP World infrastructure includes the TPTP language [28], the TPTP problem library [25], the TSTP solution library [26], the SZS ontologies [24], the Specialist Problem Classes (SPCs) and problem difficulty ratings [29], SystemOnTPTP [23] and StarExec [22], and the CADE ATP System Competition (CASC) [30]. The problem library is a large collection of Thousands of Problems for Theorem Proving – hence the name. The problem library release v9.1.0 contains over 26000 problems from over 50 different domains, written in the TPTP language. The problems are categorized into Specialist Problem Classes according to their syntactic and logical status. The TSTP solution library is the result of running numerous ATP systems on the problems in that library and collecting their output. The TPTP and TSTP libraries provide the basis for assigning a difficulty rating to each problem, according to which ATP systems are able to solve the problem.

The most salient feature of the TPTP World for this work is the TPTP language. Originally the TPTP language supported only first-order clause normal form (CNF) [35]. Over time, more complex logics were added, starting with first-order form (FOF) in TPTP release v2.0.0 [25]. Releases v3.0.0 and v4.0.0 added monomorphic typed higher-order (TH0) [32] and monomorphic typed first-order (TF0) [34] forms to the mix respectively. These got extended to their polymorphic variants TF1 and TH1 in releases v5.0.0 [2] and v6.0.0 [8]. Release v7.0.0 of the TPTP started to include extended typed first-order form (TXF) [33] which extends the typed first-order form with conditionals, let expressions, and boolean terms. All the listed extensions to the TPTP are classical in nature. This changed with the addition of non-classical typed first-order form (NTF) in release v9.0.0 [21]. A general principle of the TPTP language is: "We provide the syntax, you provide the semantics". As such, there is no a priori commitment to any semantics for each of the language forms, although in almost all cases the intended logic and semantics are well known.

Problems and solutions are built from *annotated formulae* of the form

$$language(name,\ role,\ formula,\ source,\ useful\_info)$$

The *languages* supported are `cnf` (clause normal form), `fof` (first-order form), `tff` (typed first-order form), and `thf` (typed higher-order form). The *role*, e.g., `axiom`, `lemma`, `conjecture`, defines the use of the formula. In a *formula*, terms and atoms follow Prolog conventions – functions and predicates start with a lowercase letter or are 'single quoted', and variables start with an uppercase letter. The language also supports interpreted symbols that either start with a $, e.g., the truth constants `$true` and `$false`, or are composed of non-alphabetic characters, e.g., integer/rational/real numbers such as 27, 43/92, -99.66. The logical connectives in the TPTP language are `!>`, `?*`, `@+`, `@-`, `!`, `?`, `~`, `|`, `&`, `=>`, `<=`, `<=>`, and `<~>`, for the mathematical connectives Π, Σ, choice (indefinite description), definite description, $\forall$, $\exists$, $\neg$, $\vee$, $\wedge$, $\Rightarrow$, $\Leftarrow$, $\Leftrightarrow$, and $\oplus$ respectively. Equality and inequality are expressed as the infix operators `=` and `!=`. The *source* and *useful_info* are optional.

2.2   Dependently Typed Higher-Order Logic

Dependently typed higher-order logic (DHOL) is an extension of Church's higher-order logic (HOL) [6] introduced by Rothgang et al. [17]. It takes the widely supported HOL and equips it with dependent types, i.e., types that take term arguments. As such, it is a classical and extensional type theory, as opposed to the theory used in Rocq [1,37], Lean [9], or others [3,13] that rely on an intensional type theory. Notable exceptions to this trend are PVS [19], NuPRL [7], and F* [36].

The extensionality of DHOL comes at the cost of making type checking undecidable because it must consider term equality, which may be subject to arbitrary axioms. Essentially, typing becomes undecidable if a type depends on a type for which equality is undecidable. This is because type checking t against type $a\ n$ must be done by inferring the type of t, say $a\ m$, and then checking $a\ m = a\ n$, and thus $m = n$. If all dependent type symbols depend only on types for which equality is decidable (e.g., the examples below where we only use natural numbers with Presburger arithmetic), type checking is decidable. Otherwise, e.g., when using types depending on natural numbers with Peano arithmetic, type checking is undecidable.

The gain of having judgmental and provable equality coincide is significant: It positions DHOL much closer to how mathematics is usually done in the context of ATP. The availability of dependent types allows the elegant definition of data structures such as lists of fixed-length, intervals of numbers, or vector spaces over some field. It also allows encoding constraints in the types, which can remove the need for lengthy and error-prone guards in programming and track invariants useful for theorem proving. The cost – which might seem steep at first glance – is mitigated by the ever-increasing performance of ATP systems, and the fact that in many cases the proof obligations resulting from type checking are much simpler than the original proving problem.

The changes to the TPTP syntax to accommodate DHF are small: the definition of the simple base type is changed to a type that can accept term arguments, and the simple function type $A \to B$ is changed to $\Pi x : A.B$. This makes it possible to let the result type of the function depend on the specific term of the argument.

Figure 1 gives the grammar of DHOL. A dependent base type a with arity n is written $a : \Pi x_1 : A_1, \cdots, x_n : A_n.\text{type}$, and it is a *simple* base type if $n = 0$. Declarations of this form are part of the theory against which the type checking procedure is performed. In addition to base type declarations, theories may declare constant symbols c and axioms $\triangleright F$. A context specifies typed variables and assumptions. Contexts are superficially similar to theories, but denote *local* declarations, and as such, do not contain type declarations. $\circ$ and $\bullet$ denote the empty theory and context respectively. The order in a theory or context matters because the well-typedness of declarations might depend on preceding axioms. Types, as they appear in statements and typing judgements, are either fully applied base types, (dependent) function types, or classical booleans o. Terms are built from variables/constants, lambda abstraction, application, and the usual connectives and quantifiers. Regular HOL can be recovered by omitting the **highlighted** elements – this is exactly the case when the arity of all base types is 0.

$$
\begin{array}{llr}
T, U & ::= \circ \mid T,\, a : (\boldsymbol{\Pi x : A}.)^*\textbf{type} \mid T,\, c : A \mid T,\, \triangleright F & \text{theories} \\
\Gamma, \Delta & ::= \bullet \mid \Gamma,\, x : A \mid \Gamma,\, \triangleright F & \text{context} \\
A, B & ::= a\, \boldsymbol{t_1 \cdots t_n} \mid \Pi x : A.B \mid o & \text{types} \\
t, u, F, G & ::= x \mid c \mid \lambda x : A.t \mid t\, u \mid \forall x : A.F \mid \exists x : A.F \mid F \Rightarrow G & \\
& \quad \mid F \wedge G \mid F \vee G \mid \bot \mid \top \mid \neg F \mid t =_A u & \text{terms (incl. formulae } F, G)
\end{array}
$$

Fig. 1. The grammar of DHOL

The following example encodes the familiar notion of fixed-length lists. As prerequisites, we give the usual notion of natural numbers in a simple type nat and a simple type char of characters for the elements of the lists:

$$
\text{nat} : \text{type} \qquad 0 : \text{nat} \qquad \text{suc} : \text{nat} \to \text{nat} \qquad + : \text{nat} \to \text{nat} \to \text{nat}
$$

$$
\triangleright \forall n : \text{nat}.+\, 0\, n =_{\text{nat}} n \qquad \triangleright \forall n, m : \text{nat}.+\, (\text{suc}\, n)\, m =_{nat} \text{suc}\, (+\, n\, m)
$$

$$
\text{char} : \text{type} \qquad a : \text{char} \qquad b : \text{char} \qquad \ldots
$$

Then $\text{vec}\, n$ encodes the type of fixed-length lists of characters of length n:

$$
\text{vec} : \Pi n : \text{nat}.\text{type} \quad \text{nil} : \text{vec}\, 0 \quad \text{cons} : \Pi x : \text{nat}.\text{char} \to \text{vec}\, n \to \text{vec}\, (\text{suc}\, n)
$$

$$
++ : \Pi n, m : \text{nat}.\text{vec}\, n \to \text{vec}\, m \to \text{vec}\, (+\, n\, m)
$$

Dependent Connectives. In DHOL it is desirable to make the binary connectives conjunction, implication, and disjunction dependent in the sense that the well-formedness of the second argument may assume the truth (for conjunction and implication) or the falsity (for disjunction) of the first argument. Consider the statement $a =_A b \Rightarrow f\, a =_{B(a)} f\, b$. The well-formedness of the right-hand side requires the left-hand side as a premise. More precisely, $\Gamma \vdash F : o$ resp. $\Gamma \vdash F$ expresses that F is a well-formed resp. provable formula in context Γ. The definition of well-formed formulae is:

$$\Gamma \vdash F \Rightarrow G \quad \text{if} \quad \Gamma \vdash F \text{ and } \Gamma, \triangleright F \vdash G$$
$$\Gamma \vdash F \wedge G \quad \text{if} \quad \Gamma \vdash F \text{ and } \Gamma, \triangleright F \vdash G$$
$$\Gamma \vdash F \vee G \quad \text{if} \quad \Gamma \vdash F \text{ and } \Gamma, \triangleright \neg F \vdash G$$

where the **marked** parts make the connectives dependent. The usual natural deduction proof rules of implication and conjunction are the same as for the non-dependent versions. The proof rules for disjunction are adjusted as follows:

$$\frac{\Gamma \vdash F \quad \Gamma, \triangleright \neg F \vdash G : o}{\Gamma \vdash F \vee G} \qquad \frac{\Gamma, \triangleright \neg F \vdash G}{\Gamma \vdash F \vee G} \qquad \frac{\Gamma, \triangleright F \vdash C \quad \Gamma, \triangleright \neg F, \triangleright G \vdash C}{\Gamma, \triangleright F \vee G \vdash C}$$

As usual, it is possible to choose some connectives as primitives, from which the others are defined. Rothgang et al. choose equality and implication. Contrary to HOL, they included implication because they could not define the dependent binary connectives solely from equality. For the TPTP World, it is better not to choose primitive connectives – that choice should be left to the ATP system developers. Therefore DHF extends the work by Rothgang et al. to make all connectives primitive. ATP systems can choose which connectives to treat as abbreviations, but in doing so must take the dependent nature of the connectives into account. Note that dependent connectives break the commutativity of conjunction and disjunction. While seemingly disruptive, sacrificing commutativity in this way is common practice, e.g., for short-circuit evaluation of Boolean terms in programming languages. To clarify the impact on theorem proving, Table 1 summarizes typical proof rules for FOL and their status in DHOL. Roughly speaking, all rules that do not affect the order of subformulae remain sound, while the rest of the rules require the additional check to ensure the result remains well-formed. In particular, all rules needed to perform CNF or clause normal form transformations remain available.

Developing advanced calculi for DHOL is beyond the scope of this paper. However, for example, one way to generalize resolution is to store clauses as lists $[L_1, \ldots, L_n]$ where the well-formedness of each L_i may depend on $\neg L_j$ for $j < i$. Resolving $[A, \vec{L}]$ and $[\neg A, \vec{M}]$ to $[\vec{L}, \vec{M}]$ is sound if the resolvent is well-formed, i.e., if the well-formedness of the L_i resp. M_i does not depend on $\neg A$ resp. A.

Polymorphic DHOL. DHOL as presented in the previous section and [17] is monomorphic. ATP for polymorphic DHOL, as well as proofs of properties for such an extension of the calculus, is ongoing parallel work. Polymorphic logics are already available in the TPTP language, so it is natural to offer polymorphic DHF. All the polymorphic example problems considered so far use only

Table 1. Typical proof rules for FOL and their status in DHOL

Rule	Holds in DHOL
For disjunction and conjunction	
associativity	✓
commutativity	Only if both sides are well-formed
idempotence, e.g., $A \wedge X \wedge A \Leftrightarrow A \wedge X$	✓ (Drop the *second* occurrence)
de Morgan laws	✓
distributivity of one over the other	✓
absorption, e.g., $A \wedge (A \vee B) \Leftrightarrow A$	✓
For implication	
$A \Rightarrow B \Leftrightarrow \neg A \vee B$	✓
$\neg(A \Rightarrow B) \Leftrightarrow A \wedge \neg B$	✓
$\neg(A \Rightarrow B) \Leftrightarrow \neg B \Rightarrow \neg A$	Only if both sides are well-formed
For quantifiers and equality	
all rules	✓
Common calculus rules	
classical reasoning	✓
weakening	✓
contraction	✓ (Drop the *second* occurrence)
exchange	Only if still well-formed
cut	✓
resolution	Only if the clauses remain well-formed

shallow/rank-1 polymorphism in line with the existing polymorphic first- and higher-order forms for TPTP.

Choice. Hilbert's choice operator has been part of HOL since its inception by Church [6]. As such, it is natural to include it in DHOL. This introduces some complications: Due to the usual non-emptiness constraint on types, the semantics of choice are clear in HOL. However, DHOL no longer abides by this constraint, requiring a design decision that affects well-typedness and provability. Experiments done in [16] suggest that the variant of choice dubbed "strong choice" results in more efficient automated reasoning. The eponymous characteristic of strong choice is the requirement that $\exists x : A.t$ needs to be true for $(\varepsilon x : A.t) : A$ to be well-typed. Such a requirement for typing fits well with DHOL in general, and as ATP is the main concern this is the variant of choice, as it were. The problem set described in Sect. 4 includes some examples supporting this variant.

Translation. In order to take advantage of the ATP systems available for regular HOL, Rothgang et al. define a dependency-erasure [17], and thereby a translation from DHOL into regular HOL. They also prove that this translation is sound and complete for well-typed DHOL problems. Due to this result, and the implementation of the translation into the preprocessor of the Leo-III theorem prover [20], there existed reasoning support for DHOL even before native DHOL reasoning was implemented in the Lash ATP system by Niederhauser et al. [11]. Information lost due to the erasure of term dependencies is captured in Partial Equivalence Relations (PERs) – symmetric and transitive relations on pairs of terms – with the idea that the relation is reflexive exactly for those terms that were previously of the same dependent type. The translation is shown in Fig. 2. The translation $\bar{t}$ of a term t is defined inductively on the structure of the terms. The erasure of one type declaration results in three erased declarations: the erased type, the PER constant and an axioms stating it's properties. The definition of the erasure on $\forall$- and $\exists$-quantified terms is notable as it uses a PER as guard on the argument. To see why, note that, e.g., $\forall x : A.t$ can be defined in terms of equality as $\lambda x : A.t =_{A \to o} \lambda x : A.\top$. The erasure creates a PER from

theories   contexts

$$\overline{\bar{o}} = o \qquad\qquad \overline{\bullet} = \bullet$$

$$\overline{T, D} = \overline{T}, \overline{D} \qquad\qquad \overline{\Gamma, D} = \overline{\Gamma}, \overline{D}$$

$$\overline{c : A} = c : \overline{A}, \rhd A^* \, c \, c \qquad\qquad \overline{x : A} = x : \overline{A}, \rhd A^* \, x \, x$$

$$\overline{\rhd F} = \rhd \overline{F} \qquad\qquad \overline{\rhd F} = \rhd \overline{F}$$

$$\overline{a : \Pi x_1 : A_1. \, \cdots \, \Pi x_n : A_n. \, \textbf{type}} =$$

$$\qquad a \, \textbf{type}$$

$$\qquad a^* : \overline{A_1} \to \cdots \to \overline{A_n} \to a \to a \to o$$

$$\qquad \rhd \forall x_1 : \overline{A_1}. \, \cdots \forall x_n : \overline{A_n}. \, \forall u, v : a. \, a^* \, x_1 \, \cdots \, x_n \, u \, v \Rightarrow u =_a v$$

terms and types

$$\overline{\bar{c}} = c \qquad\qquad \overline{\bar{x}} = x$$

$$\overline{\bar{o}} = o \qquad\qquad \overline{a \, t_1 \, \ldots \, t_n} = a$$

$$\overline{\Pi x : A.B} = \overline{A} \to \overline{B} \qquad\qquad \overline{\lambda x : A.t} = \lambda x : \overline{A}. \, \bar{t}$$

$$\overline{\neg t} = \neg \bar{t} \qquad\qquad \overline{t \, u} = \bar{t} \, \bar{u}$$

$$\overline{t \Rightarrow u} = \bar{t} \Rightarrow \bar{u} \qquad\qquad \overline{t =_A u} = A^* \, \bar{t} \, \bar{u}$$

$$\overline{t \wedge u} = \bar{t} \wedge \bar{u} \qquad\qquad \overline{t \vee u} = \bar{t} \vee \bar{u}$$

$$\overline{\bot} = \bot \qquad\qquad \overline{\top} = \top$$

$$\overline{\forall x : A.t} = \forall x : \overline{A}. \, A^* \, x \, x \Rightarrow \bar{t} \qquad \overline{\exists x : A.t} = \exists x : \overline{A}. \, A^* \, x \, x \wedge \bar{t}$$

PER for each type

$$o^* \, t \, u = t =_o u$$

$$(a \, t_1 \, \ldots \, t_n)^* \, u \, v = a^* \, \overline{t_1} \, \cdots \, \overline{t_n} \, u \, v$$

$$(\Pi x : A.B)^* \, t \, u = \forall x, y : \overline{A}. \, A^* \, x \, y \Rightarrow B^*(t \, x)(u \, y)$$

Fig. 2. The translation from DHOL to HOL.

this typed equality with the guarded input in the premise, and the erased term in the consequence of the implication as seen in the erasure of $\forall$.

As an example of erasure, consider the list of chars [a, b], represented by a term cons 1 a (cons 0 b nil) of type vec 2, where $0, \text{suc } 0, \text{suc } (\text{suc } 0), \ldots$ is abbreviated as $0, 1, 2, \ldots$. Applying the erasure gives cons a (cons b nil) of type vec. A predicate would be generated, establishing that this particular list is in the PER of vectors of length 2: $\text{vec}^* \ 2 \ t \ t$ where t stands for cons a (cons b nil). While one might think that unary predicates would be sufficient as a type guard, PERs becomes necessary to express the typing and equality of higher-order functions: functions are well-typed if they map well-typed inputs to well-typed outputs, and they are equal if they agree on well-typed inputs.

3 DHF

After establishing the theoretic background, this section presents the realization of DHOL in the TPTP language. Syntax and semantics are given, as well as an exposition to the problem of type checking.

3.1 Syntax

The syntax of DHF requires almost no change to the existing TPTP syntax. The TPTP language already defines the !> binder for types. In the typed TPTP language variants it is currently used for only polymorphism, e.g.,

```
cons : !>[A: $tType]: ( A > ( list @ A ) > ( list @ A ) )
```

is a type declaration for a polymorphic cons. The TPTP syntax does not forbid listing terms in the types of such variable lists. This fact is used to unobtrusively extend TPTP by dependent types. A dependent type symbol declaration is written with m terms of n types as

$$a \ : \ !>[x_1 : A_1, \ \ldots, \ x_m : A_n]:\$tType$$

or alternatively

$$a \ : \ A_1 > \ldots > A_n > \$tType.$$

Such types use the application operator @, to instantiate the terms to the dependent type:

$$a @ t_1 @ \ldots @ t_m.$$

In polymorphic problems, the variable list is prepended with the type variables, which may appear in the same binder. An example of a problem in DHF is shown in Fig. 3.

```
thf(elem_type,type,     elem: $tType ).
thf(nat_type,type,      nat: $tType ).
thf(zero_type,type,     zero: nat ).
thf(suc_type,type,      suc: nat > nat ).
thf(plus_type,type,     plus: nat > nat > nat ).
thf(list_type,type,     list: nat > $tType ).
thf(nil_type,type,      nil: list @ zero ).
thf(cons_type,type,     cons:
      !>[N: nat] : (elem > (list @ N) > (list @ (suc @ N))) ).
thf(app_type,type,      app:
      !>[N: nat,M: nat] : ((list @ N) > (list @ M) >
                            (list @ (plus @ N @ M))) ).

thf(ax1,axiom,
    ! [N: nat] : ((plus @ zero @ N) = N) ).

thf(ax2,axiom,
    ! [N: nat,X: list @ N] : ((app @ zero @ N @ nil @ X) = X) ).

thf(plus_assoc,axiom,
      ! [M1: nat,M2: nat,M3: nat] :
      ( (plus @ M1 @ (plus @ M2 @ M3))
      = (plus @ ( plus @ M1 @ M2) @ M3)) ).

thf(list_app_assoc_base,conjecture,
      ! [M2: nat,L2: list @ M2,M3: nat,L3: list @ M3] :
      ( (app @ zero @ (plus @ M2 @ M3) @ nil @
          (app @ M2 @ M3 @ L2 @ L3))
      = (app @ (plus @ zero @ M2) @ M3 @
          (app @ zero @ M2 @ nil @ L2) @ L3)) ).
```

Fig. 3. The base case of associativity of append on fixed-length lists.

3.2   Type Checking

Due to equality reflection, type checking for DHOL is, in general, undecidable. Nevertheless, problems need to be well-typed, otherwise the translation outlined in Sect. 2.2 might not be sound. Type checking in DHF thus takes on a larger role than in other logics in the TPTP World.

While performing the usual type checking procedure in DHOL, obligations of the form $a\ t_1 \cdots t_n \equiv a\ u_1 \cdots u_n$, are generated. These establish equality of the dependent base types applied to arguments $t_1 \cdots t_n, u_1 \cdots u_n$ of appropriate types. The type equality holds if all pairs t_i, u_i are equal, which depends on the available axioms. This can create interesting situations where a problem must include axioms that are not necessary for proving the conjecture itself, but are necessary for type checking it. The common example of fixed-length lists is one such example: the statement of the associativity of append is well-typed only if addition on nat is associative, and thus requires including the defining equations of addition. To prove the problem only the defining equations of appending lists are needed.

The undecidability of type checking can lead to compromises. One such compromise is "shallow type checking". When a problem file is shallowly checked, only the simply typed skeleton of the problem is considered, i.e., term arguments to types as well as dependent functions are ignored. This collapses to type checking as is done on non-dependently typed problems, and is decidable. This form of type checking is sufficient to catch many careless mistakes in the formulation of problems, and provides a basic check of issues often found in human-written DHOL problems. Examples are: mismatches in the number of arguments of a base type or function, and egregious type mismatches. Shallow type checking provides a valuable sanity check for users, especially considering the complexity that problems in DHOL forms can reach.

3.3 Semantics

As for HOL, there are two kinds of semantics for DHOL: standard models are intuitive and are the ones that are usually used; non-standard (Henkin) models are a generalization that is needed for completeness. A full account is given in the forthcoming [15], which is summarized below. The rules of DHOL, as given by Rothgang et al., already define which formulae are theorems.

Standard Models. Given a theory T, a standard model $M \in [\![T]\!]$ is a tuple providing an interpretation for every declaration in T. Similarly, given a context Γ, an assignment $\alpha \in [\![\Gamma]\!]^M$ for Γ is a tuple providing an interpretation for every declaration in Γ. These induce the interpretation function $[\![-]\!]_\alpha^M$ (with α omitted if the context is empty), which is defined inductively for all the syntax. In particular, the possible components of a model are defined by induction on declarations:

- For a type symbol with arguments $\Gamma = x_1 : A_1, \ldots, x_n : A_n$, a function $[\![\Gamma]\!]^M \to \mathcal{SET}$
- For a term symbol $c : A$, a value from $[\![A]\!]^M$
- For an axiom $\triangleright F$, a unique choice $\checkmark$ if $[\![M]\!]^F = 1$, and no choice otherwise

  For the components of an assignment:

- For a term variable $x : A$, a value from $[\![A]\!]_\alpha^M$
- For an assumption $\triangleright F$, a unique choice $\checkmark$ if $[\![M]\!]_\alpha^F = 1$, and no choice otherwise

For types and terms, the model is defined by induction in the usual way, in particular

- $[\![o]\!]_\alpha^M = \{0, 1\}$
- $[\![\Pi x : A.B]\!]_\alpha^M$ is the set of functions f mapping every $u \in [\![A]\!]_\alpha^M$ to some $f(u) \in [\![B]\!]_{\alpha^u}^M$ where α^u extends α with the value u for x

General Models. The definition of general models generalizes the Henkin models from HOL by applying methods from categorical models of type theory. First, akin to assignments for Γ, substitutions $\gamma : \Gamma \rightarrow \Delta$ as lists of terms or $\checkmark$ by induction on Γ are defined:

- For a term variable $x : A$, a term of type $\Delta \vdash A[\gamma]$
- For an assumption $\rhd F$, the unique choice $\checkmark$ if $\Delta \vdash F[\gamma]$, and no choice otherwise

Equality of contexts and substitutions is defined by applying the existing equality judgments for types and terms component-wise. For every theory T, this yields the syntactic category $\overline{\overline{[T]}}$ of T-contexts and substitutions. A general model is then defined as any pushout-preserving contravariant functor $\Phi : \overline{\overline{[T]}} \rightarrow \mathcal{SET}$. From such a Φ, an interpretation function is extracted using $\Phi(x : A)$ as the interpretation of the type A and $\Phi(t)$ as the interpretation of the term $t : A$ (seen as a substitution $x : A \rightarrow \bullet$). These general models must further satisfy $\Phi(o) = \{0,1\}$, and $\Phi \models F$ is defined as $\Phi(F) = 1$. Here the pushout-preservation essentially corresponds to the preservation of substitution, i.e., interpretation and substitution commute. The lack of any preservation of exponentials allows for a *non-compositional* interpretation of function types. This approach can be seen as a generalization of Henkin models, which also preserve substitution but do not need to interpret function types compositionally. Contrary to Henkin models, the interpretation of λ and application terms can also be non-compositional in these general models as long as substitution is preserved.

Models for Polymorphic DHOL. As mentioned above, a rank-1 polymorphic variant of DHOL is being developed in parallel work. It is straightforward to extend standard models to polymorphic DHOL. The syntax of binding a type variable corresponds to abstracting over an arbitrary set on the semantic side. In particular, the interpretation of a polymorphic term/type symbol with n type variables takes n sets as arguments. Polymorphic axioms correspond to universal quantification over sets. The definition of syntactic category and general models is expected to carry over to polymorphic DHOL as well. This has not been investigated in detail.

4   Problem Dataset

Over 100 problems in DHF format have been collected for addition to the TPTP problem library. Their classification is presented in Table 2 and discussed here (with 36 problems just for testing DHOL prover features omitted). The number of problems in each class is given in the last column. The problems concern several domains that can benefit from dependent types. While [17] shows DHOL to be sound and complete, the strength of the existing automation for this foundation (discussed in Sect. 5) still needs to be improved. For this reason, some of the harder problems were broken down into simpler subproblems that can be proven independently. Some list properties that require both induction and reasoning with dependent types are an instance of this. For example, the fact that list append is associative, `ListAppAssoc`, is split into three subproblems, showing the particular induction scheme, the proof of the base case, and the step case. These three subproblems are easier to prove than their combined version, which is also included. Some problems benefit from intermediate lemmas, e.g. the instantiation of the inductive step case. These are found in the "Lemmas" categories of Table 2.

One of the simplest classes of examples are lists that depend on their length (also called vectors, for example in the Rocq library). As the list libraries of most interactive theorem provers are substantial, it is relatively easy to experiment with many properties of dependently typed lists. Such properties include the aforementioned associativity of `append`, corollaries of this statement, or involution statements about the `reverse` function. Some of these list examples are extended to their polymorphic generalizations, which are in the "Polymorphic" categories.

The idea of expressing well-known but sometimes challenging properties extends to several other algebraic data types, such as matrices that have fixed dimensions, and lists of lists. Red-black trees are a well-known data structure for balanced trees where the invariant can be expressed using dependent types, and again several problems concerning this type are included. The `Fin` type present in several proof libraries has been manually recreated, and some problems about these are in the ROCQ category of Table 2. The collection includes the five examples from category theory that were originally presented in [17], slightly reformatted to match the TPTP syntax. To make use of the choice operator [16], several problems about dependent higher-order Skolemization are included. Choice is also used in a function definition with no fixed point, and conjectures establishing this are presented in the "no FP" category. Finally, several simple tests to evaluate the ability of provers to perform native DHOL inferences are provided.

Some of the dependent HOL problems are more interesting from a proof perspective – the deep type checking is there only to make sure the problem is well-formed. For example, for all the dependent list problems, the type checking obligations are there mostly to make sure no incorrect calls are being made, but they are relatively straightforward to discharge. It is the proof that requires more logical reasoning. Other problems, while relatively straightforward in terms of proving, are harder to type check. This is because it is possible to use dependent types to encode important properties and invariants in the type system.

5   Tools

This section discusses the tools capable of processing problems in DHF format.

Table 2. The categories of the DHF problems.

Problem Type	Problem Category	Problem Count
Monomorphic Complete	Category theory	5
	Choice basic	11
	Choice list	3
	Choice no fixed point	10
	List app assoc	3
	List app assoc corollary	1
	List app nil	4
	List of lists	1
	List reversal involution	1
	List reversal inv lemma	3
	Matrices	5
	ROCQ	3
Monomorphic Lemmas	Choice no fixed point	10
	List app assoc	5
	List app assoc corollary	5
	List reversal involution	5
	List reversal inv lemma	11
Polymorphic Complete	List app assoc poly	3
	List app nil poly	4
	List reversal involution poly	1
	Red-black tree	3
Polymorphic Lemmas	List app assoc poly	14
	List reversal involution poly	13
	Red-black tree	9

5.1 The Logic Embedding Tool

The Leo-III [20] prover includes the *Logic Embedding Tool*, which has been extended to support polymorphic DHF. The tool implements the erasure presented in Sect. 2.2, and incorporates the polymorphic extension. The tool can generate both the type checking obligations and the translated problem separately. This makes it possible to translate DHF problems into THF problems (that do not have dependent types). The embedding tool is available as NTFLET in SystemB4TPTP[2]. The embedding tool enables the use of existing higher-order ATP systems for solving DHF problems, by pipelining the output from NTFLET to a THF ATP system of the user's choosing. This has been implemented as the DT2H2X ATP systems, available in SystemOnTPTP[3].

---

[2] tptp.org/cgi-bin/SystemB4TPTP.
[3] tptp.org/cgi-bin/SystemOnTPTP.

5.2   DLash

The Lash prover [5] is a partial reimplementation of the tableaux calculus of Satallax [4], using a central term representation with perfect sharing. This design facilitated the implementation of the DLash extension of Lash, which handles DHF [11]. In addition to the erasure implementation, DLash can process monomorphic dependently typed higher-order logic with choice. As with the Logic Embedding Tool, type checking and proving can be requested separately. DLash, like Satallax, includes a strategy language used to build so-called modes. The current version includes 36 dedicated modes for dependent types, tailored to specific problem types. DLash is available in SystemOnTPTP[4].

5.3   MMT

MMT [14] is a logical framework designed to formalize and manage large collections of interconnected formal systems and their libraries, using modular theory graphs. A particular application of MMT is rapid prototyping [10], and it was the tool originally used to develop and prototype DHOL. The MMT/DHOL implementation offers reconstruction of omitted types and implicit arguments as well as parsing against user-defined notations. It can be used to interactively author and type check DHOL problems and export them in TPTP format. It uses the PER translation, and calls the Leo-III prover to discharge the resulting proof obligations. MMT is mostly useful for developing formalizations, rather than proving TPTP conjectures. Therefore, it does not provide a TPTP import at this point, but provides additional evidence of the well-typedness DHF problems.

5.4   TPTP Systems

As discussed in Sect. 2.1, TPTP includes several generic tools capable of processing problems and solutions. For DHF problems:

- TPTP4X pretty-prints DHF problems and solutions, and offers various transformations/augmentations of problems.
- BNFParser produces the abstract syntax tree from parsing a DHF problem.
- Leo-III-STC validates the syntax and types of DHF problems.
- ProblemStats outputs various syntactic measures for problems.

All these tools are available in SystemB4TPTP[5] For DHF proofs:

- ProofStats outputs various syntactic measures for DAG-structured proofs.
- IDV provides interactive viewing of proofs from DHF problems.

All these tools are available in SystemOnTSTP[6].

---

[4] tptp.org/cgi-bin/SystemOnTPTP.
[5] tptp.org/cgi-bin/SystemB4TPTP.
[6] tptp.org/cgi-bin/SystemOnTSTP.

6   Conclusion

This paper has described DHF, the dependently typed higher-order form of the TPTP language. It responds to the growing interest in dependently typed automated reasoning as exemplified by the number of TPTP problems and tools that have cropped up in the short time since DHOL was first described. It can be seen as pushing the boundary of automated theorem proving towards language features that have previously been found only in interactive provers.

DHOL problems sometimes used differing standards, which defeated the uniformity advantage that the TPTP language provides. This work unifies them, and provides over a 100 problems from different domains, benefiting from the use of dependent types. We hope that the availability of dependent types in the TPTP will stimulate research into dependently typed automated theorem proving, by making it easier to exchange and compare results. Extending existing systems with support for DHF, and improving the performance of the systems that already exist, will be important next steps. In particular, the extension of superposition-based theorem proving to dependent types is a tantalizing goal.

Acknowledgements. The authors thank Johannes Niederhauser and Colin Rothgang for granting access to their DHOL problems that are in the problem dataset. This work was supported by the ERC PoC grant no. 101156734 "FormalWeb3".

References

1. Bertot, Y., Castéran, P.: Interactive Theorem Proving and Program Development: Coq'Art: The Calculus of Inductive Constructions. Springer, Cham (2004)
2. Blanchette, J.C., Paskevich, A.: TFF1: the TPTP typed first-order form with rank-1 polymorphism. In: Bonacina, M.P. (ed.) CADE 2013. LNCS (LNAI), vol. 7898, pp. 414–420. Springer, Heidelberg (2013). https://doi.org/10.1007/978-3-642-38574-2_29
3. Bove, A., Dybjer, P., Norell, U.: A brief overview of Agda – a functional language with dependent types. In: Berghofer, S., Nipkow, T., Urban, C., Wenzel, M. (eds.) TPHOLs 2009. LNCS, vol. 5674, pp. 73–78. Springer, Heidelberg (2009). https://doi.org/10.1007/978-3-642-03359-9_6
4. Brown, C.E.: Satallax: an automatic higher-order prover. In: Gramlich, B., Miller, D., Sattler, U. (eds.) IJCAR 2012. LNCS (LNAI), vol. 7364, pp. 111–117. Springer, Heidelberg (2012). https://doi.org/10.1007/978-3-642-31365-3_11
5. Brown, C.E., Kaliszyk, C.: Lash 1.0 (system description). In: Blanchette, J., Kovács, L., Pattinson, D. (eds.) Automated Reasoning. LNAI, vol. 13385, pp. 350–358. Springer, Cham (2022). https://doi.org/10.1007/978-3-031-10769-6_21
6. Church, A.: A formulation of the simple theory of types. J. Symb. Log. **5**(2), 56–68 (1940). https://doi.org/10.2307/2266170
7. Constable, R., et al.: Implementing Mathematics with the Nuprl Development System. Prentice-Hall (1986)
8. Kaliszyk, C., Sutcliffe, G., Rabe, F.: TH1: the TPTP typed higher-order form with rank-1 polymorphism. In: Fontaine, P., Schulz, S., Urban, J. (eds.) Proceedings 5th Workshop on Practical Aspects of Automated Reasoning. CEUR Workshop

Proceedings, vol. 1635, pp. 41–55. CEUR-WS.org (2016). https://ceur-ws.org/Vol-1635/paper-05.pdf

9. de Moura, L., Ullrich, S.: The lean 4 theorem prover and programming language. In: Platzer, A., Sutcliffe, G. (eds.) CADE 2021. LNCS (LNAI), vol. 12699, pp. 625–635. Springer, Cham (2021). https://doi.org/10.1007/978-3-030-79876-5_37

10. Müller, D., Rabe, F.: Rapid prototyping formal systems in MMT: case studies. In: Miller, D., Scagnetto, I. (eds.) Logical Frameworks and Meta-languages: Theory and Practice, pp. 40–54 (2019)

11. Niederhauser, J., Brown, C.E., Kaliszyk, C.: Tableaux for automated reasoning in dependently-typed higher-order logic. In: Benzmüller, C., Heule, M.J.H., Schmidt, R.A. (eds.) Automated Reasoning. LNAI, pp. 86–104. Springer, Cham (2024). https://doi.org/10.1007/978-3-031-63498-7_6

12. Owre, S., Shankar, N.: The formal semantics of PVS. Technical report. SRI-CSL-97-2, SRI International (1997)

13. Pfenning, F., Schürmann, C.: System description: Twelf — a meta-logical framework for deductive systems. In: CADE 1999. LNCS (LNAI), vol. 1632, pp. 202–206. Springer, Heidelberg (1999). https://doi.org/10.1007/3-540-48660-7_14

14. Rabe, F.: A modular type reconstruction algorithm. ACM Trans. Comput. Log. **19**(4), 1–43 (2018)

15. Rabe, F.: Model theory for dependently-typed higher-order logic (2024). Under review, see https://kwarc.info/people/frabe/Research/rabe_dholmodels_24.pdf

16. Ranalter, D., Brown, C.E., Kaliszyk, C.: Experiments with choice in dependently-typed higher-order logic. In: Bjørner, N.S., Heule, M., Voronkov, A. (eds.) Proceedings 25th International Conference on Logic for Programming, Artificial Intelligence and Reasoning. EPiC Series in Computing, vol. 100, pp. 311–320. EasyChair (2024). https://doi.org/10.29007/2V8H

17. Rothgang, C., Rabe, F., Benzmüller, C.: Theorem proving in dependently-typed higher-order logic. In: Pientka, B., Tinelli, C. (eds.) Automated Deduction. LNAI, vol. 14132, pp. 438–455. Springer, Cham (2023). https://doi.org/10.1007/978-3-031-38499-8_25

18. Rothgang, C., Rabe, F., Benzmüller, C.: Dependently-typed higher-order logic – extended preprint (2025). https://doi.org/10.48550/arXiv.2305.15382, under review

19. Rushby, J., Owre, S., Shankar, N.: Subtypes for specifications: predicate subtyping in PVS. IEEE Trans. Softw. Eng. **24**(9), 709–720 (1998). https://doi.org/10.1109/32.713327

20. Steen, A., Benzmüller, C.: Extensional higher-order paramodulation in Leo-III. J. Autom. Reason. **65**(6), 775–807 (2021). https://doi.org/10.1007/s10817-021-09588-x

21. Steen, A., Fuenmayor, D., Gleißner, T., Sutcliffe, G., Benzmüller, C.: Automated reasoning in non-classical logics in the TPTP world. In: Konev, B., Schon, C., Steen, A. (eds.) Proceedings of the 8th Workshop on Practical Aspects of Automated Reasoning. CEUR Workshop Proceedings, vol. 3201. CEUR-WS.org (2022). https://ceur-ws.org/Vol-3201/paper11.pdf

22. Stump, A., Sutcliffe, G., Tinelli, C.: StarExec: a cross-community infrastructure for logic solving. In: Demri, S., Kapur, D., Weidenbach, C. (eds.) IJCAR 2014. LNCS (LNAI), vol. 8562, pp. 367–373. Springer, Cham (2014). https://doi.org/10.1007/978-3-319-08587-6_28

23. Sutcliffe, G.: System description: SystemOnTPTP. In: McAllester, D. (ed.) CADE 2000. LNCS (LNAI), vol. 1831, pp. 406–410. Springer, Heidelberg (2000). https://doi.org/10.1007/10721959_31

24. Sutcliffe, G.: The SZS ontologies for automated reasoning software. In: Sutcliffe, G., Rudnicki, P., Schmidt, R., Konev, B., Schulz, S. (eds.) Proceedings of the LPAR Workshops: Knowledge Exchange: Automated Provers and Proof Assistants, and the 7th International Workshop on the Implementation of Logics, no. 418, pp. 38–49. CEUR Workshop Proceedings (2008)

25. Sutcliffe, G.: The TPTP problem library and associated infrastructure. The FOF and CNF parts, v3.5.0. J. Autom. Reason. **43**(4), 337–362 (2009)

26. Sutcliffe, G.: The TPTP world – infrastructure for automated reasoning. In: Clarke, E.M., Voronkov, A. (eds.) LPAR 2010. LNCS (LNAI), vol. 6355, pp. 1–12. Springer, Heidelberg (2010). https://doi.org/10.1007/978-3-642-17511-4_1

27. Sutcliffe, G.: The logic languages of the TPTP world. Logic J. IGPL **31**(6), 1153–1169 (2023)

28. Sutcliffe, G., Schulz, S., Claessen, K., Van Gelder, A.: Using the TPTP language for writing derivations and finite interpretations. In: Furbach, U., Shankar, N. (eds.) IJCAR 2006. LNCS (LNAI), vol. 4130, pp. 67–81. Springer, Heidelberg (2006). https://doi.org/10.1007/11814771_7

29. Sutcliffe, G., Suttner, C.: Evaluating general purpose automated theorem proving systems. Artif. Intell. **131**(1–2), 39–54 (2001). https://doi.org/10.1016/S0004-3702(01)00113-8

30. Sutcliffe, G.: The CADE ATP system competition - CASC. AI Mag. **37**(2), 99–101 (2016). https://doi.org/10.1609/AIMAG.V37I2.2620

31. Sutcliffe, G.: Stepping stones in the TPTP world. In: Benzmüller, C., Heule, M.J., Schmidt, R.A. (eds.) IJCAR 2024. LNCS, vol. 14739, pp. 30–50. Springer, Cham (2024). https://doi.org/10.1007/978-3-031-63498-7_3

32. Sutcliffe, G., Benzmüller, C.: Automated reasoning in higher-order logic using the TPTP THF infrastructure. J. Autom. Reason. **3**(1), 1–27 (2010). https://doi.org/10.6092/ISSN.1972-5787/1710

33. Sutcliffe, G., Kotelnikov, E.: TFX: the TPTP extended typed first-order form. In: Konev, B., Urban, J., Rümmer, P. (eds.) Proceedings of the 6th Workshop on Practical Aspects of Automated Reasoning. CEUR Workshop Proceedings, vol. 2162, pp. 72–87. CEUR-WS.org (2018). https://ceur-ws.org/Vol-2162/paper-07.pdf

34. Sutcliffe, G., Schulz, S., Claessen, K., Baumgartner, P.: The TPTP typed first-order form with arithmetic. In: Bjørner, N., Voronkov, A. (eds.) LPAR 2012. LNCS, vol. 7180, pp. 406–419. Springer, Heidelberg (2012). https://doi.org/10.1007/978-3-642-28717-6_32

35. Sutcliffe, G., Suttner, C.B.: The TPTP problem library - CNF release v1.2.1. J. Autom. Reason. **21**(2), 177–203 (1998). https://doi.org/10.1023/A:1005806324129

36. Swamy, N., et al.: Dependent types and multi-monadic effects in F*. In: Bodik, R., Majumdar, R. (eds.) Proceedings of the 43rd Annual ACM SIGPLAN-SIGACT Symposium on Principles of Programming Languages, pp. 256–270 (2016). https://doi.org/10.1145/2837614.2837655

37. The Rocq Development Team: The Rocq reference manual – release 9.0.0 (2024). https://coq.inria.fr/doc/V9.0.0/refman

38. Trybulec, A., Blair, H.: Computer assisted reasoning with MIZAR. In: Joshi, A. (ed.) Proceedings of the 9th International Joint Conference on Artificial Intelligence, pp. 26–28. Morgan Kaufmann (1985)

Context-Aware Clause Selection Using Symbol Name Meanings in Theorem Proving

Claudia Schon$^{(\boxtimes)}$ (iD)

Trier University of Applied Sciences, Trier, Germany
c.schon@hochschule-trier.de

Abstract. When humans evaluate the validity of a logical conclusion, they naturally consider its meaning and its context, allowing them to focus on relevant information and to avoid unnecessary inferences. For example, when asked to prove that all *hammocks* are also *beds*, they will certainly not draw conclusions about *vehicles* or *weapons*. In contrast, automated theorem provers typically do not account for the contextual meaning of a conclusion when selecting inference steps. Existing heuristics for selecting the clause for the next inference step usually ignore the meaning of symbol names, overlooking valuable contextual information. As a result, in the example above, clauses with symbol names such as *weapon* or *vehicle* could well be found in the processed clauses. However, since these clauses are not required for the actual proof, they are not helpful to the prover and tend to distract from the actual proof task. In this paper, we present an approach that uses natural language processing techniques to align the selection of the clause for the next inference step with the meaning of the proof goal. Our implementation and experimental results show that this method not only increases the number of successful proofs but also reduces the number of clauses processed during proof search.

Keywords: Commonsense Reasoning · Commonsense Knowledge · Clause Selection

1 Introduction

When humans evaluate the validity of a logical conclusion, they naturally consider the context and meaning of the conclusion and avoid irrelevant inferences. This intuitive approach is in line with Daniel Kahneman's model of human cognition based on two systems [13], where system 1 represents fast, instinctive and contextual thinking, while system 2 involves slower, more deliberate and logical reasoning. In the field of automated theorem proving (ATP), current systems such as E [28] and Vampire [23] predominantly use logic-based approaches similar to system 2, usually not using the contextual insights corresponding to system 1.

© The Author(s) 2026
R. Thiemann and C. Weidenbach (Eds.): FroCoS 2025, LNAI 15979, pp. 306–323, 2026.
https://doi.org/10.1007/978-3-032-04167-8_17

For example, a human being asked to prove that all *hammocks* are also *beds* will intuitively avoid considering unrelated concepts such as *vehicles* or *weapons*. Conversely, automated theorem provers typically do not consider the contextual relevance of symbol names when selecting inference steps. Existing heuristics focus on syntactic properties without exploiting the semantic content embedded in symbol names, which can lead to the inclusion of irrelevant clauses and an inefficient proof process.

It is a key strength of human reasoning that we are able to combine both intuitive (system 1) and analytical (system 2) processes. It is therefore plausible that automated theorem proving could similarly benefit from integrating these two approaches, using the contextual understanding of system 1 alongside the logical strictness of system 2. Currently, however, the meaning of symbol names, and thus the contextual content of formulae, is not taken into account during proof search in automated reasoning.

To address this gap, we integrate statistical methods from natural language processing into the reasoning process to improve the selection of the clause for the next inference step of a theorem prover. We do this by mapping symbol names to natural language words and representing them as vectors. This allows us to measure the semantic similarity between symbols and the goal of the proof. These similarities are used to derive symbol weights, which guide the selection of the clause for the next inference step in a goal-directed way.

Our approach has been implemented and evaluated using the E theorem prover [28]. Experimental results demonstrate that taking the meaning of symbol names into account enables the prover to find more proofs. In addition, the experiments also show a reduction in the number of clauses processed during proof search, indicating a more focused and efficient proof process. This work highlights the potential of combining logic-based and statistical methods to improve automated reasoning, in line with Kahneman's theory.

The main contributions of this paper are:

– The introduction of a heuristic for determining symbol weights based on similarity to the proof goal. These weights can be used to guide the selection of the clause for the next inference step in automated theorem proving.
– An evaluation of the approach, demonstrating that taking the meaning of symbols names into account enables the prover to find more proofs and to reduce the number of clauses processed during proof search for commonsense reasoning tasks.

The paper is structured as follows: after discussing related work (Sect. 2) and preliminaries (Sect. 3), we describe how to determine symbol weights based on the similarity of the symbol names to the proof goal in Sect. 4. In Sect. 5 we present experimental results of our approach. Finally, we summarize and discuss ideas for future work in Sect. 6. This paper is a revised and extended version of our previous workshop paper [27].

2   Related Work

The selection of the clause for the next inference step has a very large influence on the performance of theorem provers. A perfect selection can make a search unnecessary, and a proof can be found directly. Most heuristics for selecting the clause for the next inference step are based on simple counting of symbols and the like [29]. In this way, weights are specified for symbols and then used to determine weights for clauses, which are used to select the clause for the next inference step.

The theorem prover E [28] allows assigning custom weights to individual symbols, enabling fine-grained control over symbol-based heuristics. This can be done by specifying a weight function with `FunWeight`[1]. Although this option allows you to set symbol weights, it does not describe how to determine them.

In [5], the selection of symbol weights is investigated. The proposed approach employs a graph neural network to predict symbol weights based on the structure of the clause normal form of the input problem. The system is trained using prior proof successes, and a novel scheme is introduced to balance positive clauses (derived from a proof) and negative clauses (not derived from a proof) during training.

Another approach is to use machine learning to derive new clause selection strategies from successful proofs [6].

The ENIGMA [10–12,32] method represents a key advancement in internal guidance within ATPs by integrating machine learning models directly into the theorem proving process to influence decisions such as clause selection. Utilizing techniques like gradient-boosted trees and recursive neural networks, ENIGMA has significantly enhanced the performance of saturation-based provers like E, particularly in large-theory settings like the Mizar Mathematical Library [4].

To the best of our knowledge, none of the currently used approaches to determining symbol weights take into account the meaning of symbol names.

The problem of premise selection, where relevant formulae for a given proof task have to be selected from a knowledge base, is related to the problem considered in this paper. Especially in the area of large mathematical libraries, there are many approaches to premise selection that rely on machine learning methods [1]. The ATP$_{BOOST}$ method improves premise selection by framing it as a binary classification task and using the XGBoost algorithm. DeepMath [9] uses neural networks for premise selection. It is worth noting that DeepMath does not use manually created features. Another notable technique uses recurrent neural networks to capture dependencies between premises [21]. In addition, the work in [22] applies the transformer architecture to premise selection, achieving superior performance compared to earlier recurrent neural network-based methods. Similarly, the transformer-based Magnushammer [16] shows significant improvements in detection success rates through effective retrieval and ranking of relevant premises.

---

[1] See the manual of E for details: https://wwwlehre.dhbw-stuttgart.de/~sschulz/WORK/E_DOWNLOAD/V_2.4/eprover.pdf.

The Semantic Web [24] is one domain where the significance of symbol names has been assessed, revealing that the semantics embedded in the names of IRIs (Internationalized Resource Identifiers) reflect a type of social semantics that aligns with the formal meaning of the referenced resource.

Regarding premise selection in commonsense knowledge bases, there are a few approaches that consider the meaning of symbol names. One such approach is Similarity SInE [8], an extension of SInE selection that uses word embeddings to account for symbol similarity. Similarity SInE ensures that all the formulae selected by SInE are included, and additionally selects formulae for symbols that are similar to those appearing in the goal. Furthermore, [26] introduces a vector-based technique for premise selection which uses a word embedding to vectorize the formulae of a knowledge base and to use vector similarity for selection purposes. The SeVEn [19] selection takes the idea of vectorizing a knowledge base one step further by using a large language model for the vectorization step. These three methods take into account the meaning of the symbol names, but they are not used to select the clause for the next inference step.

We are not aware of any approaches that use the meaning of symbols to select the clause to be used in the next reasoning step.

3   Preliminaries

We consider the following first-order logic reasoning task in this paper: given a set of formulae called the knowledge base (KB) and a goal G, the task is to show that the KB implies G. This can be reduced to showing that the conjunction of KB and $\neg G$ is unsatisfiable. To show the unsatisfiability, usually the conjunction of the KB and the negated goal are transformed into an equisatisfiable clause normal form and a contradiction is inferred from the clause set.

To achieve this contradiction, saturation-based provers organise the execution of their inferences using a given-clause algorithm as shown in Algorithm 1. This algorithm maintains two sets of clauses: The set of processed clauses and the set of unprocessed clauses. Initially, all clauses are added to the set of unprocessed clauses, and the set of processed clauses is empty. In each step, the algorithm selects a so-called given clause from the set of unprocessed clauses, adds it to the set of processed clauses, and then performs all the inferences possible with the given clause and the set of processed clauses. The resulting new clauses are added to the set of unprocessed clauses. This is repeated until either the empty clause is inferred, or the set of unprocessed clauses is empty (or a resource or time limit is reached).

The choice of the given clause (line 10 in Algorithm 1) strongly influences whether and how fast a proof is found. An unskilful choice of given clause can quickly lead to a large number of irrelevant clauses in the set of unprocessed clauses, making it difficult to find a proof. On the other hand, a skilful choice of the given clause can lead to only those inferences being made that are relevant to the proof task, so that a proof can be found directly.

To select the given clause, heuristics are usually used that assign a weight to each clause. The clause with the lowest weight is then selected as the given

---

Algorithm 1. Given Clause Algorithm

Require: Initial set of clauses *initial_clauses*
 1: *processed_set* ← {}
 2: *unprocessed_set* ← *initial_clauses*
 3: **while** True **do**
 4:    **if** empty_clause ∈ *processed_set* **then**
 5:       **return** "Proof Found"
 6:    **end if**
 7:    **if** *unprocessed_set* is empty **then**
 8:       **return** "No Proof Found"
 9:    **end if**
10:    *given_clause* ← select_clause(*unprocessed_set*)
11:    remove *given_clause* from *unprocessed_set*
12:    add *given_clause* to *processed_set*
13:    *new_clauses* ← generate_new_clauses(*given_clause*, *processed_set*)
14:    *simplified_clauses* ← simplify_clauses(*new_clauses*)
15:    **for** each *clause* in *simplified_clauses* **do**
16:       **if** *clause* ∉ *unprocessed_set* **then**
17:          add *clause* to *unprocessed_set*
18:       **end if**
19:    **end for**
20: **end while**

---

clause. Common heuristics use the age of the clause (older clauses are favoured and receive a lower weight) or are based on a weighted symbol count. These heuristics are often used in combination. The ratio of clauses selected by age to clauses selected by symbol count is called the pick-given ratio. A well-known ratio is the pick-given ratio of 5, which means that the heuristic selects the clause with the lowest weighted symbol count five times and the oldest clause once and this process is repeated continuously. There are many other heuristics for selecting clauses. See Sect. 2 for some pointers in this regard.

In the following, the set of all predicate and function symbols in a formula F is represented as $sym(F)$. In a slight abuse of notation, we use $sym(KB)$ to denote the set containing all predicate and function symbols occurring in a knowledge base KB. Furthermore, we assume that there are multiple proof tasks to solve for a given knowledge base.

3.1   Distributional Semantics

Our approach uses the meaning of the names of the function and predicate symbols. To do this, we rely on the distributional semantics of natural language. This is best explained using Firth's famous statement:

You shall know a word by the company it keeps. [7]

In other words: If we look at very large texts, we can observe that words that occur in a similar context are similar [18].

One approach in this area are word embeddings [14,15]. These are vector representations of words, usually learned using neural networks on very large amounts of text. For a given set of words V, also called a vocabulary, a word embedding is a function, $f : V \rightarrow \mathbb{R}^n$, that assigns an n-dimensional vector to each word in the vocabulary. Since our approach uses existing word embeddings and does not train new ones, we refrain from going into details on the training process of word embeddings.

It is very interesting that words with similar meanings are mapped to similar vectors. Usually, the similarity of two word vectors is calculated with the help of the cosine similarity.

Definition 1 (Cosine similarity of two vectors). *Let $u, v \in \mathbb{R}^n$, both non-zero. The cosine similarity of u and v is defined as:*

$$cos\_sim(u, v) = \frac{u \cdot v}{||u|| \, ||v||}$$

The cosine similarity of two vectors u and v takes values between -1 and 1. For exactly opposite vectors the value is -1, for orthogonal vectors the value is 0 and for equal vectors the value 1. The more similar two vectors are, the greater is their cosine similarity.

In our approach, we use a trained word embedding to determine similarities between the names of symbols in a knowledge base and the proof task. The next section describes how we do this.

4   Guiding the Reasoning Process by the Meaning of Symbol Names

Automated theorem provers usually calculate the weight of a clause from the weights of the symbols occurring in the clause. For example, the theorem prover E can be given values for weights for function and predicate symbols. These weights then determine which weights the clauses receive and therefore which clauses are preferred in the reasoning process.

We now present an approach to determine symbol weights, and thus clause weights, that uses the meaning of symbol names. As described above, we assume that there are multiple proof tasks to solve for a given knowledge base. In the following, when we talk about a knowledge base or a goal, we refer to the knowledge base or the goal in this scenario.

Our approach uses a word embedding. It is important that the word embedding fits to the domain of the knowledge base. For example if the knowledge base is Yago [31] it would be suitable to use a word embedding which was learnt on Wikipedia articles. In the following, we refer to the word embedding used, as a function $f : V \rightarrow \mathbb{R}^n$, where V is the vocabulary of the word embedding.

Figure 1 shows the first step of our approach, which determines a vector representation for all function and predicate symbols occurring in the knowledge base under consideration. To achieve this, in a first step, all function and predicate

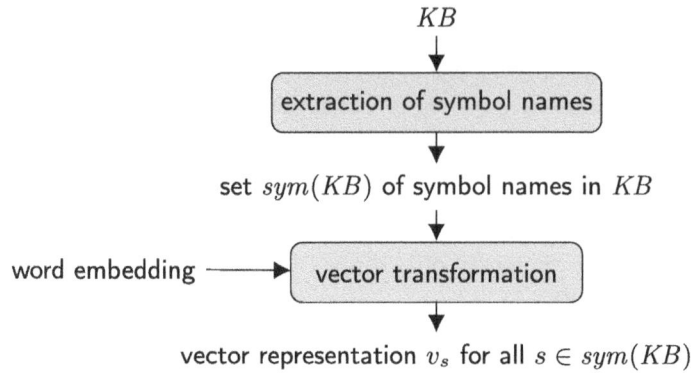

Fig. 1. Overview of the preprocessing step which determines a vector representation for all function and predicate names occurring in a knowledge base KB.

symbols are extracted from the knowledge base resulting in the set $sym(KB)$. Next, during the vector transformation, all extracted symbols $s \in sym(KB)$ are mapped to the vocabulary V of a word embedding. This mapping step is typically not trivial and highly depends on the knowledge base in use. One possibility is to build this mapping upon an existing WordNet [17] mapping for the knowledge base. WordNet is an extensive lexical database of the English language, which groups words according to their meaning and forms synonymous groups, called synsets. For example for the knowledge base Adimen SUMO [3] such a WordNet mapping is available. We do not go into detail here and refer the reader to [25] for more information on the mapping process. In the following we assume that this step is possible for all symbols extracted from the knowledge base and that there is a mapping function $map : sym(KB) \rightarrow V$ which performs this step. Once a function or predicate symbol $s \in sym(KB)$ has been assigned a word $map(s)$ from the vocabulary of the word embedding used, the vector $v_s = f(map(s))$ corresponding to the word is assigned to the symbol. This vector v_s is used as the vector representation of the symbol s. This step only needs to be performed once for a knowledge base. Therefore, it can be considered as a pre-processing step.

Since we assume that for a large number of goals it has to be proven that they are entailed from the same knowledge base, the effort of this preprocessing step is relativized.

Figure 2 provides an overview of the process of proving a goal using the symbol-name heuristic. First, a vector representation of the goal is computed for a given goal G. To do this, all function and predicate symbols are extracted from the goal leading to the set $sym(G)$ and mapped to words in the vocabulary of the word embedding used. For this, the above mentioned function map is used. It is important to use the same word embedding that was chosen for the knowledge base in the pre-processing step. The next step is to compute the vector representation for the goal: For each symbol $s \in sym(G)$ in the goal, the vector v_s of the word $map(s)$ is looked up in the word embedding. The vectors of all symbols in $sym(G)$ are summed and divided by the number of symbols in the goal resulting in vector v_G:

$$v_G = \frac{\displaystyle\sum_{s \in sym(G)} v_s}{|sym(G)|} \tag{1}$$

In other words, the vector representation of a goal corresponds to the average of the vector representations of all the symbols in the goal.

In the next step, weights for symbols in the knowledge base are computed based on the vector representations of the function and predicate symbols in the knowledge base and the vector representation of the goal. To compute the weight of a symbol $s \in sym(KB)$, we first compute the similarity of its vector representation v_s and the vector representation of the goal v_G. Cosine similarity is used for this. The values of cosine similarity are between -1 and 1. The higher the similarity of the two vectors, the higher the value. In contrast to that, symbol with a low weight are preferred by provers. Therefore, we convert the cosine similarities into weights as follows:

We assume a default weight of 1,000. From this we subtract 1,000 times the cosine similarity. The reason for setting the default weight to 1,000 is that we want to accurately incorporate the cosine similarity between v_s and v_G into the symbol weights. Since the cosine similarity of two vectors ranges from -1 to 1, multiplying this value by 1,000 and subtracting it from the default weight of 1,000 allows us to account for up to three decimal places in the similarity measure. This results in the weight of a symbol s w.r.t. the goal G as

$$weight(s, G) = 1000 - 1000 \cdot cos\_sim(v_s, v_G) \tag{2}$$

The weights of the symbols calculated in this way are now passed to the theorem prover together with the proof task. The prover calculates the weights for the clauses from the weights for the symbols and uses them to control the proof process.

5 Experimental Results

The introduced approach is implemented[2]. To evaluate the approach, we need a knowledge base with function and predicate symbols that are, or can be, mapped to natural language words. We also need a large number of proof tasks for this knowledge base. Adimen SUMO [3] is a first-order logic ontology based on the Suggested Upper Merged Ontology (SUMO) [20]. Since a mapping to WordNet synsets is available for most of the symbols of Adimen SUMO, this ontology is interesting for our evaluation. For the vectorization we use the pretrained word

---

[2] Code and all data to redo the experiments can be found in the following repository: https://gitlab.rlp.net/clsc0474908343/symbol_meaning_proof_guidance.

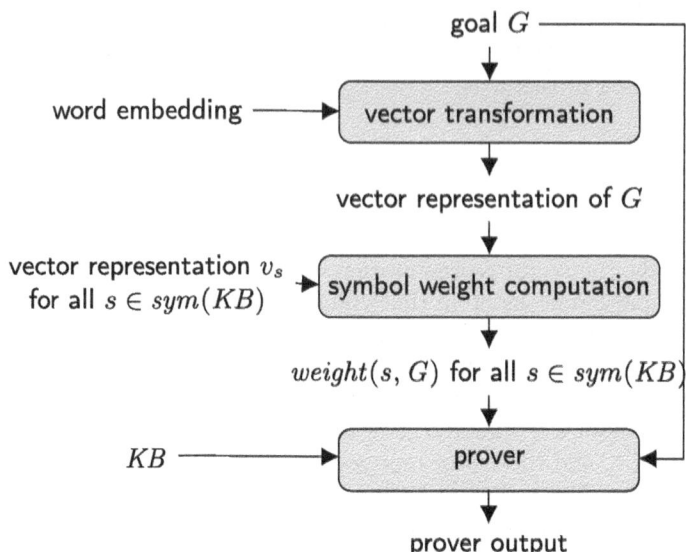

Fig. 2. Overview of the process of proving goal G from knowlege base KB using the symbol name heuristic. Note that the vector representation of KB used here was computed in the preprocessing step depicted in Fig. 1 which determines a vector representation for all function and predicate names occurring in a knowledge base KB.

embedding ConceptNet Numberbatch [30] which is well suited for the commonsense area.

The proof tasks considered in the experiments are the Adimen SUMO WhiteBoxTruthTests [2] which are a collection of automatically generated tests that were used to check and validate the Adimen-SUMO ontology. Each proof task consists of a single formula, the goal, for which it must be shown that it can be inferred from the Adimen SUMO ontology. We randomly choose two disjoint sets of 1,000 of these problems. The first of these two sets will be used to determine the best values for the parameters of the similarity-guided selection of the given clause. This set will be called the *parameter-tuning set*. The second set is disjoint from the *parameter-tuning set* and is used for the actual evaluation. This set will be called the *evaluation set*. As finding the optimal parameter values for the similarity-guided selection of clauses is similar to hyperparameter tuning in machine learning, we use a similar approach. This involves ensuring that the set of problems used for parameter selection is disjoint from the set used for the final evaluation.

The WhiteBoxTruthTests are challenging even for highly optimised theorem provers. In all our experiments, we use the theorem prover E with a timeout of

Table 1. Configurations of E considered in the experiments. For example k1000_PG5_aF corresponds to the configuration of using the symbol weights for top 1000 symbols, PickGiven = 5 without the auto parameter

Abbreviation	Description and Example
k[Num]	Uses the symbol weights of the Num symbols most similar to the conjecture. *Example:* k1000 uses the top 1000 symbols
PG[Num]	Sets the Pick Given parameter to Num, i.e., the given clause is selected Num times using similarity-guided symbol weights, after which the oldest clause is selected once. *Example:* PG5 sets PickGiven to 5
aT/aF	Indicates whether the auto parameter is enabled (aT) or not enabled (aF). *Example:* aT enables the auto parameter

10 s. We call it with different combinations of parameters[3]: We use E without any parameters as well as E with the auto parameter which allows E to choose literal selection strategy, clause evaluation heuristic, and term ordering, as well as several instantiations of the SInE algorithm automatically. The SInE algorithm is used to select formulae relevant for a given proof task. For proof tasks such as the Adimen SUMO WhiteBoxTruthTests, a selection such as SInE is usually used, since theorem provers without selection are often overwhelmed by the number and complexity of the formulas in Adimen SUMO. SInE makes the prover potentially incomplete.

Furthermore, E allows to pass weights for symbols. These weights can be used to determine which clause to use as the next given clause. As described above, to evaluate our approach we use a default weight of 1,000 for each symbol and change the weights of the k symbols that are most similar to the proof goal as given in Eq. 2. To ensure that the reasoner is refutationally complete, we alternate this given clause selection, guided by symbol weights, with the FIFO strategy, where the oldest clause is selected first. The combination of N times symbol weight guided given clause selection followed by a single selection using the FIFO strategy is called PickGiven ratio. Table 1 gives an overview of the different prover configurations used in our experiments.

5.1 Determination of Parameters on the Parameter-Tuning Set

First, we determine the most suitable parameters for similarity-guided selection of the given clause. To achieve this, we systematically varied the parameters listed in Table 1 and ran E over the 1,000 problems of the *parameter-tuning set* for each of these parameter configurations. We then recorded both the number of proofs found (see Fig. 3) and the average number of clauses processed (see Fig. 4).

---

[3] Detailed information on the different parameters used for the theorem prover E can be found in the manual which is available at: https://wwwlehre.dhbw-stuttgart.de/~sschulz/WORK/E_DOWNLOAD/V_2.4/eprover.pdf.

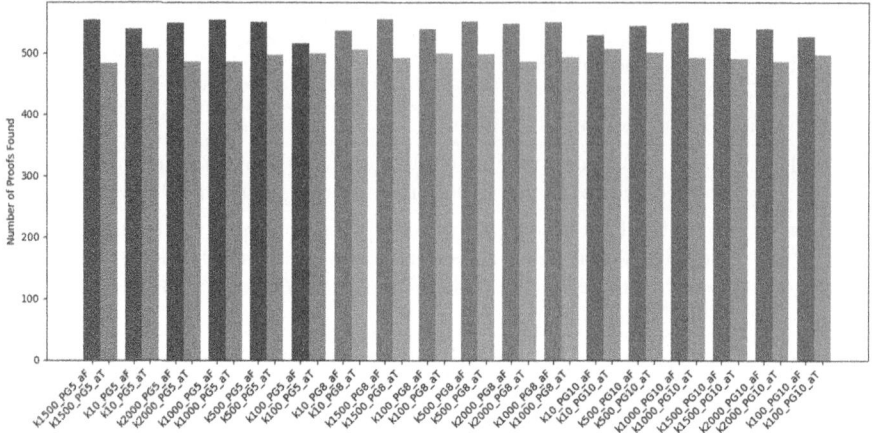

Fig. 3. Number of proofs found by E using different parameter configurations (see Table 1) on the 1,000 randomly selected problems of the *parameter-tuning set*.

Figure 3 shows the number of proofs found for the different E configurations we considered on the *parameter-tuning set*. In the graph, the bars representing the parameter configurations that differ only in whether the auto parameter is set or not are always shown directly next to each other. For all parameter configurations, we can see that the variant without the auto parameter found more proofs than the variant with the auto parameter. Therefore, in our final evaluation, we will not consider the auto parameter in combination with the similarity-guided symbol weights. Furthermore, we can see that the number of proofs found differs only slightly for parameter configurations without auto parameter. The lowest number of proofs found is 486 for the configuration k2000_PG5_aF, and the highest is 555 for k1500_PG8_aF.

As the aim of the similarity-guided selection of the given clause is to enable goal-oriented reasoning, it is interesting to examine the average number of clauses processed. The smaller the number of processed clauses, the more goal-oriented the proof. Ideally, the number of processed clauses is equal to the number of clauses in the proof, and no unnecessary conclusions have been drawn. Figure 4 shows the average number of clauses processed by the considered parameter configurations for the *parameter-tuning set* of problems. The 328 problems for which all parameter configurations have found a proof are considered here.

We observe that setting the auto parameter leads to a significantly higher number of processed clauses. For configurations without the auto parameter, the lowest average number of processed clauses (9,949) is obtained for k10_PG8_aF. The configuration k10_PG10_aF yields the highest average number of processed clauses (14,301). Examining Figs. 3 and 4 together, the parameter configurations k1000_PG5_aF and k1500_PG5_aF are also notable, both with 554 proofs found, just below the maximum of 555. The average number of clauses processed for these two configurations is also low at 10,748 and 10,440, respectively.

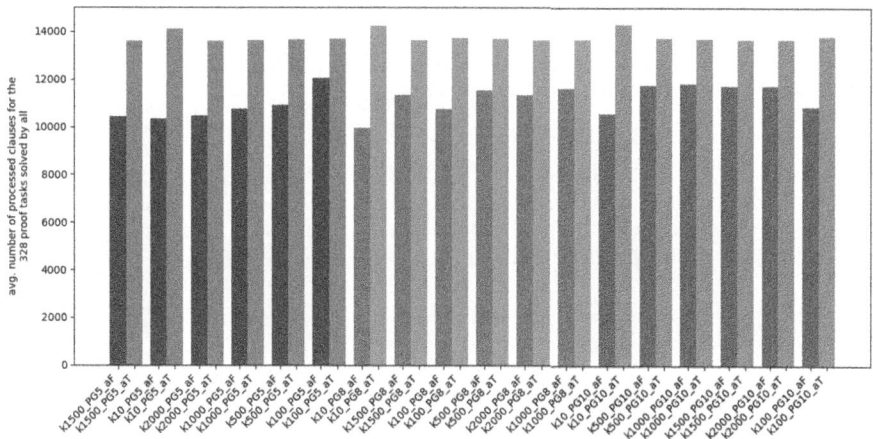

Fig. 4. Average number of clauses processed during proof search. Different parameters for E were considered (see Table 1). Problems considered were the 328 problems of the *evaluation set* for which E was able to find a proof with all considered parameter configurations.

The configuration k1500_PG8_aF, with which the highest number of proofs was found, processed an average of 13,657 clauses, placing it at the higher end of the observed range. Based on the values observed on the *parameter-tuning set*, the configurations k1500_PG8_aF, k1000_PG5_aF and k1500_PG5_aF will be examined on the *evaluation set*.

5.2 Experiments on the Evaluation Set

We now consider the parameter configurations k1500_PG8_aF, k1000_PG5_aF and k1500_PG5_aF selected on the problems of the *parameter-tuning set* in comparison to the parameter configurations aF and aT, which work without similarity-guided symbol weights. For these experiments, we use the *evaluation set* described above, which consists of 1,000 randomly selected Adimen SUMO WhiteBoxTruthTests and is disjoint from the *parameter-tuning set*.

Figure 5 shows that a higher number of proofs is found using similarity-guided symbol weights than with the parameter configurations not considering symbol meanings: While 376 and 414 proofs were found with configurations aF and aT respectively, a significantly higher number of proofs was found when using similarity-guided symbol weights: 541, 543 and 548. This suggests that the meaning of symbol names is a valuable source of information for the proof process.

As described above, the number of clauses processed is another factor to consider when evaluating our approach. The fewer clauses were processed in constructing a proof, the more targeted the process was. Ideally, only the clauses necessary for the proof would be processed. Figure 6 shows the average number

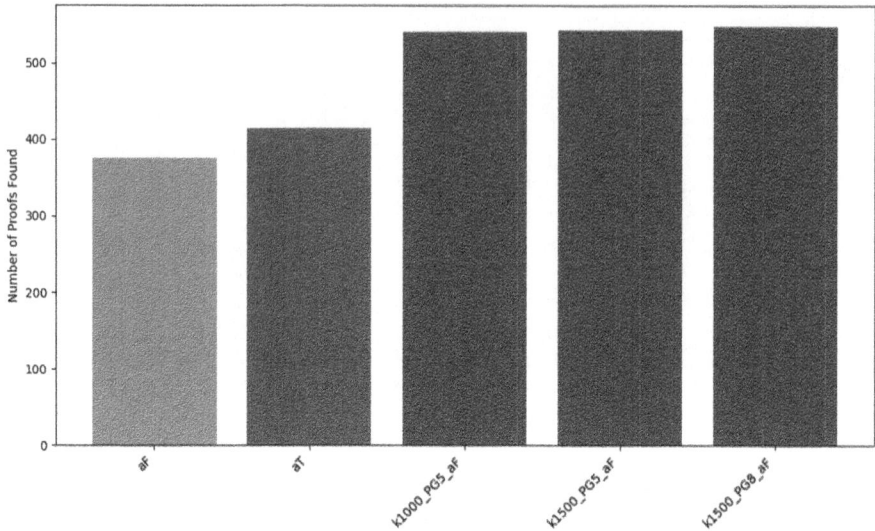

Fig. 5. Number of proofs found by E using different parameter configurations on the problems of the *evaluation set*. Parameter configurations selected in the parameter tuning step as well as parameter configurations without similarity-guided symbol weights are considered (see Table 1).

of clauses processed by each parameter configuration during proof search for the problems in the *evaluation set*. In order to make meaningful comparisons, we only consider problems that could be proven using all parameter configurations. We observe that parameter configurations aF and aT, which do not use similarity-guided symbol weights, processed an average of 17,583 and 14,548 clauses, respectively. By contrast, the configurations using similarity-guided symbol weights processed significantly fewer clauses, with averages of 10,390, 10,364 and 11,514 respectively.

Another interesting observation concerns the number of proofs found. We already observed that with the k1500_PG8_aF configuration, significantly more proofs can be found than with aT (548 proofs versus 414 proofs). However, the proofs found with parameter configuration k1500_PG8_aF are not a superset of those found with aT. There are 275 problems where both configurations find a proof. However, k1500_PG8_aF found a proof for 273 problems for which aT was not able to find a proof. Similarly there were 139 problems where aT found a proof but k1500_PG8_aF was not able to find a proof. These findings suggest that the two configurations explore different parts of the search space and follow divergent reasoning paths. To investigate this further, we compared the sizes of the proofs for the 275 problems, both configurations were able to solve. Figure 7 shows the results. There is no clear indication that one of the configurations leads to shorter proofs. On average, the size of a proof is 30 for k1500_PG8_aF and 29.5 for aT. However, we observe that the two configurations produce proofs

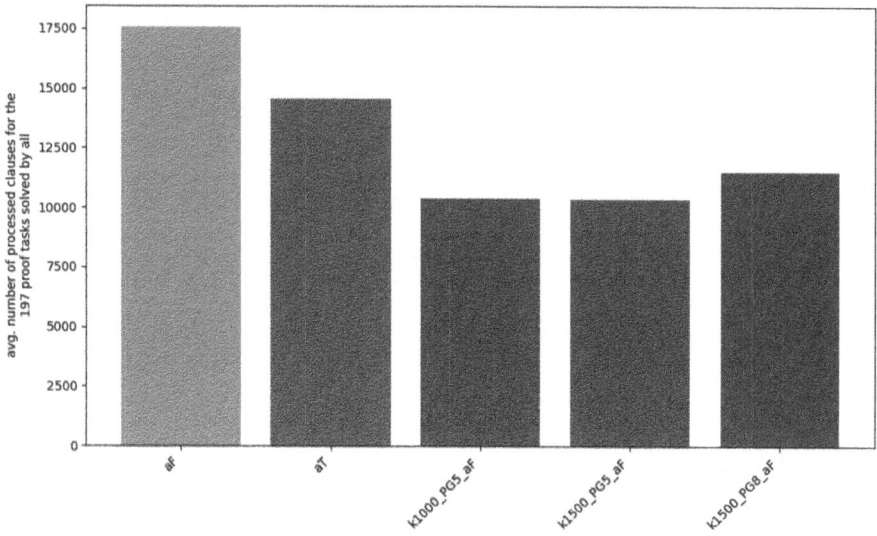

Fig. 6. Average number of clauses processed during proof search. Parameter config-urations selected in the parameter tuning step as well as parameter configurations without similarity-guided symbol weights are considered (see Table 1). Problems considered were the 197 problems of the *evaluation set* for which E was able to find a proof with all considered parameter configurations.

of different sizes for almost all problems. Therefore, they do not find the same proofs. This observation, together with the fact that each configuration solves a substantial number of unique problems indicates that the two configurations result in a different exploration of the search space. This suggests that combining these two configurations could be beneficial. However, as our experiments on the *parameter-tuning set* revealed, simply adding the `auto` parameter to the similarity-guided symbol weights deteriorates the results. Therefore, combining the two approaches will require a different approach.

6 Summary and Future Work

In this paper we have developed an approach to clause selection in automated theorem provers that aims to make the selection of the clause for the next infer-ence step more goal-directed. The approach is based on the assumption that symbols in knowledge bases have meaningful names that can be mapped to natural language words. If this assumption is correct, techniques from natural language processing can be used to determine the similarity between the proof goal and the symbols in the knowledge base. These similarities are then used to derive symbol weights that guide the selection of clauses for the next infer-ence step. The approach has been implemented and evaluated using the theorem prover E. Our experimental results show that more proofs can be found using

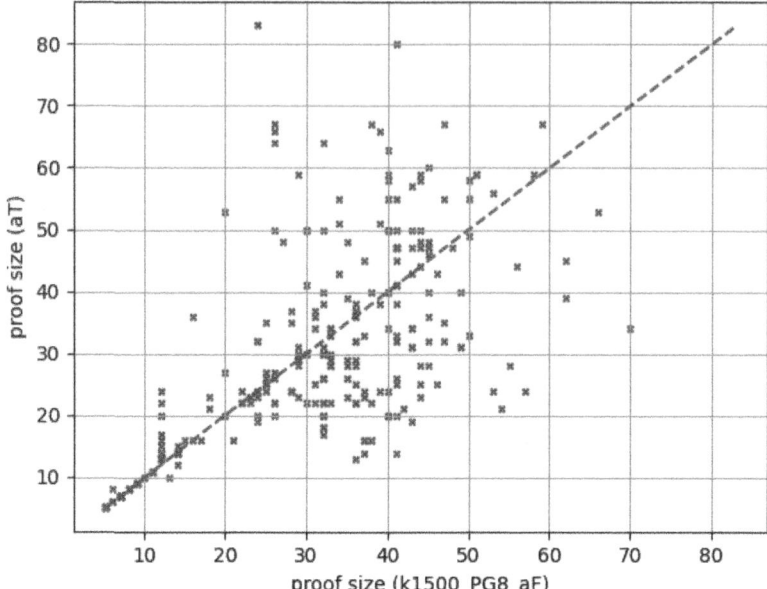

Fig. 7. Comparison of proof sizes for the 275 problems of the *evaluation set* which E was able to find a proof with parameter configuration `aT` and `k1500_PG8_aF`.

these similarity-guided symbol weights. Furthermore, we observe a reduction in the average number of clauses processed during proof search, indicating a more goal-directed and efficient proof process.

In our experiments, we have observed that the use of similarity-guided symbol weights leads to different proofs being found compared to using the `auto` parameter. This suggests that a combination of the two methods could be promising. In future work, we want to develop approaches for such a combination.

Another promising direction for future work is to evaluate the approach of similarity-guided symbol weights on mathematical problems. To make effective use of symbol similarities in this domain, we plan to employ a word embedding that has been trained specifically on mathematical texts. This would allow us to capture domain-specific semantic relationships between symbols and explore whether semantic guidance can also improve theorem proving in formalized mathematics.

References

1. Alama, J., Heskes, T., Kühlwein, D., Tsivtsivadze, E., Urban, J.: Premise selection for mathematics by corpus analysis and kernel methods. J. Autom. Reason. **52**(2), 191–213 (2014). https://doi.org/10.1007/S10817-013-9286-5
2. Álvez, J., Hermo, M., Lucio, P., Rigau, G.: Automatic white-box testing of first-order logic ontologies. CoRR abs/1705.10219 (2017). http://arxiv.org/abs/1705.10219

3. Álvez, J., Lucio, P., Rigau, G.: Adimen-sumo: reengineering an ontology for first-order reasoning. Int. J. Semant. Web Inf. Syst. **8**, 80–116 (2012)
4. Bancerek, G., et al.: Mizar: state-of-the-art and beyond. In: Kerber, M., Carette, J., Kaliszyk, C., Rabe, F., Sorge, V. (eds.) CICM 2015. LNCS (LNAI), vol. 9150, pp. 261–279. Springer, Cham (2015). https://doi.org/10.1007/978-3-319-20615-8_17
5. Bártek, F., Suda, M.: How much should this symbol weigh? A GNN-advised clause selection. In: Piskac, R., Voronkov, A. (eds.) LPAR 2023: Proceedings of 24th International Conference on Logic for Programming, Artificial Intelligence and Reasoning, Manizales, Colombia, 4-9th June 2023. EPiC Series in Computing, vol. 94, pp. 96–111. EasyChair (2023). https://doi.org/10.29007/5F4R
6. Denzinger, J., Schulz, S.: Learning domain knowledge to improve theorem proving. In: McRobbie, M.A., Slaney, J.K. (eds.) CADE 1996. LNCS, vol. 1104, pp. 62–76. Springer, Heidelberg (1996). https://doi.org/10.1007/3-540-61511-3_69
7. Firth, J.R.: Papers in Linguistics 1934–1951: Rep. Oxford University Press (1991)
8. Furbach, U., Krämer, T., Schon, C.: Names are not just sound and smoke: word embeddings for axiom selection. In: Fontaine, P. (ed.) CADE 2019. LNCS (LNAI), vol. 11716, pp. 250–268. Springer, Cham (2019). https://doi.org/10.1007/978-3-030-29436-6_15
9. Irving, G., Szegedy, C., Alemi, A.A., Eén, N., Chollet, F., Urban, J.: Deepmath - deep sequence models for premise selection. In: Lee, D.D., Sugiyama, M., von Luxburg, U., Guyon, I., Garnett, R. (eds.) Advances in Neural Information Processing Systems 29: Annual Conference on Neural Information Processing Systems 2016, Barcelona, Spain, pp. 2235–2243 (2016)
10. Jakubův, J., Urban, J.: ENIGMA: efficient learning-based inference guiding machine. In: Geuvers, H., England, M., Hasan, O., Rabe, F., Teschke, O. (eds.) CICM 2017. LNCS (LNAI), vol. 10383, pp. 292–302. Springer, Cham (2017). https://doi.org/10.1007/978-3-319-62075-6_20
11. Jakubův, J., Urban, J.: Enhancing ENIGMA given clause guidance. In: Rabe, F., Farmer, W.M., Passmore, G.O., Youssef, A. (eds.) CICM 2018. LNCS (LNAI), vol. 11006, pp. 118–124. Springer, Cham (2018). https://doi.org/10.1007/978-3-319-96812-4_11
12. Jakubuv, J., Urban, J.: Hammering Mizar by learning clause guidance (short paper). In: Harrison, J., O'Leary, J., Tolmach, A. (eds.) 10th International Conference on Interactive Theorem Proving, ITP 2019, Portland, OR, USA, 9–12 September 2019. LIPIcs, vol. 141, pp. 34:1–34:8. Schloss Dagstuhl - Leibniz-Zentrum für Informatik (2019). https://doi.org/10.4230/LIPICS.ITP.2019.34
13. Kahneman, D.: Thinking, Fast and Slow. Macmillan (2011)
14. Mikolov, T., Chen, K., Corrado, G., Dean, J.: Efficient estimation of word representations in vector space. CoRR abs/1301.3781 (2013). http://arxiv.org/abs/1301.3781
15. Mikolov, T., Sutskever, I., Chen, K., Corrado, G.S., Dean, J.: Distributed representations of words and phrases and their compositionality. In: NIPS, pp. 3111–3119 (2013)
16. Mikula, M., et al.: Magnushammer: a transformer-based approach to premise selection. CoRR abs/2303.04488 (2023). https://doi.org/10.48550/ARXIV.2303.04488
17. Miller, G.A.: WordNet: a lexical database for English. Commun. ACM **38**(11), 39–41 (1995). https://doi.org/10.1145/219717.219748
18. Miller, G.A., Charles, W.G.: Contextual correlates of semantic similarity. Lang. Cogn. Process. **6**(1), 1–28 (1991). http://eric.ed.gov/ERICWebPortal/recordDetail?accno=EJ431389

19. Jakobs, O., Schon, C.: Context-specific selection of commonsense knowledge using large language models. In: Hotho, A., Rudolph, S. (eds.) KI 2024. LNCS, vol. 14992, pp. 218–231. Springer, Cham (2024). https://doi.org/10.1007/978-3-031-70893-0_16

20. Pease, A.: Ontology: A Practical Guide. Articulate Software Press, Angwin (2011)

21. Piotrowski, B., Urban, J.: Stateful premise selection by recurrent neural networks. In: Albert, E., Kovács, L. (eds.) LPAR 2020: 23rd International Conference on Logic for Programming, Artificial Intelligence and Reasoning, Alicante, Spain, 22–27 May 2020. EPiC Series in Computing, vol. 73, pp. 409–422. EasyChair (2020). https://doi.org/10.29007/J5HD

22. Proroković, K., Wand, M., Schmidhuber, J.: Improving stateful premise selection with transformers. In: Kamareddine, F., Sacerdoti Coen, C. (eds.) CICM 2021. LNCS (LNAI), vol. 12833, pp. 84–89. Springer, Cham (2021). https://doi.org/10.1007/978-3-030-81097-9_6

23. Riazanov, A., Voronkov, A.: The design and implementation of VAMPIRE. AI Commun. **15**(2-3), 91–110 (2002). http://content.iospress.com/articles/ai-communications/aic259

24. de Rooij, S., Beek, W., Bloem, P., van Harmelen, F., Schlobach, S.: Are names meaningful? Quantifying social meaning on the semantic web. In: Groth, P., et al. (eds.) ISWC 2016. LNCS, vol. 9981, pp. 184–199. Springer, Cham (2016). https://doi.org/10.1007/978-3-319-46523-4_12

25. Schon, C.: Selection strategies for commonsense knowledge (2022). https://doi.org/10.48550/ARXIV.2202.09163

26. Schon, C.: Associative reasoning for commonsense knowledge. In: Seipel, D., Steen, A. (eds.) KI 2023. LNCS, vol. 14236, pp. 170–183. Springer, Cham (2023). https://doi.org/10.1007/978-3-031-42608-7_14

27. Schon, C.: Using the meaning of symbol names to guide first-order logic reasoning. In: Özçep, Ö.L., Rußwinkel, N., Sauerwald, K., Wolter, D. (eds.) Proceedings of the 10th Workshop on Formal and Cognitive Reasoning co-located with the 47th German Conference on Artificial Intelligence (KI 2024), Würzburg, Germany, 23 September 2024. CEUR Workshop Proceedings, vol. 3763, pp. 19–27. CEUR-WS.org (2024). https://ceur-ws.org/Vol-3763/paper2.pdf

28. Schulz, S., Cruanes, S., Vukmirović, P.: Faster, higher, stronger: E 2.3. In: Fontaine, P. (ed.) CADE 2019. LNCS (LNAI), vol. 11716, pp. 495–507. Springer, Cham (2019). https://doi.org/10.1007/978-3-030-29436-6_29

29. Schulz, S., Möhrmann, M.: Performance of clause selection heuristics for saturation-based theorem proving. In: Olivetti, N., Tiwari, A. (eds.) IJCAR 2016. LNCS (LNAI), vol. 9706, pp. 330–345. Springer, Cham (2016). https://doi.org/10.1007/978-3-319-40229-1_23

30. Speer, R., Chin, J., Havasi, C.: Conceptnet 5.5: an open multilingual graph of general knowledge. In: AAAI, pp. 4444–4451. AAAI Press (2017)

31. Suchanek, F.M., Kasneci, G., Weikum, G.: YAGO: a large ontology from Wikipedia and WordNet. Web Semant. **6**(3), 203–217 (2008). https://doi.org/10.1016/j.websem.2008.06.001

32. Suda, M.: Improving ENIGMA-style clause selection while learning from history. In: Platzer, A., Sutcliffe, G. (eds.) CADE 2021. LNCS (LNAI), vol. 12699, pp. 543–561. Springer, Cham (2021). https://doi.org/10.1007/978-3-030-79876-5_31

Specific Reasoning Procedures

When GNNs Met a Word Equations Solver: Learning to Rank Equations

Parosh Aziz Abdulla[1] , Mohamed Faouzi Atig[1], Julie Cailler[3] ,
Chencheng Liang[1(✉)] , and Philipp Rümmer[1,2(✉)]

[1] Uppsala University, Uppsala, Sweden
chencheng.liang@it.uu.se
[2] University of Regensburg, Regensburg, Germany
ph_r@gmx.net
[3] University of Lorraine, CNRS, Inria, LORIA, Nancy, France

Abstract. Nielsen transformation is a standard approach for solving word equations: by repeatedly splitting equations and applying simplification steps, equations are rewritten until a solution is reached. When solving a conjunction of word equations in this way, the performance of the solver will depend considerably on the order in which equations are processed. In this work, the use of Graph Neural Networks (GNNs) for ranking word equations before and during the solving process is explored. For this, a novel graph-based representation for word equations is presented, preserving global information across conjuncts, enabling the GNN to have a holistic view during ranking. To handle the variable number of conjuncts, three approaches to adapt a multi-classification task to the problem of ranking equations are proposed. The training of the GNN is done with the help of minimum unsatisfiable subsets (MUSes) of word equations. The experimental results show that, compared to state-of-the-art string solvers, the new framework solves more problems in benchmarks where each variable appears at most once in each equation.

Keywords: Word equation · Graph neural network · String theory

1 Introduction

A *word equation* is an equality between two *strings* that may contain variables representing unknown substrings. Solving a *word equation problem* involves finding assignments to these variables that satisfy the equality. Word equations are crucial in string constraints encountered in program verification tasks, such as validating user inputs, ensuring proper string manipulations, and detecting potential security vulnerabilities like injection attacks. The word equation problem is decidable, as shown by Makanin [33]; while the precise complexity of the problem is still open, it is know to be NP-hard and in PSPACE [38].

Abdulla et al. [11] recently proposed a Nielsen transformation-based algorithm for solving word equation problems [36]. This algorithm solves word equations by recursively applying a set of inference rules to branch and simplify the

© The Author(s) 2026
R. Thiemann and C. Weidenbach (Eds.): FroCoS 2025, LNAI 15979, pp. 327–345, 2026.
https://doi.org/10.1007/978-3-032-04167-8_18

problem until a solution is reached, in a tableau-like fashion. When multiple word equations are present, the algorithm must select the equation to process next at each proof step. This selection process is critical and heavily influences the performance of the algorithm, as the unsatisfiability of a set of equations can often be shown by identifying a small unsatisfiable core of equations. At the same time, the search tree can contain infinite branches on which no solutions can be found, so that bad decisions can lead a solver astray. The situation is similar to the case of first-order logic theorem provers, where the choice of clauses to process plays a decisive role in determining efficiency. In the latter context, several deep learning techniques have been introduced to guide theorem provers [10,16,17,27,44]. However, for word equation problems, the application of learning techniques for selecting equations remains largely unexplored.

In this work, we employ Graph Neural Networks (GNNs) [15] to guide the selection of word equations at each iteration of the algorithm. Our research complements existing techniques for learning branching heuristics in word equation solvers [11]. We refer to the selection step as the *ranking process*. For this, we enhanced the existing algorithm [11] to enable the re-ordering of conjunctive word equations. The extension preserves the soundness and the completeness (for finding solutions) of the algorithm. We refer to this extended algorithm as the *split algorithm* throughout the paper.

The primary challenge in training a deep learning model to guide the ranking process lies in managing a variable number of inputs. In our work, this specifically involves handling a varying number of word equations depending on the input. Unlike with branching heuristics, which have to handle only a fixed and small number of branches (typically 2 to 3), the ranking process must handle a variable number of conjuncts. To address this challenge, we adapt multi-classification models to accommodate inputs of varying sizes using three distinct approaches. Additionally, to effectively train the GNNs, we enhance the graph representations of word equations from [11] by incorporating global term occurrence information.

Our model is trained using data from two sources: (1) Minimal Unsatisfiable Subsets (MUSes) of word equations computed by other solvers, and (2) data extracted by running the split algorithm with non-GNN-based ranking heuristics. MUSes computed by solvers such as Z3 [35] and cvc5 [14] help detect unsatisfiable conjuncts early, enabling prompt termination and improved efficiency. When the split algorithm tackles conjunctive word equations, each ranking decision creates a branch in a decision tree. By extracting the shortest path from this tree, we obtain the most effective sequence of choices, which we then use as training data.

Moreover, we explore seven options that combine the trained model with both random and manually designed heuristics for the ranking process.

We evaluated our framework on artificially generated benchmarks inspired by [20]. The benchmarks are divided into two categories: *linear* and *non-linear*, where linear means that, within a single equation, a variable can occur only once, while non-linear allows a variable to appear multiple times. Note that this definition of linearity applies to individual equations: in systems with multiple equations, even if each equation is linear, shared variables can cause a variable to appear multiple times within the system.

Finally, we compare our framework with several leading SMT solvers and a word equation solver, including Z3, Z3-Noodler [19], cvc5, Ostrich [18], and Woorpje [20]. The experimental results show that for linear problems, our framework outperforms all leading solvers in terms of the number of solved problems. For non-linear problems, when the occurrence frequency of the same variables (non-linearity) is low, our algorithm remains competitive with other solvers.

In summary, the contributions of this paper are as follows: (i) We adapt the Nielsen transformation-based algorithm [11] to allow control over the ordering of word equations at each iteration. (ii) We develop a framework to train and deploy a deep learning model for ranking and ordering conjunctive word equations within the split algorithm. The model leverages MUSes generated by leading solvers and uses graph representations enriched with global information of the formula. We propose three strategies to adapt multi-classification models for ranking tasks and explore various integration methods within the split algorithm. (iii) Experimental results demonstrate that our framework performs effectively on linear problems, with the deep learning model significantly enhancing performance. However, its effectiveness on non-linear problems is constrained by the limitations of the inference rules.

2   Preliminaries

We first define the syntax of word equations and the concept of satisfiability. Next, we explain the message-passing mechanism of Graph Neural Networks (GNNs) and describe the specific GNN model employed in our experiments.

Word Equations. We assume a finite non-empty alphabet Σ and write Σ^* for the set of all strings (or words) over Σ. The empty string is denoted by ϵ. We work with a set Γ of string variables, ranging over words in Σ^*. The symbol $\cdot$ denotes the concatenation of two strings; in our examples, we often write uv as shorthand for $u \cdot v$. The syntax of word equations is defined as follows, where $X \in \Gamma$ ranges over variables and $c \in \Sigma$ over letters:

$$\text{Formulae } \phi ::= true \mid e \wedge \phi \qquad \text{Words } w ::= \epsilon \mid t \cdot w$$
$$\text{Equations } e ::= w = w \qquad \text{Terms } t ::= X \mid c$$

Definition 1 (Satisfiability of conjunctive word equations). *A formula ϕ is* satisfiable (SAT) *if there exists a substitution $\pi ; \Gamma \to \Sigma^*$ such that, when each variable $X \in \Gamma$ in ϕ is replaced by $\pi(X)$, all equations in ϕ hold.*

Definition 2 (Linearity of a word equation). *A word equation is called* linear *if each variable occurs at most once. Otherwise, it is* non-linear.

Graph Neural Networks. *Message Passing-based GNNs* (MP-GNNs) [23] are designed to learn features of graph nodes (and potentially the entire graph) by iteratively aggregating and transforming feature information from the neighborhood of a node. Consider a graph $G = (V, E)$, with V as the set of nodes and

$E \subseteq V \times V$ as the set of edges. Each node $v \in V$ has an initial representation $x_v \in \mathbb{R}^n$ and a set of neighbors $N_v \subseteq V$. In an MP-GNN comprising T message-passing steps, node representations are iteratively updated. The initial node representation of v at time step 0 is $H_v^0 = x_v$. At each step t, the representation of node v, denoted as H_v^t, is updated using the equation:

$$H_v^t = \eta_t(\rho_t(\{H_u^{t-1} \mid u \in N_v\}), H_v^{t-1}), \tag{1}$$

where H_u^{t-1} is the node representation of u in the previous iteration $t - 1$, and node u is a neighbor of node v. In this context, $\rho_t : (\mathbb{R}^n)^{|N_v|} \rightarrow \mathbb{R}^n$ is an aggregation function with trainable parameters (e.g., an MLP followed by sum, mean, min, or max) that aggregates the node representations of v's neighboring nodes at the t-th iteration. Along with this, $\eta_t : (\mathbb{R}^n)^2 \rightarrow \mathbb{R}^n$ is an update function with trainable parameters (e.g., an MLP) that takes the aggregated node representation from ρ_t and the node representation of v in the previous iteration as input, and outputs the node representation of v at the t-th iteration.

In this study, we employ *Graph Convolutional Networks* (GCNs) [29] to guide our algorithm due to their computational efficiency to generalize across tasks without the need for task-specific architectural modifications. In GCNs, the node representation H_v^t of v at step $t \in \{1, ..., T\}$ where $T \in \mathbb{N}$ is computed by

$$H_v^t = \text{ReLU}(\text{MLP}^t(\text{mean}\{H_u^{t-1} \mid u \in N_v \cup \{v\}\})), \tag{2}$$

where each MLP^t is a fully connected neural network, ReLU (Rectified Linear Unit) [13] is the non-linear function $f(x) = max(0, x)$, and $H_v^0 = x_v$.

3   Split Algorithm with Ranking

Split Algorithm. Algorithm 1, SPLITEQUATIONS, determines the satisfiability of a word equation formula ϕ by recursively applying inference rules from [11].

The algorithm begins by checking the satisfiability of the conjunctive formula (Line 2). If all word equations can be eliminated in this way, then ϕ is SAT. If any conjunct is unsatisfiable (UNSAT), then ϕ is UNSAT. Otherwise, the satisfiability status remains *unknown* (UKN). If ϕ is in one of the first two cases, its status is returned (Line 3).

Otherwise (Line 4), RANKEQS orders all conjuncts using either manually designed or data-driven methods. Next, the function APPLYRULES matches and applies the corresponding inference rules to generate branches—alternative prospective solving paths for the same equation. This step is called the *branching process*. Notably, rules R_7 and R_8 generate two and three branches, respectively, while all the other rules do not cause any branching.

Next, the SPLITEQUATIONS call (Line 9) recursively checks the satisfiability of each branch. Let $\{b_1, \ldots, b_n\}$ be the set of branches. The formula ϕ has status SAT if at least one branch b_i is satisfiable, UNSAT if all branches are unsatisfiable, and UKN otherwise.

Data: A formula ϕ
Result: The satisfiability status of ϕ (i.e., *SAT*, *UNSAT*, or *UKN*) and the simplified version of ϕ

```
1  begin
2  │  res ← CHECKFORMULASATISFIABILITY(φ)
3  │  if res ≠ UKN then return res, φ
4  │  else
5  │  │  φₛ = RANKEQS(φ)                                    // Ranking process
6  │  │  Branches = APPLYRULES(φₛ)                          // Branching process
7  │  │  uknFlag ← 0
8  │  │  for b in Branches do
9  │  │  │  resᵦ, φᵦ=SPLITEQUATIONS(b)
10 │  │  │  if resᵦ = SAT then  return SAT, φᵦ
11 │  │  │  if resᵦ = UKN then  uknFlag ← 1
12 │  │  if uknFlag = 1 then  return UKN, φ
13 │  │  else return UNSAT, φ
```

Algorithm 1: SPLITEQUATIONS algorithm.

Since the inference rules apply to the leftmost equation, the performance of the algorithm is strongly influenced by both the order in which branches are processed (Line 8) and the ordering of equations in ϕ (Line 5). While the impact of branch ordering has been studied in [11], this paper explores whether employing a data-driven heuristic in RANKEQS can enhance termination.

The baseline option to implement RANKEQS is referred to as **RE1: Baseline**. It computes the priority of a word equation p using the following definition:

$$
p = \begin{cases}
1 & \text{if } \epsilon = \epsilon \\
2 & \text{otherwise, if } \epsilon = u \cdot v \text{ or } u \cdot v = \epsilon \\
3 & \text{otherwise, if } a \cdot u = b \cdot v \text{ or } u \cdot a = v \cdot b \\
4 & \text{otherwise, if } a \cdot u = a \cdot v \\
5 & \text{otherwise}
\end{cases}
$$

where $a, b \in \Sigma$, and u, v are sequences of variables and letters. Smaller numbers indicate higher priority, assigning greater precedence to simpler cases where satisfiability is obvious. Word equations with the same priorities between 1 and 4 are further ordered by their length (i.e., the number of terms), with shorter equations taking precedence. For word equations with a priority of 5, the original input order is maintained. The newly created equations inherit the ranking of their parents. We refer to the split algorithm using **RE1** for RANKEQS as DragonLi. The correctness of Algorithm 1 follows directly from the soundness and local completeness of the inference rules in [11]:

Lemma 1 (Soundness of Algorithm 1). *For a conjunctive word equation formula ϕ, if Algorithm 1 terminates with the result* SAT *or* UNSAT, *then ϕ is* SAT *or* UNSAT, *respectively.*

AND-OR Tree. The search tree explored by the algorithm can be represented as an AND-OR tree, as shown in Fig. 1. The example illustrates the three paths, each placing different equations in the first position, generated by the ranking and branching process to solve the word equation $\phi = (Xb = bXX \wedge \epsilon = \epsilon \wedge X = a)$, where $a, b \in \Sigma$ and $X \in \Gamma$.

Example 1. In the first step, ϕ can be reordered in three distinct ways by prioritizing one conjunct to occupy the leftmost position (we ignore the order of the rest two equations, as their order does not influence the next rule application). Thus, the root of the tree branches into three paths. For each ranked formula, the inference rules are then applied to execute the branching process. By iterating these two steps alternately, the complete AND-OR tree is constructed. Notably, continuously selecting the leftmost branch that prioritizes $Xb = bXX$ at the root and applying the left branch of R_7 may lead to non-termination, as the length of the word equation keeps increasing. In contrast, prioritizing $X = a$ at the root results in a solution (UNSAT) at a relatively shallow depth, avoiding the risk of non-termination caused by further ranking and branching. In this case, exploring only a single branch during the ranking process suffices to determine the satisfiability of ϕ. This optimal path is highlighted with solid edges.

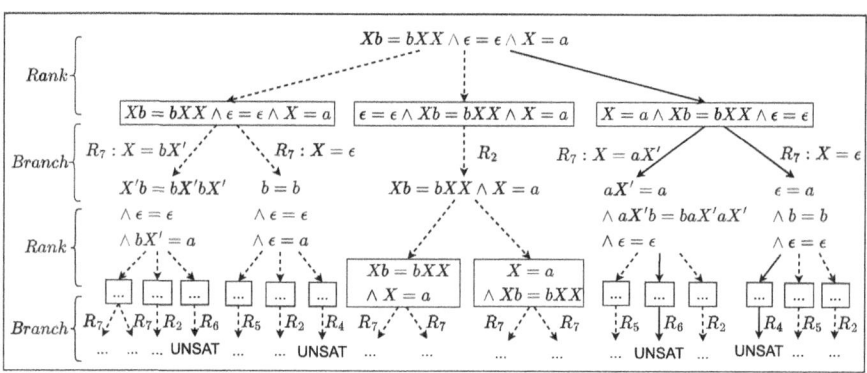

Fig. 1. AND-OR tree resulting from the word equation $Xb = bXX \wedge \epsilon = \epsilon \wedge X = a$. The formulas enclosed in boxes are generated by RANKEQS, while the formulas without boxes are obtained from APPLYRULES.

4   Guiding the Split Algorithm

This section details the training and application of a GNN model in Algorithm 1. We first describe the process of collecting training data, followed by the graph-based representation of each word equation. Next, we outline three model structures for ranking a set of word equations. Finally, we discuss methods for integrating the trained model back into the algorithm.

4.1 Training Data Collection

Assume that ϕ is an unsatisfiable conjunctive word equation consisting of a set of conjuncts $\mathcal{E}$.

Definition 3 (Minimal Unsatisfiable Set). *A subset $U \subseteq \mathcal{E}$ is a* Minimal Unsatisfiable Set *(MUS) if the conjunction of U is unsatisfiable, and for all conjuncts $e \in U$, the conjunction of subset $U \setminus \{e\}$ is satisfiable.*

We collect training data from two sources: (1) MUSes extracted by other solvers, including Z3, Z3-Noodler, cvc5, and Ostrich; and (2) formulas from the ranking process that lie on the shortest path from the subtree leading to UNSAT in the AND-OR trees. A numerical example of these two sources is provided in Sect. 5.2.

For training data from source (1), we first pass all problems to DragonLi. Next, we identify unsolvable problems and forward them to other solvers. If any solver successfully solves a problem, we select the one that finds a solution in the shortest time. This solver is then used to extract the MUS by exhaustively checking the satisfiability of all subsets of the conjuncts. Finally, each conjunct within a set of word equations is labeled based on its membership in the MUS and its length.

Formally, given a formula $\phi = e_1 \wedge \cdots \wedge e_n$, its conjuncts are denoted $\mathcal{E} = \{e_1, \ldots, e_n\}$, and an MUS $U \subseteq \mathcal{E}$. The corresponding labels of $e_i \in \mathcal{E}$ are $Y_n = \{y_1, \ldots, y_n\}$, where $y_i \in \{0, 1\}$, and their length is denoted $|e_i|$. The label y_i is computed as follows:

$$y_i = \begin{cases} 1 & \text{if } e_i \in U \text{ and } |e_i| = \min\left(\{|e| \mid e \in U\}\right), \\ 0 & \text{otherwise.} \end{cases} \tag{3}$$

We assign label 1 only to the shortest equation in the MUS, rather than labeling all MUS equations as 1 and non-MUS equations as 0, because the algorithm selects only one equation to proceed at each iteration. Our goal is to identify the most efficient choice. We assume that the shortest equation in the MUS is more likely to lead to quicker termination, as the branching process aims to reduce equation length until a form is reached where satisfiability (or unsatisfiability) can be easily concluded.

To collect training data from source (2), we pass the problems, along with the MUS extracted from other solvers, to DragonLi. If DragonLi solves the problem, multiple paths to UNSAT are generated by sequentially prioritizing each equation at the leftmost position in the ranked word equation.

Subsequently, we export and label each conjunctive word equation along the shortest path in the subtree leading to UNSAT. Formally, given a set of conjuncts $\mathcal{E} = \{e_1, \ldots, e_n\}$ of a conjunctive word equation, the corresponding labels $Y_n = (y_1, \ldots, y_n)$ are computed by

$$y_i = \begin{cases} 1 & \text{if } e_i \text{ in the shortest path of a subtree leading to UNSAT,} \\ 0 & \text{otherwise.} \end{cases} \tag{4}$$

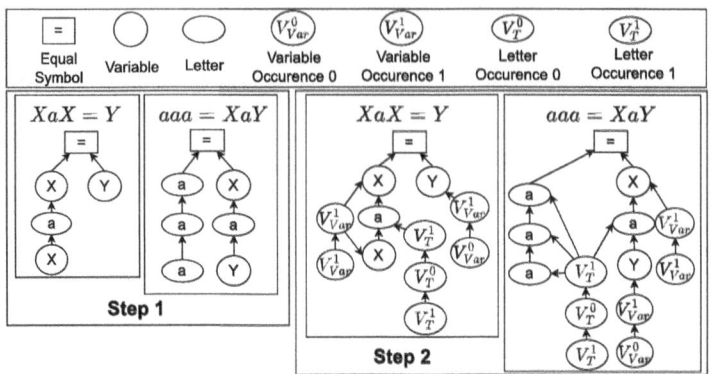

Fig. 2. The steps for constructing graph representation for the conjunctive word equations $XaX = Y \wedge aaa = XaY$ where X, Y are variables and a is a letter.

For both sources, when $\sum_{i=1}^{n} y_i > 1$, we keep the first equation with label 1 and discard the rest equations with label 1 to ensure $\sum_{i=1}^{n} y_i = 1$. When $\sum_{i=1}^{n} y_i = 0$, we discard this training data due to no positive label.

4.2   Graph Representation for Conjunctive Word Equations

The graph representation of a single word equation is discussed in [11]. However, since word equations are interconnected through shared variables, ranking them requires not only local information about individual equations but also a global perspective. By considering the entire set of word equations collectively, we can incorporate dependencies and shared structures, improving the ranking process.

To achieve this, we first represent each conjunctive word equation independently. Then, we compute the occurrences of variables and letters across all equations and integrate this global information into each individual graph representation. This enriched representation captures both the complexity of individual equations and their interactions within the system.

In details, the graph representation of a word equation is defined as $G = (V, E, v_=, V_T, V_{\text{Var}}, V_T^0, V_T^1, V_{\text{Var}}^0, V_{\text{Var}}^1)$, where V is the set of nodes, $E \subseteq V \times V$ is the set of edges, and $v_= \in V$ is a special node representing the "=" symbol. The sets $V_T \subseteq V$ and $V_{\text{Var}} \subseteq V$ contain letter and variable nodes, respectively. Additionally, V_T^0 and V_T^1 are special nodes representing letter occurrences and V_{Var}^0 and V_{Var}^1 analogously represent variable occurrences.

Figure 2 illustrates the two steps involved in constructing the graph representation of the conjunctive word equations $XaX = Y \wedge aaa = XaY$, where $\{X, Y\} \subseteq \Gamma$ and $a \in \Sigma$:

- **Step 1:** Inspired by Abstract Syntax Trees (ASTs), we begin to build the graph by placing the "=" symbol as the root node. The left and right children of the root represent the leftmost terms of each side of the equation, respectively. Subsequent terms are organized as singly linked lists of nodes.

- **Step 2:** Calculate the number of occurrences of all terms across the conjunctive word equations. In this example, $\mathrm{Occurrence}(X) = 3$, $\mathrm{Occurrence}(Y) = 2$, and $\mathrm{Occurrence}(a) = 5$. Their binary encodings are 11, 10 and 101 respectively. We encode these as sequentially connected nodes: (V_{Var}^1, V_{Var}^1) for X, (V_{Var}^1, V_{Var}^0) for Y, and (V_T^1, V_T^0, V_T^1) for a. Finally, we connect the roots of these nodes to their corresponding variable and letter nodes.

We chose binary encoding because using unary encoding would significantly increase the graph size, making computation inefficient. Higher-base encodings like ternary or decimal tend to blur structural distinctions, i.e., different values may be represented using the same number of nodes, making it hard for the graph structure to reflect meaningful differences. Binary encoding strikes a balance. It keeps the graph size manageable while preserving enough structural information for our GNN to effectively process word equations at the scale we target.

The rationale behind our other choices of graph representation for word equations, along with a discussion of alternative representations, is provided in the repository [2].

4.3   Training of Graph Neural Networks

In the function RANKEQS of Algorithm 1, equations can be ranked and sorted based on predicted rank scores from a trained model. Given a conjunctive word equation $\phi = e_1 \wedge \cdots \wedge e_n$, the model outputs a *ranking*, i.e., a list of real numbers $\hat{Y}_n = (\hat{y}_1, \ldots, \hat{y}_n)$ in which a higher value indicates a higher rank. For example, for a conjunctive word equation $e_1 \wedge e_2$, the model might output $\hat{Y}_2 = (0.3, 0.7)$, indicating that e_2 is expected to lead to a solution more quickly than e_1, and the equations should be reordered as $e_2 \wedge e_1$.

Forward Propagation. To compute this ranking, we first transform the word equations $\{e_1, ..., e_n\}$ to their graph representations $G = \{G_1, ..., G_n\}$ where $G_i = (V, E, v_=, V_T, V_{Var}, V_T^0, V_T^1, V_{Var}^0, V_{Var}^1)$. Each node $v \in V$ is first assigned an integer representing the node type: $v \in \bigcup \{V_T, V_{Var}, V_T^0, V_T^1, V_{Var}^0, V_{Var}^1\} \cup \{v_=\}$. Those integers are then passed to a trainable embedding function $\mathrm{MLP}_0 : \mathbb{Z} \to \mathbb{R}^m$ to compute all the initial node representations H_i^0 in G_i.

Equation (2) defines how node representations are updated. By iterating this update rule, we obtain the node representations $H_i^t = \mathrm{GCN}(H_i^{t-1}, E)$ for $t \in \{1, \ldots, T\}$, where the relation E is used to identify neighbors. Subsequently, the representation of the entire graph is obtained by summing the node representations at time step T, resulting in $H_{G_i} = \frac{1}{n} \sum_{i=1}^n H_i^T$.

Then, we introduce three ways to compute the $\hat{Y}_n$:

- **Task 1:** Each graph representation H_{G_i} is given to a trainable classifier $\mathrm{MLP}_1 : \mathbb{R}^m \to \mathbb{R}^2$, which outputs $\mathbf{z}_i = \mathrm{MLP}_1(H_{G_i}) = (z_1, z_2)$. The score for graph i is then computed as $y_i = softmax(\mathbf{z}_i)_1$ for $y_i \in \hat{Y}_n$ where $softmax(\mathbf{z}_i) = (\frac{e^{z_1}}{\sum_{j=1}^n e^{z_j}}, \ldots, \frac{e^{z_n}}{\sum_{j=1}^n e^{z_j}})$ and $softmax(\cdot)_1$ is the first element of $softmax(\cdot)$. It represents the probability of the class in the first index.

- **Task 2**: All graph representations in a conjunctive word equations are first aggregated by $H_G = \frac{1}{n}\sum_{i=1}^{n} H_{G_i}$. Then, we compute the score by of each graph by $y_i = softmax(\text{MLP}_2(H_{G_i}\|H_G))_1$ for $y_i \in \hat{Y}_n$ where $\text{MLP}_2 : \mathbb{R}^{2m} \to \mathbb{R}^2$ is a trainable classifier and $\|$ denotes concatenation of two vectors.
- **Task 3**: We begin by fixing a limit n of equation within a conjunctive word equation. For conjunctive word equations containing more than n word equations, we first sort them by length (in ascending order) and then trim the list to n equations. Next, we compute scores for resulting equations using $\hat{Y}_n = \text{MLP}_3(H_{G_1}, \ldots, H_{G_n})$ where $\text{MLP}_3 : \mathbb{R}^{nm} \to \mathbb{R}^n$ is a trainable classifier. Scores for any trimmed word equations are set to 0. If a conjunctive word equations contains fewer than n word equations, we fill the list with empty equations to reach n, and then compute $\hat{Y}_n$ in the same way.

Backward Propagation. The trainable parameters of the model include the weights of the embedding function MLP_0, the classifiers MLP_1, MLP_2, MLP_3, and the GCNs. Those trainable parameters are optimized together by minimizing the categorical cross-entropy loss between the predicted label $\hat{y}_i \in \hat{Y}_n$ and the true label $y_i \in Y_n$, using the equation $loss = -\frac{1}{n}\sum_{i=1}^{n} y_i \log(\hat{y}_i)$ where n is the number of conjuncts in the conjunctive word equations.

4.4   Ranking Options

In Algorithm 1, we introduce seven implementations of RANKEQS, aimed at evaluating the efficiency of deterministic versus stochastic ranking methods.

- **RE1, Baseline:** A baseline defined in Sect. 3.
- **RE2, Random:** **RE1** is first used to compute the priority of each word equation, and then equations with a priority of 5 are randomly ordered. This approach aims to add some randomness to the baseline.
- **RE3, GNN:** Equations ranked at 5 by **RE1** are then ranked and sorted using the GNN model. While this option incurs higher overhead due to frequent use of the GNN model, it provides the most fine-grained guidance.
- **RE4, GNN-Random:** Based on **RE3**, there is a 50% chance of invoking the GNN model and a 50% chance of randomly sorting word equations with a priority of 5. This option provides insight into the performance when introducing a random process into GNN-based ranking.
- **RE5, GNN-one-shot:** Based on the priority assigned by **RE1**, the GNN model is used to rank and sort equations with a priority of 5 the first time they occur, while it is managed by **RE1** in subsequent iterations. This option invokes the GNN only once to minimize its overhead, while still maintaining its influence on subsequent iterations. Ranking and sorting the word equations early in the process has a greater impact on performance than doing them later.
- **RE6, GNN-each-n-iteration:** Based on **RE3**, instead of calling the GNN model each time multiple word equations have priority 5, it is invoked only every $n = 5000$ calls to the RANKEQS function. This option explores a balance between **RE3** and **RE5**.

– **RE7, GNN-formula-length:** Based on **RE3**, instead of calling the GNN model each time multiple word equations have priority 5, it is invoked only after $n = 1000$ calls to the RANKEQS function when the length of the current word equation does not decrease. This option introduces dynamic control over calling the GNN model.

5   Experimental Results

This section describes the benchmarks and the methods used for training data collection. We also compare our evaluation data with leading solvers. The training and prediction workflow can be find in the repository [5].

5.1   Benchmarks

We initially transformed real-world benchmarks from the non-incremental QF_S, QF_SLIA, and QF_SNLIA tracks of the SMT-LIB benchmark suite [6], as well as those from the Zaligvinder benchmark suite [7], into word equation problems by removing length constraints, boolean operators, and regular expressions. However, these transformed problems were overly simplistic, as most solvers, including DragonLi, solved them easily. Consequently, we shifted to evaluating solvers using artificially generated word equation problems inspired by prior research [11,20]. We summarize the benchmarks as follows:

– **Benchmark A1:** Given a finite set of letters T and a set of variables V, the process begins by generating individual word equations of the form $s = s$, where s is a string composed of randomly selected letters from T. The maximum length of s is capped at 60. Next, substrings in s on both sides of the equation are replaced n times with the concatenation of m fresh variables from V. Here $|T| = 6$, $|V| = 10$, $n \in [0,5]$, and $m \in [1,5]$. Finally, multiple such word equations are conjoined to form a conjunctive word equation problem. The number of equations to be conjoined is randomly selected between 1 and 100. Since each replacement variable is a fresh variable from V, individual equations in the problem remain linear.
– **Benchmark A2:** This benchmark is generated using the same method as Benchmark A1; however, different parameters are employed to increase the difficulty while ensuring that the problem remains linear. Specifically, we use $|T| = 26$, $|V| = 100$, $n \in [0,16]$, and $m = 1$.
  Benchmark B: This benchmark is generated by the same method as Benchmark A1, except it does not use fresh variables to replace substrings in s. This causes a single variable to potentially occur multiple times in an equation, making the problem non-linear. The number of equations to be conjoined is randomly picked between 2 and 50, and the maximum length of s is capped at 50. In this benchmark, we use $|T| = 10$, $|V| = 10$, $n \in [0,5]$, and $m = 1$.

– **Benchmark C:** We first generate a word equation in the following format:

$$X_n a X_n b X_{n-1} \cdots b X_1 = a X_n X_{n-1} X_{n-1} b \cdots X_1 X_1 baa$$

where $X_1, ..., X_n$ are variables and a and b are letters. Then, we replace each b with one side of an individual equation generated by Benchmark A1. Finally, we join the individual equations to form a conjunctive word equation problem, with the maximum number of conjuncts capped at 100. This method ensures that the resulting benchmark is highly non-linear.

The statistics of the evaluation data for benchmarks is shown in the repository [3].

5.2 Training Data Collection

Table 1 outlines the training data collection. We generate 60,000 problems per benchmark and check their satisfiability with DragonLi. For instance, Benchmark A1 contains 1,859 unsolved problems, which are then passed to solvers such as Z3, Z3-Noodler, cvc5, and Ostrich. Together, these solvers identify 181 SAT and 1,678 UNSAT problems, with no single tool able to solve them all.

For UNSAT problems, we extract Minimal Unsatisfiable Subsets (MUSes) using the fastest solver. This yields 909 problems with extractable MUSes, as detailed in the repository [4]. We rank word equations within each problem based on their presence in the MUS and their length, then pass the ranked problems back to DragonLi. This allows DragonLi to prioritize word equations appearing in the MUS, enabling it to solve 518 new problems. Problems in the row *Have MUS* are transformed into a single labeled data (a conjunctive word equation). Problems in the row *DragonLi* using MUS are transformed into multiple labeled data, each representing a ranking process step on the shortest path to the solution.

The ranking heuristic's effectiveness varies with problem benchmarks. For Benchmarks A1 and A2, 57% to 58% of problems with MUSes are solved. In Benchmark B, the success rate drops to 20%, while for Benchmark C, the heuristic has no effect, solving 0 additional problems. Consequently, no training data or model was generated for Benchmark C.

6   Experimental Settings

To better investigate the influence of conjuncts order at a conjunctive word equations, we fixed the branch order for all inference rules. Additionally, we fixed the inference rule to the prefix version, meaning it always simplifies the word equation starting from the leftmost term.

Benchmarks were split uniformly into training, validation, and test sets, following standard deep-learning practice. We save the model from the epoch with the highest validation accuracy.

Table 1. Number of problems solved by different solvers and having extracted MUS. The row *Other solvers* shows the number of solved problem in total by Z3, Z3-Noodler, cvc5, and Ostrich where ✓, ×, and ∞ denotes SAT, UNSAT, and UKN respectively. The row *DragonLi* using MUS is the number of problems solved by DragonLi when using MUS to rank word equations in the first iteration.

Type	Linear			Non-linear			
Bench	A1		A2		B		C
Total	60000		60000		60000		60000
DragonLi	Solved	∞	Solved	∞	Solved	∞	Solved	∞
	58141	1859	50610	9390	52056	7944	31	59969
Other solvers	✓	×	✓	×	✓	×	✓	×
	181	1678	667	4167	640	7304	383	58259
Have MUS	909		1024		2996		15875
DragonLi using MUS	518		594		607		0

All training records and corresponding hyperparameters, such as a hidden layer size of 128 for all neural networks and number of message passing rounds are available in our repository [8]. For example, the experimental results for Benchmark A and Task 2 can be found in [1].

Each problem in the benchmarks is evaluated on a computer equipped with two Intel Xeon E5 2630 v4 at 2.20 GHz/core and 128GB memory. The GNNs are trained on NVIDIA A100 GPUs. We measured the number of solved problems and the average solving time (in seconds), with timeout of 300 s for each proof attempt.

6.1   Comparison with Other Solvers

Table 2 compares the results of three RANKEqs options, **RE1**, **RE2**, and **RE5** (corresponding to DragonLi, Random-DragonLi, and GNN-DragonLi), against five solvers: Z3 [35], Z3-Noodler [19], cvc5 [14], Ostrich [18], and Woopje [20].

The primary metric is the number of solved problems. In Benchmark A1, GNN-DragonLi achieves the best performance for both SAT and UNSAT problems. For Benchmark A2, GNN-DragonLi solves the most problems overall (895 problems solved), despite not being the best in either category individually GNN-DragonLi outperforms both DragonLi and Random-DragonLi, showing the effectiveness of data-driven heuristics over fixed and random heuristics.

As problem non-linearity increases (in Benchmark B), some solvers outperform all DragonLi options. For highly non-linear problems (Benchmark C), DragonLi solves almost no problems, regardless of the options. This is an effect entirely orthogonal to the ranking problem, however: for non-linear equations, substituting variables that appear multiple times can increase equation length, resulting in mostly infinite branches in the search tree. It then becomes more important

Table 2. Number of problems, average solving time, and average split counts for solvers across four benchmarks. The GNN model used in this table is trained on Task 2. Columns "UNI", "CS", and "CU" indicate uniquely solved, common SAT, and common UNSAT problems, respectively. The "-" denotes unavailable data. Each benchmark consists of 1000 problems.

Bench	Solver	Number of solved problems					Average solving time (split number)			
		SAT	UNSAT	UNI	CS	CU	SAT	UNSAT	CS	CU
A1	DragonLi	24	955	0	13	678	5.6 (244.8)	6.5 (1085.3)	5.0 (94.4)	5.7 (126.3)
	Random-DragonLi	22	944	0			5.6 (198.8)	6.3 (932.6)	5.6 (137.6)	5.7 (180.5)
	GNN-DragonLi	24	961	0			6.1 (164.7)	7.5 (1974.8)	6.1 (96.4)	6.3 (**60.5**)
	cvc5	24	952	1			0.5	0.6	0.1	0.3
	Z3	17	960	0			8.7	0.4	1.1	0.1
	Z3-Noodler	22	939	2			5.7	0.3	4.8	0.1
	Ostrich	17	931	0			15.0	5.5	8.0	4.7
	Woorpje	23	744	0			3.0	12.5	0.1	12.2
A2	DragonLi	59	824	0	3	0	8.5 (4233.4)	11.8 (1231.3)	4.7 (27.3)	-
	Random-DragonLi	44	806	1			24.7 (29779.6)	6.2 (210.9)	4.6 (27.3)	-
	GNN-DragonLi	59	836	4			8.4 (1330.6)	11.6 (1074.1)	5.9 (27.3)	-
	cvc5	**67**	142	15			0.6	56.0	0.1	-
	Z3	8	**870**	10			1.1	0.6	0.1	-
	Z3-Noodler	22	7	1			15.4	3.8	0.4	-
	Ostrich	13	18	2			24.8	38.8	8.6	-
	Woorpje	0	0	0	-	-	-	-	-	-
B	DragonLi	11	805	0	4	294	4.9 (62.5)	5.2 (81.5)	4.9 (29.2)	5.3 (82.4)
	Random-DragonLi	10	894	0			5.0 (58.7)	5.8 (295.2)	5.0 (27.25)	5.2 (73.1)
	GNN-DragonLi	11	821	0			6.5 (65.1)	6.8 (70.0)	6.5 (28.25)	6.8 (**60.2**)
	cvc5	12	915	0			0.1	0.6	0.1	0.7
	Z3	11	859	3			0.1	0.2	0.1	0.1
	Z3-Noodler	24	911	1			4.9	0.4	1.3	0.4
	Ostrich	12	**917**	2			6.9	3.7	3.3	4.2
	Woorpje	19	330	1			29.5	6.0	0.2	5.0
C	DragonLi	2	0	0	-	-	5.1 (85.5)	-	-	-
	Random-DragonLi	2	0	0	-	-	5.0 (85.5)	-	-	-
	GNN-DragonLi	-	-	-	-	-	-	-	-	-
	cvc5	0	**909**	17	-		-	46.9	-	17.3
	Z3	1	821	12	1		0.8	1.7	0.8	0.1
	Z3-Noodler	7	657	4	1	1	0.2	94.1	0.1	1.0
	Ostrich	0	61	0	-		-	77.2	-	27.1
	Woorpje	3	62	0	1		65.0	28.4	0.2	223.1

to implement additional criteria to detect unsatisfiable equations, for instance in terms of word length or letter count (e.g., [30]), which are present in other solvers. DragonLi deliberately does not include such optimizations, as we aim at investigating the ranking problem in a controlled setting.

For commonly solved problems, the average solving time provides sufficient data only for Benchmarks A1 and B (678 and 294 problems, respectively). In these cases, DragonLi shows no time advantage, partly due to its implementation in Python. Re-implementing the algorithm in a more efficient language, such as Rust [9], can yield over a 100x speedup for single word equation problems.

We also measure the average number of splits in solved problems to evaluate ranking efficiency. GNN-DragonLi demonstrates fewer average splits compared to other options, indicating higher problem-solving efficiency in Benchmarks A1 and B. Our results can be summarized as follows:

1. For linear problems, all DragonLi ranking options perform competitively, with GNN-DragonLi solving the highest number of problems.
2. For moderately non-linear problems (Benchmark B), DragonLi shows moderate performance, but the ranking heuristic offers limited benefits to GNN-DragonLi, leading to reduced performance compared to other options.
3. For highly non-linear problems (Benchmark C), DragonLi fails to solve most problems due to limitations in its calculus.
4. The current implementation of DragonLi offers no time advantage for commonly solved problems, though significant improvements are achievable by reimplementation.

Increasing training data for Benchmark A2 from 20,000 to 60,000 allowed GNN-DragonLi to solve additional problems, suggesting that larger training sets may enhance performance. An ablation study on alternative RANKEQS options is provided as an appendix in the repository [2]. All benchmarks, evaluation results, and implementation details, including hyperparameters, are available in our GitHub repository [8].

7   Related Work

Axel Thue [39] laid the theoretical foundation of word equations by studying the combinatorics of words and sequences, providing an initial understanding of repetitive patterns. The first deterministic algorithm to solve word equations was proposed by Makanin [33], but the complexity is non-elementary. Plandowski [38] designed an algorithm that reduces the complexity to PSPACE by using a form of run-length encoding to represent strings and variables more compactly during the solving process. Artur Jeż [28] proposed a nondeterministic algorithm that runs in $O(n \log n)$ space. Closer to our approach, recent research has focused on improving the practical efficiency of solving word equations. Perrin and Pin [37] offered an automata-based technique that represents equations in terms of states and transitions. This allows the automata to capture the behavior of strings satisfying the equation. Markus et al. [22] explored graph representations and graph traversal methods to optimize the solving process for word equations, while Day et al. [20] reformulated the word equation problem as a reachability problem for nondeterministic finite automata, then encoded it as a propositional satisfiability problem that can be handled by SAT solvers. Day et al. [21] proposed a transformation system that extends the Nielsen transformation [31] to work with linear length constraints.

Deep learning [24] has been integrated with various formal verification techniques, such as scheduling SMT solvers [26], loop invariant reasoning [42,43], and guiding premise selection for Automated Theorem Provers (ATPs) [27,45].

Closely related work in learning from Minimal Unsatisfiable Subsets (MUSes) includes NeuroSAT [40,41], which utilizes GNNs to predict the probability of variables appearing in unsat cores, guiding variable branching decisions for Conflict-Driven Clause Learning (CDCL) [34]. Additionally, some recent works [12,32] explore learning MUSes to guide CHC [25] solvers.

8   Conclusion and Future Work

In this work, we extend a Nielsen transformation based algorithm [11] to support the ranking of conjunctive word equations. We adapt a multi-classification task to handle a variable number of inputs in three different ways in the ranking task. The model is trained using MUSes to guide the algorithm in solving UNSAT problems more efficiently. To capture global information in conjunctive word equations, we propose a novel graph representation for word equations. Additionally, we explore various options for integrating the trained model into the algorithms. Experimental results show that, for linear benchmarks, our framework outperforms the listed leading solvers. However, for non-linear problems, its advantages diminish due to the inherent limitations of the inference rules. Our framework not only offers a method for ranking word equations but also provides a generalized approach that can be extended to a wide range of formula ranking problems which plays a critical role is symbolic reasoning.

As future work, we aim to optimize GNN overhead, integrate GNN guidance for both branching and ranking, and extend the solver to support length constraints and regular expressions for greater real-world applicability. Our framework can be generalized to handle more decision processes in symbolic methods that take symbolic expressions as input and output a decision choices.

Acknowledgement. The computations were enabled by resources provided by the National Academic Infrastructure for Supercomputing in Sweden (NAISS) at Chalmers Centre for Computational Science and Engineering (C3SE) and Uppsala Multidisciplinary Center for Advanced Computational Science (UPPMAX) partially funded by the Swedish Research Council through grant agreement no. 2022-06725. The research was also partially supported by the Swedish Research Council through grant agreement no. 2021-06327, by a Microsoft Research PhD grant, and the Wallenberg project UPDATE.

Disclosure of Interests. The authors have no competing interests to declare that are relevant to the content of this article.

References

1. DragonLi solver experimental report for benchmark a and task 2. https://github.com/ChenchengLiang/DragonLi/tree/rank/experimental_results_tables/eval_data_GNN/A1/task_2/model. Accessed 16 May 2025
2. Github repository for the ablastion study. https://github.com/ChenchengLiang/DragonLi/blob/rank/Appendix/Ablation-study.md. Accessed 30 June 2025

3. Github repository for the statistics of evaluation data. https://github.com/ChenchengLiang/DragonLi/blob/rank/Appendix/Statistics-of-evaluation-data.md. Accessed 30 June 2025

4. Github repository for the statistics of muse. https://github.com/ChenchengLiang/DragonLi/blob/rank/Appendix/Statistics-of-MUSes.md. Accessed 30 June 2025

5. Github repository for the workflow. https://github.com/ChenchengLiang/DragonLi/blob/rank/Appendix/Workflow.md. Accessed 30 June 2025

6. The satisfiability modulo theories library (SMT-LIB). https://smtlib.cs.uiowa.edu/benchmarks.shtml. Accessed 16 May 2025

7. Zaligvinder: A string solving benchmark framework. https://zaligvinder.github.io. Accessed 16 May 2025

8. DragonLi github repository branch:rank (2025). https://github.com/ChenchengLiang/boosting-string-equation-solving-by-GNNs/tree/rank. Accessed 16 May 2025

9. wordeq_solver (2025). https://github.com/tage64/wordeq_solver. Accessed 16 May 2025

10. Abdelaziz, I., et al.: Learning to guide a saturation-based theorem prover (2021). https://arxiv.org/abs/2106.03906

11. Abdulla, P.A., Atig, M.F., Cailler, J., Liang, C., Rümmer, P.: Guiding word equation solving using graph neural networks. In: Akshay, S., Niemetz, A., Sankaranarayanan, S. (eds.) Automated Technology for Verification and Analysis, pp. 279–301. Springer, Cham (2025)

12. Abdulla, P.A., Liang, C., Rümmer, P.: Boosting constrained Horn solving by unsat core learning. In: Dimitrova, R., Lahav, O., Wolff, S. (eds.) Verification, Model Checking, and Abstract Interpretation, pp. 280–302. Springer, Cham (2024)

13. Agarap, A.F.: Deep Learning using Rectified Linear Units (ReLU) arXiv:1803.08375 (2018). https://doi.org/10.48550/arXiv.1803.08375

14. Barbosa, H., et al.: cvc5: a versatile and industrial-strength SMT solver. In: Fisman, D., Rosu, G. (eds.) Tools and Algorithms for the Construction and Analysis of Systems, pp. 415–442. Springer, Cham (2022)

15. Battaglia, P.W., et al.: Relational inductive biases, deep learning, and graph networks. CoRR abs/1806.01261 (2018). http://arxiv.org/abs/1806.01261

16. Bártek, F., Suda, M.: Neural precedence recommender. In: Platzer, A., Sutcliffe, G. (eds.) CADE 2021. LNCS (LNAI), vol. 12699, pp. 525–542. Springer, Cham (2021). https://doi.org/10.1007/978-3-030-79876-5_30

17. Bártek, F., Suda, M.: How much should this symbol weigh? A GNN-advised clause selection. In: Piskac, R., Voronkov, A. (eds.) Proceedings of 24th International Conference on Logic for Programming, Artificial Intelligence and Reasoning. EPiC Series in Computing, vol. 94, pp. 96–111. EasyChair (2023). https://doi.org/10.29007/5f4r, /publications/paper/2BSs

18. Chen, T., Hague, M., Lin, A.W., Rümmer, P., Wu, Z.: Decision procedures for path feasibility of string-manipulating programs with complex operations. Proc. ACM Program. Lang. 3(POPL), 49:1–49:30 (2019). https://doi.org/10.1145/3290362

19. Chen, Y.F., Chocholatý, D., Havlena, V., Holík, L., Lengál, O., Síč, J.: Z3-noodler: an automata-based string solver. In: Finkbeiner, B., Kovács, L. (eds.) Tools and Algorithms for the Construction and Analysis of Systems, pp. 24–33. Springer, Cham (2024). https://doi.org/10.1007/978-3-031-57246-3_2

20. Day, J.D., Ehlers, T., Kulczynski, M., Manea, F., Nowotka, D., Poulsen, D.B.: On solving word equations using SAT. In: Filiot, E., Jungers, R., Potapov, I. (eds.) RP 2019. LNCS, vol. 11674, pp. 93–106. Springer, Cham (2019). https://doi.org/10.1007/978-3-030-30806-3_8

21. Day, J.D., Kulczynski, M., Manea, F., Nowotka, D., Poulsen, D.B.: Rule-based word equation solving. In: Proceedings of the 8th International Conference on Formal Methods in Software Engineering, FormaliSE 2020, pp. 87–97. Association for Computing Machinery, New York (2020). https://doi.org/10.1145/3372020.3391556

22. Diekert, V., Lohrey, M.: Word equations over graph products. In: Pandya, P.K., Radhakrishnan, J. (eds.) FSTTCS 2003. LNCS, vol. 2914, pp. 156–167. Springer, Heidelberg (2003). https://doi.org/10.1007/978-3-540-24597-1_14

23. Gilmer, J., Schoenholz, S.S., Riley, P.F., Vinyals, O., Dahl, G.E.: Neural message passing for quantum chemistry. CoRR abs/1704.01212 (2017). http://arxiv.org/abs/1704.01212

24. Goodfellow, I.J., Bengio, Y., Courville, A.: Deep Learning. MIT Press, Cambridge (2016). http://www.deeplearningbook.org

25. Horn, A.: On sentences which are true of direct unions of algebras. J. Symb. Log. **16**(1), 14–21 (1951). https://doi.org/10.2307/2268661

26. Hůla, J., Mojžíšek, D., Janota, M.: Graph neural networks for scheduling of SMT solvers. In: 2021 IEEE 33rd International Conference on Tools with Artificial Intelligence (ICTAI), pp. 447–451 (2021). https://doi.org/10.1109/ICTAI52525.2021.00072

27. Jakubův, J., Chvalovský, K., Olšák, M., Piotrowski, B., Suda, M., Urban, J.: ENIGMA anonymous: symbol-independent inference guiding machine (system description). In: Peltier, N., Sofronie-Stokkermans, V. (eds.) IJCAR 2020. LNCS (LNAI), vol. 12167, pp. 448–463. Springer, Cham (2020). https://doi.org/10.1007/978-3-030-51054-1_29

28. Jeż, A.: Recompression: a simple and powerful technique for word equations (2014). https://arxiv.org/abs/1203.3705

29. Kipf, T.N., Welling, M.: Semi-supervised classification with graph convolutional networks. In: 5th International Conference on Learning Representations, ICLR 2017, Toulon, France, 24–26 April 2017, Conference Track Proceedings. OpenReview.net (2017). https://openreview.net/forum?id=SJU4ayYgl

30. Kumar, A., Manolios, P.: Mathematical programming modulo strings. In: Formal Methods in Computer Aided Design, FMCAD 2021, New Haven, CT, USA, 19–22 October 2021, pp. 261–270. IEEE (2021). https://doi.org/10.34727/2021/ISBN.978-3-85448-046-4_36

31. Levi, F.W.: On semigroups. Bull. Calcutta Math. Soc. **36**(141–146), 82 (1944)

32. Liang, C., Rümmer, P., Brockschmidt, M.: Exploring representation of horn clauses using GNNs. In: Konev, B., Schon, C., Steen, A. (eds.) Proceedings of the Workshop on Practical Aspects of Automated Reasoning Co-located with the 11th International Joint Conference on Automated Reasoning (FLoC/IJCAR 2022), Haifa, Israel, 11–12 August 2022. CEUR Workshop Proceedings, vol. 3201. CEUR-WS.org (2022). https://ceur-ws.org/Vol-3201/paper7.pdf

33. Makanin, G.S.: The problem of solvability of equations in a free semigroup. Math. Sb. (N.S.) **103(145)**(2(6)), 147–236 (1977)

34. Marques-Silva, J., Sakallah, K.A.: Grasp: a search algorithm for propositional satisfiability. IEEE Trans. Comput. **48**, 506–521 (1999). https://api.semanticscholar.org/CorpusID:13039801

35. de Moura, L., Bjørner, N.: Z3: an efficient SMT solver. In: Ramakrishnan, C.R., Rehof, J. (eds.) TACAS 2008. LNCS, vol. 4963, pp. 337–340. Springer, Heidelberg (2008). https://doi.org/10.1007/978-3-540-78800-3_24

36. Nielsen, J.: Die Isomorphismen der allgemeinen, unendlichen Gruppe mit zwei Erzeugenden. Mathematische Annalen **78**, 385–397 (1917). https://api.semanticscholar.org/CorpusID:119726936

37. Pin, J.E., Perrin, D.: Infinite Words: Automata, Semigroups, Logic and Games. Elsevier (2004). https://hal.science/hal-00112831

38. Plandowski, W.: Satisfiability of word equations with constants is in PSPACE. In: 40th Annual Symposium on Foundations of Computer Science (Cat. No. 99CB37039), pp. 495–500 (1999). https://doi.org/10.1109/SFFCS.1999.814622

39. Power, J.F.: Thue's 1914 paper: a translation. CoRR abs/1308.5858 (2013). http://arxiv.org/abs/1308.5858

40. Selsam, D., Bjørner, N.: Neurocore: guiding high-performance SAT solvers with unsat-core predictions. CoRR abs/1903.04671 (2019)

41. Selsam, D., Lamm, M., Bünz, B., Liang, P., de Moura, L., Dill, D.L.: Learning a SAT solver from single-bit supervision. In: 7th International Conference on Learning Representations, ICLR 2019, New Orleans, LA, USA, 6–9 May 2019. OpenReview.net (2019). https://openreview.net/forum?id=HJMC_iA5tm

42. Si, X., Dai, H., Raghothaman, M., Naik, M., Song, L.: Learning loop invariants for program verification. In: Bengio, S., Wallach, H., Larochelle, H., Grauman, K., Cesa-Bianchi, N., Garnett, R. (eds.) Advances in Neural Information Processing Systems, vol. 31. Curran Associates, Inc. (2018)

43. Si, X., Naik, A., Dai, H., Naik, M., Song, L.: Code2Inv: a deep learning framework for program verification. In: Lahiri, S.K., Wang, C. (eds.) CAV 2020. LNCS, vol. 12225, pp. 151–164. Springer, Cham (2020). https://doi.org/10.1007/978-3-030-53291-8_9

44. Suda, M.: Improving ENIGMA-style clause selection while learning from history. In: Platzer, A., Sutcliffe, G. (eds.) CADE 2021. LNCS (LNAI), vol. 12699, pp. 543–561. Springer, Cham (2021). https://doi.org/10.1007/978-3-030-79876-5_31

45. Wang, M., Tang, Y., Wang, J., Deng, J.: Premise selection for theorem proving by deep graph embedding. In: Proceedings of the 31st International Conference on Neural Information Processing Systems, NIPS 2017, pp. 2783–2793. Curran Associates Inc., Red Hook (2017)

A Finite Abstraction of Real-Valued Functions for Complete Reasoning About Influence

Sören Möller[1]([⊠])[ID], Florian Bruse[2][ID], and Martin Lange[1][ID]

[1] Theoretical Computer Science/Formal Methods, University of Kassel, Kassel, Germany
soeren.moeller@uni-kassel.de
[2] TUM School of Computation, Information and Technology, Technical University of Munich, Munich, Germany

Abstract. We consider the reasoning problem of logical consequence between simple statements about the behaviour of continuous functions on certain intervals, representing the way that variables influence each other. Automated reasoning for such statements has applications in formal modelling of classroom experiments in natural sciences. A previous attempt, employing a simple proof system for this reasoning task, is known to be incomplete and unlikely to be extendable to obtain completeness for arbitrary experiments. Here we develop an algebraic approach in the form of an abstraction of the uncountable space of finite collections of continuous, real-valued functions, connected by a composition principle, into finitely many representatives of equivalence classes. We show that this is sufficient for the reasoning task at hand. The approach achieves completeness under very reasonable restrictions of the involved statements, extending what has previously been achieved using proof-theoretic means, and yields an upper bound of coNP.

Keywords: formal modelling · hybrid systems · formal reasoning · completeness

1 Introduction

Formal reasoning forms the basis for automated solutions to many decision problems [9,14], especially when they can be seen as instances of classic logical problems like validity or logical consequence: given a set of formulas Ψ and a single formula φ, is it the case that $\Psi \models \varphi$, i.e. do all models of Ψ also satisfy φ? Calculi and algorithms are continuously developed for formal reasoning tasks involving various kinds of logics from general purpose ones like First-Order Logic [15], Higher-Order Logic [1], etc. to specific-purpose ones like program logics [8], description logics [2], temporal logics [7], etc.

Here we are concerned with automated reasoning for logical consequence in a very specific and very simple logic that makes assertions about particular hybrid systems. These comprise collections of continuous, real-valued functions, each of

© The Author(s) 2026
R. Thiemann and C. Weidenbach (Eds.): FroCoS 2025, LNAI 15979, pp. 346–363, 2026.
https://doi.org/10.1007/978-3-032-04167-8_19

which is associated with a pair of elements of an underlying finite, partial order of so-called *variables*. A function $\mathcal{F}_{a,b} : \mathbb{R} \to \mathbb{R}$, associated with the variable-pair (a, b), models dynamic behaviour. However, this does not necessarily model the evolution of some value over time (as it is the case in e.g. hybrid automata [10]), but it models the dependency of b-values on a-values where a and b are arbitrary variables. Thus, it models the way that variable a *influences* variable b. Influence as an abstract concept between a discrete set of variables can naturally form a partial order, in particular it should clearly be transitive: if altitude (Alt) influences air pressure (AP) and air pressure influences oxygen saturation (Ox) then Alt also influences Ox. In particular, $\mathcal{F}_{\mathsf{Alt,Ox}}$ is determined by $\mathcal{F}_{\mathsf{Alt,AP}}$ and $\mathcal{F}_{\mathsf{AP,Ox}}$, imposing constraints on valid combinations of functions and excluding arbitrary collections. The valid collections are called *experiments* for reasons to become clear below when we discuss the motivation for this reasoning task.

Anti-symmetry of influence – the inability of two variables to mutually influence each other – is arguably not such a natural requirement. For instance, pressure, temperature and volume of a gas all influence each other mutually. We impose anti-symmetry as a technical requirement, restricting the domain of application slightly but not unreasonably. This restriction is needed to obtain a decision procedure for the reasoning problem under consideration.

The "formulas" of the logic under consideration here are simple atomic statements about observable, abstract behaviour of influence on certain intervals, e.g. "*air pressure decreases steadily from 1bar to 0.8bar at altitudes between 0m and 2000m*". A set of such statements is called a *scheme*, and it describes valid influence behaviour between the underlying variables, formally described as the satisfaction of such statements by an experiment in the sense above. The reasoning problem we study then is: given such a scheme $\mathcal{C}$ and another statement H, called the *hypothesis*, does $\mathcal{C} \models H$ hold?

The motivation for this study stems from a particular application, namely the intention to digitalise classroom experiments in natural sciences, in particular biology. As part of standard high school curricula to instigate scientific reasoning, students devise experiments and hypotheses and test them empirically. Virtualisation of this process has advantages [11,17], e.g. by extending the range of experiments that can be done in classrooms, perhaps involving dangerous substances or those of limited accessibility, infeasible time scales, etc. This requires sound, complete and efficient automated reasoning techniques, though.

The use of a formal system from logic or computer science for formal modelling of biological processes is not new (cf. [3,16,18]), not even w.r.t. the special aspect of variable influence [6]. Our work here combines not only aspects of formal modelling and biological systems but also demands imposed by didactics. The reason for studying simple statements only, for example, is their potential use in a suitable learning tool that cannot require 8th graders for instance to possess knowledge in formal logic.

The first approach at providing automated support for the problem of logical consequence between schemes and hypotheses was a proof-theoretic one, called the *Calculus of Influence* (CoI) [5]. It tries to capture the relation '$\models$' by a finite set of proof rules. This is sound and polynomial-time computable, but unfortunately complete only for very restricted forms of partial orders of the underyling variable set. In this paper we present an algebraic approach based on an abstraction of the uncountably many experiments described by schemes into finitely many representatives of equivalence classes. This abstraction is faithful w.r.t. logical consequence, leading to a reasoning algorithm that achieves completeness without restrictions on the underlying partial orders.

The paper is organised as follows. In Sect. 2 we introduce the involved concepts like experiments, schemes, consequence etc. formally. In Sect. 3 we intuitively develop an equivalence relation on experiments that possesses the properties mentioned above, which opens up the path for an algorithmic approach to the consequence relation between schemes and hypotheses. In Sect. 4 we develop this approach for flat partial orders, i.e. those in which transitivity plays no role. This is simply done to separate the technical developments into two steps, first focussing on the discretisation of continuous functions. This is then lifted in Sect. 5 to non-flat orders, there focussing on the issues arising with function composition. We conclude in Sect. 6 with remarks on further work in this area. Technical proofs have been moved to the appendix for space considerations.

2   Preliminaries

Influences and Influence Experiments. Let $\mathcal{V} = \{a, b, \ldots\}$ be a finite set of *variables* ordered by some partial order $\leq$. For a variable $a \in \mathcal{V}$, $\text{Post}(a) := \{b \in \mathcal{V} \mid a < b$ and there is no $b' \in \mathcal{V}$ s.t. $a < b' < b\}$ are all its *successors*. The set of *predecessors*, denoted by $\text{Pre}(a)$, is defined analogously. An *interval* is a $[x, y] \subseteq \mathbb{R}$ such that $x \leq y$ as usual.

An *influence* is a continuous function $f : \mathbb{R} \to \mathbb{R}$ with domain $\text{dom}(f) = [x, y]$ for some $x, y \in \mathbb{Q}$. For $x \notin \text{dom}(f)$, we define $f(x) = \bot$. Furthermore, we assume that $\bot$ is absorbing under composition, i.e. $f(g(x)) = \bot$ whenever $g(x) = \bot$ for all $x \in \mathbb{R}$.

The *behaviour* of an influence on a (sub-)domain $[x, y] \subseteq \text{dom}(f)$ is *monotonic* ($\nearrow$) if $f(z) \leq f(z')$, *antitonic* ($\searrow$) if $f(z) \geq f(z')$, *constant* ($\to$) if $f(z) = f(z')$ for all $x \leq z \leq z' \leq y$, and *arbitrary* ($\rightsquigarrow$) otherwise.

Behaviours are naturally ordered: $\to$ is a special case of $\nearrow$ and of $\searrow$, and these are special cases of $\rightsquigarrow$ in turn. We use $q \prec q'$ to indicate that q is a special case of q'. We write $f|_{[x,y]} \preceq q$ with $q \in \{\nearrow, \searrow, \to, \rightsquigarrow\}$ to indicate that f exhibits behaviour q on $[x, y]$, and $f|_{[x,y]} = q$ if $f|_{[x,y]} \preceq q$ and $f|_{[x,y]} \not\preceq q'$ for any $q' \prec q$.

The *range* of an influence f on $[x, y]$ is $\text{rng}_{[x,y]}(f) = \{f(z) \mid x \leq z \leq y\}$.

Definition 1. *A $\mathcal{V}$-influence experiment $\mathcal{F}$ is a collection of influences $\mathcal{F}_{a,b}$ for each pair of variables $a, b \in \mathcal{V}$ such that $a < b$. Moreover, $\mathcal{F}$ must satisfy the coherence property: for all $a, b, c \in \mathcal{V}$ with $a < b < c$ and all $x \in \mathbb{R}$, we have $(\mathcal{F}_{b,c} \circ \mathcal{F}_{a,b})(x) = \mathcal{F}_{a,c}(x)$.*

Example 1. The $\mathcal{V}$-influence experiment $\mathcal{F}$ illustrated in Fig. 1 depicts the relationships between the variables *Altitude* (Alt) in meters, *Air Pressure* (AP) in kPa, and *Oxygen* (Ox) in percent, using orange lines to indicate the influences

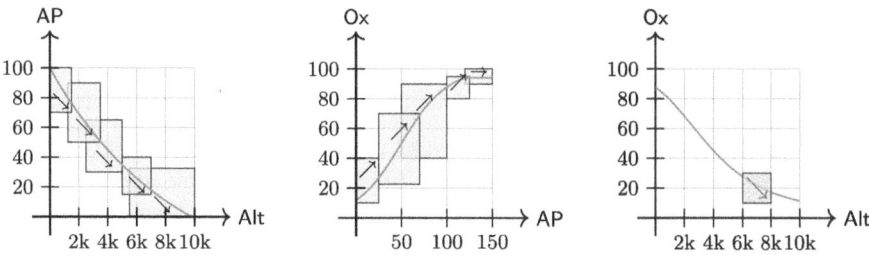

Fig. 1. Example of an experiment (orange), scheme (grey), and hypothesis (red). (Color figure online)

between them. Specifically, $\mathcal{F}$ captures the influences of altitude on air pressure and air pressure on oxygen levels. We obtain the influence of altitude on oxygen levels via the coherence property, i.e. $\mathcal{F}_{\mathsf{Alt,Ox}} = \mathcal{F}_{\mathsf{Alt,AP}} \circ \mathcal{F}_{\mathsf{AP,Ox}}$.

Statements and Influence Schemes. Let $\mathcal{V}$ be as above. A $\mathcal{V}$-statement is a 5-tuple $S = (a, [x,y], q, [l,u], b)$, typically written as $a \xrightarrow{[x,y]\, q\, [l,u]} b$, where $a, b \in \mathcal{V}$ are variables s.t. $a < b$, $\mathrm{dom}(S) = [x,y]$ is the statements's *domain*, $\mathrm{rng}(S) = [l,u]$ is the statements *range*, and $q \in \{\nearrow, \searrow, \rightarrow\}$ is the statements' *behaviour*. It abstractly describes the gradient of influences as functions on the domain as mapping into the range either monotonically ($\nearrow$), antitonically ($\searrow$) or in a constant fashion $\rightarrow$. The behaviour $\rightsquigarrow$ is disallowed in such statements. Intuitively, the statement S asserts that the influence $\mathcal{F}_{a,b}$ of a $\mathcal{V}$-influence experiment $\mathcal{F}$ is defined on $\mathrm{dom}(S)$, must only take values in $\mathrm{rng}(S)$ on that domain, and behaves just as q asserts.

More formally, influence f *satisfies* S, written $f \models S$, if

- $[x,y] \subseteq \mathrm{dom}(f)$,
- $\mathrm{rng}(f) \subseteq [l,u]$, and
- $f|_{[x,y]} \preceq q$.

Definition 2. *A $\mathcal{V}$-(influence) scheme $\mathcal{C}$ is a finite set of $\mathcal{V}$-statements. For a scheme $\mathcal{C}$ and $a, b \in \mathcal{V}$, let $\mathcal{C}_{a,b} := \{S \mid S = a \xrightarrow{I\, q\, I'} b \in \mathcal{C}$ for some $I, q, I'\}$.*

We lift the semantics of a single statement to the semantics of an influence scheme. Given a $\mathcal{V}$-influence scheme $\mathcal{C}$ and a $\mathcal{V}$-influence experiment $\mathcal{F}$, we say that $\mathcal{F}$ satisfies $\mathcal{C}$, written $\mathcal{F} \models \mathcal{C}$, if $\mathcal{F}_{a,b} \models S$ for all $S = a \xrightarrow{I\, q\, I'} b \in \mathcal{C}$.

Example 2. Figure 1 depicts, besides a particular $\mathcal{V}$-influence experiment $\mathcal{F}$ using orange lines as described in Example 1, a $\mathcal{V}$-influence scheme $\mathcal{C}$. Each statement $a \xrightarrow{[x,y]\, q\, [l,u]} b \in \mathcal{C}$ is represented by a grey rectangle spanning from (x,l) to (y,u) in the corresponding influence diagram with variable names a and b, and behaviour q is indicated by the label inside the rectangle.

Using this visual interpretation, we can verify that $\mathcal{F} \models \mathcal{C}$ holds by inspecting the diagram for each pair of variables $(\mathsf{Alt}, \mathsf{AP})$, $(\mathsf{AP}, \mathsf{Ox})$, and $(\mathsf{Alt}, \mathsf{Ox})$. We confirm that, for each of these, the corresponding influence is defined on all relevant domains, only takes values within the rectangles, and behaves as indicated by the labels inside the rectangles.

Hypothesis Validation. We aim to validate hypotheses such as *"does the oxygen level decrease to levels of 10% to 30% at altitudes between 6 and 8 km?"* relative to the theory of behaviour of variables described by an influence scheme. Such a hypothesis asserts properties as a $\mathcal{V}$-statement does, but it may or may not make a statement on the behaviour of the function in question. Formally, a *hypothesis* is simply a special $\mathcal{V}$-statement, typically written as H, that may state behaviour $\rightsquigarrow$. Satisfaction of a hypothesis H by an influence F, written $F \models H$, is defined as it is for $\mathcal{V}$-statements.

This provides the model-theoretic machinery for the reasoning problem "does a given hypothesis follows from a scheme?" to be well-defined.

Definition 3. *A hypothesis H follows* from *a $\mathcal{V}$-influence scheme $\mathcal{C}$, written $\mathcal{C} \models H$, if for all $\mathcal{V}$-influence experiments $\mathcal{F}$ with $\mathcal{F} \models \mathcal{C}$ we have $\mathcal{F} \models H$.*

Example 3. Consider the $\mathcal{V}$-influence experiment $\mathcal{F}$ and the $\mathcal{V}$-influence scheme $\mathcal{C}$ shown in Fig. 1. The statement $H = \mathsf{AP} \xrightarrow{[6000,8000] \searrow [10,30]} \mathsf{Ox}$ is a formalisation of the hypothesis given above. It is visualised in Fig. 1 as a red box to distinguish it from the grey boxes representing the scheme.

It is straightforward to see that $\mathcal{F}_{\mathsf{Alt,Ox}} \models H$, and hence $\mathcal{F} \models H$, holds. However, this does not imply that $\mathcal{C} \models H$ holds, as there may be $\mathcal{V}$-influence experiments $\mathcal{F}'$ with $\mathcal{F}' \models \mathcal{C}$ such that $\mathcal{F}'_{\mathsf{Alt,Ox}} \not\models H$, for example when $\mathcal{F}'_{\mathsf{Alt,Ox}}$ takes values in $[40, 50]$ on the domain of $[6000, 8000]$.

We aim to give an algebraic characterisation of logical consequence between schemes and hypotheses, i.e. to provide a sound and complete decision procedure for the following problem SCHEMEENTAILMENT over a given variable set $\mathcal{V}$:

> **given:**   a $\mathcal{V}$-influence scheme $\mathcal{C}$, a hypothesis H
> **decide:** does $\mathcal{C} \models H$ hold?

As a syntactic convention, we write $\mathcal{C} \cup H$ instead of $\mathcal{C} \cup \{H\}$ in the following.

3   Indistinguishable Experiments

In general, there are uncountably many influence experiments that satisfy a given influence scheme, given that a statement is a rather coarse representation of uncountably many continuous, real-valued functions. Hence, SCHEMEENTAILMENT cannot be solved by exhaustive search. A promising idea is to formalize logical consequence of schemes and statements into a calculus and to show completeness of this calculus. This works in certain instances, but in general this approach suffers from the complex interactions that the coherence property induces alongside chains in the variable order, sometimes even in a backwards fashion [5]. We therefore follow a different approach: we reduce SCHEMEENTAILMENT to a

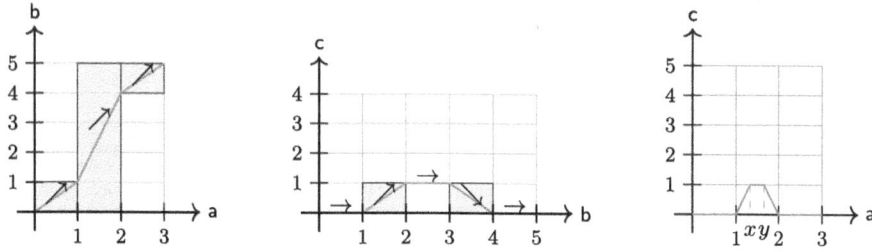

Fig. 2. An influence scheme that enforces behaviour $\rightsquigarrow$.

corresponding problem in a discrete space. This is achieved by combining sets of influence experiments into finitely many equivalence classes according to a yet-to-be-defined equivalence relation.

A first intuition behind this uses the fact that a scheme (and a hypothesis) may only "talk about" finitely many points, namely those mentioned as the borders of the domain or range of a statement. The exact values of an influence strictly between such boundary points are not important, only their abstract behaviour. This approach will be refined later, but we illustrate the idea first.

Example 4. Consider the scheme $\mathcal{C} = \{a \xrightarrow{[1,2] \nearrow [0,2]} b\}$ and the hypothesis $a \xrightarrow{[1,2] \rightarrow [0,1]} b$. It is easy to see that e.g. the influence $\mathcal{F}_{a,b}(x) = 2$ defined on $[0,2]$ refutes $\mathcal{C} \models H$. However, we can divide the set of all influences that satisfy $\mathcal{C}$ into seven different classes, tabulated below:

behaviour on $[1,2]$	image of $\mathcal{F}_{a,b}$ on $[1,2]$
constant	$[0,0]$, $[1,1]$, $[2,2]$, or $[i,i]$ with $0 < i < 1$ or $1 < i < 2$
strictly monotonic	$[i,j]$ with $0 \le i < j \le 1$, $1 \le i < j \le 2$ or $i < 1 < j$

It is not hard to verify that each of these classes can be realized by an actual influence, and that these seven classes partition the set of all influences that satisfy $\mathcal{C}$. Moreover, either all influences from a class satisfy H, or none does, so this partitioning is a congruence w.r.t. H. We conclude that $\mathcal{C} \not\models H$, since the influences in at least one of these classes satisfy $\mathcal{C}$, but not H.

These seven classes are not defined arbitrarily, but following two criteria: (I) the *actual* range of the influence on the interval $[1,2]$, compared to one of the integers that appears as a bound on the b-axis (i.e. 0, 1 or 2), and (II) the actual behaviour of the influence on the interval $[1,2]$.

If $\mathcal{C}$ had been $\{u \xrightarrow{[0,1] \nearrow [0,1]} b, a \xrightarrow{[1,2] \rightarrow [0,2]} b\}$, it would not suffice to look at the behaviour on the interval $[1,2]$, even though H is restricted to it. In fact, we would have generated 20 equivalence classes since there are five options for the behaviour of an influence on the domain $[1,2]$ (the five constant options above), and another four for the behaviour on $[0,1]$ (the four options where the actual range is in $[0,1]$). Of course, some of them do not form a proper influence (e.g. the function that is constant 0 on $[0,1]$ and constant 2 on $[1,2]$). This illustrates that we have to look at the whole scheme in order to ensure that each class is inhabited.

In the presence of a nontrivial chain $a < b < c$ in the variable order, the approach needs to be refined, though.

Example 5. Consider the scheme

$$C = \{a \xrightarrow{[0,1] \nearrow [0,1]} b,\, a \xrightarrow{[1,2] \nearrow [0,5]} b,\, a \xrightarrow{[2,3] \nearrow [4,5]} b,\, b \xrightarrow{[0,1] \rightarrow [1,1]} c,$$
$$b \xrightarrow{[1,2] \nearrow [0,1]} c,\, b \xrightarrow{[2,3] \rightarrow [1,1]} c,\, b \xrightarrow{[3,4] \searrow [0,1]} c,\, b \xrightarrow{[4,5] \rightarrow [0,0]} c\}$$

depicted in Fig. 2 with an influence that satisfies it. Due to the construction of the scheme, the image of $\mathcal{F}_{a,b}$ on $[1,2]$ must include the entire interval $[1,4]$. On the other hand, $\mathcal{F}_{b,c}$ must describe a convex pattern on $[1,4]$, moving upwards from 0 to 1 between 1 and 2, staying constant between 2 and 3, and moving downwards from 1 to 0 between 3 and 4. Hence, the influence $\mathcal{F}_{a,c}$ must describe a similar pattern on $[1,2]$.

This behaviour in Example 5 produces two problems:

- The behaviour of any $\mathcal{F}_{a,c}$ on $[1,2]$ can only be described as $\rightsquigarrow$, even though influence schemes cannot have $\rightsquigarrow$ in their statements. Hence, such behaviour can crop up as a logical consequence of seemingly innocuous statements.
- The categorisation of influence schemes alongside the bounds of the scheme described above does not work in the presence of nontrivial variable chains. For example, $\mathcal{C}' = \mathcal{C} \setminus \{a \xrightarrow{[2,3] \nearrow [4,5]} b\}$ does not force the above convex pattern on $\mathcal{F}_{a,c}$. However, such a pattern still satisfies $\mathcal{C}'$ whence it must be considered because any influence experiment that satisfies $\mathcal{C}$ also satisfies $\mathcal{C}'$.

However, the above approach of categorising functions alongside the bounds mentioned in a scheme and a hypothesis does not fail completely. While $\mathcal{F}_{a,c}$ describes the convex pattern within the interval $[1,2]$, and, hence, has behaviour $\rightsquigarrow$, this does not mean that the behaviour of $\mathcal{F}_{a,c}$ is completely arbitrary. In fact, any influence that satisfies $\mathcal{C}$ must describe exactly this behaviour, and for every such influence, there are points $x \le y \in (1,2)$ that mark beginning, respectively the end of the top constant part of the convex pattern (also depicted in Fig. 2). Where exactly they sit depends on the concrete influence, but they must exist and $1 < x < y < 2$ must be true. Moreover, the influence is monotonic between 1 and x, constant between x and y, and antitonic between y and 2.

Hence, the idea of categorising influence experiments into finitely many equivalence classes needs to be refined by introducing such undefined, but constrained *points of interest*, that (I) are derived (heriditarily) from the bounds of the scheme and (II) partition the influence in question into pieces that resort to behaviour which is stronger than $\rightsquigarrow$ again.

Next, we outline the intuition and essential properties that such equivalence relations should satisfy. However, the precise definition and construction of these equivalence relations, and how to handle the coherence property in the presence of variable chains, are non-trivial and form the core contributions of this work. These are detailed in Sect. 4 and Sect. 5.

The above considerations gives rise to the following, refined idea: given an input to the problem SCHEMEENTAILMENT, i.e. an influence scheme $\mathcal{C}$ and a hypothesis H, for each pair of variables a, b with $a < b$, compute an equivalence relation $\sim_{C,H,a,b}$ that satisfies the following properties:

1. (Finiteness) The index of $\sim_{C,H,a,b}$ is finite and the classes are effectively enumerable.
2. (Congruence w.r.t. C) If $\mathcal{F}_{a,b} \sim_{C,H,a,b} \mathcal{G}_{a,b}$, then $\mathcal{F}_{a,b} \models C_{a,b}$ if and only if $\mathcal{G}_{a,b} \models C_{a,b}$.
3. (Congruence w.r.t. H) $\mathcal{F}_{a,b} \sim_{C,H,a,b} \mathcal{G}_{a,b}$ and $H = a \xrightarrow{I \, q \, I'} b$, then $\mathcal{F}_{a,b} \models H$ if and only if $\mathcal{G}_{a,b} \models H$.
4. (Coherence) For all $c \in \mathcal{V}$ with $b < c$, if $\mathcal{F}_{a,b} \sim_{C,H,a,b} \mathcal{G}_{a,b}$ and $\mathcal{F}_{b,c} \sim_{C,H,b,c} \mathcal{G}_{b,c}$, then $\mathcal{F}_{a,c} \sim_{C,H,a,c} \mathcal{G}_{a,c}$.

The first three properties have been discussed above. The last property, Coherence, is a crucial sanity condition that filters out influence classes that do not match each other, i.e. that cannot satisfy the coherence property.

The structure of experiments allows us to lift these relations on influences to a relation on experiments, by defining $\mathcal{F} \sim_{C,H} \mathcal{G}$ if $\mathcal{F}_{a,b} \sim_{C,H,a,b} \mathcal{G}_{a,b}$ for all $a, b \in \mathcal{V}$ with $a < b$. This yields an algorithm to determine whether $C \models H$.

1. For all $a, b \in \mathcal{V}$ with $a < b$ but no c with $a < c < b$, compute the equivalence classes of $\sim_{C,H,a,b}$. Remove all uninhabited (due to discontinuities) classes.
2. Combine the equivalence classes of $\sim_{C,H,a,b}$ for all $a, b \in \mathcal{V}$ with $a < b$ to obtain the equivalence classes of $\sim_{C,H}$.
3. Remove equivalence classes that do not satisfy C.
4. Check whether all remaining classes do satisfy H and return **true** if yes, or else return **false** if this fails for some class.

The first and second step work because there are only finitely many equivalence classes of $\sim_{C,H,a,b}$, which can be effectively enumerated. The second step requires the coherence property to be satisfied, which is possible due to the requirement of Coherence above. The third step is possible since all experiments in the same equivalence class are indistinguishable with respect to C (Congruence w.r.t. C), hence we must only check for one experiment in each equivalence class whether it satisfies the respective sub-scheme. Finally, the last step works as equivalent experiments are indistinguishable with respect to H (Congruence w.r.t. H).

The most challenging requirement on the equivalence relations is Coherence. It involves complex and fine-grained reasoning about the equivalence classes. Hence, in Sect. 4 we focus on schemes defined over *flat* variable orders, i.e. orders where there are no variable chains of the form $a < b < c$, whence Coherence is satisfied vacuously and a formalisation of the informal discussion above suffices. The assumption of flatness is then lifted in Sect. 5.

4   Completeness for Flat Schemes

In this section, we assume the underlying variable order to be *flat*, i.e. there are no $a, b, c \in \mathcal{V}$ such that $a < b < c$. Experiments over a flat variable order are more general than just a single influence, as they may contain multiple influences, but these are unrelated by the coherence property.

Definition 4. *Let C be a V-influence scheme, let H be a hypothesis, and let $a \in V$. Then p is an a-boundary point if*

- *there is $S \in C_{a,b} \cup H$ for some $a < b$ with $S = a \xrightarrow{[x,y]\, q\, [l,u]} b$ and $p = x$ or $p = y$, or*
- *there is $S \in C_{b,a} \cup H$ for some $b < a$ with $S = b \xrightarrow{[x,y]\, q\, [l,u]} a$ and $p = l$ or $p = u$.*

We write $\mathrm{bds}_a(C \cup H)$ for the set of all a-boundary points of C and H.

Note that $\mathrm{bds}_a(C \cup H)$ is naturally ordered via the order of the reals, whence we can refer to the ith such point (tacitly assuming that such an ith point exists).

Given a V-influence scheme C and a hypothesis H, we consider influences to be equivalent if they behave in the same way w.r.t. all boundary points, formalised as follows.

Definition 5. *Let C be a scheme and let H be a hypothesis. Let f be an influence from a to b, $[x, y] \subseteq \mathrm{dom}(f)$, $\mathrm{rng}_{[x,y]}(f) = [l, u]$. Then the value range of f is $\mathrm{vrng}_{[x,y]}(f) = [l', u']$ where $l' = \max\{p \in \mathrm{bds}_b(C \cup H) \mid p \leq l\}$ and $u' = \min\{p \in \mathrm{bds}_b(C \cup H) \mid p \geq u\}$.*

Combining this definition with the intuition explained in the previous section, we obtain the following definition of the equivalence of influences.

Definition 6. *Let C be a V-influence scheme, $a, b \in V$ such that $a < b$, H be a hypothesis, f, g be influences from a to b.*

Then f is equivalent to g w.r.t. H and C, written $f \sim_{C,H,a,b} g$, if for all x, x' that are the ith and $i + 1$st point in $\mathrm{bds}_a(C \cup H)$ for some i, we have $[x, x'] \not\subseteq \mathrm{dom}(f)$ and $[x, x'] \not\subseteq \mathrm{dom}(g)$, or

1. *$[x, x'] \subseteq \mathrm{dom}(f)$ and $[x, x'] \subseteq \mathrm{dom}(g)$,*
2. *$\mathrm{vrng}_{[x,x']}(f) = \mathrm{vrng}_{[x,x']}(g)$, and*
3. *$f|_{[x,x']} = g|_{[x,x']}$.*

This formalises the above idea that two influences are equivalent if they have (i) the same range w.r.t. the b-boundary points on each interval introduced by a-boundary points, and (ii) the same actual behaviour, or equivalently are both undefined on such an interval.

It is not hard to verify that $\sim_{C,H,a,b}$ is an equivalence relation. This leaves the requirements collected in Sect. 3 to be shown.

Lemma 1. *Let C be a V-influence scheme and H be a hypothesis. Let $a < b$. Then the index of $\sim_{C,H,a,b}$ is finite and the classes are effectively enumerable.*

Proof (Sketch). Since the V-influence scheme C is finite, there are only finitely many boundary points for a and b. Between consecutive a-boundary points, only finitely many value ranges and behaviours are possible. All options can be effectively enumerated, excluding combinations where value ranges within segments are conflicting. □

The two congruence requirements (w.r.t. $\mathcal{C}$ and H) are closely related; we therefore consider them together.

Lemma 2. *Let $\mathcal{C}$ be a $\mathcal{V}$-influence scheme, H be a hypothesis and f and g be influences from a to b such that $f \sim_{\mathcal{C},H,a,b} g$. For any $S \in \mathcal{C}_{a,b} \cup H$, we have $f \models S$ iff $g \models S$.*

Proof (Sketch). Each class of $\sim_{\mathcal{C},H,a,b}$ contains more information than any $\mathcal{V}$-statement in $\mathcal{C} \cup H$, and hence, it suffices to combine this information to verify that all influences in a given class satisfy a given $\mathcal{V}$-statement. □

We lift the definition of $\sim_{\mathcal{C},H,a,b}$ to influence experiments in the expected way.

Definition 7. *Let $\mathcal{C}$ be a flat $\mathcal{V}$-influence scheme and H be a hypothesis. $\mathcal{F}$ and $\mathcal{G}$ are equivalent with respect to $\mathcal{C}$ and H, written $\mathcal{F} \sim_{\mathcal{C},H} \mathcal{G}$, if for all $a, b \in \mathcal{V}$ such that $a < b$, it holds that $\mathcal{F}_{a,b} \sim_{\mathcal{C},H,a,b} \mathcal{G}_{a,b}$.*

It is straightforward to see that finiteness and the congruences extend from $\sim_{\mathcal{C},H,a,b}$ to $\sim_{\mathcal{C},H}$. Coherence holds trivially. Hence, as described in Sect. 3, decidability of SCHEMEENTAILMENT for flat schemes follows.

Theorem 1. SCHEMEENTAILMENT *is decidable for flat $\mathcal{V}$-influence schemes in polynomial time.*

Proof (Sketch). Given a flat $\mathcal{V}$-influence scheme $\mathcal{C}$ and a hypothesis H, the equivalence relation $\sim_{\mathcal{C},H}$ has finitely many classes, as follows from Lemma 1 and the finiteness of $\mathcal{V}$. Thus, we can enumerate all equivalence classes, discard those that do not satisfy the $\mathcal{V}$-influence scheme $\mathcal{C}$, and check whether any of the remaining classes satisfy the hypothesis H. Both steps are possible by Lemma 2.

Although this naive exhaustive enumeration does not yield a polynomial-time algorithm, a more refined approach guided by the structure of H permits a more efficient exploration of the search space. Specifically, for flat schemes, such a hypothesis-driven procedure ensures polynomial-time decidability. □

It should be noted that this is already known from [5]. However, the approach outlined above is more general and carries further, to be seen in the next section.

5 Completeness for General Schemes

Now we consider schemes over an arbitrary order that is not necessarily flat. When chains of the form $a < b < c$ are allowed, coherence does not hold automatically. This makes reasoning more challenging. Recall from Sect. 3 that the logic of function composition can force influences to exhibit behaviour that can only be described as $\rightsquigarrow$. In Sect. 3, we already saw a potential remedy: to look at more points.

We refine the notion of boundary points twice, first to so-called *turning points*, which formalise the idea that the slope of an influence from a to b may be so steep that it crosses several b-boundary points between two a-boundary points. The points on the a-axis where this happens are the turning points. While their exact position is not necessarily the same for two equivalent influences, their existence and relative position are (i.e. influences without such a steep slope may not exhibit such turning points). The notion of turning points works backwards on the variable order: b-boundary points (and, in fact, b-turning points) induce a-turning points, and so forth.

However, refining boundary points into turning points does not suffice. We later refine the concept further into so-called *points of interest* that also carry information forward alongside the variable order. We then obtain an equivalence relation define analogously to that in Sect. 4, but using points of interest instead of boundary points, which yields the desired decision procedure.

Turning Points. Above we said that a turning point is the point on the a-axis on which an influence from a to b crosses a b-boundary point (actually, a b-turning point). However, that point may not be unique, not even on an interval on which a function is strictly monotonic, since it can remain constant for a time. Hence, we introduce the following notation:

- $\mathrm{vfst}_{[x,y]}(f,p) = \min\{z \mid x \le z \le y, f(z) = p\}$
- $\mathrm{vlst}_{[x,y]}(f,p) = \max\{z \mid x \le z \le y, f(z) = p\}$

Definition 8 (Turning Points). *Let $\mathcal{C}$ be a $\mathcal{V}$-influence scheme and be H a hypothesis. Let $\mathcal{F}$ be a $\mathcal{V}$-influence experiment and $a \in \mathcal{V}$. Then p is an a-turning point if p is an a-boundary point, or*

1. *there is $b \in \mathrm{Post}(a)$ with $\mathrm{Post}(b) \ne \emptyset$,*
2. *there are adjacent a-boundary-points $x < y$ with $[x,y] \subseteq \mathrm{dom}(\mathcal{F}_{a,b})$,*
3. *there is a b-turning point t with $t \in \mathrm{rng}_{[x,y]}(\mathcal{F}_{a,b})$, and*
4. *$p = \mathrm{vfst}_{[x,y]}(\mathcal{F}_{a,b}, t)$ or $p = \mathrm{vlst}_{[x,y]}(\mathcal{F}_{a,b}, t)$.*

We write $\mathrm{tp}_a(\mathcal{F}, \mathcal{C}, H)$ for the set of a-turning points.

The definition matches the intuition above: a turning point is a point on the a-axis such that $\mathcal{F}_{a,b}$ reaches an important point on the b-axis (i.e. a b-turning point, which includes b-boundary points) for the first or last time on an interval induced by two adjacent a-boundary points.

The definition is inductive in a top-down fashion along the influence order: turning points for a variable a are defined based on the turning points of its successors $b \in \mathrm{Post}(a)$. For maximal variables (i.e. those with no successors), the important points on the b-axis are simply the b-boundary points. For non-maximal variables, the important points are the inductively constructed b-turning points.

We illustrate the concept with an example. Consider the $\mathcal{V}$-influence experiment $\mathcal{F}$ depicted in Fig. 3, and assume that $\mathcal{C}$ and H are given s.t. $\mathrm{bds}_c(\mathcal{C} \cup H) = \{0, 1, 2\}$. As d is maximal w.r.t. $<$, by definition, we have $\mathrm{tp}_d(\mathcal{F}, \mathcal{C}, H) = \mathrm{bds}_d(\mathcal{C} \cup H)$, and hence also $\mathrm{tp}_c(\mathcal{F}, \mathcal{C}, H) = \mathrm{bds}_c(\mathcal{C} \cup H)$. The intuition here is that there is no influence in the experiment that can be composed with $\mathcal{F}_{c,d}$, whence it suffices to look at the boundary points of d and c.

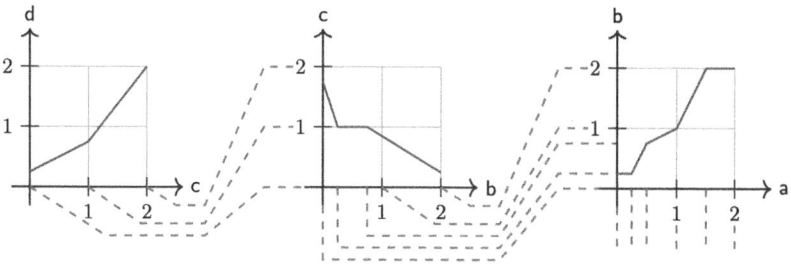

Fig. 3. Example showing the construction of turning points.

Now consider $tp_b(\mathcal{F}, \mathcal{C}, H)$. Since the composition of $\mathcal{F}_{b,c}$ with $\mathcal{F}_{c,d}$ yields $\mathcal{F}_{b,d}$, we have to consider potential subdivisions of the b-axis to ensure that the latter function has behaviour stronger than $\leadsto$ between two b-turning points. Hence, such points are introduced on the b-axis whenever $\mathcal{F}_{b,c}$ crosses a c-turning point, for example at roughly 0.2 and 0.8. The same process is repeated to obtain $tp_a(\mathcal{F}, \mathcal{C}, H)$ (cf. Fig. 3 for details).

Note that, for nonlinear variable orders, e.g. those of the form $a < b < c$ and $a < d < e$, the definition yields a-turning points derived from $tp_b(\mathcal{F}, \mathcal{C}, H)$ and from $tp_d(\mathcal{F}, \mathcal{C}, H)$.

Points of Interest. The introduction of turning points does not suffice to cover all peculiarities introduced by the presence of function composition, together with the requirement of coherence. Consider Fig. 4. It shows an experiment consisting of f and g (in black and blue), and one consisting of f and g' (in black and red). The influences g and g' are equivalent w.r.t. to the definition from Sect. 4, even with turning points in place of boundary points. However, their compositions are clearly not equivalent under any sensible definition, since one of them is constant and the other is not.

The reason for this problem is that g and g' behave differently on the interval $[0.5, 1.5]$ on the b-axis generated by $f(0)$ and $f(1)$. The red function g' is constant there, but the blue function g is not. As a consequence, we extend the concept of turning points into that of *points of interest*, which are obtained by projecting turning points (actually, points of interest) forward alongside the variable order, just as turning point are projections backwards alongside that order.

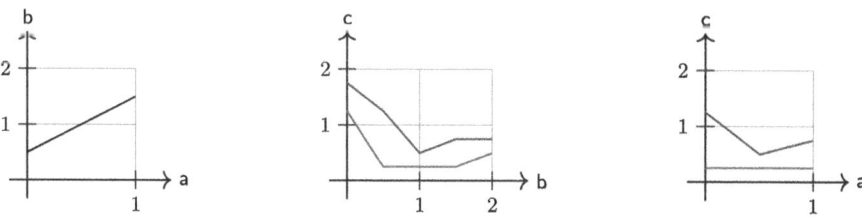

Fig. 4. Influence composition: f (left), g and g' (middle), and $g \circ f$, $g' \circ f$ (right)

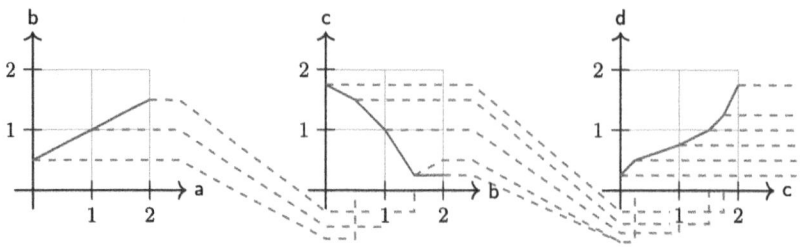

Fig. 5. Example showing the construction of points of interest.

Definition 9 (Points of Interest). *Let C be a $\mathcal{V}$-influence scheme, H be a hypothesis, $\mathcal{F}$ be a $\mathcal{V}$-influence experiment and $b \in \mathcal{V}$. Then p is a b-point of interest with respect to C, H and $\mathcal{F}$ if p is a b-turning point, or if there is an a-point of interest p' s.t. $p = \mathcal{F}_{a,b}(p')$. We write $\mathrm{poi}_b(\mathcal{F}, C, H)$ for the set of b-points of interest.*

The definition is inductive in a bottom-up fashion along the influence order: points of interest for a variable b are defined from the turning points of b, and also they are propagated forward via the functions $\mathcal{F}_{a,b}$ from points of interest of predecessor variables a. This means a point of interest for b is either a b-turning point, or the image of an a-point of interest under $\mathcal{F}_{a,b}$.

Again, we illustrate the concept by means of an example. Consider the previous example depicted in Fig. 4. The points of interest for a, b, c, and d can be computed in a bottom-up fashion. To keep the visualization concise, we base the construction on $\mathrm{bds}(C \cup H)$ instead of $\mathrm{tp}_a(\mathcal{F}, C, H)$ for each variable $a \in \mathcal{V}$.

Since a is minimal w.r.t. the variable order, the a-points of interest are simply the a-boundary points (actually, the a-turning points).

We obtain $\mathrm{tp}_b(\mathcal{F}, C, H)$ as the set of the $\mathcal{F}_{a,b}(x)$ where $x \in \mathrm{tp}_b(\mathcal{F}, C, H)$. We iterate this for c and d, each based on the points of interest of the predecessor variable. Note that, as for the turning points, in non-linear variable orders a variable projects points of interests on all its successors w.r.t the variable order (Fig. 5).

Equivalence of Experiments. We now lift the definitions of $\sim_{C,H,a,b}$ and $\sim_{C,H}$, based on boundary points (cf. Definitions 6 and 7) to their natural refinement based on points of interest.

Recall that sets such as $\mathrm{poi}_a(\mathcal{F}, C, H)$ can be viewed as ordered lists, using the order on the reals. Hence, we can speak of e.g. the ith a-point of interest (with the tacit assumption that i is such that this point exists). The following definition formalises the idea that two influence experiments have the same structure of points of interest (w.r.t. a scheme and a hypothesis), i.e. the same number of points of interest for each variable, and these points connect to points of interest for other variables in the same manner.

Definition 10. *Let C be a $\mathcal{V}$-influence scheme, H be a hypothesis, $\mathcal{F}$ and $\mathcal{G}$ be $\mathcal{V}$-influence experiments. Assume that the following holds for all $a \in Vars$:*

1. *We have* $|\operatorname{poi}_a(\mathcal{F}, \mathcal{C}, H)| = |\operatorname{poi}_a(\mathcal{G}, \mathcal{C}, H)|$.
2. *Let* x *be the* i*th point in* $\operatorname{poi}_a(\mathcal{F}, \mathcal{C}, H)$, *let* x' *be the* i*th point in* $\operatorname{poi}_a(\mathcal{G}, \mathcal{C}, H)$.
   (a) *If* $p \in \operatorname{bds}_a(\mathcal{C} \cup H)$ *is an* a*-boundary point, then* $p = x$ *iff* $p = x'$.
   (b) *If* $b \in \operatorname{Pre}(a)$, y *is the* j*th point in* $\operatorname{poi}_b(\mathcal{F}, \mathcal{C}, H)$ *and* y' *is the* j*th point in* $\operatorname{poi}_b(\mathcal{G}, \mathcal{C}, H)$, *then* $x = \mathcal{F}_{b,a}(y)$ *iff* $x' = \mathcal{F}_{b,a}(y')$.
   (c) *If* $b \in \operatorname{Post}(a)$, y *is the* j*th point in* $\operatorname{poi}_b(\mathcal{F}, \mathcal{C}, H)$, y' *is the* j*th point in* $\operatorname{poi}_b(\mathcal{G}, \mathcal{C}, H)$, *and if* z_1, z_2 *are the* k*th and* $k+1$*st points in* $\operatorname{tp}_a(\mathcal{F}, \mathcal{C}, H)$ *and* z'_1, z'_2 *are the* k*th and* $k+1$*st points in* $\operatorname{tp}_a(\mathcal{G}, \mathcal{C}, H)$, *then* $x = \operatorname{vfst}_{[z_1,z_2]}(\mathcal{F}_{a,b}, y)$ *iff* $x' = \operatorname{vfst}_{[z'_1,z'_2]}(\mathcal{G}_{a,b}, y')$, *and* $x = \operatorname{vlst}_{[z_1,z_2]}(\mathcal{F}_{a,b}, y)$ *iff* $x' = \operatorname{vlst}_{[z'_1,z'_2]}(\mathcal{G}_{a,b}, y')$.

Then $\mathcal{F}$ *and* $\mathcal{G}$ *are* order equivalent *w.r.t.* $\mathcal{C}$ *and* H, *written* $\equiv^{\leq}_{\mathcal{C},H}$.

The intuition here is the following: item 1 says that both experiments have the same number of a-points of interest. Item 2 says that corresponding a-points of interest match the same boundary points (subitem 2a) that they get mapped to corresponding b-points of interest (subitem 2b), and they are induced by the same crossing of turning points on the b-axis.

This definition does not force $\mathcal{F}$ and $\mathcal{G}$ to be equivalent in the stricter sense, i.e. they can still have functions with e.g. different actual variable ranges or actual behaviours. However, the desired equivalence is now easy to formalise based on order equivalence.

Definition 11. *Let* $\mathcal{C}$ *be a* $\mathcal{V}$*-influence scheme*, H *be a hypothesis*, $\mathcal{F}$ *and* $\mathcal{G}$ *be order-equivalent* $\mathcal{V}$*-influence experiments, and* $a, b \in \mathcal{V}$ *with* $a < b$. *Assume that the following holds for all* x_1, x_2 *that are the* i*th and* $i+1$*st points in* $\operatorname{poi}_a(\mathcal{F}, \mathcal{C}, H)$ *and all* x'_1, x'_2 *that are the* i*th and* $i+1$*st points in* $\operatorname{poi}_a(\mathcal{G}, \mathcal{C}, H)$:

1. $[x_1, x_2] \subseteq \operatorname{dom}(\mathcal{F}_{a,b})$ *iff* $[x'_1, x'_2] \subseteq \operatorname{dom}(\mathcal{G}_{a,b})$.
2. $\mathcal{F}_{a,b}|_{[x_1,x_2]} = \mathcal{G}_{a,b}|_{[x'_1,x'_2]}$.
3. *Let* y_1, y_2 *be the* j*th and* k*th points in* $\operatorname{poi}_b(\mathcal{F}, \mathcal{C}, H)$ *and let* y'_1, y'_2 *be the* j*th and* k*th points in* $\operatorname{poi}_b(\mathcal{G}, \mathcal{C}, H)$, *where* $j \leq k$. *Then* $\operatorname{rng}_{[x_1,x_2]}(\mathcal{F}_{a,b}) = [y_1, y_2]$ *iff* $\operatorname{rng}_{[x'_1,x'_2]}(\mathcal{G}_{a,b}) = [y'_1, y'_2]$.

Then $\mathcal{F}_{a,b}$ *and* $\mathcal{G}_{a,b}$ *are* equivalent *w.r.t.* $\mathcal{C}$, a, b *and* H, *written* $\mathcal{F}_{a,b} \equiv_{\mathcal{C},H,a,b} \mathcal{G}_{a,b}$.
$\mathcal{F}$ and $\mathcal{G}$ are equivalent *w.r.t.* $\mathcal{C}$ *and* H, *written* $\mathcal{F} \equiv_{\mathcal{C},H} \mathcal{G}$, *if* $\mathcal{F}_{a,b} \equiv_{\mathcal{C},H,a,b} \mathcal{G}_{a,b}$ *for all* $a < b$.

The intuition here is that $\mathcal{F}_{a,b}$ and $\mathcal{G}_{a,b}$ are defined on the same intervals w.r.t. their a-points of interest (item 1), have the same actual behaviour on intervals between corresponding pairs of a-points of interest (item 2), and their value ranges on corresponding intervals (w.r.t. a-points of interest) are corresponding intervals (w.r.t. b-points of interest).

It remains to show that $\equiv_{\mathcal{C},H}$ possesses the properties given in Sect. 3. We first establish the finiteness and congruence properties, which follow by arguments similar to those in Lemma 1 and Lemma 2.

Lemma 3. *Let C be a V-influence scheme, H be a hypothesis.*

1. *The index of $\equiv_{C,H}$ is finite and the equivalence classes can be effectively enumerated.*
2. *For any V-influence experiments F and G such that $F \equiv_{C,H} G$ and any $S \in C \cup H$, it holds that $F \models S$ if and only if $G \models S$.*

Proof (Sketch). Item 1 follows from the fact that the set of points of interest remains finite and enumerable, yielding only finitely many ways in which experiments can behave between these points. Item 2 relies on the fact that that each equivalence class of $\equiv_{C,H}$ captures strictly more information than any individual V-statement in $C \cup H$. This allows us to combine the available information in a class and verify whether all V-influence experiments within it satisfy a given V-statement. □

Additionally, we have to show that coherence holds. This step is more involved and requires verifying that the conditions of Definition 11 ensure enough transitivity to guarantee Coherence.

Lemma 4. *Let C be a V-influence scheme, H be a hypothesis and F and G be V-influence experiments. Then for all $a, b, c \in V$ such that $a < b < c$, it holds that if $F_{a,b} \equiv_{C,H,a,b} G_{a,b}$ and $F_{b,c} \equiv_{C,H,b,c} G_{b,c}$ then $F_{a,c} \equiv_{C,H,a,c} G_{a,c}$.*

Proof (Sketch). From the equivalence classes of $\equiv_{C,H,a,b}$ and $\equiv_{C,H,b,c}$, we know the exact behaviour of $F_{a,b}$ between a-points of interest and of $F_{b,c}$ between b-points of interest. Furthermore, the values of $F_{a,b}$ on a-points of interest are themselves b-points of interest.

Thus, the range of $F_{a,c}$ between consecutive a-points of interest is uniquely determined by composing the ranges of $F_{a,b}$ and $F_{b,c}$, and likewise, the behaviour of $F_{a,c}$ between consecutive a-points of interest is fully determined by composing the behaviours of $F_{a,b}$ and $F_{b,c}$.

Applying the same arguments to G, and by considering that G and F behave equally w.r.t. their points of interest, it follows that $F_{a,c} \equiv_{C,H,a,c} G_{a,c}$. □

From the previous lemmas, we obtain the desired decidability of SCHEMEEN-TAILMENT, following the decision procedure outlined in Sect. 3.

Theorem 2. SCHEMEENTAILMENT *is in* coNP.

Proof (Sketch). Given a V-influence scheme C and a hypothesis H, we provide a polynomial-sized witness P verifying that $C \not\models H$.

The witness consists of lists of pairs $P_{a,b}$ for each $a, b \in V$ with $a < b$, mapping a-points of interest to b-points of interest. If $(x, y) \in P_{a,b}$, this imposes $F_{a,b}(x) = y$, with monotonicity assumed between points.

Verifying that the induced V-influence experiment F is a counterexample can be done in polynomial time:

- Coherence is checked via Lemma 4.
- Satisfaction of C and violation of H follow from Lemma 3(2).

It remains to bound the witness size. By construction, the number of points of interest per $a \in \mathcal{V}$ is at most exponential in $|\mathcal{V}|$. Since $\mathcal{V}$ is fixed in the input, the total size of $\mathcal{P}$ remains polynomial.   □

6 Conclusion

This paper is concerned with a very particular reasoning problem which arises from an attempt to formalise models and tasks occurring in natural sciences classes, especially in designing and conducting experiments, with an overall aim to provide digitalisation support for such learning scenarios. We have extended previous work based on a simple proof system, known as the *Calculus of Influence* (CoI) [5], in the sense that the algebraic approach to the underlying reasoning problem presented here lifts several structural restrictions which need to be imposed on schemes in order for CoI to provide sound and complete reasoning.

The acute reader may have noticed two restrictions on schemes that have been imposed here, and that were not imposed for CoI: here, the domain of scheme statements cannot contain infinities as interval bounds. This is simply done for simplicity. Statements like $\underset{}{\llcorner^{[0,\infty]} \nearrow^{[0,1]}}$ could be handled by replacing infinities by sufficiently large numbers. Second, we drew a distinction between scheme statements and hypotheses: arbitrary behaviour can only be stated in hypotheses. Technically, schemes with arbitrary behaviour are too weak to categorise their models in terms of equivalences of finite index, since the coherence property could demand an arbitrary amount of turning points. While this restriction slightly weakens this approach mathematically, we argue that from an application point of view arbitrary behaviour in schemes is unnatural anyway. Its main purpose is to allow hypotheses to be formalised even when pupils' knowledge about experiments is only partial, i.e. when they can predict the range of influences for instance, but not necessarily its monotonicity or antitonicity.

Further work is going into two directions: a reasoner for influence needs to be integrated into educational software which allows experiments to be designed and conducted virtually. It remains to be seen what the best practical approaches for solving SCHEMEENTAILMENT are, perhaps based on the use of SMT solvers or an on-the-fly, goal-directed search.

Moreover, the model of influence schemes studied here does not cover arbitrary scenarios in experiments in natural sciences. Many biological or chemical processes are only triggered by the combination of several variables. This happens, for example, in gene transcription which may only occur in the presence of multiple transcription factors, cf. [12]. Chemical reactions often only proceed when a substrate and a co-factor are presence, for instance Acetaldehyde requires Ethanol and NAD^+, cf. [13]. Also, the use of specific, interpreted variables like time [4] may require specific reasoning principles. All in all, the theory of formal models for reasoning about influence in phenomena studied in natural sciences largely remains to be explored further.

References

1. Andrews, P.B.: Classical type theory. In: Robinson, A., Voronkov, A. (eds.) Handbook of Automated Reasoning, pp. 965–1007. North-Holland (2001). https://doi.org/10.1016/B978-044450813-3/50017-5

2. Baader, F., Calvanese, D., McGuinness, D.L., Nardi, D., Patel-Schneider, P.F. (eds.): The Description Logic Handbook: Theory, Implementation, and Applications. Cambridge University Press (2003)

3. Bortolussi, L., Policriti, A.: Hybrid systems and biology. In: International School on Formal Methods for the Design of Computer, Communication and Software Systems, pp. 424–448. Springer (2008)

4. Bruse, F., Kastaun, M., Lange, M., Möller, S.: The calculus of temporal influence. In: Proceedings of 30th International Symposium on Temporal Representation and Reasoning, TIME 2023. LIPIcs, vol. 278, pp. 10:1–10:19. Schloss Dagstuhl - Leibniz-Zentrum für Informatik (2023). https://doi.org/10.4230/LIPICS.TIME.2023.10

5. Bruse, F., Lange, M., Möller, S.: Formal reasoning about influence in natural sciences experiments. In: Proceedings of 29th International Conference on Computed-Aided Deduction, CADE 2023. LNCS, vol. 14132, pp. 153–169. Springer, Cham (2023)

6. De Ory, I., Romero, L.E., Cantero, D.: Modelling the kinetics of growth of acetobacter aceti in discontinuous culture: influence of the temperature of operation. Appl. Microbiol. Biotechnol. **49**(2), 189–193 (1998)

7. Demri, S., Goranko, V., Lange, M.: Temporal Logics in Computer Science. Cambridge Tracts in Theoretical Computer Science. Cambridge University Press (2016). http://www.cambridge.org/core_title/gb/434611

8. Harel, D., Kozen, D., Tiuryn, J.: Dynamic Logic. MIT Press (2000)

9. Harrison, J.: Handbook of Practical Logic and Automated Reasoning. Cambridge University Press (2009)

10. Henzinger, T.A.: The theory of hybrid automata. In: Proceedings of 11th Annual IEEE Symposium on Logic in Computer Science, pp. 278–292. IEEE (1996)

11. Hillmayr, D., Ziernwald, L., Reinhold, F., Hofer, S., Reiss, K.: The potential of digital tools to enhance mathematics and science learning in secondary schools: a context-specific meta-analysis. Comput. Educ. **153**, 103897 (2020)

12. Panne, D., Maniatis, T., Harrison, S.C.: Crystal structure of ATF-2/c-Jun and IRF-3 bound to the interferon-beta enhancer. EMBO J. **23**, 4384–4393 (2004). https://doi.org/10.1038/sj.emboj.7600453

13. Plapp, B.V.: Conformational changes and catalysis by alcohol dehydrogenase. Arch. Biochem. Biophys. **493**(1), 3–12 (2010). https://doi.org/10.1016/j.abb.2009.07.001

14. Robinson, J.A., Voronkov, A. (eds.): Handbook of Automated Reasoning (in 2 volumes). Elsevier and MIT Press (2001)

15. Smullyan, R.M.: First-Order Logic. Springer (1968)

16. Steggles, L.J., Banks, R., Wipat, A.: Modelling and analysing genetic networks: from boolean networks to petri nets. In: Priami, C. (ed.) CMSB 2006. LNCS, vol. 4210, pp. 127–141. Springer, Heidelberg (2006). https://doi.org/10.1007/11885191_9

17. Sumatokhin, S., Petrova, O., Serovayskaya, D., Chistiakov, F.: Digitalization of school biological education: problems and solutions. In: SHS Web of Conferences, vol. 79, p. 01016. EDP Sciences (2020)

18. Theocharopoulou, G., Bobori, C., Vlamos, P.: Formal models of biological systems. In: Proceedings of 2nd World Congress on Genetics, Geriatrics and Neurodegenerative Disease, GeNeDis 2016, Advances in Experimental Medicine and Biology, vol. 987, pp. 325–338. Springer (2017)

Proof Checking

Checking Linear Integer Arithmetic Proofs in Lambdapi

Alessio Coltellacci[ID] and Stephan Merz[✉][ID]

University of Lorraine, CNRS, Inria, LORIA, Nancy, France
alessio.coltellacci@inria.fr, stephan.merz@loria.fr

Abstract. Modern SMT solvers can generate proofs of unsatisfiability so that the result can be checked independently. A dependable approach to verify these proofs is to reconstruct them within a proof assistant. In previous work, the SMT checker Carcara was extended to reconstruct SMT proofs in Lambdapi—a proof assistant designed for interoperability, supporting the import and export of proofs for integration with other proof assistants such as Rocq, Lean, or HOL-Light. Whereas that work was limited to SMT theories without arithmetic, we here present an extension that enables the reconstruction of SMT proofs involving linear integer arithmetic.

Keywords: SMT · Alethe · integer arithmetic · Lambdapi · normal form · proof by reflection

1 Introduction

SMT solvers have become capable of producing proofs of unsatisfiability, enabling independent verification of correctness without relying on the solver's implementation. This development addresses the growing need for trustworthy verification in safety-critical applications and for using SMT solvers as backends of skeptical proof assistants that do not trust the solver. Alethe [2,24] is an established SMT proof format supported by the solvers cvc5 and veriT. In our previous work [12], we extended the Alethe proof checker and elaborator Carcara [1] to reconstruct Alethe SMT proofs within the Lambdapi proof assistant, thereby ensuring their validity. Lambdapi [18] is a proof assistant based on the $\lambda\Pi$-calculus modulo rewriting [13], a logical framework [17] that extends the λ-calculus with dependent types and user-defined rewrite rules. This foundation allows Lambdapi to serve as a framework for formalizing various logical systems. Designed with interoperability in mind, Lambdapi can import and export proofs, facilitating integration with other proof assistants such as Rocq [26], Lean [20], and HOL-Light [9].

However, our prior work was limited to proofs expressed within the logic of Uninterpreted Functions (UF). In the present work, we extend this approach to support the reconstruction of proof steps involving linear integer arithmetic (LIA). In the context of LIA, the SMT solver determines unsatisfiability by analyzing formulas composed of integer variables, linear arithmetic operations,

© The Author(s) 2026
R. Thiemann and C. Weidenbach (Eds.): FroCoS 2025, LNAI 15979, pp. 367–385, 2026.
https://doi.org/10.1007/978-3-032-04167-8_20

and logical connectives. This process typically relies on techniques such as Simplex methods adapted for integers and cutting-plane methods to establish the unsatisfiability of linear constraints [11,14]. Our main contribution is the implementation of an automatic decision procedure to verify these proof steps, using proof by reflection [10,16].

The remainder of this paper is organized as follows. In Sect. 2, we provide an overview of Lambdapi and present the structure of Alethe proof certificates for linear arithmetic. Then, in Sect. 3, we describe how we leverage Carcara's elaboration process to reconstruct linear integer arithmetic steps, even when coefficient annotations are missing. Section 4 introduces our encoding of SMT linear arithmetic within Lambdapi, while Sect. 5 presents an automatic decision procedure, based on proof by reflection, to verify these arithmetic steps. An empirical evaluation of our approach is provided in Sect. 6. We review related work in Sect. 7, and we conclude in Sect. 8.

2   Background

2.1   An Overview of Lambdapi

Lambdapi is an implementation of $\lambda\Pi$ modulo theory $(\lambda\Pi/\equiv)$ [18], an extension of the Edinburgh Logical Framework $\lambda\Pi$ [17] that is based on a simply typed λ-calculus with dependent types. $\lambda\Pi/\equiv$ adds user-defined higher-order rewrite rules. Its syntax is given by

Universes	$u ::= \texttt{TYPE} \mid \texttt{KIND}$
Terms	$t, v, A, B, C ::= c \mid x \mid u \mid \Pi\, x : A, B \mid \lambda\, x : A, t \mid t\, v$
Contexts	$\Gamma ::= \langle\rangle \mid \Gamma, x : A$
Signatures	$\Sigma ::= \langle\rangle \mid \Sigma, c : C \mid \Sigma, c := t : C \mid \Sigma, t \hookrightarrow v$

where c is a constant, x is a variable such that the sets of constants and variables are disjoint, and C is a closed term. *Universes* are constants used to verify if a type is well-formed – more details can be found in [17, §2.1]. $\Pi\, x : A, B$ is the dependent product (we write $A \to B$ when B does not depend on x), $\lambda\, x : A, t$ is an abstraction, and $t\, v$ is an application. A *(local) context* Γ is a finite sequence of variable declarations $x : A$ introducing variables and their types. A *signature* Σ representing the global context is a finite sequence of *assumptions* $c : C$, indicating that constant c is of type C, *definitions* $c := t : C$, indicating that c has value t and type C, and *rewrite rules* $t \hookrightarrow v$ such that $t = c\, v_1 \ldots v_n$ where c is a constant.

The relation $\hookrightarrow_{\beta\Sigma}$ is generated by β-reduction and by the rewrite rules of Σ. The relation $\hookrightarrow^*_{\beta\Sigma}$ denotes the reflexive and transitive closure of $\hookrightarrow_{\beta\Sigma}$, and the relation $\equiv_{\beta\Sigma}$ (called *conversion*) the reflexive, symmetric, and transitive closure of $\hookrightarrow_{\beta\Sigma}$. The relation $\hookrightarrow_{\beta\Sigma}$ must be confluent, i.e., whenever $t \hookrightarrow^*_{\beta\Sigma} v_1$ and $t \hookrightarrow^*_{\beta\Sigma} v_2$, there exists some w such that $v_1 \hookrightarrow^*_{\beta\Sigma} w$ and $v_2 \hookrightarrow^*_{\beta\Sigma} w$, and it must preserve typing, i.e., whenever $\Gamma \vdash_\Sigma t : A$ and $t \hookrightarrow_{\beta\Sigma} v$ then $\Gamma \vdash_\Sigma v : A$ [5].

A Lambdapi typing judgment $\Gamma \vdash_\Sigma t : A$ asserts that term t has type A in the context Γ and the signature Σ. The typing rules of $\lambda\Pi/\equiv$ are those of $\lambda\Pi$ [17,

§2], except for the rule (Conv), given below, that identifies types modulo $\equiv_{\beta\Sigma}$ instead of just modulo β-reduction.

$$\frac{\Gamma, \vdash_\Sigma B : u \quad \Gamma \vdash_\Sigma t : A \quad A \equiv_{\beta\Sigma} B}{\Gamma \vdash_\Sigma t : B} \text{(Conv)}$$

In our encoding presented in [12], we employ Tarski-style universes [19] where types are represented by elements of a base type and interpreted via a decoding function. We define the constant $\texttt{Prop} : \text{TYPE}$ for the type of propositions and the decoding function $\texttt{Prf}^c : \texttt{Prop} \to \text{TYPE}$ that maps each proposition to TYPE. This is necessary because Lambdapi does not support quantification over a variable of type TYPE: it is not possible to assign the type $\Pi X : \text{TYPE}, (X \to \texttt{Prop}) \to \texttt{Prop}$ to the universal quantifier $\forall$. To circumvent this, we have the constant $\texttt{Set} :$ TYPE for the types of object-terms, and a decoding function $\texttt{El} : \texttt{Set} \to \text{TYPE}$ that embeds Set into TYPE. This allows us to define the universal quantifier as $\forall : \Pi x : \texttt{Set}, (\texttt{El}\ x \to \texttt{Prop}) \to \texttt{Prop}$. To quantify over propositions, we further define a constant $o : \texttt{Set}$ and add the rewrite rule $\texttt{El}\ o \hookrightarrow \texttt{Prop}$. This encoding is well-established in the literature on systems formalized in Lambdapi [7].

2.2 Alethe Proofs

The Alethe proof trace format [2] for SMT solvers comprises two parts: the trace language based on SMT-LIB and a collection of proof rules. Traces witness proofs of unsatisfiability of a set of constraints. They are sequences $a_1 \ldots a_m\ t_1 \ldots t_n$ where the assumptions a_i correspond to the constraints of the original SMT problem being refuted, each t_i is a clause inferred from previous elements of the sequence, and t_n is $\bot$ (the empty clause). In the following, we designate the SMT-LIB problem as the *input problem*.

```
1 (set-logic LIA)
2 (declare-const x Int)
3 (declare-const y Int)
4 (assert (= x 2))
5 (assert (= 0 y))
6 (assert (or (< (+ x y) 1) (< 3 x)))
7 (check-sat)
8 (get-proof)
```

Listing 1.1. Input problem.

```
1  (assume a0 (or (< (+ x y) 1) (< 3 x)))
2  (assume a2 (= 0 y))
3  (assume a1 (= x 2))
4  (step t1 (cl (< (+ x y) 1) (< 3 x)) :rule or :premises (a0))
5  (step t2 (cl (not (< 3 x)) (not (= x 2))) :rule la_generic :args (1/1 -1/1))
6  (step t3 (cl (not (< 3 x))) :rule resolution :premises (a1 t2))
7  (step t4 (cl (< (+ x y) 1)) :rule resolution :premises (t1 t3))
8  (step t5 (cl (not (< (+ x y) 1)) (not (= x 2)) (not (= 0 y)))
9         :rule la_generic :args (1/1 1/1 -1/1))
10 (step t6 (cl) :rule resolution :premises (t5 t4 a1 a2))
```

Listing 1.2. Proof of unsatisfiability of the input problem of listing 1.1.

We will use the input problem shown in Listing 1.1 with its Alethe proof (found by cvc5) in Listing 1.2 as a running example to introduce Alethe concepts and illustrate our reconstruction of linear arithmetic step in Lambdapi.

Overview of the Alethe Trace format. An Alethe proof trace inherits the declarations of the corresponding input problem. All symbols (sorts, functions, assertions, etc.) declared or defined in the input problem remain declared or defined. Furthermore, the syntax for terms, sorts, and annotations uses the syntactic rules defined in SMT-LIB [3, §3] and the SMT signature context defined in [3, §5.1 and §5.2]. In the following we will represent an Alethe step as

$$i \;.\; \boxed{\Gamma} \;\triangleright\; l_1 \ldots l_n \quad (\; \boxed{\mathcal{R}} \;\; \boxed{p_1 \ldots p_m}\;) \;\; \boxed{a_1 \ldots a_r} \tag{1}$$

index ↑   ↑context ↑clause   ↑rule   ↑premises   ↑arguments

A step consists of an index $i \in \mathbb{I}$ where $\mathbb{I}$ is a countable set of indices such as a0, t1), and a clause representing the disjunction of literals $l_1, \ldots, l_n$. Steps that are not assumptions are justified by a proof rule $\boxed{\mathcal{R}}$ that depends on a possibly empty set of premises $\{\boxed{p_1, \ldots, p_m}\} \subseteq \mathbb{I}$ that only contains earlier steps such that the proof forms a directed acyclic graph. A rule might also depend on a list of arguments $a_1, \ldots, a_r$ where each argument a_i is either a term or a pair (x_i, t_i) for a variable x_i and a term t_i. The interpretation of the arguments is rule-specific. The context $\boxed{\Gamma}$ of a step is a list $c_1, \ldots, c_l$ where each element c_j is either a variable or a variable-term tuple denoted $x_j \mapsto t_j$. Therefore, steps with a non-empty context contain variables x_j that appear in l_i and will be substituted by t_j. Proof rules $\boxed{\mathcal{R}}$ include theory lemmas and **resolution**, which corresponds to hyper-resolution on ground first-order clauses.

We now have the key components for explaining the proof in Listing 1.2. The proofs starts with **assume** steps a0, a1, a2 that restate the assertions from the input problem. Step t1 transforms the disjunction a0 into a clause by using the Alethe rule **or**. Steps t2 and t5 are tautologies introduced by the main rule **la_generic** in Linear Real Arithmetic (LRA) logic and also used in LIA logic, where $l_1, l_2, \ldots, l_n$ represent linear inequalities. The **Real** terms in LRA and LIA logic are built over the **Real** and **Int** signatures from SMT-LIB with free variables, but containing only linear atoms; that is atoms of the form d, (* d x), or (* x d) where x is a free variable and d is an integer or rational constant. A linear inequality is an expression of the form

$$\sum_{i=0}^{n} c_i \times t_i + d_1 \bowtie \sum_{i=n+1}^{m} c_i \times t_i + d_2 \tag{1}$$

where $\bowtie \in \{=, <, >, \leq, \geq\}$, $m \geq n$, c_i, d_1, d_2 are either **Int** or **Real** constants, and where c_i and t_i have the same sort for all i. Checking the validity of the clauses t2 and t5 in Listing 1.2 amounts to checking the unsatisfiability of a system of linear (in)equations e.g. $x < 3$ and $x = 2$ in t2. Coefficients for each

Table 1. Linear arithmetic rules in Alethe supported in our encoding.

Rule	Description
la_generic	Tautologous disjunction of linear inequalities
lia_generic	Tautologous disjunction of linear integer inequalities
la_disequality	$t_1 \approx t_2 \lor \neg(t_1 \geq t_2) \lor \neg(t_2 \geq t_1)$
la_totality	$t_1 \geq t_2 \lor t_2 \geq t_1$
la_mult_pos	$t_1 > 0 \land (t_2 \bowtie t_3) \rightarrow t_1 * t_2 \bowtie t_1 * t_3$ and $\bowtie \in \{<, >, \geq, \leq, \approx\}$
la_mult_neg	$t_1 < 0 \land (t_2 \bowtie t_3) \rightarrow t_1 * t_2 \bowtie_{inv} t_1 * t_3$
la_rw_eq	$(t \approx u) \approx (t \geq u \land u \geq t)$
comp_simplify	Simplification of arithmetic comparisons
arith-int-eq-elim	$(t \approx s) \rightarrow t \geq s \land t \leq s$
arith-refl-geq	$t \geq t \rightarrow \top$
arith-refl-lt	$t < t \rightarrow \bot$
arith-refl-leq	$t \leq t \rightarrow \top$
arith-elim-leq	$t \leq s \rightarrow s \geq t$
arith-elim-gt	$t > s \rightarrow \neg(t \leq s)$
arith-leq-norm	$t \leq s \rightarrow \neg(t \geq s + 1)$
arith-geq-norm1	$t \geq s \rightarrow (t - s) \geq 0$
arith-geq-norm2	$t \geq s \rightarrow -t \leq -s$
arith-geq-tighten	$\neg(t \geq s) \rightarrow s \geq t + 1$
arith-poly-norm	polynomial normalization
evaluate	evaluate constant terms

inequality are passed as arguments e.g. $(\frac{1}{1}, \frac{1}{1})$ in t2. Steps t3 and t4 apply the
`resolution` rule to the premises a1, t2 (respectively t1 and t3). Finally, the
step t6 concludes the proof by generating the empty clause $\bot$, denoted as (cl)
in Listing 1.2. Notice that the contexts Γ of each step are all empty in this
proof.

Linear Arithmetic in Alethe. Proofs for linear arithmetic steps use a number of rules listed in Table 1, such as `la_totality` that asserts totality of the
ordering $\leq$. Besides arithmetical tautologies, the table also contains simplification rules, indicated with the symbol $\rightarrow$. Following our encoding of Alethe
in Lambdapi as described in [12], the linear arithmetic rules `la_disequality`,
`la_totality`, and `la_mult_*` are implemented as lemmas. We do not support
the remaining arithmetic simplification rules, including the `la_tautology` rule
from Alethe. This omission is primarily due to the fact that cvc5 extends Alethe
with the RARE simplification rules [21], which it uses in place of the original ones. Consequently, we support the RARE rules prefixed by `arith-*`, as
listed in Table 1, and we have selectively implemented those that appear in the
proof traces of the benchmarks discussed in Sect. 6. In addition, support for the

evaluate rule is provided through the work described in Sect. 4, and support for arith-poly-norm is realized through the normalization approach explained in Sect. 5.

A different approach is taken for the rules la_generic and lia_generic, as they describe an algorithm. While the la_generic rule is primarily intended for LRA logic, it is also applied in LIA proofs when all variables in the (in)equalities are of integer sort. A step of the rule la_generic represents a tautological clause of linear inequalities. It can be checked by showing that the conjunction of the negated inequalities is unsatisfiable. After the application of some strengthening rules, the resulting conjunction is unsatisfiable, even if Int variables are assumed to be Real variables. Although the rule may introduce rational coefficients, they often reduce to integers—as shown in List. 1.2, where the coefficients are $(\frac{1}{1}, \frac{1}{1})$. Cases where coefficients cannot be reduced to integers are rare in practice, however, we reduce them to integers by *clearing denominators* with their least common denominator. Let $\varphi_1, \ldots, \varphi_n$ be linear inequalities or their negations, but different from $s_1 \approx s_2$ and $a_1, \ldots, a_n$ rational numbers, then an la_generic step has the general form

$$i. \triangleright \varphi_1, \ldots, \varphi_n \quad \text{la\_generic } [a_1, \ldots, a_n]$$

The constants a_i are of sort Real. To check the unsatisfiability of the conjunction $\neg\varphi_1 \wedge \ldots \wedge \neg\varphi_n$, one performs the following steps for each literal.

1. If φ_i is of the form $s_1 \geq s_2$ or $\neg(s_1 < s_2)$, then let $\psi_i = s_2 > s_1$. If φ_i is of the form $s_1 > s_2$ or $\neg(s_1 \leq s_2)$, then let $\psi_i = s_2 \geq s_1$. If φ_i is of the form $s_1 < s_2$ or $\neg(s_1 \geq s_2)$, then let $\psi_i = s_1 \geq s_2$. If φ_i is of the form $s_1 \leq s_2$ or $\neg(s_1 > s_2)$, then let $\psi_i = s_1 > s_2$. If φ_i is of the form $\neg(s_1 \approx s_2)$, then let $\psi_i = s_1 \approx s_2$. This step produces a positive literal that is equivalent to $\neg\varphi_i$ and that only contains the operators $>$, $\geq$, and $\approx$.
2. Replace $\psi_i = \sum_{j=0}^{k_i} c_j^i \times t_j^i + d_1^i \bowtie \sum_{j=k_i+1}^{m_i} c_j^i \times t_j^i + d_2^i$ by the literal $\left(\sum_{j=0}^{k_i} c_j^i \times t_j^i \right) - \left(\sum_{j=k_i+1}^{m_i} c_j^i \times t_j^i \right) \bowtie d_2^i - d_1^i$.
3. Now ψ_i has the form $s_1^i \bowtie d^i$. If all variables in s_1^i are integer-sorted then replace $s_1^i > d^i$ by $s_1^i \geq \lfloor d^i \rfloor + 1$, respectively, replace $s_1^i \geq d^i$ by $s_1^i \geq \lfloor d^i \rfloor + 1$ if d is not an integer.
4. If all variables of ψ_i are integer-sorted and the coefficients $a_1 \ldots a_n$ are in $\mathbb{Q}$, then $a_i :- a_i \times lcd(a_1 \ldots a_n)$ where lcd is the least common denominator of $\{a_1, \ldots, a_n\}$.
5. If $\bowtie$ is $\approx$, then replace ψ_i by $\sum_{j=0}^{m_i} a_i \times c_j^i \times t_j^i = a_i \times d^i$, otherwise replace ψ_i by $\sum_{j=0}^{m_i} |a_i| \times c_j^i \times t_j^i \bowtie |a_i| \times d^i$.
6. Finally, the sum of the resulting literals is trivially contradictory,

$$\sum_{i=1}^{n} \sum_{j=1}^{m_i} c_j^i * t_j^i \bowtie \sum_{i=1}^{n} d^i$$

The operator $\bowtie$ is $=$ if all operators are $=$, $>$ if all are either $\approx$ or $>$ (but at least one operator is different from $\approx$), and $\geq$ otherwise. Finally, the sum on the left-hand side is 0 and the right-hand side is > 0 (or ≥ 0 if $\bowtie$ is $>$).

The above algorithm is adapted from the Alethe specification [2], except that we clarified step 1: the subsequent steps in the original algorithm are designed for $>$ and $\geq$ and do not clearly address how to handle $<$ and $\leq$. Additionally, we added step 4 in order to ensure that our construction is independent of $\mathbb{Q}$.

Example 1. Consider the following `la_generic` step in the logic `QF_UFLIA` with the uninterpreted function symbol `(f Int)`:

```
1 (step t11 (cl (not (<= f 0)) (<= (+ 1 (* 4 f)) 1))
2   :rule la_generic :args (1/1 1/4))
```

The algorithm then performs the following steps:

$$-f \geq 0,\ 4 \times f > 0 \qquad \text{(Steps 1 and 2)}$$
$$-f \geq 0,\ 4 \times f \geq 1 \qquad \text{(Step 3)}$$
$$\text{Replace arguments } [\frac{1}{1}, \frac{1}{4}] \text{ by } [4, 1] \text{ due to clearing denominators} \qquad \text{(Step 4)}$$
$$|4| \times (-f) \geq |4| \times 0,\ |1| \times 4 \times f \geq |1| \times 1) \qquad \text{(Step 5)}$$
$$-4 \times f + 4 \times f \geq 1 \qquad \text{(Step 6)}$$

Which simplifies to the contradiction $0 \geq 1$.

Remark 1. The operator `to_real` is used in the `LIA` theory to embed integers into the reals. As a result, a proof for a problem formulated in `LIA` may involve reasoning over real numbers. Since our approach does not support the `Real` theory, we do not attempt to reconstruct such proofs and instead let the translation process fail in this case.

Quantifiers in Linear Arithmetic. The Alethe format defines rules for quantifier instantiation, Skolemization, substitution, and other manipulations of bound variables. For instance, the rule `forall_inst` is used to express quantifier instantiation. It produces a unit clause with a formula of the form $(\neg \forall \bar{x},\ \varphi) \vee (\varphi[\bar{t}])$, where φ is a term containing the free variables $\bar{x}$, and each term t is a ground term of the same sort as the corresponding variable x. Accordingly, an Alethe proof will first instantiate the quantifier to produce a ground term, enabling subsequent arithmetic steps such as those involving `la_generic` or `lia_generic` to operate solely on ground terms.

3   Elaborating lia_generic Steps

The rule `lia_generic` is similar to `la_generic`, but the SMT solver does not provide the coefficients, i.e. $[a_1 \ldots a_r]$ is empty. We decided to leverage the elaboration process of `lia_generic` performed by Carcara, as doing otherwise would require implementing Fourier-Motzkin elimination for integers, as done in [4,22], hence reimplementing work that was already done by the solver.

Carcara considers `lia_generic` steps as holes in the proof, given that "their checking is as hard as solving" [1, §3.2]. To address this, Carcara invokes an external SMT solver, such as cvc5, or any tool capable of reading SMT-LIB input and producing Alethe proofs, and attempts to generate an Alethe proof that avoid using `lia_generic`. Suppose the resulting proof still includes a `lia_generic` step. In that case, Carcara repeats the process for up to three iterations, merging the final results if a complete proof without any `lia_generic` steps is eventually found. The proof is then imported and validated, replacing the original step.

Example 2 (Sketch of lia_ generic elaboration). Consider a step S (Listing 1.3) concluding the clause $\neg l_1 \lor \ldots \neg l_n$ where all l_i are inequalities and proved by `lia_generic` rule.

```
1    (step S (cl (not l1) ... (not ln)) :rule lia_generic)
```

Listing 1.3. Elaborated proof

Carcara will generate an SMT-LIB problem asserting $l_1, \ldots, l_n$ and invoke the solver cvc5 on it, expecting an Alethe proof of the unsatisfiability of $l_1 \land \cdots \land l_n$ that does not use `lia_generic`. Carcara will check this subproof and then replace the original step by a proof of the form shown in Listing 1.4.

```
1  (anchor :step S.t_m+1)
2  (assume S.h_1 l1)
3  ...
4  (assume S.h_n ln)
5  ...
6  (step S.t_m (cl false) :rule ...)
7  (step t.t_m+1 (cl (not l1) ... (not ln) false) :rule subproof)
8  (step t.t_m+2 (cl (not false)) :rule false)
9  (step S (cl (not l1) ... (not ln))
10        :rule resolution :premises (S.t_m+1 S.t_m+2))
```

Listing 1.4. Elaboration of `lia_generic`

In Listing 1.4, steps `S.h_1` until `S.t_m` are imported from the cvc5 proof. As a result the `lia_generic` step `S` in the original proof (Listing 1.3) will have been replaced by a detailed justification whose correctness can be independently established by Carcara.

4   Encoding of Linear Integer Arithmetic in Lambdapi

The definition of integers in Lambdapi that we use appears in Fig. 1. It follows a common encoding found in many other theories, including the one adopted in the Rocq standard library [26]. First, the type $\mathbb{P}$ is an inductive type representing strictly positive integers in binary form. Starting from 1 (represented by the constructor H), one can add a new least significant digit via the constructor O (digit 0) or the constructor I (digit 1). The type $\mathbb{Z}$ represents integers in

$\mathbb{P}$: TYPE	$\mathbb{Z}$: TYPE	Comp : TYPE	$\mathbb{B}$: TYPE
| H : $\mathbb{P}$	| Z0 : $\mathbb{Z}$	| Eq : Comp	| true : $\mathbb{B}$
| O : $\mathbb{P} \to \mathbb{P}$	| ZPos : $\mathbb{P} \to \mathbb{Z}$	| Lt : Comp	| false : $\mathbb{B}$
| I : $\mathbb{P} \to \mathbb{P}$	| ZNeg : $\mathbb{P} \to \mathbb{Z}$	| Gt : Comp	
pos : Set	int : Set	comp : Set	bool : Set
El pos $\hookrightarrow \mathbb{P}$	El int $\hookrightarrow \mathbb{Z}$	El comp $\hookrightarrow$ Comp	El bool $\hookrightarrow \mathbb{B}$

Fig. 1. Type definitions for binary positive number, integers, comparison and Booleans.

$+ : \mathbb{Z} \to \mathbb{Z} \to \mathbb{Z}$ $\doteq : \mathbb{Z} \to \mathbb{Z} \to$ Comp

$\text{Z0} + y \hookrightarrow y$ $\text{Z0} \doteq \text{Z0} \hookrightarrow \text{Eq}$

$x + \text{Z0} \hookrightarrow x$ $\text{Z0} \doteq \text{Zpos} \_ \hookrightarrow \text{Lt}$

$(\text{Zpos } x) + (\text{Zpos } y) \hookrightarrow (\text{Zpos (add } x \ y))$ $\text{Z0} \doteq \text{Zneg} \_ \hookrightarrow \text{Gt}$

$(\text{Zpos } x) + (\text{Zneg } y) \hookrightarrow (\text{sub } x \ y)$ $\text{Zpos} \_ \doteq \text{Z0} \hookrightarrow \text{Gt}$

$(\text{Zneg } x) + (\text{Zpos } y) \hookrightarrow (\text{sub } y \ x)$ $\text{Zpos } p \doteq \text{Zpos } q \hookrightarrow \text{cmp } p \ q$

$(\text{Zneg } x) + (\text{Zneg } y) \hookrightarrow \text{Zneg (add } x \ y)$ $\text{Zpos} \_ \doteq \text{Zneg} \_ \hookrightarrow \text{Gt}$

$\text{Zneg} \_ \doteq \text{Z0} \hookrightarrow \text{Lt}$

$\text{Zneg} \_ \doteq \text{Zpos} \_ \hookrightarrow \text{Lt}$

$\text{Zneg } p \doteq \text{Zneg } q \hookrightarrow \text{cmp } q \ p$

isEq : Comp $\to \mathbb{B}$	isLt : Comp $\to \mathbb{B}$	isGt : Comp $\to \mathbb{B}$
isEq Eq $\hookrightarrow$ true	isLt Eq $\hookrightarrow$ false	isGt Eq $\hookrightarrow$ false
isEq Lt $\hookrightarrow$ false	isLt Lt $\hookrightarrow$ true	isGt Lt $\hookrightarrow$ false
isEq Gt $\hookrightarrow$ false	isLt Gt $\hookrightarrow$ false	isGt Gt $\hookrightarrow$ true

$\leq : \mathbb{Z} \to \mathbb{Z} \to \text{Prop} := \lambda x, \lambda y, \neg(\text{istrue}(\text{isGt}(x \doteq y)))$ istrue : $\mathbb{B} \to$ Prop

$< : \mathbb{Z} \to \mathbb{Z} \to \text{Prop} := \lambda x, \lambda y, (\text{istrue}(\text{isLt}(x \doteq y)))$ istrue true $\hookrightarrow \top$

$\geq : \mathbb{Z} \to \mathbb{Z} \to \text{Prop} := \lambda x, \lambda y, \neg(x < y)$ istrue false $\hookrightarrow \bot$

$> : \mathbb{Z} \to \mathbb{Z} \to \text{Prop} := \lambda x, \lambda y, \neg(x \leq y)$

Fig. 2. Definitions for operators over $\mathbb{Z}$.

binary form. An integer is either zero (with constructor Z0) or a strictly positive number Zpos (coded as a $\mathbb{P}$) or a strictly negative number Zneg. We make use of Lambdapi's builtin mechanism to enable decimal notation for numeric values, allowing us to write, e.g., 2 instead of ZPos(OH). We also introduce enumeration types Comp and $\mathbb{B}$ representing comparison operators and Booleans.

In order to enable quantification over elements of these types, we introduce constants such as int : Set that represent codes for these types along with a rule for rewriting codes to their corresponding types, for example El int $\hookrightarrow \mathbb{Z}$. Figure 2 introduces operations on these types, including addition ($+$) and comparison ($\doteq$) over $\mathbb{Z}$. The auxiliary operations add, sub, and cmp implement addition, subtraction, and comparison for binary positive numbers; their definitions are not shown here for space restrictions. We also define the operations of multiplication ($*$) and subtraction ($-$) over $\mathbb{Z}$. We will refer to the rewriting rules defining these operations as $\rightarrow_{\mathbb{Z}}$ and $\rightarrow_{\mathbb{P}}$ (for operations on $\mathbb{Z}$ and $\mathbb{P}$) in the following sections. The confluence of these rewriting rules has been proven using CSI [27]. We leverage these rewriting rules to perform the constant folding required by the `evaluate` rule, enabling the final proof step to be discharged by reflexivity.

Finally, we define inequality operators for $\mathbb{Z}$ as binary predicates by reducing them to the decidable comparison $\doteq$. They reduce to $\top$, $\bot$ (or negated) by applying rules of $\rightarrow_{\mathbb{Z}}$ and $\rightarrow_{\mathbb{P}}$. For example, $1 < 2 \hookrightarrow \texttt{istrue(isLt}(1 \doteq 2)) \hookrightarrow \texttt{istrue(isLt(Lt))} \hookrightarrow \texttt{istrue(true)} \hookrightarrow \top$.

We use this encoding of integer operations for extending our existing embedding of Alethe proofs in Lambdapi [12]. In particular, the SMT sort **Int** is mapped to `El int`, and the arithmetic operations of SMT to their counterparts in the Lambdapi encoding. The following section describes how we leverage this representation of integers in Lambdapi to simulate the algorithm presented in Sect. 2.2 for checking applications of the rule `la_generic`.

5   Reconstruction of Linear Arithmetic for LIA Logic

Proof by reflection [10] is a technique for writing certified procedures for automated reasoning. It reduces the validity of a logical statement to a symbolic computation. Let $P : Z \rightarrow \texttt{Prop}$ be a predicate over a data type Z and $f : Z \rightarrow \texttt{bool}$ be a function such that the following theorem holds:

$$\texttt{f\_correct} : \forall z : Z, (f\ z = \texttt{true}) \rightarrow (P\ z)$$

If $f\ z$ reduces to `true`, then the proof term `f_correct` z (`refl bool true`) with $\texttt{refl} : \Pi A : \texttt{Set}, \Pi x : \texttt{El}\ A, \texttt{Prf}^c(x = x)$, constitutes a proof of predicate $(P\ z)$. In step 6 of checking an application of rule `la_generic`, the primary challenge lies in reasoning modulo associativity and commutativity when manipulating expressions over $\mathbb{Z}$. The key idea is to provide a normalization function that transforms a $\mathbb{Z}$ expression into a canonical form.

5.1   Representation

The procedure is based on an algebraic group structure, denoted as $\mathbb{G}$ defined in Fig. 3, which represents linear polynomials. The base type for its elements is $\mathbb{G} : \text{TYPE}$. The unary operator `cst` injects constants from $\mathbb{Z}$ into $\mathbb{G}$. The term `var` $c\ x$ is intended for representing expressions $c \times x$ that appear as constituents of linear inequalities, where c is an integer coefficient and x a $\mathbb{Z}$ term, in particular a variable. The constructor `mul` represents the multiplication of an element of $\mathbb{G}$ by a constant. The constructor `opp` corresponds to unary minus. Lastly, the constructor $\oplus$ represents the addition of two elements of $\mathbb{G}$.

$\mathbb{G} : \textbf{TYPE}$ $\Uparrow : \mathbb{Z} \to \mathbb{G}$ $\Downarrow : \mathbb{G} \to \mathbb{Z}$

$| \oplus : \mathbb{G} \to \mathbb{G} \to \mathbb{G}$ $\Uparrow \texttt{Z0} \hookrightarrow (\textbf{cst}\ \texttt{Z0})$ $\Downarrow (\textbf{cst}\ c) \hookrightarrow c$

$| \ \textbf{var} : \mathbb{Z} \to \mathbb{Z} \to \mathbb{G}$ $\Uparrow \texttt{ZPos}\ c \hookrightarrow (\textbf{cst}\ (\texttt{ZPos}\ c))$ $\Downarrow \textbf{opp}\ x \hookrightarrow\ \sim (\Downarrow x)$

$| \ \textbf{mul} : \mathbb{Z} \to \mathbb{G} \to \mathbb{G}$ $\Uparrow \texttt{ZNeg}\ c \hookrightarrow (\textbf{cst}\ (\texttt{ZNeg}\ c))$ $\Downarrow \textbf{mul}\ c\ x \hookrightarrow c \times (\Downarrow x)$

$| \ \textbf{opp} : \mathbb{G} \to \mathbb{G}$ $\Uparrow (x + y) \hookrightarrow (\Uparrow x) \oplus (\Uparrow y)$ $\Downarrow x \oplus y \hookrightarrow (\Downarrow x) + (\Downarrow y)$

$| \ \textbf{cst} : \mathbb{Z} \to \mathbb{G}$ $\Uparrow (\sim x) \hookrightarrow \textbf{opp}\ \Uparrow x$ $\Downarrow (\textbf{var}\ c\ x) \hookrightarrow c \times x$

$\textbf{grp} : \textbf{Set}$ $\Uparrow ((\texttt{ZPos}\ c) * x) \hookrightarrow \textbf{mul}\ (\texttt{ZPos}\ c)\ (\Uparrow x)$

$\textbf{El grp} \hookrightarrow \mathbb{G}$ $\Uparrow ((\texttt{ZNeg}\ c) * x) \hookrightarrow \textbf{mul}\ (\texttt{ZNeg}\ c)\ (\Uparrow x)$

$\Uparrow (x * (\texttt{ZPos}\ c)) \hookrightarrow \textbf{mul}\ (\texttt{ZPos}\ c)\ (\Uparrow x)$

$\Uparrow (x * (\texttt{ZNeg}\ c)) \hookrightarrow \textbf{mul}\ (\texttt{ZNeg}\ c)\ (\Uparrow x)$

$\Uparrow (x * \texttt{Z0}) \hookrightarrow (\textbf{cst}\ 0)$

$\Uparrow (\texttt{Z0} * x) \hookrightarrow (\textbf{cst}\ 0)$

$\Uparrow x \hookrightarrow (\textbf{var}\ 1\ x)$

Fig. 3. Definition of $\mathbb{G}$ Algebra and its reification ($\Uparrow$) and denotation ($\Downarrow$) functions.

Lambdapi provides modifiers for supporting associative and commutative operations, ensuring that terms are systematically transformed into a canonical form w.r.t. a builtin ordering relation [6,8]. We declare the operator $\oplus$ as associative commutative, ensuring that expressions involving sums of elements of $\mathbb{G}$ are systematically canonicalized.

5.2 Associative Commutative Normalization

The transformation to canonical form implemented in Lambdapi ensures that sum expressions of the form

$$(\textbf{var}\ c_1\ x_1) \oplus (\textbf{cst}\ k_1) \oplus (\textbf{var}\ c_2\ x_2) \oplus \cdots \oplus (\textbf{cst}\ k_m) \oplus \cdots \oplus (\textbf{var}\ c_n\ x_n)$$

will be normalized such that any pair of terms $(\textbf{var}\ c\ x)$ and $(\textbf{var}\ d\ x)$ involving the same variable x are placed next to each other, and all $(\textbf{cst}\ k)$ will be placed at the left before the first variable $(\textbf{var}\ c\ x)$. We will use the rewriting rules shown in Fig. 4 for reducing $\mathbb{G}$ expressions. Notably, the resulting normal forms do not contain the constructors $\texttt{mul}$ and $\texttt{opp}$, as the associated rewrite rules eliminate them in favor of $\textbf{var}, \textbf{add}$ and $\textbf{cst}$.

Definition 4. *The $\leq$ builtin total order on $\mathbb{G}$-terms is defined as follows: Terms are ordered such that $cst(c_1) \leq cst(c_2) < (\textbf{var}\ c\ x)$ for any constants $c_1 \leq c_2$ and any variable term $(\textbf{var}\ c\ x)$. For variable terms, $(\textbf{var}\ c\ x) \leq (\textbf{var}\ d\ y)$ if either $x < y$, or $x = y$ and $c \leq d$. Let $\to\!\!\!\!\!\to^{AC}$ be the relation mapping every term t to its unique AC-canonical form denoted $[t]$.*

Two terms t and u are AC-equivalent (written $t \simeq_{AC} u$) iff their AC-canonical forms are equal.

$$(\textbf{var } c_1 \ x) \oplus (\textbf{var } c_2 \ x) \hookrightarrow (\textbf{var } (c_1 + c_2) \ x) \tag{2}$$

$$(\textbf{var } c_1 \ x) \oplus ((\textbf{var } c_2 \ x) \oplus y) \hookrightarrow (\textbf{var } (c_1 + c_2) \ x) \oplus y \tag{3}$$

$$(\textbf{cst } c_1) \oplus (\textbf{cst } c_2) \hookrightarrow (\textbf{cst } (c_1 + c_2)) \tag{4}$$

$$(\textbf{cst } c_1) \oplus ((\textbf{cst } c_2) \oplus y) \hookrightarrow (\textbf{cst } (c_1 + c_2)) \oplus y \tag{5}$$

$$(\textbf{cst } 0) \oplus x \hookrightarrow x \tag{6}$$

$$x \oplus (\textbf{cst } 0) \hookrightarrow x \tag{7}$$

$$\textbf{opp } (\textbf{var } c \ x) \hookrightarrow (\textbf{var } (-c) \ x) \tag{8}$$

$$\textbf{opp } (\textbf{cst } c) \hookrightarrow (\textbf{cst } (-c)) \tag{9}$$

$$\textbf{opp } (\textbf{opp } x) \hookrightarrow x \tag{10}$$

$$\textbf{opp } (x \oplus y) \hookrightarrow (\textbf{opp } x) \oplus (\textbf{opp } y) \tag{11}$$

$$\textbf{opp } (\textbf{mul } k \ x) \hookrightarrow \textbf{mul } (-k) \ x \tag{12}$$

$$\textbf{mul } k \ (\textbf{var } c \ x) \hookrightarrow (\textbf{var } (k * c) \ x) \tag{13}$$

$$\textbf{mul } k \ (\textbf{opp } x) \hookrightarrow \textbf{mul } (-k) \ x \tag{14}$$

$$\textbf{mul } k \ (x \oplus y) \hookrightarrow (\textbf{mul } k \ x) \oplus (\textbf{mul } k \ y) \tag{15}$$

$$\textbf{mul } k \ (\textbf{cst } c) \hookrightarrow (\textbf{cst } (k * c)) \tag{16}$$

$$\textbf{mul } c_1 \ (\textbf{mul } c_2 \ x) \hookrightarrow \textbf{mul } (c_1 * c_2) \ x \tag{17}$$

Fig. 4. Rewrite system on canonical forms.

Definition 5. *The relation* $\longrightarrow_{\Sigma}^{AC}$ *is defined as* $\hookrightarrow_{\Sigma} \twoheadrightarrow^{AC}$, *where* Σ *contains the rewrite rules of Figs. 2 and 4.*

An $\longrightarrow_{\Sigma}^{AC}$ step is a standard $\hookrightarrow_{\Sigma}$ step with syntactic matching followed by AC-canonicalization. We now prove that the relation $\longrightarrow_{\Sigma}^{AC}$ terminates and is confluent.

Lemma 6. *The relation* $\longrightarrow_{\Sigma/AC} = \simeq_{AC} \hookrightarrow_{\Sigma} \simeq_{AC}$ *of matching modulo AC, which contains* $\longrightarrow_{\Sigma}^{AC}$, *terminates.*

Proof. AProVE [15] automatically proves the termination of $\longrightarrow_{\Sigma/AC}$. □

Lemma 7. $\longrightarrow_{\Sigma}^{AC}$ *is locally confluent on AC-canonical terms.*

Proof. We show that every critical pair is joinable using $\longrightarrow_{\Sigma}^{AC}$ and confluence of $\rightarrow_{\mathbb{Z}}$ and $\rightarrow_{\mathbb{P}}$. □

We compare two $\mathbb{Z}$-terms t_1 and t_2 wrt $\longrightarrow_{\Sigma}^{AC}$ by reifying them into their corresponding $\mathbb{G}$-terms, denoted $[g_1]$ and $[g_2]$, using the reification function $\Uparrow$, and normalizing them using $\twoheadrightarrow^{AC}$. Following the reduction rules specified in Fig. 4, we can then compare their corresponding $\mathbb{Z}$-terms by applying the denotation function $\Downarrow$. To validate this procedure, it is necessary to establish the correctness of the following diagram, formally expressed by Theorem 8.

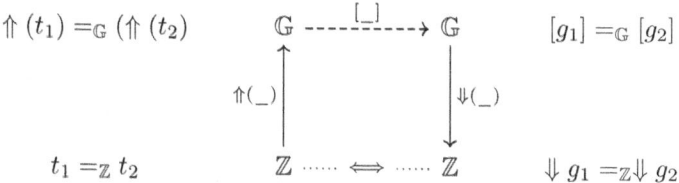

Theorem 8 (Correctness of normalization). *For all $\mathbb{G}$-terms t, we have* $(\Downarrow [t]) = (\Downarrow t)$ *where $[t]$ is the AC-canonical form of t with respect to $\longrightarrow_{\Sigma}^{AC}$.*

Proof. The proof proceeds by induction on t, and the key case is the one where $t = t_1 \oplus t_2$. We have to show that $\Downarrow [t_1 \oplus t_2] = (\Downarrow t_1) + (\Downarrow t_2)$. By the induction hypothesis, we have $\Downarrow [t_1] = \Downarrow t_1$ and $\Downarrow [t_2] = \Downarrow t_2$. Hence,

$$(\Downarrow t_1) + (\Downarrow t_2) = (\Downarrow [t_1]) + (\Downarrow [t_2]) = \Downarrow ([t_1] \oplus [t_2])$$

It remains to show that $\Downarrow ([t_1] \oplus [t_2]) = \Downarrow [t_1 \oplus t_2]$. Now, $[t_1]$, $[t_2]$, and $[t_1 \oplus t_2]$ are terms built solely from cst, var, and $\oplus$ since the remaining operators have been eliminated by applying the rules in Fig. 4, and the terms on both sides of the equation contain the same multisets of subterms. The two terms are therefore identified by AC-canonicalization. □

We make use of Lemma 9 to embed $\mathbb{Z}$-terms into $\mathbb{G}$ for normalization and subsequent comparison. In addition, we leverage this normalization process to support the arith-poly-norm rule.

Lemma 9 (Conversion). *For all $x : \mathbb{Z}$, we have $x = (\Downarrow (\Uparrow x))$.*

Proof. By induction on x. We consider the three cases: $x = \text{ZPos}(n)$, $x = \text{ZNeg}(n)$, and $x = \text{Z0}$. In each case, $\Uparrow (x)$ yields the corresponding constant (cst x), and by definition of the denotation function, $x = \Downarrow ((\text{cst } x))$. Hence, $x = (\Downarrow (\Uparrow x))$ in all cases. □

```
1  opaque symbol t2: Prf● ((¬ (3 < x) ∨ᶜ ¬ (x = 2)) ∨ ∎) {
2      apply ∨ᶜᵢ1;
3      rewrite Zinv_lt_eq;
4      rewrite Z_diff_gt_Z0_eq (∾ 3) (∾ x);
5      rewrite Z_diff_eq_Z0_eq (x) 2;
6      rewrite Zgt_le_succ_r_eq ((∾ 3) - (∾ x)) 0;
7      rewrite Zmult_ge_compat_eq 1 ((∾ 3) - (∾ x)) ((0 + 1));
8      rewrite Zmult_eq_compat_eq (∾ 1) (x - 2) 0;
9      rewrite imp_eq_or; apply ⇒ᶜᵢ; assume H0; apply ¬ᶜᵢ; assume H1;
10     set H0l' := (1 * ((∾ 0) - (∾ x))); set H0r' := (1 * (0 + 1));
11     set H1l' := ((∾ 1) * (x - 2)); set H1r' := ((∾ 1) * 0);
12     have H1': Prfᶜ (H1l' ≥ H1r') { refine Z_eq_implies_ge H1 }; remove H1;
13     have contra : Prfᶜ ((⇓ (⇑ (H0l' + H1l'))) ≥ (⇓ (⇑ (H0r' + H1r')))){
14         rewrite ⇓_⇑; rewrite ⇓_⇑;
15         apply (Zsum_geq_s H0l' H0r' H1l' H1r' H0 H1');
16     };
17     apply (⇒ᶜₑ' contra); apply ⊤ᶜᵢ;
18 };
```

Listing 1.5. Lambdapi proof of Listing 1.2

Table 2. Benchmark results.

Logic	Benchmark	Samples	Proofs	Elaborate	Translate	Check
LIA	tptp	36	36 - 0 - 0	36 - 0	36 - 0 - 0	28 - 8 - 0
	Ultimate	153	120 - 0 - 33	73 - 47	68 - 5 - 0	50 - 18 - 0
	Svcomp'19	27	27 - 0 - 0	25 - 2	0 - 25 - 0	0
	psyco	50	48 - 0 - 2	48 - 0	43 - 0 - 5	0 - 37 - 6
QFLIA	SMPT	1568	1529 - 39 - 0	1497 - 32	1476 - 0 - 21	804 - 638 - 34
	rings	294	70 - 1 - 223	49 - 21	49 - 0 - 0	7 - 0 - 42
	CAV2009	85	85 - 0 - 0	19 - 66	19 - 0 - 0	19 - 0 - 0
UFLIA	sledgeh	1521	1343 - 0 - 178	1278 - 65	1258 - 13 - 7	711 - 467 - 80
	tokeneer	1732	1732 - 0 - 0	1689 - 43	1689 - 0 - 0	1482 - 197 - 10

We present in Listing 1.5 the translation of Step t2 from Listing 1.2 using our Carcara module. The `rewrite Zinv_lt_eq` step at line 3 performs the normalization from Step 1, rewriting $\neg(3 < x)$ as $\neg(\sim 3 >\sim x)$. The lemmas `Z_diff_gt_Z0` and `Z_diff_eq_Z0_eq` (lines 4–5) implement Step 2. Since the goal involves a $>$ inequality, Step 3 applies with the lemma `Zgt_le_succ_r_eq` (line 6). The coefficients $[\frac{1}{1}, -\frac{1}{1}]$ from Step 4 are trivially cast to $\mathbb{Z}$ and applied in lines 7–8. To express all inequalities uniformly, remaining equalities are rewritten as $\geq$ using `Z_eq_implies_ge` (line 12). Finally, Step 6 derives the contradiction by summing inequalities from lines 13 to 17.

6 Evaluation

Our benchmark suite shown in Table 2 is composed of files from the SMT-LIB benchmarks[1]. The suite includes a total of 5,466 samples drawn from 9 benchmark categories spanning three SMT-LIB logics: LIA, QFLIA, and UFLIA that correspond to those covered by our method. Within the logics QFLIA and UFLIA, we prioritized benchmarks with the most significant number of available samples. Table 2 provides a detailed breakdown of the benchmarks and the corresponding results. The *Logic* column indicates the SMT theory used, while the *Benchmark* column lists abbreviated benchmark names. The column *Samples* describes the number of problems available with status *unsat*. Each of the columns *Proofs*, *Translate*, and *Check* reports a triple in the format success - error - timeout, representing respectively the number of successful executions, failed attempts, and timeouts. The *Proofs* column reports the number of proofs generated by cvc5[2] that do not contain the `to_real` cast operator. The *Elaborate* column shows a pair of values: the number of proofs that were successfully elaborated by Carcara, and the number that failed. Only proofs successfully elaborated by Carcara are considered for translation. The *Translate* column gives

---

[1] https://smtlib.cs.uiowa.edu/benchmarks.shtml.
[2] cvc5 version 1.2.1-dev.144.38fcc340e5 [git 38fcc340e5 on branch main].

Table 3. Lambdapi checking times in milliseconds.

Bench	Min	Q1	Mean	Q3	Max
tptp	240	262	263	267	336
Ultimate	82	96	100	111	346
SMPT	52	55	55	56	293
rings	670	704	773	826	1197
CAV2009	54	296	403	498	683
sledgeh	53	166	354	552	1594
tokeneer	55	60	61	248	753

the number of proof traces successfully translated into Lambdapi proofs, while the *Check* column indicates the number of these translated proofs that were successfully type-checked by Lambdapi.

We enforced a timeout of 30 s for cvc5 to find a proof and 30 s for the translation step with Carcara. No timeout was imposed during the elaboration step, as the runtime is negligible. A timeout of 20 s was set for Lambdapi when type-checking the final proofs to ensure that proof verification remains as fast as possible.[3]

All nine benchmarks demonstrated consistently reliable proof generation, with few or no timeouts, except for the *rings* benchmark. The elaboration phase was generally robust, except in the *Ultimate* benchmark, where an error in the elaborator caused failures. For LIA, performance in the translation and checking stages was mixed. In particular, for *Svcomp'19* and *psyco*, no or few proofs could be translated or verified, mainly due to currently unsupported simplification rules involving the ite operator. The QFLIA benchmarks exhibited more reliable proof checking in *SMPT* and *CAV2009*, while only a small number of proofs from the *rings* benchmark were successfully checked. The errors encountered during the elaboration of the *CAV2009* come from a bug in the elaborator. Since the samples in this benchmark are derived from a common base problem while increasing in size, the bug propagated across all samples that depend on the same base instance. The limited success with checking proofs in the *rings* category is due to the presence of la_generic terms with hundreds of uninterpreted variables; the current normalization mechanism, described in Sect. 5.2, relies on a built-in term ordering that is not sufficiently efficient in this setting. Benchmarks under UFLIA performed better throughout the pipeline. Most proofs were successfully generated and elaborated, and a large portion were translated and verified by Lambdapi, particularly in the *tokeneer* dataset. The higher number of errors in *SMPT* and *sledgeh* is primarily due to unsupported RARE rules related to the QF_UF logic, as well as unhandled cases in the evaluate rule for LIA and QF_UF.

---

[3] All benchmarks were executed in parallel using GNU parallel [25] with an Apple silicon M2.

Table 3 reports the Lambdapi proof-checking times in milliseconds, presenting the minimum, first quartile (Q1), mean, third quartile (Q3), and maximum durations for each benchmark. In most cases, the checking time remains below one second.

7   Related Work

The reconstruction for Alethe proofs produced by the veriT solver has been implemented within Isabelle/HOL [23] to enhance the reconstruction success rate compared to Z3. Concerning linear arithmetic reasoning, they also follow the algorithm described in Sect. 2.2, relying on Isabelle's simplifier (which supports reasoning modulo associativity and commutativity) for normalizing expressions.

Besson [4] introduces a modular framework for integrating SMT solvers with the Rocq proof assistant, emphasizing the generation and efficient verification of proof certificates directly within Coq. His approach enables fast, reflexive proof checking using Nelson-Oppen-style theory combination, and it supports both Linear Integer Arithmetic (LIA) and Linear Real Arithmetic (LRA) logics. To efficiently generate Farkas certificates for LA, the technique relies on the Simplex algorithm, while for LIA, a variant of the Omega test [22] is adopted. The technique has been evaluated on SMT-LIB 2 benchmarks using the Z3 solver.

Compared to these approaches, which demonstrate stronger scalability in handling larger and more complex systems of inequalities, our method does not yet scale as well, in particular for cases that require significant arithmetic simplification. As shown in Sect. 6, performance degrades on benchmarks such as *rings*, where large instances of rule `la_generic` are generated. Nevertheless, our framework offers the advantage of supporting proof export from Lambdapi to other systems. This interoperability enables the reuse of valid SMT proofs in external environments such as Rocq.

8   Conclusion

We presented an extension of Carcara's [1][4] translation module [12] for reconstructing arithmetic reasoning steps in Alethe proof traces involving linear arithmetic reasoning in the foundational proof assistant Lambdapi [18]. The translation module enables the export of an Alethe proof, together with its input problem, parsed and elaborated by Carcara, into a Lambdapi file that can be independently verified using the Lambdapi compiler and the Lambdapi library included in Carcara, which encodes Alethe logic. Building on this module, our extension introduces support for exporting arithmetic proof steps and extends the Lambdapi Alethe library to incorporate integer arithmetic proof rules. Our method includes a ring solver inspired by the computational reflection techniques described in [10,16].

---

[4] https://github.com/NotBad4U/carcara/tree/lambdapi-translate.

We have shown that this allows us to reconstruct several thousand SMT proofs that originate from the SMT-lib Benchmarks. To the best of our knowledge, this is the first work to automatically solve arithmetic goals in Lambdapi. Nonetheless, the current implementation does not yet scale well in arithmetic-heavy cases. As future work, we plan to improve Lambdapi's built-in normalization mechanism to better handle such cases. We also intend to extend our work to support rational and real arithmetic, enabling verification of broader fragments of linear arithmetic (LRA) theories. This will in particular require an encoding of rational and real arithmetic in Lambdapi and their normalization function, based on the *gcd* operator, as a basis for implementing proof by reflection.

References

1. Andreotti, B., Lachnitt, H., Barbosa, H.: CARCARA: an efficient proof checker and elaborator for SMT proofs in the Alethe format. In: Sankaranarayanan, S., Sharygina, N. (eds.) TACAS 2023. LNCS, vol. 13993, pp. 367–386. Springer, Cham (2023). https://doi.org/10.1007/978-3-031-30823-9_19
2. Barbosa, H., Fleury, M., Fontaine, P., Schurr, H.J.: The Alethe proof format an evolving specification and reference (2024). https://verit.gitlabpages.uliege.be/alethe/specification.pdf
3. Barrett, C., Fontaine, P., Tinelli, C.: The SMT-LIB standard: version 2.7. Technical report, Department of Computer Science, The University of Iowa (2017–2024). https://smt-lib.org/papers/smt-lib-reference-v2.7-r2025-07-07.pdf
4. Besson, F.: Fast reflexive arithmetic tactics the linear case and beyond. In: Altenkirch, T., McBride, C. (eds.) TYPES 2006. LNCS, vol. 4502, pp. 48–62. Springer, Heidelberg (2007). https://doi.org/10.1007/978-3-540-74464-1_4
5. Blanqui, F.: Type safety of rewrite rules in dependent types. In: 5th International Conference on Formal Structures for Computation and Deduction (FSCD 2020). Leibniz International Proceedings in Informatics (LIPIcs), vol. 167, pp. 13:1–13:14 (2020)
6. Blanqui, F.: Encoding type universes without using matching modulo associativity and commutativity. In: Felty, A.P. (ed.) 7th International Conference on Formal Structures for Computation and Deduction (FSCD 2022). Leibniz International Proceedings in Informatics (LIPIcs), vol. 228, pp. 24:1–24:14 (2022)
7. Blanqui, F., Dowek, G., Grienenberger, E., Hondet, G., Thiré, F.: Some axioms for mathematics. In: 6th International Conference on Formal Structures for Computation and Deduction (FSCD 2021). Leibniz International Proceedings in Informatics (LIPIcs), vol. 195, pp. 20:1–20:19. Schloss Dagstuhl – Leibniz-Zentrum für Informatik, Dagstuhl (2021)
8. Blanqui, F., Hardin, T., Weis, P.: On the implementation of construction functions for non-free concrete data types. In: De Nicola, R. (ed.) ESOP 2007. LNCS, vol. 4421, pp. 95–109. Springer, Heidelberg (2007). https://doi.org/10.1007/978-3-540-71316-6_8
9. Blanqui, F.: Translating HOL-light proofs to Coq. In: Proceedings of 25th Conference on Logic for Programming, Artificial Intelligence and Reasoning. EPiC Series in Computing, vol. 100, pp. 1–18 (2024)
10. Boutin, S.: Using reflection to build efficient and certified decision procedures. In: Abadi, M., Ito, T. (eds.) TACS 1997. LNCS, vol. 1281, pp. 515–529. Springer, Heidelberg (1997). https://doi.org/10.1007/BFb0014565

11. Bromberger, M., Sturm, T., Weidenbach, C.: A complete and terminating approach to linear integer solving. J. Symb. Comput. **100**, 102–136 (2020). https://doi.org/10.1016/J.JSC.2019.07.021
12. Coltellacci, A., Merz, S., Dowek, G.: Reconstruction of SMT proofs with Lambdapi. In: Proceedings of the 22nd International Workshop on Satisfiability Modulo Theories Co-located with the 36th International Conference on Computer Aided Verification (CAV 2024). CEUR Workshop Proceedings, vol. 3725, pp. 13–23. CEUR-WS.org, Montreal (2024)
13. Cousineau, D., Dowek, G.: Embedding pure type systems in the lambda-pi-calculus modulo. In: Della Rocca, S.R. (ed.) TLCA 2007. LNCS, vol. 4583, pp. 102–117. Springer, Heidelberg (2007). https://doi.org/10.1007/978-3-540-73228-0_9
14. Dutertre, B., de Moura, L.: Integrating simplex with DPLL(T). Technical report CSL-06-01, SRI International (2006). https://yices.csl.sri.com/papers/sri-csl-06-01.pdf
15. Giesl, J., et al.: Proving termination of programs automatically with AProVE. In: Demri, S., Kapur, D., Weidenbach, C. (eds.) IJCAR 2014. LNCS (LNAI), vol. 8562, pp. 184–191. Springer, Cham (2014). https://doi.org/10.1007/978-3-319-08587-6_13
16. Grégoire, B., Mahboubi, A.: Proving equalities in a commutative ring done right in Coq. In: Hurd, J., Melham, T. (eds.) TPHOLs 2005. LNCS, vol. 3603, pp. 98–113. Springer, Heidelberg (2005). https://doi.org/10.1007/11541868_7
17. Harper, R., Honsell, F., Plotkin, G.D.: A framework for defining logics. J. ACM **40**, 143–184 (1993). https://api.semanticscholar.org/CorpusID:13375103
18. Hondet, G., Blanqui, F.: The new rewriting engine of Dedukti. In: 5th International Conference on Formal Structures for Computation and Deduction (FSCD 2020). Leibniz International Proceedings in Informatics (LIPIcs), vol. 167, pp. 35:1–35:16. Schloss Dagstuhl – Leibniz-Zentrum für Informatik, Dagstuhl (2020)
19. Martin-Löf, P.: Intuitionistic type theory (1980)
20. Moura, L., Ullrich, S.: The lean 4 theorem prover and programming language. In: Platzer, A., Sutcliffe, G. (eds.) CADE 2021. LNCS (LNAI), vol. 12699, pp. 625–635. Springer, Cham (2021). https://doi.org/10.1007/978-3-030-79876-5_37
21. Nötzli, A., Barbosa, H., Niemetz, A., Preiner, M., Reynolds, A., Barrett, C., Tinelli, C.: Reconstructing fine-grained proofs of rewrites using a domain-specific language. In: FMCAD 2022, pp. 65–74 (2022). https://doi.org/10.34727/2022/isbn.978-3-85448-053-2_12
22. Pugh, W.: The Omega test: a fast and practical integer programming algorithm for dependence analysis. In: Proceedings of the 1991 ACM/IEEE Conference on Supercomputing, pp. 4–13 (1991)
23. Schurr, H.-J., Fleury, M., Desharnais, M.: Reliable reconstruction of fine-grained proofs in a proof assistant. In: Platzer, A., Sutcliffe, G. (eds.) CADE 2021. LNCS (LNAI), vol. 12699, pp. 450–467. Springer, Cham (2021). https://doi.org/10.1007/978-3-030-79876-5_26
24. Schurr, H.J., Fleury, M., Barbosa, H., Fontaine, P.: Alethe: towards a generic SMT proof format (extended abstract). In: Electronic Proceedings in Theoretical Computer Science, vol. 336, pp. 49–54 (2021)
25. Tange, O.: GNU parallel 20250322 (2025). https://doi.org/10.5281/zenodo.15071920. GNU Parallel is a general parallelizer to run multiple serial command line programs in parallel without changing them
26. The Rocq Development Team: The Rocq reference manual – release 9.0.0 (2025). https://rocq-prover.org/doc/V9.0.0/refman/index.html

27. Zankl, H., Felgenhauer, B., Middeldorp, A.: CSI – a confluence tool. In: Bjørner, N., Sofronie-Stokkermans, V. (eds.) CADE 2011. LNCS (LNAI), vol. 6803, pp. 499–505. Springer, Heidelberg (2011). https://doi.org/10.1007/978-3-642-22438-6_38

Certifying rlive: A New Proof Strategy for Liveness Model Checking

Giulia Sindoni$^{(\boxtimes)}$ ⓘ, Alberto Griggio$^{(\boxtimes)}$ ⓘ, and Stefano Tonetta$^{(\boxtimes)}$ ⓘ

Fondazione Bruno Kessler, Trento, Italy
{gsindoni,griggio,tonettas}@fbk.eu

Abstract. SAT-based model checking has become a prominent app-roach to the verification of temporal properties. However, while invari-ant model checking can produce simple proofs based on induction, proof generation for SAT-based model checking of liveness properties is much more complex.

In this paper, we focus on a recently developed algorithm, called rlive, which has been proved quite effective in practice. rlive tries to find a coun-terexample with a series of reachability checks, while iteratively blocking shoals, i.e., set of states that cannot be extended with fair paths. Despite the complexity of the algorithm, we show that the shoals are sufficient to generate a proof in a deductive system for temporal properties. We imple-ment the approach in an existing certifying model checking framework based on the PVS theorem prover, and we experimentally evaluate it on liveness verification problems from the hardware model checking compe-tition, generating proofs using the nuXmv model checker and checking them with PVS.

1 Introduction

Applying formal methods as a tool for certifying high-assurance and safety-critical systems demands for verification tools that are capable of providing a high level of confidence in their outcomes.

A model checker generally offers a straightforward "yes" or "no" answer when addressing a verification problem. When the answer is "no" the model checker provides a counterexample as supporting evidence. No such evidence is usually given when the answer is "yes". Moreover, the growing complexity of model checkers themselves has made it increasingly important to obtain certificates from their process. The idea of certifying model checking [19] is to generate certificates as a byproduct of the verification. These certificates, often in the form of deductive proofs, serve to build trust in the verification results by providing additional evidence of correctness.

In this paper we consider problem of certifying the liveness checking problem, denoted $\mathcal{M} \models \mathbf{FG}q$ where $\mathbf{FG}q$ intuitively means that, in any satisfying trace, q eventually holds in all the future states. More specifically, we focus on rlive [30], a new SAT-based model-checking algorithm for the verification of liveness prop-erties of finite-state symbolic transition systems, which has been proved quite

© The Author(s) 2026
R. Thiemann and C. Weidenbach (Eds.): FroCoS 2025, LNAI 15979, pp. 386–403, 2026.
https://doi.org/10.1007/978-3-032-04167-8_21

effective in practice. rlive tries to find a counterexample with a series of reachability checks, while iteratively blocking a set of shoals, i.e. set of states that cannot reach a $\neg q$-state infinitely often.

We show that, despite the complexity of this algorithm, the shoals are sufficient to generate certifying proofs for the liveness property in a deductive system. The shoals are easily provided by the model checker, in the case where this has verified that the model satisfies the liveness property.

Our starting point is the approach presented in [15], describing a method for the generation of liveness checking certificates using the k-liveneess algorithm [9]. The key idea of k-liveness is it prove that a liveness property holds, by bounding how many times q can be false. For any valid liveness property in a finite-state transition system, there exists a bound k such that q can become false at most k times in any trace. The algorithm incrementally searches for this bound ($k = 0, 1, 2, \ldots$), using a SAT-based safety checker to verify each bound until one succeeds. In this paper, we adapt and generalise the certification procedure for k-liveness of [15] to make it applicable also to rlive. We then extend our previous work of [28], where we presented a theorem prover based certification framework for invariant properties, to handle liveness proofs.

More specifically, we make the following contributions:

1. The formalisation of new temporal deductive rule capturing rlive. We formally prove the correctness and completeness of the rule. This rule is a generalisation of the temporal rule for k-liveness presented in [15]. The correctness result is proved within a deductive proof system developed in the PVS specification language [26], so that it can be used within an automated proof strategy.

2. The development of a proof strategy for certifying the success of the model checking answer "yes", when the model checker has used rlive to show that the model satisfies the liveness property. This strategy only takes as input the set of shoals, which are created during the model checking stage.

We experimentally evaluate our approach on liveness verification problems from the hardware model checking competition, generating proofs using the nuXmv model checker [7] and checking them with PVS.

Outline. The rest of the paper is organised as follows. Section 2 provides an overview of related work. Section 3 introduces notation and background notions. Section 4 describes our contribution at formalising rlive as a temporal deductive rule and at generating proofs for certifying liveness checking results using rlive. Section 5 reports an evaluation of the prototype implementation of the proof strategy on a standard set of benchmarks for liveness checking. Section 6 concludes the paper.

2   Related Work

This work builds upon the concepts first presented in [15], where it was shown how to exploit the k-liveness algorithm to extend proof generation capabilities for invariant checking to cover full linear-temporal logic (LTL) properties, with little overhead for the model checker. The work shows how k-liveness can be formalised as a temporal deductive rule and its correctness proved within a complete axiomatic system for LTL from [13]. However, in that case no theorem prover was used to check the proof generated by the model checker.

In [28] the authors fill this gap by presenting a novel approach for certifying model checking results exploiting a theorem prover, namely PVS, and a theory of temporal deductive rules that can support various kinds of transformations and simplifications of the original model, such as 2-phase abstraction and temporal decomposition. This work was however restricted in that it can only handle the proof of invariant properties.

The present work builds upon the theorem-prover based approach from [28], by showing how to certify model checking results for liveness properties, specifically when the model checker uses the newly introduced rlive algorithm to prove the property at issue. Even though rlive looks as a very different algorithm from k-liveness, the proof of the first turns out to be a generalisation of the latter presented in [15].

A different approach to certification is presented in [31], where a formal framework designed to certify model checking results based on k-induction is described. The core of this certification process is the creation of a witness circuit which simulates the original circuit, and which includes an inductive invariant that serves as a proof certificate. This approach is extended further in [4] and [12]. The framework is however limited to the certification of invariants, and doesn't consider liveness or general LTL properties.

A relevant approach to certifying the correctness of liveness properties specifically is presented in [16]. The authors present a variant of the liveness-to-safety algorithm [1], and transform the liveness property into a safety property using a reduction. Then they get a proof for that safety property. However, this reduction has to be trusted as correct, and the proof does not target the original system, but the result of the reduction. In our work, we produce a temporal proof of the fact that the original system satisfies the property, so that only the theorem prover performing the proof, and not the model checking algorithms used, has to be trusted.

Other approaches concerning the generation of proofs from model checking results include [22,23], [17] and [10], but they are mainly theoretical, and no implementation is available, to the best of our knowledge. In contrast, our certification procedure has been implemented within a theorem prover framework, and specifically targets the rlive algorithm.

3   Background and Preliminaries

We operate within the framework of Boolean (propositional) logic, using the standard concepts of satisfiability, validity, interpretations, and models. We use lowercase Latin letters x, v (possibly with subscripts or primes) to denote propositional variables. Similarly, uppercase Latin letters X, V represent sets of variables. Uppercase Latin letters $\mathcal{I}, T$, as well as lowercase Latin and Greek letters

q, ϕ, ψ, are used to denote formulae, while uppercase Greek letters Γ and Δ and Π represent sets of formulae.

3.1   Transitions Systems

We take into account systems modeled by state transition structures, implicitly represented by propositional formulae. A *transition system* $\mathcal{M}$ is a triple $\langle X, \mathcal{I}, T \rangle$, where X is a set of (propositional) *state variables*, $\mathcal{I}(X)$ is a formula representing the *initial states*, and $T(X, X')$ is a formula representing the system's *transition relation*. The states of $\mathcal{M}$ are (complete) assignments to the variables in X. We denote by Σ_X the set of states. A state $s \in \Sigma_X$ is a model for a propositional formula ψ, denote by $s \models \psi(X)$, if substituting the values of s into ψ, the formula ψ evaluate to *True*. Next states, i.e., those reached after a transition, are represented as assignments to primed state variables X'. A *path* of $\mathcal{M}$ is an infinite sequence of states $s_0, s_1, \ldots$ such that $s_0 \models \mathcal{I}$, and for all $i \geq 0$, $s_i, s'_{i+1} \models T$. Given a path $\pi := s_0, s_1, \ldots$ we denote with $\pi[i]$ the state s_i.

3.2   Linear Temporal Logic

Linear Temporal Logic (LTL) was introduced by Pnueli [24] for the specification and verification of reactive systems. Formulae of LTL are constructed from a set of *propositional variables* X using the usual *logical connectives* ($\neg$, $\wedge$, $\vee$) and some *temporal operators* $\mathbf{X}$ ("next"), $\mathbf{F}$ ("eventually"), $\mathbf{G}$ ("always") and $\mathbf{U}$ ("until"). LTL formulae are interpreted in terms of paths, i.e., sequences of states of a transition system. Their semantics is also extended to states and whole transition systems.

Given a transition system $\mathcal{M} = \langle X, \mathcal{I}, T \rangle$, a path $\pi := s_0, s_1, \ldots$ in $\mathcal{M}$, an index i and a formula ψ over X, we define $\pi, i \models \psi$, i.e. that π satisfies ψ in i, as follows:

- $\pi, i \models \top$ and $\pi, i \not\models \bot$.
- For each $p \in X$, $\pi, i \models p$ iff $\pi[i] \models p$.
- $\pi, i \models \neg\psi$ iff $\pi, i \not\models \psi$.
- $\pi, i \models \psi_1 \wedge \psi_2$ iff $\pi, i \models \psi_1$ and $\pi, i \models \psi_2$.
- $\pi, i \models \psi_1 \vee \psi_2$ iff $\pi, i \models \psi_1$ or $\pi \models \psi_2$.
- $\pi, i \models \mathbf{X}\psi$ iff $\pi, i+1 \models \psi$.
- $\pi, i \models \mathbf{F}\psi$ iff $\pi, j \models \psi$ for some $j \geq i$.
- $\pi, i \models \mathbf{G}\psi$ iff $\pi, j \models \psi$ for every $j \geq i$.
- $\pi, i \models \psi_1\mathbf{U}\psi_2$ iff $\pi, j \models \psi_2$ for some $j \geq i$ and $\pi, k \models \psi_1$ for every $i \leq k < j$.

Finally, $\pi \models \psi$ iff $\pi, 0 \models \psi$. Given a propositional formula q over X, we call the *liveness checking problem*, denoted by $\mathcal{M} \models \mathbf{FG}q$, the problem to check $\pi \models \mathbf{FG}q$ for all paths π of $\mathcal{M}$. $\mathbf{FG}q$ intuitively means that, in any path of $\mathcal{M}$, q eventually holds in all the future states. Therefore the condition $\neg q$ can only be visited a finite number of times. Dually, a counterexample of $\mathbf{FG}q$ is an infinite path where $\neg q$ is visited an infinite number of times, i.e. there is a trace satisfying $\mathbf{GF}\neg q$. Since we are working in the finite-state case, such a counterexample must be a lasso-shaped path, i.e. an infinite sequence of states consisting of a finite prefix leading to a cycle that repeats forever. The general model checking problem, denoted by $\mathcal{M} \models \phi$ where ϕ is an LTL formula, can be reduced to the liveness checking problem $\mathcal{M} \times \mathcal{A}_{\neg\phi} \models \mathbf{FG}q$ following the standard automata-theoretic approach [29], where $\neg q$ is the Buchi acceptance condition of $\mathcal{A}_{\neg\phi}$.

3.3   Liveness Checking with rlive

rlive is a recent algorithm for verifying liveness properties in finite-state symbolic transition systems [30]. It can be seen as a variant of k-liveness [9] that explores the state-space in a depth-first search manner. Like other approaches, rlive reduces the liveness checking to a sequence of safety checks. Algorithm 1 describes how rlive is implemented using a generic invariant-checking engine. The key innovation is that rlive builds counterexamples to $\mathbf{FG}q$ incrementally through a recursive, depth-first search process, rather than directly searching for lasso-shaped counterexamples. When looking for counterexamples, rlive first finds a path from the initial states to a $\neg q$-state, i.e. a state that satisfies $\neg q$. This happens in the first iteration of the while-loop at line 4, Algorithm 1, where $\neg C$ and $\neg C'^1$ both evaluate to $\top$. The state s, line 5, is the first $\neg q$-state met. Notice that if such a state is not reachable, then $\mathbf{G}q$ is proved and so is $\mathbf{FG}q$. Then it searches for additional $\neg q$-states from the successors of each discovered $\neg q$-state (line 9). During this process, either of the following outcomes occurs:

1. a previously visited $\neg q$-state is met again, creating a lasso-shaped counterexample that violates the liveness property (lines 11-12), or
2. the search reaches a point where no more $\neg q$-states can be reached. In this case, rlive obtains an inductive invariant, the *shoal*, from the safety checker, which describes the set of states from which $\neg q$ can be visited a finite number of times only (lines 15-16). Clearly, no state in the shoal belongs to a counterexample trace.

Hence, the shoals are used to restrict future searches by blocking parts of the system state space. The algorithms excludes the states in C from the transition system by adding the constraint $\neg C \wedge \neg C'$ to T (lines 4 and 9). Additionally, the states to be searched are no longer simply $\neg q$-states, but states in $T^{-1}(\neg C) \cap \neg q$ (lines 4 and 9), i.e. $\neg q$-states that also have successors outside the shoal C, to exclude $\neg q$-states that are proved not to be part of the counterexample. This procedure continues until either all the reachable $\neg q$-states are eliminated, proving the property (line 18), or a lasso-shaped counterexample is found (lines 11-12).

---

[1] We remark that for a formula A, the primed notation A' represents the set of states that are immediate successors to states satisfying A. This is semantically equivalent to the LTL next operator $\mathbf{X}$ introduced in Sect. 3.2.

Algorithm 1: rlive algorithm [30].

```
1  Procedure rlive(X, I, T, FGq) begin
2      C := ⊥
3      B := empty stack of states
4      while check-invariant(X, I, T ∧ (¬C ∧ ¬C'), T⁻¹(¬C) → q) is Unsafe do
5          s := final state of get-counterexample()
6          B.push(s)
7          while B is not empty do
8              s := B.top()
9              if check-invariant(X, T(s), T ∧ (¬C ∧ ¬C'), T⁻¹(¬C) → q) is
                   Unsafe then
10                 t := final state of get-counterexample()
11                 if t ∈ B then
12                     return Unsafe
13                 B.push(t)
14             else
15                 inv := get-inductive-invariant()
16                 C := C ∨ inv
17                 B.pop()
18     return Safe
```

3.4   Theorem Proving in PVS

The Prototype Verification System (PVS) [20] is a specification language integrated with a theorem prover. The PVS theorem prover is interactive, but it also supports strategies development [21] and a batch mode [18], so that proofs can be run automatically. PVS uses a sequent-style [14] proof representation. A PVS sequent is an object of the form $A_1, A_2, A_3, \ldots \vdash B_1, B_2, B_3, \ldots$, where formulae A_i make the antecedent and formulae B_j make the consequent. The sequent above asserts that "if all the A's are true, then at least one of the B's is true". Hence, the sequent means the same as: $(A_1 \wedge A_2 \wedge A_3 \ldots) \to (B_1 \vee B_2 \vee B_3 \ldots)$.

The prover builds a proof tree that starts with $\vdash A$, where A is the theorem to be established. A proof is accomplished when all the leaves are recognised as true: this occurs if any antecedent is the same as any consequent $(C, \Gamma \vdash C, \Delta)$, if any antecedent is false $(False, \Gamma \vdash \Delta)$, or if any consequent is true $(\Gamma \vdash True, \Delta)$. Other sequents can be recognised as true using more powerful inferences [26].

3.5   A Shallow Embedding of LTL into PVS

In [28] we present a formalisation of LTL into PVS, following a shallow embedding approach [5,25].

In the PVS theory shallow_ltl we declare the type *trace* as all mappings from natural numbers to states. An *LTL formula* is a function that takes a trace and a natural number, and returns a boolean PVS type (*True* or *False*), which is the truth-value of the formula at point on the trace. A *state* is an object of any type, and it is an explicit parameter of shallow_ltl.

```
shallow_ltl[State: TYPE+]: THEORY
BEGIN
Trace: TYPE = ARRAY[nat -> State]
ltlformula: TYPE = [Trace -> [nat -> bool]]
```

Examples of definition of propositional and LTL operators within our theory[2] follow, where P is an LTL formula.

```
NOT(P)(trace: Trace)(t: nat): bool = NOT P(trace)(t);
NEXT(P)(trace: Trace)(t: nat): bool = P(trace)(t+1);
GLOBALLY(P)(trace: Trace)(t: nat): bool = FORALL (t0: nat): t0 >= t IMPLIES
    P(trace)(t0);
```

An LTL formula P is *valid* if it is true at the initial state of any trace. A stronger notion of validity, called *global validity*, is when the formula is true at any state of any trace.

```
|=(trace:Trace, t:nat, P): bool = P(trace)(t)
valid(P): bool = FORALL (trace: Trace): |=(trace, 0, P)
valid_all(P): bool = FORALL (trace: Trace): FORALL (t: nat): |=(trace, t, P)
```

The full theory `shallow_ltl` can be found in a dedicated repository [27].

4   Certifying Liveness Properties Using rlive

Consider the liveness checking problem $\mathcal{M} \models \mathbf{FG}q$, where $\mathcal{M} = \langle X, \mathcal{I}, T \rangle$ and q is a propositional formula over X. With an abuse of notation, we consider T also an LTL formula, identifying x' with $\mathbf{X}(x)$ for every variable $x \in X$. In order to prove $\mathcal{M} \models \mathbf{FG}q$, we provide a proof of $(\mathcal{I} \wedge \mathbf{G}T) \rightarrow \mathbf{FG}q$, following the same approach as in [15].

4.1   A New Temporal Deductive Rule for Liveness

In order to prove $(\mathcal{I} \wedge \mathbf{G}T) \rightarrow \mathbf{FG}q$, we use the following inference rule denoted with RL

$$\frac{P_i \quad P_0 \quad Pk_1 \quad Pp_1 \quad \dots \quad Pk_n \quad Pp_n}{\mathcal{I} \wedge \mathbf{G}(T) \rightarrow \mathbf{FG}q} \text{ RL}$$

The premises of the rule RL are:

$P_i := (\mathcal{I} \wedge \mathbf{G}T \wedge \mathbf{G}\neg C) \rightarrow \mathbf{G}q$
$P_0 := \mathbf{G}(C_0 \leftrightarrow \bot)$
$Pk_1 := \mathbf{G}((C_0 \vee C_1) \wedge T \rightarrow \mathbf{X}(C_0 \vee C_1))$
$Pp_1 := \mathbf{G}((C_0 \vee C_1) \wedge T \wedge \neg q \rightarrow \mathbf{X}(C_0))$
$\dots$
$Pk_n := \mathbf{G}((C_0 \vee \dots \vee C_n) \wedge T \rightarrow \mathbf{X}(C_0 \vee \dots \vee C_n))$

---

[2] PVS allows overloading of built-in symbols. In the definition above the first NOT is our defined LTL operator, which creates an LTL formula and whose semantics is defined via the boolean PVS operator NOT.

$$Pp_n := \mathbf{G}((C_0 \vee \ldots \vee C_n) \wedge T \wedge \neg q \to \mathbf{X}(C_0 \vee \ldots \vee C_{n-1}))$$

where $C := C_0 \vee C_1 \vee \ldots \vee C_n$.

Intuitively, P_i means that any trace of $\mathcal{M}$ satisfies that either a state in the shoal will be met eventually, or q is an invariant - being the formula $(\mathcal{I} \wedge \mathbf{G}T \wedge \mathbf{G}\neg C) \to \mathbf{G}q$ equivalent to $(\mathcal{I} \wedge \mathbf{G}T) \to (\mathbf{F}C \vee \mathbf{G}q)$. If the latter is the case, then $\mathbf{F}\mathbf{G}q$ holds and the liveness property is therefore verified. Thus we need to cover the case where a shoal state is met eventually ($\mathbf{F}C$).

We consider the additional premises of RL, P_0, Pk_1, Pp_1, ..., Pk_n, Pp_n. P_0 simply states that the shoal is initially empty. Each premise Pk_i ($1 \leq i \leq n$) states that the invariant $C_0 \vee \cdots \vee C_i$ incrementally built is inductive. Each premise Pp_i ($1 \leq i \leq n$) states that if we are in a state where $C_0 \vee \cdots \vee C_i$ and $\neg q$ both hold, following the transition T, the next state will belong to at least one shoal that was added to C before C_i itself, i.e. to $C_0 \vee \ldots \vee C_{i-1}$. This means that once in the shoal, we do not exit it, and that the search space can be incrementally restricted, as long as we keep visiting a $\neg q$-state. Notice that Pk_1 is equivalent to $\mathbf{G}(C_1 \wedge T \wedge \neg q \to \bot)$: states in C_1 cannot reach $\neg q$-states at all. C_1 represents the first non-empty set of states added to C by the algorithm.

A formal proof of the fact that rlive contains the information necessary to prove premises P_i, and Pk_i, Pp_i for $1 \leq i \leq n$ is given in Sect. 4.3.

RL as a Generalisation of k-liveness Rule. In the temporal proof for k-liveness from [15] we have formulae $\alpha_0, \ldots, \alpha_{k+1}$, that keep count of the number of times the fairness condition $\neg q$ is reached. Assuming by contradiction that we will keep reaching $\neg q$, eventually α_{k+1} is reached. This final formula expresses a contradiction as $\neg q$ can be visited at most k times by the k-liveness algorithm [9]. Thus, any path starting from $\mathcal{I}$ can visit $\neg q$ finitely many times only (concluding $\mathbf{F}\mathbf{G}q$).

RL generalises this k-liveness rule, in the sense that it can be used to build proofs for k-liveness, but the premises are more relaxed to cover more general proofs. In particular, given the α's conditions from k-liveness, RL can be used to perform a k-liveness proof as in [15].

Given $n = k + 1$, we can establish this mapping: each k-liveness condition α_i for $0 \leq i \leq k+1$ maps to C_{k-i+1}, so specifically α_{k+1} maps to C_0, both formulae expressing a contradiction, α_k maps to C_1 and so on through the sequence up α_1 mapping to C_k and α_0 mapping to C_{k+1}. $C = C_0 \vee \ldots \vee C_n = \alpha_{k+1} \vee \ldots \vee \alpha_0$. Given this mapping, we can prove that if the premise P_i of k-liveness holds, which states that $\mathcal{I} \to \mathbf{F}(\alpha_0)$, than the corresponding P_i of RL holds too, as α_0 implies C using the mapping above. Moreover it is possible to prove by induction that, given this mapping, if each Pk_i and Pp_i premises from k-liveness hold, then so do the corresponding premises for RL.

Thus, RL can be used in alternative to the rule defined in [15] for k-liveness, but the premises are more relaxed to accommodate the proof of rlive. In particular, it provides a more general first premise P_i, and weaker premises Pk_i than the corresponding premises of k-liveness. In the k-liveness rule, $P_i := \mathcal{I} \to \mathbf{F}(\alpha_0)$, i.e., from the initial state we can reach α_0 and start counting. In RL we need to consider the alternative possibility that the shoal stays empty (FC is false), thus concluding $\mathbf{G}q$. The Pk_i premises from RL allows to transition from a C_i to any shoal with a lower index, whilst in the k-liveness rule a state from α_i is required to either remain in α_i (when q holds) or transition to the immediate successor condition α_{i+1}.

4.2   Correctness of the Rule

Let us denote the set of formulae $\{Pk_1, Pp_1, \ldots, Pk_n, Pp_n\}$ simply with Π. The full formalisation and proof of correctness of RL has been done in PVS in our theory `lemmas_shallow_ltl` [27], in the form of a validity statement: for all formulae $\mathcal{I}$, T, q and C we proved that $valid((P_i \wedge P_0 \wedge \Pi) \to (\mathcal{I} \wedge \mathbf{GT} \to \mathbf{FG}q))$. The schema of the proof is as follows, and we refer to [27] for the fine-grained proof.

$$\cfrac{\cfrac{\cfrac{P_i}{(\mathcal{I} \wedge \mathbf{GT}) \to (\neg \mathbf{G}\neg C \vee \mathbf{G}q)}}{(\mathcal{I} \wedge \mathbf{GT}) \to (\mathbf{F}C \vee \mathbf{G}q)} \qquad [\mathcal{I} \wedge \mathbf{GT}]}{\mathbf{F}C \vee \mathbf{G}q}$$

If $\mathbf{G}q$ is the case:

$$\cfrac{\cfrac{\cfrac{\mathbf{G}q}{\mathbf{FG}q}}{}}{(\mathcal{I} \wedge \mathbf{GT}) \to \mathbf{FG}q}$$

Let us now consider the second possibility: $\mathbf{F}C$.

$$\cfrac{\cfrac{\mathrm{RLB}\ \cfrac{\mathbf{F}C \quad \Pi \quad [\mathcal{I} \wedge \mathbf{GT}] \quad [\mathbf{GF}\neg q]}{\mathbf{F}C_0} \qquad \cfrac{P_0}{\mathbf{G}\neg C_0}}{\cfrac{\perp}{\neg \mathbf{GF}\neg q}}}{\cfrac{\mathbf{FG}q}{(\mathcal{I} \wedge \mathbf{GT}) \to \mathbf{FG}q}}$$

Notice that the main step to prove the correctness of RL is the following deduction rule

$$\mathrm{RLB}\ \cfrac{\mathbf{F}C \quad \Pi \quad \mathcal{I} \wedge \mathbf{GT} \quad \mathbf{GF}\neg q}{\mathbf{F}C_0}$$

This rule states that if we are on a trace where the shoal C is eventually entered, and where $\neg q$ holds infinitely often then, considering the additional premises Π of RL, we are bound to enter the last shoal C_0. As shown in the proof sketch above, the assumption of the fact that $\neg q$ holds infinitely often is used to perform a proof by contradiction, and it is negated when the contradiction is reached. Also RLB has been formalised and proved in PVS within our theory `lemmas_shallow_ltl` [27]. The proof RLB uses the KLB rule from [15], which is the main step for the deduction of their temporal rule for k-liveness. This is because, as explained earlier, RL is a generalisation of this rule.

4.3 Completeness for rlive

In this section, we show that the rule is complete to provide a proof for the property proved by rlive, in the sense that rlive can be easily extended to generate the premises of the rule.

The C_i are the inductive invariants that are generated by performing a series of invariant checks on variations of the original transition system. Thus, initially $C := C_0$ is empty ($C_0 = \bot$, from line 2 of Algorithm 1). New shoals are added in disjunction and at the i-th iteration $C = C_{\leq i} := C_0 \vee \ldots \vee C_i$ (lines 15-16). At each iteration (lines 8-17), rlive proves that the new C_{i+1} shoal is an inductive invariant for the modified transition $T \wedge \neg C_{\leq i} \wedge \neg C'_{\leq i}$ and that it implies the invariant $T \wedge \neg C'_{\leq i} \to q$ (line 9). We can prove that this is sufficient to prove the premises Pk_n and Pp_n from Sect. 4.2.

Theorem 1. *Assume that for all i, $0 \leq i < n$, the following holds:*

$$\models (C_{i+1} \wedge T \wedge \neg C_{\leq i} \wedge \neg C'_{\leq i}) \to C'_{i+1} \tag{1}$$

$$C_{i+1} \wedge \neg q \wedge T \wedge \neg C'_{\leq i} \models \bot \tag{2}$$

Then for all i, $0 \leq i < n$, the following implications are valid:

$$((C_{\leq i} \vee C_{i+1}) \wedge T) \to (C'_{\leq i} \vee C'_{i+1}) \tag{3}$$

$$((C_{\leq i} \vee C_{i+1}) \wedge T \wedge \neg q) \to C'_{\leq i} \tag{4}$$

Proof. We prove (3) by induction on i. Since $C_{\leq i} = \bot$ in case $i = 0$, the base case of (3), what we want to prove says that $(C_1 \wedge T) \to (C'_1)$, which is exactly the assumption (1) with $i = 0$.

Let us consider the step case of the induction. By inductive hypothesis we know that $(C_{\leq i} \wedge T) \to (C'_{\leq i})$. By (1), we have that $\neg C_{\leq i} \wedge C_{i+1} \wedge T \to C'_{\leq i+1}$. From these two, we can deduce that the same holds for $((C_{\leq i} \vee C_{i+1}) \wedge T) \to (C'_{\leq i} \vee C'_{i+1})$, that is 3.

We now prove (4). From (3), we have that $((C_{\leq i}) \wedge T) \to (C'_{\leq i})$. From (2), we deduce that $(C_{i+1} \wedge T \wedge \neg q) \to C'_{\leq i}$. From these two, we can deduce that $((C_{\leq i} \vee C_{i+1}) \wedge T \wedge \neg q) \to C'_{\leq i}$, that is (4).   □

Similarly, we can prove that the information provided by the algorithm rlive is sufficient to prove the initial premise P_i. The idea is that C represents the final shoals returned by the rlive algorithm and the algorithm proves that P_i holds. The last invariant check at line 4 of Algorithm 1 returns an invariant, let us call it ψ, that is inductive for the modified transition $T \wedge \neg C \wedge \neg C'$, and such is that it implies the invariant $T \wedge \neg C' \to q$.

Theorem 2. *Assume that the following holds:*

$$\models \psi \to (T \wedge \neg C' \to q) \tag{5}$$

$$\models \mathcal{I} \wedge \mathbf{G}(T \wedge \neg C) \to \mathbf{G}\psi \tag{6}$$

Then the following implication is valid:

$$\mathcal{I} \wedge \mathbf{G}(T \wedge \neg C) \to \mathbf{G}q \tag{7}$$

Proof. From 5 and 6 it immediately follows that $\mathcal{I} \wedge \mathbf{G}(T \wedge \neg C) \rightarrow \mathbf{G}(T \wedge \neg C' \rightarrow q)$. This is equivalent to $\mathcal{I} \wedge \mathbf{G}(T \wedge \neg C) \rightarrow \mathbf{G}(q \vee \neg T \vee C')$. From this we can easily prove that $\mathcal{I} \wedge \mathbf{G}(T \wedge \neg C) \rightarrow \mathbf{G}q$ which is 7. This final step has been verified in PVS, since it is an essential proven lemma of our proof strategy presented in Sect. 4.5. Having proven it definitively, we can reuse it throughout our approach. For the detailed proof, we refer to [27], where the proven lemma appears under the name `stronger_ind_proof_2`. □

These proofs give an alternative demonstration of the correctness of the rlive algorithm, when the property is proved correct, using the rule RL. The proofs are given here for completeness of the presentation. However, to avoid trusting the implementation of the rlive algorithm and in the spirit of certifying model checking, we set a certification process in which we use a theorem prover to check the certificates generated by the model checker, as detailed in the following section.

4.4   Certification Process

Our certification process goes through three main stages:

1. The model checking stage, where we run the model checker and we dump the inductive invariants C making the shoals and the final invariant ψ as described in Sect. 4.3. These are the parameters required by the proof strategy described in the next section.
2. The theory generation phase, where a PVS theory is generated with the relevant specification of the model $\mathcal{M}$, the property to be proved, the parameters, the claim of the main theorem and the PVS proof-script with the strategy to be run to prove the main theorem.
3. The PVS proof which generates the proof certificate. Each proof uses the PVS strategy presented in the next sections, and follows a consistent pattern for all liveness checking problems $\mathcal{M} \models \mathbf{FG}q$. The proof consists of two key components: a *structural part* and a *proof obligations discharging part*. The structural part involves applying LTL definitions and the temporal deductive rules which we have proved *once and for all* as PVS lemmas, such as the lemmas for rlive RL. This part remains identical regardless of the specific model and property being certified. The proof obligations discharging part focuses on proving the propositional implications at the leaves of the proof tree and it is accomplished using the PVS built-in SAT solver (PVS uses the SMT solver Yices [11]). The critical aspect of the proof lies in this discharge of the proof obligations by Yices, as these proof steps confirm that the model $\mathcal{M}$ satisfies the necessary premises for applying RL, thereby validating the conclusion of $\mathcal{M} \models \mathbf{FG}q$. We remark that, alternatively to a SAT solver, purely syntactic and resolution based methods can be used in this stage of the proof strategy to discharge the propositional implication leaves. In PVS such methods are `prop` or `bdd-simp` [26]. However, for large formulae, they do not scale as well as a SAT solver. A full example of a proof using RL, on a concrete transition system and liveness property, can be found at [27] (`rlive_example_proof_output`).

4.5   A Proof Strategy for Liveness Checking

Given a model $\mathcal{M} = \langle X, \mathcal{I}, T \rangle$, a liveness property q and a formula C representing the shoal, which is provided by the model checking stage, a proof strategy for certifying liveness results utilises the temporal deductive rule RL (as presented above) as a proven lemma, and then proceeds to discharge each of its premises P_i, P_0 and Π.

The strategy takes the sequence of formulae $C_0, \ldots, C_n$, whose disjunction makes the shoal, as explicit parameters. The model checker provides an additional parameter formula, let us call it ψ. As we will see later, this is the inductive invariant that will be used to accomplish the proof of the premise P_i.

The proof tree starts with the goal: $\vdash valid(\mathcal{I} \wedge \mathbf{G}T \rightarrow \mathbf{FG}q)$. The strategy splits in two branches: **Branch 1**, where the premise P_i is added to the set of assumptions, and **Branch 2** where P_i is added to the set of conclusions, to be proved. In practice we make use of the PVS rule Case which allows us to assume a formula and subsequently prove this formula to be true [26].

Branch 1 in turns splits into two branches: **Branch 1.1** where the remaining premises P_0 and Π's are added to the set of assumptions, and **Branch 1.2** where P_0 and Π's are added to the set of conclusions, to be proved.

On **Branch 1.1** RL is added to the set of assumptions as a proven lemma, with appropriate substitution for the formulae representing the shoal C, $\mathcal{I}$, T and the liveness property q within the RL premises P_i, P_0 and Π. The sequent at the leaf of **Branch 1.1** has this form:

$$
\begin{array}{r|l}
\text{-1} & valid(P_i \wedge P_0 \wedge \Pi \rightarrow (\mathcal{I} \wedge \mathbf{G}T \rightarrow \mathbf{FG}q)) \\
\text{-2} & valid(P_i) \\
\text{-3} & valid(P_0 \wedge \Pi) \\
\hline
1 & valid(\mathcal{I} \wedge \mathbf{G}T \rightarrow \mathbf{FG}q)
\end{array}
$$

which is clearly provable after expanding the definition of "*valid*" and some simple symbolic manipulation. This concludes the proof of **Branch 1.1**.

The strategy turns then to **Branch 1.2**, where the premises P_0, Pk_1, Pp_1, $\ldots$, Pk_n, Pp_n have to be discharged. After expanding the definition of the *Globally* operator $\mathbf{G}$, which is the main operator of each of these premises, they can all be discharged by rewriting $\mathcal{I}$, T, q and each C_i for $0 \le i \le n$ with the appropriate formulae from the theory at issue, and by using the PVS SAT solver Yices to prove the propositional implications at the resulting leaves. This completes the proof of **Branch 1.2**.

The strategy turns to **Branch 2**, where premise P_i has to be discharged. We remind the reader that $P_i := \mathcal{I} \wedge \mathbf{G}T \wedge \mathbf{G}\neg C \rightarrow \mathbf{G}q$. This is a invariant claim equivalent to $\mathcal{I} \wedge \mathbf{G}(T \wedge \neg C) \rightarrow \mathbf{G}q$. P_i expresses that the formula q is an invariant for the model $\hat{\mathcal{M}} = \langle X, \mathcal{I}, \hat{T} \rangle$ with $\hat{T} := T \wedge \neg C \wedge \neg C'$. Since formula q is not necessarily inductive w.r.t. $\hat{\mathcal{M}}$, we need an invariant formula ψ, that is inductive and that will imply the proof of the invariant claim in P_i. The model checker is able to produce such an inductive invariant as the result of the invariant check contained within the rlive algorithm, as described in Sect. 4.3. (line 4 of Algorithm 1). It then passes this as a parameter for the proof strategy, together with the shoal formula C. In order to prove P_1, the proof strategy applies a subroutine for proving invariants using inductive invariants. This subroutine strategy takes the formula ψ as parameter and carries out a proof of P_1. This strategy is an adaptation of the strategy for proving invariant presented in [28]. This completes the proof of **Branch 2**.

Our PVS implementation of this strategy can be found at [27], together with a full example of a proof using this strategy.

5   Experimental Evaluation

In this section, we present the experimental evaluation of our proposed methodology, assessing the effectiveness, efficiency, and robustness of our approach through a series of comprehensive tests run on publicly available benchmarks sets. We describe the experimental setup, including the hardware and software configurations, the datasets used, and the specific metrics considered for the evaluation. We also provide a detailed analysis of the results obtained.

Setup. We have implemented our proof generation and certification procedure on top the model checking tool nuXmv [7]. The tool takes as input a model in Aiger [2] format, and produces the inductive invariants making the shoal and the inductive invariant ψ described in Sect. 4.5, as Aiger combinational circuits expressed over the state variables of the model.

We then apply a simple Python script to translate the input model and the generated invariants into a PVS theory. We make the script available (together with the rest of the our toolchain) at [27]. The Python script is relatively simple, and it can be verified through standard software verification methodologies. This was adapted from our work from [28] to include generation of theories for liveness checking. The overhead of this translation stage (namely, stage 2 of the certification process described in Sect. 4.4) is negligible, and therefore not included in the results evaluation where we only compare the model checking stage and the proof generation stage.

Benchmark Set. For our evaluation, we have collected a total of 53 distinct problem instances from different families, stemming from previous Hardware Model Checking Competitions (HWMCC) [3]. These 53 instances are the safe instances that could be successfully proved by nuXmv in the time limit of 1200 s. All benchmarks, certificates, and run logs have been made available for reference [27].

Results. The nuXmv runs were carried out on a computer cluster, on a queue consisting of 4 nodes with identical hardware specifications. Each node is equipped with an Intel Xeon CPU 6226R processor operating at 2.9 GHz, with 32 CPU cores and 16 GB of memory. These jobs were managed by SLURM with a memory limit of 4 GB and a wall-time limit of 1200 seconds per experimental run.

PVS experiments were conducted using PVS8.0[3] on the set of benchmarks described above, on the same cluster and in the same setup mentioned above, with a memory limit of 8 GB and a wall-time limit of 3600 s per run.

The results demonstrate the effectiveness of the prototype implementation, integrating our rlive proof strategy described in Sect. 4.5 within the existing certifying model checking framework based on PVS [28]: of the 53 total test cases, 41 in total were successfully proved by PVS within the allotted time and memory constraints, whilst remaining 12 cases exceeded the available memory resources.

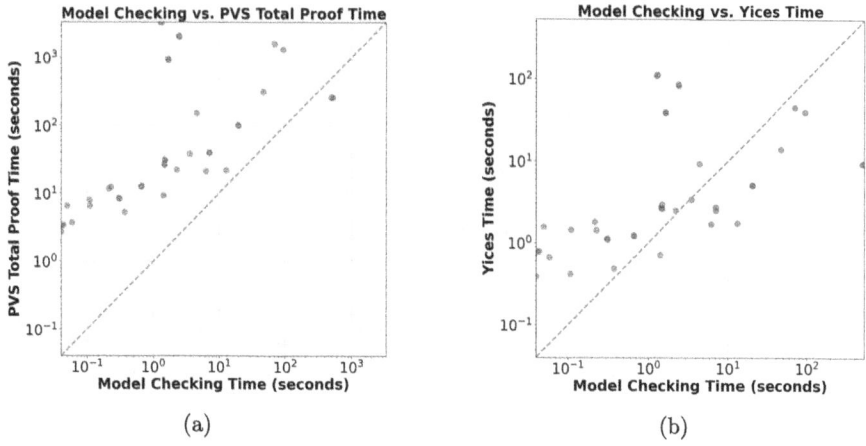

Fig. 1. Comparison between model checking verification and PVS certification times, considering overall certification times (a) and just SAT solver times (b).

Figure 1 presents preliminary results comparing model checking instances verification times, i.e. the time taken by the model checker to verify that an instance model satisfies a liveness property using the rlive algorithm (this is stage 1 of the certification process described in Sect. 4.4), against the certification times of PVS, i.e. the time taken by PVS to prove the corresponding theorem (this is stage 3 of the certification process described in Sect. 4.4). Figure 1a accounts for all the PVS certification contributions whereas Fig. 1b focuses on just Yices SAT solver times. Figure 1a shows that almost all data points lie significantly above the diagonal dashed line indicating that PVS total proof time is consistently

---

[3] We modified the PVS Makefile configuration to increase resource allocations. The SBCL_SPACE_SIZE parameter was increased from 6 GB to 30 GB, and SBCL_STACK_SIZE was increased from 8 MB to 32 MB.

higher than the model checking verification time for the same problems. Figure 1b shows that Yices times are generally closer to the diagonal line, suggesting that the proof-obligation discharging part of the proof is more efficient than the rest of the steps performed in the PVS proofs.

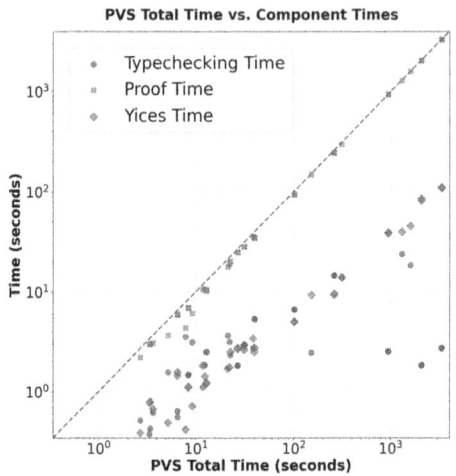

Fig. 2. Times breakdown for PVS-based runs.

To better understand the reasons behind this gap, we further analysed the breakdown of execution times for different operations within PVS. Figure 2 illustrates the total certification time divided into three components: *type-checking time*, the time spent verifying semantic constraints, determining expression types, and resolving names, *proof-checking time*, the time spent executing the actual steps of the proof strategy and *SAT-solving time*, the time of the proof-checking time spent on calls to the SAT solver Yices. Our analysis reveals that PVS performance bottlenecks occur primarily within proof steps other than the Yices solver component. When processing theories with numerous shoals formulae, PVS spends disproportionate time on fundamental logical operations, such as logical operators' expansion. For n shoals, expanding basic LTL operators like 'AND' requires approximately n separate expansion operations, each triggering cascading expansions of nested 'OR' operations. These operations, as well as operations of installing and rewriting definitions, involve substantial hidden costs. PVS performs additional typechecking and book-keeping during these operations. This explains the significant gap between Yices processing time and proof time observed in our performance analysis.

While our analysis indicate scaling limitations in the current prototype implementation, it is important to emphasise that the primary contribution of this work is the theoretical foundation and correctness of our proof strategy for rlive. The prototype serves its intended purpose: demonstrating that the strategy is sound and functional by successfully certifying the tested benchmarks. The PVS based framework could be implemented using alternative certification tools or optimised versions of PVS tailored to this problem domain. As proposed in [28], future work will address these scaling concerns.

6   Conclusions and Future Work

In this paper we have considered rlive [30], a new SAT-based model-checking algorithm for the verification of liveness properties of finite-state symbolic transition systems. We have shown that, despite the complexity of the algorithm, the shoals provided by the model checker are sufficient to generate proof certificates in a deductive system for temporal properties, and that even though rlive and k-liveness seem two very different algorithms, in terms of temporal rules the first can be seen a generalisation of the second, as it is presented in [15]. We have formalised the rule for rlive, proved its correctness and completeness, and developed a proof strategy that uses this rule to certify liveness checking results. We have implemented our strategy as a prototype in an existing certifying model checking framework [28] based on PVS, and tested the implementation on a set of benchmarks from the hardware model checking competition.

We see several directions for future work, such as extending the certifying model checking approach to other liveness checking algorithms such as liveness-to-safety [1] and FAIR [6]. It would also be interesting to investigate the possibility of a proof strategy that encompasses all these liveness checking algorithms. We would also like to generalise the current proof strategy for rlive to account for multiple fairness constraints, as it is done for k-liveness in [15], since our approach is currently limited to a single fairness condition (namely $\neg q$). Since proofs are easily composed, it is a very feasible next step to consider the generation of proofs that combine multiple transformation techniques with liveness proofs, as it is done in [15] for k-liveness. Some of these transformations, such as temporal decomposition and phase abstraction, are already certifiable using the theorem prover based approach from [28]. We would also like to consider generalisations to the infinite-state transition system and SMT (Satisfiability Modulo Theories) based model checking, since rlive has recently been generalised to handle this type of transition systems [8].

Acknowledgments. The authors acknowledge the support of the PNRR project FAIR - Future AI Research (PE00000013), under the NRRP MUR program funded by the Next Generation EU and in particular the activity of technology transfer "nuXmv - Towards Market Readiness".

References

1. Biere, A., Artho, C., Schuppan, V.: Liveness checking as safety checking. Electron. Notes Theor. Comput. Sci. **66**(2), 160–177 (2002)
2. Biere, A., Heljanko, K., Wieringa, S.: AIGER 1.9 and beyond. Technical Report 11/2, Institute for Formal Models and Verification, Johannes Kepler University, Altenbergerstr. 69, 4040 Linz, Austria (2011)

3. Biere, A., Jussila, T.: The Model Checking Competition Web Page, http://fmv.jku.at/hwmcc

4. Biere, A., Yu, E., Froleyks, N.: Stratified certification for k-induction. In: Proceedings of the 22nd Conference on Formal Methods in Computer-Aided Design–FMCAD 2022, vol. 3, p. 59. TU Wien Academic Press (2022)

5. Boulton, R.J., et al.: Experience with embedding hardware description languages in HOL. In: TPCD, vol. 10, pp. 129–156 (1992)

6. Bradley, A.R., Somenzi, F., Hassan, Z., Zhang, Y.: An incremental approach to model checking progress properties. In: 2011 Formal Methods in Computer-Aided Design (FMCAD), pp. 144–153. IEEE (2011)

7. Cavada, R., et al.: The NUXMV Symbolic Model Checker. In: Biere, A., Bloem, R. (eds.) CAV 2014. LNCS, vol. 8559, pp. 334–342. Springer, Cham (2014). https://doi.org/10.1007/978-3-319-08867-9_22

8. Cimatti, A., Griggio, A., Johannsen, C., Rozier, K.Y., Tonetta, S.: Infinite state liveness checking with rlive. In: Proceedings of the 37th International Conference on Computer Aided Verification (CAV 2025) (2025). To be published

9. Claessen, K., Sörensson, N.: A liveness checking algorithm that counts. In: 2012 Formal Methods in Computer-Aided Design (FMCAD), pp. 52–59. IEEE (2012)

10. Dax, C., Hofmann, M., Lange. M.: A proof system for the linear time μ-calculus. In: FSTTCS 2006: Foundations of Software Technology and Theoretical Computer Science: 26th International Conference, Kolkata, India, December 13-15, 2006. Proceedings 26, pp. 273–284. Springer (2006)

11. Dutertre, B., De Moura, L.: The yices smt solver. Tool paper at http://yices.csl.sri.com/tool-paper.pdf, 2(2), 1–2 (2006)

12. Froleyks, N., Yu, E., Biere, A., Heljanko, K.: Certifying phase abstraction. In: International Joint Conference on Automated Reasoning, pp. 284–303. Springer (2024)

13. Gabbay, D., Pnueli, A., Shelah, S., Stavi, J.: On the temporal analysis of fairness. In: Proceedings of the 7th ACM SIGPLAN-SIGACT symposium on Principles of programming languages, pp. 163–173 (1980)

14. Gentzen, G.: Untersuchungen über das logische schließen. i. Mathematische zeitschrift, 35 (1935)

15. Griggio, A., Roveri, M., Tonetta, S.: Certifying proofs for sat-based model checking. Formal Methods Syst. Des. 57(2), 178–210 (2021)

16. Kuismin, T., Heljanko, K.: Increasing confidence in liveness model checking results with proofs. In: Haifa Verification Conference, pp. 32–43. Springer (2013)

17. Kupferman, O., Vardi, M.Y.: From complementation to certification. Theor. Comput. Sci. 345(1), 83–100 (2005)

18. Munoz, C.A.: Batch proving and proof scripting in PVS. Technical report, National Institute of Aerospace (2007)

19. Namjoshi, K.S.: Certifying model checkers. In: Berry, G., Comon, H., Finkel, A. (eds.) CAV 2001. LNCS, vol. 2102, pp. 2–13. Springer, Heidelberg (2001). https://doi.org/10.1007/3-540-44585-4_2

20. Owre, S., Rushby, J.M., Shankar, N.: PVS: a prototype verification system. In: International Conference on Automated Deduction, pp. 748–752. Springer, 1992

21. Owre, S., Shankar, N.: Writing PVS proof strategies. In: Design and Application of Strategies/Tactics in Higher Order Logics (STRATA 2003), number CP-2003-212448 in NASA Conference Publication, pp. 1–15 (2003)

22. Peled, D., Pnueli, A., Zuck, L.: From falsification to verification. In: International Conference on Foundations of Software Technology and Theoretical Computer Science, pp. 292–304. Springer (2001)

23. Peled, D., Zuck, L.: From model checking to a temporal proof. In: International SPIN workshop on model checking of software, pp. 1–14. Springer (2001)

24. Pnueli, A.: The temporal logic of programs. In: 18th Annual Symposium On Foundations of Computer Science (sfcs 1977), pp. 46–57. IEEE (1977)

25. Rushby, J.: PVS embeddings of propositional and quantified modal logic. arXiv preprint arXiv:2205.06391 (2022)

26. Shankar, N., Owre, S., Rushby, J.M., Stringer-Calvert, D.W.J.: PVS prover guide. Comput. Sci. Lab. SRI Int. Menlo Park, CA 1, 11–12 (2001)

27. Sindoni, G., Griggio, A., Tonetta, S.: Certifying-rlive-25. https://gitlab.fbk.eu/gsindoni/Certifying_Rlive_25. Accessed 15 May 2025

28. Sindoni, G., et al.: Giulia Sindoni, et al.: A theorem prover based approach for sat-based model checking certification. In: Automated Deduction-CADE- 35: 30th International Conference on Automated Deduction, Stuttgart, Germany, 2025, Proceedings 30 (2025). To be published

29. Vardi, M.Y.: An automata-theoretic approach to linear temporal logic. In: Logics for concurrency: structure versus automata, pp. 238–266 (2005)

30. Xia, Y., Cimatti, A., Griggio, A., Li, J.: Avoiding the shoals-a new approach to liveness checking. In: International Conference on Computer Aided Verification, pp. 234–254. Springer (2024)

31. Yu, E., Biere, A., Heljanko, K.: Progress in Certifying Hardware Model Checking Results. In: Silva, A., Leino, K.R.M. (eds.) CAV 2021. LNCS, vol. 12760, pp. 363–386. Springer, Cham (2021). https://doi.org/10.1007/978-3-030-81688-9_17

Author Index

R. Thiemann and C. Weidenbach (Eds.): FroCoS 2025, LNAI 15979, pp. 405–406, 2026.
https://doi.org/10.1007/978-3-032-04167-8

The manufacturer's authorised representative in the EU is Springer
Nature Customer Service Centre GmbH, Europaplatz 3, 69115 Heidelberg,
Germany. If you have any concerns regarding our products, please
contact ProductSafety@springernature.com

Printed and bound by CPI Group (UK) Ltd, Croydon, CR0 4YY

28/04/2026

02098524-0008